DUMBARTON OAKS
MEDIEVAL LIBRARY

Jan M. Ziolkowski, General Editor

POEMS

VENANTIUS FORTUNATUS

DOML 46

Poems

Venantius Fortunatus

Edited and Translated by

MICHAEL ROBERTS

Dumbarton Oaks
Medieval Library

Harvard University Press
Cambridge, Massachusetts
London, England
2017

Library of Congress Cataloging-in-Publication Data
Names: Fortunatus, Venantius Honorius Clementianus, approximately
540–approximately 600, author. | Roberts, Michael, 1947 September 16 —
editor, translator. | Container of (expression): Fortunatus, Venantius
Honorius Clementianus, approximately 540–approximately 600. Poems.
Selections. 2017. | Container of (expression): Fortunatus, Venantius
Honorius Clementianus, approximately 540–approximately 600. Poems.
Selections. English. 2017.
  Title: Poems / Venantius Fortunatus ; edited and translated by Michael
Roberts.
  Other titles: Dumbarton Oaks medieval library ; 46.
  Description: Cambridge, Massachusetts : Harvard University Press,
2017. |
  Series: Dumbarton Oaks medieval library ; 46 | Includes bibliographical
references and index. | Texts in Latin with English translations on facing
pages; introduction and notes in English.
  Identifiers: LCCN 2016048601 | ISBN 9780674974920 (alk. paper)
  Subjects: LCSH: Fortunatus, Venantius Honorius Clementianus,
approximately 540–approximately 600 —Translations into English. |
Merovingians — Poetry. | France — History —To 987 — Poetry.
  Classification: LCC PA8310.F7 A2 2017 | DDC 871/.02 —dc23 LC record
available at https://lccn.loc.gov/2016048601

Contents

Introduction   *vii*

PREFACE   1

BOOK 1   11

BOOK 2   67

BOOK 3   121

BOOK 4   211

BOOK 5   277

BOOK 6   347

BOOK 7   419

BOOK 8   489

BOOK 9   555

BOOK 10   605

BOOK 11   705

APPENDIX   759

FIGURE POEMS   827

CONTENTS

Abbreviations   *831*

Note on the Text   *833*

Notes to the Text   *835*

Notes to the Translation   *841*

Bibliography   *895*

Index   *899*

Introduction

Venantius Honorius Clementianus Fortunatus, to give him his full name, was born in Duplavis, modern Valdobbiadene, near Treviso, sometime in the 530s.[1] After receiving the literary education traditional in late antiquity in the schools of Ravenna, he began his career as poet in northern Italy with the first two poems in his collection, written probably for Bishop Vitalis of Altinum. In the mid-560s, though, for reasons that remain obscure, he traveled to Merovingian Gaul, where in 566 he wrote an epithalamium for the marriage in Metz of the Austrasian king Sigibert and his Visigothic bride Brunhild (6.1). All the rest of his poetry was written in Gaul for or about figures in his adopted homeland.

In addition to the two poems he wrote for the royal couple (6.1 and 6.1a), a number of compositions on the bishops of northern Gaul contained in Books 2 and 3 probably date to this early period (2.11–13, 3.11–15, 3.23, and 3.23a; also 9.9). Subsequently, Fortunatus moved to Paris, as evidenced by his panegyric to King Charibert (6.2), who died in 567. There too he must have struck up a friendship with Ragnemod (3.26), who was later to become bishop of Paris (9.10), succeeding Germanus, who is the subject of one of Fortunatus's poems (2.9) and of a prose *Vita* after his death. From Paris, Fortunatus seems to have moved on to Tours, where

he made the acquaintance of Bishop Eufronius (3.1–3). Finally, his travels took him to Poitiers, where he encountered Radegund, founder of the Convent of the Holy Cross, and her abbess Agnes. He was to settle in Poitiers for the rest of his life, though his poetry bears witness to occasional further journeys, for instance, to Bordeaux, Toulouse, and Nantes. In the late 580s he once more traveled to the royal court at Metz of Sigibert's son, Childebert II, and of his widow, Brunhild (10.7–9). Scholars generally assume that he accompanied Gregory of Tours, his friend and patron, to Metz in 588, though neither author mentions the other in writing of the trip. Little is known of Fortunatus's later life. His last datable poem (10.14, dating to 591) celebrates the election of Plato as bishop of Poitiers. Fortunatus was to be his successor (he had become a priest earlier during his time in Gaul). His two prose exegetical works (10.1 and 11.1), on the Lord's Prayer and the Creed, probably date to his episcopate. It is generally assumed that he died in the early years of the seventh century.

The manuscripts of Fortunatus's poetry, with one exception, divide his works into eleven books. Books 1 to 7 were published together at the urging of Gregory of Tours, as the dedicatory letter to the collection makes clear, probably in 576 or soon thereafter. Subsequently, Fortunatus published a second collection, consisting of Books 8 and 9. The last two books were most probably collected for publication after his death.[2] One manuscript, *Parisinus lat.* 13048, does not follow the normal book divisions and preserves some poems not found in other manuscripts. Friedrich Leo published these works as an *Appendix* to his edition. They largely derive in some way from Fortunatus's relationship with Rade-

gund and the Convent of the Holy Cross. Fortunatus also wrote, sometime between 573 and 576, a hexameter *Vita Sancti Martini,* again dedicated to Gregory (not included in the present translation), and a number of prose saints' lives.[3]

As Wilhelm Meyer pointed out,[4] the first collection of Fortunatus's poetry shows a careful ordering by status of the addressees or subject of the poems: Books 1 to 3 and 5 are addressed to figures in the church or deal with religious matters; Books 6 and 7 are addressed to secular figures. There is also a tendency to order poems within and between books by the status of the addressee: Book 3 begins with bishops and ends with deacons; Book 6 is largely devoted to royalty, first male, then female, but ends with a pair of letters to the powerful rector of Provence, Dynamius. Book 7 then continues this progression, giving prominence to three figures important in the Austrasian kingdom, Gogo, Lupus, and Jovinus, all of whom Fortunatus got to know at the royal court in Metz when he first arrived in Gaul. Book 4 stands apart and is made up entirely of epitaphs, but it too shows the same ordering principle, from church to secular figures, and in the latter group from men to women and children. Later books show less pronounced patterns of order, though Book 8 gathers poems dedicated to the Convent of the Holy Cross, its founder, Radegund, and its abbess, Agnes (1–10), along with a succession of poems to Fortunatus's chief patron, Gregory of Tours (11–21), thereby bringing together the two figures, Radegund and Gregory, with whom he was most closely associated during his time in Gaul.

Fortunatus adopts a variety of tones in his poetic corpus, but characteristically praise of his subject or addressee plays a prominent role, especially in his first published collection.

The subjects run the gamut of the great and the good in Merovingian society, from substantial panegyrics of kings (6.2, Charibert; 9.1, Chilperic) to less ambitious compositions on bishops or other clergy that rehearse their virtues, including charitable, preaching, and building activities. Within such episcopal praise poems, three figures stand out as recipients of small dossiers of compositions. Leontius of Bordeaux receives fourteen poems (1.6 and 1.8–20), including epigrams celebrating his building or restoring of churches (1.6 and 1.9–13), a more conventional panegyric (1.15), and three poems (1.18–20) describing villas owned by the bishop and the landscape in which they are set that convey a sense of the status of the villa owner and the order and prosperity his episcopal oversight provides.[5] (Fortunatus was later to write Leontius's epitaph [4.10].) A second figure is Felix of Nantes, who is the subject or addressee of seven poems along with a prose letter (3.4–10 and 5.7). They include a complementary pair of poems on the dedication of Felix's cathedral in Nantes (3.6 and 3.7) and a poem celebrating the baptism of Saxon converts by the bishop at Easter (3.9) that with its evocation of the mood of Easter morning and its hymn to the risen Christ demonstrates impressively Fortunatus's poetic range.

Gregory of Tours is the third bishop who figures prominently in Fortunatus's corpus. But his role is different from that of the other two. The majority of poems to or about Gregory are epistolary in form (5.8–17, 8.11–21, 9.6 and 9.7, 10.12a). Although they include many complimentary remarks about Gregory, they are not for the most part primarily praise poems. The closest Fortunatus comes to pure panegyric is the poem he wrote for Gregory's entry into the

episcopate of Tours in 573 (5.3), perhaps marking his first acquaintance with Gregory.[6] For the most part Gregory played the role of literary patron. Fortunatus dedicated both his first collection of poems and the *Vita Sancti Martini* to the bishop of Tours. Gregory in return provided Fortunatus with gifts, including a small estate by the river Vienne (8.19 and 8.20). Gregory also could request compositions from the poet: for instance, epigrams for his newly restored cathedral (10.6) or a poem in the Sapphic meter (9.6 and 9.7). The exchanges between the two imply mutual respect but also a difference of status, with Gregory as the superior.

A second group of poems takes as its subject the women of the Convent of the Holy Cross in Poitiers, its founder Radegund, Thuringian princess and former wife of Chlothar I, and Agnes, her abbess. The poems in Book 8 celebrate Radegund as a royal ascetic, in a manner that is consistent with, if not as extreme as, the portrait Fortunatus paints in his prose life of the saint. The poems of Book 11 and the *Appendix,* however, largely epistolary in nature, depart from this orthodox view to present a more intimate picture of relations between Fortunatus and the two women, whom the poet prefers to present as a family, with Radegund as mother and Agnes and himself as siblings. Fortunatus also wrote a number of poems in the interest of the convent (for example, 8.1, 8.4) or conveying greetings from the two women. His longest elegiac poem (8.3), in praise of Christian virginity, probably marks the consecration of Agnes as abbess of the convent. He also celebrated the convent's acquisition in 569 of fragments of the holy cross with a group of poems (2.1, 2.2, and 2.6) that include the hymns *Pange, lingua* (2.2), and *Vexilla regis* (2.6), which were to be his best-known

works because of their acceptance into the liturgy. In connection with the same event, the *Appendix* includes a poem of thanks written on Radegund's behalf to the emperor Justin II and the empress Sophia for their gift of relics of the cross (*App.* 2). Three figure poems also incorporate an image of the cross (2.4, 2.5, and 5.6a), and, in the case of the first two, take as their subject its praise.

Despite being the author of a four-book hagiographic epic on the life of Saint Martin, Fortunatus rarely ventures into narrative in his shorter poems. The most common exception is precisely for poems of hagiographic content narrating martyrdoms (Saturninus of Toulouse, 2.7; Maurice and the Theban Legion, 2.14) or saints' miracles (Saint Medard, 2.16; Saint Lawrence, 9.14; Saint Martin, 1.5 and 10.6). The corpus also contains two lengthy poems with a large element of narrative. One, the elegy for Galswintha (6.5), describes the departure of that Visigothic princess from her Spanish homeland to marry the Frankish king Chilperic, her journey, and the laments of her nurse, sister, and mother at her death. The second (*App.* 1), written in the person of Radegund, seeks news of her cousin Amalfred at the Byzantine court and recalls the tragic history of their childhood in Thuringia.[7] In both poems, as in his elegy on Christian virginity, where the virgin expresses her longing for her bridegroom Christ, Fortunatus demonstrates a penchant for adopting the persona of a grieving woman separated from a loved one in the manner of Ovid's *Heroides*.

Preserved among Fortunatus's poems are eight letters in prose (3.1, 3.2, and 3.4; 5.1 and 5.6; 10.2–4)—nine, if the dedicatory letter to Gregory is included—and two prose treatises (10.1 and 11.1), the first, on the Lord's Prayer, incomplete.[8] Of the 270 poems in the collection—one poem

(*Epistulae Austrasicae* 14) is separately transmitted—all but ten are in elegiac couplets. The exceptions are the hymn *Vexilla regis* (2.6) and a hymn celebrating the restoration of Bishop Leontius to his see (1.16), both in iambic dimeters; *Pange, lingua* (2.2), in trochaic tetrameters catalectic; a poem in Sapphics written at Gregory's request (9.7); the three figure poems (2.4, 2.5, and 5.6a), the epithalamium for Sigibert and Brunhild (6.1), and a poem to Felix of Nantes (5.7), all in hexameters;[9] and one text (*App.* 11) that appears to be an incomplete draft of a poem.

In Fortunatus's hands the elegiac couplet becomes an efficient medium for communicating praise or making a spiritual or rhetorical point. For instance, in a relatively undistinguished poem (3.11.9–14), Fortunatus rehearses the praise of Nicetius of Trier:

> Dum tibi restrictus maneas et largus egenis,
>   quod facis in minimis te dare crede Deo.
> Captivus quicumque redit sua limina cernens
>   ille lares patrios, tu capis inde polos.
> Hic habet exul opem, ieiunans invenit escas;
>   qui venit esuriens hinc satiatus abit.

In living with frugality to yourself, but generosity to the poor, what you do for the least, believe that you give to God. Every captive who returns and sees once more his threshold gains again his father's house, but you from that gain heaven. Here the exile wins assistance, the hungry finds his food; the person who arrives famished departs from here filled.

As is regularly the case in classical elegiacs, each couplet is a self-contained unit of sense. But Fortunatus goes fur-

ther. In the vast majority of cases each line of his poems is an independent syntactical unit. Furthermore, it is often the case, as exemplified by the present passage, that each verse is again divided into two clauses, with the division typically at the central caesura, or break in the line.[10] Fortunatus's poetry shows a marked liking for figures of diction—antithesis, paronomasia (play on words), rhyme, and alliteration—and these regularly serve to articulate further the structure of the verse, by setting the two halves of the line off against each other in sound and sense. In the present passage four of the six lines contain antitheses: "frugality to yourself: generosity to the poor; for the least: to God; his father's house: heaven; arrives famished: departs filled." The rhyme between the two halves of the pentameter in line 12 is particularly characteristic. Reydellet has observed that although Fortunatus's elegiacs show a slightly lower percentage of pentameters with such rhymes than the works of Ovid and Propertius, his practice stands out because while in classical poetry the rhyme is normally occasioned by the agreement of noun and adjective, in Fortunatus's typically there is no such accord and regularly the rhymed words are in separate clauses, as in the present case.[11] I have argued elsewhere that the effect of these changes in the elegiac couplet is to provide aural cues to the structure of the verse and thereby make it perceptible as poetry for an audience that was no longer sensitive to differences of quantity.[12] In the present passage this predictable structure produces a hymn-like litany of the bishop's virtues. Fortunatus's poetry generally displays a delight in verbal play and an alliterative inventiveness that can present challenges for the translator. Earlier in the Nicetius poem, for instance, is the line *cui*

moritur mundus non moriture manes (3.11.6). The best I can manage is the tame "the world is dead to you, but you will never die," sacrificing the alliteration.

All Fortunatus's poetry shows his taste for epigrammatic point and for figures of diction. But it accommodates a variety of subjects and tones. His poetry includes a number of attractive passages of natural description: for instance, of the exultation of the world at the coming of spring and Easter (3.9); of a parched summer landscape and the new birth of spring (both in 7.8); and of the river Gers, dried up in summer, but subject to sudden flash floods (1.21). Elsewhere there are shorter descriptions of the seasons or accounts of buildings and landscapes. In a different register he describes the brilliance of heaven, emphasizing the holy company gathered there, in passages that suggest parallels with the mosaics of Ravenna.[13] In general, Fortunatus makes great use of the language of light, not only of objects, but also of the natural world, and of human virtues and status—especially of an individual's power to nurture and protect—as well as of the faculties of sight and life.

One of the most engaging features of Fortunatus's poetry is his sense of humor, which is typically self-deprecating. The closest he comes to an invective is denunciation of a cook, who allegedly commandeered a boat from Fortunatus (6.8.7–20). The cook is very much a stock character, however, and the poem overall is a rueful account of the chapter of accidents Fortunatus suffered and praise of those who tried to help him. More typically humor derives from the poet's supposed appetite for food and drink. After indulging in a lavish banquet provided by Mummolenus, an important figure at Sigibert's court, Fortunatus suffers an attack of in-

digestion that he compares, in Virgilian language, to a storm at sea or the blast of bellows (7.14.25–34). When provided rich fare by Radegund and Agnes, he eagerly scoffs the lot (11.9.13–14; compare 11.20.5–6). Another poem finds him fighting sleep in his attempt to write to the two women. His compositional skills are impaired, he tells us, by drinking too much (11.23). In all these cases it would be unwise to take the poems too literally. But they do give insight into Fortunatus's sense of humor, which was apparently shared by his correspondents.

Fortunatus also has a way with metaphor. Both his poem to Mummolenus and the description of the meal provided by Radegund and Agnes speak of the fare presented to the poet in terms of landscape: in the first case, mountain, valley, and river (7.14.17–22); in the second, mountains surrounding a garden (11.9.9–14). The word *sal* (salt) recurs often in his poem in a metaphorical sense as a literary term, referring to spiritual eloquence or rhetorical substance (not wit, as in classical authors). Fortunatus rings a number of changes on the basic idea of the seasoning of speech, exploiting the polysemy of the word, which can also refer by metonymy to the sea.[14] To take one last example, Fortunatus elaborates on the Horatian metaphor of poetic composition as metalworking but gives it an unexpected twist when he, the poet, becomes the metal worked on by an affectionate appeal from the Parisian clergy (2.9.7–16).[15]

Thanks to his schooling in Ravenna, Fortunatus displays familiarity with a range of classical authors. As is always the case for late antique poets, Virgil is the strongest presence, but among the Augustan poets Horace and Ovid are also influential, while Fortunatus reveals knowledge too of the first-century authors most commonly read in late antiquity,

Lucan and Statius, Martial and Juvenal. From the postclassical period Claudian, Ausonius and Sidonius all find echoes in his verse. He also shows familiarity with the most important Christian Latin poets of the period. His *Vita Sancti Martini* enumerates as writers of Christian narrative poetry Juvencus, Sedulius, Orientius, Prudentius, Paulinus (of Nola and of Périgueux, he confuses the two), Arator, and Avitus (*VSM* 1.14–25). Of that group Sedulius exerts by far the strongest influence on Fortunatus's poetry, especially in the *Vita Sancti Martini*. Of prose texts the Bible naturally is regularly evoked; Fortunatus is capable of paraphrasing quite closely biblical texts in verse.

Comparisons with biblical figures sometimes serve to enhance Fortunatus's praise of his subjects, a role in earlier writers frequently played by figures from myth. For instance, in his combination of royalty and holiness, Childebert I is a second Melchesidech (2.10.19–22); Felix of Nantes, in building his cathedral, outdoes Solomon and his temple (3.6.1–10). Myth, by contrast, plays a limited role in Fortunatus's corpus, though there are occasional examples when writing to his most familiar or learned correspondents: a poem to Jovinus enumerates mythical figures who despite their stature nevertheless were subject to death (7.12); a prose letter to Felix of Nantes (3.4) displays mythological learning in response to a letter from that bishop of high literary finish. His first datable poem of those written in Gaul (6.1), the epithalamium for Sigibert and Brunhild, is an outlier in this respect. In the manner traditional for late antique epithalamia, the poem employs a mythological framing narrative. Cupid and Venus promote the match and fly to earth to deck the bridal chamber and sing the virtues of the happy couple. It is telling that Fortunatus was never again to write a poem

so closely allied to the traditions of late antique secular poetry and the use of myth as a prestigious idiom of praise. Myth is entirely absent from his other royal poems. Instead, he forged a functional idiom, with some affinities to the style of verse epigraphy,[16] well suited to poetry of praise in the cultural context of Merovingian Gaul, where the audience typically lacked the literary education to understand more sophisticated forms of composition. Fortunatus's expertise lay in meeting the expectations of those who commissioned his poems by presenting the powerful of the Merovingian world in the way they wished to be represented and in an idiom that was readily accessible. But despite the constraints on expression caused by the circumstances of reception in sixth-century Gaul, he created a flexible poetic style that was capable of giving voice to a variety of subjects and tones. Fortunatus's mastery of the short praise poem was to secure him an admiring readership in the Carolingian period, when his name was added to the canon of Christian Latin poets he himself had first formulated.[17]

The present volume is the first English translation of all twelve books of Fortunatus's poetry. The only poem omitted is the hexameter *Vita Sancti Martini*. Several selections of his poetry exist already. In preparing my own translation, I have most frequently consulted the edition and translation of Marc Reydellet in the Budé series and the parallel text and Italian translation of Stefano di Brazzano, though I differ from their understanding of the text in some places.[18] My aim has been to produce a readable and accurate version of Fortunatus's Latin, without slavishly following the structure of the Latin when it would produce uncomfortable

English. I hope that the reader will find it immediately accessible. The notes to the translation primarily serve to facilitate such reading by providing extra help when needed. For the most part they make no claim to advance scholarship on Fortunatus or to give detailed historical background.

I should like to express my gratitude to Gregory Hays, Danuta Shanzer, and Michael Winterbottom, members of the editorial board of DOML, whose careful reading of my manuscript in its final stages improved it in many ways. Needless to say, remaining errors and infelicities are all my own doing. My gratitude too to Jan Ziolkowski for his invitation to contribute to the series and his enthusiasm for the project over the years I have been working on it. Finally, special thanks to Raquel Begleiter, Assistant Managing Editor of the series, for her unfailing patience and helpfulness in bringing my manuscript to publication.

Notes

1 The conclusion to Fortunatus's verse *Vita Sancti Martini* (4.661–703) contains a certain amount of biographical information. For more detailed treatments of Fortunatus's biography and discussion of contested points, see Brennan, "The Career of Venantius Fortunatus," 49–78; George, *Venantius Fortunatus,* 18–34; Reydellet, *Venance Fotunat, Poèmes,* 1:vii–xxviii; and Di Brazzano, "Profilo biografico di Venanzio Fortunato," 37–72.

2 I have given the most commonly accepted version of the publication history of Fortunatus's poetry, but some points are contested. In particular, George, "Venantius Fortunatus: The End Game," 32–43, has argued that Fortunatus was responsible for the publication of Books 10 and 11 as well.

3 Edited by Bruno Krusch, *Venanti Honori Clementiani Fortunati presbyteri Italici opera pedestria. Monumenta Germaniae Historica. Auctores Antiquissimi* 4.2 (Berlin, 1885).

4 Wilhelm Meyer, *Der Gelegenheitsdichter Venantius Fortunatus,* Abhandlungen der königlichen Gesellschaft der Wissenschaften zu Göttingen, phil.-hist. Klasse, N.F. 4.5 (Berlin, 1901), 25.

5 For this interpretation see Roberts, *The Humblest Sparrow,* 71–82.

6 Many scholars assume Fortunatus must have met Gregory earlier, but there is no evidence for such a meeting. The convent at Poitiers depended heavily on the support of the bishop of Tours, so it was in the women's interest for Fortunatus to establish good relations with the new bishop on their behalf.

7 A second poem (*App.* 3), written to another relative in the East, Artachis, reveals that he has sent her the news that Amalfred had died.

8 Poem 5.6, to Syagrius of Autun, accompanies a figure poem, seeking the bishop's help in the release of a captive. The poems 5.5 and 8.12 each come with a short prose letter addressed to Gregory of Tours.

9 The epithalamium has an elegiac preface, following a common practice in late antique poetry. In addition to the figure poems the corpus contains an abecedarian poem (1.16), three acrostic poems (3.5, 8.5, and 9.5), and two epanaleptic poems (*versus reciproci,* 3.30 and 8.2).

10 Line 11 varies this pattern somewhat, with a fourth-foot caesura and with a participial expression rather than a separate clause occupying the second half of the line.

11 Reydellet, *Venance Fortunat, Poèmes,* 1:lxvi–lxviii.

12 Roberts, *The Humblest Sparrow,* 322–24. The phonetic changes in Latin in the period mean that in lines 11 and 14 there would be assonance between the final vowels of *redit* and *cernens* and of *esuriens* and *abit.*

13 The best examples are 8.3.1–42 and 10.7.15–30. Such passages are a feature of Fortunatus's *Vita Sancti Martini.*

14 See, for instance, 3.8.18, 5.1.3, and 7.1.24.

15 Horace, *Ars Poetica* 291 and 441. Fortunatus reverts to the same metaphor in the *Vita Sancti Martini* (4.18–23), where he uses it more conventionally.

16 See Blomgren, "Fortunatus cum elogiis collatus," 95–111.

17 Alcuin, *Versus de patribus, regibus et sanctis Euboricensis ecclesiae* 1552; Theodulf of Orleans, *Carmina* 45.14.

18 For bibliographical details of these editions, see the list of abbreviations. Both are equipped with valuable notes.

PREFACE

Acuminum suorum luculenta veteris aetatis ingenia qui na-
tura fervidi, curatura fulgidi, usu triti, auso securi, ore freti,
more festivi, praeclaris operibus celebraturi posteris stu-
pore laudanda reliquere vestigia, certe illi inventione pro-
vidi, partitione serii, distributione librati, epilogiorum calce
iucundi, colae fonte proflui, commate succiso venusti, tro-
pis, paradigmis, periodis, epichirematibus coronati pariter
et cothurnati tale sui canentes dederunt specimen ut adhuc
nostro tempore quasi sibi postumi vivere credantur etsi non
2   carne, vel carmine. Quos licet sors fine tulerit, tamen cum
dicta permanent vivaci memoriae de mortuis aliquid mors
reliquit nec totum usquequaque sepelivit in tumulo cui re-
stat liberum, ut vel lingua vivat in mundo. Hoc nesciens
avara mors auferre cum funere quod per ora viventium de-
functos videt currere si non pede, poemate. In hoc tamen
melius superata mors invida, si se sermone senserit et mer-

The brilliant intellects of ancient times, who, inspired by
nature, burnished by culture, polished by practice, confi-
dent in boldness, assured in speech, lively in character, and
destined for distinction by their brilliant works, left to pos-
terity a record of their keen intelligence worthy of awe-
struck praise, certainly by their facility in invention, their
assurance in division, their discrimination in arrangement,
the charm of their concluding statements, the fluent profu-
sion of their clauses, and the charming concision of their
phrasing, garlanded and elevated by tropes, examples, peri-
ods, and epicheiremes, gave such an impression of them-
selves in their song that still in our times they are believed to
survive themselves and live on, if not in flesh then in verse.
Though fate has carried them off at the last, nevertheless, 2
as long as their words remain, death has left something of
the dead to live in memory and has been unable for ever to
bury completely in the tomb anyone whose tongue at least
can still live on in the world. Greedy death has no power to
abolish with the grave the sight of the dead still circulating
on the tongues of the living, in poetry if not in person. Yet
envious death is conquered all the more effectively if it feels

3

3 cede bis victam. Sed sicut hos quos clarae linguae iactitat lux illustres, quorum fuerat aperte damnum pati dicta celari, qui pomposae facundiae florulenta germina nisi misissent in publicum, fecerant peculatum, merito famae radii per qua-qua traxerunt, ut peragrantes omnia, quotquot magis car-mina locis innotescerent, laus augeret, ita fit eis consultius si occulantur taciti, qui fastidiri poterunt revelati; nec tantum sit exprobrabile nesciri quod horreat quam patesci quod urat minorisque dispendii celata videatur inscitia quam pro-lata, quia illic obstat pudor ne prodatur notitia, hic audacia proditur ut ingerat notam.

4 Unde, vir apostolice, praedicande papa Gregori, quia viritim flagitas ut quaedam ex opusculis imperitiae meae tibi transferenda proferrem, nugarum mearum admiror te amore seduci, quae cum prolatae fuerint nec mirari pote-runt nec amari, praesertim quod ego impos de Ravenna progrediens Padum, Atesim, Brintam, Plavem, Liquentiam, Teliamentumque tranans, per Alpem Iuliam pendulus mon-tanis anfractibus, Dravum Norico, Oenum Breonis, Liccam Baiuaria, Danuvium Alamannia, Rhenum Germania transi-ens ac post Mosellam, Mosam, Axonam et Sequanam, Lige-rem et Garonnam, Aquitaniae maxima fluenta, transmit-tens, Pyrenaeis occurrens Iulio mense nivosis paene aut

itself twice vanquished, by words and by renown. But in the   3
case of those to whom the brilliance of their fine elo-
quence lends distinction, whose words cannot be concealed
without clearly inflicting a loss, who would have defrauded
the public if they had not published the flowering growth of
their rich eloquence, rightly the rays of fame have spread
their reputation everywhere so that praise extolled them
in their universal dispersion, wherever their poetry became
well known. On the other hand, in the case of those who
will be scorned if put on show, it is wiser if they are kept in
secret and silence. So it should not be as reprehensible for
what would arouse distaste to be unknown as for what of-
fends to be revealed. Let the loss be less when ignorance
is concealed rather than revealed, since in the former case
shame prevents notice being taken whereas in the latter a
display of brazenness inflicts notoriety.

Therefore, apostolic man and venerable bishop Gregory,   4
as you urgently demand that I produce and send to you
some of the works of my unskilled hand, I marvel that you
are enticed by love of my trifles, which, once they have been
revealed, can neither inspire admiration nor love. All the
more so because I wrote them in a daze, for the most part
either on horseback or half-awake, during my journey from
Ravenna, when I navigated the Po, Adige, Brenta, Piave,
Livenza, and Tagliamento, traveled through the Julian Alps
suspended on mountain passes, crossed the Drava in Nori-
cum, the Enn among the Breuni, the Lech in Bavaria, the
Danube in Alamannia, and the Rhine in Germany, and af-
ter the Moselle, the Meuse, the Aisne, and the Seine, passed
the Loire and the Garonne, the greatest of Aquitaine's riv-
ers, to arrive at the Pyrenees, still snowcapped in the month

equitando aut dormitando conscripserim, ubi inter barbaros longo tractu gradiens aut via fessus aut crapula brumali sub frigore Musa hortante nescio gelida magis an ebria novus
5 Orpheus lyricus silvae voces dabam, silva reddebat. Quid inter haec extensa viatica consulte dici potuerit censor ipse mensura, ubi me non urguebat vel metus ex iudice vel probabat usus ex lege nec invitabat favor ex comite nec emendabat lector ex arte, ubi mihi tantundem valebat raucum gemere quod cantare apud quos nihil disparat aut stridor anseris aut canor oloris, sola saepe bombicans barbaros leudos arpa relidens, ut inter illos egomet non musicus poeta sed muricus deroso flore carminis poema non canerem sed garrirem, quo residentes auditores inter acernea pocula salute bibentes insana Baccho iudice debaccharent. Quid ibi fabre dictum sit ubi quis sanus vix creditur, nisi secum pariter insanitur, quo gratulari magis est si vivere licet post bibere, de quo convivam thyrsicum non fatidicum licet exire, sed fatuum? Cum quantum ad mei sensus intellegentiam pertinet, quia se pigra non explicat, brutae animae ipsa ieiuna sunt ebria?

6   Hinc est quod latens opusculum, etsi minus videtur esse famosum, plus liberum, quia de examinatione non habet quod tam trepidet privatum quam publicum. Unde necessarie angusti sensus ingenium se mensuret censore quod est mittendum sub iudice. Sed quoniam humilem impulsum alacriter, acrius renitentem, sub testificatione divini myste-

of July; when in my lengthy progress among the barbarians, exhausted by the journey or hungover, in the winter chill, at the urging of a Muse whose coldness was perhaps matched by her drunkenness, I, a new lyric Orpheus, gave voice to the forest and the forest echoed it back. Judge for yourself 5 what on this long journey could be properly expressed when I had neither fear of a critic to impel me, nor the law of usage to test me, nor the goodwill of a companion to encourage me, nor a skillful reader to correct me, when a rough croak was as valued as a song among those who could not discriminate between a goose's honking and a swan's singing, often only on their harps strumming barbarian lays, so that among them I was not a poet of the Muses but like a mouse, nibbling on the blossoms of verse, and did not perform a poem but prattled it, while my listeners sat back among their maple-wood cups, crazily toasted each other in drink, and reveled under the jurisdiction of Bacchus. What can be artistically expressed where a person is hardly thought in his right mind unless he joins the general madness, where it is a cause for satisfaction if one continues living after a drinking bout, from which the thyrsus-wielding reveler departs not prophetic but pathetic? When, as far as I can estimate, because the insensate spirit cannot in its slowness express itself, its very fasts are drunken?

This is why a secret work, though it seems to lose fame, 6 gains in freedom, because if kept private rather than published it does not have the same cause to fear criticism. And so a talent of limited capacity must evaluate itself if it is to be submitted to critical scrutiny. But, though in my humility I vigorously resisted your eager persuasion, since you insistently urge me, calling on the divine mystery and invoking

rii et splendore virtutum beatissimi Martini coniurans hortaris sedulo ut contra pudorem meum deducar in publicum, me meis frivolis arbitrem scabrosi operis ignorantiam confitente, quod aliis poscentibus patefacere distuli, oboediendo cedo virtuti. Hanc saltim obtemperanti vicissitudinem repensurus, ut quia haec favore magis delectantur quam iudice, aut tibi tantummodo innotescentia relegas aut intimorum auribus tecum amicaliter quaeso conlatura committas.

VENANTI HONORI CLEMENTIANI
FORTUNATI, PRESBYTERI ITALICI

the brilliance of the blessed Martin's miracles, to swallow my embarrassment and to appear in public, I give way in obedience to your virtue and reveal what when others demanded I put off revealing, though in full knowledge of the triviality of my work and recognizing its roughness and lack of intelligence. At least you will compensate me with this reward for my obedience, that since these poems give more pleasure because of the goodwill of the reader than by critical judgment, either you will read them over but keep the knowledge to yourself or entrust them only, I beg, to the care of an audience of close acquaintances in a spirit of friendship.

VENANTIUS HONORIUS CLEMENTIANUS
FORTUNATUS, ITALIAN PRIEST

BOOK ONE

I

Ad Vitalem episcopum Ravennensem

Antistes Domini, meritis in saecula vivens,
    gaudia qui Christi de grege pastor habes,
cum te Vitalem voluit vocitare vetustas,
    noverat aeternum te meruisse diem,
5 dignus apostolica praefulgens mente sacerdos,
    qui sacer Andreae tam pia templa locas.
Quam bene pro meritis Domini consedit in aula,
    per quem digna Deo est aedificata domus!
Sumpsisti a Domino culmen cui culmina condis;
10 qui tibi digna dedit reddis honore vicem.
Emicat aula potens solido perfecta metallo,
    quo sine nocte manet continuata dies.
Invitat locus ipse Deum sub luce perenni,
    gressibus ut placidis intret amando lares.
15 Qui loca das populis, Dominum quo semper adorent,
    ut capiant veniam te facis esse viam.
Gratia, mens, animus, bonitas, dilectio plebis,
    et gradus et pietas te dedit esse patrem.
Prosperitas se vestra probat, quae gaudia supplens
20 intulit egregios ad tua vota viros.
Dux nitet hinc armis, praefectus legibus illinc;
    venerunt per quos crescere festa solent.

I

To Vitalis, bishop of Ravenna

Bishop of the Lord, by your virtues living forever, who take
joy in shepherding the flock of Christ, when your parents in
the past chose to call you Vitalis, they knew that you de-
served to win eternal light, a worthy priest, shining with the   5
spirit of the apostles, who piously built for Andrew so holy a
church. How rightly for his virtues he occupies the hall of
the Lord, by whom was founded an abode fit for God! You
have been raised up by the Lord for whom you raise up a
building, and repay with honor him who gave you your due.   10

The mighty church is aglow, finished with panels of metal,
where without any night day is always present. With its per-
petual light the very site bids welcome to God, that he may
lovingly enter his home with gracious step. In granting the   15
people a place continually to worship the Lord you make
yourself the way for them to receive pardon. Your kindness,
your spirit and character, your goodness and your love of the
people, your status and your holiness gave you your role as
their father. Your success is self-evident, for crowning your
happiness it has brought men of distinction to fulfill your   20
vows. Here shines a duke, brilliant in arms, there a prefect,
skilled in the laws; all have assembled who customarily en-
hance a celebration. So that you may not want for honor,

Ne tibi desit honor, populum Deus auxit opimum,
    qui vidit sensum hoc voluisse tuum.
25 Mysterium fidei complevit vota petenti.
    Felix cui Dominus quae cupis ipsa vehit!
Plurima divino celebres sollemnia dono
    atque Dei florens templa locando colas.

2

Versus de templo domni Andreae quod aedificavit Vitalis episcopus Ravennensis

Quisquis ad haec sancti concurris limina templi,
    si venias supplex, hic prece sumis opem.
Quam sacer antistes Vitalis condidit arcem,
    culmine quae celso est tempore ducta brevi,
5 fundavit, struxit, dotavit, deinde dicavit
    et meruit templi solvere vota sui.
Quo veneranda pii requiescunt viscera Petri,
    qui meruit solus clave ligare polos;
Paulus apostolica simul hac retinetur in aula,
10   seductor quondam qui modo doctor ovat;
hanc sacer Andreas propriam sibi vindicat arcem
    et cum fratre pio participata regit;
haec sua tecta replet Laurentius igne sereno,
    cui pia flamma dedit luce perenne diem;

God has exalted a noble people, for he saw that this was your heartfelt wish. The mystery of faith accomplished your will in response to your prayer. Happy are you to whom the Lord brings just what you want! By divine favor may you celebrate many ceremonies, and may you prosper to found and nurture churches of God. 25

2

Verses on the church of Lord Andrew built by Vitalis, bishop of Ravenna

All you who hurry to the threshold of this sacred church, if you come as a suppliant, by prayer you will receive aid here. The structure that the holy bishop Vitalis erected, which in a short time was brought to a great height, he founded, 5 built, endowed, then dedicated and duly paid his vow to raise this church. There rest the venerable relics of holy Peter, who alone won the right to secure heaven with his key; in this apostolic hall Paul also finds a place, once a tempter, 10 but who now rejoices to be called teacher; this structure saintly Andrew lays claim to for himself and rules over it in the company of his holy brother; Laurence too fills this building of his with a tranquil fire, to whom a holy flame

15   Vitali domus ista placet, qui vivus harenis
      defossus meruit perdere mortis iter;
   sunt loca Martini qui texit veste tonantem:
      ne magis algeret, se spoliare dedit;
   ecce Vigili arx est quem rustica turba peremit:
20   unde mori voluit, mors magis ipsa fugit;
   incolit haec pariter Marturius atque Sisennus,
      quos genus atque fides et tenet una salus;
   sanctus Alexander felixque Cicilia pollent,
      quos meritis omnes una corona manet.
25   Haec bonus antistes Vitale urguente Iohannes
      condidit egregio viscera sancta loco.
   O nimium felix, aeternum in lumen iture,
      cuius vita suo proficit ista Deo!

3

De basilica domni Stephani

Gloria celsa pios Domini circumdat amicos,
      quorum diffuso vivit in orbe decus.
Pertulit hic martyr pro Christo orientis in axe;
      ecce sub occasu templa beatus habet.
5   Fundatus virtute Dei, de morte triumphans
      excepit lapides cui petra Christus erat.

granted the gift of day with eternal light; this is a dwell- 15
ing favored by Vitalis, who buried alive in the earth won
for himself the right to overcome the journey to death; the
place holds Martin too, who clothed in his cloak the Lord:
he caused himself to be stripped so as not to endure further
chill; here is the shrine of Vigilius, whom a crowd of coun-
trymen slaughtered: because of his willingness to die, in- 20
stead death itself took flight; together Marturius and Sisen-
nus take up their dwelling in this place, whom a single family,
faith, and salvation unite; holy Alexander and the blessed
Cecilia lend their powerful presence: all these a single crown
awaits for their merits. These the good bishop John at Vi- 25
talis's urging laid up as holy relics in this venerable site. O
how very happy you are, destined to enter eternal light,
whose actions in this life work to benefit his God!

3

On a church of Lord Stephen

Lofty fame encompasses the saintly friends of the Lord,
whose glory lives on throughout the wide world. This martyr
suffered for Christ in eastern climes; but, see, the holy man
has churches in the West. Firm-founded on the strength of 5
God, in triumph over death he whose rock was Christ en-

Gens Iudaea ferox, Stephanum quem perdere credis,
  etsi carne, tamen nescit honore mori.
Ille tenet palmam meritis, tu crimine poenam;
10   possidet ille polos, tu magis ima petis.
Haec sacra Palladius levitae templa locavit,
  unde sibi fiat non peritura domus.

4

De basilica Sancti Martini

Emicat aula decens venerando in culmine ducta,
  nomine Martini sanctificata Deo,
cui vitae merito fiducia tanta coruscat
  ut populis tribuat quod pia vota rogant.
5 Extulit hanc Faustus devoto corde sacerdos,
  reddidit et Domino prospera dona suo.

dured a hail of stones. Cruel race of the Jews, the Stephen
you believe you are killing, though he is dead in the flesh, yet
in glory he cannot die. He earns the palm for his merits,
you earn punishment for your crime; he wins residence in   10
heaven, but you rather are bound for the depths. Palladius
established this holy church for the deacon so he could win
for himself a house that will not perish.

4

On a church of Saint Martin

This beautiful church is aglow, raised to a venerable height,
made sacred to God by the name of Martin. By the virtue of
his life, so brilliant is his influence that he grants to the peo-
ple what their holy prayers seek. Bishop Faustus raised this   5
church up in the devotion of his heart and rendered to his
Lord these beneficent gifts.

5

In cellulam Sancti Martini
ubi pauperem vestivit rogante
Gregorio episcopo

Qui celerare paras, iter huc deflecte, viator;
    hic locus orantem cautius ire docet.
Exul enim terris, caeli incola, saepe solebat
    clausus Martinus hinc aperire polos.
5 Aede sub hac habitans heremi secreta tenebat,
    per medios populos anachorita potens.
Hic se nudato tunica vestivit egenum:
    dum tegit algentem, plus calet ipse fide.
Tum vili tunica vestitur et ipse sacerdos
10   processitque inopi tegmine summus honor.
Qui tamen altaris sacra dum mysteria tractat,
    signando calicem signa beata dedit,
namque viri sacro de vertice flamma refulsit,
    ignis et innocui surgit ad astra globus,
15 ac brevibus manicis, fieret ne iniuria dextrae,
    texerunt gemmae qua caro nuda fuit;
bracchia nobilium lapidum fulgore coruscant
    inque loco tunicae pulchra zmaragdus erat.
Quam bene mercatur cui, dum vestivit egenum,
20   tegmine pro tunicae bracchia gemma tegit!

5

For the cell of Saint Martin where he clothed a poor man, written at the request of Bishop Gregory

Though you are about to hurry by, traveler, turn your steps here; this place instructs the devotee to slow his pace. For it was often his custom, as an exile on earth, but a citizen on high, for Martin, though enclosed, from here to lay open the sky. When he lived in this dwelling he practiced desert se- 5
clusion as a powerful hermit, though surrounded by people. Here he stripped off and clothed a poor man with his tunic: in clothing the chilled, he grew warmer himself by his faith. Then he dressed himself in a worthless tunic, despite being a bishop, and the highest dignity stepped forth in mean at- 10
tire. Yet when at the altar he was performing the holy Mass, in blessing the cup he revealed blessed miracles, for from the man's holy head a flame burst forth and a ball of harm-less fire rose to the stars. His sleeves were short, but jewels 15
clothed him where the flesh was bare, to prevent his hand being injured; his arms glittered with the radiance of pre-cious stones, and a beautiful emerald took the place of his tunic. What a happy exchange, for when he clothed the poor man, jewels covered the arms in exchange for the tu- 20

Tu quoque qui caelis habitas, Martine precator,
    pro Fortunato fer pia verba Deo.

Ad Gregorium
Imperiis parere tuis, pie care sacerdos,
25   quantum posse valet, plus mihi velle placet.

6

De basilica Sancti Martini

Qui cupit aeterna sociari in sede beatis,
    hos sibi participes per pia vota facit
nec patitur differre diu quod oportet agendo,
    cum bona quae dederit haec sua lucra putet.
5   Condidit ergo arvis delubra Leontius alma,
    talibus officiis intret ut ipse polos.
Martini meritis et nomine fulta coruscant,
    quem certum est terris signa dedisse poli,
qui leprae maculas medicata per oscula purgans
10   pacis ab amplexu morbida bella tulit.
Haec tamen ingenio sunt aedificata perito,
    quo nihil egregius gloria laudis eget.
Additur ad specimen locus ipse quod eminet arvis
    elatoque iugo colle tumente patet.

nic's covering! So too you who dwell in the heavens, Martin, our intercessor, on behalf of Fortunatus convey to God holy words of prayer.

To Gregory

To obey your commands, holy and beloved bishop, what- 25
ever power I have falls short of my will to comply.

6

On a church of Saint Martin

He who desires to join the blessed in their eternal abode by his holy vows associates those men with himself, nor does he long delay in performing the actions he must take, since the goods that he gives away he considers his gain. And so Leon- 5
tius set up in the country a welcoming shrine so that by such services he might make his own way to heaven. It shines out brightly, firm in the name and merits of Martin, for he, it is certain, on earth gave intimations of heaven. Cleansing the stains of leprosy by his curative kisses, with the embrace of 10
peace he banished wars waged by disease.

This building was the work of a man of talent and skill; the glory of praise needs no greater distinction than that. The site itself adds to its appeal, as high over the fields it

15 Altius educto sub se tenet omnia dorso
   et quacumque petit, deliciosa videt.
   A longe adveniens oculo vicinus habetur;
   iungitur aspectu dissociante loco.
   Quo fessus rapitur visu invitante viator;
20   si pede defecerit, lumine tractus adit.
   Quae Placidina sacris ornavit culmina velis,
   certantesque simul hic facit, illa colit.

7

In honorem basilicae
Sancti Martini quam aedificaverunt
Basilius et Baudegundis

Discite, mortales, fidei nihil esse quod obstet,
   cum sacra templa Dei flumine fixa manent.
Pulchra per angustos ut surgeret aula meatus,
   etsi mons vetuit, praebuit unda locum;
5 ut famularetur domui vaga lympha supernae,
   cursibus antiquas ars nova subdit aquas.
Cum Baudegunde quo mente Basilius una
   hoc renovans priscum reddit et auget opus.

stands out on the lofty slopes of a swelling hill. On a high, 15
extended ridge it overlooks all below, and everywhere it
looks the prospect is delightful. When a person approaches
from afar his eyesight makes him seem close; he draws near
in vision though far off in location. The weary traveler finds
energy in the inviting sight; though his feet grow tired, he 20
advances, drawn on by his eyes. Placidina decked out the
structure with sacred hangings; together in rivalry he built
the church, she decorated it.

7

In honor of a church
of Saint Martin that
Basil and Baudegund built

Learn, mortals, that nothing can be an obstacle to faith,
since a holy church of God stands fixed and firm in a river.
For a splendid basilica to rise up in a narrow defile, though a
mountain forbade it, a river provided the space; for the wan- 5
dering wave to pay service to the heavenly abode, a new art
constrained in their course the waters of old. There Basil, of
one mind with Baudegund, restored anew the ancient struc-

Sic, Martine, tuus honor amplus ubique meretur
10   ut loca nulla negent, quo tibi festa sonent.
Talibus officiis pacatus, opime sacerdos,
    quorum vota vides, redde benigne vicem.

8

De basilica Sancti Vincenti ultra Garonnam

Tempore vita brevis meritis fit longior almis
    angustosque dies tendit honore fides.
Post finem sine fine manet mens dedita Christo,
    linquens turbam hominum stat sociata Deo.
5   Hac ope suffultus Vincentius extat in aevum,
    gloria martyrii cuius opima viret,
vertice succiso rapuit qui ex morte triumphum
    et nova de terris proles ad astra volat.
Credidit unde necem, sancto dedit hostis honorem
10   percussorque magis morte perenne iacet:
Vicerat ille miser, hunc si iugulare nequisset,
    nam abstulit unde caput, contulit inde polum.
Huius amore novo pia vota Leontius explens,
    quo sacra membra iacent, stagnea tecta dedit,

ture and enlarged it. So, Martin, your abundant glory everywhere merits that no place refuse to let your festivities 10
ring out. In gratitude for such services, glorious bishop, recompense generously those whose vows you see performed.

8

On a church of Saint Vincent beyond the Garonne

The brief time of life grows longer by a man's saintly virtues, and faith with its glory extends the short span of days. After life's end a mind dedicated to Christ lives on endlessly; leaving the mass of humanity, it stands in the company of God. Secure in this blessing, Vincent lives on forever, the glory 5
of his martyrdom abundant and fresh; though his head was cut off, he snatched triumph from death, and from earth he flew in a new birth to the stars. His enemy thought he was bringing death, but he brought the saint glory and the exe- 10
cutioner instead lies low in perpetual death. That wretch would have triumphed if he had not been able to cut his throat, for by taking off his head he took him off to heaven.

Out of fresh love for this man, Leontius, fulfilling a pious

15 et licet eniteat meritis venerabile templum,
   attamen ornatum praebuit iste suum.
Praemia succedant operanti longa salutis,
   huius ut obsequiis culmina sancta micent.

9

Item de basilica
Sancti Vincenti Vernemetis

Cultoris Domini toto sonus exiit orbe
   nec locus est, ubi se gloria celsa neget,
sed cuius meritum scimus percurrere mundum,
   huius ubique viri surgere templa decet.
5 Ecce beata nitent Vincenti culmina summi,
   munere martyrii qui colit astra poli,
promptus amore pio quae papa Leontius olim
   condidit eximio consolidata loco.
Nomine Vernemetis voluit vocitare vetustas,
10   quod quasi fanum ingens Gallica lingua refert.
Auspicii praemissa fides erat arce futura,
   ut modo celsa domus staret honore Dei.
Hic etiam sanctus, Domini suffultus amore,
   virtutis summae signa tremenda dedit.
15 Nam cum templa Dei praesul de more dicavit,
   martyris adventu daemonis ira fugit:

vow, donated a roof of tin where his revered relics lie, and   15
though the sacred church gleams brightly with the saint's
virtues, yet Leontius too brought to it his own decoration.
May this benefactor enjoy the reward of extended good
health, so that the holy edifice may shine by his services.

9

Again on the church of Saint Vincent at Vernemet

The renown of the Lord's devotee has spread all through the
world, and there is nowhere glory refuses to exalt him; in-
deed, it is proper that everywhere churches should be raised
up for a man whose virtue we know traverses the world.
Look, here the blessed roofs of mighty Vincent shine out,   5
who as reward for martyrdom inhabits the starry heavens.
Bishop Leontius, impelled by holy love, established this
structure on a firm foundation at an excellent site. The peo-
ple of the past chose to dub it by name Vernemet, which in   10
the Gallic tongue conveys the sense great shrine. With this
omen a pledge was made of a building that was to come, that
soon a lofty house would stand there in honor of God. Here
too the saint, sustained by the love of the Lord, gave daunt-
ing proofs of his high power. For when according to custom   15
the bishop dedicated God's church, at the coming of the
martyr a demon's rage took to flight: a sick man, suffering a

redditur incolumis quidam de peste maligna,
    cui vidisse pii templa medella fuit.
Emicat aula potens divino plena sereno,
20   ut merito placeat hic habitare Deo.
Nunc specie suadente loci ac virtutis honore
    evocat hic populos hinc decus, inde salus.
Qui plebem accendit venerandae conditor arcis,
    talibus officiis praemia iusta metet.

10

De domno Nazario

Culmina conspicui radiant veneranda Nazari,
    cuius membra solum, spiritus astra tenet,
Semine terrigeno terrenis usibus exsors,
    inmortale bonum pulvere natus homo,
5   nil carnale volens, sed Christi praemia poscens,
    sanguine de proprio victima digna Deo.
Haec tibi templa, sacer, devota Leontius offert
    maioremque suam hinc cupit esse domum.
Hic prius angusto fabricata est machina gyro,
10   quo neque tunc poterat plebs veneranda capi,
deiectamque solo rursus fundavit ab imo
    et dedit haec quae nunc amplificata placent.

cruel disease, was made sound; the mere sight of the saint's
sanctuary served as cure. The mighty church is aglow, filled
with a calm, divine light, so that rightly here God is pleased   20
to make his abode. Now the beauty of the site and the glory
of its miracles attract the people; two forces summon them,
its splendor and its healing powers. May the founder of this
sacred building, inspiration of his people, reap just rewards
for such services as these.

10

On the Lord Nazarius

The sacred roofs of brilliant Nazarius spread their glow; his
body occupies the earth, but his spirit the stars. Created
from earthly seed but alien to earthly practices, he was a
man born from dust but enjoying immortal blessing, desir-   5
ing nothing fleshly, but seeking the rewards of Christ, with
his own blood a sacrifice worthy of God. Leontius offers
this church, holy man, dedicated to you, and in so doing de-
sires a greater house for himself. Here previously a structure
was built of narrow compass, where the holy congregation   10
then could not be housed. He razed it to the ground, built
it again from its foundations, and provided this enlarged
building which now wins applause.

II

De basilica domni Dionysi

Qui cupis egregii structorem noscere templi,
    tam pia non patiar vota latere tibi.
Longius hinc olim sacra cum delubra fuissent
    et plebs ob spatium saepe timeret iter,
5 exiguam dederat hic praesul Amelius arcem,
    Christicolam populum nec capiente loco.
Quo vitae claudente diem dehinc prole graduque
    venit ad heredem hoc opus atque locus,
fundavitque piam hanc papa Leontius aulam,
10 obtulit et Domino splendida dona suo.
Quam venerandus habet propriam Dionysius aedem,
    nomine sub cuius sanctificata nitet,
qui fervente fide, Christi solidatus amore,
    vertice subposito colla secanda dedit.
15 Membrorum contemptor erat cupiendo coronam,
    vile putans quicquid ferret amore Dei.
Ut moritura caro donum immortale pararet,
    vulnera dilexit, sed caritura nece.
Hostili occurrens gladio se misit Olympo;
20 unde mori voluit, vota salutis habet.
Nec angusta prius subtraxit fana sacerdos,
    haec nisi perficeret quae modo culta placent,
assidue in prisco peragens cerimonia templo,
    donec rite sequens consolidasset opus.

II

On a church of the Lord Dionysius

For you who wish to know the builder of this fine church, I will not allow such holy wishes to remain hidden. Seeing that once the holy shrine had been further from this place and that because of the distance the people often dreaded the journey, Bishop Amelius established here a small foundation, though its site did not accommodate all the Christian people. When he brought to a close the course of his life, then by birth and status, this task and this site devolved upon his heir, and Bishop Leontius set up here this holy church and offered brilliant gifts to his Lord. This shrine revered Dionysius possesses as his own, from whose name it wins sanctity and luster. For he in the fervor of his faith, firm-founded on the love of Christ, bowed his head and offered his neck to be severed. In coveting a crown he had contempt for his limbs, thinking but slight whatever he endured for God's love. So that flesh soon to die might win a deathless prize, he welcomed wounds that were to bring him no death. By meeting the enemy's sword he consigned himself to heaven; because he wished to die, he fulfilled his wish for salvation. Nor did the bishop remove the cramped shrine until he had completed what now charms with its finery, continuing dutifully to perform in the old church the proper rites, until in due order he had completed work on its successor.

12

De basilica Sancti Bibiani

Digna sacerdotis Bibiani templa coruscant,
    quo si iusta petis, dat pia vota fides.
Quae praesul fundavit ovans Eusebius olim,
    ne tamen expleret raptus ab orbe fuit.
5 Cui mox Emerius successit in arce sacerdos,
    sed coeptum ut strueret, ferre recusat onus.
Qui precibus commisit opus tibi, papa Leonti,
    cuius ad hoc votum iugiter instat amor.
Ultro tale decus tibi se servavit agendum,
10   nec nisi tu fueras qui loca sacra dares.
O meritum iusti mansurum in luce perenni,
    per quem se cupiunt templa verenda coli!
Sacra sepulchra tegunt Bibiani argentea tecta,
    unianimis tecum quae Placidina dedit.
15 Quo super effusum rutilans intermicat aurum
    et spargunt radios pura metalla suos.
Ingenio perfecta novo tabulata coruscant
    artificemque putas hic animasse feras.
Sed cui vos animo donaria tanta dedistis,
20   hic agat ut vobis stet diuturna salus,
nec dubitent qui digna ferunt, sibi magna rependi,
    dum quoque pro parvis reddat opima Deus.

12

On the church of Saint Bibianus

The brilliance of this church is worthy of Bishop Bibianus; if you make just requests here, faith fulfills your holy prayers. In the past Bishop Eusebius with joy laid its foundations, but he was taken from this world and unable to finish the work. Soon Emerius succeeded him in the eminence of the 5 bishopric, but he balked at the task of completing the building. By his prayers, though, he consigned to you, Bishop Leontius, this duty and in the fulfillment of this charge you show constant love and devotion. Such a distinction readily reserved itself for you to perform it; no one but you could 10 have provided this sacred site. How the merit of the just man will endure in perpetual light, by whom holy churches themselves long to be venerated!

   Silver coating covers the sacred tomb of Bibianus, the gift of Placidina, of one mind with you. Laid upon it the sheen 15 of gold intermingles its glimmer, and the unalloyed metal spreads widely its rays. A paneled ceiling of novel and ingenious construction lends luster; you'd think here the artist had brought wild animals to life. May the saint to whom you have given wholeheartedly such gifts assure that your salva- 20 tion is firm established forever, and may those who bring worthy offerings not doubt they will receive great rewards, since even for small services God renders rich recompense.

13

De basilica Sancti Eutropis

Quantus amor Domini maneat tibi, papa Leonti,
    quem sibi iam sancti templa novare monent!
Eutropitis enim venerandi antistitis aula
    conruerat senio dilacerata suo,
5 nudatosque trabes paries vacuatus habebat,
    pondere non tecti, sed male pressus aquis.
Nocte sopore levi cuidam veniente ministro
    instauratorem te docet esse suum.
Pro mercede tui meruit magis ille moneri;
10   o felix de quo fit pia cura Deo!
Nunc meliore via viruit renovata vetustas
    et lapsae fabricae flos redivivus adit.
Aetas accessit, sed haec iuvenescit honore;
    unde senes fieret, iunior inde redit.
15 Hic scalptae camerae decus interrasile pendit:
    quos pictura solet, ligna dedere iocos.
Sumpsit imagineas paries simulando figuras:
    quae neque tecta prius, haec modo picta nitent.
Urbis Santonicae primus fuit iste sacerdos
20   et tibi qui reparas iure priora dedit.
Cum sua templa tenet sanctus habitando quiete,
    instauratori reddet amore vicem.

13

On the church of Saint Eutropius

How great a love is in store for you, Bishop Leontius, from
the Lord, when now already the saints bid you restore their
temples! For the church of the revered bishop Eutropius,
broken down by old age, had tumbled into ruins, walls were 5
laid bare and beams were exposed, caused to collapse not by
the weight of the ceiling but by damp. At night, the saint in-
structed one of the clergy, who was only lightly asleep, that
you were to be his restorer. It was in honor of you that he
was honored with the message. O happy the man who en- 10
joys God's loving concern!

Now the old, made new, is refreshed and improved, and
the flower of its fallen fabric comes back to life once more.
Its age has increased, but that age has the glory of youth;
from its very years it returns all the younger. Here is sus- 15
pended a beautifully worked carved ceiling: wood has pro-
vided the pleasure that a picture usually provides. The wall
has received images that imitate figures: what once was not
even covered, now is radiant with paintings.

This man was the first bishop of the city of Saintes, and 20
to you who revive him he has rightly granted primacy. Now
the saint occupies his shrine, dwelling there in peace; out of
love he will pay recompense to his restorer.

14

De calice Leonti episcopi

Summus in arce Dei pia dona Leontius offert,
  votis iuncta sacris et Placidina simul.
Felices quorum labor est altaribus aptus,
  tempore qui parvo non peritura ferunt.

15

De Leontio episcopo

Inter quos genuit radians Aquitanicus axis,
  egregiis meritis culmina prima tenes.
Civibus ex Gallis supereminet alta potestas;
  tu potior reliquis et tibi nemo prior.
5 Praecedis multos nulli minor atque secundus
  nec superest aliquid quod dare possit honor.
Qui cum se primo vestivit flore iuventus,
  parvus eras annis et gravitate senes.
Versus ad Hispanas acies cum rege sereno,
10 militiae crevit palma secunda tuae,

14

On a chalice of Bishop Leontius

Supreme in the high service of God, Leontius presents holy offerings, and along with him Placidina, his companion in sacred vows. Happy are those who devote their efforts to the altars and in a brief period of time carry off imperishable rewards.

15

On Bishop Leontius

Among those to whom the brilliant clime of Aquitaine gave birth, you hold first rank by your outstanding merits. Your lofty power overtops all the citizens of Gaul; you surpass all others; none is superior to you. You take precedence over 5 many, subordinate and second to none, and nothing is left that honor can bestow upon you. When your youth was clothed in its first flowering, you were a child in years, but old in dignity. You campaigned against Spain with your serene king and won a second palm for your service in war. 10

cuius primitiae tanto placuere relatu,
    ut meritis esset debitus iste gradus,
nec poterant subito tibi culmina celsa parari,
    haec nisi digna tuum promeruisset opus.
15 Nobilitate potens praecellis, papa Leonti,
    clarus ab antiquis, si numerentur avi.
Nam genus et proavi vel quicquid in ordine dicam,
    per proceres celsos currit origo vetus.
Tempora diffugiunt et stat tamen aula parentum
20   nec patitur lapsum te reparante domus.
Nobilitas longos non inclinavit in annos,
    cui magis ascensum proles opima dedit.
Inclita progenies ornavit luce priores,
    heredis radio splendet origo patrum.
25 De radice sua vestita est flore vetustas,
    quam merito vestrae laudis obumbrat honor.
Quamvis non aliquis potior modo possit haberi,
    tu tibi praecedis amplificando patres.
Emicat altus apex generosa stemmata pandens,
30   cuius apud reges unica palma patet.
Ecclesiae nunc iura regis, venerande sacerdos;
    altera nobilitas additur inde tibi.
Pontificalis apex quamvis sit celsus in orbe,
    postquam te meruit, crevit adeptus honor.
35 Aula Dei et pastor vicibus sibi praemia reddunt:
    illi tu ornatum, spem dedit illa tibi.
Munere divino pariter floretis utrique:
    tu mercede places, illa decore nitet.
Tertius a decimo huic urbi antistes haberis,
40   sed primus meritis enumerandus eris.

Your first acts won so much acclaim in the telling that by
your merits you won this high status as your due, nor could
lofty eminence have been bestowed on you so quickly if
your actions had not deserved this fitting reward. Bishop 15
Leontius, you excel in the prestige of nobility, distinguished
by the lengthy roll call of your ancestral line. For family and
descent, every generation I can number, trace from ancient
beginnings a succession of noble patricians. The seasons
pass, yet your family's halls stand firm, and your house suf- 20
fers no decline with you to bolster its fortunes. Its nobil-
ity has not diminished over the long sequence of years, but
rather its splendid offspring has caused it to rise. A famous
scion has adorned his predecessors with his light, and his
forefathers' ancestry shines with the radiance of their heir.
The family's past is adorned with a flower sprung from its 25
own roots, a past that the glory of your praise rightly over-
shadows. While no one else now can be held your superior,
by increasing your ancestors' honor you even excel yourself.
Your high distinction shines out, revealing your noble de-
scent; because of it you enjoy unique acclaim among royalty. 30

But now you hold sway over the church, revered bishop;
from that a second nobility accrues to you. Although episco-
pal distinction is exalted in the world, after it laid claim to
you, that honor you attained grew in status. The church of 35
God and its shepherd provide each other with mutual bene-
fits: you have given it adornment, it has given you hope. By
God's bounty each of you flourishes equally: you please by
your generosity, it gleams in its beauty. You are accounted
the thirteenth bishop of this city, but because of your merits 40
you will have to be numbered first. You recalled the ancient

Templa vetusta Dei revocasti in culmine prisco
   postque suum lapsum nunc meliora placent;
flore iuventutis senio fugiente coruscant
   et tibi laeta favent, quo renovante virent.
45 Ut tu plus ageres, incendia tecta cremarunt
   et nunc laude tua pulchrius illa micant,
Nullaque flammicremae senserunt damna ruinae,
   quae modo post ignes lumine plena nitent.
Credo quod ex sese voluissent ipsa cremari
50   ut labor ille tuus haec meliora daret.
Post cineres consumpta suos tenuesque favillas
   sic solet et phoenix se renovare senes.
Instaurata etiam sacri est baptismatis aula,
   quo maculas veteres fons lavat unus aquis.
55 Ecce beata sacrae fundasti templa Mariae,
   nox ubi victa fugit semper habendo diem.
Lumine plena micans imitata est aula Mariam:
   illa utero lucem clausit et ista diem.
Nec solum hic, sed ubique micant tua templa, sacerdos,
60   inter quae plaudens Santonus illa docet.
Qui loca das populis, ubi Christum iugiter orent,
   unde salus veniat te facis esse viam.
Ecclesiaeque domus crescente cacumine pollet
   et probat esse tuum, quod modo culta placet.
65 Fecisti ut libeat cunctos huc currere cives
   et domus una vocet quicquid in urbe manet.
Ornasti patriam cui dona perennia praestas,
   tu quoque dicendus Burdegalense decus.
Quantum inter reliquas caput haec super extulit urbes,
70   tantum pontifices vincis honore gradus.

churches of God to their former eminence, and after their collapse they now are more pleasing than ever. They glitter with the flower of youth, all old age fled, and joyfully sound your acclaim, by whose work of restoration they thrive. To 45 add to your efforts, fire burned down their roofs, but now to your credit they gleam all the finer. They felt no loss from the fiery destruction, since now after the flames they shine full of light. I believe of their own free will they wished to be burned so that now your efforts could bring them these 50 benefits. Even so, when it is burned up, reduced to ashes and fine powder, the phoenix is accustomed to renew itself in old age. The hall of a sacred baptistery also has been restored, where a single spring cleanses ancient stains with its waters. Here you have founded a holy church to the blessed 55 Mary, where night is bested and flees, and it is always day. The glittering church full of light is an imitation of Mary: she enclosed light in her womb, it encloses day.

Not only here, but everywhere your churches shine forth, my bishop; among others the citizen of Saintes rejoices to 60 tell the same tale. You give the people sites where they can constantly pray to Christ, and so make yourself the path from which salvation can come. The house of the church gains prestige as it gains in height, and shows that its present finery is all due to you. You have brought it about that all 65 citizens gladly assemble here, and this one home summons to it the whole of the city. By the undying gifts you give it, you have beautified your homeland, you who also deserve to be called the glory of Bordeaux. As high as it has raised its head above all other cities, so you surpass other bishops 70

Inferiora velut sunt flumina cuncta Garonnae,
    non aliter vobis subiacet omnis apex.
Rhenus ab Alpe means neque tantis spumat habenis,
    fortior Hadriacas nec Padus intrat aquas;
75 Danuvius par est, quia longius egerit undas;
    haec ego transcendi, iudico nota mihi.
Muneribusque piis dotasti altaria Christi,
    cum tua vasa ferunt viscera sancta Dei.
Nam cruor et corpus, Domini libamina summi,
80   rite ministerio te tribuente venit.
O felix cuius ditat pia templa facultas,
    cui res ista magis non peritura manet!
Non aerugo teret mordaci dente talentum
    nec contra haec fures arma dolosa movent,
85 et data res vivit, facit et bene vivere dantem;
    cum moritur terris, ducitur inde polis.
Haec possessor habet quicquid transmiserit ante;
    sola tenet secum quae prius ire facit.
Haec tibi templa dabunt et vasa sacrata, sacerdos,
90   et quicquid reliquum nec numerare queo.
Ecclesiae culmen per tempora longa gubernes
    et mercede pia fructus ubique mices.
Cogor amore etiam Placidinae pauca referre,
    quae tibi tunc coniunx, est modo cara soror.
95 Lumen ab Arcadio veniens genitore refulget,
    quo manet augustum germen, Avite, tuum.
Imperii fastus toto qui rexit in orbe,
    cuius adhuc pollens iura senatus habet.

in the status of your office. Just as all rivers are inferior to
the Garonne, so every eminence is subordinate to you. The
Rhine issuing from the Alps does not foam with such great
vehemence, nor the Po enter more forcefully the Adriatic
sea; the Danube is its equal, for its waters have longer to 75
flow; I have crossed them; I judge of things about which I
know. With your holy donations you have enriched the al-
tars of Christ, since your vessels contain the sacred body of
God. For it is by your gift that the blood and the body, offer-
ings of the Lord on high, are present at the proper fulfill- 80
ment of the rite. O happy is he whose wealth enriches holy
churches! All the more does he retain his possessions, des-
tined never to perish. Rust will not wear away his talent with
its corrosive bite, nor do thieves turn treacherous weapons
against these gifts. Property given both lives on and causes 85
the giver to live in contentment; when he dies on earth, he is
conducted from there to the heavens. He keeps in his pos-
session whatever he has sent on before him and retains for
himself only what he caused to go on ahead. These blessings,
my bishop, your churches and your sacred vessels will give
you, and all your other gifts that I am unable even to num- 90
ber. May you direct the high eminence of the church for
many long years, and be resplendent everywhere in enjoy-
ment of a holy reward.

I am obliged by my love to say a few words too of Pla-
cidina, who once was your wife, but now is your dear sis-
ter. From the light of her father Arcadius she derives her 95
own splendor, for in her survives, Avitus, your imperial fore-
runner. He held imperial sway throughout the whole world,
with an authority the still powerful senate possesses. If you

Humani generis si culmina prima requiras,
100   semine Caesareo nil superesse potest.
Sed genus ipsa suum sensus moderamine vicit,
        cuius ab eloquio dulcia mella fluunt,
cara, serena, decens, sollers, pia, mitis, opima,
        quae bona cuncta gerit, quicquid honore placet.
105   Moribus, ingenio, meritorum luce coruscans
        ornavit sexum mens pretiosa suum.
      Plurima cur referam quantis sit praedita rebus,
        quae potuit votis nupta placere tuis?
Augeat haec vobis vitam cui templa dedistis
110   culminibusque suis culmina vestra tegat.

16

Hymnus de Leontio episcopo

Agnoscat omne saeculum
        antistitem Leontium,
        Burdegalense praemium,
        dono superno redditum.
5   Bilinguis ore callido
        crimen fovebat invidum,
        ferens acerbum nuntium
        hunc iam sepulchro conditum.

seek the highest pinnacle of the human race, nothing can 100
excel the blood of an emperor. But she herself by her modest
demeanor has surpassed her descent, for from her speech
the sweetness of honey flows. Beloved and calm, comely,
clever, pious, gentle, and generous, she displays every virtue
that wins favor and regard. Splendid in her character and 105
her nature, in the brilliance of her merits, her precious mind
is an ornament of her sex. Why should I enumerate at length
the qualities that she displays, when she was able to win your
favor in marriage as your wife? May she to whom you dedi-
cated a church enhance both your lives and protect your 110
eminence with her own.

16

Hymn on Bishop Leontius

Let every age pay honor to Bishop Leontius, the glory of
Bordeaux, restored by divine favor.

A deceiver with treacherous tongue hatched a hateful 5
crime, bringing the bitter news that he was already laid in

Celare se non pertulit
10   qui triste funus edidit;
      etsi nocere desiit,
      insana vota prodidit.
Deceptus arte noxia
      cassata deflet crimina,
15   dum quae putabat tristia
      conversa sunt in gaudia.
Exempla saeva protulit,
      calcanda cuncto tempore,
      ut iam sibi conscriberet
20   decreta vivo antistite.
Fucata res haec contigit,
      vitanda casto pectore,
      superstite ut praesumeret
      post fata quod vix debuit.
25 Gravat sacerdos ordinem
      qui episcopatum sic petit;
      praecepta qui conplectitur,
      fugit honoris ambitum.
Hoc si cui sit debitum,
30   coactus ascendat gradum,
      non se petente callide,
      sed dante Christi munere.
Ineptus est quis ipse se
      praeferre vult ecclesiae,
35   nam rem sacratam sumere
      electio divina sit.
Karus sacerdos ordinem
      Hilarius non ambiit,
      Martinus illud effugit,
40   Gregorius vix sustulit.

48

his tomb. The man who reported the sad death was not able   10
to conceal himself long; although he had ceased to do harm,
he betrayed his maddened intent. Thwarted in his wicked
plan he lamented his failed crimes, since what he thought   15
would produce grief had actually turned to joy. He set an evil
example to be spurned for all time in composing his own
decrees while the bishop was still alive. This act of decep-   20
tion took place, alien to every honest heart, to dare with the
bishop still living what was hardly permissible were he dead.
A priest impairs his order who seeks to be bishop in this   25
way; he who embraces right practice avoids contending for
honors.

The man to whom this falls as his due should assume the   30
rank against his will, not through his own cunning canvass-
ing, but by the bountiful gift of Christ. Foolish is he who by
his own efforts seeks to win preferment in the church, for   35
the assumption of a sacred office should be a choice made
by God. The beloved bishop Hilary did not contend for of-
fice, Martin positively fled from it, and Gregory reluctantly   40

Leges refutant ambitum,
  invasor omnis pellitur;
  quod respuunt praetoria
  vitet nefas ecclesia.
45 Maligna erant certamina
  de sede non tamen sua.
  Quae nec pati desiderat
  non inferat mens inproba.
  Nec longiore tempore
50   versantur in hoc murmure;
  dum cogitant succedere,
  redit sacerdos qui fuit.
  Orante plebe protenus,
  dum nemo credit, redditur.
55   Quae confluunt post tristia
  maiora sunt haec gaudia.
  Plausu favebat civitas,
  cui redit felicitas,
  orbata quem defleverat
60   patrem recepit anxia,
  Quem vix putabat redditum,
  praeventa voto prospero.
  Res mira quando cernitur,
  solet stupere visio.
65 Recolligit rector gregem
  errore captum semitae.
  Pastoris arce cognita
  gavisa sunt ovilia.
  Sumpsit gradum quo tempore,
70   regressus est eo die.
  Quis non superno munere
  hoc contigisse praedicet?

endured it. The laws condemn self-seeking, every usurper
is expelled; the act that palaces reject the church should
shrink from as a crime. The contention was malicious for a   45
see not even his own. A wicked mind should not inflict what
it does not wish itself to suffer.

But men were not for too long a time caught up in such   50
speculations, for while they were planning his succession, he
who was their bishop returned to them. The people prayed
continuously; though no one believed, he was restored. All   55
the greater are those joys that after grief come flooding
in. The citizens, whose happiness had been restored, cele-
brated with applause; the father whose loss they had be-
wailed though still perturbed they welcomed home; sur-   60
prised by their prayers' fulfillment, they scarcely thought he
was restored. Whenever a miracle is seen, sight customarily
feels amazement. Their ruler reassembled his flock, which   65
had been tricked into straying from the path. The sheepfold
was overjoyed when it recognized the eminence of its shep-
herd. He returned on the very day on which he had received   70
his office. Who would deny that this occurred by the bounty
of God on high? In the past, when he was elected, the peo-

Tantum nec ante praemium
    plebi fuit, cum factus est,
75   laetata quantum tunc fuit,
    quando recepit praesulem.
Venite, cives, plaudite
    et vota votis addite,
    cui facta sunt miracula,
80   servent eum caelestia.
Χρς sereno lumine
    circumvolet quem reddidit,
    ut trina crescat gratia
    mercede, vita, gloria.
85 Ymnum canendo concrepet
    quisquis Deo non invidet:
    laus eius est qui praesulem
    de mortis ore retrahit.
Zelante fido pectore
90   tam vera dici non pudet.
    Haec parva nobilissimo
    papae damus Leontio.

17

Ad Placidinam

Munera parva nimis, pia, suscipe quaeso libenter,
    quae magis ipsa decens munus in orbe micas.
Fluctibus e mediis ut haec daret insula vobis,
    oceanus tumidas murmure pressit aquas.

ple's satisfaction was not as great as their joy at this time   75
when they welcomed back their prelate.

Gather round, you citizens, and applaud, and add present
prayers to past, that the heavens preserve the man for whom
these miracles were performed. May Christ wreathe with   80
radiant light the man he has restored so that he may increase
in threefold grace, in good works, life, and glory. Let all who   85
are not enemies of God sound out this hymn in song. It
sings the praise of him who saved the bishop from death's
jaws. There is no shame to tell such truth in fervent faith of   90
heart. We bring this modest offering to Leontius, noblest
bishop.

17

To Placidina

Receive, I beg, O holy one, my all too modest gifts with fa-
vor, for you are more becoming, a brilliant ornament in the
world. For an island to make you this present from the midst
of the waves, the ocean suppressed its heaving and murmur-

5 Quae loca dum volui properans agnoscere ponti,
     a Borea veniens reppulit unda furens.
  Prosperitas ut vestra tamen se plena probaret,
     obtulit in terris quod peteretur aquis.

18

De Bissonno villa Burdegalensi

  Est locus, aestifero quamvis sit tempore fervor,
     quo viret assidue flore refectus ager:
  Respirant croceis depicta coloribus arva,
     fragrat odoriferis blandior herba comis.
5 Incola Bissonnum vocat hunc de nomine prisco
     (milia septem urbs hinc Burdegalensis abest),
  qua possessor amans praetoria grata locavit,
     partibus atque tribus porticus aequa subit.
  Straverat ipsa solo senio rapiente vetustas,
10   perdiderat vultum forma decora suum.
  Haec meliore via revocat labor ille Leonti,
     quo praesente domos nulla ruina premit.
  Nunc quoque prosperius velut aula sepulta resurgit
     et favet auctori vivificata suo.

ing waters. When I wished in my eagerness to explore this 5
stretch of the sea, the frenzy of the breakers rolling in from
the North drove me back. But your good fortune exhibited
itself in abundance, for it brought to sight on land what was
sought in the water.

18

On the Villa of Bissonum,
in the Bordelais

There is a spot where even in the boiling heat of summer
the land is always green, made fresh with flowers. The fields
are scented, spangled with saffron coloring, the turf breathes
odors and entices with its scented grasses. The natives call 5
this place Bissonum from an ancient name (Bordeaux is sit-
uated seven miles away). Here its loving owner has built a
charming residence, where a well-proportioned portico ad-
vances on three sides. Time had laid the building low as old
age took its toll, its pleasing form had lost its former beauty. 10
But Leontius by his efforts set it on recovery's path; when
he is present, ruin does not threaten any dwelling. Now too
the halls, once as if entombed, rise anew still finer, and re-

15   Reddidit interea prisco nova balnea cultu,
      quo recreant fessos blanda lavacra viros.
   Hic referunt nutrisse lupos deserta tenentes:
      intulit hic homines, expulit unde feras.

19

De Vereginis villa Burdegalensi

Inter opima ferax qua volvitur unda Garonnae,
   Vereginis ripis vernat amoenus ager.
Hic brevis ascensus leni subit aggere clivum,
   carpit et obliqua molle viator iter.
5 Altior a planis arvis minor eminet altis,
    nec humilis nimium necve superbit apex.
Colle sedet medio domus aedificata decenter,
    cuius utrumque latus hinc iacet, inde tumet.
Machina celsa casae triplici suspenditur arcu,
10   quo pelagi pictas currere credis aquas.
Exilit unda latens vivo generata metallo
    dulcis et inriguo fonte perennis aquae,
Quo super accumbens celebrat convivia pastor
    inclusoque lacu pisce natante bibit.
15 Nunc renovanda venit papae mercede Leonti,
    quem dominum longo tempore culta cupit.

stored to life they celebrate their patron. At the same time 15
he returned new baths to their former splendor, where the
enticing pools refresh weary people. Here they say in a
wilderness wolves were once raised: he drove out animals
from here and brought men in.

19

On the villa of Vereginis, in the Bordelais

Where in a rich landscape the fertile stream of the Garonne
flows, at Vereginis verdant fields bring charm to its banks.
Here a short climb ascends the slope by a gentle path, and
the traveler takes an easy slanting course. Its summit stands 5
higher than the plain below, less high than the tops, nei-
ther too low-lying nor too proud. On midslope the villa sits,
a splendid edifice; on one side the land falls away, on the
other it rises up. The lofty structure of the building is raised
on triple arches; you imagine the seawaters painted there 10
are actually flowing. A hidden watercourse bursts forth into
life from the native rock in a running spring of sweet, ever-
flowing water. Above it reclines the shepherd to celebrate
his banquets, and he drinks as fish swim in an enclosed pool
below. The villa now seeks renewal from the generosity of 15
Bishop Leontius, whom in its new finery it wishes long to be
its master.

20

De Praemiaco villa Burdegalensi

Quamvis instet iter retraharque volumine curae,
    ad te pauca ferens carmine flecto viam.
Captus amore tui numquam memoranda tacebo
    te neque praetereo praetereundo locum;
5 Cui quae digna loquar? Si syllaba quarta recedat,
    Praemiacum pollens, praemia nomen habes.
Deliciis obsessus ager viridantibus arvis
    et naturalis gratia ruris inest.
Condita quo domus est, planus tumor exit in altum,
10 nec satis elato vertice regnat apex.
Qua superincumbens locus est devexus in amnem,
    florea gemmato gramine prata virent.
Leniter adpulsus quotiens insibilat Eurus,
    flexa supinatis fluctuat herba comis.
15 Hinc alia de parte seges flavescit aristis
    pinguis et altricem palmes opacat humum.
Piscibus innumeris non deficit unda Garonnae,
    et si desit agris fruges, abundat aquis.
Sed te quaerebant haec munera tanta, Leonti;
20 solus defueras qui bona plena dares.
Nam quod pulchra domus, quod grata lavacra nitescunt,
    consolidatorem te cecinere suum.
Ut tamen adquirant adhuc fabricanda decorem,
    temporibus longis haec tua dona regas.

20

On the villa of Praemiacum, in the Bordelais

Although my journey beckons and I am recalled by a burden of care, I turn aside from my course to make you a small of-fering in song. In my devoted love for you I shall never be silent about what should be spoken, and I do not pass you by as I pass by the place. What should I say worthy of it? If ⁵ the fourth syllable is removed, powerful Praemiacum, you are named a premier location. The land is full of delights, the fields are green, and the countryside there has a natural beauty. The villa is set where a hill, rising to a height, flat-tens out; though of no great elevation, the summit domi- ¹⁰ nates the scene. Where the elevated site slopes down to the river, flowered meadows bloom, green with jeweled grass. Whenever the east wind rustles and gently blows, plants bend and wave, turning up their leaves. Elsewhere a harvest ¹⁵ grows golden ears of grain, and a fertile vine-branch shades the fostering earth. In fish beyond number the Garonne's stream never fails; if crops were to fail the fields, its waters still are full. But these great gifts lacked you alone, Leontius; only you were needed to make the good things complete. ²⁰ Because your beautiful house and charming baths shine in splendor, in this they have sung your praise, who made firm their fabric. But so that what is still to be built possess its own beauty, may you disburse these gifts of yours for long years to come.

21

De Egircio flumine

Laus tibi forte minor fuerat, generose Garonna,
    si non exiguas alter haberet aquas.
Lubricat hic quoniam tenuato Egircius haustu,
    praefert divitias paupere fonte tuas.
5 Denique dissimilem si conparet ullus utrumque,
    hic ubi fit rivus, tu, puto, Nilus eris.
Te famulans intrat, sed hunc tua regna refrenant;
    Gallicus Euphrates tu fluis, iste latet.
Nam quantum oceanum tumidus tu cursibus auges,
10   iste tuas tantum crescere praestat aquas.
Torrida praesertim cum terris incubat aestas
    ac sitiente solo tristis anhelat ager,
cum Titan radiis ferventibus exarat arva
    et calor ignifero vomere findit humum,
15 languidus arentes fugiens vix explicat undas
    et cum pisce suo palpitat ipse simul.
Flumine subducto vacuatas lambit harenas,
    sedibus in propriis exul oberrat aquis.
In limo migrante lacu consumitur amnis
20   terraque fit sterilis quo fuit unda rapax.
Deficiunt usto solacia cuncta rigoris,
    nomine cum proprio tristis et aeger eget.
Forte viator iter gradiens non invenit haustus.
    Unde alios recreet qui sitit ipse sibi?

21

On the river Gers

Perhaps, noble Garonne, your glory would have been less-
ened, if another river did not have a meager course of wa-
ter. Because here the Gers slips along with a diminished vol-
ume, it draws attention to your riches by its impoverished
supply. Indeed if one compares the two unlike rivers, where   5
this is a stream, you, I think, will be the Nile. It is your sub-
servient tributary, you hold sway over it; you are the Euphra-
tes of Gaul, it merely anonymous. For it causes your waters
to grow only as much as with your swelling current you aug-   10
ment the sea.

In particular, when the scorching summer heat lies heavy
on the land and the fields pant in distress, their soil parched
and dry, when Titan furrows the earth with his fiery rays and
his heat splits the ground with a plowshare of fire, its slug-   15
gish flow in retreat scarcely ripples the dried up waters and
river, and it gasps for breath along with its fish. Without any
flowing stream it licks the exposed sands, and exiled in its
own home it aimlessly trickles along. As pools become mud
the river dries up, and barren earth replaces the whirling wa-   20
ters. In its scorched state it can bring no solace for hard-
ship, for sad, sick, and true to its name, the Gers is indigent.
When a traveler chances to pass that way he can find no wa-
ter to drink. How can it refresh others when it thirsts itself?

25   Se cupit infundi fluvius, si porrigis undas,
      si tamen est fluvius quem madefactat homo.
     Gurgitis inpressas labens rota signat harenas
      atque resudantes orbita sistit aquas.
     Si venias equitando viam sub tempore cancri,
30   vix tamen insidens ungula mergit equi.
     Vidimus exiguum de limo surgere piscem,
      qui retinente luto naufragus errat humo.
     Nec fluvius nec campus adest nec terra nec unda;
      piscibus inhabilem nullus arare potest.
35   Sola palude natans querulos dat rana susurros;
      piscibus exclusis advena regnat aquis.
     At si forte fluat tenuis de nubibus imber,
      vix pluit in terris, iam tumet iste minax.
     Ingentes animos parva de nube resumit;
40   fit subito pelagus qui fuit ante lacus.
     Turbidus incedens undis eget ipse lavari,
      semper inaequalis qui nihil aut satis est.
     Non ripis contentus agit conpendia cursus;
      quod de monte bibit per sata plena vomit.
45   Vertice torrenti rapitur quasi more tyranni;
      indignatus iter munera vastat agri.
     Discurrit seges in fluvium, stat piscis in arvo:
      ordine perverso messe natante iacet.
     Quae fuerant ovibus donantur pascua ranis,
50   prata tenent pisces et trahit unda pecus.
     Obtinet expulsus stabulum campestre silurus;
      plus capitur terris quam modo piscis aquis.
     Sarcula quos foderent agros male retia miscent;
      figitur hic hamus quo stetit ante palus.

If you offer water, the stream wants to be wetted by it; that   25
is, if you can call it a stream whose moisture a human pro-
vides. A wheel passing over marks the sand of the riverbed
with its impress, and the track blocks the waters that are
seeping up. If you come that way on horseback in the season
of Cancer, the tread of the horse's hoof scarcely sinks into   30
the ground. I have seen a tiny fish emerge from the slime,
caught in the mud, a shipwrecked vagrant on land. There is
neither river nor field there, neither land nor water; though
fish cannot live there, equally no one can plow. Only the frog   35
swimming in the mire sounds its plaintive croaks; with the
fish sent into exile, an interloper rules over the waters. But if
even a light shower falls from the clouds, as soon as the rain
hits the earth, the river is swollen and threatening. It re-
ceives great force from a small cloud and suddenly what was   40
just a pool becomes a sea. The turbulent course of its waters
itself needs to be cleansed, its flow always excessive, either
nothing or too much. Not content with its banks, its cur-
rent takes short cuts, and pours out on teeming cropland
what it drinks in from the hills. Like some tyrant it speeds   45
along in a whirling torrent; scorning its bed, it lays waste the
bounty of the fields. The harvest floats off in the flood, fish
settle on farmland: in a topsy-turvy world the crops swim,
the fish lies flat. What once was pasturage for sheep is now
handed over to frogs, fish occupy the meadows and waters   50
carry off the herd. The catfish, in exile, finds lodging in the
plain; more fish are caught on land than shortly before in
the wave. Fishing nets now sow confusion in the fields where
once harrows dug, and a hook sticks its catch where before

55 Sors una est piscis, siccent aut flumina crescant:
      nunc residet limo, nunc iacet exul agro.
   Sed cur triste diu loquimur de gurgite parvo?
      uritur et verbis, nec recreatur aquis.
   Sufficiat flagrare sibi. Cur addo vapores
60   atque bis aestivum crescere tempus ago?
   Unica sed tandem damus haec solacia laudis,
      quod tribuit pisces evacuatus aquis.

there was marsh. It is all the same for the fish, whether the 55
river rises or dries: in one case it's stuck in the mud, in the
other exiled on land.

But why do I waste so much complaint on an insignifi-
cant stream? It's scorched by my words, but not replenished
by waters. Enough that it burn on its own. Why do I in-
crease the temperature and cause the onset of a second sum- 60
mer heat? Yet after all I can provide one compensatory
praise, that when drained of water it yet serves up fish.

BOOK TWO

I

De cruce Domini

Crux benedicta nitet, Dominus qua carne pependit
    atque cruore suo vulnera nostra lavat,
mitis amore pio pro nobis victima factus
    traxit ab ore lupi qua sacer agnus oves,
5 transfixis palmis ubi mundum a clade redemit
    atque suo clausit funere mortis iter.
Hic manus illa fuit clavis confixa cruentis
    quae eripuit Paulum crimine, morte Petrum.
Fertilitate potens, o dulce et nobile lignum,
10   quando tuis ramis tam nova poma geris!
Cuius odore novo defuncta cadavera surgunt
    et redeunt vitae qui caruere diem.
Nullum uret aestus sub frondibus arboris huius,
    luna nec in noctem sol neque meridie.
15 Tu plantata micas secus est ubi cursus aquarum
    spargis et ornatas flore recente comas.
Appensa est vitis inter tua brachia, de qua
    dulcia sanguineo vina rubore fluunt.

I

On the cross of the Lord

The blessed cross shines bright, where the Lord incarnate hung and with his own blood washes clean our wounds, where gentle in his loving mercy he became a sacrifice for us and, a holy lamb, saved his sheep from the jaws of the wolf, where with pierced hands he ransomed the world from destruction and by his own death closed off the path to mortality. Here that hand that rescued Paul from wrongdoing, Peter from death was pierced with bloody nails.

O sweet and noble wood, excelling in your fertility, since you bear on your branches such unaccustomed fruit! At your novel scent the bodies of the dead rise up and those who were without the light of day return to life. Under the leaves of this tree no one will be scorched by the heat, neither by the moon at night nor the sun at midday. You gleam brightly, planted beside flowing waters, and fan out your foliage adorned with fresh blossoms. On your arms was hung the vine from which there flows a sweet vintage of bloodred hue.

2

In honore sanctae crucis

Pange, lingua, gloriosi proelium certaminis
et super crucis tropaeo dic triumphum nobilem,
qualiter redemptor orbis immolatus vicerit.

De parentis protoplasti fraude factor condolens,
5 quando pomi noxialis morte morsu corruit,
ipse lignum tunc notavit, damna ligni ut solveret.

Hoc opus nostrae salutis ordo depoposcerat,
multiformis perditoris arte ut artem falleret
et medellam ferret inde, hostis unde laeserat.

10 Quando venit ergo sacri plenitudo temporis,
missus est ab arce patris natus orbis conditor
atque ventre virginali carne factus prodiit.

Vagit infans inter arta conditus praesepia;
membra pannis involuta virgo mater alligat
15 et pedes manusque, crura stricta pingit fascia.

Lustra sex qui iam peracta tempus implens corporis,
se volente natus ad hoc, passioni deditus
agnus in crucis levatur immolandus stipite.

Hic acetum, fel, harundo, sputa, clavi, lancea;
20 mite corpus perforatur, sanguis, unda profluit,
terra, pontus, astra, mundus quo lavantur flumine.

2

In honor of the holy cross

Sing, my tongue, of the battle in the famous contest and tell
of the trophy of the cross and of its glorious triumph, how
the redeemer of the world, though sacrificed, was yet victo-
rious.

The Creator, grieving for the crime of our first-formed
father, when by the bite of the fatal fruit he fell in death, 5
then picked out wood to remedy the harm that wood had
caused. The plan of our salvation had demanded that this
take place, so that by his art he should foil the art of the
shape-shifting destroyer, and secure healing from the very
source from which our enemy had worked harm.

When, then, the fullness of sacred time arrived, the son, 10
the world's creator, was sent from his father's heaven and in-
carnate in human flesh, came forth from a virgin's womb.
He cried, a baby, cradled in the confines of a manger; his
virgin mother wrapped his limbs in swaddling clothes, and 15
bands drawn tight adorned his feet, hands, and legs.

But after the passing of thirty years, the term of his life in
the flesh, of his own free will, born for this purpose, surren-
dered to the Passion, he was raised up, a lamb for sacrifice,
on the tree trunk of the cross. Here were vinegar, gall, a
reed, and spittle, nails, a spear; his gentle body was pierced; 20
blood and water flowed, by whose flood are cleansed the
earth, sea, stars, the world.

Crux fidelis, inter omnes arbor una nobilis,
nulla talem silva profert flore, fronde, germine,
dulce lignum, dulce clavo dulce pondus sustinens!

25 Flecte ramos, arbor alta, tensa laxa viscera,
et rigor lentescat ille quem dedit nativitas,
ut superni membra regis mite tendas stipite.

Sola digna tu fuisti ferre pretium saeculi
atque portum praeparare nauta mundo naufrago,
30 quem sacer cruor perunxit fusus agni corpore.

3

Item versus in honore sanctae crucis vel oratorii domus ecclesiae apud Toronos

Virtus celsa crucis totum recte occupat orbem,
    haec quoniam mundi perdita cuncta refert,
quodque ferus serpens infecit felle veneni,
    Christi sanguis in hac dulce liquore lavat,
5 quaeque lupi fuerant raptoris praeda ferocis
    in cruce restituit virginis agnus oves.
Tensus in his ramis, cum plantis brachia pandens,
    ecclesiam stabilit pendulus ipse cruce,
hoc pius in ligno reparans deperdita pridem,
10   quod vetiti ligni poma tulere boni.

Faithful cross, supremely noble tree above all others, no forest produces your like in flower, fruit, and foliage, sweet wood with sweet nails holding up a sweet burden. Flex your 25 branches, lofty tree, relax your tight-stretched flesh, and let the hardness native to you assume a softness, to extend on gentle trunk the limbs of the heavenly king.

You alone were worthy to bear the ransom of the earth and as sailor prepare a harbor for the shipwrecked world, whom the sacred blood anointed, shed from the body of the 30 lamb.

3

Again, verses in honor of the holy cross and of a chapel in the episcopal palace of Tours

The lofty power of the cross rightly spreads over the globe, since it restores all that was lost in the world, and by it what the cruel serpent tainted with the bitterness of poison the blood of Christ washes clean in a sweet stream. With the 5 cross the virgin's lamb rescues the sheep, who once had been the prey of the fierce, ravening wolf. Extended on these branches, spreading hands and feet, though hanging aloft on the cross, he firmly founded the church, mercifully restoring by this wood what had long been lost, the blessings the 10

Addita quin etiam virtutum flamma coruscat,
  dona quod obsequiis crux parat ipsa suis.
Denique sancta cruci haec templa Gregorius offert.
  Dum pallas cuperet signa gerendo crucis,
15 dona repente dedit divina potentia Christus
  mox fuit et voti causa secuta pii.
Pallia nam meruit, sunt quae cruce textile pulchra
  obsequiisque suis crux habet alma cruces,
serica quae niveis sunt agnava blattea telis,
20 et textis crucibus magnificatur opus.
Sic cito pontifici dedit haec devota voluntas,
  atque dicata cruci conscia vela placent.
Unde salutifero signo tibi, clare sacerdos,
  hoc cui complacuit reddere magna valet.

4

Item de signaculo sanctae crucis

Dius apex carne effigians genetalia limi
vitali terrae conpingit sanguine gluten.
Luciferax auras animantes affluit illic:
conditur enixans Adam factoris ad instar.
5 Exiluit protoplasma solo, res nobilis usu,
dives in arbitrio radianti lumine; dehinc
ex membris Adae vas fit tum virginis Evvae;
carne creata viri dehinc copulatur eidem,

fruit of that forbidden wood had annulled. What is more, the flame of further miracles burns bright, for the cross in its own right bestows gifts on its worshipers.

So Gregory dedicated to the cross this holy church. When he wanted coverings bearing the sign of the cross, Christ in his divine power swiftly gave him a gift and his pi- 15 ous prayer quickly took effect. For he won for himself beautiful fabric, woven with crosses: the blessed cross provides crosses for its devotees. It is of fresh purple silk with snow-white threads; the embroidered crosses give glory to the 20 work. So a devout disposition quickly gave this present to the bishop; the fabric won approval when dedicated to the cross that it shared. And therefore by its saving sign, glorious bishop, he whose favor this won can give you great rewards.

4

Again, on the sign of the cross

The divine majesty, shaping in flesh the generative properties of mud, constructed a compound of earth and animating blood. The bringer of light then inspired it with life-giving breath: Adam was born, modeled after the image of his creator. He sprang from the earth, first-formed, a crea- 5 ture noble in purpose, rich in his powers in the brilliant light; and then from the limbs of Adam was made a vessel for the virgin Eve; created from the body of the man, she is

ut paradyssiaco bene laetaretur in horto.
10 Sed de sede pia pepulit temerabile guttur,
serpentis suasu pomi suco atra propinans.
Insatiatrici morti fames accidit illinc.
Gavisurus ob hoc caeli fluis arce locator,
nasci pro nobis miseraris et ulcere clavi
15 in cruce configi. Tali malagmate inunctis
una salus nobis ligno agni sanguine venit.
Iucunda species! In te pia bracchia Cristi
affixa steterunt et palma beabilis, in hac
cara caro poenas inmites sustulit haustu.
20 Arbor suavis agri, tecum nova vita paratur.
Electa ut visu, sic e crucis ordine pulchra
lumen, spes, scutum gereris livoris ab ictu.
Immortale decus nece iusti laeta parasti.
Una omnem vitam sic, crux, tua causa rigavit,
25 imbre cruenta pio. Velis das navita portum,
tristia summerso mundasti vulnera clavo.
Arbor dulcis agri, rorans e cortice nectar,
ramis de cuius vitalia crismata fragrant,
excellens cultu, diva ortu, fulgida fructu,
30 deliciosa cibo et per poma suavis in umbra.
En regis magni gemmantem et nobile signum!
Murus et arma viris, virtus, lux, ara precatu,
pande benigna viam, vivax et fertile lumen.
Tum memor adfer opem nobis, e germine David
35 in cruce rex fixus iudex cum praeerit orbi.

then joined to him as wife to enjoy in blessedness the garden of paradise. But reckless gluttony drove them out of their happy abode, as they took a fatal draft from the juice of the fruit at the serpent's persuading. From that moment death had an appetite that was insatiable. For this reason, destined to rejoice, Creator, you descend from heaven's heights, and in your pity suffer to be born for us and be fastened on the cross with wounding nails. For us, anointed with so fine a salve, there comes but one salvation, from the wood by the blood of the lamb. A joyous sight! On you the merciful arms of Christ, his sacred hands, were pinned and raised upright, and here his precious flesh endured to drain the cup of cruel pains. Dear tree of the field, with you a new life comes into being. Excelling in your appearance, lovely in the plan of the cross, as light, hope, shield you are taken up against the blows of jealousy. Joyfully you brought about undying glory through the death of the just. In this way, cross, you were the single cause that watered all of life with a holy shower of blood. As sailor you give anchorage to men's sails, you have cleansed their grievous wounds with your drenched nails. Sweet tree of the field, exuding nectar from your bark, from whose branches the life-giving unction takes its fragrance, you are splendid in finery, divine in your birth, and brilliant in your produce, delicious in your sustenance, sweet with your fruits in your shade.

Behold the jeweled and noble standard of the great king! Bulwark and weaponry for men, power, light, and altar for prayer, be kind and reveal the way, fruitful and life-giving lamp. Remember and bring aid to us, when the king from David's blood, once nailed to the cross, presides over the world as judge.

A lateribus:

Dulce decus signi, via caeli, vita redempti.
In cruce mors Christi curavit mortua mundi.

Crux ipsa:

Crux pia, devotas Agnen tege cum Radegunde,
tu Fortunatum fragilem, crux sancta, tuere.
Vera spes nobis ligno, agni sanguine, clavo,
arbor suavis agri, tecum nova vita paratur.

5

Extorquet hoc sorte Dei veniabile signum
rusticulas laudes viventi reddere flatu
in me qui regit ire lutum plasmabile numen.
Portio viventum, curatio fausta medellae,
5 exclusor culpae, Trinitas effusa, creator,
cuius honor, lumen, ius, gloria, regna, coaeve
. . .

Infra:

Sic pater et genitus, sic sanctus spiritus unus.

A lateribus:

Eripe credentes, fidei decus, arma salutis.
Munere, Criste, tuo removetur causa reatus.

On the sides:

Sweet beauty of the sign, path to heaven, life of the redeemed. On the cross the death of Christ healed the mortality of the world.

The cross itself:

Holy cross, guard your devoted servants Radegund and Agnes, and protect too, sacred cross, Fortunatus in his weakness. Our true hope lies in the wood, the blood of the lamb, and the nails; sweet tree of the field, with you new life is acquired.

5

This merciful sign by God's design demands that I render praise, however awkward, with living breath, to the divinity who in me caused the mud to take on shape. Patron of the living, beneficent performer of healing, remitter of fault, far-reaching Trinity, Creator, to whom are honor, brilliance, power, glory, and kingdom, O coeternal ... 5

On the bottom:

So the Father, the Son, and the Holy Spirit are one.

On the sides:

Glory of the faith, weapon of salvation, rescue believers. Christ, by your bounty the claims of sin are abolished.

Crux ipsa:

Dulce mihi lignum, pie, maius odore rosetis.
Dumosi colles, lignum generastis honoris.
Ditans templa Dei, crux, et velamen adornas.
Ex fidei merito magnum, pie, reddis Abraham.

6

Hymnus in honore sanctae crucis

Vexilla regis prodeunt,
    fulget crucis mysterium,
    quo carne carnis conditor
    suspensus est patibulo.
5 Confixa clavis viscera,
    tendens manus, vestigia
    redemptionis gratia
    hic inmolata est hostia.
Quo vulneratus insuper
10   mucrone diro lanceae,
    ut nos lavaret crimine
    manavit unda et sanguine.
Impleta sunt quae concinit
    David fideli carmine,
15   dicendo nationibus
    "regnavit a ligno Deus."

The cross itself:

O merciful one, to me this wood is sweet, excelling in its scent gardens of roses. Hills, though thorny, you have given birth to this honored wood. Cross, you enrich the church of God and decorate its hangings. For the merit of his faith, merciful one, you magnify Abraham.

6

Hymn in honor of the holy cross

The standards of the king advance, the mystery of the cross shines clear, for there in flesh flesh's creator was hung upon a gibbet. His body pierced with nails, his arms and legs 5 extended, to bring redemption he was sacrificed as victim here. And here he suffered a further wound from a spear's 10 cruel point; to cleanse us from the stain of sin he shed water and his blood. Thereby the prophecy was fulfilled that David sang in truthful verse, by proclaiming to all the world: 15 "God has reigned from wood."

Arbor decora et fulgida,
   ornata regis purpura.
   Electa digno stipite
20   tam sancta membra tangere!
Beata cuius brachiis
   pretium pependit saeculi!
   Statera facta est corporis
   praedam tulitque Tartari.
25 Fundis aroma cortice,
   vincis sapore nectare,
   iucunda fructu fertili
   plaudis triumpho nobili.
Salve ara, salve victima
30   de passionis gloria,
   qua vita mortem pertulit
   et morte vitam reddidit.

7

De domno Saturnino

Ianua celsa poli terra pulsante patescit
   et recipit natos quos generavit humus.
Admiranda haec est occasio facta salutis,
   ut de morte sua praemia lucis emant.
5 Saturninus enim cupiens se nectere Christo
   carnali in habitu noluit esse diu,
vincula corporei dissolvere carceris optans,
   plenius ut Domino se sociaret homo.

O glorious and shining tree, adorned with purple of a king, and chosen worthy with your trunk to touch so sacred 20 a body. Happy is it on whose arms there hung the ransom of the world! It became the balance for his body and deprived Tartarus of its prey. From your bark you diffuse a scent, in 25 taste you surpass nectar, and delighting in your fertile fruit you rejoice in a famous triumph.

Hail altar, hail victim for the glory of your passion, by 30 which life endured death and by death restored life.

7

On Lord Saturninus

The lofty door of heaven opens wide when earth knocks and receives its sons whom the soil brought to birth. This is a remarkable opportunity offered for salvation, that men may purchase by their death the prize of light. For Saturninus in 5 his desire to bind himself to Christ did not wish to be long clothed in flesh, seeking instead to loose the bonds of his bodily prison so that, though a man, he could more fully join his Lord.

Tempore maturo cum iam spes esset adulta,
10   sumpserunt pretium vota beata suum,
dumque sacerdotio frueretur in urbe Tolosa
      et populis Christum panderet esse Deum,
ostendens verbis, addens miracula factis,
      ut quod sermo daret consequeretur opus,
15 gentiles animas rapiens de fauce tyranni
      subdebat regi qui dedit arma sibi.
Sed vitiata malis et plebs infecta venenis,
      curari effugiens, aegra iacere volens,
comprendit male sana virum, ad capitolia duxit,
20   atque suo medico vulnera plura dedit.
Pro pietate dolum, pro melle venena rependens
      contra tutorem noxia bella movet.
Subligat indomiti sanctum ad vestigia tauri
      et stimulat, fieret ne fuga tarda feri.
25 Pessima mens hominum, diri nova bestia monstri!
      Nec tauri indomiti sufficit ira tibi?
Naturae rabidae feritatem adiungere nosti;
      quod per se nescit te stimulante furit.
Turba cruenta nocens, huius te vulnere perdis;
30   etsi non illi, parcere disce tibi.
Hinc ferus impatiens mox curva per avia raptus
      passim membra pii fudit in urbe viri.
Tum mulier collegit ovans et condidit artus,
      una sed famula participante sibi.
35 Haec fuit insignis rapiendae causa coronae,
      gloria martyrii sic celebrata nitet.
Ante sepulchra pii dantur modo dona salutis
      et corpus lacerum corpora multa fovet.

When in the fullness of time his hope had reached frui-
tion, his happy vows now received their due reward. While   10
he held the office of bishop in the city of Toulouse and an-
nounced to his people that Christ was God, showing it by
his words, adding miracles by his deeds, so that what his
speech preached was achieved in action, rescuing pagan   15
souls from the jaws of the tyrant, he was making them sub-
jects of the king who gave him his weapons. But the peo-
ple, corrupted by evil and tainted by poison, shunning heal-
ing and preferring to lie sick, in their frenzy seized the holy
man, led him to the capitol, and inflicted many wounds on   20
their own physician. Returning treachery for devotion and
venom for honey, they waged wicked war on their protector.
They bound the saint to the hindquarters of an unbroken
bull and goaded it so the wild beast's flight would not be
slow.

O the supreme wickedness of the human mind, an un-   25
natural beast, a terrible prodigy! Was the anger of an unbro-
ken bull not enough for you? You found a way to increase the
intensity of its natural ferocity; the rage it lacks itself you
provide by your goading. Bloody, guilty mob, by wounding
this man you destroy yourself; if you won't spare him, learn   30
to spare yourself. So the animal in its rage quickly charging
in twisting career scattered the limbs of the holy man ev-
erywhere in the city. Then a woman joyfully gathered and
buried his bodily remains, with only a single servant sharing
in the task. This was the illustrious cause of his winning the   35
crown; the glory of his martyrdom enjoys such brilliant re-
nown. Before the holy man's tomb to this day gifts of heal-
ing are granted, and his torn body now brings relief to many
bodies.

Dic ubi, mors inimica, iaces, ubi victa recumbis,
40   quando vides sancti funere vota dari?
Quem male credebas obitu finire salutem,
    dat vitam multis et tenet ipse suam.
Huc captiva cubas quo te regnare putabas;
    invadendo peris teque furendo necas.
45 Te tua poena premit, tua te fera vincula torquent,
    quos dare vis gemitus ipsa ferendo gemis.
Martyr ovans caelos retinet, tu livida tristis;
    mors inimica tibi, Tartara nigra colis.
Florigera nunc sede manet sine fine beatus
50   inter odoratos ture calente choros.
Non aliquas metuit placato iudice causas,
    praemia sed miles victor habenda petit.
Digna triumphantem quae restat palma sequetur;
    pro te, Christe, mori est gloria, vita, quies.

8

De Launebode qui aedificavit templum Sancti Saturnini

Laudibus humanis reliquorum corda resultent,
    at mihi de iustis commemorare vacet.
Nam pietatis opus, victores texere libris,
    admonet ingenium res ratione duplex:

Tell me, hostile Death, where do you lie, where do you
sink down defeated, when you see that prayers are answered   40
by the dead body of the saint? The man you wrongly be-
lieved by his demise had brought his life to an end gives life
to many while retaining it for himself. Where you thought
to rule supreme you succumb in captivity; by your aggres-
sion you perish, by your frenzy you kill yourself. The pun-   45
ishment you inflict afflicts you, your cruel chains are your
own torture, in your own suffering you groan the groans you
wanted to provoke. The martyr joyfully occupies heaven,
you mournfully the gloom; Death, you are your own enemy,
black Tartarus is your home. Now he lives a life of endless
bliss in a flower-strewn abode among choirs scented by the   50
warm breath of incense. He had won over his judge and
feared no charge, but as a victorious soldier sought to re-
ceive his reward. A palm as due prize awaits him in his tri-
umph; to die for you, Christ, is glory, life, and peace.

8

On Launebod, who built the church of Saint Saturninus

Let others' hearts resound with praise of humankind; my
task will be to celebrate the just. Two different reasons
prompt my spirit to an act of piety, to weave in books ac-

5   una quod est habilem de magnis magna fateri,
      nam bona qui reticet criminis auctor erit;
   altera causa monet quoniam succensus amore
      et meliora cupit qui sua facta legit.
   Saturninus enim martyr venerabilis orbi
10   nec latet egregii palma beata viri,
   qui cum Romana properasset ab urbe Tolosam
      et pia Christicoli semina ferret agri,
   tunc vesana cohors Domini comprendit amicum
      instituitque pii membra terenda trahi.
15   Implicitus tauri pede posteriore pependit,
      tractus in oblicum dilaceratus obit.
   Hac ope de terris animam transmisit Olympo;
      o felix cuius funere mors moritur!
   Sed locus ille quidem quo sanctus vincula sumpsit
20   nullius templi fultus honore fuit.
   Launebodis enim post saecula longa, ducatum
      dum gerit, instruxit culmina sancta loci.
   Quod nullus veniens Romana gente fabrivit,
      hoc vir barbarica prole peregit opus,
25   coniuge cum propria Berethrude, clara decore
      pectore quae blando clarior ipsa nitet.
   Cui genus egregium fulget de stirpe potentum,
      addidit ornatum vir venerando Deum.
   Quae manibus propriis alimonia digna ministrat:
30   pauperibus tribuens se satiare cupit.
   Indefessa spem Christi per templa requirit,
      iugiter excurrens ad pietatis opus.
   Nudos veste tegit, sitienti pocula profert,
      se magis aeterno femina fonte replet.
35   Proficit hoc etiam, quidquid gerit illa, marito,
      anxia pro cuius vota salute facit.

counts of victors: the first that it is proper to proclaim great 5
things of the great, for he will be the perpetrator of a crime
who keeps silent about good deeds; the second reason ad-
vises that, inflamed by love, those who read such men's
deeds desire to better themselves.

Now Saturninus is a martyr honored all through the
world; the noble man's glorious palm is common knowledge. 10
When he hurried from the city of Rome to Toulouse and
brought the holy seeds for fields devoted to Christ, then the
maddened crowd laid hands on this friend of the Lord and
caused the saint's limbs to be dragged to their destruction.
Bound to the bull's hind hooves he hung there, dragged in a 15
sidelong course, mutilated he died. By this recourse he sent
his soul from earth to heaven; happy is he by whose death
death dies itself!

But yet the place where the holy man took on his bonds
was not distinguished by the honor of a church. So after 20
long ages Launebod, in the office of duke, constructed a sa-
cred building on the spot. The work that no one descended
from the Roman race performed, a man of barbarian ances-
try brought to completion with his wife Beretrud, distin- 25
guished by her beauty, but still more brilliant by her sweet-
ness of heart. Her noble line gains luster from powerful
ancestors, a distinction her husband's devotion to God in-
creased. From her own hands she dutifully distributes alms:
by giving to the poor she seeks to satisfy herself. Unwearied 30
she pursues her hope in Christ from church to church, con-
tinually busying herself with works of piety. The naked she
covers with clothing, to the thirsty she provides drink, but
sates herself still more from an eternal spring. What is more, 35
whatever she does also profits her husband, for whose salva-

Dux meritis in gente sua qui pollet opimis
    celsus ubique micans nobilitatis ope,
sed quamvis altum teneat de stirpe cacumen,
40   moribus ipse suos amplificavit avos.
Ergo pari voto maneant in saecula iuncti
    et micet ambobus consolidatus amor.

9

Ad clerum Parisiacum

Coetus honorifici decus et gradus ordinis ampli,
    quos colo corde, fide, religione patres,
iam dudum obliti desueto carmine plectri
    cogitis antiquam me renovare lyram.
5 En stupidis digitis stimulatis tangere cordas,
    cum mihi non solito currat in arte manus.
Scabrida nunc resonat mea lingua rubigine verba
    exit et incompto raucus ab ore fragor.
Vix dabit in veteri ferrugine cotis acumen
10   aut fumo infecto splendet in aere color.
Sed quia dulcedo pulsans quasi malleus instat
    et velut incudo cura relisa terit
pectoris atque mei succenditis igne caminum,
    unde ministratur cordis in arce vapor,

tion she anxiously offers up prayers. The duke who excels among his people by his abundant merits is everywhere resplendent, exalted by his high nobility. But although he derives from his ancestry lofty status, he has himself by his   40 character glorified his ancestors. Therefore may they remain united from age to age in common vows and may a firm-founded love shine on them both.

9

To the clergy of Paris

Honorable and glorious company and members of a noble order, fathers whom I revere in heart, faith, and devotion, though my song is long disused and my plectrum forgotten, you compel me to take up my former lyre once again. See,   5 you are urging me to pluck with awkward fingers the strings, although my unpracticed hand has no skill in playing. Now the words my tongue sounds out are scaled with rust, and a harsh din emerges from my tuneless mouth. A whetstone will hardly restore sharpness amid ingrained corrosion; when smoke stained, the color in bronze scarcely retains its   10 glow. But because your sweet friendship like a hammer insistently strikes, and like a resilient anvil your affection wears me down, because you fire the furnace of my feelings with your flames, from which heat passes to the sanctum of my

15 obsequor hinc, quia me veluti fornace recoctum
　　artis ad officium vester adegit amor.
Celsa Parisiaci clerus reverentia pollens,
　　ecclesiae genium, gloria, munus, honor,
carmine Davitico divina poemata pangens,
20　cursibus assiduis dulce revolvit opus.
Inde sacerdotes, leviticus hinc micat ordo,
　　illos canities, hos stola pulchra tegit,
illis pallor inest, rubor his in vultibus errat,
　　et candunt rutilis lilia mixta rosis;
25 illi iam senio, sed et hi bene vestibus albent,
　　ut placeat summo picta corona Deo.
In medio Germanus adest antistes honore,
　　qui regit hinc iuvenes, subrigit inde senes.
Levitae praeeunt, sequitur gravis ordo ducatum;
30　hos gradiendo movet, hos moderando trahit.
Ipse tamen sensim incedit, velut alter Aaron,
　　non de veste nitens, sed pietate placens:
non lapides, coccus, cidar, aurum, purpura, byssus
　　exornant humeros, sed micat alma fides.
35 Iste satis melior veteri quam lege sacerdos,
　　hic quia vera colit quod prius umbra fuit.
Magna futura putans, praesentia cuncta refellens,
　　antea carne carens quam caro fine ruens,
sollicitus quemquam ne devoret ira luporum,
40　colligit ad caulas pastor opimus oves.
Assiduis monitis ad pascua salsa vocatus,
　　grex vocem agnoscens currit amore sequax.
Miles ad arma celer, signum mox tinnit in aures,
　　erigit excusso membra sopore toro.

heart, I obey you because your love has compelled me, as if   15
reworked in a forge, to fulfill my duty by my art.

The high and powerful dignity of the Parisian clergy, the
church's spirit, glory, bounty, honor, singing sacred poems
to the strains of David, performs in constant services its   20
sweet duty. Here priests, there the ranks of deacons shine;
white hair clothes one group, fine vestments the other. One
is pale, ruddiness tinges the others' complexions, and white
lilies mingle with crimson roses; age makes one group white,   25
their fine clothing the other, so that they form a multicol-
ored garland, pleasing to God on high. Germanus, the hon-
ored bishop, is present in their midst, here directing the
young, there uplifting the old. The deacons go ahead, the
solemn order of priests follows his lead; the first he impels   30
by his step, the second he draws on by his rule. The bishop
himself moves slowly like a second Aaron, not brilliant in
his dress, but comely in his holiness. Precious stones and
scarlet, priestly headdress, gold, purple, and linen—none of
these adorn his shoulders, but kindly faith shines from him.
He is better by far than was the priest of the old law, for he   35
worships the truth, while before there was only a shadow.
Believing in future glory and rejecting all present things, al-
ready free of the flesh before his flesh meets its end in death,
taking care that the wolves in their fury not devour anyone,
as a trusty shepherd he gathers his sheep to his fold. Sum-   40
moned by constant admonitions to his eloquent pastures,
his flock, recognizing his voice and prompted by love, comes
running.

A soldier swift to arms, as soon as the bell rings in his
ears, he shakes off sleep and lifts his body from the bed.

45 Advolat ante alios; mysteria sacra requirens,
    undique quisque suo templa petendo loco.
Flagranti studio populum domus irrigat omnem
    certatimque monent, quis prior ire valet.
Pervigiles noctes ad prima crepuscula iungens,
50   construit angelicos turba verenda choros.
Gressibus exertis in opus venerabile constans
    vim factura polo cantibus arma movet.
Stamina psalterii lyrico modulamine texens,
    versibus orditum carmen amore trahit.
55 Hinc puer exiguis attemperat organa cannis,
    inde senis largam ructat ab ore tubam:
cymbalicae voces calamis miscentur acutis
    disparibusque tropis fistula dulce sonat.
Tympana rauca senum puerilis tibia mulcet
60   atque hominum reparant verba canora lyram.
Leniter iste trahit modulus, rapit alacer ille;
    sexus et aetatis sic variatur opus.
Triticeas fruges fervens terit area Christi,
    horrea quandoquidem construitura Dei,
65 voce creatoris reminiscens esse beatos
    quos Dominus vigiles, dum redit ipse, videt.
In quorum meritis, animo, virtute fideque
    tegmine corporeo lumina quanta latent!
Pontificis monitis clerus, plebs psallit et infans,
70   unde labore brevi fruge replendus erit.
Sub duce Germano felix exercitus hic est.
    Moyses, tende manus et tua castra iuvas.

He flies before the rest; they, eager for the holy rites, make 45
their way to the church from every side, each to his place.
That house inspires the whole people with a burning desire,
and in rivalry they compete for who can get there first. Con-
tinuing their nightlong vigils till the first coming of dawn,
the holy congregation forms an angelic choir. With vigorous 50
step and firm devotion to their sacred task, they wield the
weapons of song to storm the ramparts of heaven. Interlac-
ing the threads of the psalter with musical refrain, they lov-
ingly weave a tapestry of song from the warp of verse. The 55
young tune their voices to the slender reeds, while the old
blare the full trumpet blast from their mouths: sounds of
the cymbal mingle with the shrill pipes, and to different
notes the flute sounds sweetly. Youth's piping moderates the
harsh percussion of the old, and human voices raised in song 60
make music like a lyre. One measure leisurely lingers, an-
other swiftly passes; in this way the office is varied by ages
and sexes. The busy threshing floor of Christ separates the
harvest of wheat, who in the future will make up the grana-
ries of God, bringing to mind the words of the Creator, that 65
blessed are they whom the Lord sees awake when he makes
his return. In their merits and minds, their virtues and faith,
how bright are the lights concealed by the cloak of the body.
Instructed by their bishop, the clergy, people, and children
sing psalms; though the effort is slight, it will bear ample 70
fruit. Here is a happy army under the leadership of Germa-
nus. Moses, stretch out your hands and bring aid to your
forces.

IO

De ecclesia Parisiaca

Si Salomoniaci memoretur machina templi,
    arte licet par sit, pulchrior ista fide.
Nam quaecumque illic veteris velamine legis
    clausa fuere prius, hic reserata patent.
5 Floruit illa quidem vario intertexta metallo,
    clarius haec Christi sanguine tincta nitet;
illam aurum, lapides ornarunt, cedrina ligna,
    huic venerabilior de cruce fulget honor.
Constitit illa vetus ruituro structa talento:
10   haec pretio mundi stat solidata domus.
Splendida marmoreis attollitur aula columnis,
    et quia pura manet, gratia maior inest.
Prima capit radios vitreis oculata fenestris
    artificisque manu clausit in arce diem.
15 Cursibus Aurorae vaga lux laquearia complet
    atque suis radiis et sine sole micat.
Haec pius egregio rex Childeberthus amore
    dona suo populo non moritura dedit.
Totus in affectu divini cultus adhaerens
20   ecclesiae iuges amplificavit opes;
Melchisedech noster merito rex atque sacerdos
    complevit laicus religionis opus.

10

On the cathedral of Paris

If one calls to mind the structure of Solomon's temple, this building, though its equal in art, is finer in faith. For whatever there was formerly concealed under the covering of the ancient law here stands plainly revealed. That structure was 5 brilliant in the intermingling of its varied materials, but this shines brighter, for it is dyed with the blood of Christ. That one gold, precious stones, beams of cedar adorned; this one derives greater reverence and glory from the luster of the cross. That former temple was built and established by wealth that must fail; this house is firmly founded on the 10 ransom of the world. Its brilliant nave is raised up on columns of marble, and because it remains unsullied, the greater is its beauty. Through glass windows, as through eyes, it catches first the sun's rays, and by an artist's skill it keeps the daylight enclosed in the building. At dawn's com- 15 ing shifting light floods the paneled ceiling, and even without the sun it glitters with its own sunbeams.

The pious king Childebert in his excelling love presented to his people these undying gifts. Wholly devoted to the love of divine worship, he ceaselessly enlarged the wealth of 20 the church; our Melchisedech, rightly titled king and priest, though a layman, fulfilled a religious office. While reigning

Publica iura regens ac celsa palatia servans,
   unica pontificum gloria, norma fuit.
25 Hinc abiens illic meritorum vivit honore;
   hic quoque gestorum laude perennis erit.

II

De baptisterio Magantiae

Ardua sacrati baptismatis aula coruscat,
   quo delicta Adae Christus in amne lavat.
Hic pastore Deo puris grex mergitur undis,
   ne maculata diu vellera gestet ovis.
5 Traxit origo necem de semine, sed pater orbis
   purgavit medicis crimina mortis aquis.
Hanc tamen antistes Sidonius extulit arcem,
   qui Domini cultum templa novando fovet.
Struxit Berthoarae voto complente sacerdos,
10   quae decus ecclesiae cordis amore placet.
Catholicae fidei splendor, pietate coruscans,
   templorum cultrix, prodiga pauperibus
seminat unde metat fruges, spargendo recondens;
   terrenis opibus non moritura parat.
15 Filia digna patri te, Theudebercthe, reformans,
   rexisti patriam qui pietate patris

over the people, he looked to the palace on high; for the
bishops he was both preeminent glory and model. After de-   25
parting from here he lives in heaven honored for his virtues,
but here too he will be eternal by the fame of his actions.

II

On the baptistery of Mainz

A lofty hall of sacred baptism brilliantly glistens, where
Christ in his stream washes away the sins of Adam. Here
with God as shepherd a flock is plunged in a cleansing flood,
so that the sheep no longer wear a long-stained fleece. Men's   5
ancestry carried death with it by inheritance, but the father
of the world cleansed these mortal crimes with his healing
waters. So Bishop Sidonius, who prospers the Lord's wor-
ship by restoring churches, raised on high this building. The
bishop achieved the work in fulfillment of a vow of Ber-
thoara, who, as the church's glory, wins favor by her heart's   10
devotion. Brilliance of the Catholic faith, radiant in her ho-
liness, patron of churches, and generous to the poor, she
sows to reap from there a harvest, storing up by distribut-
ing; by earthly possessions she wins things that will never
die. A daughter worthy of her father, she replicates you,   15
Theudebert, who ruled your country with paternal love and

et comitante fide revocasti ex hoste triumphos,
    sed capti pretio mox rediere tuo.
Ecclesiae fultor, laus regum, pastor egentum,
20   cura sacerdotum, promptus ad omne bonum,
cuius dulce iugum nullus gemuisse fatetur,
    vivis adhuc meritis rex in amore tuis.

12

De basilica Sancti Georgi

Martyris egregii pollens micat aula Georgi,
    cuius in hunc mundum spargitur altus honor.
Carcere, caede, fame, vinclis, site, frigore, flammis
    confessus Christum duxit ad astra caput,
5 qui virtute potens orientis in axe sepultus
    ecce sub occiduo cardine praebet opem.
Ergo memento preces et reddere vota, viator;
    obtinet hic meritis quod petit alma fides.
Condidit antistes Sidonius ista decenter;
10   proficiant animae quae nova templa suae.

bolstered by your faith won victories over the enemy, with captives soon returning home that you had ransomed. Supporter of the church, glory of kings, shepherd of the needy, protector of bishops, quick to perform every good deed, under whose sweet yoke no man can say he ever groaned, by your virtues you live still a king in their love.

   20

12

On the church of Saint George

The mighty church of the noble martyr George is aglow, a saint whose high honor spreads as far as this realm. Through prison, beatings, hunger, chains, thirst, cold, and flames, making confession of Christ, he raised his head up to the stars. Strong in his powers, though buried in eastern climes, behold, here under western skies he proffers his aid. Therefore be mindful, traveler, to give him your prayers and your vows; here true faith secures by his merits the petitions it makes. Bishop Sidonius founded this building with fitting display; may this new church win due profit for his soul.

   5

   10

13

De oratorio Trasarici

Lucida perspicui nituerunt limina templi,
    quo capit haud dubiam spem veneranda fides.
Haec est aula Petri, caelos qui clave catenat,
    substitit et pelagus quo gradiente lapis.
5 Sedibus his Paulus habitat, tuba gentibus una,
    et qui praedo prius, hic modo praeco manet.
Martini domus est, Christum qui vestit egentem,
    regem tiro tegens et homo iure Deum.
Ecce sacerdotis sacri micat aula Remedi,
10   qui tenebras mundi liquit et astra tenet.
Cultor opime Dei, templum, Trasarice, locasti;
    has cui persolvis reddet amator opes.

14

De sanctis Agaunensibus

Turbine sub mundi cum persequebantur iniqui
    Christicolasque daret saeva procella neci,
frigore depulso succendens corda peregit
    rupibus in gelidis fervida bella fides.

13

On the chapel of Trasaricus

The threshold of the radiant church has won a brilliant luster, where pious faith receives hopes that brook no doubt. This is the hall of Peter, who confines the sky with his keys, and at whose step sea became solid stone. Paul occupies this abode too, sole clarion to the nations; a man who once was a persecutor, but now is a preacher. It is the house of Martin, who clothed Christ as a poor man, a raw recruit cloaking a king and a man rightly covering God. See, too, the hall of the holy bishop Remedius is aglow, who has left the darkness of the world to occupy the stars. Trasaricus, noble devotee of God, you have set up a church; this wealth you expend, its recipient will pay back to you in love.

14

On the saints of Agaune

In turbulent times for the world when wicked men were engaged in persecution and a violent storm was consigning Christians to slaughter, faith, dispelling the cold and inflaming men's hearts, waged heated warfare among frozen crags.

5   Quo, pie Maurici, ductor legionis opimae
     traxisti fortes subdere colla viros,
quos positis gladiis armasti dogmate Pauli
     nomine pro Christi dulcius esse mori.
Pectore belligero poterant qui vincere ferro,
10   invitant iugulis vulnera cara suis.
Hortantes se clade sua sic ire sub astra
     alter in alterius caede natavit heros.
Adiuvit rapidas Rhodani fons sanguinis undas
     tinxit et Alpinas ira cruenta nives.
15 Tali fine polos felix exercitus intrans,
     iunctus apostolicis plaudit honore choris.
Cingitur angelico virtus trabeata senatu;
     mors fuit unde prius, lux fovet inde viros.
Ecce, triumphantum ductor fortissime, tecum
20   quattuor hic procerum pignora sancta iacent.
Sub luteo tumulo latitat caeleste talentum
     divitiasque Dei vilis arena tegit,
qui faciunt sacrum paradisi crescere censum,
     heredes Domini luce perenne dati.
25 Sidereo chorus iste throno cum carne locandus,
     cum veniet iudex, arbiter orbis, erit.
Sic pia turba simul festinans cernere Christum,
     ut caelos peteret, de nece fecit iter.
Fortunatus enim per fulgida dona Tonantis,
30   ne tenebris crucier, quaeso feratis opem.

There, holy Maurice, as commander of a noble legion, you 5
persuaded brave men to bend the neck; their swords laid
aside, you armed them with the teaching of Paul: that it is
sweeter to die for the name of Christ. Although their spirits
were warlike and they could have conquered by the sword,
they courted wounds and welcomed them to their throats. 10
With mutual encouragement to mount to the stars by their
deaths the heroes swam in each other's gore. Springs of
blood augmented the whirling waters of the Rhone, and an-
ger, bloodred, dyed the Alpine snows. By such a death the 15
happy host has entered into heaven and, joined to apos-
tolic choirs, rejoices in its glory. Virtue in consular finery is
encircled by a senate of angels; from the same source that
brought their deaths, light now brings the men comfort.

See, most valiant leader of the triumphant soldiery, here 20
lie with you the holy relics of four lords. Under a grave of
earth lies hidden the talent of heaven, and worthless loam
provides covering for God's riches, who cause the sacred
treasury of paradise to swell, heirs of the Lord, endowed
with eternal light. That choir will take its place in the flesh 25
by the throne of heaven when the judge and lord of the
world makes his return. So the holy company, with one ac-
cord hurrying to look upon Christ, made death a path for
themselves to reach up to heaven. I, Fortunatus, now beg by
the glorious bounty of God that you grant me your aid that I 30
may not be tormented by darkness.

15

De Sancto Hilario

Si Hilarium quaeris qui sit cognoscere, lector,
    Allobroges referunt Pictavios genitum.
Cum populum regeret divina mente sacerdos,
    servabat legis foedera sollicitus.
5   Improbus ut vidit plebes quod scinderet error,
    Graecorum virus protulit in medium,
vipereo promunt semper qui ex corde venena,
    filius ut dicunt quia est creatura Dei,
quis magis auxilium praestat sapientia mundi,
10   de ingenito genitum quae negat esse Deum;
quam male complexus, cupiens calcare prophetas,
    Arrius infelix cum retinet crepuit.
Egregius doctor, veterum monumenta secutus,
    quem Stephanus vidit comprobat esse Deum.
15   Victus amore Dei contempto principe mundi
    intemerata fides pertulit exilium.
In patre, qui potens Deus est, cognoscere natum
    divinis tantum vocibus insinuat.
Perpetuum lumen Christum Dominumque Deumque
20   bis senis populos edocet esse libris.

15

On Saint Hilary

Reader, if you wish to discover who Hilary is, the Allobroges report that he was born in Poitiers. When with a divine spirit he ruled over his people as bishop, he conscientiously observed the ordinances of the law. When he saw that 5 wicked error was dividing the people, he exposed the venom of the Greeks, who always spew poison from their serpentine heart, saying that the Son is the creation of God. Worldly wisdom provided them with further reinforcement, in denying that one born of one unborn is God; this 10 Arius unwisely embraced, eager to trample the prophets, for the wretched man, in clinging to it, burst asunder. The noble teacher, following writings of old, demonstrated that it was God that Stephen saw. Possessed by the love of God, scorn- 15 ing the prince of the world, his faith unshaken, he endured an exile. That the Son is to be recognized in the Father, who is God all-powerful, he taught by relying only on divine pronouncements. That Christ is perpetual light, Lord, and God he laid out for the people in twelve books. 20

16

De Sancto Medardo

Inter Christicolas quos actio vexit in astris
    pars tibi pro meritis magna, Medarde, patet,
qui sic vixisti terrenis hospes in oris
    ut caelos patriam redderes esse tuam.
5 Exilium tibi mundus erat caenosa caventi
    et modo te gaudet cive manente polus.
Exutus tenebris, vestitus tegmine lucis,
    post obitum frueris liberiore die,
de tellure satus factus possessor Olympi
10   et matrem linquens cum patre laeta tenes.
Humani victor vitii super astra triumphas
    atque cremans carnem das animae requiem.
Te inter mundanos vepres gradiente fatemur
    calcatis spinis promeruisse rosas.
15 Flore refectus ager suaves tibi fundit odores;
    balsama, tura replent quae paradisus habet.
Cauta per angustum figens vestigia callem,
    sic dedit arta tibi semita lucis iter.
(Lata voluptatum via, quae submergit Averno,
20   dulcia carnis alens mortis amara parat.)
Hoc numquam sacros flexisti tramite gressus,
    nec potuere tuos prava tenere pedes.
Durum iter ad laudes, gravior via ducit in altum:
    quo labor est potior, gloria maior erit.

16

On Saint Medard

Among those Christians who were raised by their deeds to the stars, a great role is assigned to you, Medard, for your virtues, who so lived as an alien in the confines of earth that you demonstrated heaven was your true native land. The 5
world was an exile for you, you shunned its pollution; now heaven rejoices, having you as its citizen. Divested of darkness, clothed in a mantle of light, after your death you enjoy more freely the day. Born from the earth, you have become an occupant of heaven; leaving your mother behind, with 10
your father you experience bliss. Vanquisher of human vice, you triumph above the stars, and in sacrificing the flesh, you win rest for your soul.

As you journeyed through the briers of this world, this we declare: by trampling its thorns underfoot, you won the reward of roses. Lands vivid with flowers pour out for you 15
their sweet perfumes; you enjoy the balsam and frankincense that paradise possesses. Because you carefully kept your footsteps on the narrow track, a straitened pathway provided you a way to the light. (The road of pleasures is broad that plunges one into Avernus; it fosters delights of 20
the flesh, but leads to the bitterness of death.) You never turned your holy progress from this path, nor could wickedness detain your footsteps. The path to praise is hard, the road that leads on high more difficult: where the labor is heavier, the glory will be greater.

25   Quae prius incipiam sacri miracula facti,
       cum, quidquid facias, omnia prima micent?
     Dum fuit ad superos humano in corpore vita,
       ex oculis fugiens lux tibi cordis erat.
     Si caecus venit, rapuit palpando salutem;
30   in mediis tenebris fulsit aperta dies.
     Qui voluit furti causa penetrare latenter,
       te religante sedet, te reserante fugit.
     Fur sine perfectu voto deceptus inani
       omnia restituens crimina fraudis habet.
35   Nam semel ut molles carpserunt palmitis uvas,
       non valuere gradus inde referre foris;
     nec potuit raptor pedibus subducere praedam,
       raptori abduxit sed sua praeda pedes.
     Ergo suis laqueis coepit miser esse ligatus:
40   venerat ut caperet, captus at ipse fuit;
     nec tetigit mustum, sed iniqua mente rotatur;
       antea quam biberet, ebria turba iacet.
     Incepit servare magis quam ferre racemos
       et datus est custos qui cupit esse rapax,
45   donec, sancte, tuis verbis iussisses abire;
       ut furtum impleret, doctus ab hoste redit.
     Quae manet haec animi pietas, sanctissime praesul,
       laedentem auxilio qui facis ire tuo?
     Tintinnum rapit alter inops, magis improbus ille,
50   qui iumentorum colla tenere solet,
    absconditque sinu, faeno praecludit hiatum,
       et tenet ipse manu, ne manifestet opus.
     Te veniente, sacer, causas patefecit opertas,
       tinnitu incipiens iam quasi furta loqui.

With what miracle among your holy deeds shall I first 25
make a start, when whatever you do makes a prior claim
by its brilliance? While your life was spent in human body
among the living, loss of sight from the eyes was a special
concern for you. If a blind man approached, by touch he
won healing; in the middle of his darkness shone the clear 30
light of day. A burglar who wanted to make a break-in in se-
cret was forced to sit when you bound him, but fled when
you freed him. The thief, empty-handed, was thwarted of
his futile intent; he gave everything back, but retained the
guilt for his deceit. For once he had plucked the soft grapes 35
from the vine, he could not move one step from that spot;
the robber could not get away with his loot on foot, but the
loot deprived the robber of the use of his feet. And so the
wretch was caught fast by the snares he himself had set: he 40
had come to take, but he himself was taken. He touched no
wine, but his wicked mind was set spinning; before he could
drink, he was prostrate in drunken confusion. He found
himself protecting, not carrying off, the clusters of grapes,
and the would-be thief took on the role of guard, until, holy 45
one, you gave him the order to leave; he returned home in-
structed by his enemy how to achieve his theft's purpose.
How great is the mercy you hold in your heart, most holy
bishop, who dismiss with your aid one who would do you
harm?

A second man, poor, but more wicked than the first, stole
a bell of the kind that customarily hangs on the necks of cat- 50
tle. He hid it in his clothing, stopped up its opening with
straw, and kept his hand on it so that his action would not be
revealed. But on your arrival, holy one, it revealed the secret
crime; with its ringing it began, as it were, to denounce the

55   Nil valet abscondi, nil claudi nilve teneri;
     facundo strepitu prodidit omne malum.
  Pandebat propriam veluti sub iudice causam,
     nil de fure timens, liberiore sono.
  Indicat, accusat, convincit, damnat, acerbat;
60   te praesente tamen non licet esse reum.
  Absolvis furem solitae pietatis amore,
     addens et monitus, cautus ut intret iter,
  praecipiens querulam secum portare rapinam,
     ne vacua tristis spe remearet inops.
65   Hinc tamen, ut potero, cum raptus ab orbe fuisses,
     quae dederis populis signa verenda loquar.
  Cum pia composito veherentur membra feretro,
     substratus meruit caecus habere diem.
  Anxius ille sacra lumen suscepit ab umbra
70   et tua mors illi lucis origo fuit;
  dumque sepulchra darent, oculi rediere sepulti
     et sopor ille tuus hunc vigilare facit.
  Cum fugis a mundo, datur illi lumine mundus;
     te linquente die hunc fugiunt tenebrae.
75   Antiqui vultus lucem stupuere modernam
     et veteri fabricae prima fenestra venit.
  Compedibus validis alter manicisque ligatus
     mox tetigit templum, ferrea vincla cadunt.
  Tam grave fragmentum—dolor est vel cernere poenam—
80   pondera tot miseros sustinuisse pedes!
  Si conexa forent, elephantum solvere possent
     nec poterat rigidos ipse movere gradus.

theft. Nothing can be concealed, nothing stopped up, noth- 55
ing held in check; by its eloquent clamor it betrayed the
whole evil act. As though before a judge, it laid out the facts
of its case in ringing tones, having no fear of the thief. It
arraigns, accuses, convicts, sentences, and intensifies the
crime; but when you are present no one can be truly guilty. 60
You acquit the thief out of love and your accustomed mercy,
adding your injunctions that he show care in pursuing his
journey, instructing him to take with him the stolen goods
that were his accuser, lest saddened by his thwarted hopes
he return home in poverty.

From this point, as best I can, I will tell of your remark- 65
able miracles, granted to your people when you had been
carried off from this world. When your holy limbs were car-
ried and laid out on a bier, a blind man, prostrating himself,
won the gift of sight. In his grief he was illumined by the
holy man's shade, and your death was for him the source of 70
light. While they were entombing you, his entombed eyes
were restored, and that sleep of yours caused this man to
awake. While you flee the world, he wins the world with his
sight; as the daylight takes its leave of you, darkness flees
away from him. His elderly features were astonished at the 75
new light, and for the first time a window opened in the
aged frame.

Another man, bound by strong handcuffs and fetters,
no sooner reached the church than his iron chains fell off.
So heavy were the pieces—just to see that torment was a
cause of pain! To think his suffering feet had endured such 80
weights! If the pieces were joined up, they could hobble
even an elephant and it would not be able to move forward,
held in their grip. The man's experience was no different

Non minus est illi quae subvertente procella
    litoribus Libycis anchora fracta iacet.
85 Poena quidem gravior cecidit crescente triumpho:
    vincere rem saevam gloria maior erat.
Non habuit tot vincla pati miser ille ligatus,
    sed tua quo virtus plus mereretur opus.
Cum solidarentur non sic strepuere catenae,
90   ceu tinniverunt, cum crepuere ferae.
Quae fuit illa prius nimiis male vincta catenis
    iam tibi, qui solvis, libera dextra favet.
Lignea vincla gerens alter confugit ad aulam,
    quae simili merito scissa repente cadunt.
95 Nec mora, vix tetigit sacrati limina templi,
    fit tonitrus caelis, arma ferendo tibi.
Grandia divisi ceciderunt pondera ligni,
    et qui gessit onus corruit ipse simul.
Expavit subito de libertate recepta
100   atque magis timuit quando solutus erat.
Quae ratio fuerit, cecidit cur pronus in arvis?
    Gaudia magna quidem saepe timere solent.
Dum stupet unde salus laceris est reddita plantis,
    admirante animo membra soluta fluunt.
105 Inde v•tus mulier, pariter nascente periclo,
    vulnere naturae mortua membra tulit.
Inclusos digitos morbo glomerante tenebat
    nec poterat ducto pollice fila dare.
Secum nata quidem, sed non sua, dextra pependit;
110   corpore iuncta suo res aliena fuit.
Tempore sed tardo est, cum iam spes fracta iaceret,
    ante tuos tumulos vivificata manus.
Sic inopinatum commendat gratia votum;
    desperata salus dulcior esse solet.

than when by the force of a storm an anchor lies broken
on the African shores. For the harsh punishment fell away, 85
while the triumph increased: the glory was all the greater for
conquering such cruelty. The wretched prisoner would not
have had to bear so many shackles, were it not to provide
scope for your virtue to work further its effect. When forged
the cruel chains did not resound as loudly as they rang when 90
they cracked. The hand that before was firmly bound by
many chains, now freed, salutes you who released it.

A second man fled to your sanctuary, wearing wooden
shackles, which by a like miracle suddenly split and fell.
Without any delay, scarcely had he reached the holy shrine's 95
threshold when there was thunder in the heavens, bring-
ing you reinforcements. The wood broke apart and its heavy
weights fell away; at the same time the one who was bearing
the load fell to the earth as well. He was struck with sud-
den fright at receiving the gift of freedom and feared all the 100
more when he had been released. What was the reason why
he fell headlong to the turf? Men often are accustomed to
feel fear at great causes of joy. When this man was aston-
ished at how health was restored to his mutilated feet, his
mind was in awe, and his limbs gave way and collapsed.

Next an old woman, her suffering arising from her years, 105
by a natural infirmity lost all life in her limbs. Her fingers
were turned in on themselves, knotted by disease, and she
could not draw out threads and spin them with her thumb.
The hand was hers since birth, but it hung at her side, no
part of her; though attached to her body, it was a foreign ob- 110
ject. After a long period of time, when now all hope lay shat-
tered, before your tomb life was restored to her hand. Such
bounty won favor for an unexpectedly fulfilled prayer; when
health comes unlooked for it is customarily all the sweeter.

115 Mobilis ergo venit digitis torpentibus umor
   et dispensatus fluxit in ungue vigor.
Arida nervorum sese iunctura tetendit
   agnovitque suum vena soluta locum.
Apta ministeriis incepit palma moveri,
120   servitium discens libera dextra fuit.
Nec tantum profugos pietas tua reddidit artus;
   reddidit et victum pensa trahente manu.
Eripuisti aliam simili de peste puellam
   membraque restituens plus animae tribuis.
125 Desponsata viro mortali lege iacebat,
   nunc thalamis Christi virgo dicata micat.
Sponsa quidem radiat cum virginitate modesta,
   spe meliore fruens, nupta tenenda polis.
Nec fructus uteri sterilis deperdit honesti;
130   flore pudicitiae mater habenda placet:
acquirit cunctos natum quae non habet unum
   progeniemque sibi gignit amore Dei.
Inde pari morbo deflenda infantia parvae
   in lucem veniens membra necata trahit.
135 Mors et origo simul misero processit ab alvo,
   extinctam generans mater anhela manum.
Commendata tuo rediit medicata sepulchro;
   quod de matre perit, de tumulo recipit.
Dum iacet alter inops, visu caligine clauso,
140   caecus nec misero lumine lumen erat—
longa nocte oculos quarto iam mense premebat,
   in lucem obscurus, vivus imago necis—

Then with moisture came motion to her paralyzed fingers, 115
and the strength bestowed on her flowed to her fingernails.
The dried-up texture of her sinews stretched itself out, and
her veins cleared and recognized their proper place. Her
whole palm, now suited to its function, began to move; in 120
learning to serve, her hand gained its freedom. Your holiness
not only restored her fugitive limbs; it also restored her live-
lihood, for now her hand could work the wool.

You also rescued another girl from a similar disease;
though healing her limbs, you more greatly benefited her
soul. She once was betrothed to a husband and lay sick un- 125
der mortality's law; now she is a radiant virgin, consecrated
to the bridal chamber of Christ. She still is betrothed, but
modest and brilliant in her virginity, enjoying a better hope,
destined to be a bride in heaven. She is not barren nor has
lost the fruit of an honorable womb, but in the flower of her 130
chastity she holds the high status of a mother. She acquires
all as her children who has not one single child, and gives
birth to her own offspring in the love of God.

Again a baby girl, because of the same sickness, a woeful
sight, on her entry into the light brought with her limbs that
were dead. Birth and death together emerged from that ill- 135
fated womb, when the mother in her labors gave birth to a
hand that lacked life. When entrusted to your grave, she re-
turned from it cured; what she lost from her mother she re-
gained from your tomb.

When another, a poor man, was stricken, his vision ob-
scured by a mist, blinded and wretched, without any light in 140
his eyes—for four months now he had closed his eyes in a
long–drawn-out night, plunged in darkness in the daylight, a
living image of death—in his sleep you instructed him with

vocibus hunc medicis monuisti tempore somni,
    tenderet ut velox ad tua templa gradum.
145 Mox veniente die, sed non sibi forfice pressa,
    enituit Christi vertice tonsus ovis.
Detrahit hic crines nitidos ut haberet ocellos
    et mercante coma munera lucis emat.
Qui titubante gradu tractus pervenit ad aulam.
150   Per biduum recubans ante sepulchra fuit.
Tertia lux rediens nocturnas solverat umbras,
    et caeco occurrit sic revocata dies.
Undique limitae cecidere a fronte tenebrae;
    sanguinis unda rigat, luminis atra lavat.
155 Sicca lucerna novo flagrante refulsit olivo
    obtinuitque suum lux peregrina locum.
Quid referam mutis qui verbo verba dedisti?
    Quod gravat eiciens, quod iuvat omne locas.
Cuncta nec enumero, tua me praeconia vincunt;
160   etsi non potui, velle fuisse vide.
En tua templa colit nimio Sigibercthus amore,
    insistens operi promptus amore tui.
Culmina custodi qui templum in culmine duxit,
    protege pro meritis qui tibi tecta dedit.
165 Haec, pie, pauca ferens ego Fortunatus amore,
    auxilium posco; da mihi vota, precor.

your healing commands to make his way with all speed to
your sanctuary. Soon when the day dawned, no scissors hav-   145
ing been used, he shone forth a sheep of Christ with his
head shorn. He sacrificed his locks to win eyes that gleamed
bright and at the price of his hair to buy the present of light.
Brought there with faltering step he made his way to the
shrine. For two days he lay on the ground in front of the   150
tomb. The third dawn had returned and dispersed the shad-
ows of night; in the same way the blind man experienced the
recurrence of day. Darkness was diminished and entirely fell
away from his brow; a flood of blood ran down, it cleansed
his eyes' black night. Their lamp, once dry, burned bright   155
with a fresh source of oil, and a light formerly alien took up
its own proper residence.

Why should I speak of how with a word you gave words
to the mute? You expel whatever is burdensome, whatever
is beneficial you bestow. I do not tell all your deeds, your
praise exceeds my powers; although I had not the capacity,   160
be sure that I had the will. See here, Sigibert in his great love
does honor to your church, urgently forwarding the work,
impelled by his love of you. Preserve his high eminence who
built your church to its height, and guard in accordance with
his deserts the one who gave you this abode. In offering   165
these few verses, holy one, out of love, I, Fortunatus, ask
your aid; grant me my prayer, I beg.

BOOK THREE

I

Ad Eufronium episcopum Turonensem

DOMINO SANCTO ET MERITIS
APOSTOLICO DOMNO ET DULCI PATRI
EUFRONIO PAPAE FORTUNATUS

Ante paucorum dierum volubilitatem transcursam, deferente praesentium portitore, venerabilis oris vestri salutare colloquium a me caelesti pro munere significo fuisse perceptum. Quod ea aviditate, teste rerum creatore, complexus sum, qua et vestrum piissimum animum circa meam humilitatem iugiter approbavi profusum et me supplicem multis repletum beneficiis agnosco devotum. Qui quamvis in altera commorer civitate, novit Deus quia vobis absens sum tantummodo loco, non animo, et quocumque fuero, intra me vos clausos habebo. Vere dico, non est illud cor carneum ubi vestrae animae non recipitur miranda dulcedo, sed est marmore durior si tantae caritatis non amplectitur blandimentum. Nam quis de te tam congrua praedicet quam mens vere sancta deposcit? Aut quis suo sic satisfaciat animo, ut vestrum sicut condecet digne prodat affectum? Qui in terra sic humilis es, ut habites erectus in caelis et inclinando ad in-

To Eufronius, bishop of Tours

I send to you to tell you that just a few days have elapsed in their course since a letter of greeting from your reverend lips was received by me, brought by the carrier of the present letter, like a gift from heaven. I embraced it, the creator of the universe bear witness, with that enthusiasm with which I have always welcomed the generosity of your most kindly spirit to my humility, and as a suppliant richly endowed with your many attentions, I avow my devotion to you. For though I live in another city, God knows I am absent from you only in location, not in spirit, and wherever I am I shall have you locked in my inner being. I speak the truth. That heart is not made of flesh that does not admit the wonderful sweetness of your soul, and it is harder than marble if it does not embrace the charm of so great affection. For who could praise you in a fashion appropriate to what your truly saintly character demands? Or who could be sufficiently assured as to properly portray your feelings in a fitting manner? Such is your humility on earth that you live

fima te sublevari facias ad excelsa, ut iam agnoscaris, qui Christi humilitatem libenter amplecteris, de eius regni munere quid habebis. Quoniam, sicut ipsius mandata sunt, qui se parvulum inter homines vult videri magnificum se elatus respiciet in supernis. Unusquisque qualiter desiderat et expugnat.

3   Ego vero gratulor in corde domni Eufronii dilectionem domni mei sensisse Martini. Quapropter multiplici me prece apostolatui et sanctae caritati vestrae commendans, rogo per ipsum domnum Martinum, cuius frueris participato consortio, ut apud eum memorari praecipias me famulum et devotum, quatenus quid apud eum meritis praevaletis in meae humilitatis protectione iugiter ostendatis. Ora pro me, domine sancte et apostolice, peculiaris domne et pater.

2

Ad eundem

DOMINO SANCTO MIHIQUE IN DEO PECULIARI
PATRONO EUFRONIO PAPAE FORTUNATUS

Copiosam et superabundantem pectoris vestri dulcedinem, quam circa devotionem personae meae vestram beatitudinem, pater amantissime, fateor impendisse, quis illam ut dignum est vel corde possit concipere vel sermone

raised aloft in the heavens, and by demeaning yourself to the lowest level you cause yourself to be lifted up to the heights, so that now it is recognized what you who willingly embrace the humility of Christ will receive from the bounty of his kingdom. For, in accordance with his decrees, he who wants to be seen as a child among men, when raised to heaven will see himself exalted. As each man desires, so he gains his end.

As for me, I rejoice to have felt in the heart of lord Eu- 3 fronius the love of my lord Martin. And therefore, commending myself with many prayers to your apostolate and your saintly affection, I ask by this same lord Martin, whose colleagueship you enjoy, that you bid me, his devoted servant, be kept in his memory so that you may continually show the power you have with him by your virtues through the protection of my humility. Pray for me, saintly and apostolic lord, my special father and master.

2

To the same man

FORTUNATUS TO BISHOP EUFRONIUS, MY
SAINTLY LORD AND SPECIAL PATRON IN GOD

Who could fitly either conceive in his heart or express in language that abundant and overflowing sweetness of your spirit that, most loving father, I confess your blessedness

valeat explicare? Quae tanto me sibi vinculo admirandae ca-
ritatis astrinxit ut nec unius horae spatio ab illo mihi videar
separari conspectu, quem et si praesentem non video, atta-
men intra pectoris habitaculum retineo conditum et reclau-
2 sum. Quis enim tuae pietati peculiaris non rcdditur, in quo
tantae bonitatis beneficia continentur? Aut quem ad tuam
dulcedinem non ducas invitum, cuius probavimus animum
ineffabili caritate profusum? Qua autem illud admirati-
one complectar, cum te sic video cunctos diligere, ac si
unumquemque de proprio visus sis latere generasse?

3   Quis vero filiorum superbus esse desideret, ubi te pa-
trem et doctorem tantae humilitatis agnoscit? Aut, quamvis
summo nobilitatis descendat de culmine, cum te sic respicit
supplicem, non se tuis vestigiis in terra provolutus extendit?
Vere dico, si tumidum superbia deicit, vos multum est lauda-
bilis humilitas quod erexit. Quis denique illic esse possit ira-
cundus aut turbidus, ubi sacerdos et pontifex tam placidus
es inventus? Scit enim totus sine rapacitate grex vivere ubi
vivendi tranquillitas discitur a pastore.

4   Quid de rebus reliquis referam, in quibus te sic inpendis
in singulis, ut lauderis in cunctis? Quae tamen etsi imitari
non possumus, vel vidisse quod imitari deceat congaude-
mus.

5   Quapropter dominationi et sanctitati vestrae peculiariter
me commendans rogo et obtestor—sic ille domnus meus
Martinus sua intercessione obtineat, ut cum ipso iuxta me-

bestowed on devotion to my person? It has so bound me to itself by ties of extraordinary affection that not even for the space of an hour do I seem separated from the sight of that one whom, even if I do not see him present before me, yet I keep stored away and enclosed in the dwelling of my heart. Who indeed is not specially attached to your kindness, in   2 whom are displayed charitable acts of such goodness? Or whom would you not attract even against his will to your sweetness whose mind, as we have experienced, overflows with love past description? With what sense of wonder shall I embrace the fact that I observe you love everyone as if you seemed to have begotten each of them from your own loins?

Which of your sons could wish to be proud when he sees   3 you are a father and teacher of such great humility? Even if he is descended from the highest summit of the nobility, when he sees you a suppliant in this way, will he not stretch himself out on the ground and fall before your feet? I speak the truth. If pride casts down the arrogant, then it is much to your credit that humility has raised you up. In fact who could be angry or disputatious when you, their priest and bishop, are discovered to be so mild? For the whole flock knows how to live without greed when it learns a peaceful mode of life from its shepherd.

What shall I say about the rest of your actions, in which   4 you so exert yourself in each case that you win praise in them all? And though we are not able to imitate them, yet we rejoice that we can at least see what is worthy of imitation.

Therefore I commend myself in particular to your lord-   5 ship and sanctity and ask and beseech—so may my lord Martin secure by his intercession that the divine mercy es-

rita vestra in luce perpetua vos conlocet divina misericor-
dia–ut pro me humili filio et servo vestro ad eius beatum
sepulcrum orare digneris et pro peccatorum meorum remis-
6 sione pius intercessor accedas. Eos vero qui vestri sunt
omnes domnos et dulces meos reverenter saluto. Domnum
meum per omnia dulcissimum, filium vestrum Aventium,
pro me multipliciter supplico salutari. Domno meo Felici
episcopo, si per vos venit, me benigno animo commendari
deposco. Ora pro me.

3

Ad eundem

Quamvis pigra mihi iaceat sine fomite lingua
   nec valeam dignis reddere digna viris,
attamen, alme pater, Christi venerande sacerdos,
   Eufroni, cupio solvere parva tibi.
5 Debeo multa quidem, sed suscipe pauca libenter;
   sit veniale precor quod tuus edit amor.
Ecclesiae lampas sub te radiante coruscat,
   lumine pontificis fulget ubique fides.
Gratia praecellens sincero in pectore vernat;
10   quo nullus dolus est Israhelita vir es.

tablish you with him according to your merits in light ever-
lasting—that you see fit to pray for your humble son and
servant at his blessed tomb and that as merciful intercessor
you approach him for the remission of my sins. I greet with   6
due reverence all those lords and sweet friends of mine who
are of your company. I beg that my lord, in every respect
most sweet to me, your son Aventius, receive many greet-
ings on my behalf and I ask that, if you have the opportu-
nity, through your generosity of spirit I be commended to
my lord, Bishop Felix. Pray for me.

3

To the same man

Though my tongue lies idle and lacks inspiration, and I can-
not give worthy return to men of great worth, yet, kindly fa-
ther, venerable bishop of Christ, I wish, Eufronius, to pay
my small homage to you. Though I owe you much, yet re-   5
ceive this small offering with goodwill; may you be lenient, I
beg, to what my love for you expresses. The lamp of the
church gleams brightly, reflecting your radiance; in your
episcopal light faith everywhere shines forth. Surpassing
grace flowers in the purity of your heart; you are an Israelite   10

Immaculata tibi feliciter actio currit:
  ut penetres caelos, haec via pandit iter.
Dulcia colloquii sine fuco dicta refundis;
  non sic mella mihi quam tua verba placent.
15 Quidquid habet sensus, hoc lingua serena relaxat,
  pectore sub vestro fraus loca nulla tenet,
qui sine felle manes in simplicitate columbae
  nec serpens in te dira venena fovet.
Advena si veniat, patriam tu reddis amatam
20 et per te proprias hic habet exul opes.
Si quis iniqua gemit, tristis hinc nemo recedit,
  sed lacrimas removens laetificare facis.
Martinus meritis hac vos in sede locavit;
  dignus eras heres qui sua iussa colis.
25 Ille tenet caelum, largo dans omnia voto;
  iunctus eris Christo hunc imitando virum.
Non perit hic vestrum qui grex ad ovile recurrit,
  candida nec spinis vellera perdit ovis,
non lupus ore rapit praedam pastore vigente,
30 sed fugit exclusus non lacerando greges.
Haec tibi lux maneat longos, venerande, per annos
  atque futura dies lucidiora ferat.

in whom there is no deceit. Your deeds are unsullied and bear happy results; this is the path that opens your way to the heavens. In your conversation you pour out sweet words without guile; even honey does not give me the pleasure your words do. Whatever your senses conceive, your calm 15 tongue expresses; in your breast no falsehood finds a place for itself; with the innocence of a dove you are quite without rancor, and the serpent does not harbor in you his dread poison. If a foreigner comes, you represent to him his beloved homeland, and through you, though an exile, he has suc- 20 cor here. Whoever laments an injustice never departs from here sad, but you remove his tears and cause him to be happy. Martin by his merits settled you in this see; you were a worthy heir, who put into practice his precepts. He occu- 25 pies heaven, granting all favors with generous intent; you will join Christ's company by taking this man as model. The flock that returns to your fold does not perish, nor does the sheep damage its white fleece with thorns; when the shepherd is vigilant the wolf does not seize any prey in its jaws, but is shut out and flees without mauling the flocks. May 30 this life's light, revered sir, remain for you for many a long year, and may a future day bring you brighter things to come.

4

Ad Felicem episcopum Namneticum

DOMINO SANCTO ET
APOSTOLICA SEDE DIGNISSIMO DOMNO ET
PATRI FELICI PAPAE FORTUNATUS

Oscitantem me prope finitima pelagi, blandimento natura-
lis torporis illectum, et litorali diutius in margine decu-
bantem subito per undifragos vestri fluctus eloquii quasi
scopulis incurrentibus elisa salis spargine me contigit irro-
rari. Sed ad primos evigilandi stimulos infundi poteram, non
tamen excitari. Qui adhuc more solito graviter obdormi-
tans, tandem aliquando inter crepitantia verborum vestro-
2 rum tonitrua vix surrexi. Igitur cum considerarem dicta sin-
gula de more tubarum clangente sermone prolata et sidereo
quodammodo splendore perfusa, velut coruscantium radio-
rum perspicabili lumine mea visi estis lumina perstrinxisse
et soporantes oculos, quos mihi aperuistis tonitruo, clausis-
tis corusco. Tantus enim exercitati claritate colloquii vestrae
linguae iubar effulsit, tanta se renidentis eloquentiae lux vi-
bravit, ut converso ordine mihi videretur verbis radiantibus
ab occidentali parte te loquente sol nasci.

4

To Felix, bishop of Nantes

FORTUNATUS TO BISHOP FELIX,
MY SAINTLY LORD AND FATHER,
MOST WORTHY OF HIS APOSTOLIC SEE

I was yawning away by the seacoast, enticed by the seduction of my natural sloth, and lounging over-long on the edge of the shore, when suddenly I had the experience of being soaked by the rolling breakers of your eloquence as if by salt spray sent up by a barrier of rocks. At this first summons to wake up, I got a good drenching, but could not be roused. Still, as is my habit, deeply asleep, I finally with a struggle raised myself amid the booming thunderstorm of your language. And so when I pondered all your words, expressed 2 with the resonance of trumpets and suffused with an almost starlike radiance, you seemed to have dazzled my vision with, as it were, the brilliant light of the sun's bright rays, and my sleeping eyes, which you had opened with your thunder, you closed with your flash. For so greatly in the clarity of your practiced discourse did the splendor of your language shine forth, and so greatly did the light of your scintillating eloquence flare, that in a reversal of nature by the radiance of your words when you spoke the sun seemed to rise in the West.

3   Credebam enim quasi sopho Pindarico compactus tetras-
trophos pedestri glutine suggillatus et ac si enthymematum
parturiens catenatum vinculum fecunda fluxisset oratio spi-
ris intertexta sophismate peregrino. Denique quantum ad
profunditatem vestrae dictionis attinet, feceratis igno-
rantem per sermonum compitos velut inter cautes Echina-
das oberrare, nisi a vobis ipsis lampas praeviatrix itineris oc-
currisset.

4   Quod vero vestris inseruistis epistulis vocem meam nec
acclamatione laudum superatam in ultimo orbis angulo per-
sonasse, haec ipsa dum relego, coepi me mirari vestro subito
crevisse colloquio qui favorem proprio non mererer ornatu,
gavisus usque adeo affectu fautoris erigi qui me recognos-
5   cerem ingenii qualitate substerni. O quantum caritas prae-
valet, cum illud lingua laudantis adicit quod laudati vena
subducit! Optandum est siquidem, ut de me humillimo tali
credatur testi potius quam auctori. Non enim Polydeucen
suae commendasset venae salientis ubertas, nisi Smyrnaei
fontis fatidico latice fuisset attactus.

6   Illud itaque quod dixistis, in ultimo orbis angulo quasi
vestram habitare praesentiam, satis hoc fieri iustum est,
ut de vobis mihi credatis qui de me vobis credi blandius sua-
detis, quoniam loca, quamvis regione ultima, te cive sunt
prima. Nam si personae merito urbes sibi vindicant princi-
patum, nulli per vos est ille locus inferior, ubi quidquid de

I believed that like a four-strophe poem composed with 3
the skill of Pindar but supplied with a setting of prose your
fertile speech, as if generating a linked series of en-
thymemes, issued forth with well-turned phrases interwo-
ven and with more-than-native skill. In sum, as far as the
subtlety of your composition goes, you would have caused
an ignorant man to lose his way through the byways of your
language as if among the rocky Echinades, if a lamp had not
been provided by you yourself to guide the way.

As for your including in your letter that my voice, not 4
drowned out by shouts of praise, rang out in the furthest
corner of the world, when I read this I begin to be astounded
that by your words my reputation has suddenly grown,
though I did not deserve any credit for my own fluency,
while rejoicing that I was so exalted by the partiality of an
admirer, though I recognized I was far your inferior in qual-
ity of intellect. How strong is the force of affection, when 5
the eloquence of a praiser can add what the praised person's
talent subtracts! For it is to be hoped that in the case of my
great humility credence be given to a witness of such stand-
ing rather than to the author himself. For his rich and over-
flowing talent would not have won fame for Polydeuces, if
he had not been sprinkled by the prophetic waters of the
font of Smyrna.

As to the fact that you said that your powerful self lives as 6
it were in the furthest corner of the world, it is only right
that you believe me about you, who persuasively argue that
you be believed about me, when I say that your location, al-
though geographically distant, enjoys primacy with you as
its citizen. For if cities claim first rank by personal merit,
that place because of you is inferior to none, where what-

laude requiritur Felix actibus pontifex est assertor. Denique non Cecaumene rabida nec ursae situs frigoribus intertextus respirat, sed per vos mutatis sedibus assiduo Favoni sibilo modulante vernatur.

7   Hoc etiam, quod sanctitas vestra conqueritur, me invento Turonis parva prolixitate potitam se fuisse colloquiis, cum me e contra pudeat in brevi spatio prodidisse inscitiam, sed latere tanti gratiam pontificis acquisitam, tamen, si nostri animi partes considerare velitis, quamvis protracto spatio

8   aspectu vestro fruerer, incitari poteram, non expleri. Quis enim semel odore suavium rosarum afflatus vel satiatum quandoque se iudicet vel patiatur reddere fastidentem, cum, si diuturnius fuissemus incomminus, tanto magis dilectione succenderer, quanto plus agnoscerem quem amarem?

9   Quod enim intulistis: "Si Ligerem vobiscum ascendissem, secundis fluctibus Namnetas occurrissem," novi quidem, te mihi Canobo, Cherucis accersientibus myoparonem prae-petem, catus arte armoniaca tutus inter Symplegadas se mordentes exissem et, si res exigeret, plausu creperegico Oetam Tirynthiacum Pindo respirante pulsassem.

10   Qua vero aviditate illud me creditis perlegisse (quod vos intexere mera caritas imperavit) quod dixistis: "Nec si Vulsci venissent in solacio, me vobis abripere valuissent?" Credite, quantum meus animus inspicit, ipsa vix Roma tantum mihi dare ad auxilia poterat quantum praestitistis in verba. Nec

ever is the subject of praise Felix by his actions demon-
strates as its bishop. In sum neither the raging torrid zone
nor the cold climes of the Bear breathe their influence, but
through you the landscape changes and it is spring, with the
continual tuneful whispering of the west wind.

As to your sanctity's complaint that when you met me at 7
Tours you had enjoyed my conversation for too short a time,
though I on the contrary am ashamed that I revealed my ig-
norance in so brief a period and that the gratitude I felt to-
ward so great a bishop was not displayed, still if you want to
consider my attitude of mind, even if I enjoyed your counte-
nance for an extended period of time, I could be stimulated
but never satisfied. For who, when once he has breathed the 8
sweet scent of roses, ever either judges himself sated or lets
himself become blasé? For if we had been in close proximity
for longer, the more I got to know the man I loved, the more
I would be inflamed with affection.

As for your remark, "If I had set sail on the Loire with 9
you, I would have reached Nantes on favoring waves," I
know well that with you as my Canobus and the Cherusci
requisitioning their swift galleys for me, skilled in the art of
music I would have passed safely through the Symplegades
that clash against each other and, if necessary, would have
made Tirynthian Oeta resound with my ringing chant, while
Pindus sounded the echo.

With what eagerness do you think I read your words, 10
which nothing but affection induced you to insert: "Not
even if the Volsci had come to your aid, could they have
snatched me away from you?" Believe me, as far as I can
see, Rome itself could hardly give as much in physical aid
as you have provided in your language. Nor in my opinion is

apud me plus aliquid est factis impendere, quam vota volun-
tatis offerre. Nam alloquii refluente dulcedine nihil opus est
plus egere.

11 Quod vero facetiis addidistis, "nisi sollicitatus laudibus
rusticus calamus non turnasset," licet talis cultor Christicola
feracissima iugera saepius exaravit, attamen nuper illum,
id est vos, confiteor ludos ithyphallicos Amphioneo barbito
reboasse.

12 Hoc quoque quod delectabiliter adiecistis me domnae
meae Radegundae muro caritatis inclusum, scio quidem
quia non ex meis meritis, sed ex illius consuetudine, quam
circa cunctos novit impendere, collegistis, et quantum in
mea persona panegyricum poetice tangitis, tantum in eius
laudes historiam retulistis. Tamen in verbis vestris illud rele-
gere merui quod in eius gratia iam percepi. Sed qui de me
parvo magna depingitis, quaeso, de magnis maxima praedi-
cetis.

13 Quapropter dominationi et sanctitati vestrae me humili
supplicatione commendans deprecor per Dominum re-
demptorem animarum nostrarum, qui vos praedestinatos
sua facturus est in luce consortes, ut me in sanctis orationi-
bus pietatis intuitu dignemini memorare. Magnum enim
erit spei meae auxilium a vobis obtinere quod posco.

Si veniant linguae pariter Graeca atque Latina,
    pro meritis nequeunt solvere cuncta tuis.
Laudibus obsessus, votis venerandus haberis;
    felix qui sensus luce perennis eris!

it any better to devote oneself to actions than to pledge one's feelings in words. For when the sweetness of communication is in full flow, there is no need to ask for more.

As for your further pleasantry, "If, inspired by your praise, 11 my countrified pen had not turned out verses," though such a Christian cultivator had often tilled the most fertile of fields, yet I recognize that he, by whom I mean you, had recently struck up playful ithyphallics on Amphion's lyre.

As to your further delightful comment that I am secured 12 by the wall of my mistress Radegund's loving affection, I am well assured that you inferred this not from my merits but from her practice, which she habitually shows toward everyone, and as in my case you strike a panegyric note with poetic license, so in praise of her you reported plain facts. Yet still in your words I had the experience of reading what from her kindness I had already received. But you who depict my lowly person in great terms, proclaim, I beg, a great subject in the highest terms.

Therefore commending myself to your lordship and holi- 13 ness in humble entreaty, I pray by the Lord, redeemer of our souls, who will make you predestined to share in his light, that you see fit to make mention of me in your holy prayers with kindly intent. For it will be a great comfort to my good hope to obtain what I request from you.

Even if the languages of Greek and Latin should both join together, they would not be able to do your virtues full justice. Encompassed by praise, you are revered in prayers; happy are you who will be eternal in the light of your spirit!

5

Item ad Felicem episcopum
ex nomine suo

Fida salus patriae, Felix spe, nomine, corde,
    Ordo sacerdotum quo radiante micat,
Restituis terris quod publica iura petebant,
    Temporibus nostris gaudia prisca ferens.
5 Vox procerum, lumen generis, defensio plebis,
    Naufragium prohibes hic ubi portus ades.
Actor apostolicus qui iura Britannica vincens,
    Tutus in adversis, spe crucis arma fugas.
Vive decus patriae, fidei lux, auctor honoris,
10   Splendor pontificum, noster et orbis amor.

6

Item ad Felicem episcopum
de dedicatione ecclesiae suae

Cum Salomon coleret generosi encaenia templi,
    Israhel electos fecit adesse viros.
Levitas, proceres, pueros, iuvenesque senesque
    undique certatim regia pompa trahit.

5

Again to Bishop Felix,
incorporating the poet's name

Trusted salvation of your country, happy in hope, name, and heart, in whose brilliance the order of bishops gains luster, you restore to the land all that public justice aspired to, bringing to our times the rejoicing of old. Voice of the no- 5 bles, light of your family, defense of the people, where you are present as a harbor you keep off all shipwreck.

Apostolic in your actions, you suppress Breton power, and secure in hard times, with trust in the cross you put weapons to flight. Long life to you, ornament of your coun- 10 try, light of the faith, bringer of glory, illuminator of the bishops, beloved by us and the world.

6

Again to Bishop Felix,
on the dedication of his cathedral

When Solomon was celebrating the dedication of his great temple, he caused the chief men of Israel to attend. From every side in eager haste the royal parade assembled Levites,

5 Mactantur vituli, tauri iugulantur ad aras,
      et populi in votis gaudia caedis erant.
  Nunc vero assurgit ritu placitura beato
      tempore decurso iustior ara Deo.
  Prospera quae populis Felix modo festa ministrans
10   exsuperat rebus gesta priora novis.
  Convocat egregios sacra ad sollemnia patres,
      quo stat vera salus et fugit umbra vetus:
  docti clave Petri caelos aperire petenti
      ac monitis Pauli noscere clausa poli.
15 Ne lupus intret oves neu morbus inulceret agnos
      hinc sunt custodes, inde medella gregis,
  quorum vox refluens populo de fonte salutis,
      ut bibat aure fidem, porrigit ore salem.
  Inter quos medios Martini sede sacerdos
20   Eufronius fulget metropolita sacer,
  plaudens in sancta fratrum coeunte corona
      et sua membra videns fortior exstat apex.
  Laetius inde caput, quia sunt sua viscera secum;
      ecclesiae iuncto corpore crescit honor.
25 Domitianus, item Victorius, ambo columnae,
      spes in utrisque manens pro regionis ope.
  Domnulus hinc fulget meritis, Romacharius inde,
      iure sacerdotii cultor uterque Dei.
  En spectata diu, data nunc memoranda per aevum,
30   votis plena piis fulget in urbe dies,
  in qua promeruit sua gaudia cernere pastor
      officioque sacro reddere vota Deo,

nobles, boys, young men and old. Calves are sacrificed, bulls 5
slaughtered on the altars, and as the people wished, there
was reveling in bloodshed. But now in the course of time
with happy ritual, a more fitting altar for God rises up, des-
tined to please. Felix in now providing this joyful festival
for his people surpasses the deeds of the past with his new 10
achievements. He calls revered fathers to this holy ceremo-
nial, where true salvation is established, and the old shadow
flees: they have the skill to open heaven with Peter's key to a
petitioner, and by the precepts of Paul to ponder the secrets
of the skies. So that a wolf does not get among the sheep 15
and disease does not scar the lambs, they act both as protec-
tion and as healing for their flocks; their voice gushing forth
for the people from the spring of salvation provides salu-
tary eloquence from the mouth so they may drink faith with
their ears. Among them in the middle on the seat of Mar-
tin the bishop, the holy metropolitan Eufronius, radiates 20
his light, rejoicing in the saintly band of brothers collected
around him; in viewing his limbs as their head he stands
out still greater. The head takes special pleasure because his
members are with him; his glory increases when the body
of the church is conjoined. Domitianus and Victorius were 25
there, twin pillars of the church, each the abiding hope for
the prosperity of their regions. Here Domnulus shone forth
with his merits, and there Romacharius, each by virtue of
episcopal office a devotee of God.

See, the long awaited day has arrived, granted now but
to be remembered forever, a day full of holy prayers and ra- 30
diating bright light in the city, on which the shepherd won
the reward of seeing the joys he wished for and fulfilling
his vows to God in performing his holy office. For a long

tempore qui longo adventu pendebat in isto,
    despiciens aliud–hoc erat omnis amor–
35 omnia tuta timens suspecto in tramite vitae,
    ne prius iret iter quam daret ista Deo.
Saepius occultans suspiria lassa trahebat,
    cederet ut Dominus hoc properare decus.
Anxius incerto curarum fasce laborans,
40   dum votum spectat, pondera tempus erant.
Sed iam festus adest, solvatur sarcina curae,
    laetitiae cumulus triste repellat onus.
Prospera dans populis et gaudia larga per urbem,
    Felix, felici cum grege pastor age.
45 Hinc te pontifices circumdant, inde ministri;
    cingit te totum hinc honor, inde favor.
Clericus ecce choris resonat, plebs inde choraulis;
    quisque tuum votum qua valet arte canit.
Tarda fuere tibi, quia fit mora semper amanti;
50   res sublimis enim tarda, sed ampla venit.
Nunc Domini laudes inter tua classica canta
    et Trinitatis opem machina trina sonet.
Adde medullata in templis holocausta sacerdos,
    quo diuturna mices hostia pura Deo.

time he remained in suspense at the outcome of his venture, disregarding everything else—this was his entire aspiration. When all seemed secure, he was afraid on the treacherous journey of life that he would complete his course before giving this gift to God. Often in secret he would heave weary sighs in prayer that the Lord would allow this honor quickly to take place. While he anxiously endured suffering under the uncertain burden of cares, the passage of time weighed upon him as he looked to fulfill his vow. But now that the festal day is here, let the burden of care be lifted, and let the full measure of joy drive off the weight of grief. Granting good times to the people and abundant happiness in the city, Felix, be a shepherd and with that bring felicity to your flock. On one side bishops flank you, on the other are the deacons; you are entirely surrounded by glory and by acclaim. Look, the clergy ring out in their choirs and the people join with their voices; each sings of your achievement with all the skill they can muster. Progress was slow for you, because all is slow for a lover; for a great work is long in the making, but brings ample reward. Now with your trumpets sing the praises of the Lord, and let the threefold structure hymn the Trinity's power. As bishop furnish in your sanctuary the richness of burned offerings, so that you may long shine as a pure offering for God.

7

In honore eorum quorum ibi reliquiae continentur

Siderei montes, speciosa cacumina Sion,
    a Libano gemini flore comante cedri,
caelorum portae, lati duo lumina mundi,
    ore tonat Paulus, fulgurat arce Petrus.
5   Inter apostolicas radianti luce coronas
    doctior hic monitu, celsior ille gradu.
Per hunc corda hominum reserantur et astra per illum;
    quos docet iste stilo, suscipit ille polo.
Pandit iter caeli hic dogmate, clavibus alter;
10   est via cui Paulus, ianua fida Petrus.
Hic petra firma manens, ille architectus habetur;
    surgit in his templum, quo placet ara Deo.
Uno fonte pares medicata fluenta rigantes,
    restingunt avidam dulce liquore sitim.
15   Fortia bella gerens quisquis cupit astra tenere,
    rex dedit hos proceres militis esse duces.
Gallia, plaude libens, mittit tibi Roma salutem;
    fulgor apostolicus visitat Allobrogas;
a facie hostili duo propugnacula praesunt,
20   quos fidei turres urbs caput orbis habet.
Hi radiant oculi pretioso in corpore Christi,
    lumine qui proprio cetera membra regunt.

7

In honor of those whose relics are contained there

Mountains starlike in radiance, beautiful heights of Sion, twin cedars of Lebanon, rich in flower and foliage, gates to the heavens, double lights of the wide world, Paul has thunder in his voice, Peter lightning from his throne. Among the crowns of the apostles with their brilliant light, one is more learned in teaching, the other higher in status. By one the hearts of men are laid open, by the other the stars; those whom one instructs with his pen, the other receives into heaven. One opens the path to the skies with his doctrine, the other with his keys; to whom Paul is the way, Peter is the faithful door. Peter is the firm-founded rock, while Paul acts as the architect; on these rises a church, where is an altar pleasing to God. From a single spring the pair pour out their healing waters, and with its sweet liquid slake a burning thirst. Our sovereign Lord has granted that these princes be the leaders in battle for all who by waging fierce wars desire to lay hold of the stars. Gaul, rejoice with full heart, for Rome sends you salvation; the bright light of the apostles has come to the Allobroges. You have won two bulwarks to face the enemy's assaults, whom the city that is capital of the world possesses as towers of the faith. These are the brilliant eyes in the precious body of Christ, who direct with their light all the rest of his limbs.

Munere Felicis caeli cape, Gallia, fruges
    pontificisque tui vota beata cole,
25 cuius castus amor dedit hanc in honore superno
    ecclesiae nuptae dote perenne domum.
Vertice sublimi patet aulae forma triformis,
    nomine apostolico sanctificata Deo.
Quantum inter sanctos meritum supereminet illis,
30   celsius haec tantum culmina culmen habent.
In medium turritus apex super ardua tendit
    quadratumque levans crista rotundat opus.
Altius, ut stupeas, arce ascendente per arcus
    instar montis agens aedis acumen habet.
35 Illic expositos fucis animantibus artus
    vivere picturas arte reflante putas.
39 Ire redire vides radio crispante figuras
40   atque lacunar agit quod maris unda solet.
37 Sol vagus ut dederit per stagnea tecta colorem,
38   lactea lux resilit, cum rubor inde ferit.
41 Fulgorem astrorum meditantur tecta metallo
    et splendore suo culmina sidus habent.
Luna coronato quotiens radiaverit ortu,
    alter ab aede sacra surgit ad astra iubar.
45 Si nocte inspiciat hanc praetereundo viator,
    et terram stellas credit habere suas.
Tota rapit radios, patulis oculata fenestris.
    Et quod mireris hic foris, intus habes.
Tempore quo redeunt tenebrae, mihi dicere fas sit,
50   mundus habet noctem, detinet aula diem.
Dextera pars templi meritis praefulget Hilari,
    compare Martino consociante gradum.

By Felix's bounty, Gaul, receive the fruits of heaven and
welcome the happy fulfillment of your bishop's vows, whose   25
chaste love presented in honor of the Most High this house
as perpetual dowry for his bride the church. The shape of
the church, lofty in height, extends in three parts, made sa-
cred to God by the names of the apostles. Their virtue ele-
vates them as far above the saints as the tops of these roofs   30
out-top any other. In its midst a towering pinnacle rises up
on high, its elevated summit rounding off a rectangular
structure. An amazing sight, arch rises on arch in ascending
height, a church like a mountain comes to a peak. There col-   35
ors bring life to limbs on display; you'd think the pictures
were living, animated by art. You see the figures come and go   39
in the undulating sunlight; the paneled ceiling behaves like   40
the waves of the sea. When the errant sun brings color to   37
the roofs of tin, its rays strike red, but reflect as milky light.   38
Roofs sheathed in metal mimic the gleam of stars, and in   41
their brightness their tops have an astral glow. When the
moon shines forth in its haloed rising, another beam mounts
to the stars from the holy church. If a traveler passing by   45
night turns to look this way, he thinks the earth too has its
own constellations. The whole building ensnares the light,
with wide-open windows like eyes, and what you wonder
at from outside, you enjoy when within. At the time when
the darkness returns, if I may so say, the world experiences   50
night, the church retains the day.

The right side of the building shines bright with the vir-
tues of Hilary; Martin was his partner and his companion in

Gallia sic proprios dum fudit ubique patronos,
    quos hic terra tegit, lumina mundus habet.
55 Altera Ferreoli pars est, qui vulnere ferri
    munere martyrii gemma superba nitet.
Obtulit haec Felix, ut sit magis ipse sacerdos,
    Christe, tuum templum, qui tibi templa dedit.

8

Item ad eundem in laude

Illuxit festiva dies, me gaudia cogunt
    ut quod plebs poterat, solus amore loquar.
Ultima quamvis sit regio Armoricus in orbe,
    Felicis merito cernitur esse prior.
5 Miserunt similes Oriens et Gallia sortes:
    illa micat radiis solis et ista tuis.
Nam splendore novo sua munera quisque ministrat:
    tu fers oceano lumen et ille rubro;
denique si sensus clara pro lampade fulget,
10   ingenium vestrum luminis instar habet.
Maxima progenies, titulis ornata vetustis,
    cuius et a proavis gloria celsa tonat.
Nam quicumque potens Aquitanica rura subegit
    extitit ille tuus sanguine, luce parens.

rank. While Gaul in this way sends a flood of its patrons in every direction, the world wins as its lights those whom the earth here conceals. The other side holds Ferreolus, who by the stroke of a sword glistens as a glorious jewel in reward for his martyrdom. Felix made this offering so that he, your bishop, who gave you a temple, would himself thereby become your temple, Christ. 55

8

Again to the same person, in his praise

The festive day has dawned, the mood of joy compels me to speak alone in love what the people would otherwise have said. Although the region of Armorica is the most remote in the world, because of Felix's virtue it is reckoned to be supreme. To both the East and Gaul has been allotted a similar 5 fortune: the first flames with the rays of the sun, the other with rays from you. For each of you bestows your gifts with an unequaled brilliance: you illuminate the ocean, it sheds light on the Red Sea. And so if character shines brightly like a lamp, your nature then is just like a beacon. 10

Your family is most lofty, adorned with ancient glories; even from remote ancestry its high fame resounds. For every powerful man who cultivated the Aquitanian country-

15 Germinis antiqui venerabile culmen in orbe,
   laudibus in cuius militat omne decus,
   flos generis, tutor patriae, correctio plebis,
   eloquii flumen, fons salis, unda loquax,
   semita doctrinae, ius causae, terminus irae,
20   cuius in ingenium hic nova Roma venit.
   Illic quod poterat per plures illa docere,
   te contenta suo Gallia cive placet.
   Ornamenta geris gemino fulgentia dono
   et te concelebrant hinc opus, inde genus.
25 Sed qui terrena de nobilitate nitebas,
   ecclesiam nunc spe nobiliore regis.
   Cuius ad ornatum, bone cultor, iugiter instans,
   ut iam multa Deo splendida dona dares,
   nupsisti ecclesiae, felicia vota iugasti,
30   hanc qui matronam dote potente reples;
   cuius in amplexu ducis sine crimine vitam,
   altera nec mulier corde recepta fuit.
   Hanc oculis, animo retines et corde pudico;
   unde tibi nupsit, castior inde manet.
35 Illa tibi prolem peperit, sed corpore virgo,
   et populum gremio fudit amata tuo.
   Ecce tuos natos divina ex coniuge sumptos,
   et modo te gaudent quos patris umbra tegit.
   Proque salute gregis pastor per compita curris,
40   exclusoque lupo tuta tenetur ovis.
   Insidiatores removes vigil arte Britannos;
   nullius arma valent quod tua lingua facit.
   Tu quoque ieiunis cibus es, tu panis egenti;
   quae sibi quisque cupit, hic sua vota videt.

side was a relative of yours in blood and in distinction. Per- 15
fection of an ancient race, held in honor in the world,
in whose praise every glory plays an active role, flower of
your family, protector of your country, director of the peo-
ple, river of eloquence, spring of good seasoning, articulate
flood, straight path of teaching, justice in law, stayer of
wrath, in your talent a new Rome finds its way here. Con- 20
tent with you alone as its citizen, Gaul excels in what in
Rome it took many teachers to impart. You sport distinc-
tions that shine with a double gift, and are recommended
both by your actions and your descent.

But though you once won glory from earthly nobility, you 25
now direct the church with still nobler hope. Constantly
attentive to its adornment, O excellent patron, so that al-
ready you have given many splendid gifts to God, you mar-
ried the church, joined with it in wedded felicity, and you 30
bestow on this wife a generous dowry. In her embrace you
live a life without fault, and no other woman has been re-
ceived in your heart. You keep her in your sight, in your
mind and modest breast; from the act of marrying you she
then becomes more chaste. She has borne you an offspring, 35
though in body a virgin, and beloved by you has entrusted a
whole people to your embrace. Look, here are your children
received from a wife who's divine; because of you now they
rejoice, protected under a father's shade. For the safety of
the flock as their shepherd you patrol the crossroads; by 40
shutting out the wolf the sheep are rendered secure. Watch-
ful in your care you banish the assaults of the Bretons; no
one can match in arms all that your tongue can do. You are
food for the hungry, you are bread for the needy; the desires
each person has for himself, he sees here those wishes ful-

45 Divitias proprias in pauperis ore recondis,
    largas mendici ventre reponis opes.
Tempore quo veniet Christus, tunc omnia vobis
    iudicis in facie sacculus iste refert.
Sit tibi fixa salus numerosos ampla per annos,
50   perpetuo Felix nomine, mente, fide.

9

Ad Felicem episcopum de pascha

Tempora florigero rutilant distincta sereno
    et maiore poli lumine porta patet.
Altius ignivomum solem caeli orbita ducit,
    qui vagus oceanas exit et intrat aquas.
5 Armatis radiis elementa liquentia lustrans,
    adhuc nocte brevi tendit in orbe diem.
Splendida sincerum producunt aethera vultum
    laetitiamque suam sidera clara probant.
Terra favens vario fundit munuscula fetu,
10   cum bene vernales reddidit annus opes.
Mollia purpureum pingunt violaria campum,
    prata virent herbis et micat herba comis.
Paulatim subeunt stellantia lumina florum
    arridentque oculis gramina tincta suis.
15 Semine deposito lactans seges exilit arvis,
    spondens agricolae vincere posse famem.

filled. You store up your own riches in feeding the mouths of 45
the poor, and you invest great wealth in the bellies of beg-
gars. At the time when Christ makes his return, before the
face of the judge treasure there will repay all those actions of
yours. May your health remain strong, resilient through nu-
merous years, happy, Felix, forever in name, mind, and faith. 50

9

To Bishop Felix on Easter

The season is aglow, spangled with flowers under a cloud-
less sky, and the gate of heaven lies open with fuller light.
Higher in the sky the fiery sun's path extends; in wandering
course it leaves, then reenters the ocean waters. Illuminat- 5
ing with its piercing rays the liquid-clear elements, it spreads
day through the world, though night still briefly stays. The
bright heavens reveal their cloudless countenance, while the
stars, still clear, bear witness to their gladness. The earth in
joy pours forth a bountiful variety of offspring, when the 10
year has brought back the full wealth of spring. Soft beds
of violets paint the fields purple, meadows are green with
grass, plants gleam with foliage. Gradually the starry lights
of flowers appear and smile on the grass they color with
their eyes. From the sown seed milky-rich crops spring forth 15
in the field, promising to the farmer that he can conquer

Caudice desecto lacrimat sua gaudia palmes;
    unde merum tribuat, dat modo vitis aquam.
Cortice de matris tenera lanugine surgens,
20   praeparat ad partum turgida gemma sinum.
Tempore sub hiemis foliorum crine revulso,
    iam reparat viridans frondea tecta nemus:
myrta, salix, abies, corylus, siler, ulmus, acernus,
    plaudit quaeque suis arbor amoena comis.
25 Construitura favos apes hinc alvearia linquens,
    floribus instrepitans poplite mella rapit.
Ad cantus revocatur aves, quae carmine clauso
    pigrior hiberno frigore muta fuit.
Hinc filomela suis attemperat organa cannis
30   fitque repercusso dulcior aura melo.
Ecce renascentis testatur gratia mundi
    omnia cum Domino dona redisse suo.
Namque triumphanti post tristia Tartara Christo
    undique fronde nemus, gramina flore favent.
35 Legibus inferni oppressis super astra meantem
    laudant rite Deum lux, polus, arva, fretum;
qui crucifixus erat, Deus ecce per omnia regnat,
    dantque creatori cuncta creata precem.
Salve, festa dies, toto venerabilis aevo,
40   qua Deus infernum vicit et astra tenet.
Nobilitas anni, mensum decus, arma dierum,
    horarum splendor, scripula, puncta fovens,
Hinc tibi silva comis plaudit, hinc campus aristis,
    hinc grates tacito palmite vitis agit.
45 Si tibi nunc avium resonant virgulta susurro,
    has inter minimus passer amore cano.
Christe, salus rerum, bone conditor atque redemptor,
    unica progenies ex deitate patris,

hunger. When shoots are pruned the stock weeps for joy, and the vine produces liquid now to furnish wine later. Rising with soft down from the bark of its mother, the swelling 20 bud prepares its womb for offspring. In winter time the canopy of leaves was stripped, but now the greening wood regains its covering of foliage: myrtle, osier, fir, hazel, willow, elm, and maple, each tree, fair in its foliage, joins the celebration. Here the bee now leaves the hives to build its 25 combs, and buzzing round the flowers steals honey on its legs. The bird awakes again to song that, its music stopped, had been voiceless, duller from the winter cold. Here the nightingale tunes its voice with its piping, and the breeze 30 grows sweeter with the reechoed song.

Behold, the beauty of the reborn world declares that all God's gifts have returned with their Lord. For as Christ celebrates his triumph after the gloom of Tartarus, on every side the wood with leaves, the grass with flowers acclaim him. As he passes beyond the stars, the laws of hell over- 35 thrown, light, heaven, fields, and wave give God due praise. He who had been crucified, look, now as God reigns over all, and all creation utters a prayer to its creator. Greetings, holy day, revered for the whole of time, when God con- 40 quered hell and took possession of the stars. Ennobler of the year, glory of the months, and bulwark of the days, illuminator of hours, nourisher of minutes and seconds, here the forest acclaims you with its leaves, here the field with its crops, and here the vine gives thanks to you with its silent shoots. If thickets now ring with the gentle whispering of 45 birds, I, the humblest sparrow, among them sing from love.

Christ, salvation of the world, its gracious creator and redeemer, sole offspring of the divinity of the Father, ineffably

irrecitabiliter manans de corde parentis,
50   verbum subsistens et penetrare potens,
aequalis, concors, socius, cum patre coaevus,
      quo sumpsit mundus principe principium,
aethera suspendis, sola congeris, aequora fundis,
      quaeque locis habitant quo moderante vigent,
55 qui genus humanum cernens mersisse profundo,
      ut hominem eriperes es quoque factus homo;
nec voluisti etenim tantum te corpore nasci,
      sed caro quae nasci pertulit atque mori.
Funeris exequias pateris vitae auctor et orbis;
60   intras mortis iter dando salutis opem.
Tristia cesserunt infernae vincula legis
      expavitque chaos luminis ore premi.
Depereunt tenebrae Christi fulgore fugatae
      et tetrae noctis pallia crassa cadunt.
65 Pollicitam sed redde fidem, precor, alma potestas;
      tertia lux rediit, surge, sepulte meus.
Non decet ut humili tumulo tua membra tegantur
      neu pretium mundi vilia saxa premant.
Indignum est, cuius clauduntur cuncta pugillo,
70   ut tegat inclusum rupe vetante lapis.
Lintea tolle, precor, sudaria linque sepulchro;
      tu satis es nobis et sine te nihil est.
Solve catenatas inferni carceris umbras
      et revoca sursum quidquid ad ima ruit.
75 Redde tuam faciem videant ut saecula lumen;
      redde diem, qui nos te moriente fugit.
Sed plane implesti remeans, pie victor, ad orbem.
      Tartara pressa iacent nec sua iura tenent.
Inferus insaturabiliter cava guttura pandens,
80   qui rapuit semper, fit tua praeda, Deus:

originating from the heart of your parent, existing as Word 50
with all-penetrating power, his equal and companion, har-
monious and coeternal with the Father, under whose reign
the world had its beginning, you hold up the sky, you amass
the earth, make flow the sea, and by your governance make
their inhabitants flourish, who seeing that the human race 55
was submerged in the depths, were made man yourself to
rescue man from that fate. Not only were you willing to be
born in bodily form, but the flesh which suffered birth also
suffered death. Creator of life and the world, you endure the
rituals of burial, and enter upon the path of death bringing 60
the blessing of salvation. The cruel bonds of the infernal law
gave way, and chaos feared extinction when confronted by
light. Darkness perishes, put to flight by Christ's brilliance,
and the thick cloak of loathsome night falls to the ground.

But fulfill the promise you made, I beg, O merciful power; 65
the third day has come, arise, my entombed lord. It is not
right that your body should be contained in a humble tomb,
or that worthless rocks should constrain the ransom of the
world. It is unfitting that you, in whose hand all things are
held, should be kept enclosed by a stone, a boulder blocking 70
the way. Remove the linen wraps, I pray, leave the handker-
chief in the tomb; you are sufficient for us and without you
there is nothing. Free the enchained shades of the infernal
prison and call up again whatever fell down to the depths.
Bring back your countenance that the world may see the 75
light; bring back the day, which fled us with your death.

But this you have clearly fulfilled in returning to the
world, holy conqueror. Tartarus is overthrown, and pros-
trate no longer has power. Hell, its gaping throat insatiably
yawning wide, has become your captive, God, that always 80

eripis innumerum populum de carcere mortis
  et sequitur liber quo suus auctor adit.
Evomit absorptam trepide fera belua plebem
  et de fauce lupi subtrahit agnus oves.
85 Hinc tumulum repetens, post Tartara carne resumpta,
  belliger ad caelos ampla tropaea refers:
quos habuit poenale chaos, iam reddidit in te,
  et quos mors peteret, hos nova vita tenet.
Rex sacer, ecce tui radiat pars magna triumphi,
90 cum puras animas sancta lavacra beant.
Candidus egreditur nitidis exercitus undis
  atque vetus vitium purgat in amne novo.
Fulgentes animas vestis quoque candida signat
  et grege de niveo gaudia pastor habet.
95 Additur hac Felix consors mercede sacerdos,
  qui dare vult Domino dupla talenta suo.
Ad meliora trahens gentili errore vagantes,
  bestia ne raperet, munit ovile Dei.
Quos prius Evva nocens infecerat, hos modo reddit
100 ecclesiae pastos ubere, lacte, sinu.
Mitibus alloquiis agrestia corda colendo,
  munere Felicis de vepre nata seges.
Aspera gens Saxo, vivens quasi more ferino;
  te medicante, sacer, belua reddit ovem.
105 Centeno reditu tecum mansura per aevum
  messis abundantis horrea fruge reples.
Immaculata tuis plebs haec vegetetur in ulnis,
  atque Deo purum pignus ad astra feras.
Una corona tibi de te tribuatur ab alto,
110 altera de populo vernet adepta tuo.

used to take captives. You snatch countless people from the prison of death; they follow freely where their creator leads. The fierce beast fearfully vomits out the people it has swallowed, and the lamb rescues his sheep from the jaws of the wolf. Then returning to the tomb, after Tartarus resuming 85 flesh once more, a warrior, you carry to heaven glorious victory trophies. The punishment of hell has surrendered in you those it once possessed; new life is now theirs, whom death was seeking.

Holy king, behold, a great part of your triumph shines forth, when the sacred bath sanctifies souls and makes them 90 pure. An army in white steps out from the shimmering waters and washes away the old fault in a new stream. White clothing too displays the brightness of souls, and their shepherd takes joy in his snow-white flock. Bishop Felix in their 95 company shares in the reward, for he wished to present to his Lord double his talents. Bringing to the better course those wandering in pagan error, he fortified God's fold so that the beast would not carry them off. Those whom Eve first infected with her sin he now restores, suckled by the 100 rich milk of the Church's breast. By cultivating savage hearts with gentle words, thanks to Felix a crop grows up from the thorns. A hard race the Saxons, living like wild animals, but when you heal them, holy one, the beast surrenders your sheep. Reaping a hundredfold return that will stay with you 105 for ever, you fill the granaries with the fruit of a bountiful harvest. May this your people flourish spotless in your embrace, and may you carry them aloft to the stars before God as a holy pledge. May one crown be granted to you from on high for your own deserts and another flourish spring-fresh 110 for your service to your people.

10

De domno Felice Namnetico, cum fluvium alibi detorqueret

Cedant antiqui quidquid meminere poetae;
    vincuntur rebus facta vetusta novis.
Includi fluvios si tunc spectasset Homerus,
    inde suum potius dulce replesset opus.
5 Cuncti Felicem legerent modo, nullus Achillem,
    nomine sub cuius cresceret artis honor,
qui probus ingenio mutans meliore rotatu
    currere prisca facis flumina lege nova.
Aggere composito removens in gurgite lapsum,
10   quo natura negat, cogis habere viam.
Erigis hic vallem, subdens ad concava montem,
    et vice conversa haec tumet, ille iacet.
Altera in alterius migravit imagine forma:
    mons in valle sedet, vallis ad alta subit.
15 Quo fuit unda fugax, crevit pigro obice terra,
    et quo prora prius, huc modo plaustra meant.
Collibus adversis flexas superinvehis undas
    et fluvium docilem monte vetante trahis.
Qua rapidus flueret, veniens celer amnis obhaesit
20   et subito nato colle retorsit iter.
Quae prius in praeceps veluti sine fruge rigabant,
    ad victum plebis nunc famulantur aquae.

10

On Lord Felix of Nantes,
when he diverted a river

Let ancient poets with the tales they tell step aside; the
deeds of the past are put in the shade by recent achieve-
ments. If in his day Homer had seen the courses of streams
dammed, he would have preferred that subject to fill his
sweet work. Everybody would be reading of Felix now, none 5
of Achilles, and under that name the fame of the poet's art
would increase, for beneficent in your skill, effecting change
for the better, you cause the former river-course to run by a
new dispensation. By erecting a highway and diverting the
flow in a fresh stream, where nature denies it, you compel a 10
road to exist. You raise up a valley here and hollow out a
mountain; in a reversal of roles the one swells, while the
other subsides. Each shape has taken on the outline of the
other: the mountain settles in a valley, the valley mounts to
the heights. Where once water rapidly flowed, behind a re- 15
straining barrier land has grown up, and where once boats,
now wagons wend their way. With the hills as a barrier you
channel the water in a curved course from above, and be-
cause of the mountain's obstruction you direct an obedient
stream. Where once it flowed apace, the swift stream has
come to a halt and at the hill that has suddenly sprung up 20
has redirected its course. The waters that previously ran
headlong seemingly without bringing fruit now offer their

Altera de fluvio metitur seges orta virorum,
    cum per te populo parturit unda cibum.
25 Qualiter incertos hominum scis flectere motus,
    qui rapidos fontes ad tua frena regis?
Stet sine labe tibi, Felix, pia vita per aevum,
    cuius ad imperium transtulit unda locum.

II

De Nicetio episcopo Treverensi

Splendor, apex fidei, venerabile mente Niceti,
    totius orbis amor pontificumque caput,
summus apostolico praecellens pastor ovili,
    auxisti meritis quidquid honoris habes.
5 Divino insistens operi terrena relinquis;
    cui moritur mundus, non moriture manes.
Vita brevis cunctis, sed non brevis illa beatis;
    cum bona non pereant, iure perennis eris.
Dum tibi restrictus maneas et largus egenis,
10   quod facis in minimis te dare crede Deo.
Captivus quicumque redit sua limina cernens
    ille lares patrios, tu capis inde polos.
Hic habet exul opem, ieiunans invenit escas;
    qui venit esuriens hinc satiatus abit.

service to bring sustenance to the people. Men reap a second crop produced by the stream, when because of you waters provide food for the people. How skilled are you in 25 shaping the uncertain impulses of men, who control with your bridle even fast-moving streams? Felix, may your holy life remain always firm without stain, at whose command water changed its location.

II

On Nicetius, bishop of Trier

Brilliant, preeminent in faith, Nicetius of venerable mind, beloved of all the world, supreme among the bishops, greatest of shepherds, excelling in care of your apostolic fold, you have enhanced with your merits whatever honor you receive. Intent on God's work, you leave behind you earthly 5 things; the world is dead to you, but you will never die. Life is brief for all, but it is not brief for the blessed; since good deeds do not die, you will rightly be eternal. In living with frugality to yourself, but generosity to the poor, what you do 10 for the least, believe that you give to God. Every captive who returns and sees once more his threshold gains again his father's house, but you from that gain heaven. Here the exile wins assistance, the hungry man finds his food; the per-

15 Tristibus imponis curas purgando querellas,
   et sanat cunctos una medella viros.
   Pauperis hinc lacrimas desiccas gaudia praestans:
   qui prius ingemuit, vota salutis habet.
   Te pascente greges numquam lupus abripit agnos;
20   sunt bene securi quos tua caula tegit.
   Templa vetusta Dei revocasti in culmine prisco
   et floret senior te reparante domus.
   Hic populis longos tribuas pia vota per annos
   et maneas pastor, ne lacerentur oves.

12

Item de castello eiusdem super Mosella

Mons in praecipiti suspensa mole tumescit
   et levat excelsum saxea ripa caput.
Rupibus expositis intonsa cacumina tollit
   tutus et elato vertice regnat apex.
5 Proficiunt colli quae vallibus arva recedunt;
   undique terra minor vergit et iste subit:
quem Mosella tumens, Rodanus quoque parvulus ambit
   certanturque suo pascere pisce locum.
Diripiunt dulces alibi vaga flumina fruges;
10   haec tibi parturiunt, Mediolane, dapes.

son who arrives famished departs from here filled. You take 15
on the cares of the grief-stricken, wiping away their sorrows;
you bring health to everyone, their single source of healing.
You dry the tears of the poor and bring them rejoicing; he
who once groaned aloud now gains his wish for wellbeing.
With you as shepherd of the flock the wolf never snatches
the lambs; those whom your sheepfold protects enjoy per- 20
fect security of mind. You have restored the ancient church
of God to its former heights, and the building, though aged,
flourishes through your repair. May you fulfill here the pious
wishes of your people for many years and remain their shep-
herd, so that your sheep suffer no mauling.

12

Again on the castle of the same bishop above the Moselle

A mountain swells up, hanging over a steep cliff, and a rocky
riverbank lifts high its head. On its prominent crags for-
ested heights stand out; its summit in lofty eminence reigns
secure. The land which slopes from the valley augments the 5
hill; everywhere the low-lying land falls away and the moun-
tain looms above. The swelling Moselle and the tiny Dhron
embrace this spot and vie to feed it with their native fish.
Elsewhere rivers in flood destroy the welcome harvests, but, 10

Quantum crescit aquis, pisces vicinius offert:
 exhibet hinc epulas unde rapina venit.
Cernit frugiferos congaudens incola sulcos,
 vota ferens segeti fertilitate gravi.
15 Agricolae pascunt oculos de messe futura;
 ante metit visu quam ferat annus opem.
Ridet amoenus ager tectus viridantibus herbis,
 oblectant animos mollia prata vagos.
Hoc vir apostolicus Nicetius ergo peragrans
20 condidit optatum pastor ovile gregi.
Turribus incinxit ter denis undique collem;
 praebuit hic fabricam, quo nemus ante fuit.
Vertice de summo demittunt brachia murum,
 dum Mosella suis terminus extet aquis.
25 Aula tamen nituit constructa cacumine rupis
 et monti imposito mons erit ipsa domus.
Complacuit latum muro concludere campum
 et prope castellum haec casa sola facit.
Ardua marmoreis suspenditur aula columnis,
30 qua super aestivas cernit in amne rates.
Ordinibus ternis extensaque machina crevit
 ut, postquam ascendas, iugera tecta putes.
Turris ab adverso quae constitit obvia clivo,
 sanctorum locus est, arma tenenda viris.
35 Illic est etiam gemino ballista volatu,
 quae post se mortem linquit et ipsa fugit.
Ducitur irriguis sinuosa canalibus unda,
 ex qua fert populo hic mola rapta cibum.
Blandifluas stupidis induxit collibus uvas;
40 vinea culta viret quo fuit ante frutex.

Mediolanus, these two streams provide banquets for you. The fuller the waters become, the closer the supply of fishes; from the cause of destruction comes the display of a meal. The locals rejoice to see the fertile plow land, and make their prayers for a crop of rich abundance. Farmers feed their eyes on the harvest to come and first reap with their glance the wealth the year will bring. 15

The pleasant countryside beams in its green cloak of vegetation and soft meadows delight the minds that range over them. The apostolic man Nicetius in roaming this land founded as shepherd a welcome sheepfold for his flock. He surrounded the hill on every side with thirty towers, and created a structure where previously forest had stood. From the topmost summit arms extend as walls, while the Moselle marks their limit with its waters. A palace shone out, constructed on the top of the rock; placed on a mountain, the building will itself be a mountain. He chose to surround a broad plateau with walls, and this dwelling alone almost constitutes a castle. A lofty hall is supported on columns of marble; from there in summer is a view of the boats on the river. The structure extends in width over three wings, so that, after you climb up, you imagine the roofs cover acres. Opposite is a tower that meets you as you climb the slope; it is the abode of saints, an arsenal for arming men. There is also a ballista there of double shot, which leaves death behind itself and itself flees. Water is conducted along winding irrigation channels, by which a mill here is powered that brings food to the people. He has clothed the astonished hills with sweet-juiced grapes; where once there was scrub, 40

Insita pomorum passim plantaria surgunt
    et pascunt vario floris odore locum.
Haec tibi proficiunt quidquid laudamus in illis,
    qui bona tot tribuis, pastor opime gregis.

13

Ad Vilicum episcopum Mettensem

Gurgite caeruleo pelagus Mosella relaxat
    et movet ingentes molliter amnis aquas;
lambit odoriferas vernanti gramine ripas
    et lavat herbarum leniter unda comas.
5 Hinc dextra de parte fluit qui Salia fertur,
    flumine sed fluctus pauperiore trahit.
Hic ubi perspicuis Mosellam cursibus intrat,
    alterius vires implet et ipse perit.
Hoc Mettis fundata loco speciosa coruscans
10   piscibus obsessum gaudet utrumque latus.
Deliciosus ager ridet vernantibus arvis;
    hinc sata culta vides, cernis at inde rosas.
Prospicis umbroso vestitos palmite colles;
    certatur varia fertilitate locus.
15 Urbs munita nimis, quam cingit murus et amnis,
    pontificis merito stas valitura magis.
Vilicus, aetheriis qui sic bene militat armis,
    stratus humi genibus te levat ille suis.

a green vineyard is tended. Everywhere fruit orchards are planted and grow; they fill the area with the varied scent of blossoms. All we praise in this redound to your credit, you who bestow so many blessings, noble shepherd of the flock.

13

To Vilicus, bishop of Metz

With sky-blue eddies the Moselle unwinds its flood and gently rolls its ample waters in its course. It licks the scented banks of spring-green grass, and softly washes the leaves of plants that it passes. On the right side flows the river called 5 the Seille, but it brings a current of poorer flow. Here where it joins the Moselle with its crystal stream, it augments another's strength, but loses its own. Metz, founded in this spot, radiant and beautiful, rejoices that both its flanks 10 are rich in fish. The smiling countryside charms with burgeoning fields; on one side you see crops growing, on the other roses. Ahead you look at hills clothed with shady vine boughs; fertility in varying forms stages a contest in this place.

City, though strongly fortified with wall and river, you 15 stand still stronger by the merits of your bishop. Vilicus, staunch fighter with heavenly weapons, by prostrating himself on his knees, raises you up. When humbly throwing

Unde humilis terris te proicis, alme sacerdos,
20   orando hinc patriae ducis ad astra caput.
Fletibus adsiduis acquiris gaudia plebi;
    pastoris lacrimis laetificantur oves.
Ictibus invalidis quamvis minitetur iniquus,
    tu quibus es murus, vulnera nulla timent,
25   et licet incluso lupus insidietur ovili,
    te custode gregis nil ibi praedo nocet.
Oblectas populos vultu sine nube sereno
    cunctorumque animos gratia blanda fovet.
Si poscat novus hospes opem, tu porrigis escas,
30   invenit et proprios ad tua tecta lares.
Dum satias querulum, magis obliviscitur illas
    quas habet in patriis finibus exul opes.
Qui sua damna refert, gemitus subducis ab ore;
    gaudia restituens tristia cuncta fugas.
35   Protegis hinc nudos, illinc tu pascis egentes;
    nil tibi reddit inops, reddit amore Deus.
Horrea praemittis, melius tua condita servans:
    quas sic diffundis dat paradisus opes.
Culmina templorum renovasti, Vilice cultor:
40   cum veniet Dominus, stat labor ecce tuus.
Commissum video non suffodisse talentum,
    sed magis aptatum multiplicatur opus.
Longius extensos peragas tam digna per annos
    et maneat semper nomen, opime, tuum.

yourself to the ground, kindly bishop, by praying you raise 20
your country's head to the stars. You win joys for your peo-
ple by your indefatigable weeping; by the tears of their shep-
herd your sheep are made glad. Although the malign one
threatens with unavailing blows, those whose wall you are
need have no fear of wounds, and though the wolf plots 25
snares for your enclosed sheepfold, with you as guardian of
the flock, that robber can do no harm there. You delight
your people with your clear and cloudless countenance, and
your warm affection wins the hearts of all. If a new arrival is
looking for aid, you provide him with food, and he discovers 30
a home for himself under your roof. When you satisfy his
woes, in exile he comes to forget the possessions he still has
in his native country. You remove from his lips all laments in
returning to him what he's lost; by restoring his joys, you put
to flight all grief. You protect the naked, and you feed those 35
in need; the poor pay you nothing back, but God pays you in
his love. You send ahead your provisions, so keeping your
possessions better in store; the wealth you distribute in this
way, paradise will give in return. Devout Vilicus, you have re-
built churches to their full height; when the Lord returns, 40
they stand here witness to your labors. I see you have not
buried the talent entrusted to you, but multiplied it is put to
a more suitable use. May you perform such worthy deeds for
many years to come, and may your name, O excellent one,
live on forever.

13a

Item ad eundem

Pastor opime gregis, cunctis tua pabula prosunt;
  qui satias animas, quam bene membra foves!
Sic avidos reddis convivas nectare lactis,
  ut scutella levet quod cocleare solet.

13b

Item ad eundem

Currit ovis repetens a te sua pascua, pastor.
  Qui cibus esse soles, da mihi panis opem.

13c

De pictura vitis in mensa eius dictum

Vitibus intextis ales sub palmite vernat
  et leviter pictas carpit ab ore dapes.
Multiplices epulas meruit conviva tenere:
  aspicit hinc uvas, inde Falerna bibit.

13a

Again to the same man

Noble shepherd of the flock, your pasturing profits all; how well you nurture the body, who also satisfy souls! You make your guests so hungry with the nectar of your milk, it takes a dish to serve what is normally only a spoonful.

13b

Again to the same man

A sheep hurries up, requesting pasturage from you, its shepherd. Grant me the succor of bread, for your role is to be food for all.

13c

On a picture of a vine, spoken at his table

In the interlacing vines under a tendril a bird is frolicking; with its beak it gently picks the food that is pictured there. The dinner guest enjoys receiving double sustenance: here he sees grapes, but he also drinks Falernian.

13d

De piscibus in mensa eius

Retia vestra, pater, oneroso pisce redundant:
   apparet Petri vos meruisse vices.

14

De pontifice Carentino Coloniae

Carentine, decus fidei, deitatis amice,
   nomine de proprio care, perennis amor,
pontificem pollens Agripina Colonia praefert,
   frugiferis agris digne colone Dei.
5   Si videas aliquos quacumque ex gente creatos,
   quamvis ignotos mox facis esse tuos.
Quos semel affectu astringis pietate paterna
   ulterius numquam dissociare potes,
nec subito veniens veluti fugitiva recedit,
10   sed concessa cito gratia fixa manet.
Verba Dei complens sicut te diligis ipsum,
   a te ita diligitur proximus omnis homo.
Vocis apostolicae sectator dignus haberis,
   quae caros animos praeposuit fidei.

13d

On fish at his table

Your nets, Father, overflow with a heavy catch of fish; it is clear you have just claim to be the successor of Peter.

14

On Bishop Carentinus of Cologne

Carentinus, glory of the faith and friend of the divinity, dear, as your name implies, eternal object of love, the powerful city of Cologne proudly proclaims you its pontiff, worthy cultivator for God in its fruitful fields. Whomever you see, 5 whatever their nationality, though you don't know them, you soon make them yours. Once you have bound anyone in affection with your paternal kindness, you never are able to part from them again, nor does the loving tie, though quickly formed, then retreat like a fugitive, but though 10 swiftly entered into, it yet remains firmly established. Fulfilling the words of God, in the same way that you love yourself, so is every neighbor loved by you. You are deemed a worthy follower of the words of the apostle, who gave pref-

15 Tranquillus, placidus, mitis, sine nube serenus,
      cui rabies mundi nil dominare potest,
   pectora cunctorum reficis dulcedine verbi,
      laetificas vultu tristia corda tuo.
   Pauperibus cibus es, sed et esurientibus esca,
20   rite pater populi dando salutis opem.
   Aurea templa novas pretioso fulta decore;
      tu nites unde Dei fulget honore domus.
   Maioris numeri quo templa capacia constent,
      alter in excelso pendulus ordo datur.
25 Sollicitat pia cura gregis te, pastor opime;
      nil lupus ab stabulis quo vigilante rapit.
   tempora longaevo teneas felicia tractu
      et per te Domini multiplicentur oves.

15

De Igidio episcopo Remorum

Actibus egregiis venerabile culmen, Igidi,
   ex cuius meritis crevit honore gradus,
subtrahor ingenio, compellor amore parato
   laudibus in vestris prodere pauca favens.
5 Namque reus videor tantis existere causis,
   si solus taceam quidquid ubique sonat.
Sed quamvis nequeam digno sermone fateri,

erence to charity of mind over faith. Calm, peaceful, mild, 15
and cloudlessly serene, over whom the madness of the world
can have no power, you refresh the breasts of all with the
sweetness of your word, you gladden grieving hearts with
your countenance. You are food for the poor and nourish-
ment for the hungry, bestowing as true father of the people 20
the alms of salvation. You restore churches in gold, fit them
out with costly decoration, and gain distinction from the ra-
diant beauty of God's house. To provide churches that can
accommodate greater numbers of people, a second floor is
erected, suspended on high. A holy concern for your flock 25
occupies you, noble shepherd; with you on guard, the wolf
steals nothing from your stables. May you enjoy happy times
in a long stretch of life, and may the sheep of the Lord find
increase by your efforts.

15

On Aegidius, bishop of Reims

Aegidius, high eminence revered for your noble deeds, from
whose virtues your office has grown in glory, I am restrained
by my failings, but compelled by my ready love for you to
speak in your praise a few admiring words. For I would seem 5
culpable before such a weighty subject, if I alone should
keep silent about all that sounds forth everywhere. But
although I cannot express myself in appropriate language,

da veniam voto me voluisse loqui.
Exiit in mundo gestorum fama tuorum
10   et meritis propriis sidus in orbe micas.
Clarior effulges quam Lucifer ore sereno;
    ille suis radiis, tu pietate nites.
Nil lupus insidiis cauto subducit ovili
    te pastore sacro pervigilante gregem.
15 Facundo eloquio caelestia dogmata fundis;
    ecclesiae crevit te monitore domus.
Pontificis studio correctio plebis haberis;
    ne tenebrae noceant, semita lucis ades.
Cunctorum recreas animos dulcedine verbi;
20   qui satias epulis, pascis et ore greges.
Praecepta implentur, non solo pane cibamur;
    delicias capimus quas tua verba ferunt.
Ut gaudet corpus cui mitior esca paratur,
    sic animae gaudent si tua lingua sonet.
25 Haeresis ira cadit forti te milite Christi;
    adquiris regi qui dedit arma tibi,
qui purgas spinis agros sermone colente,
    et mundata Deo surgit ubique seges.
Qui venit huc exul tristis, defessus, egenus,
30   hic recipit patriam te refovente suam.
Quae doluit tollis, gemitus in gaudia vertens,
    exilium removes, reddis amore lares.
Pauper habere cibum, meruit quoque nudus amictum;
    invenit hic semper, quae bona quisque cupit.
35 Consultum tribuis generaliter omnibus unum;
    qui populi pater es, tot pia rite regis.
Haec tibi vita diu Domino tribuente supersit
    atque futura micet lucidiore die.

pardon me for my good intentions, my willingness to speak of you.

The fame of your actions has gone forth through the world, and you glitter with your virtues, a star in the fir- 10 mament. With unclouded countenance you shine brighter than the morning star; it gleams with its rays, but you with your holiness. The wolf with his snares steals nothing from the well-guarded fold, when you, its saintly shepherd, keep watch over the flock. With your fluent eloquence you pour 15 forth the teachings of heaven; the family of the church has increased under your instruction. In your episcopal devotion you are deemed the people's corrector; you are their path of light so the darkness works no harm. You refresh the souls of all with the sweetness of your word; you satisfy 20 with food, and also pasture your flock with your voice. The teaching is fulfilled, we are not fed by bread alone; we enjoy the delicacies that your words bring to us. As the body rejoices that is served with choicer meals, so souls rejoice if your tongue gives voice. The fury of heresy falls before you, 25 Christ's valiant soldier; you make gains for the king who gave you your arms. You clear fields of thorns, tilled by your preaching, and everywhere a purified harvest springs up for God. The exile who comes here, grieving, weary, and needy, rediscovers in your protection his own native land. You re- 30 move his sorrows, turning his mourning to joy, you banish exile, you lovingly provide him a home. The poor can get food and the naked also get clothing; here everyone always finds the blessings he wants. You provide a single consola- 35 tion, universally bestowed on all; father of your people, you dutifully perform so many holy deeds. By the gift of the Lord may this life of yours long continue, and may it in the future shine with a still more brilliant light.

16

Ad Hilarium

Lux sincera animi, semper mihi dulcis Hilari,
    quamvis absentem quem mea cura videt,
cuius honestus amor tantum mea corda replevit
    ut sine te numquam mente vacante loquar,
5 versibus exiguis mandamus vota salutis;
    quae dedit affectus sint tibi cara, precor.

17

De Bertechramno episcopo, cum elevaretur in currum

Curriculi genus est memorat quod Gallia raedam:
    molliter incedens orbita sulcat humum;
exiliens duplici biiugo volat axe citato
    atque movet rapidas iuncta quadriga rotas.
5 Huc ego dum famulans comitatu iungor eodem
    et mea membra cito dum veherentur equo,
pontificisque sacri Bertechramni actus honore
    comprendente manu raptus in axe levor.
Qualiter implumes fetus pia mater hirundo

16

To Hilary

Unclouded light of my soul, always sweet to me, my Hilary, whom my affection sees though you are far away, for whom my virtuous love has so filled my heart that when I speak my mind is never apart from you, in modest verses I send my   5 wishes for your good health; may this gift of affection be dear to you I pray.

17

On Bishop Bertram, when the poet was raised into his carriage

There is a kind of chariot that the Gauls call a coach: in its smooth running it traces a track on the earth; propelled by a double two-horse team, it flies with speeding axle, and as a four-horse chariot it wheels rapidly along. When I in atten- 5 dance here joined this very company, and my body kept pace with them on a swift horse, I received an honor from the holy bishop Bertram, who seized me, snatched me up, and put me on his car. As a devoted mother swallow tends her

10   confovet et placide pinnula tensa tegit,
       sic bonitate potens, affectu dives opimo
          in proprium pastor molle sedile locat.
       Nec solum amplectens pia mens, sed diligit omnes,
          unde magis populis unicus extat amor.

18

Item ad eundem
de opusculis suis

   Ardua suscepi missis epigrammata chartis
      atque cothurnato verba rotata sopho.
   Percurrens tumido spumantia carmina versu,
      credidi in undoso me dare vela freto.
5 Plana procellosos ructavit pagina fluctus
      et velut oceanas fonte refudit aquas.
   Vix modo tam nitido pomposa poemata cultu
      audit Traiano Roma verenda foro.
   Quid si tale decus recitasses in aure senatus?
10   Stravissent plantis aurea fila tuis.
   Per loca, per populos, per compita cuncta videres
      currere versiculos plebe favente tuos.
   Sed tamen in vestro quaedam sermone notavi
      carmine de veteri furta novella loqui;

unfledged offspring and her plumage spreads lovingly to   10
protect them, so rich in charity and endowed with abun-
dant goodwill, the shepherd set me on his own soft seat.
Nor does his affectionate heart embrace me alone, but he
loves all, and so all the more for his people he is their single
beloved.

18

Again to the same person, about his compositions

I have received in the letter you sent your excellent epi-
grams and the words you wield with such high-sounding
skill. Navigating your poems that foam with your verses'
swell, I believed I was launching my sails onto the surging
sea. Your page, though flat, threw up stormy breakers, and   5
from your spring poured forth ocean-like waves. Scarcely
now are magnificent poems of such brilliant refinement
heard in the forum of Trajan by the venerable city of Rome.
What if you had recited such a masterpiece in the senate's
hearing? They would have spread before your footsteps   10
threads of gold. Through every land and people, on every
highway you would see your verses hastening to popular ap-
plause. But yet still I detected in the language of your verse
certain novel expressions stolen from the poems of the past,

15 ex quibus in paucis superaddita syllaba fregit
    et pede laesa suo musica cloda gemit.
Nunc, venerande pater, prece, voto, voce saluto,
    commendans animum supplice corde meum.
Sit tua vita diu, cuius modulante Camena
20   cogimur optatis reddere verba iocis.

19

Ad Agricolam episcopum

Praesul, honoris apex, generis fideique cacumen,
    cultor agri pollens, pastor opime gregis,
cum mea terra manu meruit genitoris arari,
    reddatur nati vomere culta sui.
5 Nam pater, affectu dulci memorabilis orbi,
    me vobiscum uno fovit amore duos.
Corde parens, pastu nutrix, bonus ore magister,
    dilexit, coluit, rexit, honesta dedit.
Ille pio studio sulcata novalia sevit;
10   quod pater effudit hoc mihi semen ale.

in which in some few cases an extra syllable has caused a   15
break so that maimed in its foot the halting meter groans
aloud. But now, my revered father, in prayer, vow, and voice I
greet you, entrusting to you my spirit with suppliant heart.
May your life be long, by whose tuneful Muse we are com-   20
pelled to send back words in welcome sport.

19

To Bishop Agricola

Bishop, eminent in status, high glory of your family and
faith, prime cultivator of your fields, noble shepherd of your
flock, since my soil had the good fortune to be plowed by
the hand of your father, may it be brought into cultivation
by the plowshare of his son. For your father, remembered   5
with sweet affection by the world, embraced the two of us,
you and me, with a single love. In heart a parent, in suste-
nance a nurse, in speech a good teacher, he loved and cared
for, guided, and taught the right. With holy zeal he sowed
the tilth he furrowed; the seed your father sowed now culti-   10
vate in me.

20

Ad Felicem episcopum Biturigum, scriptum in turrem eius

Quam bene iuncta decent, sacrati ut corporis agni
    margaritum ingens aurea dona ferant!
Cedant chrysolitis Salomonia vasa metallis:
    ista placere magis ars facit atque fides.
5 Quae data, Christe, tibi Felicis munera sic sint
    qualia tunc tribuit de grege pastor Abel,
et cuius tu corda vides, pietate coaeques
    Siraptae merito quae dedit aera duo.

21

Domino sancto atque apostolicis actibus praeconando, domno pio et peculiariter dulci in Christo, patri Avito papae Fortunatus humilis

Officiis intente piis, pater urbis Avite,
    gloria pontificum noster et altus amor,
per quem plebs, regio, peregrinus et hospes aluntur,
    in quo cuncta capit quae sibi quisque cupit,

20

To Felix, bishop of Bourges, written for his pyx

How fitting a combination, that a golden offering should enclose the mighty pearl that is the sacred body of the lamb! Let the vessels of Solomon fashioned of chrysolite concede the palm; both art and faith make these vessels of yours more pleasing. May the gifts that Felix gives to you, Christ,   5 in this way be such as Abel the shepherd once brought from his flock, and may you who see his heart compare him in devotion with the merit of the woman who at Sarepta gave her two mites.

21

Fortunatus in humility to my father Bishop Avitus, saintly lord, worthy of praise for his apostolic actions, holy lord and particularly dear in Christ

Devoted to your holy duties, Avitus, father of your city, ornament of bishops and our own dearest love, by whom a region and its people, foreigner and stranger are fed, in whom

5 ex opere immeritus merui pia dona patroni,
      ne minimam pascens immemor esses ovem.
   Qui trahis ore greges aeterna ad pabula Christi,
      qualiter hinc vivant est quoque cura tui.
   Semper et absentes praesens tua protegit ala;
10   quo pede non curris, munere totus ades.
   Muneribus vestris Agnes . . . aut Radegundis
      multiplici orantes fomite vocis agunt.
   Ad caelos penetranda seras, pater alte, talenta,
      quae centena suo tempore culta metas.
15 Per Dominum regemque bonum precor, aulice praesul,
      ut Fortunati sis memor, alme, tui.

22

Ad eundem

Paruimus iussis, sacer ac venerande sacerdos
   et pater, imperiis, dulcis Avite, tuis,
garrulitate levi potius stridente cicuta
   quam placeat liquido nostra camena melo.
5 Sed tamen, ut veniam tribuas, pietatis amator
      intende obsequium nec trutinato sophum.
   Munere pro magno modicus haec parvula solvo;
      pensetur votis, est cui lingua rudis.

everyone acquires all he desires, though undeserving in deed, I have won kindly gifts from my patron, so that you do not forget to feed even your humblest sheep. With your preaching you bring your flocks to the eternal pastures of Christ, and you make it your concern how they live here too. Your ever-present wing shelters even those who are absent; in your bounty you are fully present where on foot you do not go. For your generosity Agnes . . . and Radegund together voice prayers, fired by many motives to speak. May you sow, eminent father, talents that will rise to the heavens, for you to reap what you've nurtured a hundredfold in its due season. By the good Lord and King, I pray, courtly bishop, that you remember your Fortunatus, kindly one.

22

To the same man

I have done your bidding, saintly and venerable bishop, and, sweet father Avitus, obeyed your commands. My muse pipes shrilly with idle prattling rather than giving pleasure with a tuneful song. But yet you love to be charitable, so, to forgive me, give me credit for obedience and do not weigh my skill. For your great generosity in my modesty I make this slight return; let him whose tongue is awkward be judged by his intent.

22a

Item ad eundem

Virtutum quid celsa fides mereatur honoris,
    summe sacerdotum, dulcis Avite, probas,
qui nectens animos cunctorum in amore beato
    post te, care pater, pectora capta trahis.
5 Sed tamen inter eos, tua quos dulcedo replevit,
    promptus in affectu portio maior agor.
Lumen dulce meum, patriae vigor, altor egentum,
    spes peregrinorum, ductor honorque patrum,
si mea vox iugi resonaret acumine carmen,
10 laude minor loquerer, maior amore, pater.
Maxima sed nostri datur haec occasio voti
    vel memorare tuum nomen, opime, sacrum.
Commendantur item vestrae pietatis amori
    Agnes voce humili cum Radegunde pari.
15 Larga salutiferos vigeat tibi vita per annos,
    nam tua quae fuerit fit mea, care, salus.

22a

Again, to the same man

The honor that high regard for a person's virtues inspires, greatest of bishops, sweet Avitus, you demonstrate, who binding the spirits of all in a sanctified love, dear father, draw in your train their captive hearts. But yet among those   5 who are suffused with your sweetness, in my devoted affection I enjoy a special role. My own sweet light, pillar of your country, nourisher of the needy, hope for foreigners, chief and renown of our fathers, even if my voice rang out in a song of continual distinction, my words would fall short in   10 your praise, father, though excelling in love. But this opportunity is offered most favorably to fulfill my wish and to commemorate, noble one, your holy name. In addition Agnes with humble voice, and her companion Radegund are commended to your loving generosity of heart. May your   15 life flourish abundantly for many healthful years, for your good health, dear one, is mine as well.

23

De domno Agerico episcopo de Vereduno

Urbs Vereduna, brevi quamvis claudaris in orbe,
    pontificis meritis amplificata places.
Maior in angusto praefulget gratia gyro,
    Agerice, tuus quam magis auxit honor.
5 Plurima magnarum fudisti semina laudum,
    quae matura operis fertilitate metes.
Tempore praesenti victum largiris egenis,
    unde futura dies centuplicabit opes.
Dogmatis arcani reseras penetralia pastor,
10   nec solum dapibus, pascis et ore greges.
Templa vetusta novas pretiosius et nova condis;
    cultior est Domini te famulante domus.
Egregios fontes sacri baptismatis exples;
    tam pia divino fonte repletus agis.
15 Candida sincero radiat haec aula sereno
    et si sol fugiat, hic manet arte dies.
Ad nova templa avide concurrunt undique plebes
    et tribuis populis plus in amore Deum.
Te solamen inops meruit, te nudus amictum,
20   et solus cunctis potus et esca manes.
Felix qui meritis, aeternae lucis amator,
    tempore tam modico non moritura paras.

23

On Lord Ageric, bishop of Verdun

City of Verdun, although you are enclosed in a circum-
scribed orbit, by the virtues of your bishop you are enlarged
in renown. In its narrow circuit its luster shines the greater,
which your fame, Ageric, has increased all the more. You 5
have sowed many seeds of greatly praiseworthy deeds,
which you will reap when your work grows ripe to fruition.
In the present moment you bestow means of living on the
poor, for which a future time will increase your wealth a
hundredfold. As shepherd you reveal the innermost details
of mystical teachings and feed your flock not only with food, 10
but with speech. You renew old churches to greater splen-
dor, new ones you found; the house of the Lord is finer with
you as his servant. You bring to completion noble fonts for
the sacred rite of baptism; such holy deeds you perform, re-
plete with a font divine. This church shines brilliant with 15
clear, pure light, and if the sun departs, the daylight remains
here by art. From everywhere congregations eagerly gather
to the new sanctuaries, and in your love you make your peo-
ple a still greater gift of God. The poor find in you their con-
solation, the naked clothing, and alone you are food and 20
drink for all. Devotee of the eternal light, happy are you who
by your merits in so brief a time win an immortal reward.

23a

Item de Agerico episcopo de Vereduno

Phoebus ut elatum suspendit in aethera currum
    purus et igniferum spargit ubique iubar,
effusis radiis totum sibi vindicat orbem,
    montes, plana replens, ima vel alta tenet.
5 Sic, praesul, splendore animi cum sole coruscas;
    ille suis radiis fulget et ipse tuis.
Agerice sacer, cuius sermone colente
    ecclesiae segetes fertilitate placent,
terrenis sterilis rebus, fecunde supernis,
10   humana spernens, dives iture polis,
illecebris mundi mundus, lasciva repellens,
    nil cui subripuit carnis amarus amor,
lubrica culpa perit neque mors de crimine gaudet,
    cum tua delictis libera membra vides.
15 In templis habitando piis sic purus haberis,
    ut tua corda, pater, sint pia templa Dei.
Eligit in tali Christus se vase recondi;
    quam sibi purgavit possidet ipse domum.
Non dolus in labiis, nec sunt fera nubila mentis;
20   sinceris animis vernat in ore dies.
Doctilocum flumen salienti fonte refundis
    et sensus steriles voce rigante foves.
Ardua caelorum pandis mysteria terris,
    per quem plus Dominum scit, timet, orat, amat.

23a

Again on Ageric, bishop of Verdun

When Phoebus raises his lofty chariot to the heavens, and
with pure light scatters over all his fiery beam, with his
spreading rays he lays claim to all the world; filling moun-
tains and flatlands, he possesses both high and low. So,   5
bishop, with the brilliance of your soul you gleam like the
sun; he shines with his rays and you with yours. Saintly
Ageric, by the cultivation of whose preaching the church's
harvest brings joy with its fruitfulness, barren in worldly af-
fairs, but fertile in the celestial, scorning human concerns,   10
destined for wealth in heaven, proof against the entice-
ments of the world, shunning all wantonness, for whom the
bitter lure of the flesh has no allure, treacherous sin gives
way and death takes joy in no crime, when you see that your
body is free of all faults. By your dwelling in holy shrines you   15
become so pure that your heart, my father, is a holy shrine of
God. Christ himself chooses to be confined in such a vessel;
the dwelling he cleansed for himself he takes as his own.
There is no deceit on your lips nor are there lowering clouds
in your mind; your spirit is clear and daylight beams from   20
your face. You pour a stream of learning from your babbling
spring, and animate barren minds with the waters of your
voice. You expound on earth the high secrets of heaven; by

25 Dogmate divino, praesul facunde, triumphas,
       dans pastor monitis ne premat error oves.
    Deliciis reficis quas caelum, arva, unda ministrat,
       et satiat populos hinc cibus, inde fides.
    Sumit pauper opem, tristis spem, nudus amictum;
30   omnia quidquid habes omnibus esse facis.
    Hic tibi longa salus maneat, licet inde futura,
       atque diu, pastor, pro grege vota feras.

24

Ad virum venerabilem
Anfionem presbyterum

    Vir pietate calens, blanda dulcedine vernans,
       cuius in aspectu mens pretiosa micat,
    quem prius ut merui cognoscere lumine vultus,
       conspexi sensus lumen inesse tibi,
5   Anfion, mihi care pater, venerande sacerdos,
       atque meo semper corde tenendus amor,
    qui quemcumque novum videas facis esse propinquum;
       si genus ignores, fit tibi mente parens.
    Provocat alloquio cunctos iucunda voluntas,
10   cogis et unianimes iugiter esse tuos.

you more get to know, fear, worship, and love the Lord. You   25
win victory, eloquent prelate, with your divine teaching, as
a shepherd who by your preaching keep your sheep from
straying. You refresh with the delicacies heaven, earth, and
sea provide, and both food and faith bring your people satis-
faction. The poor receive aid, the grieving hope, the naked
clothing; everything that you have you put at the disposal of   30
everyone. May you long enjoy wellbeing here, even though
later you will do so in heaven, and, shepherd, may you long
offer prayers for your flock.

24

To a venerable man,
the priest Anfion

Figure of warm generosity, radiant with enchanting sweet-
ness, in whose visage your precious intellect shines forth, as
soon as I got to know you by my faculty of vision, I saw that
in you there were brilliant faculties of mind, Anfion, father   5
dear to me and venerable priest, always to be embraced as
my love in my heart, who make every stranger you see your
intimate; even if you do not know his family, he still be-
comes your relative at heart. The sympathetic charm of your
speech is attractive to all, and you compel them to be always   10

Ingenio vivax, sensus moderamine firmus,
    pondere consilii fixus ubique manes,
qui bene cauta regis maturae frena senectae,
    cui quem praestat honor scis moderare gradum.
15 Promptus ad omne decus larga bonitate redundas,
    cui se coniungit quisquis in urbe venit.
Profluus humane frugem venientibus offers
    et tua fit populis omnibus una domus.
Verbis quippe suis quem papa Leontius effert,
20   iudicio tanti credimus ista viri.

25

Ad Paternum abbatem
de codice emendato

Paruimus tandem iussis, venerande sacerdos,
    nominis officium iure, Paterne, regens,
qui propriis meritis ornans altaria Christi
    tam prece quam voto das placitura Deo.
5 Supplico, cede tamen, si quid me forte fefellit;
    nam solet iste meas error habere manus.
Obtineat supplex modo pagina missa salutis
    haec quoque cum relegis me memorare velis.

true in their devotion to you. Lively of intellect, steadfast
under reason's control, by the solidity of your judgment you
everywhere stand firm, who with prudent caution guide the
reins of ripe old age, and know the way to wield the rank
that honor grants you. Quick to perform every good deed, 15
you overflow with generous bounty; whoever comes to the
city allies himself to you. Liberal in your charity, you offer
food to new arrivals, and your house becomes a single home
for all peoples. Since Bishop Leontius sings your praises
with his words, we believe what he says, trusting so great a 20
man's judgment.

25

To Abbot Paternus,
on a corrected manuscript

I have finally fulfilled your orders, holy priest, Paternus,
who duly perform the calling of your name. Adorning the al-
tar of Christ with your own special virtues both in prayer
and vow, you offer what is pleasing to God. I beg you, give 5
pardon if any mistake has escaped me, for such an error ha-
bitually afflicts my writing. May the page I send as greeting
by its pleas now achieve that when you read it over you call
me to mind.

26

Ad Rucconem diaconum,
modo presbyterum

Altaris Domini pollens, bone Rucco, minister,
    hinc tibi festinus mando salutis opus.
Nos maris oceani tumidum circumfluit aequor,
    te quoque Parisius, care sodalis, habet.
5 Sequana te retinet, nos unda Britannica cingit;
    divisos terris alligat unus amor.
Non furor hic pelagi vultum mihi subtrahit illum
    nec boreas aufert nomen, amice, tuum.
Pectore sub nostro tam saepe recurris amator,
10   tempore sub hiemis quam solet unda maris.
Ut quatitur pelagus quotiens proflaverit eurus,
    stat neque sic animus te sine, care, meus.
Blanda serenato tempestas pectore fervet
    atque ad te varia mobilitate trahit.
15 Sed memor esto mei votumque repende petenti
    ut pariter paribus det sua dona Deus,
humanam mentem Christi quo gratia ditet
    ac Domino nostro sensus et ora vacent.

26

To Deacon Rucco,
now priest

Good Rucco, mighty servant of the altar of the Lord, from here in haste I dispatch the duty of greeting. The heaving surface of the ocean washes round me, while Paris holds you, dear friend, in its keep. The Seine is your dwelling 5 place, mine circled by the Breton tide: one love binds us together, though we are geographically apart. The fury of the deep does not steal from me your countenance here, nor the north wind carry off your name, my friend. To my heart you return as often, my dear one, as the sea-wave to the shore in 10 stormy weather. As the sea tosses when the east wind blows, so my mind, dear friend, is agitated without you. A pleasurable storm seethes in my tranquil heart and draws me to you with varying speed. But be mindful of me and grant the wish 15 I am seeking so that God give his gifts to the two of us together, and that Christ's grace enrich our human minds, and we devote to God our thoughts and voices.

27

Ad archidiaconum de Meldis

Si mihi vel vestros licuisset cernere vultus,
    munere pro tanto plurima verba darem..
Direxit nobis mustum tua cara voluntas;
    et dulces animos dulcia dona probant.
5 Quem non vidisti promptus satiare parasti;
    quid facias illi qui tibi notus adest?
Det tibi larga Deus, qui curam mente fideli
    de grege pontificis, magne minister, habes.

28

Ad Iohannem diaconum

Pignus amicitiae semper memorabile nostrae
    versibus exiguis, care Iohannis, habe,
ut cum me rapiunt loca nunc incognita forsan,
    non animo videar, dulcis, abesse tuo.
5 Anthemium patrem per te, venerande, saluto,
    cuius in affectu consolidatus agor.

27

To the archdeacon of Meaux

If I only had the opportunity to see you face to face, I would
spend many words in thanks for your wonderful gift. Your
kind benevolence has dispatched to me wine, a sweet gift,
proof of your sweetness of character. You were quick to sat- 5
isfy a person you'd never seen; what would you do for some-
one who was well known to you? May God grant you his
bounty, who minister with faithful attention to the needs of
the bishop's flock, noble deacon.

28

To Deacon John

As a pledge of our friendship, always firm in memory, dear
John, receive from me these slender verses, so that when
now unknown lands call me, perhaps, away, I do not seem
distant, sweet one, from your heart. Through you I send 5
greeting, revered one, to Father Anthemius, in whose affec-
tions I have a confirmed place. Likewise the name of Hilary,

Hilarium pariter nobis in amore tenacem
  insero carminibus, quem mea corda colunt.
Perpetuo maneas meritis felicibus aevo;
10   haec quoque cum relegis me memorare velis.

29

Ad Anthimium diaconum

Suscipe versiculos, Anthimi, pignus amantis,
  quos tibi sincero pectore fudit amor.
Cum tua blanditus retineret lumina somnus
  lassaque fecisset membra iacere toro,
5 dum dubito, pecco, nolens vexare quietum:
  sic mea culpa tui causa soporis erit.
Discedo tacitus, veluti fur, indice nullo
  nec dixi amplectens: "frater amate, vale."
Non licuit mandata animo committere caro
10   nec tenuit verbis hora vel una tuis.
Testificor Dominum mihi fortiter esse molestum,
  quod sic abscedo nec tua dicta fero.
Sed cui plura volens poteram tunc dicere praesens
  nunc faciat paucis pagina missa loqui.
15 Haec tamen ante Deum rogo te mihi munera praestes,
  omnibus ut semper carus ubique mices.
Nemo mihi vestem, denaria nemo ministret,
  quod dulcedo monet, hoc mihi nemo neget.

bound to me in love, whom in my heart I hold dear, I include in my poem. For your excelling virtues may you live in life eternal, and when you read this over may you call me to mind. 10

29

To Deacon Anthemius

Accept as pledge of my devotion, Anthemius, these slight verses, which are the outpourings of love from a sincere heart. When sleep with its charms cast its spell on your eyes and laid your weary body to rest on its bed, in my hesitation 5 I did wrong, unwilling to disturb your rest; in this way your sleep will be the cause of my sin. I slipped away in silence like a thief with no parting sign, without an embrace and the words "beloved brother, farewell." I had no chance to impart a message to your dear soul nor even the extent of one 10 hour for your words. As the Lord is my witness, it caused me great grief to depart as I did without speaking with you. But the many things I wished to say to you then in person now this page that I send allows me to say in brief compass. This 15 gift I request before God that you grant to me, that always and everywhere your affection shine out for all. Though no one give me clothing, and no one give me money, let no one deny to me the feeling that sweetness inspires.

30

Ad Sindulfum diaconum

Frater amore Dei, digno memorabilis actu,
    pectore fixe meo frater amore Dei,
carpe libenter iter quod ducit ad aetheris aulam;
    altius ut surgas, carpe libenter iter.
5 Fer patienter onus neque te pia sarcina lasset;
    unde manet requies, fer patienter onus.
Subdere colla decet, quia sunt iuga dulcia Christi:
    quo mereamur opem, subdere colla decet.
Qui sua rura colit solet horrea plena tenere
10   nec ieiunus erit qui sua rura colit.
Per mare nauta volat quo multa pecunia crescat;
    mercibus ut placeat per mare nauta volat;
non timet ille necem rabie turbante procellae:
    ut lucretur opes non timet ille necem.
15 Miles ad arma venit quaerens per vulnera palmam;
    ut redeat victor, miles ad arma venit.
Proelia sume libens mihi tu quoque, care sodalis;
    unde triumphus erit, proelia sume libens.
Quisquis amore venit nescit se ferre laborem;
20   nemo labore iacet quisquis amore venit.
Carmina parva ferens tibi debita reddo salutis;
    des meliora, precor, carmina parva ferens.

30

To Deacon Sindulf

Brother in the love of God, distinguished by your noble actions, deep set in my heart's affection, brother in the love of God, with joy pursue the journey that leads to the heavenly court; to mount up on high with joy pursue the journey. Patiently support your load, let not your holy burden tire you; to secure the repose that awaits you patiently support your load. It is right to bend the neck for the yoke of Christ is sweet; to win the reward it is right to bend the neck. Who farms his own fields is used to having full granaries; he will experience no hunger who farms his own fields. The sailor wings over the sea to increase his great wealth; to win favor with his wares the sailor wings over the sea. He has no fear of death, though the storm boils and rages, to make more money he has no fear of death. The soldier takes up arms, seeking by wounds the palm; to return in victory the soldier takes up arms. Enter the fray in good heart, you too, my dear companion; from it you will win a triumph, enter the fray in good heart. Whoever journeys in love is oblivious to any suffering; no one is defeated by suffering, whoever journeys in love. In offering my small poem I send you the greeting I owe; may you send back better, I beg, in offering my small poem.

BOOK FOUR

I

Epitaphium Eumeri
episcopi civitatis Namneticae

Quamvis cuncta avido rapiantur ab orbe volatu,
  attamen extendit vita beata diem,
nec damnum de fine capit cui, gloria, vivis
  aeternumque locum missus ad astra tenet.
5 Hoc igitur tumulo requiescit Eumerius almo,
  per quem pontificum surgit opimus honor.
Stemmate deducit fulgens ab origine culmen
  et meritis priscos crescere fecit avos.
Emicuit populis geminum memorabile donum:
10 inde gradu iudex, hinc pietate pater.
Dulcis in eloquio, placidus moderamine sacro,
  in cuius sensu perdidit ira locum,
alterius motus patienti pectore vicit;
  ut levitas laesit, hoc gravitate tulit.
15 Si quis ab externis properavit sedibus hospes,
  mox apud hunc proprios sensit habere lares.
Hic habitare volens patriis rudis exul ab oris
  oblitus veterem huius amore patrem.
Gaudenti arrisit, probat is se cernere flentem;
20 alterius lacrimas mox facit esse suas.

I

Epitaph of Eumerius,
bishop of the city of Nantes

Although all things are snatched from the world in greedy
flight, yet a blessed life prolongs a person's days, and the
man for whom you, glory, live receives no harm from death,
but enjoys a place in eternity, exalted to the stars. And so in 5
this sacred tomb Eumerius finds his rest, by whom the high
office of bishops gains in eminence. In his family origins he
traced a brilliant distinction and by his virtues caused his
ancestors to gain merit. Renowned he shone forth as a twin
boon for his people: in status a judge, in kindness a father. 10
Sweet in his speech, and peaceable in holy governance, in
his character anger had lost all hold. He calmed others' emo-
tions with his patience of spirit; with dignity he bore all that
vanity inflicted. If a stranger traveled from distant parts, im- 15
mediately with the bishop he felt he'd found home. Wishing
to settle here a recent exile from his native shores soon for-
got his old father in his love for his new one. He had smiles
for the joyful and showed his regard for the sorrowing; the 20

Partitus cum ventre vices pietate magistra,
    unde tulit luctus, mox ibi vota dedit.
Pauperibus dives censum transfudit egenis,
    ante bonus tribuit quam peteretur opem.
25 Semina iactavit centeno pinguia fructu,
    cui modo de reditu messis adulta placet.
Unica cura fuit, cunctos ut viseret aegros,
    ipse quibus medicus vixit et ipse cibus.
Extulit ecclesiae culmen; quod restitit unum
30   venit ad heredem, qui cumularet opus.
Felix ille abiit, Felicem in sede reliquit,
    heredis meritis vivit in orbe pater.

2

Epitaphium domni Gregori episcopi civitatis Lingonicae

Postquam sidereus disrupit Tartara princeps,
    sub pedibus iusti, mors inimica, iaces.
Hoc veneranda sacri testatur vita Gregori,
    qui modo post tumulos intrat honore polos.
5 Nobilis antiqua decurrens prole parentum,
    nobilior gestis nunc super astra manet.
Arbiter ante ferox, dehinc pius ipse sacerdos,
    quos domuit iudex fovit amore patris.

tears of another he quickly claims as his own. Sharing the lot
of the hungry at the prompting of charity, when exposed to
grief he quickly gave what was wanted. Rich to the poor, he
dispersed his wealth to the needy, a good man he bestowed
his bounty before being asked. He cast seeds rich with a   25
hundredfold fruit; now the harvest is ripe and he enjoys the
return. His special care it was to visit every one of the sick;
he spent his life as their physician and sustenance. He raised
up a lofty church; the single task that remained fell to his   30
successor, to complete the work. He passed away in felicity,
and left Felix in his see; in the virtues of his successor the
father still lives on earth.

2

Epitaph of Lord Gregory, bishop of the city of Langres

Now that the celestial prince has broken the bonds of Tarta-
rus, you lie prostrate, hateful death, under the feet of the
just. To this the venerable life of saintly Gregory bears wit-
ness, who now after the tomb enters the heavens in glory.
Noble and descended from ancient ancestral stock, but no-   5
bler by his actions, he now dwells beyond the stars. Once a
strict judge, but thereafter a holy bishop, those whom he
disciplined as judge he loved as father. For thirty-two years

Triginta et geminos pie rexit ovile per annos
10   et grege de Christi gaudia pastor habet.
Si quaeras meritum, produnt miracula rerum,
     per quem debilibus fertur amica salus.

3

Epitaphium domni Tetrici episcopi civitatis Lingonicae

Palma sacerdoti, venerando Tetrice cultu,
     te patriae sedes, nos peregrina tenent.
Te custode pio numquam lupus abstulit agnum,
     nec de fure timens pascua carpsit ovis,
5 sex qui lustra gerens et per tres insuper annos
     rexisti placido pastor amore gregem.
Nam ut condirentur divino corda sapore,
     fudisti dulcem iugiter ore salem.
Summus amor regum, populi decus, arma parentum,
10   ecclesiae cultor, nobilitatis honor,
esca inopum, tutor viduarum, cura minorum,
     omnibus officiis omnia, pastor, eras.
Sed cui praebebat varie tua cura medellam,
     funere rectoris plebs modo triste gemit.
15 Hoc tamen, alme pater, speramus: dignus in astris
     qualis honore nites, hic pietate probes.

he devotedly ruled over his sheepfold and as its shepherd 10
took pleasure in herding Christ's flock. If you wish to know
his virtuousness, his miracles bear witness: by him the boon
of healing is bestowed on the infirm.

3

Epitaph of Lord Tetricus, bishop of the city of Langres

Paragon of the priesthood, Tetricus, worthy of reverence,
you reside in your homeland, we are in exile on earth. Under
your holy tutelage no wolf ever carried off a lamb, no sheep
feared capture as it grazed in the pasture; for thirty years 5
and an additional three more, you guided your flock as a
calm and loving shepherd. In order that their hearts be sea-
soned by a heavenly savor, you constantly poured from your
mouth a sweet salted flood. High favorite of kings, pride of
the people, stronghold of kin, promoter of the church and 10
glory of the noble, food for the needy, protector of widows,
guardian of the young, you were, shepherd, in every duty all
in all. But the people to whom in various ways your care
brought healing now sorrowfully grieve for the death of
their leader. Still this we hope for, kindly father, that re- 15
warded in heaven you show here by your compassion how
you shine with glory there.

4

Epitaphium domni Galli episcopi civitatis Arvernae

Hostis inique, Adam paradiso fraude repellis;
    ecce Deus famulos praestat adire polos.
Invide, sic tua mors homini meliora paravit:
    tu expellis terris, hic dat et astra suis.
5 Testis et antistes Gallus probat ista beatus,
    nobilis in terris, dives eundo polis.
Qui Christi auxilio fultus nec adultus in annis,
    se maiora petens odit amore lares.
Effugit amplexus patrios matremque relinquit;
10   qui monachum regeret, quaeritur abba parens.
Illic tiro rudis generoso coepit ab aevo
    militiae Domini belliger arma pati.
Quintiano demum sancto erudiente magistro
    pulchrius est auro corde probatus homo.
15 Inde palatina regis translatus in aula,
    Theuderice, tuo vixit amore pio.
Mox ubi destituens terras petit astra magister,
    cessit discipulo cura tuenda gregem.
Pontificatus enim moderans ita rexit habenas
20   pastor ut officiis esset, amore pater,
mansuetus, patiens, bonus, aequus, amator, amandus,
    non erat offensae, sed locus hic veniae.
Si qua supervenit, facta est iniuria virtus;
    unde furor poterat, inde triumphus erat.

4

Epitaph of Lord Gallus, bishop of the city of Clermont in the Auvergne

Cruel foe, though you expel by your guile Adam from paradise, see, God grants to his servants to rise to the sky. Jealous one, this death you bring improved the state of man: you drive them out from earth, he gives to his faithful the stars. As witness and bishop, blessed Gallus proves this is so, noble 5 on earth, rich in his journey to heaven. Leaning on Christ's assistance, though not yet full-grown in years, seeking to better himself he lovingly shunned his home. He fled his father's embrace and left behind him his mother; he sought as 10 parent an abbot to direct him as monk. There an unformed novice he began in his youthful nobility to endure battles as a warrior in the service of the Lord. Then next when instructed by holy Quintianus his teacher, he was proved a man finer than gold in his heart. From there he was moved 15 to the royal palace court, where he lived enjoying your devotion and love, Theuderic. Soon when his teacher quit the earth and rose to the stars, the responsibility for protecting the flock fell to his pupil. With such good judgment did he govern the reins of the episcopate that he was a shepherd in 20 his duties, but a father in love. Mild, patient, virtuous, and just, loving and beloved, he had no truck with anger, but only with forgiveness. If any offense occurred, the slight became an occasion for virtue; from what could have aroused

25 Plebem voce fovens quasi natos ubere nutrix,
       dulcia condito cum sale mella rigans,
    hoc opus exercens praesciit dona futuri,
       se pastore nihil posse perire gregi.
    Sic pater ecclesiam regit in quinquennia quinque,
30   vix terdena tamen lustra superstes agens.
    Hinc meliore via sanctum ad caelestia vectum
       non premit urna rogi, sed tenet ulna Dei.

5

Epitaphium Ruriciorum
episcoporum civitatis Limovecinae

    Invida mors, rabido quamvis miniteris hiatu,
       non tamen in sanctis iura tenere vales.
    Nam postquam remeans domuit fera Tartara Christus,
       iustorum meritis sub pede victa iaces.
5   Hic sacra pontificum toto radiantia mundo
       membra sepulchra tegunt, spiritus astra colit.
    Ruricii gemini flores, quibus Aniciorum
       iuncta parentali culmine Roma fuit.
    Pectore vena loquax, mundano culta sapore,
10   venit ad aetherios lingua colenda libros.
    actu, mente, gradu, spe, nomine, sanguine nexi,
       exultant pariter hinc avus, inde nepos.

wrath, instead he won a triumph. Nurturing his people with
his words as a nurse does children with her breast, sending
streams of sweet honey with his eloquence, in performing
this work he foreknew the future reward, that with him as
shepherd his flock could suffer no loss. So as a father he gov-
erned the church for twenty-five years, though scarce sixty-
five years was the span of his life. From here the holy man
was borne on a better journey to heaven; no funeral urn con-
fines him, but he is embraced in the arms of God.

25

30

5

Epitaph of the Ruricii,
bishops of the city of Limoges

Envious death, although you threaten with ravenous jaws,
yet over the holy you can hold no power. For after Christ by
his return brought cruel Tartarus to heel, you lie underfoot,
vanquished by the virtues of the just. Here with a brilliance
that sends its rays through all the world a tomb conceals the
bishops' holy limbs, their spirit joins the stars. The Ruricii
are a double bloom, to whom Rome is related by ancestral
ties of nobility through the family of the Anicii. In their
hearts was a stream of eloquence, refined with a worldly sa-
vor, but their tongues turned to heavenly books for their
nurture. In action, thought, and status, in hope, name, blood
connected, grandson and grandfather, they share a common

5

10

Tempore quisque suo fundans pia templa patroni
    iste Augustini, condidit ille Petri.
15 Hic probus, ille pius, hic serius, ille serenus,
    certantes pariter quis cui maior erit,
plurima pauperibus tribuentes divite censu
    misere ad caelos quas sequerentur opes.
Quos spargente manu redimentes crimina mundi
20   inter apostolicos credimus esse choros.
Felices qui sic de nobilitate fugaci
    mercati in caelis iura senatus habent.

6

Epitaphium Exoci
episcopi civitatis Limovecinae

Quamvis pontificem premeret tremebunda senectus,
    attamen haec voluit plebs superesse patrem,
aut si naturae mutari debita possent,
    pro pastore suo grex properasset iter.
5 Sed quia non licuit, populum spes consulat illa,
    quod hunc pro meritis vexit ad astra fides.
Immaculata Deo conservans membra pudore
    Exocius meruit iam sine fine diem,
pectore sub cuius regnans patientia victrix;
10   fluctibus in tantis anchora sensus erat.

joy. Each in his lifetime built a sacred shrine to his patron:
one founded a church to Augustine, the other a church to
Peter. One was virtuous, the other pious, one was grave, the   15
other calm; they engaged in a mutual contest each to outdo
the other. Bestowing richly on the poor from their abundant
wealth, they sent on to heaven a treasure they were to fol-
low. By redeeming the crimes of the world by their generous
bounty we believe they take their place among the apostles.   20
Happy are they who in exchange for fleeting nobility have
bought senatorial status in heaven.

6

Epitaph of Exocius, bishop of the city of Limoges

Although the tremors of old age were afflicting their bishop,
yet the people wanted their father still to live, or if the debt
due to nature could be transferred, his flock would have
sped on that course in place of their shepherd. But as that   5
could not be, let this assurance console the people, that his
faith, as he deserved, has transported him to the stars. In
keeping his body in chastity unstained for God, Exocius has
won now a daylight without end; in his heart patience main-
tained triumphant sway; good judgment served as his an-   10

Felle carens animus, placida dulcedine pastus,
    nesciit offensis ira referre vices.
Templorum cultor, recreans modulamine cives,
    vulneribus patriae fida medella fuit.
15 Qui tria lustra gerens in pontificatus honore
    pergit ad antiquos plebe gemente patres.
Non decet hunc igitur vacuis deflere querellis,
    post tenebras mundi quem tenet aula poli.
Militiam peragens, capiens nova praemia regis,
20   pro Fortunato supplice funde precem.
Obtineas votis, haec qui tibi carmina misi,
    ut merear claudi quandoque clave Petri.

7

Epitaphium Chaletrici
episcopi civitatis Carnotenae

Illacrimant oculi, quatiuntur viscera fletu
    nec tremuli digiti scribere dura valent,
dum modo, qui volui vivo, dabo verba sepulto
    carmine vel dulci cogor amara loqui.
5 Digne tuis meritis, Chalacterice, sacerdos,
    tarde note mihi, quam cito, care, fugis!
Tu patriam repetis, nos triste sub orbe relinquis:
    te tenet aula nitens, nos lacrimosa dies.

chor in the stormy waves of life. His mind lacked bitterness,
it fed on the sweetness of peace, and was incapable of an-
swering insults with anger. Patron of churches, by tuneful
eloquence refreshing his people, he was a sure source of
healing for the wounds of his country. For fifteen years he   15
occupied the office of the episcopate, then to the grief of his
people went to join his forefathers. No cause, then, to weep
for this man with empty tears, whom after this world's dark-
ness the court of heaven holds.

After performing your service, receiving fresh rewards
from your king, give voice to a prayer for Fortunatus your   20
petitioner. May you win by your prayers that I, who have
sent you this poem, gain one day admittance by the key of
Saint Peter.

7

Epitaph of Chaletricus,
bishop of Chartres

Tears fill my eyes, weeping shakes my inmost being, and my
trembling fingers cannot shape the painful words, as now I
address you in the tomb, not, as I'd wished, alive and am
forced to speak of what's bitter in sweet song. Chaletricus,   5
by your virtues worthy to be bishop, too late known to me,
how quickly, my dear friend, you flee! You return to your
homeland, but leave us in the sad world below; bright halls
possess you, but us only tearful day.

Ecce sub hoc tumulo pietatis membra quiescunt
10   dulcior et melli lingua sepulta iacet:
forma venusta, decens, animus sine fine benignus,
   vox suavis, legem promeditata Dei,
spes cleri, tutor viduarum, panis egentum,
   cura propinquorum, totus ad omne bonum;
15   organa psalterii cecinit modulamine dulci
   et tetigit laudi plectra beata Dei,
cautere eloquii bene purgans vulnera morbi,
   quo pascente fuit fida medella gregi.
Sex qui lustra gerens, octo bonus insuper annos,
20   ereptus terrae iustus ad astra redis.
Ad paradisiacas epulas te cive reducto
   unde gemit mundus gaudet honore polus,
et quia non dubito quanta est tibi gloria laudum,
   nec debes fleri, talis amice Dei.
25   Haec qui, sancte pater, pro magnis parva susurro,
   pro Fortunato, quaeso, precare tuo.

8

Epitaphium Cronopi
episcopi civitatis Petrocoricae

Si terrena, sacer, quondam tibi cura fuisset,
   carmine plus lacrimas, quam modo verba darem.
Sed quia tu mundus nec sunt tibi crimina mundi,
   nos gaudere mones qui sine morte manes.

See, here in this grave his holiness's body finds rest, and 10
his tongue sweeter than honey lies entombed. His body was
graceful and elegant, his mind unfailingly kind, and his voice
sweet, well-versed in the law of God; hope of the clergy, pro-
tector of widows, bread of the needy, guardian of his rela-
tives, wholehearted for everything good, with sweet tune- 15
fulness he sang the music of the psalms and took up in praise
the happy plectrum of God, cleansing the wounds of disease
with the cauterizing iron of eloquence; with him as their
shepherd his flock could be certain of healing. You lived, a
good man, for thirty years, and eight more in addition, then 20
snatched from earth you return, being just, to the stars. You
go back to the banquet of paradise where you are a citi-
zen; what causes the world to grieve brings joy to heaven
in honoring you, and because I do not doubt the great glory
of your virtues, there is no need for weeping, such is your
friendship with God. Holy father, pray for your Fortunatus, 25
I beg, who whisper so feebly of your great deserts.

8

Epitaph of Cronopius,
bishop of the city of Périgueux

If, holy man, you had made earthly things in the past your
care, in this poem tears now would outnumber words, but
because you are unstained, free from the taint of the world,
you bid us be joyful, for you abide released from death.

5 Antistes pietate calens, venerande Cronopi,
      membra sepulchra tegunt, spiritus astra tenet.
  Ordo sacerdotum cui fluxit utroque parente,
      venit ad heredem pontificalis apex.
  Hunc tibi iure gradum successio sancta paravit,
10   ut quasi iam merito debitus esset honor.
  Nobilis antiquo veniens de germine patrum,
      sed magis in Christo nobilior merito,
  sic vultu semper placidus ceu mente serenus,
      pectore sincero frons sine nube fuit.
15 Cuius ab eloquio nectar per verba fluebat,
      vinceres ut dulces ore rigante favos.
  Nudorum tu vestis eras, algentis amictus;
      qui ad tua tecta fugit, tectus et ipse redit.
  Divitias omnes inopum sub ventre locasti,
20   unde tibi semper viva talenta manent.
  Esuriens epulum, sitiens te sumere potum,
      cernere te meruit tristis et exul opem.
  Implesti propriis viduatam civibus urbem
      videruntque suos te redimente lares.
25 Quam lupus ab stabulis tulerat frendente rapina,
      te pastore gregis reddita plaudit ovis.
  Templa exusta celer revocasti in culmine prisco;
      hinc tua sed caelis stat sine labe domus.
  Ipse bis octono vixisti in corpore lustro;
30   nunc tibi pro meritis est sine fine dies.

Bishop, fervent in your holiness, worshipful Cronopius, a 5
tomb encloses your body, your spirit dwells in the stars.
From both parents you trace a long line of priests; episcopal
rank comes to you as a family inheritance. Holy succession
procured for you this title as of right, so that the honor was 10
due to you as if you'd already won it. Noble in the antiquity
of your descent from your forefathers, but still more noble
by your merit in Christ, always as calm in your countenance
as serene in your mind, your brow was cloudless, your heart
unconstrained. From your eloquence nectar coursed through 15
your words so that in the streams from your mouth you out-
did the sweetness of honeycombs. You were clothing for the
naked and cloak for the cold; all who came to your address
returned home dressed. You invested all your wealth in the
bellies of the needy, as return for which you receive talents 20
that will live forever. The hungry can turn to you as food, the
thirsty as drink, and the grieving and exiled see in you their
support. You have repopulated a city stripped of its own cit-
izens, and homes have seen again their occupants, ransomed
by you. The sheep the wolf's furious assault snatched from 25
the stalls with you as the flock's shepherd is joyfully re-
stored. Scorched churches you have swiftly returned to their
former glory; for this you have a dwelling in heaven without
stain. You have lived here in body twice forty years; now for 30
your virtues you enjoy day without end.

9

Epitaphium Leonti episcopi anterioris civitatis Burdegalensis

Ultima sors avido graviter properavit hiatu,
    pastorem rapiens qui fuit arma gregis.
Hoc recubant tumulo venerandi membra Leonti,
    quo stetit eximium pontificale caput.
5 Quem plebs cuncta gemens confusa voce requirit:
    hinc puer, hinc iuvenis deflet, et inde senes.
Defensoris opem hic omnis perdidit aetas,
    et quantum coluit nunc lacrimando docet.
Nemo valet siccis oculis memorare sepultum,
10   qui tamen in populo vivit amore pio.
Egregius, nulli de nobilitate secundus,
    moribus excellens, culmine primus erat.
Hic pietate nova cunctis minor esse volebat,
    sed magis his meritis et sibi maior erat.
15 Quo praesente viro meruit discordia pacem,
    expulsa rabie corda ligabat amor.
Ecclesiae totum concessit in ordine censum
    et tribuit Christo quod fuit ante suum.
Ad quem pauper opem, pretium captivus habebat;
20   hoc proprium reputans quod capiebat egens.
Cuius de terris migravit ad astra facultas,
    et plus iste Deo quam sibi vixit homo,
cordis in amplexu retinens et pectore plebem,
    diceret ut populum se generasse patrem.

9

Epitaph of Leontius the Elder, bishop of the city of Bordeaux

With hungry gorge death's final hour has come in cruel haste, snatching away the shepherd, the bulwark of his flock. In this tomb reposes the body of venerable Leontius, by whom was exalted the high status of the bishopric. For him all the people long with mingled cries of grief: here a child is weeping, here a young man, there an old. All ages hereby have lost the support of their protector, and show with their present tears how great was their reverence for him. No one can speak with dry eyes of him now in his tomb, who yet lives on in the devoted love of the people. Of outstanding merit, second to none in nobility, he was distinguished in character and first in high status. By a new kind of piety he wished to be lower than all, but rather by this virtue exceeded even himself. In this man's presence dissension yielded to peace, rage was banished, and love bound hearts together. He handed over to the church the whole of his possessions, and granted to Christ what previously had been his own. In him the poor had sustenance, the captive his ransom; he believed he still retained what the needy had received. From the earth his wealth took flight up to the stars and though a man he lived more for God than himself, holding his folk in his heart's embrace to his breast, so that they said that he as their father had given birth to his peo-

25 Namque suos cives placida sic voce monebat
        confitereris ut hunc ad sua membra loqui.
    Ingenio vigilans, dives quoque dogmate Christi,
        et meruit studio multiplicare gradum.
    Largior in donis absens sibi iunxit amantes
30   et quo non fuerat, munere notus erat.
    Principibus carus huiusque amor unicus urbis,
        festinans animis omnibus esse parens.
    Lustra decem pollens, septem quoque vixit in annos,
        mox urguente die raptus ab orbe fuit.
35 Sed quis cuncta canat, cum tot bona solus habebat?
        Nunc uno in tumulo plurima vota iacent.
    Haec tibi parva nimis, cum tu merearis opima,
        carmina Theudosius praebet amore tuus.

10

Epitaphium Leonti episcopi sequentis civitatis Burdegalensis

    Omne bonum velox fugitivaque gaudia mundi,
        prosperitas hominum quam cito rapta volat!
    Malueram potius cui carmina ferre salutis,
        perverso voto flere sepulchra vocor.
5   Hoc recubant tumulo venerandi membra Leonti,
        quem sua pontificem fama sub astra levat.
    Nobilitas altum ducens ab origine nomen,
        quale genus Romae forte senatus habet,

ple. For he instructed his citizens with so soothing a voice 25
that you would declare he was addressing limbs of his own.
Attentive in intellect, rich too in the teaching of Christ, he
was successful through his energy in advancing his status.
Generous in gift giving, even absent he won over friends and 30
where he had not been he was known by his bounty. Favorite
of princes, singularly beloved by this city, he exerted him-
self to be everyone's spiritual parent. He lived in full vigor
for fifty years, with seven too in addition, but then, as time
pressed on, he was snatched from this world. Who could 35
hymn all his virtues, when one man possessed so many? Now
in a single tomb a multitude of prayers lies buried. These
all too humble verses, though you deserve a rich offering,
Theudosius presents to you, your devotee in love.

10

Epitaph of Leontius the Younger, bishop of the city of Bordeaux

Everything good is fleeting and the joys of the world pass by,
how swiftly human prosperity is snatched away and takes
flight! The man to whom I would rather have sent poems of
greeting, my hopes overturned, I'm summoned to mourn
over his grave. In this tomb reposes the body of venerable 5
Leontius, the bishop whom his fame raises up to the stars.
His nobility derives from his ancestry a lofty title, a family
such as might belong to the senate at Rome, and although

et quamvis celso flueret de sanguine patrum,
10   hic propriis meritis crescere fecit avos.
Regum summus amor, patriae caput, arma parentum,
    tutor amicorum, plebis et urbis honor,
templorum cultor, tacitus largitor egentum,
    susceptor peregrum distribuendo cibum.
15   Longius extremo si quis properasset ab orbe,
    advena mox vidit, hunc ait esse patrem;
ingenio vivax, animo probus, ore serenus,
    et mihi qualis erat pectore flente loquor.
Hunc habuit clarum qualem modo Gallia nullum;
20   nunc humili tumulo culmina celsa iacent.
Placabat reges, recreans moderamine cives:
    gaudia tot populis, heu, tulit una dies.
Lustra decem felix et quattuor insuper annos
    vixit, et a nostro lumine raptus obit.
25   Funeris officium, magni solamen amoris,
    dulcis adhuc cineri dat Placidina tibi.

II

Epitaphium Victoriani
abbatis de monasterio Asanae

Quisquis ab occasu properas huc, quisquis ab ortu,
    munus in hoc tumulo quod venereris habes.
Respice ditatum caelesti dote talentum,
    cuius semper habet pectoris arca Deum.

he was descended from a distinguished line of ancestors, he 10
increased the prestige of his forbears by his own merits. He
was supreme favorite of kings, distinction of his country,
stronghold of kin, protector of friends, glory of the peo-
ple and city, promoter of churches, silent benefactor of the
needy, supporter of strangers by distributing to them food.
If anyone traveled a long journey from a far distant land, 15
though a foreigner, on seeing the bishop he called him his
father. He was lively in intellect, honest in character, calm
in his countenance—I tell how he was to me with a tearful
heart. Gaul now has no one to match in distinction the man
it once had; high eminence now lies low in a humble tomb. 20
He won over kings, refreshing the citizenry with his gov-
ernance; alas, one day deprived the people of so many joys.
For fifty years he lived, with a further four in addition, then
snatched from our sight he passed away. This funeral rite 25
and consolation for the great love she bears Placidina pres-
ents in abiding affection to your ashes.

II

Epitaph of Victorianus, abbot of the monastery of Asan

Whoever journey here from the West, whoever from the
East, find in this tomb a prize worthy of veneration. Ob-
serve this talent enriched by heavenly bounty, which always

5   Religionis apex, vitae decus, arma salutis,
      eximius meritis, Victorianus adest,
   dignum opus exercens qui fructificante labore,
      cunctis, non soli vixit in orbe sibi.
   Plurima per patriam monachorum examina fundens,
10   floribus aeternis mellificavit apes.
   Lingua potens, pietas praesens, oratio iugis;
      sic fuit ut iam tum totus ad astra foret.
   Plura salutiferis tribuens oracula rebus,
      saepe dedit signis vita beata fidem.
15 Bis senis rexit patrio moderamine lustris
      rite Deo placitas pastor opimus oves.
   Calle sequens recto sacra per vestigia Christum,
      nunc fruitur vultum quem cupiebat amor.

12

Epitaphium Hilari presbyteri

Omnes una manet sors irreparabilis horae,
   cum venit extremus lege trahente dies.
Sic furit ira necis neque nos fugit orbita mortis;
   pulvere facta caro est, non nisi pulvis erit.
5 Haec tamen insignes animas spes non vacua pascit,
   quod qui digna gerit de nece nulla timet.
Hoc iacet in tumulo venerandus Hilarius actu,
   corpore qui terras et tenet astra fide.

holds God in the treasury of its heart. Supreme in religion, 5
glory of life, warrior for salvation, distinguished by his vir-
tues, Victorianus is here, who, performing a worthy task
with productive labor, lived his life in the world for all, not
just for himself. Distributing through his fatherland numer-
ous hives of monks, he provided his bees honey from eternal 10
flowers. Powerful of tongue, ever-ready with charity, unre-
lenting in prayer, he acted as one already wholly in the stars.
He expended many prayers in actions of healing and in the
blessedness of his life by miracles often inspired faith. For 15
twice thirty years as their noble shepherd he ruled his sheep
with paternal governance, who rightly won favor with God.
He followed Christ on the straight path tracing his holy
footsteps, and now enjoys the countenance that in love he
had longed for.

12

Epitaph of the priest Hilary

A single fate of the irrevocable hour awaits all, when the last
day comes, subject to mortality's law. So rages the anger of
death and we cannot escape its onset; of dust flesh is created
and nothing but dust will it be. Yet this not idle hope nour- 5
ishes souls of distinction, that he whose deeds are worthy
need have no fear of death.

There lies in this tomb Hilary, venerable in his actions,
who in body occupies the earth, but in his faith the stars. A

Vir bonus, egregia de nobilitate refulgens,
10   inter honoratos germinis altus apex,
conubio iunctus simili, sed coniuge rapta
      stans in amore Dei; non fuit alter amor.
Utilis in propriis, doctus moderamine legis,
      cuius iudicium pondere libra fuit,
15 iustitiam tribuens populis examine recto:
      vendita res pretio non fuit ulla suo.
Funeris officio lacrimans Euantia caro
      contulit haec genero maesta sepulchra suo.

13

Epitaphium Servilionis presbyteri

Quamvis longa dies, brevis hic et hospita lux est;
      sola tamen nescit vita beata mori.
Hoc igitur tumulo Servilio clausus habetur,
      nobilis et merito nobiliore potens.
5   Ipse palatinam rexit moderatius aulam
      commissaeque domus crescere fecit opes.
Presbyter inde sacer mansit venerabilis urbi
      servitioque Dei libera vita fuit.
Orphanus hic patrem, viduae solacia deflent,
10   unde magis caelis gaudia vera tenet.
Pontificem genitum vidit dehinc munere Christi;
      raptus ab orbe quidem laetus ad astra redit.

good man, conspicuous in his eminent nobility, among dis- 10
tinguished ancestors the lofty pinnacle of his family, joined
in a well-matched marriage, but, once his wife was taken
from him, constant in his love of God; he had no other love.
Efficient in his own affairs and skilled in the handling of
the law, whose judgment was equable, well-weighted and
balanced, he meted out justice to the people with impartial 15
proceedings: no case was bought by making him payment.
In performing the funeral Evantia has tearfully bestowed
this sad burial on her beloved son-in-law.

13

Epitaph of the priest Servilio

However long the day, our light here is but a short sojourn;
only a blessed life is capable of transcending death. Enclosed
in this tomb, then, Servilio is concealed, noble but empow-
ered by his still more ennobling virtue. He governed the 5
royal palace with moderation, and caused the wealth of the
household in his care to grow. Then as holy priest he re-
tained the regard of his city, and in service to God enjoyed
freedom in life. While here on earth the orphan weeps for
his father and widows for their comforter, for this reason all 10
the more he enjoys true bliss in heaven. Here too he saw his
son made bishop by Christ's favor; when carried off from
this world he joyfully returned to the stars.

14

Epitaphium domni Praesidi

Vita brevis hominum, sed non brevis illa piorum,
    dum migrante die prosperiora tenent.
Qui meruere magis de carcere carnis euntes
    post tenebras mundi luce perenne frui.
5 Ex quibus hic recubans meritis Praesidius almis
    carne tenet tumulum, spiritus igne polum.
Pectore de proprio Christi responsa rigando
    multorum extinxit fonte fluente sitim.
Invitans instanter oves ad pascua regis,
10   distribuit dulcem fratribus ore salem.
Nam quotiens monachus peccati est vulnere fixus,
    missus ad artificem, certa medella fuit.
Ibat ad abbatem famulans sanctumque magistrum
    discipulus humilis, qui fuit ante tumens.
15 Talibus officiis intentus amore Tonantis
    inter et angelicos fulget honore choros.

14

Epitaph of Lord Praesidius

The life of humans is short, but not short that of the holy,
for when the light passes away, they gain a greater reward.
Their deserts are more as they pass from the bonds of the
body after this world's darkness to enjoy the eternal light.
Among them here reposes Praesidius of saintly virtues; in   5
flesh he is in the tomb, but his fiery spirit is in heaven. Chan-
neling from his own breast the teachings of Christ, he has
quenched the thirst of many from his streaming spring. Ur-
gently summoning his sheep to the pastures of the king, he   10
shared with the brothers the sweet salt of his eloquence. For
whenever a monk was transfixed by the wound of a sin, he
was sent to this master and his healing was secure. When in
obedience he went before his abbot and holy teacher, a pu-
pil became humble who previously had been arrogant. De-   15
voted to such services in love of the Lord he now shines in
glory among angel choirs.

15

Epitaphium Boboleni diaconi

Innumeris hominum subiecta est vita periclis
   casibus et variis sors inimica premit.
Nam recubando toro Bobolenus, honore diacon,
   dum fruitur somno, mors rapit atra virum:
5 hostis in insidiis securo caede securis
   percutiens cerebrum fecit obire dolo.
Dic, tibi quid prodest scelus hoc peragendo, nefande?
   Ille Deo vivit, tu moriture peris.
Martyris ille decus meruit, tu damna latronis;
10   hinc sibi palma placet, sed tibi poena manet.

16

Epitaphium Attici

Quamvis longa seni ducatur in ordine vita,
   cum venit extremum, nil valet esse diu.
Sed quia nemo fugit, nisi terram terra recondat,
   lege sub hac cunctos sors rapit una viros.
5 Celsus in hoc humili tumulo iacet Atticus ille,
   qui dabat eloquio dulcia mella suo,

15

Epitaph of the deacon Bobolenus

The life of mankind is exposed to innumerable dangers, and
hostile fate with various misfortunes presses it hard. For
when Bobolenus, in office a deacon, was reclining in bed, as
he was enjoying his sleep, black death snatched him away:
an enemy assailant unexpectedly with a blow from an ax   5
struck him on the skull and treacherously caused him to die.
Say, how do you benefit from performing this crime, wicked
one? He lives in God, you, destined for death, are lost.
He has won the glory of a martyr, you a theif's damnation;
the palm gives pleasure to him, but for you there remains   10
only pain.

16

Epitaph of Atticus

Although the life of an old man extends for a long time,
when the last moment comes, longevity alters nothing. But
because no one escapes without earth reclaiming earth, un-
der this law one destiny carries off all men. In this lowly   5
tomb lies the exalted Atticus, who dispensed in his speech
the sweetness of honey; with pleasing rhythms he employed

inpendens placidam suavi modulamine linguam,
    pacificusque suus sermo medella fuit.
Cuius abundantem venerata est Gallia sensum
10   excoluitque senem semper honore patrem.
Clarus ab antiquis, spes nobilitatis opimae,
    sufficiens propriis nulla rapina fuit,
dogmata corde tenens plenus velut arca libellos;
    quisquis quod voluit fonte fluente bibit,
15   consilio sapiens, animo pius, ore serenus,
    omnibus ut populis esset amore parens.
Sic venerabilibus templis, sic fudit egenis,
    mitteret ut caelis quas sequeretur opes.

17

Epitaphium Arcadi iuvenis

Omne bonum velox fugitivo tempore transit;
    quae placitura videt, mors magis illa rapit.
Hic puer Arcadius, veniens de prole senatus,
    festinante die raptus ab orbe iacet.
5 Parvula cuius adhuc freno se vinxerat aetas
    ut teneris annis surgeret ipse senes.
Eloquio torrens, specie radiante venustus,
    vincens artifices et puer arte rudis.
Quo me, forma, rapis laudes memorare sepulti?

a soothing tongue, and his peacemaking language was itself
a healing. Gaul held his rich intelligence in reverence and   10
always honored him when he was old as its father. Distin-
guished in ancient line, pride of the thriving nobility, in pos-
sessions amply endowed, he practiced no rapacity. He kept
his heart full of doctrines as a bookcase holds books; every-
one drank what he wished from his flowing source. He was   15
wise in counsel, pious in spirit, cloudless of countenance, so
that to all the people he was a parent in love. He so lavished
money on venerable churches, so alms on the poor, that he
sent on to heaven a treasure he was to follow.

17

Epitaph of a young man, Arcadius

Every good thing is transient, it passes with the fleeting of
time; death seizes especially on things that it sees will give
pleasure. Here the boy Arcadius, descended from a senato-
rial line, lies buried, prematurely snatched from the world.
His still tender age had so subjected itself to a curb that   5
though young in years, he was maturing into an old man. His
eloquence was rapid, he charmed with his radiant beauty,
and surpassed the experts, a boy untrained in art. Where
are you taking me, beauty, to sing the praise of the dead?

10   Singula si memores, plus lacrimanda mones.
        Sed quoniam nulla maculatus sorde recessit,
          nulli flendus erit quem paradisus habet.

18

Epitaphium Basili

Impedior lacrimis prorumpere nomen amantis
    vixque dolenda potest scribere verba manus.
Coniugis affectu cogor dare pauca sepulto:
    si loquor, adfligor; si nego, durus ero.
5 Qui cupis hoc tumulo cognoscere, lector, humatum,
    Basilium illustrem maesta sepulchra tegunt,
cuius blanda pio recreabat lingua relatu
    et dabat eloquio verba benigna suo.
Hinc doctrina rigans, illinc dulcedo redundans
10   ornavit radio, lux geminata, virum.
Regis amor, carus populis, ita pectore dulcis
    ut fieret cunctis in bonitate parens,
tranquillus, sapiens, iucundus, pacis amicus,
    nullaque quo stabat semina litis erant.
15 Hunc consultantem legati sorte frequenter
    misit ad Hispanos Gallica cura viros.
Sufficienter habens numquam fuit arma rapinae;
    non propriis eguit, non aliena tulit.

Each detail you recall means more tears must be shed. But 10
because he departed defiled by no stain, no one should
mourn him, for paradise is his home.

18

Epitaph of Basil

Tears prevent me from pronouncing the name of a loved
one, and my hand can scarcely write painful words. A wife's
affection compels me to speak a few words to him in the
grave; if I speak, I suffer, if I refuse, I shall be cruel. Reader, 5
if you desire to know who is interred in this tomb, this
mournful grave contains Basil, a man of distinction, whose
winning tongue and kindly speech brought cheer and with
their eloquence gave voice to words of affection. The waters
of his learning, his overflowing sweetness adorned this man 10
with their beams, in a twofold light. He was beloved of the
king, dear to the people, and of so warm a heart that by his
kindness he became the parent of all, calm, wise, engaging, a
lover of peace; where he took his stance, no inkling of con-
flict arose. Frequently Gallic concerns dispatched him in 15
the role of an envoy to the people of Spain to negotiate with
them. He had enough for himself, he never used force to
plunder; he did not lack for possessions, he did not steal

Ecclesias ditans, loca sancta decenter honorans,
20   pauperibus tribuens dives ad astra subit.
Annis bis denis cum Baudegunde iugali
        iunxit in orbe duos unus amore torus.
Qui tamen undecimo lustro cito raptus ab aevo
        post finem terrae regna superna petit.
25 Non iam flendus eris humana sorte recedens,
        dum patriam caeli, dulcis amice, tenes.

19

Epitaphium Arachari

Partu terra suo fraudem non sustinet ullam:
        quae dedit haec recipit debita membra luto.
Hic vergente suo situs est Aracharius aevo,
        sex qui lustra gerens raptus ab orbe fuit.
5   Ipse palatina refulsit clarus in aula
        et placito meruit regis amore coli.
Omnia restituit mundo quae sumpsit ab ipso;
        sola tamen pro se quae bene gessit habet.

those of others. By enriching churches and beautifying places of holiness, by giving to the poor he rose wealthy to 20 the stars. For twice ten years with his wife Baudegund, one bed joined the two in love in this world. But now in his fifty-fifth year he has been suddenly snatched from life, and, after his farewell to earth, has gone to the kingdom above. There 25 will be no call to weep for you as you depart the human lot, since, sweet friend, you dwell in a fatherland in heaven above.

19

Epitaph of Aracharius

In its bringing to birth the earth incurs no loss: the body that is owed to clay is a gift it takes back. Here after failing health Aracharius is laid to rest, who lived thirty years, then was taken from the world. In the royal palace he shone with 5 conspicuous brilliance, and won the regard of the king and his affectionate love. All that he took from the world he restored, he only keeps for himself the good deeds he performed.

20

Epitaphium Brumachi

Quisquis in hoc tumulo cineres vis nosse sepulti,
    Brumachius quondam fulsit in orbe potens.
Quem sensu, eloquio legati nomine functum,
    dum remeat patriae, sors inimica tulit.
5 Finibus Italiae raptus, sed Frigia coniunx
    detulit huc cari funus amando viri.
Ceu vivum coluit cui grata est umbra mariti:
    coniugibus castis ipsa favilla placet.
Ipse quater denos permansit in orbe per annos;
10 mox obit et magnum parva sepulchra tegunt.

21

Epitaphium Avoli

Inriguis Avolum lacrimis ne flete sepultum,
    qui propriis meritis gaudia lucis habet.
Nam si pensentur morum pia gesta suorum,
    felix post tumulos possidet ille polos.
5 Templa Dei coluit, latitans satiavit egentem;
    plenius illa metit quae sine teste dedit.

20

Epitaph of Brumachius

All you who wish to know whose ashes are buried in this tomb, his name is Brumachius, once a brilliant force in this world. He fulfilled the role of envoy with good sense and eloquence, but when he was returning to his homeland, cruel fate carried him off. He died in the land of Italy, but Frigia   5 his devoted wife brought back here the body of her dearly loved husband. She honored him as if living, holding dear the shade of her spouse; for virtuous wives the very ashes are treasured. He remained in this world for a period of forty years, then died and a small tomb encloses a great man.   10

21

Epitaph of Avolus

Do not let tears flow or weep for Avolus who is buried, for he by his own personal virtues is rejoicing in the light. For if his holy actions and character are weighed in the balance, he now inhabits heaven, happy beyond the grave. He honored   5 the churches of God, gave alms to the needy in secret; he

Nobilitate potens, animo probus, ore serenus,
    plebis amore placens, fundere promptus opes,
non usurae avidus, licet esset munere largus,
10   plus nihil expetiit quam numerando dedit.
Nil mercedis egens, merces fuit una salutis:
    quod minus est pretio, proficit hoc merito.
Luce perenne fruens felix cui mortua mors est,
    quem non poena premit, vita superna manet.

22

Epitaphium Innocentum

Hoc iacet in tumulo non flenda infantia fratrum,
    quos tulit innocuos vita beata viros.
Uno utero geniti simili sunt sorte sepulti
    et pariter natos lux tenet una duos.
5 Lotus fonte sacro prius ille recessit in albis,
    iste gerens lustrum ducitur ante Deum.
Nomine sed primus vocitatus rite Iohannes,
    alter, Patricius, munere maior erat,
de cuius merito se plurima signa dederunt.
10   Felices animae, quae pia vota colunt!
Hic etiam felix genetrix requiescit eorum,
    quae meruit partu lumina ferre suo.

fully now reaps what he gave unobserved. Powerful in nobil-
ity, honest in character, cloudless in countenance, well-liked
for his love of the people, quick to expend his wealth, with
no greed for usury, though generous in his bounty, he sought   10
for no more than in giving he paid out. He had no need of
profit, his sole profit was salvation; the less he won in pay-
ment, the more he gained in merit. He is happy in enjoy-
ment of eternal light, for to him death is dead; no punish-
ment oppresses him, but life on high awaits him.

22

Epitaph of Innocents

There lies in this tomb, no cause for tears, a pair of infant
brothers, whom a life of blessedness carried off still in their
innocence. Born from one womb they experience in the
grave a like fate, and after sharing a birth one light holds
them both. Bathed in the holy font one departed first,   5
dressed in white; the other lived five years then was brought
before God. The first of the two was duly named John, the
second, Patrick, was greater in his gifts; of his qualities
numerous signs gave evidence. Happy the souls that holy   10
prayers honor! Here too their fortunate mother takes her
rest, who in her childbirth succeeded in bringing forth
lights.

23

Epitaphium Iuliani

Condita sunt tumulo Iuliani membra sub isto,
    cuius in aeternum vivere novit honor.
Mercator quondam, conversus fine beato,
    raptus ab hoc mundo crimine liber homo.
5 Collegit nimium, sed sparsit egentibus aurum:
    praemisit cunctas quas sequeretur opes.
Sollicitus quemcumque novum prospexit in urbe;
    hunc meruit veniens exul habere patrem.
Pascere se credens Christum sub paupere forma,
10   ante omnes apud hunc sumpsit egenus opem.
Nec solum refovens sed dona latendo ministrans
    amplius inde placet quod sine teste dedit.
Felicem censum qui fratris migrat in alvo
    et vivos lapides aedificare potest!
15 Extulit hunc tumulum genitoris honore Iohannes,
    qui modo divinis fungitur officiis.
Qualiter hic vivo serviret amore parenti,
    cum nati pietas ipsa sepulchra colit!

23

Epitaph of Julian

Beneath this tomb is laid to rest the body of Julian, whose glory is able to live for eternity. Once a merchant, but happily converted at the last, when snatched from this world he was free of all crime. He amassed large quantities of gold, 5 but gave it out to the needy, and sent in advance all his wealth he was to follow. Whenever he saw with concern a newcomer to the city, that exile won the honor of having him as a father. He believed he was feeding Christ in the persons of the poor; the needy above all received from him 10 sustenance. Not only providing comfort but also giving gifts in secret, he pleased all the more because he did so without witness. Happy the wealth that is transformed by the stomach of a brother and is able to build with living stones! John, 15 who now performs the duties of holy office, raised up this tomb in honor of his father. With what love he must have attended his parent when alive, when his filial devotion pays such honor even to his grave!

24

Epitaphium Orienti

Non hic nostra diu est fugienti tempore vita,
    quae sub fine brevi, vix venit, inde redit.
Ecce caduca volant praesentia saecula mundi;
    sola fides meriti nescit honore mori.
5 Clauditur hic pollens Orientius ille sepultus,
    cui palatina prius mansit aperta domus.
Consiliis habilis regalique intimus aulae
    obtinuit celsum dignus in arce locum.
Vir sapiens, iustus, moderatus, honestus, amatus
10   hoc rapuit mundo quod bene gessit homo,
sexaginta annis vix implens tempora lucis,
    coniuge Nicasia, qua tumulante cubat,
cuius castus amor colit ipsa sepulchra mariti,
    nec placitura homini se dedit esse Dei.

25

Epitaphium Theudechildae reginae

Quamvis aetatis senio iam flecteret annos,
    multorumque tamen spes cito rapta fuit.
Si precibus possent naturae debita flecti,
    plebs ageret lacrimis hanc superesse sibi.

24

Epitaph of Orientius

Our life here is not long as time rapidly passes; in a brief span no sooner has life come than it's gone. See how the present ages of the world fade and fly by; only faith with the glory of virtue cannot die. Here the great Orientius lies enclosed in his tomb, to whom previously the royal palace remained ever open. Adept at counsel and an intimate in the king's court by merit he acquired lofty rank in high circles. A man wise, just, temperate, honorable, and beloved, he took with him from this world all his good actions, completing his time in the light in scarcely sixty years. Nicasia was his wife, who erected the tomb where he is resting, whose chaste love does honor still to the grave of her husband and instead of pleasing man has devoted herself to the service of God.

25

Epitaph of Queen Theudechild

Although her years were now in decline with the advance of age, the hope of many was too soon carried off. If the debt owed to nature could be affected by prayers, the people with

5 Gaudia quanta inopum tumulo sunt clausa sub isto
     votaque quot populis abstulit una dies!
Inclita nobilitas genitali luce coruscans,
     hic properante die Theodechilde iacet.
Cui frater, genitor, coniunx, avus atque priores
10   culmine succiduo regius ordo fuit.
Orphanus, exul, egens, viduae nudaeque iacentes
     matrem, escam, tegmen hic sepelisse dolent.
Unica res placuit cumulo mercedis opimae:
     antea cuncta dedit quam peteretur opem,
15 occultans sua dona suis neu forte vetarent,
     sed quae clausa dedit, iudice teste docet.
Templorum Domini cultrix, pia munera praebens,
     hoc proprium reputans quidquid habebat inops.
Una mori sors est et terrae reddere terram;
20   felix cui meritis stat sine fine dies.
Actibus his instans, aeterna in luce relata,
     ter quino lustro vixit in orbe decus.

26

Epitaphium Vilithutae

Omne bonum velox fugitivaque gaudia mundi;
     monstrantur terris et cito lapsa ruunt.
Ut dolor adquirat vires cum perdit amantem,
     ante placere facit, durius inde premit.

their tears would have secured her survival. How many joys 5
of the poor were shut up in that tomb, how many prayers
did that one day take from the people! Of high nobility, brilliant in the light of her birth, Theudechild with the passing
of time lies buried here. Her brother, her father, her husband, her grandfather and forefathers made up a royal dy- 10
nasty, a powerful succession. The orphan, the exile, the
needy, widows and women lying naked grieve that their
mother, their food, and their clothing is buried here. One
thing won favor as the culmination of her generous almsgiving: she made all her donations before any help was requested. She hid all her gifts from her family in fear they 15
would forbid them, but what she gave in secret, she declares
before the divine judge. She honored the churches of the
Lord and made pious benefactions, thinking whatever the
poor received remained in her possession. To die is the universal lot, to give back earth to earth. Happy is she who en- 20
joys by her virtues a day that is endless! Active in charitable
deeds, then carried off to eternal light, she lived for seventy-
five years gloriously in this world.

26

Epitaph of Vilithuta

Everything good is fleeting and the joys of the world are
transient; no sooner do they appear on earth, they collapse
and fall into ruin. For pain to increase in force when it destroys a lover, it first causes pleasure, to torture then more

5 Heu lacrimae rerum, heu sors inimica virorum,
   cur placitura facis quae dolitura rapis?
Vilithute decens, Dagaulfi cara iugalis,
   coniugis amplexu dissociata iacet.
Corpore iuncta toro, plus pectore nexa marito,
10   lucis in occasu vincula rupit amor.
Tempora cui poterant adhuc in flore manere,
   principium vitae finis acerbus habet.
Sanguine nobilium generata Parisius urbe,
   Romana studio, barbara prole fuit.
15 Ingenium mitem torva de gente trahebat;
   vincere naturam gloria maior erat.
Numquam maesta manens, vultu nova gaudia portans,
   nubila fronte fugans, corde serena fuit.
Fudit ab ore iubar species redimita decore,
20   protulit et radios forma venusta suos.
Stirpe sua reliquas superavit pulchra puellas
   et rosea facie lactea colla tulit.
Splendida conspectu meliori pectore fulsit,
   digna micans animo nec pietate minor.
25 Cui quamvis nullus hac in regione propinquus,
   obsequio facta est omnibus una parens,
divinis intenta bonis, alimenta ministrans,
   qua mercede magis se satiasse videt.
Haec data post obitum faciunt quoque vivere functam;
30   forma perit hominum, nam benefacta manent.
Corpora pulvis erunt et mens pia floret in aevo;
   omnia praetereunt praeter amare Deum.

cruelly. Alas for the tears of the world, alas, destiny, for your 5
hostility to men, why do you make pleasing what will bring
pain when you carry it off?

Beautiful Vilithuta, beloved wife of Dagaulf, lies in the
grave, far from her spouse's embrace. She was joined in mar-
riage in body, but more tightly bound to her husband in
heart; with the setting of the light love broke those bonds 10
apart. She could expect years still remaining for her in the
flower of youth, but a cruel termination overtook her at her
life's beginning.

Born in the city of Paris, descended from the blood of
nobles, she was Roman in her attainments, barbarian in her
family. Though from a fierce race, she acquired a gentle 15
character; all the greater was her glory for overcoming na-
ture. She never appeared sad, but showed joy ever-new on
her face, she banished clouds from her brow, in heart she re-
mained serene. Wreathed in grace her presence radiated its
own beams from her face and her charm and beauty emitted 20
rays of light of their own. In her fairness she surpassed all
other girls of her race and under her rosy complexion she
had a neck as white as milk. Although she was radiant to
look at, she shone with a still finer heart, fittingly brilliant in
mind, but no less so in holiness. Though she had in this re- 25
gion not a single kinsman, by her attentions this one woman
became the relative of all. Distributing nourishment, but
with her eye on heavenly rewards, by this act of charity she
finds she has rather fed herself. After death these gifts cause
her to live even when dead; human beauty perishes, but 30
benefactions remain. Bodies will become dust, but a holy
mind flourishes forever; everything is transient except lov-
ing God.

Orphana tunc aviae studiis adolevit opimae
    inque loco natae neptis adulta fuit.
35 Tertius a decimo ut hanc primum acceperat annus,
    traditur optato consociata viro,
nobilitas in gente sua cui celsa refulsit
    atque suis meritis additur alter honor.
Dulcis, ovans, alacris, studiis ornata iuventus;
40   quod natura nequit, littera prompta dedit.
Tres meruere tamen iuncti superesse per annos
    coniugioque suo corde ligante frui.
Ambo pares animo, voto, spe, moribus, actu
    certantesque sibi mente, decore, fide.
45 Tempore iam certo est enixa puerpera prolem,
    damno feta suo, quae pariendo perit.
Abripuit teneram subito mors invida formam,
    annos quippe duos, lustra gerendo tria.
Sic animam generans anima spoliatur et ipsa,
50   spem peperit luci luce negante sibi.
Exemplum sed triste dedit fetura parenti:
    unde redire solet, deficit inde genus.
Tertius esse pater cupiens, heu, solus habetur:
    crescere quo numerus debuit, ecce cadit.
55 Nam partus cum matre perit, nascendo sepultus,
    nil vitale trahens, natus in ore necis.
Plus fuerant soli, si tunc sine prole fuissent;
    addita posteritas abstulit id quod erat.
Infaustis votis genitus de funere matris
60   et genetrix nato mortis origo fuit.
Alter in alterius letali sorte pependit,
    inque vicem sibi mox ambo dedere necem.

Made an orphan, she grew up in the care of a wealthy grandmother and though a granddaughter grew up just as a daughter. As soon as she reached the age of thirteen years she was handed over in marriage to the husband she wished for, who received luster from the lofty nobility of his own race and was endowed with a second glory by his own virtues, a young man of sweet temper, high-spirited, vigorous, accomplished in his studies; what nature denied him, his learning readily provided. For three years they were able to live together in union and to enjoy their marriage bound by ties of the heart. The two were alike in spirit, wishes, hopes, character, and actions and vied with one another in mind, propriety, and devotion. Then after a fixed period of time in labor she gave birth to a child; her pregnancy caused her destruction, childbirth was her demise. In a moment envious death snatched away her delicate beauty; she had lived just fifteen years, with a further two in addition. In this way in producing a life her own life was taken from her, she brought a source of hope to the light, a light she herself was denied. So the childbirth provided an unhappy lesson for a parent; a family may suffer a loss from where it usually receives gain. The father wanted to make up three but, alas, he is left on his own; the number that should have increased, here is diminished. For the child died along with his mother, its birth was a burial, it gave no signs of life, but was born in the jaws of death. They alone would have been more, if they had then been childless; the addition of offspring subtracted what already was there. A birth took place with unhappy auspices, the death of a mother, and a mother in turn was the cause of death of her son. Each was implicated in the fatal destiny of the other and they mutually both

Sed sensit graviora dolens pater atque maritus,
   qui gemit uno obitu se sepelisse duos.
65 Pro vixdum genito lacrimas iam soluit humato;
   vidit quod fleret, non quod haberet amor.
Tristitiae cumulum tribuit cui rapta iugalis,
   dans longas lacrimas tempore nupta brevi.
Consultum tamen illud habet de coniuge coniux,
70   huic quia mercedis non vacuatur opus.
Nam quod ad ornatum potuit muliebre videri
   ecclesiis prompte pauperibusque dedit.
Hic nulla ex illis rebus peritura reliquit,
   ut modo praemissas dives haberet opes.
75 Quam bene distribuens sine se sua noluit esse!
   Nam quae larga dedit, haec modo plena metit.
Condidit ergo sibi quidquid porrexit egenti
   et quos sumpsit inops hos habet illa cibos.
Felices quos nulla gravant de morte secunda
80   nec faciunt poenis subdita membra feris!
Dulcibus inlecebris qui non sibi condit amarum
   nec per carnem animam vult sepelire suam,
sed casta pietate manens sine crimine vitae,
   illius in luce hac praemia lucis emit.
85 Tempore quam parvo lacrimas aut colligit amplas
   aut, cui vita nitet, gaudia longa capit!
Hac de morte levis dolor est; nam durius illud,
   hic quem viventem Tartara nigra tenent.
Infelix quisquis maculosis actibus usus
90   ante redemptorem se laqueasse videt,
nubibus invectus cum venerit arbiter orbis
   et tuba terribilis commovet arma polis!

brought about their demise. The father and husband felt grief all the greater, since he mourned at one passing the burial of two. For one scarcely born he sheds tears on his grave; love saw what to weep for but not what to hold. But the loss of his wife brought his sorrows to their peak; their marriage had been brief, but his tears lasted long. 65

This consolation at least he had, husband for wife, that in acts of charity she was in no way deficient. For whatever could serve for the adornment of women she readily gave away to churches and the poor. She left none of those perishable things down here behind her, so as now to be rich with the wealth she sent on ahead. How well she distributed alms, without wanting her possessions to leave her! For what she gave out in abundance, now she harvests in full. She stored up for herself whatever she provided the needy and the food the poor received she keeps for as her own. 70 75

Happy are they whom no fear of the second death burdens and who make their limbs subject to no fierce punishments! The man who stores up no bitterness for himself with sweet temptations nor seeks to entomb his soul with fleshly pursuits, but remains faultless in his life and pure in his piety, purchases in this light the rewards of the light to come. How brief is the time when either he amasses an abundance of tears or, if his life is spotless, secures longlasting joys! For such a death the grief is slight; far harder is the case of one who while living here falls into the power of dark Tartarus. 80 85

Unhappy are all those whose actions are stained with corruption, who see in the presence of their redeemer that they have been caught, when he comes carried on clouds to be judge of the world and the dread trumpet sounds the war 90

His venit Helias, illis in curribus Enoch,
    anteviando suos hinc Petrus, hinc Stephanus:
95 flore puellarum rosea stipante corona
    inter virgineos prima Maria choros:
hinc mater, hinc sponsa Agnes, Tecla dulcis, Agathe
    et quaecumque Deo virginitate placet.
Tunc ibi quis terror caeli adsistente senatu?
100   Quid dicturae animae iudicis in facie?
Mox aut poena manet miseros aut palma beatos;
    quisque suae vitae semina iacta metit.
Sunt dicturi alii: "cade mons et comprime corpus,"
    sed iussi colles ferre sepulchra negant.
105 Cogentur minimi quadrantem solvere nummi;
    nemo pedem removet quo sua culpa trahit.
Spe vacui paleae similes mittentur in ignes;
    pascendis flammis fit caro nostra cibus.
Vivunt ad poenas aeterno ardente camino;
110   ut cruciet gravius, mors mala non moritur.
Ne fessi recreent animas longo igne crematas,
    porrigit, heu, nullas flammiger amnis aquas.
Parte alia, meritis felicibus alta tenentes,
    fulgebunt iusti sol velut arce poli.
115 Digni lumen habent, damnati incendia deflent;
    illos splendor alit, hos vapor igne coquit.
Res est una quidem, duplici sed finditur actu:
    nam cremat indignos quo probat igne pios.
Aeterna radiant paradisi in luce beati
120   cum facie Christi regna tenendo sui.
Gratia quanta manet, vultus qui aspexerit illos,
    quantus honor hominum, posse videre Deum!

cry to heaven! On one chariot comes Elijah, on another one
Enoch, at the head of their columns move Peter and Ste-
phen; encircled by a rosy crown, the flower of maidenhood,   95
Mary, takes first place in the choirs of virgins. Here is the
mother, here the bride Agnes, sweet Thecla, and Agatha,
and all who win favor with God by their virginity. Then what
will be their terror in face of the senate of heaven? What can   100
the souls say in the presence of their judge? In an instant ei-
ther pain awaits the wretched or the palm the blessed; each
reaps the seeds that in his lifetime he sowed. Some will say
then: "Fall, mountain, and destroy my body," but the moun-
tains, though bidden, will refuse them burial. They will be   105
compelled to pay to the very last farthing; no one takes a
step back from where his sins are impelling him. Deprived
of hope they will be thrown into the fire like chaff; our flesh
becomes the food with which the flames are fed. They live
on for punishment in the eternally blazing furnace; to tor-   110
ture them further, dread death does not die. So that when
weary they do not refresh their souls burned by long fires, a
river of flame, alas, denies them all water. In another loca-
tion, raised on high by their prospering virtues, the just will
shine like the sun in the vault of the heavens. The deserv-   115
ing possess light, the damned weep at the flames; brilliance
nourishes one group, the other heat cooks in the fires. A
single force is involved, but divided with double effect, for
the fire that burns the unworthy proves the just. In the eter-
nal light of paradise the blessed shine brightly, occupying in   120
his sight the kingdom of Christ.

How marvelous the reward, to cast eyes on that counte-
nance, what honor for men, to be able to see God! If to see a

Si nimis erigitur fragilem qui cernit amicum,
    qualiter exultet qui videt ora Dei!
125 Lilia, narcissus, violae, rosa, nardus, amomus,
    quidquid odorifero germine mittit Arabs
iudicis in vultu, florentia lumina, vernant,
    sed super haec Domini suavior efflat odor.
Nam quantum obsceno melior lux aurea plumbo,
130   tantum tura Deo cedit et omnis odor;
quantum nocte dies distat, sol lampade lunae,
    factori cedunt sic sua facta suo.
Cum vero iusti tanto splendore fruantur,
    congaudent nimium se caruisse mori.
135 De tenebris migrasse favent in luce perenni,
    et magis ad bona tot tardius isse dolent.
Tu quoque ne lacrimis uras pia fata iugalis,
    cui modo creduntur huc meliora dari.
Nam si deplores meritis quae vivit opimis.
140   coniugis ipse bonis invidiosus eris,
praesertim quam sensu, animo, tibi corpore iunctam
    cum Christo semper corde fuisse refers.
Post Domini vultus ad te si iussa rediret,
    fleret in hunc mundum se revocare gradum.
145 Carius illa diem retinet quem perdere nescit
    quam hunc quem timuit fine sequente sibi.
Nec grave funus agas cunctis natura quod offert,
    quod cum principibus participatur inops.
Nullum paupertas, non eripit ampla facultas,
150   hoc commune simul dives, egenus habet.
Nam puer atque senes, niger, albus, turpis, honestus,
    debilis et fortis, mitis et asper obit.

frail mortal friend arouses great joy, how he will rejoice who
sees the face of God! Lilies, narcissus, violets, rose, nard,   125
and balsam, whatever Arabia sends from its garden of scents,
all bloom in the judge's features flowerlike and bright, yet
the scent of the Lord breathes still sweeter than these. For
as much as the sheen of gold outdoes the vileness of lead, so   130
much are incense and every other scent inferior to God. As
day is distinct from night and the sun from the light of the
moon, so the whole of his creation gives place to its creator.
And so when the just experience splendor so great, they re-
joice very much to have avoided dying. They are happy to   135
have left darkness for the light everlasting and grieve rather
to have come to such pleasures too late.

You too should not disparage your wife's holy fate with
your tears, for we are assured she now is granted a better
existence there. For if you lament one who lives on by her
abundant merits, you will be found envious of the happiness   140
your wife enjoys, especially as you declare that she who was
joined to you in thought, mind, and body was always at one
in heart with Christ. If she were commanded to return to
you after sight of the Lord, she would weep to retrace her
steps back to this world. She clings more dearly to the light   145
that she cannot lose than to this daylight that she feared be-
cause of the imminence of its end. Do not be oppressed by
death, which nature brings to all, the common lot of the
poor and of princes. Poverty exempts no one nor do abun-
dant resources; all share in this together both the rich and   150
the needy. For young and old, black, white, evil and good,
weak and strong, gentle and cruel, all of them die. To this

Huc sapiens stolidus, probus improbus, . . . omnis
  plenior exiguus, parvus et altus adit.
155 Tardius aut citius currit sors ista per omnes;
  dissimili merito mors trahit una viros.
Non decet ergo graves pro coniuge fundere fletus
  de cuius meritis te dubitare negas.
Felices nimium hic qui sine crimine praesunt,
160 qui melius discunt vivere post obitum.

27

Epitaphium Eufrasiae

Si pietatis opus numquam morietur in aevo,
  vivis pro merito, femina sancta, tuo.
Inclita sidereo radians, Eufrasia, regno,
  nec mihi flenda manes, cum tibi laeta places.
5 Terrae terra redit, sed spiritus astra recepit;
  pars iacet haec tumulo, pars tenet illa polum.
Corpore deposito, leviori vecta volatu,
  stas melior caelo, quam prius esses humo.
Carnis iniqua domans, de te tibi facta triumphans,
10 ad patriae sedes civis opima redis.
Ardua nobilitas proavorum luce coruscans,
  plus tamen es meritis glorificanda tuis.
Vir cui Namatius—datus inde, Vienna, sacerdos—

the wise and the foolish, honest and wicked, . . . men of sub-
stance and of slim means, the humble and the high, all come.
With fast pace or slow sooner or later this destiny over-   155
comes all; a single death carries off humans, however differ-
ent their deserts. It is not right therefore to shed bitter tears
for a wife about whose virtues, as you say, you have not a
doubt. Most happy are those who live here without sin, for   160
they are learning to live a better life after death.

27

Epitaph of Eufrasia

If works of piety never die but are eternal, holy woman, you
live because of your virtues. Fair in fame, Eufrasia, you shine
bright in the heavenly kingdom, and give me no reason to
weep, since you are happy and content. Earth returns to   5
earth, but your spirit has gained the stars; one part lies here
in the tomb, the other occupies heaven. Shedding the body,
borne upward in more buoyant flight, you win a better place
in heaven than previously you had here on earth. Subduing
the sins of the flesh, and triumphing over yourself, you re-   10
turn an honored citizen to your native abode. High is your
nobility, illuminated by brilliant ancestors, but for your own
virtues you are to win greater glory. Your husband was Na-
matius — subsequently, Vienne, your bishop — but when your

coniuge defuncto consociata Deo.
15   Exulibus, viduis, captivis, omnia fundens,
      paupertate pia dives ad astra subis.
Aeternum mercata diem sub tempore parvo,
      misisti ad caelos quas sequereris opes.
Sed rogo per regem paradisi gaudia dantem,
20   pro Fortunato supplice funde precem.
Obtineas votis, haec qui tibi carmina misi
      ut merear claudi quandoque clave Petri.

28

Epitaphium Eusebiae

Scribere per lacrimas si possent dura parentes,
      hic pro pictura littera fletus erat.
Sed quia lumen aquis non signat nomen amantis,
      tracta manus sequitur qua iubet ire dolor.
5   Nobilis Eusebiae furibundi sorte sepulchri
      hic, obscure lapis, fulgida membra tegis.
Cuius in ingenio seu formae corpore pulchro
      arte Minerva fuit, victa decore Venus.
Docta tenens calamos, apices quoque figere filo,
10   quod tibi charta valet hoc sibi tela fuit.
Dulcis in Eusebii iam desponsata cubile,
      vivere sed tenerae vix duo lustra licet.

husband died, you devoted yourself to God. After giving all   15
that you had to exiles, widows, and prisoners, rich in holy
poverty you mounted up to the stars. In a brief period of
time you bought yourself eternal light, and sent ahead to the
heavens treasure you were to follow. But I ask in the name of
the king who bestows the joys of paradise, for Fortunatus   20
your suppliant please offer a prayer. May you obtain by your
request that I who sent you this poem win the right in the
future to be shut in by Peter's key.

28

Epitaph of Eusebia

If parents could write in tears the pains they suffer, in this
case their grief would be a text as good as a picture. But be-
cause the eye with its waters cannot inscribe the name of a
loved one, the track of a hand follows the course grief bids it
go. Here, gloomy stone, in the rapacious fate of the grave   5
you enclose the radiant body of noble Eusebia. In her intel-
ligence and in her physical beauty of figure she was a Mi-
nerva in art, Venus was outdone by her grace. Skilled as she
was with a pen and in stitching letters with thread, the role   10
paper plays for you, her weaving performed for her. Already
betrothed to the bed of gentle Eusebius, delicate as she was,
she was granted scarcely ten years to live. She so surpassed

Ut stupeas iuvenem, sensum superabat anilem;
se quoque vincebat non habitura diu.
15 Conteriturque socer cui nata generque recedit;
haec letalis obit, ille superstes abit.
Sit tamen auxilium, quia non es mortua Christo;
vives post tumulum virgo recepta Deo.

the intelligence of age that you were amazed at her youth; though not destined to live long, she even surpassed herself. The father-in-law to be was distraught, who had lost a 15 daughter and son-in-law; she had met her death, but he survived and left. Let him take as a consolation that you are not dead to Christ; you will live on after the tomb as a virgin welcome to God.

BOOK FIVE

I

Ad Martinum episcopum Galliciae

DOMINO SANCTO ATQUE APOSTOLICO
ET IN CHRISTI REGIS EXERCITU POST DUCEM
PAULUM PRIMIPILO MARTINO EPISCOPO
FORTUNATUS

Felici propulsa flatu recreabilis opinionis vestrae nostras aures aura demulsit et molli blandita lapsu sibilo crepitante, paradisiaci horti odoramenta saburrans, suavium florum nuntia nares ipsas aromate respirante suffivit, admodulanter indicans, sicut ad orientem Eden a principio, ita decurso saeculo alterum ad occasum Deus plantasset Elysium, in quo fortior Adam, id est Martius Martinus, inexpugnabilis accola, Christi fide ditior viveret perpetuo servante mandato, quem non tam ad auram Dominus revisendum post meridiem pergeret, quam ipse vir factus paradisus inter perspicui cordis zmaragdinas plateas et vernantis operis inumbrantes corymbos (non quod ficus tegeret, sed fructus ornaret) inambulantis in se beati redemptoris adhaesura vestigia cohercet fide figente. Unde nec ad momentum pii

To Bishop Martin of Galicia

FORTUNATUS TO BISHOP MARTIN, HOLY AND
APOSTOLIC LORD AND SENIOR CENTURION
UNDER THE COMMAND OF PAUL IN CHRIST
THE KING'S ARMY

The restorative breeze of your thoughts, propelled by a favorable wind, has charmed my ears, enticing by its gentle gliding with a whispering refrain, and, breathing the scents of the garden of paradise, redolent of sweet flowers has filled my nostrils with its fragrant scent, tunefully showing that just as in the beginning God planted Eden in the East, so with the lapse of time he has planted a second Elysium in the West for a braver Adam, that is Martin the martial, its invincible inhabitant, to live there richer in his faith in Christ in perpetual observance of the law. It was not so much that the Lord should come to visit him in the breeze after midday, but that he himself should become paradise and among the emerald-paved pathways of his transparent heart and the shade-giving tendrils of his prolific works (not those that fig leaves cover but those that fruit bedecks), holding them fast by faith he should bring to a halt the steps

conditoris laberetur praesentia, quia nec in atomo plasma notaretur in culpa, sed per illas beatitudines velut odori nemoris inlectus deliciis et vernulam dominus et verna dominum possideret, utpote cum, alternante sibi concatenati dulcedine, nec iste fugaretur admissu nec ille fraudaretur amplexu.

2   Hinc inhiantibus animis, medullis aestuantibus, oculis suspectis, palmis extensis, fervens magis quam sitiens praestolabar epistolae vestrae magna, si vel parva nubecula madidanti vellere bibulus umectarer, desiderii conscius, vota voto praeveniens, si quid de vobis certissime vel per undas mobiles fixa mihi littera nuntiaret, ita ut ariditatem meam conloquii vestri temperaturus imber sic inrigaret, paginam

3   ne deleret. Quo tamen providentiae divinae consulto per filium vestrum, venerandum mihi Domitium, sancta caritate refertam suscepi crescens epistolam quae, ut vos nostis arte conpacta, ut ego sensi flore confecta, bibentem se potius quam legentem fere per singulos apices pigmentato affamine inebriatura dives pauperem propinavit et, ut ita dixerim, quasi Falerni nobilis ipso me prius odore pincernante supplevit, gemina dicendi fruge congesta, condita sale, melle perfusa, permixta blanditie cum vigore, meque peregrini poculi quantum desuetum plus avidum dum pars inli-

of the blessed redeemer who was walking in him, there to remain. So not for a moment was the presence of the holy Creator to fail because not for a second was his creation at fault, but in the midst of that blessedness, as though enticed by the charms of a fragrant grove, the master was to possess the servant and the servant the master, for, locked together by the sweetness of mutual affection, neither the one was banished from his lord's presence nor the other deprived of his servant's embrace.

Therefore my spirits agog, my heart in a passion, with eyes upraised and hands held out, afire with eagerness rather than parched, I awaited the great tidings of your letter to see if I in my thirst would be moistened though even by a small cloudlet and my fleece become damp, fully aware of my longing, my wishes outstripping what I wished for, in the hope that a letter, traveling secure even over the shifting waves, would bring to me the surest news of you so that the rain shower of your speech would assuage my dryness and water me without erasing your writing. In accordance, then, with the plan of divine providence I received with swelling pride by the hands of your son Domitius, a person revered by me, your letter full of holy affection, which, as you have the skill, is artistically constructed, and, as I experienced, is composed with flowers of language. As I drank it down rather than read it, its rich draft threatened to intoxicate me in my poverty at almost every stroke with its highly-colored speech and, I might say, the promise of its very bouquet, as though of a fine Falernian, gave me satisfaction first, replete as it was with a double endowment of language, seasoned with salt and drenched in honey, a mixture of charm and forcefulness. The more unfamiliar it was the greedier I

cet, pars deterret (in ancipiti posito conviva rusticulo nec sustinente magna bibente), consentio dulcedini qui cedo virtuti.

4   Hoc igitur fluente dono venit ad me, fateor, per cana ponti fons poculi, venit, pater optime, per salsum mare quod sitim restingueret, venit Oceanitide miscente e fluctu mera dulcedo, cuius liquor non fauce tenus saperet, sed arcana mulceret, quippe quod non carnem foveris tali potu, sed spiritum. Unde, ut vere prosequar, huius uva palmitis nobis si-
5   tim prorogat, dum propinat. Hac inopina fruge delapsa per gurgitem primus iste mihimet venit fructus e fluctibus. Detulit puppis illa reliquis forsan alumen, mihi vestri conloquii certe lumen, commercium tali discrepante mercatu, quod aliis illud ad pretium, hoc nobis inemptum: illinc restinguitur, hinc purgatur, illud inficit, hinc nivescit.

6   Quid loquar de periodis, epichirematibus, enthymemis, syllogismisque perplexis? Quo laborat quadrus Maro, quo rotundus Cicero. Quod apud illos est profundum, hic profluum, quod illic difficillimum, hic in promptu. Comperi paucis punctis quoniam quo volueris colae pampinosae diffundis propagines, quod vero libuerit acuti commatis falce succidis, ut cauti vinitoris studio moderante nec in hoc luxurians germinet umbra fastidium et illuc tensa placeat pro-
7   pago cum fructu. Nam quod refertis in litteris post Stoicam

was for this unaccustomed brew—I was partly enticed and partly daunted (in a quandary like a country guest at a banquet with no head for fine drink)—but I give way to its sweetness as I give place to you in goodness.

With this fluent gift, then, there came to me, I confess, on the foam of the deep a draft for my cup, there came, best of fathers, on the salty sea an assuager of thirst, there came pure sweetness from the waves, an Oceanid brew, whose liquid did not impart flavor only as far as my throat, but soothed my innermost parts, since with such a potion you did not warm the flesh but the spirit. And so, to tell the truth, the grape of this vine prolongs my thirst as it is drunk. When this bounty came to me unexpectedly on the billows, for the first time I enjoyed gain from the main. That ship has perhaps brought others alum, but to me without doubt it has brought your luminous speech in a quite different kind of transaction, because the others had to pay for their goods, but mine came unbought: one extinguishes fires, the other purifies, one is used in dyeing, the other bleaches snow-white.

Why need I mention periods, epicheiremes, enthymemes, and complex syllogisms? In this way Virgil strives for his compact style and Cicero his rolling periods. What with them is profound is here prolific, what is there very difficult is here easy to understand. I have found in a few instances that when you want you extend the tendrils of a clause like a far-spreading vine, but at will you cut back with the pruning hook of a sharp, concise phrase so that by deploying the skill of an experienced vintner in the one case the abundance of shade does not generate aversion and in the other the compact growth attracts with its fruit. Moreover when you say that in my literary studies after the severe

Peripateticamque censuram me theologiae ac theoriae tiro-
cinio mancipatum, agnosco quid amor faciat, cum et non
merentes exornat. Cur tamen, bone pater, in me reflectis
quod tuum est ac de me publice profers quod tibi priva-
tum est, cum prima sint vobis nota et secunda domestica?
Nam Plato, Aristoteles, Chrysippus, vel Pittacus cum mihi
vix opinione noti sint nec legenti, Hilarius, Gregorius, Am-
brosius, Augustinusque vel si visione noti fierent, dormi-
tanti: et ego vere senserim, eo quod copiae artium apud vos
velut in commune diversorium convenerunt, ipsa vobis te-
nacius quae sunt caelo propinquius, quia non oblectamini
tam pompa dogmatum quam norma virtutum. Unde procul
dubio caelestium clientela factus es Cleantharum.

8   Sed quid ego haec autumo, dulcissime pater et vere
Christi discipule, qui, ad instar Samaritani vinum miscens
et oleum aegroto decubanti, blandum mihi malagma por-
rexisti, mercedem pii operis relaturus cum venerit qui se
stabulario aera pensare debiti repromisit, custodiens in vo-
bis, pontifex summe, quod contulit, sciens suis oculis hoc
placere dignissime, quod ipsam apud te vincit dignatio dig-
nitatem?

9   Quapropter sacratissimae, sincerissimae atque clemen-
tissimae apostolicae coronae vestrae plantas supra meum
pectus stratus inponens et ultimus ego membra subdita vel

doctrine of the Stoic and Peripatetic schools I have devoted myself to training in theology and abstract thought, I recognize the effect of love, since it praises even the undeserving. But why, good father, do you attribute to me what belongs to you and pronounce publicly of me what is private to you, since the first group is well-known to you and the second your intimates? For while Plato, Aristotle, Chrysippus, and Pittacus are scarcely known to me by reputation, without my having read them, as for Hilary, Gregory, Ambrose, and Augustine, even if they became known to me by observation, it was when I was drowsy. And indeed I truly realize, because the multitude of the arts have met in you as if in their common lodging-place, that the nearer things are to heaven the closer you cling to them, for the ostentation of learning gives you less delight than the pattern of what is virtuous. Therefore without a doubt you have taken your place in the retinue of the Cleantheses in heaven.

But why do I say this, sweetest father and true disciple 8 of Christ, who, in the manner of the good Samaritan combining wine and oil for one who was lying sick, have proffered me a soothing poultice, destined to be repaid for your kindly action when he comes who promised to pay the sum of the debt to the innkeeper? You keep secure, supreme bishop, the gift he bestowed on you, knowing it very properly is pleasing in his eyes that for you his favor outstrips all status.

For this reason laying my breast prostrate under the feet 9 of your most pure and merciful apostolic dignity and in my humility even making my limbs a stool for your feet, commending myself in this way with eager longing to your holi-

pedum vestrorum recubatorium faciens, ita vestrae pietati avido desiderio me commendans, deposco in Domino ut inter peccatorem et redemptorem mundi alter quodammodo mediator accedens levigato delicto, probe pater, reprobum reconcilies post reatum. Et quia vestris litteris fiduciae pignus accepi, pietati vestrae filias et famulas Agnem et Radegundem una mecum devote earum desiderio mandato commendo, communiter supplicantes, ut apud domnum Martinum pro nobis verba faciens tam fidus intercessor accedas qualis apud Dominum ipse tunc promptus extitit, cum cadaver exanimum non prius dimitteret quam mors mortuum dimisisset—est enim ratio consequens, ut per vos illinc nobis redeat spes patrocinii, quia ad vos hinc prodiit pars patroni—coram Domino supplicans, pie pater, ut in gratia vestra receptus vel apud eos, qui vestri sunt, commendatus sentiam tam oratione quam carmine te doctore regi, genitore diligi, duce progredi, tutore muniri. Praesentium vero portitorem famulum vestrum vere mihi bonum Bonosum pietati vestrae supplex accedens nec prius relaxans pedes quam, dulcis pater, promiseris, qua valeo prece supplex commendo. Qui interventu sanctorum cum vobis sospes occurrerit absentis vota praesens exsolvens, illud prius obtineam ut quis quam primum huc commeat, me celebris verbi vestri gaudia festiva respergant.

Martini meritis cum nomine nobilis heres,
    pro Fortunato, quaeso, precare Deum.

ness, I pray in the Lord's name that coming forward as, as it were, a second intermediary between a sinner and the redeemer of the world you may lighten my sin, good father, and win reconciliation for a culprit after a crime. And because with your letters I have received a guarantee to trust in you, I devoutly commend to your holiness along with myself your daughters and servants Agnes and Radegund in accordance with their expressed desire, all of us together entreating that before lord Martin you speak on our behalf and come forward as just as trusty an intercessor as he showed himself to be when without hesitation he did not abandon a lifeless corpse until death had quit the dead. For it is logically consistent that the hope of patronage should come to us from where you are through you, because from where we are the function of a patron came to you. Before the Lord I entreat, holy father, that I be received in your grace and commended to those close to you and that I feel that I am guided both in prose and in verse by you as a teacher, loved by you as a father, advanced by you as a leader, and guarded by you as a protector. In the pose of a supplicant and without releasing your feet until you have given your promise, sweet father, I commend with all the force of prayer I can muster the bearer of this present letter Bonosus, your servant and true to his name, a good man to me. When he has with the protection of the saints reached you safely and in your presence given voice to my wishes in my absence, may I first ensure that as soon as anyone makes the journey here, I may revel with joy in the shower of your abundant language.

Noble inheritor of the merits of Martin and of his name, pray to God for Fortunatus, I beg.

2

Item ad eundem

Lumen apostolicum cum spargeret una triades
    exciperetque novum mundus honore diem,
ut tenebras animae lux sementiva fugaret
    et claram hauriret mens oculata fidem,
5 redditur avulsis spinis urbs Romula princeps,
    principis egregii vomere culta Petri.
Paulus ad Illyricos Scythicas penetrando pruinas
    dogmate ferventi frigora solvit humi.
Mattheus Aethiopos adtemperat ore vapores
10   vivaque in exusto flumina fundit agro.
Bellica Persidis Thomae subiecta vigori
    fortior efficitur victa tiara Deo.
Lurida perspicuo datur India Bartholomaeo;
    Andreae monitis extat Achaia seges.
15 Ne morer adcelerans, Martini Gallia prisci
    excellente fide luminis arma capit.
Martino servata novo, Gallicia, plaude;
    sortis apostolicae vir tuus iste fuit.
Qui virtute Petrum praebet tibi, dogmate Paulum,
20   hinc Iacobi tribuens, inde Iohannis opem.
Pannoniae, ut perhibent, veniens e parte Quiritis
    est magis effectus Gallisueba salus.
In sulcum sterilem vitae plantaria sevit,
    quo matura seges fertilitate placet.
25 Heliae meritis alter redit imber aristis,
    munera roris habens, ne premat arva sitis.

2

To the same man

When a single Trinity was spreading the light of the apostles, and the world was receiving with honor a new day, so that the generative light was putting to flight the darkness from souls and clear-eyed minds were drinking in the brightness of faith, the primacy of the city of Romulus was 5 restored, its thorns uprooted, when cultivated by the plowshare of the noble primate Peter. Paul traveling as far as Illyria and braving Scythian frosts with the warmth of his teaching melted the cold on the ground. Matthew moderated with his words the Ethiopian heat and poured living 10 waters onto the dried up fields. Warlike Persia, when exposed to the energy of Thomas, became stronger, its tiara conquered by God. Dusky India was handed over to brilliant Bartholomew; by the teachings of Andrew a harvest sprung up in Greece. Not to slow the pace of my catalog, 15 from the surpassing faith of the elder Martin Gaul received the weapons of light.

Reserved for a new Martin, Galicia, rejoice; that man of yours was of apostolic rank. He brings you by his virtue a Peter and by his teaching a Paul, granting you the assistance 20 of both a James and a John. He came, as we're told, from Roman Pannonia, but has become, rather, the salvation of Galician Sueves. In the barren furrows he sowed the first shoots of life, from which a ripe harvest with its fertility wins favor. By the same power as Elijah's a second rain fell 25 on the crops, bringing the gift of dew, so drought would not

Neu iaceant stupidis arentia iugera sulcis,
    influit inrigue fonte perennis aquae.
In ramis heresis fidei pia germina fixit,
30   quodque oleaster erat pinguis oliva viret.
Quae stetit exilis viduatis frondibus arbor
    iam paritura cibum floret honore novo.
Inponenda focis sine spe ficulnea tristis
    praeparat ad fructum stercore culta sinum.
35 Palmitis uva tumens, avium laceranda rapinis,
    hoc custode bono non perit una lacu.
Rebus apostolicis direxit vinitor antes,
    arva ligone movens, falce flagella premens.
Ex agro Domini labruscam excidit inertem
40   atque racemus adest quo fuit ante frutex.
De satione Dei zizania vulsit amara,
    surgit et aequalis laetificata seges.
Martino servata novo, Gallicia, plaude:
    sortis apostolicae vir tuus iste fuit.
45 Pastoris studio circum sua saepta recurrens,
    ne lupus intret oves, servat amore greges.
Supportante manu trahit ipse ad pabula Christi
    montibus instabilem, ne voret error, ovem.
Cuius vox refluens plebi de fonte salubri
50   ut bibat aure fidem, porrigit ore salem.
Hosti damna quidem, domino pia vota paravit
    et commissa sibi dupla talenta refert,
vocem euangelicam expectans operarius almus,
    ut sibi dicatur, "Servule, perge, bone.
55 Quando fidelis enim mihi supra pauca fuisti,
    supra multa nimis constituendus eris.
Ecce tui Domini modo gaudia laetior intra

strangle the fields. So the land not dry up and its furrows
not be infertile, from a spring of eternal water he flowed in
an irrigating stream. On the boughs of heresy he grafted the
holy shoots of faith; what was once the oleaster, becomes   30
the green, rich olive. The tree that once stood bleak and
shorn of leaves now blooms in new splendor, soon to pro-
duce food. The blighted, barren fig tree, due to be consigned
to the fire, tended and manured prepares to embrace its
fruit. The swelling grapes on the vine shoot, the prey of rav-   35
aging birds, with this good man to protect them, are entirely
preserved for the vat. On the apostolic estate as dresser he
has drawn up the vine rows, working the land with a hoe,
pruning the tendrils with a hook. From the fields of the
Lord he has cut out the unfruitful wild vine and where once   40
was just scrub, there now are grape clusters. From the land
God has sowed he has uprooted harsh tares, and a flour-
ishing crop has grown up to one height.

Reserved for a new Martin, Galicia, rejoice; that man of
yours was of apostolic rank. Patrolling his territory with a   45
shepherd's concern, he lovingly protects his flock so the
wolf will not visit his sheep. He cradles in his hands and
takes to the pastures of Christ a sheep astray in the moun-
tains so error does not consume it. His voice flows from a
saving spring upon the people; so they drink in the faith   50
with their ears, he proffers salt from his mouth. To the en-
emy he has brought loss, but to the Lord his holy prayers,
and he pays back double the talents that were entrusted to
him, an honest laborer waiting to hear the words of the Gos-
pel, for it to be said to him, "Good servant, go on your way.
Since you have been faithful to me in a few things, you will   55
be set by me over very many. Lo, enter in happiness now the

proque labore brevi magna parata tibi."
Auditurus eris vocem, Martine, beatam,
60   sed Fortunati sis memor ipse tui.
Quaeso precare, pater, videam tua gaudia tecum;
        sic placeas Regi poste patente Petri.
Cum Radegunde humili supplex, pie, postulat Agnes,
        ut commendatae sint tibi, sancte pater,
65   et crescente choro per carmina sancta sororum
        complaceant Domino, te duce mite, suo,
atque adscita sibi servetur ab urbe Genesi
        regula Caesarii praesulis alma pii,
qui fuit antistes Arelas de sorte Lerini,
70   et mansit monachus pontificale decus.
Sedulitate patris proprias tuearis alumnas,
        ut tibi proficiat hae bona si qua gerant.
Unde illustre caput cingas diademate pulchro
        et grates dignas pro grege pastor agas.

3

Ad cives Turonicos
de Gregorio episcopo

Plaudite, felices populi, nova vota tenentes,
        praesulis adventu reddite vota deo.
Hoc puer exertus celebret, hoc curva senectus,
        hoc commune bonum praedicet omnis homo.

joys of the Lord; in exchange for brief struggles great rewards await you."

You are destined, Martin, to hear these blessed words, but be mindful of your own Fortunatus. Pray, I beg, father, that I see your joys with you; so may Peter's portal part and you please the King. Agnes with humble Radegund begs in supplication, holy one, that they be commended to you, saintly father, and as the choir of sisters swells in holy song, may they with you as gentle guide be pleasing to their Lord, and may the rule adopted from the city of Genesius be observed, the sacred rule of the holy pontiff Caesarius, who was bishop of Arles, from the ranks of Lérins, and remained a monk, despite his pontifical glory. With the care of a father may you protect your own foster-daughters, so that whatever good they do redound to your credit. For this may you bind your fair head with a beautiful diadem and give fitting thanks on behalf of your flock as its shepherd.

60

65

70

3

On Bishop Gregory
to the citizens of Tours

Rejoice, happy people, your prayers are newly answered; your bishop has come, give thanks to God. Let the vigorous young extol this, let bent old age, and let every person pro-

5   Spes gregis ecce venit, plebis pater, urbis amator;
        munere pastoris laetificentur oves.
    Sollicitis oculis quem prospera vota petebant
        venisse aspiciant, gaudia festa colant.
    Iura sacerdoti merito reverenter adeptus,
10   nomine Gregorius, pastor in urbe gregis.
    Martino proprium mittit Iulianus alumnum
        et fratri praebet quod sibi dulce fuit.
    Quem patris Egidii Domino manus alma sacravit,
        ut populum recreet, quem Radegundis amet.
15 Huic Sigibercthus ovans favet et Brunichildis honori;
        iudicio regis nobile culmen adest.
    Quo pascente greges per pascua sancta regantur
        et paradisiaco germine dona metant,
    immaculata pii qui servet ovilia Christi,
20   ne pateant rabidis dilaceranda lupis.
    Pervigili cura stabulum sine labe gubernet
        commissumque gregem nulla rapina gravet.
    Muniat inclusos pretiosi velleris agnos
        atque soporantes protegat ipse vigil.
25 Florea divino pinguescat vinea cultu
        et matura suo sit speciosa botro,
    fructibus aeternis ut compleat horrea caeli,
        unde animae vivo fonte fluenta bibant,
    ne sitis excruciet; digito quam Lazarus udo
30   ignem ut leniret, tunc petebatur opem.
    Sed magis in gremio Abrahae vernante locandas
        pastor oves placido ducat ad astra sinu,
    ut bene commisso sese duplicante talento
        introeat Domini gaudia vera sui.

claim this universal good. See, the hope of the flock is com- 5
ing, father of the people, lover of the city; let his sheep be
gladdened by the gift of a shepherd. They sought him with
yearning gaze and favoring prayers; let them now watch his
arrival and make joyful holiday. Rightly and with due rever-
ence he has won the bishop's office; his name is Gregory, a 10
shepherd for the city and its flock. Julian is sending his own
foster-son to Martin, and offering to a brother what was
dear to himself. The blessed hand of father Aegidius conse-
crated him to the Lord, to relieve the people, for Radegund
to love. Sigibert with joy supports this election and Brun- 15
hild too; by the king's judgment a noble eminence is here
among us.

With Gregory as pastor may the flocks be tended in the
holy pastures, and may they reap their rewards in the mead-
ows of paradise. May he keep the sheepfolds of merciful
Christ undefiled so they not be exposed to being torn apart 20
by ravening wolves. With watchful care may he govern his
flawless sheepfold, and may the flock in his charge suffer
no depredations. May he pen in and protect his lambs with
their costly fleeces, and though they sleep, himself stand
guard awake. May the flowering vineyard grow fertile with 25
God's tending and ripen in beauty with its clusters of grapes,
to fill with eternal fruit the storerooms of heaven, so that
thereby souls may drink the streams from a living fountain
and thirst not torture them; a fiery thirst that Lazarus once
was asked to help assuage with dampened finger. Rather 30
may the sheep find a place in Abraham's verdant bosom, and
their shepherd bring them to the stars in his kindly em-
brace, so that by doubling the talent faithfully entrusted to

35 laetus agat sub clave Petri, per dogmata Pauli
        inter sidereos luce micante choros,
    fortis Athanasius, qua clarus Hilarius adstant,
        dives Martinus, suavis et Ambrosius,
    Gregorius radiat, sacer Augustinus inundat,
40   Basilius rutilat Caesariusque micat.
    Quorum gesta sequens et dicta fideliter implens
        perpetuae vitae participatus ovet,
    atque coronatus digna mercede laborum
        obtineat miles Regis in arce locum.

4

Item versus in natalicio Gregori episcopi, cum antiphonam dicere rogaretur, in mensa dictum

    Martini meritis per tempora longa, Gregori,
        Turonicum foveas pastor in urbe gregem.
    Conciliis sacris sis norma et vita piorum
        exemploque tuo crescat adeptus honor.
5   Lumen apostolicum populis tua lingua ministret
        et caeli donum te radiante micet.

him he may enter the true joys of his Lord. May he live hap- 35
pily where Peter holds the key and Paul is the teacher among
star-bright choirs in brilliance of light, in the company of
brave Athanasius and famous Hilary, rich Martin and sweet
Ambrose, where Gregory shines and holy Augustine pours
his learning, Basil glitters and Caesarius gleams. After fol- 40
lowing their deeds and faithfully fulfilling their words, may
he rejoice to join them in eternal life, and crowned with a
fitting reward for his labors, may he as a soldier win a place
in the citadel of the King.

4

Verses on the anniversary of Bishop Gregory, when he was asked to say the antiphons, spoken at the table

With the merits of Martin, Gregory, for a long time to come
may you protect your flock in the city of Tours as its shep-
herd. In sacred councils may you be the standard and model
for the life of the holy, and by your example may the honor
you have won grow in prestige. May your tongue bring to 5
the peoples the light of the apostles, and the gift of heaven
shine forth in your radiant beam.

5

Item ad eundem de Iudaeis conversis per Avitum episcopum Arvernum

DOMINO SANCTO ET MERITIS
APOSTOLICIS PRAECONANDO DOMNO
ET IN CHRISTO PATRI GREGORIO
PAPAE FORTUNATUS

Instigas, pater optime, seria curiositate, sincera tamen dulcedine, carmine elinguem proloqui et currere pigrum versu pedestri atque de laude laudabilis et apostolici viri domni Aviti pontificis ex eventu occasionis inlatae etsi non aliqua compte, saltim comiter praelibare, cum in me non inveneris quod dictionis luculentia diligeres, sed deleres et, ut ipse mei sum conscius, habeas apud nos non quod tam probes quam reprobes, praesertim cum instans portitor per verba singillatim hianti fauce cadentia quasi gravis exactor non me tam fenora solvere cogeret quam pensaret. Sub quo, licet illum praeceps iter inpingeret, mihi interanhelanti vix licuerit respirare, tamen praeceptis vestris, licet inpliciter expeditis, paremus devoti potius quam placemus, vobis reputaturi ne-

2

5

To the same man on the conversion of Jews by Avitus, bishop of Clermont

FORTUNATUS TO BISHOP GREGORY,
MY SAINTLY LORD, WORTHY OF RENOWN
FOR YOUR APOSTOLIC VIRTUES,
AND MY FATHER IN CHRIST

You press me, best of fathers, with genuine urgency yet true affection to express myself, though tongue-tied, in poetry and, though slothful, to run in pedestrian verse, and if not with good style at least with good intent to touch on the praise of the praiseworthy and apostolic man, the lord bishop Avitus, taking advantage of the opportunity that is offered. And this, though you have not found in me anything to love because of its brilliance of diction, but instead to remove, and, as I am well aware, what you receive from me will not win your approval as much as your disapproval, all the more so since an insistent letter carrier like a pressing debt collector does not so much compel me to pay what I owe as weigh it out in words that fall one by one from gaping jaws. In these circumstances, though his urgent need 2 to depart was driving him on and though I with irregular gasps can scarcely catch my breath, yet out of devotion I comply with rather than do justice to your commands, however difficult their expression, uncertain whether to attrib-

scio magis an tempori, quod illi hoc iniungitur qui non habebat apud se nec modum nec spatium. Sed obsequella morigeri, servitute devoti, quod a vobis in laude praedicti pontificis amore praecipitur honore cantetur.

In venerabilibus famulis operator opime,
  condecet ut semper laus tua, Christe, sonet,
inspirans animum, votum effectumque ministrans,
  et sine quo nullum praevalet esse bonum,
5 lumine perspicuo fecundans pectora vatum,
  ut populis generent viscera sancta fidem,
supra candelabrum positi, quorum ore corusco
  dogmatis igne micans luceat alma domus,
et velut est oculus capitis qui dirigit artus,
10 sic pia pastoris cura gubernet oves.
Pectora pontificum ditans virtute superna,
  tu Deus omnipotens, summe, perennis apex,
spiritus alme, sacri labiis infusus Aviti,
  per famulum loqueris, crescat ut ordo gregis.
15 Qui non contentus numero quem accepit ab illo,
  vilicus hic domini dupla talenta refert.
Plebs Arverna etenim, bifido discissa tumultu,
  urbe manens una non erat una fide.
Christicolis Iudaeus odor resilibat amarus
20 obstabatque piis impia turba sacris.
Extollens cervix Domini iuga ferre recusans,
  sic tumidis animis turget inane cutis.
Quos in amore Dei monitabat saepe sacerdos,
  ut de conversis iret ad astra seges,
25 sed caligosi recubans velaminis umbra
  pectora taetra premens cernere clara vetat.

ute it to you or the situation that a person who had neither the wherewithal nor the time receives this instruction. But in compliant obedience and devoted service let what you lovingly commissioned in praise of the above-mentioned bishop be sung in his honor.

Christ, performer of abundant works through your venerable servants, it is fitting your praise should always resound. You inspire the spirit, supply wish and fulfillment, and without you no good thing can prevail, making fertile 5 the hearts of prophets with clear-shining light so that their holy wombs bring faith to birth among peoples. They are set on a candlestick, and from their brilliant speech the holy house shines bright in the fiery glow of their teaching, and as it is the eye in the head that controls the limbs, so let 10 the shepherd's devoted care govern his sheep. You enrich the hearts of the bishops with power from above, almighty God, most high, forever supreme; Holy Spirit, distilled on the lips of saintly Avitus, you speak through your servant to swell the ranks of his flock. Not content with the number he 15 had received from his lord, this steward is returning double the number of talents. For the Arvernian people, torn apart by a rancorous schism, all inhabited the one city, but were not of one faith. The distasteful odor of the Jews recoiled from the Christians, and the unholy company opposed the 20 holy rites. Their arrogant neck refused to support the yoke of the Lord, and with this swelling pride their skin was foolishly distended. The bishop in the love of God often tried to recall them so a harvest of converts would mount to the stars, but the shade of the dark veil that encompassed them, 25 oppressing their foul hearts, stopped them seeing clear.

Venerat ergo dies Dominus qua est redditus astris
    ac homo sidereum pendulus iit iter.
Plebs armante fide Iudaica templa revellit
30   et campus patuit quo synagoga fuit.
Tempore quo Christi repedavit ad alta potestas,
    ille quod ascendit, res inimica ruit.
Hic tamen antistes Moysei lege rebelles
    alloquitur blande, quos dabat ira truces:
35 "Quid facis, o Iudaea cohors nec docta vetustas?
    Ut vitam renoves, credere disce senes.
Lactea canities sapiat maiora iuventae;
    sensum pone gravem quo puerile fuit.
Non pudeat meliora sequi vel tarda veternus;
40   corpore deficiens crescat honore senes.
Est Deus, alta fides, unus trinus et trinus unus;
    personis propriis stat tribus unus apex.
Nam pater et genitus, quoque sanctus spiritus idem:
    sic tribus est unum ius, opus, ordo, thronus.
45 Legifer hoc reboat, patriarcha hoc credit Abraham;
    hinc pater est nobis, est quia nostra fides.
Tres videt aequales, unum veneratus adorat;
    unum voce rogat, tres quoque pelve lavat.
Sic patruo similis Loth suscipit hospes euntes;
50   quos cibat in Sodomis, hi rapuere Segor.
Cum a Domino Dominus pluit igni triste Gomorrae,
    filius et pater est, a Domino Dominus.
Qui tuus, ipse meus stat conditor atque creator;
    huius plasma sumus qui est trinitate Deus.
55 Unius estis oves, heu, cur non uniter itis?
    Sit rogo grex unus, pastor ut unus adest.

And so the day had dawned on which the Lord returned to the stars, and as a man made his way on high to the heavens. The people, armed by their faith, tore down the shrine of the Jews and where once there was a synagogue, now 30 there was an open plain. At the season when Christ in his power reascended to heaven, because he rose on high, the hostile forces were brought low. At this moment, then, the bishop addressed in gentle tones those rebels in the Mosaic law whom anger made fierce: "What are you doing, you 35 band of Jews, venerable but unschooled? Though you are old, learn to believe, and so renew your life. Milk-white hair should have more wisdom than the young; replace your former childishness with mature beliefs. Age should not be ashamed to adopt the better course, however late; as an old 40 man fails in body he should gain in respect. God is one in three and three in one—such is our profound faith; a single eminence exists in three distinct persons. For the Father and Son and the Holy Spirit too are the same: so in three there is one power, one agency, one rank, one throne. The 45 lawgiver proclaims this, the patriarch Abraham believes this; this is why he is our father, because this is our faith. He saw three men of like age, but he bowed down to worship just one; he addressed one in speech, but he washed three from his basin. In the same way as his uncle, Lot, received travelers as their host; he gave them food in Sodom, they 50 took him away to Segor. When the Lord rained grim fire 'from the Lord' on Gomorrah, this means the Father and Son, a Lord 'from the Lord.' He is your originator and creator, as he is mine; we are the creation of him who is God in the Trinity. You are the sheep of one master, alas, why do you 55 not walk in unison? Let there be one flock I beg, as there is a

Rennuis? An recolis quod canna Davitica pangit
   quodque prophetali virgine fetus agit?
In cruce transfixus palmis pedibusque pependit,
60   sed corrupta caro non fuit ex tumulo.
Post triduum remeans sanat nos vulnere longo:
   quod rediit caelis, testis et ista dies.
Crede meis aut crede tuis, convicta senectus;
   si fugis ac trepidas, nec legis ista legens.
65 Protrahimus verbum brevitatis tempore longum;
   aut admitte preces aut, rogo, cede loco.
Vis hic nulla premit, quo vis te collige liber;
   aut meus esto sequax aut tuus ito fugax.
Redde, colone, locum, tua duc contagia tecum:
70   aut ea sit sedes, si tenet una fides."
Haec pia verba viris miti dedit ore sacerdos,
   ut sibi quo libeat semita cordis eat.
Ast Iudaea manus, stimulante furore rebellis,
   colligitur, rapitur, conditur inde domo.
75 Christicolae ut cernunt tunc agmina manzara iungi,
   protinus insiliunt qua latet ille dolus.
Si fremerent, gladiis sentirent iusta cadentes:
   vivere quo possint aut daret arma fides.
Legati occurrunt vati mandata ferentes:
80   "Nos Iudaea manus iam tua caula sumus.
Ne pereant, adquire Deo qui vivere possunt.
   Si mora fit, morimur et tua lucra cadunt.
Tende celer gressum. Properes nisi praepete cursu,
   funera natorum sunt tibi flenda, pater."
85 Fletibus his victus rapitur miserando sacerdos
   ut ferat adflictis rite salutis opem.

single shepherd. You refuse? Do you remember the refrain
David's pipe sang, and what the child of a virgin, as prophe-
sied, performs? He hung on the cross, his hands and feet
pierced, but his flesh suffered no harm from the tomb. Af-   60
ter three days he returned and healed us of our longstand-
ing wound; this very day bears witness that he returned to
heaven. Believe my arguments or believe your own, elders
convicted of error; if you are fleeing in fear, you are not re-
ally reading the things that you read. I am dragging out a   65
long speech, but the time is short; either accede to my
prayers or withdraw, I ask you, from this place. Here no
force compels you, you are free to take yourself off where
you wish; either follow and join me or flee and go on your
way. Newcomer, give place and take your infection with you,
or let this be your abode, if you adopt one faith." The bishop   70
addressed in gentle tones these holy words to the crowd so
that their heart might follow whichever path it desired.

But the band of the Jews possessed by fury resisted; they
joined together, hurried off, and shut themselves up in a
house. When the Christians saw that the bastard troops   75
were gathered, they immediately sallied forth to where that
guile was in hiding. If they raised a disturbance, they would
experience justice, falling by the sword; alternatively faith
would give them the weapons by which they could live. En-
voys came to the bishop, bringing a message to deliver: "We,   80
the company of Jews, now belong to your sheepfold. Lest
they perish, win over to God our people, who thereby
can live. If there is any delay we die and your profit is lost.
Quickly start on your journey. If you do not hurry with ur-
gent pace, you will have to weep, father, for the death of
your children." Overwhelmed by these tears the bishop, full   85
of pity, hastened off duly to bring the help of salvation to

Perveniunt quo clausa loco fera turba latebat,
   quae occurrens lacrimis ingerit ore preces:
"Mens est tarda boni Iudaica iura tenenti;
90   lucem sero videt praetereunte die.
Sic oculis cordis velum est ab origine tensum
   caecus ut ignoret quo via recta vocet.
Sed tandem sequimur, pastor, quo saepe monebas,
   qui sale tam dulci currere cogis oves.
95 Credentes iam crede tuos nec fallere falsis.
   Nos lavacrum petimus, sit tibi praesto lacus.
Sensimus effectu quod agebas rite precando,
   quod per te hominem nos Deus ipse monet."
Hinc trahit ad lucem quos texerat umbra negantes
100   militiaeque novae Rex aperibat iter.
Agmina conveniunt quondam diversa sub unum
   partibus et geminis fit Deus unus amor.
Hinc oleare ovium perfunditur unguine vellus
   aspersuque sacro fit gregis alter odor.
105 Ecce dies aderat qua spiritus almus ab alto
   missus apostolicis fluxit in ora viris.
Res sacra ruricolas, urbanos excitat omnes
   certatimque aditus ad pia festa terunt.
Abluitur Iudaeus odor baptismate divo
110   et nova progenies reddita surgit aquis.
Vincens ambrosios suavi spiramine rores,
   vertice perfuso chrismatis efflat odor.
Ingenti numero celebratur pascha novellum
   ac de stirpe lupi progenerantur oves.
115 Excepit populus populum, plebs altera plebem;
   germine qui non est, fit sibi fonte parens.

their suffering. They came to where the savage crowd was
enclosed hiding, who met him with tears and urgent expres-
sion of prayers: "The mind that clings to the Judaic law is
slow to grasp the good, but late it sees the light, even when   90
day is ending. In such a way from the first has a veil been
stretched over the eyes of the heart, that in blindness a man
is ignorant of where the right path summons him. But at last
we follow, father, where you often urged us to go, who with
such sweet salt compel your sheep to make haste. Now be-   95
lieve that we are yours and we believe, that we are not false
or faking. We ask for baptism, do you make ready the font.
We have felt by the results what you brought about by due
prayer, for through you, though only a man, God speaks to
us himself." In this way he brought to the light those deniers
who lived in the shade, and the King showed the way to a   100
new soldiery. Previously separate forces came together as
one, and for the two sides God has become their one love.
In this way the fleece of the sheep is anointed richly with oil,
and by holy aspersion their flock acquires a new odor.

Now, see, the day was on hand when the Holy Spirit from   105
on high was sent down and flowed into the mouths of the
apostles. The holy ceremony attracted all country and city
dwellers alike and eagerly they tread the roads leading to the
sacred festival. The odor of the Jews was washed away by di-
vine baptism, and a new offspring emerged, restored, from   110
the waters. Surpassing ambrosial distillations in its sweet ex-
halation, the chrism breathed its scent over their anointed
heads. In large numbers this new form of Easter was cele-
brated, and from the family of the wolf sheep were brought
to birth. People gave welcome to people, a second group   115
welcomed the first; though no relation by race, they became

Undique rapta manu lux cerea provocat astra
    credas ut stellas ire trahendo comas.
Lacteus hinc vestis color est, hinc lampade fulgor,
120   ducitur et vario lumine picta dies,
Nec festiva minus quam tunc fuit illa coruscans,
    diversis linguis quae dedit una loqui.
Quis, rogo, pontificis fuit illic sensus Aviti,
    quam validus fervor, cum daret ista deo?
125 Inter candelabros radiabat et ipse sacerdos,
    diffuso interius spiritus igne micans.
Tum sibi qualis erat tam vera holocausta ferendo,
    cum libeat vivo hostia viva Deo?
Si patriarcha placet, quoniam natum obtulit unum,
130   qui tantos offert quam placiturus erit?
Moyses non valuit fidei quos subdere nostrae
    qui Christo adquirit quod sibi munus erit?
Fudit aromaticum Domini libamen ad aram
    incensumque novum misit ad astra Deo.
135 Obtinuit votum, quia iunxit ovile sub uno,
    et grege de niveo gaudia pastor habet.

Haec inculta tibi reputa, pater alme Gregori,
    qui Fortunato non valitura iubes.
Adde quod exiguum me portitor inpulit instans
140   et datur in spatiis vix geminata dies.
Novimus affectu potius quo diligis illum;
    hinc quem corde vides semper et ore tenes.
Hoc tibi nec satis est, huius quod es ipse relator;
    conpellis reliquos plaudere voce sibi.
145 Non fuit in vacuum, quod te provexit alumnum;
    sic cui mente fidem reddis amore vicem.

so by the baptismal font. On every side candles snatched up
in the hand rivaled stars with their light so you would think
they were comets leaving a trail behind them. Here is the
milk-white color of clothing, here the brightness of lamps,
and the day is celebrated illuminated by different forms of   120
light. It was no less joyful than was that brilliant day that
gave to different tongues the power to speak as one.

What were the feelings then, I wonder, of the bishop Avi-
tus, how strong his passion, when he gave that gift to God?
Among the candlesticks the bishop himself gave off light,   125
gleaming with the fire of the spirit that spread within him.
What were his thoughts when he presented so true a sacri-
fice, for a living offering is pleasing to the living God? If the
patriarch won favor for offering his only son, how much fa-   130
vor will he win who offers so many? What reward will he win
who won over to Christ those whom Moses could not enlist
for our faith? He poured a fragrant libation on the altar of
the Lord and sent to the stars a new incense for God. He   135
obtained his wish, for he brought unity in one single sheep-
fold, and as shepherd rejoices in his snow-white flock.

For these artless words you must take the blame, good fa-
ther Gregory, for you ordered Fortunatus to do what cannot
be done. What is more your letter carrier insistently pressed
me in my inadequacy and I was scarcely given two days of   140
time. I know with what affection you love that bishop; be-
cause you see him in your heart, you always have him on
your lips. It is not even enough for you that you are his pro-
moter; you compel others also to give voice to his praises. It   145
was not for nothing that he advanced you, his foster-child;
you pay him back in love, as you do in loyalty of spirit. May

Annuat Omnipotens longo memoraliter aevo
    ut tu laus illi, laus sit et ille tibi.
Me quoque vos humilem pariter memoretis utrique
150   et pro spe veniae voce feratis opem.

6

Ad Syagrium episcopum Augustidunensem

DOMINO SANCTO ET APOSTOLICA
SEDE DIGNISSIMO DOMNO
SYAGRIO PAPAE FORTUNATUS

Torpore vecordis otii, quo mens ebria desipit diutina tabe morbescente brutiscens, et velut ignavi soporis hebetante marcore suffectus, negotii indulti nulla mordente cura dormitans, cum videretur scilicet tam lectio neglegi quam usus abuti neque nancisceretur quicquam occasionis ex themate quod digereretur in poesi, et, ut ita dictum sit, nihil vellere- tur ex vellere quod carminaretur in carmine, intra me quo- dammodo me ipsum silentio sarcofagante sepeliens, et, cum nulla canerem, obsoleto linguae plectro aeruginavissem, tan- dem nec opinato concaptivo meo, sed tamen ut arbitror ves- trae felicitatis ad me sorte delato, quis, unde, quidve deferat dum percontor, de fili calamitate suae necessitatis, meae

the Almighty grant that in the memory of long ages he bring praise to you, as you bring praise to him. Me too, your humble servant, may you both equally remember and bring aid with your advocacy to my hope for forgiveness. 150

6

To Syagrius, bishop of Autun

FORTUNATUS TO BISHOP SYAGRIUS,
MY SAINTLY LORD,
MOST WORTHY OF HIS APOSTOLIC SEE

Infected by the lethargy of insensate leisure, in which the drunken mind wanders dulled by the long onset of a corrupting sickness, and by a debilitating apathy like that of torpid sleep, I was drowsy without any involvement in a pressing issue to stimulate me, for my reading seemed to be as neglected as my practice went to waste, I found no opportunity from any subject that could be turned into poetry, and, so to speak, no fleece could be sheared to card into verse. I was buried within myself by my own silence as if in a coffin and, since I had no songs to sing, the plectrum of my tongue had rusted over with disuse, till at last a fellow captive of mine was brought to me unexpectedly, but, as I be-

conpassionis, vestrae mercedis causas, indice singultu vix laxante, prorupit. Quo voce intercepta tam viscerum maerore quam luminum flumine dum loqui non permittitur, ipso silentio patrem lacrimae fatebantur, quia, dum anxius in verbo genitor pendet nec exprimit, tacente faucis organo pupilla fletibus loquebatur. Tantum est in caritate natura quod praevalet ut parens ante se prodat affectu quam labio.

2   Fluebant igitur lumina suggestionem suam blandito ploratu conpunctam, ut etiam quamvis crudelem redderent lamenta clementem. Inrigabant lacrimae tam semen miseriae quam frugem misericordiae. Uno fonte manabant res maeroris et muneris, uno luctus et merces, ut unus rigans oculis alter bibens auribus quod iste torcularet in fletu ille apothecaret in fructu. Itaque signo singulti fecit se intellegi mens

3 captivi et quasi speculariter traxit maeror in facie qui videbatur angor in corde. Unde inter tacentes causa rerum cognita, dum apud me valuit hoc fari quod flere, videbatur affectus mire sine lingua sic loqui.

4   Igitur cum me moveret lamentabilis concivis tam iactura quam patria, cum cernerentur vultus patris pietatis imbre perfundi, ut paene totus et ipse in alieno affectu migrarem,

lieve, by the destiny of your good fortune and when I asked him who he was, where from, and what his business was, he burst forth with the story of his son's misfortune, the grounds for his distress, my compassion, and your charitable action, though his telltale sobs scarcely let him get out a word. And when he was unable to speak because his voice was stifled both by this grief of the heart and by the floods from his eyes, his weeping by its very silence bore witness to his paternity, since, as a grief-stricken father, his words failed and could not find expression and though his throat's instrument was silent, his pupils spoke with their tears. So strongly does nature prevail in affection that a parent reveals himself with his feelings before he does with his lips.

In this way the stream from his eyes sent a message made 2 forceful by the appeal of his grief, so that his mourning would render even the most cruel merciful. His tears watered not just the seed of his grief but the fruit of pity. From one spring flowed the qualities of both grief and relief, from one both lamentation and reward, so that while one ran from the eyes, the other drank with the ears, and while one pressed out tear juice, the other stored it for use. And so by 3 the sign of a sob the mind of the captive made itself understood and like a mirror the distress on his face reflected the anguish in his heart. In this way without saying anything the situation was understood and since for me his tears were as good as speech, his feelings seemed wonderfully to speak for themselves though unvoiced.

Therefore since my wretched fellow citizen moved me 4 both by his loss and his homeland and since the sight of his face drenched in showers of paternal devotion caused me to surrender myself almost entirely to the emotions of an-

lacrimantes oculi querellas mihi fixerunt ad vicem incausti
et admirabili modo aqua, quae delere solet, per fletus scrip-
sit. Quis enim flenti non crederet quem lapis non genuit?
Quem non humanitas flecteret quem partus tigridis non ef-
fudit, cum lentiscat blanditiis cursus pardi, virtus apri, dens
5 leonis et moles elephanti? Qui tandem sedato querellarum
strepitu doloris sui prosperum te designat antidotum, scili-
cet dum aeger mente sibi poscit medellam, si se dignanter
inpendat, vestra lingua sit malagma. Quo loquente media
per verba me miscens, mihi de vobis credulus fidem feci ho-
mini ex hoc per me te consuli, se non flere.

6 Restabat tamen conici, utrumne pro redemptione dirige-
rem, quod suboles valeret, an quod vobis proficeret. De
conpendio cogitans, ne vilitate pretii depretiaretur tibi
merces captivi; illud certe metuens, si caperetur in nummo,
res periret in talento, praesertim cum desiderem, thesauros
ex aequo te tuo frui cum martyre.

7 Quid vero pro munere modicitas proferret? Cum in elec-
tione cunctarer, venit in mentem lethargico dictum Flacci
Pindarici: "pictoribus atque poetis quaelibet audendi sem-
per fuit aequa potestas." Considerans versiculum, si quae
vult artifex permiscet uterque, cur non, etsi non ab artifice,
misceantur utraque ut ordiretur una tela simul poesis et pic-
tura?

8 Dehinc cum pro captivo velim versu suggerere, attendens
quae fuerint tempora redemptoris, quoto nos suae aetatis

other, his dripping eyes have inscribed on me his woes in the manner of ink and in a miraculous fashion water, which is accustomed to erase, has written with tears. For who not born of a stone would refuse to believe someone weeping? Who, unless a tigress gave him birth, would not feel fellow feeling, seeing that the speed of a leopard, the strength of a boar, the tooth of a lion, and the bulk of an elephant are moderated by blandishments? May your tongue be a poultice for that man who at last has calmed the storm of his laments and identifies you as the sovereign remedy for his grief, that is, while sick in mind he seeks healing for himself, provided he conducts himself properly. While he was speaking I interrupted the man in mid-sentence and with full confidence in you I made a promise to him that you would be consulted by me on this matter, and his tears would end.

It remained to determine what I should send for the ransom, what a son was worth or what would benefit you? In thinking of profit I feared that the worth to you of the captive would be diminished by a low valuation. I was certainly afraid that if the payment were in cash, wealth in heavenly talents be forfeited, especially since I desired you to enjoy treasure equally with your martyr.

What then should my modesty offer as a gift? As I was hesitating to decide, in my inertia the words of Pindaric Horace came to mind: "Painters and poets have always enjoyed equal sanction to dare anything." In pondering the verse I wondered, if each artist intermingles whatever he wants, why should not their two practices be intermingled, even if not by an artist, so that a single web be set up, simultaneously a poem and a painting?

Accordingly when I wished to make representations for the captive in verse, bearing in mind the lifetime of the Re-

315

anno Christus absolverit, totidemque versiculis texerem
carmen quot litteris, hac protenus operis difficultate repul-
sus aut magis difficulter inclusus tam metri necessitate
quam litterarum epitome quid facerem, quo prodirem?
Nova calculatione angustus mihi numerus angustias dilata-
vit, quia praefixo termino non erat nec ubi se prolixitas ex-
cuteret aut brevitas angularet, nec evagari propter descen-
dentes versus frenante repagulo orditura permisit. In quo
quippe exordio supercrescente apice non licuit vel solvere
vel fila laxare ne numerum transiliens erratica se tela turba-
9 ret. Hinc cura commoveor, ut duo per capita, duo ex obli-
quo, unus vero per medium descendentes integri versiculi
legerentur. Altera pars restiterat, quam inter omnes litteram
meditullio conlocarem, quae sic reciperet omnem ut offen-
deret neminem.

10 Igitur huius telae cum licia numero collegissem, ut texere
coeperam, et se et me fila rumpebant: incipiens ego opere
propter absoluturum ligari, atque mutata vice, dum captivi
solvere lora cupio, me catena constringo. Nam huius opus-
culi quae sit hinc conicitur difficultas: ubicumque volueris,
si addis, crescit linea; subtrahis, perit gratia; mutas, non
11 consonant capita. Figis nec fugis litteram. Itaque cum pen-
deret haec tela versibus laqueata, ut si duo transirem, adhuc
tria non fugerem, ego incautus passer quasi mentita per nu-
bila incurri pantheram, quia quod cavere volebam huc pinna

deemer and Christ's age when he set us free, I wove a poem
of just that number of verses and letters. Consequently what
was I to do or where was I to go, deterred, as I was, immedi-
ately by the difficulty of the task or rather in difficulties be-
cause inhibited by the constraints of meter and the restraint
on the number of letters? By a novel calculus the limit on
numbers expanded my limitations, because once a bound-
ary was set amplitude could not give itself room nor brev-
ity be constricted and because of the check imposed by the
verses read vertically the texture allowed no free movement.
For in this weave it was not possible to disrupt or slacken
the threads by adding a letter lest by exceeding the number
it throw the web into disarray. And so I carefully strove that   9
two complete verses be read at the either end, two diago-
nally, and one running through the middle. A further ele-
ment remained, what letter I should set among them all in
the very middle that would be so welcoming to everyone as
to offend no one.

Accordingly, after I had computed numerically the strands   10
of this web, once I started to weave, the threads broke both
themselves and me. I began to be bound by a task under-
taken for a man to be freed and, with a reversal of roles, I
enchained myself as I sought to remove the captive's ties.
The difficulty of this task can be estimated from the follow-
ing: if you add whenever you wish, the line grows in length;
subtract, and it loses its charm; make changes and the acros-
tics are awry. You set a letter in place and you cannot escape
it. And so when this web was set as a trap for me in verse, so   11
that, if I escaped two times, I would not evade a third, like
a reckless sparrow I flew through deceptive clouds into a
net, because I was caught by the wing in what I sought to

ligabar, aut magis, ut dictum sit, velut plumis inlitis quinqui-
fida viscatura tendebar, inter haec illud me commovens,
quod tale non solum feceram, sed nec exemplo simili tra-
hente ducebar.

12   His incertus et trepidus, ipsa novitate suspensus utrumne
temptarem quae numquam adgressus sim an cautius respue-
rem quam incaute proferrem, tamen, licet invitus, loquor
paene quae nescio et tu me vincis amore, ne vincar ab opere.
Ecce exigis a me et quod in me vix invenis; violentiam facis
qui tuus, non rebellis est; extorques nec repelleris: amor
13   blandus tyrannus est. Ut hoc pararem commercii, per incer-
tum pelagi rudis nauta vela suspendi; affectu raptus deferor
per fluctus et scopulos. Urgues me praecipitem per ignota
transire. Quid est quod non obtineas? Sicut amas, sic impe-
ras.

14   Habes igitur opus sic uno textu quadratum, ut sit legendo
quinquifidum, et cum sint triginta tres tam versus quam lit-
terae ad similitudinem Christi carnalis aetatis, qua nos ab-
solvit unus resurgens, adhuc duo per capita, duo ex obliquo,
unus quoque per medium legitur in descensu. Unde fit ut se
finito versu littera non finiret, quia etsi in directo pervenit
ad terminum, tamen cursus illi superest in descensu, quia
15   adhuc coniungitur in finali versiculo. In meditullio autem
parvi huius opusculi illam fiximus litteram quae inter viginti

avoid, or rather, I might say, with feathers, as it were, be-
smeared I was held by the fivefold birdlime snare. In these
circumstances I was concerned that I had not only under-
taken such a task but that I had no similar guiding example
to follow.

Made uncertain and fearful by these considerations, in 12
doubt because of its very novelty whether I should under-
take what I had never attempted or cautiously reject my in-
cautious project, yet, however unwillingly, I speak in a fash-
ion of which I am virtually ignorant. You overcome me by
love so that I not be overcome by the task. See, you are even
demanding from me what you scarcely find in me; you are
exerting duress on one who is devoted to you, not in revolt;
you extort and find no resistance: love is a seductive tyrant.
To secure this merchandise, though an inexperienced sailor, 13
I raised my sails on the treacherous deep; swept away by af-
fection I was borne through the waves and past rocks. You
bid me venture headlong into the unknown. What wish will
you fail to obtain? Your command has the strength of your
love.

You have, then, a work in the form of a square, one single 14
text, but able to be read in five ways, and while there are
both thirty-three verses and as many letters after the model
of Christ's age in the flesh, when by his resurrection he alone
set us free, a further two are read at the sides, two diago-
nally, and one in the middle from top to bottom. As a conse-
quence the text is not finished when the poem is finished,
because although from a linear reading it has come to an
end, there remains a sequence to be read vertically, since
that still comes together in the final line. In the middle 15
of this small work, however, I have set that letter which is

tres numeratur permedia ac tantas ante se respicit quantas
et post se transilit, quia concurrentibus versibus et dividitur
tota et manet integra res divisa. Littera vero quae tinguitur
in descendenti versiculo et tenetur in uno et currit in altero
et, ut ita dicatur, et stat pro stamine et pro trama currit in
tramite, ut esse potest in pagina licia litterata.

16   Ne tamen causa nos oneret quod velut Aragnaea arte
videmur picta fila miscere, quod vobis compertum est in
Moysi prophetae libris, polymitarius artifex vestes texuit
sacerdotis. Unde, cum desit hic coccinum, res est texta de
minio. Versus autem ex obliquo descendentes ab angulis ra-
tione stant, etsi positione succlinant. Qualiter autem conexi
sint singulive quid continent satis est prudentiae sine indice
rem probare.

17   In summa, commendato me piae beatitati et exuberanti
vestrae dulcedini, tribuentes petita confidenti vicarietate
servitii, si placet, hoc opere parieti conscripto pro me ostia-
rio pictura servet vestibulum. Ora pro me.

numbered in the middle of the twenty-three and looks forward to as many as it leaves behind it, because where the verses come together the whole is divided but in that division retains its unity. But each letter that is colored in the vertical verse both retains its place in one sequence and enters into another and, so to speak, stands as a strand and goes ahead as a thread, so that the page becomes a lettered loom.

Lest we be troubled that we seem to intertwine colored 16 threads with the art of an Arachne, in the books of the prophet Moses, as you well know, an artist in embroidery wove the priestly vestments. So since there is no scarlet here, the text has been woven with red. The verses, however, that run from the corners downward at an angle are stable in meaning, if inclined in stance. For the intelligent it is sufficient to judge how they are connected or what each contains without any markers.

To conclude, commending myself to your holy blessed- 17 ness and overflowing sweetness, may you grant what I seek in full confidence of reciprocal service and may this work be written on a wall, if it please you, and in place of me as doorkeeper may the painting stand guard over your entrance hall. Pray for me.

6a

Augustidunensis, opus tibi solvo, Syagri

Dius apex Adam ut fecit, dat somnia, donec
avulsa costa plasmata est Eva nec impar:
felices pariter, diploide lucis operti,
ore coruscantes inter pia rura iugales.
5   Ripae iucundae nari grata aura redibat,
turis deliciae saturabant ubere flatu.
Una fovens ambos florosa sede voluptas,
nota bonis regio pascebat Tempe beatos.
At cum tam magno pollerent maius honore—
10   tota hominum mire parebat terra duorum—
occultus mendax mox exerit arma veneni:
serpens elatus, zelator, larveus hostis,
atrox innocuos evincens felle nocenti,
collisit suasu quos gratia diva bearat.
15   Et homo de terra tum denuo decidit illuc
reptantisque dolo Eoo is excluditur ortu.
Hac nati morimur damnati lege parentum.
At Deus excellens aie et de lumine lumen
e caeli solio dum munera providet ultro,
20   castae carne rudi vivax introiit agnus.
Prodiit inde salus matutinive lucerna
intactae partu lux eruit excita mundum.
A patre iure Deus, homo dehinc carneus alvo,

6a

Syagrius of Autun, I give this work to you as payment

When the supreme divinity had created Adam, he put him
to sleep, until Eve was formed from a rib he removed, nor
was she ill-matched. Both were happy, both were covered in
a cloak of light, a married couple, radiant in countenance, 5
in a blessed land. An alluring breath was wafted to their nos-
trils from a pleasant riverbank and the charm of incense
filled them with its rich fragrance. A shared pleasure sus-
tained them both in their flowery abode; a Tempe, known
for its delights, nurtured the happy pair. But when with so 10
great glory their power was supreme—amazingly the whole
earth obeyed two human beings—the dissembling deceiver
quickly deployed his poisonous weapons: the proud serpent,
the envious one, the diabolic enemy, cruelly outwitting the
innocent with his fatal venom, destroyed with his persua- 15
sion those whom divine grace had blessed. Man, born from
the earth, then once again fell back there and was excluded
from the eastern realm by the serpent's guile. We are born
under sentence of death by this law of our parents. But when
God, always holy and preeminent, light of the light, sponta- 20
neously from his heavenly throne made ready his bounty,
the living lamb in the flesh entered a chaste innocent. Salva-
tion then was born, a lamp for the morning, from a virgin's
childbed a light arose and rescued the world. Truly God

ut nos eriperet, vili se detrahit auctor.
25 O Regis venale caput, quod de cruce fixit,
    telo, voce, manu malfactus verbere, felle,
    ac tu hac solvis captivos sorte, Creator:
    Sero vera data est vitalis emptio morte,
    ymnos unde Deo loquor absolvente reatu.
30 At vos, aeternae suffulti laude coronae,
    Gallorum radii, vobis quo fulgeat et nox,
    rumpite lora iugis et sumitis arma diei;
    ipsave libertas vos liberat atque beabit.

    Da Fortunato, sacer, haec pia vota, Syagri.
    Captivos laxans Domini meditatio fies.
    Cristus se misit cum nos a morte revexit.

    Dulce Dei munus quo merx te, care, coronet.
    Cara Deo pietas animam dat de nece solvi.

7

Item ad Felicem episcopum Namneticum

Sentio, summe pater, lumen venerabile cunctis,
urbis dulce caput, mihi nomen amabile, Felix,
amplectens quem corde gero pietatis in ulnis,
pondus suave meum (nec onus gravat istud amantem).
5 Cur humilem me, summe, vocas loca visere blanda

from the Father, then a man in the flesh from a womb, in 25
order to save us the Creator brought himself low. O head of
the King, sold for a price, who hung on the cross, you too,
Creator, maltreated by weapon, voice, hand, blows, and gall,
set captives free by this your lot. Life-giving true redemp-
tion came late by this death, for which I offer hymns to 30
God, my sins forgiven. But you, exalted by the glory of an
eternal crown, bright radiance of Gaul, in order that night
too may shine for you, break the bonds of subjection and
take up the weapons of light; freedom itself frees you and
will make you blessed.

Saintly Syagrius, grant to Fortunatus these holy wishes.
By freeing the captives you will become an imitation of the
Lord. Christ offered himself when he brought us back from
death.

The gift of God is sweet; dear friend, may he crown you
with it as your reward. Holiness beloved by God sets a soul
free from death.

7

Again to Felix, bishop of Nantes

I feel, Felix, highest of fathers, light revered by all, sweet
head of the city and name loved by me, whom embracing
in heart I bear in the arms of devotion, that my burden is
sweet—such a load does not weigh down a lover. Why, most 5
high one, do you summon lowly me to visit the pleasant

quae te, care, tenent? Tecum modularer in illis,
qua tua rura lavat vitrea Liger algidus unda.
Cariaci speciosus ager devexus in amnem,
hinc ubi flumen aquis recreat, hinc pampinus umbris,
10   et crepitans Boreas pineta comata flagellat.
Uber nempe solum, piscoso litore pulchrum,
sed Fortunato facies tua reddit amoenum.

8

Ad Gregorium episcopum post itiner

Culmen honoratum, decus almum, lumen opimum,
    pastor apostolicae sedis amore placens,
amplectende mihi semper, sacer arce, Gregori,
    nec divulse animo, vir venerande, meo,
5   gaudeo quod rediit Turonis antistes honore
    laetificorque mihi te remeasse patrem.
plaudimus instanter communia vota tenere
    civibus et patriae te revocasse diem.
Praesentem famulum mecum commendo, sacerdos,
10   optantes longe vos moderare gregem.

haunts that where you, my friend, reside? There I would make music with you, where the chill Loire washes your land with its crystalline stream. The beautiful estate of your Cariacum slopes down to the river, where on one side the stream refreshes with its waters, on the other the vine with its shade, and the crack of the north wind flails the needles 10 of the pine groves. Your land is certainly fertile and lovely, with a strand rich in fish, but for Fortunatus it is your face that lends it its charm.

8

To Bishop Gregory after a journey

Honored eminence, saintly glory, source of abundant light, shepherd of the apostolic see, winning affection with love, always to be held in my embrace, sacred in status, Gregory, and never torn from my heart, a man worthy to be revered, I am happy that the bishop of Tours has returned in full 5 honor and feel joy for myself that you, their father, have come back. I heartily rejoice that the community's wishes prevail, and that you have brought daylight back to the citizens and land. The present servant, bishop, I commend to you along with myself; we share a wish that you long direct 10 your flock.

8a

Ad eundem

Officiis generose piis, pater alme Gregori,
    mente salutifera qui petis astra palam,
et quicumque tuis monitis animatur inermis,
    militiae sacrae victor habebit opem.
5 Commendans humilem famulum me solvo salutem
    semper amore pio, vir benedicte Deo.
Pagina si brevis est, non est brevis ardor amantis,
    nam plus corda colunt quam mea verba canunt.

8b

Ad eundem
pro libro praestito

Carmina diva legens proprioque e pectore condens,
    participans aliis fit tibi palma, parens.
Haec quoque quae pridem tribuisti pastor ovili
    grates persolvens debite laudo libens.
5 Vos tamen hinc maneant donaria celsa Tonantis,
    qui sacras inopi distribuistis opes.

8a

To the same man

Kindly father Gregory, ennobled by your sacred office, who plainly are bound for the stars, with a spirit that dispenses salvation; whoever is inspired by your teachings, though unarmed, will win the aid of holy warfare and be victorious. Commending myself as your humble servant I offer greeting in perpetual love and devotion, good sir, blessed by God. Though my page is brief, the passion of my love has no abbreviation, for my heart is more devoted than my words can sing.

5

8b

To the same man, for the present of a book

Reading sacred songs and composing them by your inspiration, you win a palm in common with others, my father. For those too which you gave in the past, as shepherd to his fold, I gladly give thanks, pay the due debt of praise. But may you win lofty rewards for these from the high Lord, for you have

5

Quae cum percontare queam, pro munere tanto
    tunc magis ore meo gratia vestra sonet.
Praesentem famulum Prodomerem, summe sacerdos,
10   commendo supplex, dulcis amore pater.
Cui sua concedens iustae moderamine librae,
    crescat honore Dei palma futura tibi.

9

Ad eundem
pro invitatione

Invitas pietate patris, sacer, ire, Gregori,
    qua Domini Turonis pascis amore greges,
quo sacer antistes meritis Martinus opimis
    quas prius obtinuit, has tibi cessit oves,
5 nunc quoque per caulas et florea pascua Christi
    rite gubernantes ducitis ambo greges.
Sed mihi vim faciens vester modo frater honore,
    ad vos ne properem, nempe retorsit iter.
Saepe rogans voto, mandato, et missile verbo,
10   et coniuratus sum sibi pollicitus.
Vir bonitate placens et pastor pacis amator,
    foederis ob studium sit veniale, precor.
Vos quoque sed genitae propriae, venerande, salutant;
    ast ego commender, quaeso, beate pater.

distributed holy aid to one in need. When I can read them
through, then for so generous a gift let my gratitude sound
more loudly on my tongue.

I commend to you, supreme bishop, with my prayers the   10
present servant Prodomeres, O sweet and beloved father.
By granting to him his due, as weighed on the scales of jus-
tice, may the palm you will enjoy increase with honor from
God.

9

To the same man,
in response to an invitation

Holy Gregory, with the devotion of a father you invite me to
journey to where in Tours you lovingly pasture the flock of
the Lord, where the saintly bishop Martin, rich in his mer-
its, has entrusted to you the sheep he formerly won. Now   5
too through the sheepfolds and flowering pastures of Christ
you both lead your flocks as dutiful guides. But recently
your brother in status, exerting pressure on me, forbade my
journey, so that I could not hasten to you. I made frequent
requests, in person, by messenger, and by letter I sent, and   10
I even made a promise to him on my oath. You who win
favor by your goodness, shepherd, lover of peace, because
of your love of harmony may my behavior be pardonable, I
pray. Your daughters too send greetings to you, venerable sir;
may I too, blessed father, I beg, win commendation.

10

Ad eundem
pro commendatione mulieris

Summe pater patriae, specimen pietatis opimae,
  dulce caput Turonis, religionis apex,
iugiter alta sequens, clementi corde Gregori,
  unde animae decus est huc ratione petens,
5 quam commendasti venientem, celse sacerdos,
  hanc redeuntem ad te suscipe more patris.
Sis quoque longaevus cunctorum, care, recursus,
  et mihi vel reliquis sit tua vita seges.

11

Ad eundem de itinere suo

Iugiter opto libens, sacer amplectende Gregori,
  cernere vos oculis, quaerere litterulis.
Dulce videre mihi, at si desit copia cerni,
  spes erit oranti vel dare verba patri.
5 Nuper ab aspectu decedens concite vestro
  per glaciem vitreas me loquor isse vias,
sed crucis auxilio, Martino operante patrono,

10

To the same man,
in recommendation of a woman

Highest father in the land, model of abundant piety, sweet
primate of Tours, supreme in religion, who always set your
sights on high, Gregory of merciful heart, seeking by your
reason here what brings glory to the soul, lofty bishop, take   5
to yourself as a father this woman returning to you, whom
you recommended to me when she came here. May you also,
dear friend, be a long-lived refuge for all, and may your life
be a rich harvest for me and for others.

11

To the same man, on his journey

It is always my heartfelt desire, saintly and cherished Greg-
ory, to see you with my eyes, to seek you with my letters.
Sweet it is to see you, but if the opportunity for sight is
denied, I will hope at least to express my requests in words
to my father. When recently I departed hastily from your   5
presence, I can tell you that I traveled on roads glassy with
ice, but by the aid of the cross and the efficacy of Martin,

perveni ad matres salvus, opime pater.
  Quae vos multiplici veneranter honore salutant;
10   ast ego pro reditu vota salutis ago.

12

Ad eundem salutatoria

Summe sacerdotum, bonitatis opima facultas,
  culmen honore tuo, lumen amore meo,
officiis venerande sacris, pietatis alumne,
  pignore amicitiae corde tenende meae,
5 florens in studiis et sacra in lege fidelis,
  semper agens animae dona futura tuae,
te, pater, ergo precans terram, freta, sidera testor,
  ut velis ore sacro me memor esse tuum.

13

Ad eundem pro pomis et graphiolis

Officiis generose piis, sacer arce Gregori,
  absens fis praesens munere, summe pater,
qui mihi transmittis propria cum prole parentes,

my patron, I came home safely to my mothers, noble father. They respectfully with manifold honor send you their greetings, but I because of my return send wishes for your wellbeing. 10

12

To the same man, in greeting

Highest of bishops, rich resource of goodness, eminent in your status, brilliant in my love, revered for your sacred office, fostered by holiness, who by the bond of friendship win a place in my heart, flourishing in studies and faithful in the 5 sacred law, always pursuing the future rewards of your soul, you, father, I therefore beseech, by the earth, sea, and stars, that in your holy prayers you remember me, your own.

13

To the same man, for apples and cuttings

Gregory, sacred in status, ennobled by your holy office, although you are absent, highest father, you are present in your gift. You have sent me parents along with their off-

insita cum fructu, surcula, poma simul.
5   Det Deus omnipotens meritorum fruge repletus
    mala legas avide quae paradisus habet.

14

Ad eundem
de commendatione puellae

Cum graderer festinus iter, pater alme Gregori,
    qua praecessoris sunt pia signa tui—
quod fertur convulsa iacens radicitus arbor
    Martini ante preces exiluisse comis,
5   quae fidei merito nunc stat spargendo medellas,
    corpora multa medens, cortice nuda manens—
fletibus huc <lugent> genitor genetrixque puellam,
    voce implendo auras et lacrimando genas.
Figo pedem, suspendo aurem; mihi panditur ore
10   vix per singultus vendita nata suos.
Quaero adhuc; questus perhibet nullo indice furto
    furti ex obiectu hanc pater ire iugo;
se voluisse dare et iurantes ordine testes
    nomine quemque tenens, nec potuisset egens.
15   Non aderat iudex, erat accusator adurguens.
    Hic ego quid facerem, posse vetante, sacer?

spring, grafts with their fruit, cuttings together with apples. May almighty God grant that, replete with the reward for 5 your virtues, you greedily pluck the fruit that paradise provides there.

14

To the same man,
in recommendation of a girl

As I was hurrying on my way, kindly father Gregory, where there is evidence of your predecessor's holiness—for they say that a tree lying flat with its roots torn out at the prayers of Martin burst forth in foliage, and now by the virtue of 5 his faith stands tall dispensing healing, curing many bodies, though quite bereft of bark—here I encountered a father and mother in tears for their daughter, filling the air with their voices and their cheeks with tears. I halt my step, I cock my ear; with difficulty through their sobs I make out 10 their story: a daughter sold into slavery. I continue my questions; the father laments, though without evidence of theft she lost her freedom: theft was the charge. He wanted to provide witnesses, taking the oath in due order—everyone was listed by name—but he was poor and could not. There 15 was no judge there to hear the case, only a vehement accuser. What could I have done, holy father, I have no power?

"Si pius hic," dixi, "praesens Martinus adesset,
    nil permisisset perdere pastor ovem."
Sed tamen invalui recolens te, summe sacerdos,
20   spem praecessoris qui pietate refers.
Discute, distringe ac, si sit secus, eripe dulcis,
    et pater adde gregi; hanc quoque redde patri.
Me simul officio famulum tibi, care, subactum
    protege perfugio, pastor opime, pio.

15

Item ad eundem de commendatione peregrini

Vir bone, pro meritis adipiscens culmen honoris,
    nobile praesidium, pontificale caput,
quem gradus et genium fructu pietatis opimo
    dignius adtollunt amplificante Deo,
5   ut tibi sit famulans memoratus amore benigno,
    Fortunati humilis te, pater, orat apex.
Hic peregrinus item laetetur, summe sacerdos,
    pastorem et patriam te meruisse suam.

"If saintly Martin were present here with us," I said, "he, as a shepherd, would not allow his sheep to be lost." But then I remembered you and gained heart, most high bishop, for in 20 your holiness you recall the trust your predecessor inspired. With affection question them, examine the case, and if you find differently, come to the rescue; holy father, add to your flock; restore this girl to her father. Me too, your dutiful and devoted servant, dear as you are, shelter, noble shepherd, with your merciful protection.

15

To the same man, in recommendation of a stranger

Man of virtue, by your merits acquiring the highest of honors, noble protector, supreme in episcopal status, whom position and talent with the rich fruit of your holiness worthily advance, in receiving honor from God, the words of For- 5 tunatus the lowly beg you, father, that you remember your servant with kindly love. May this stranger likewise rejoice, highest bishop, that he has won you as his shepherd and his homeland.

16

Ad eundem salutatoria

Pastor honoris apex, venerabilis arce sacerdos
    et decus alme patrum, religionis amor,
gloria pontificum, meriti pia palma Gregori,
    assurgente gradu nobile iure caput,
5   Fortunatus, opem tribui qui poscit Olympi,
    per te, care pater, quo mereatur age.

17

Item ad eundem salutatoria

Visitat a vobis dignanter epistula currens
    me, sacer antistes, vir pietate pater.
Hanc avidus capiens oculis animoque recurro,
    sospite te gaudens, quod referebat apex.
5   Longius huc vestro sub nomine, papa Gregori,
    pagina me recreet missa salutis ope.

16

To the same man, in greeting

Shepherd most high in status, bishop revered for your rank,
saintly glory of the prelates, embodying the love of religion,
renown of pontiffs, and holy palm of virtue, Gregory, with
your lofty position you rightly hold noble preeminence.
Bring it about, dear father, by your agency that Fortunatus is   5
found worthy to get his wish to win the aid of heaven.

17

To the same man, in greeting

In haste from you a letter has graciously paid me a visit,
saintly bishop, man of holiness and father to me. Greed-
ily taking it in my grasp, I examined it with my eyes and
my mind, rejoicing that you are well, news that the letter
brought. For a long time may pages carrying your name, fa-   5
ther Gregory, bring me relief here, carrying the boon of a
greeting.

18

Dominis sanctis atque apostolicis in Christo patribus ecclesiae pontificibus Fortunatus

Gloria pontificum, veneratio Christicolarum,
  norma sacerdotum, culmen et orbis honor,
qui loca perspicitis propriae mercedis amore,
  succurrendo viris vester ut extet apex,
5 ecce venit praesens Italus, peregrinus et hospes;
  cernens pastores ne, precor, erret ovis.
Qualiter ad patriam properet, solacia poscit.
  Inveniat munus vos vagus, exul, inops.
Me Fortunatum proprium pietate parentum
10   conciliate polo, quaeso, precando Deum.

19

Ad Aredium abbatem

Opto, benigne pater, verbo tibi ferre salutem,
  si minus hinc oculo cernere te valeo.
Est etenim vestri tantus mihi cultus honoris
  ut pro me occurrat hinc tibi missus apex.

18

Fortunatus to my saintly lords and apostolic fathers in Christ, bishops of the Church

Glory of bishops, for Christians an object of reverence, model for prelates, pinnacle and honor of the world, who keep watch over your sees out of love for performing good works, so aiding your people that your eminence shows clear, here comes before you an Italian, a foreigner and 5 guest; when he sees his shepherds, I pray, let him not be a sheep astray. He is seeking assistance to hasten back to his homeland. An exile, adrift and in need, may he find you bountiful to him. With the devotion of parents win the favor of heaven for your own Fortunatus. I beg, by praying to 10 God.

19

To Abbot Aredius

I desire, kindly father, to bring to you greetings in words, seeing that I cannot look at you here with my eyes. For indeed so great is the devotion I have for your honor that a letter from here finds its way to you in place of my per-

5   Quaeso, beate, tamen per dulcia pabula Christi:
      me quoque commemores, cum dabis ore preces.
   Munera credo Dei tribui mihi, pastor Aredi,
      si Fortunati sis memor, alme, tui.
   Pro me etiam sanctam genetricem, care, salutans,
10   cum redit iste puer, redde loquentis opem.
   Vos itidem genitae propriae, pater ample, salutant,
      Agnes amore pio cum Radegunde simul.

son. Blessed one, I beg of you, by the sweet nourishment of 5
Christ, that you call me to mind too when you give voice
to your prayers. I believe gifts from God will be granted to
me, my shepherd Aredius, if you remain mindful, kindly sir,
of your devoted Fortunatus. Greet also for me, dear friend,
your saintly mother, and when this servant returns, dispatch 10
to me the boon of your words. In like fashion your own
daughters, noble father, salute you, Agnes along with Rade-
gund, in devoted love.

BOOK SIX

I

De domno Sigiberctho rege

Vere novo tellus fuerit dum exuta pruinis,
    se picturato gramine vestit ager,
longius extendunt frondosa cacumina montes
    et renovat virides arbor opaca comas;
5 promittens gravidas ramis genitalibus uvas,
    palmite gemmato vitis amoena tumet.
Praemittens flores gracili blandita susurro,
    deliciosa favis mella recondit apes.
Progeniem reparans casto fecunda cubili,
10   artifices natos gignere flore cupit.
Nexibus apta suis pro posteritatis amore
    ad fetus properans garrula currit avis.
Semine quisque suo senio iuvenescit in ipso;
    omnia dum redeunt gaudia mundus habet.
15 Sic modo cuncta favent, dum prosperitate superna
    regia Caesareo proficit aula iugo.
Ordine multiplici felicem in saecula regem
    undique cinxerunt lumina tanta ducum.
Culmina tot procerum concurrunt culmen ad unum;
20   Mars habet ecce duces, pax habet ecce decus.
Cunctorum adventu festiva palatia fervent;

I

On the lord and king Sigibert

With the coming of spring, when the earth has thrown off the frost, the land clothes itself with new many-colored growth, the mountains stretch upward their foliage-covered peaks, and trees, now shady, bring forth fresh, green leaves; the pleasant vine swells with gemlike buds on its shoots, 5 promising bulging grapes for the boughs that will give them birth. Sipping the flowers and charming with their delicate humming, bees store in their combs the sweet-tasting honey. Prolific in producing new offspring by chaste reproduction, they desire to bring forth from flowers the children they 10 create. Primed to mate out of love for a new generation, the twittering bird eagerly rushes to give birth. Each creature grows youthful by breeding, even though it be old; when all things return, the world experiences joy. In the same way 15 all things rejoice when with heaven-sent good fortune the royal palace is graced by a union worthy of emperors. In serried ranks around the king, the favorite of fortune forever, have gathered together his dukes, so many brilliant lights. So many eminent nobles convene at his single eminence; see, Mars has his lords, but peace has its rewards. When 20 all arrive the palace is alive with festivity; the people see

349

coniugio regis gens sua vota videt.
Vos quorum inrigui fontis meat unda, favete:
iudicio vestro crescere parva solent.

25 Felicem, sol, pande diem radiisque serenis
sparge comas, thalamos sincero lumine conplens.
Sigibercthus ovans, ad gaudia nostra creatus,
vota facit, qui nunc alieno liber amore
vincula cara subit, cuius moderante iuventa
30 conubium mens casta petit lasciva retundens;
ad iuga confugit cui nil sua subripit aetas.
Corde pudicus agens, rector tot gentibus unus,
et sibi frena dedit, sed quod natura requirit
lege maritali amplexu est contentus in uno,
35 quo non peccat amor, sed casta cubilia servans
instaurat de prole lares, ubi luserit heres.
    Torsit amoriferas arcu stridente sagittas
forte Cupido volans; terris genus omne perurit,
nec pelagus defendit aquis; mox vilia corda
40 subdit, vulgus iners. Tandem dehinc sensus opimi
regis anhelantem placidis bibit ossibus ignem
molliter incumbens et inhaesit flamma medullis.
Regalis fervebat apex, nec nocte sopora
cordis erat requies, oculis animoque recurrens
45 ad vultus quos pinxit Amor mentemque fatigans
saepe per amplexum falsa sub imagine lusit.
    Mox ubi conspexit telo superante Cupido
virginea mitem torreri lampade regem,
laetus ait Veneri: "Mater, mea bella peregi.

their wishes fulfilled by the marriage of their king. Be well-disposed, you from whose spring there flows a quickening stream; your good opinion customarily makes small things grow.

Illuminate, sun, this happy day and with your unclouded 25 rays spread wide your tresses, filling the bridal chamber with transparent light. Sigibert, who was born to bring us joy, in exultation is celebrating his marriage. Free as he is from other loves he now takes on welcome bonds; his youth exerts restraint and his chaste mind desires marriage, rejecting 30 all wantonness; his youth exercises no allure, but he seeks out a wedding. Modest in spirit, one sole ruler for so many peoples, on himself too he has set checks and, as nature demands, according to marital law is content with a single embrace. Thereby his love does not sin but, preserving a chaste 35 marriage bed, refreshes with children his house where an heir is to play.

Once winged Cupid has discharged his love-bearing arrows with the hiss of his bow, he sets fire to all creatures on earth; even the waters of the sea provide no protection; next he subdues common hearts, the idle populace. Only finally 40 then did the senses of a noble king drink in his untroubled bones the seething fire and the flame, coming gently on him, settled in his innermost being. His royal eminence was afire and not even in the sleep of night did his heart find rest, as with his eyes and his mind he returned continually to the 45 face that Love had painted and he exhausted his spirit with frequent empty embraces, deceived by a phantom.

As soon as Cupid saw that his weapons were victorious and the gentle king was being scorched by a virginal torch, he joyfully said to Venus: "Mother, I have completed my

50 Pectore flagranti mihi vincitur alter Achilles,
Sigibercthus amans Brunichildae carpitur igne,
quae placet apta toro, maturis nubilis annis,
virginitas in flore tumens, conplexa marito
primitiis placitura suis, nec damna pudoris
55 sustinet, unde magis pollens regina vocatur.
Hoc quoque virgo cupit, quamvis verecundia sexus
obstet. Amata viri dextra leviore repellit
ignoscitque sibi culpas quas intulit ignis.
Sed modo laeta veni quoniam te vota requirunt."
60   Mox Venus ambrosio violas admiscet amomo,
demetit ungue rosas gremioque recondit avaro,
et pariter levibus fregerunt nubila pinnis.
Ut venere simul thalamos ornare superbos,
hinc Venus egregiam praeponere coepit alumnam,
65 inde Cupido virum, nubentibus ambo faventes,
et litem fecere piam. Sic deinde Cupido
matri pauca refert: "Tibi quem promisimus hic est,
Sigibercthus, amor populi, lux nata parentum,
qui genus a proavis longo tenet ordine reges
70 et reges geniturus erit, spes gentis opimae,
quo crevit natale decus, generosa propago,
ac melior de stirpe redit famamque priorum
posteritas excelsa fovet: hic nomen avorum
extendit bellante manu, cui de patre virtus
75 quam Nablis ecce probat, Toringia victa fatetur,
proficiens unum gemina de gente triumphum—

campaign. A second Achilles has been conquered by me, his 50
breast aflame, Sigibert is in love, he is wracked by a fiery pas-
sion for Brunhild. She has won his approval, who is well-
suited to wed, of ripe, marriageable age, a virgin growing
into bloom, and, when embraced by her husband, sure to
please with her first favors; because she bears no mark on 55
her honor, she wins all the more the title of a mighty queen.
The maiden desires this too, although the modesty of her
sex inhibits her. Beloved by this man, she resists with weak-
ened force and forgives in her own mind the failings that
passion induces. So come now with joy, for the wedding
needs you to be present."

Immediately Venus mingled violets with fragrant balsam, 60
broke off roses with her nail, and stored them up in her ea-
ger bosom. Together the gods broke through the clouds on
their light wings. When they arrived as one to bring luster to
the proud marriage ceremony, Venus for her part began to
promote the merits of her noble foster-child and Cupid of 65
the groom, both favoring one of the bridal couple, and they
enacted a well-meaning dispute. Cupid then addressed as
follows a few words to his mother: "Here is the one I prom-
ised you, Sigibert, the love of his people, born to be a light
for his kinsmen, who traces in his ancestry a long line of
kings from his forefathers and will in future bring to birth 70
kings himself, hope of a powerful race, who has increased
the glory of his line, a child of noble descent, but who out-
does his ancestry and in him an excellent posterity swells
the fame of those who have gone before. With warlike hand
he enlarges his ancestors' renown, showing the courage of
his father, which the Naab bears witness to, conquered 75
Thuringia proclaims, a courage that successfully achieved a

de Theudebertcho pietas venit patrueli.
Reddidit iste duos, pro ambobus sufficit unus.
Cardinis occidui dominans in flore iuventae,
80 iam gravitate senes tenerosque supervenit annos.
Legem naturae meruit praecedere factis:
quamvis parva tamen nulli minor imperat aetas.
Qui sensum mature regit generosior hic est,
quisquis in angusto fuerit moderatior <aevo>.
85 Sic fovet hic populos ipsis intrantibus annis
ut pater et rex sit, nullum gravet, erigat omnes.
Nulla dies sine fruge venit: nisi congrua praestet,
perdere plura putat, si non concesserit ampla.
Gaudia diffundit radianti lumine vultus;
90 nubila nulla gravant populum sub rege sereno.
Pectore maturo culpas indulget acerbas:
unde alii peccant, ignoscendo iste triumphat.
Doctus enim quoniam prima est in principe virtus
esse pium, quia semper habet qui parcere novit.
95 Corrigit ipse prius quod poscit ut alter emendet;
qui sibi censura est reliquos bene lege coercet.
In quo digna manent quidquid de rege requiras,
solus amat cunctos et amatur ab omnibus unus."
    Incipit inde Venus laudes memorare puellae:
100 "O virgo miranda mihi, placitura iugali,
clarior aetheria, Brunichildis, lampade fulgens,
lumina gemmarum superasti lumine vultus.
Altera nata Venus regno dotata decoris,
nullaque Nereidum de gurgite talis Hibero
105 oceani sub fonte natat, non ulla Napaea

single triumph over two nations—the devotion of Theude- bert to his uncle came to his aid. But Sigibert embodies the two men; though one man, he equals them both. Lord of the western climes in the flower of his youth, already an elder in 80 dignity, he surpasses his tender years. By his actions he has been able to transcend nature's law: although his years are few, yet his authority is second to none. Whoever at a young age displays unusual self-restraint and control of his senses beyond his years wins special nobility. He so nurtures his 85 people even in these early years as to be their father and king, oppressing no one, supporting them all. No day passes without benefit: if he does not dispense proper largesse, if he does not make lavish gifts, he believes that he suffers the most loss. He spreads rejoicing by the bright light of his countenance; no clouds shroud his people when the king's 90 face is clear. In the maturity of his heart he pardons griev- ous crimes; from the faults of others he wins a triumph by forgiveness. For he was taught that the prime quality in a prince is to be merciful, because he who knows how to for- give never goes wanting. He first corrects in himself what he 95 asks others to mend; because he is strict with himself, he successfully constrains others by law. In him are found what- ever you could properly desire of a king. He alone loves ev- eryone and alone is loved by all."

Venus then began to praise the virtues of the girl: "O 100 maiden marvelous to me, soon to delight your husband, who shine brighter than the torch of the heavens, you surpass, Brunhild, in the luster of your countenance the luster of jewels. By birth a second Venus, endowed with sovereignty over beauty, none of the Nereids that swims in the Spanish wave, in the ocean waters is your match, no nymph of the 105

pulchrior, ipsa suas subdunt tibi flumina nymphas.
lactea cui facies incocta rubore coruscat,
lilia mixta rosis. Aurum si intermicet ostro,
decertata tuis numquam se vultibus aequant.
110 Sapphirus, alba, adamans, crystalla, zmaragdus, iaspis
cedant cuncta: novam genuit Hispania gemmam.
Digna fuit species, potuit quae flectere regem."
    Per hiemes validasque nives Alpenque Pyrenen
perque truces populos vecta est duce rege sereno
115 externis regina toris. Super ardua montis
planum carpis iter: nil obstat amantibus umquam
quos iungi divina volunt. Quis crederet autem
Hispanam tibimet dominam, Germania, nasci
quae duo regna iugo pretiosa conexuit uno?
120 Non labor humanus potuit tam mira parare,
nam res difficilis divinis utitur armis.
Longa retro series regi hoc vix contulit ulli;
difficili nisu peraguntur maxima rerum.
    Nobilitas excelsa nitet, genus Athanagildi,
125 longius extremo regnum qui porrigit orbi,
dives opum quas mundus habet populumque gubernat
Hispanum sub iure suo pietate canenda.
Cur tamen egregii genitoris regna renarrem,
quando tuis meritis video crevisse parentes?
130   Quantum, virgo micans, turbas superare videris
femineas, tantum tu, Sigibercthe, maritos.
Ite diu iuncti membris et corde iugati,
ambo pares genio, meritis et moribus ambo,
sexum quisque suum pretiosis actibus ornans,
135 cuius amplexu sint colla conexa sub uno,
et totos placidis peragatis lusibus annos.

woods more beautiful, the very rivers confess their nymphs inferior to you. Your milk-white face dazzles dyed with red, lilies and roses mixed. If gold were to mingle its glitter with purple, in a contest it never would rival your countenance. Sapphire, pearl, diamond, crystal, emerald, jasper, let all give place; Spain has given birth to a new jewel in you. Such was your beauty it deserved to sway the heart of a king."

Through storms and heavy snow, over the Pyrenees range, and amid savage peoples she traveled under the guidance of the serene king, a queen for a foreign bed. Though over mountain summits you journey on the flat: nothing ever obstructs lovers whose union divinity favors. Who would have believed, Germany, that in Spain was born a mistress for you who united two thriving kingdoms under a single yoke? No human effort could produce such a miracle; such a difficult task needs divine weaponry. Scarcely any king in history's long annals has been granted such a thing; the greatest achievements are attained only after hard struggle.

She is of high nobility and brilliance, the daughter of Athanagild, who extends his kingdom far to the extremities of the world, rich in the wealth that the world provides, and who under his sway governs the Spanish people with a devotion worthy of song. But why should I tell of an excellent father's kingdom, when I see that by your virtues your family has grown in prestige?

As far, brilliant maiden, as you excel the mass of women, so far do you, Sigibert, surpass all husbands. May you advance, long joined in body and united in heart, both equal in character, in merits and manners both equal, each ornamenting your sex with your laudable actions. May you encircle one another's necks in a single embrace and spend all your years in peaceful amusements. May each desire what

110

115

120

125

130

135

357

Hoc velit alterutrum quidquid dilexerit alter.
Aequa salus ambobus eat duo pectora servans;
unus amor vivo solidamine iunctus alescat.
140   Auspiciis vestris cunctorum gaudia surgant;
pacem mundus amet, victrix concordia regnet.
Sic iterum natis celebretis vota parentes
et de natorum teneatis prole nepotes.

1a

Item de Sigiberctho rege et Brunichilde regina

Victor, ab occasu quem laus extendit in ortum
  et facit egregium principis esse caput,
quis tibi digna ferat? Nam me vel dicere pauca
  non trahit ingenium, sed tuus urguet amor.
5   Si nunc Vergilius, si forsitan esset Homerus,
  nomine de vestro iam legeretur opus.
Sigibercthe potens, generosis clare triumphis,
  hinc nova te virtus praedicat, inde genus.
Cuius rapta semel sumpsit Victoria pinnas
10   et tua vulgando prospera facta volat.
Saxo et Thoringus resonat, sua damna moventes,
  unius ad laudem tot cecidisse viros.
Quod tunc ante aciem pedibus prior omnibus isti,
  hinc modo te reges unde sequantur habes.

the other delights in, and both share a health that keeps safe
two hearts; may one love, held firm by a living bond, sus-
tain you. Under your auspices may everyone's happiness in-   140
crease; may the world embrace peace, may victorious har-
mony reign. So again may you celebrate as parents your chil-
dren's wedding, and may you have grandchildren, your own
children's offspring.

1a

Again, on King Sigibert and Queen Brunhild

Conqueror, whose renown praise carries from West to East,
bringing distinction to your princely person, who could
make worthy offerings to you? For my abilities do not in-
duce me to say even a few words, though my love urges me
on. If a Virgil now was alive or even perhaps a Homer, a work   5
written about you already would be read.

Great Sigibert, famed for your glorious triumphs, both
your special valor and your lineage proclaim your fame.
Your Victory, once won, has taken wings and in flight   10
spreads abroad your successes. Saxon and Thuringian la-
ment, mourning their losses, that so many men have fallen
to bring praise to just one. Because once you advanced on
foot before all in the battle line, now other kings have a rea-

15 Prosperitate nova pacem tua bella dederunt
        et peperit gladius gaudia certa tuus.
    Plus tamen ut placeas, cum sit victoria iactans,
        tu magis unde subis, mitior inde manes.
    Est tibi summus honor, sed mens praecessit honorem,
20   moribus ut vestris debitor extet apex.
    Iustitiae cultor pietatis amore coruscas;
        quod te plus habeat, certat utrumque bonum.
    Lingua, decus, virtus, bonitas, mens, gratia pollent;
        ornarent cunctos singula vestra viros.
25 Cunctorum causas intra tua pectora condis,
        pro populi requie te pia cura tenet.
    Omnibus una salus datus es, quibus ordine sacro
        tempore praesenti gaudia prisca refers.
    Catholico cultu decorata est optima coniux;
30   ecclesiae crevit te faciente domus.
    Reginam meritis Brunichildem Christus amore
        tunc sibi coniunxit, hanc tibi quando dedit.
    Altera vota colens melius quia munere Christi,
        pectore iuncta prius, plus modo lege placet.
35 Rex pie, reginae tanto de lumine gaude:
        adquaesita bis est quae tibi nupta semel,
    pulchra, modesta, decens, sollers, <pia>, grata, benigna,
        ingenio, vultu, nobilitate potens.
    Sed quamvis tantum meruisset sola decorem,
40   ante tamen homini, nunc placet ecce Deo.
    Saecula longa micans cara cum coniuge ducas,
        quam tibi divinus consociavit amor.

son to follow behind you. Your wars have brought peace, 15
with a newfound prosperity, and your sword has given rise to
dependable joys. To win greater affection, though victory is
boastful, the more you rise, the gentler you remain. Your
rank is the highest, but your mind has transcended rank, so 20
that your eminence owes a debt to your character.

Devoted to justice, you shine bright with your love for
mercy; each virtue fights a contest, to determine which is
to have preeminence in you. Great in tongue, glory, virtue,
goodness, mind, and charm, any one of your qualities would
be enough to adorn all other men. You cherish the interests 25
of all within your breast, in dutiful devotion to the people's
relief. To all you have been granted as their single salvation
and by divine ordinance in the present moment you bring
them back the joys of the past.

Your excellent wife is adorned with the Catholic faith; by 30
your actions the house of the Church has been strength-
ened. Brunhild is your queen by her merits, for Christ in his
love then joined her to himself when he gave her to you. Per-
forming her vows better a second time, because by the gift
of Christ, though formerly united in heart, now she pleases
still more by her faith. Good king, rejoice in the brilliant 35
light of your queen: she has twice been won, though married
to you only once, a beautiful and modest woman, graceful,
clever, pious, charming, and generous, and well-favored in
her character, looks, and nobility. But although just in her
own person she would have merited high honor, yet first she 40
won favor with a man, but now, see, she pleases God. May
you pass long and brilliant years with your dear wife, whom
divine love has joined in alliance with you.

361

2

De Chariberctho rege

Inclita magnarum processit gloria rerum
    et de rege pio sparsit ubique decus,
quem gravitate, animo, sensu, moderamine legum
    praedicat occiduus sol oriensque virum,
5 qui quadripertitis mundi sub partibus amplis
    fructificante fide semina laudis habet,
hinc cui barbaries, illinc Romania plaudit:
    diversis linguis laus sonat una viri.
Dilige regnantem celsa, Parisius, arce,
10 et cole tutorem qui tibi praebet opem.
Hunc modo laeta favens avidis amplectere palmis,
    qui iure est dominus, sed pietate pater.
De Childeberctho veteres compesce dolores;
    rex placidus rediit, qui tua vota fovet.
15 Ille fuit mitis, sapiens, bonus, omnibus aequus;
    non cecidit patruus, dum stat in orbe nepos.
Dignus erat heres eius sibi sumere regnum,
    qui non est illo, laude loquente, minor.
Charibercthus adest, qui publica iura gubernans
20 tempore praesenti gaudia prisca refert.
In tantum patruo se prodidit esse sequacem
    ut modo sit tutor coniugis iste nepos,
qui Childebercthi retinens dulcedine nomen,
    eius natarum est frater et ipse pater,
25 quae bene defensae placido moderamine regis
    in consobrino spem genitoris habent.

2

On King Charibert

The glory of his great deeds has advanced in renown and spread everywhere the praise of a devoted king, a man who wins acclaim from the setting to the rising sun for dignity, character, good sense, and his exercise of justice, who in the four wide regions of the world lays the seedbed of praise, made fruitful by faith. Here barbarians, there Romans applaud him; in different tongues one song of praise rings out. Love your ruler, Paris, in his lofty eminence and cherish your protector who provides you with aid. Embrace him now with eager hands and joyous acclaim; he is by law your lord, but your father by devotion.

Put an end to your former grief for Childebert; a new, pacific king has come, who forwards your desires. Childebert was gentle, wise, and good, and just to all; the uncle has not passed away, while his nephew remains in the world. His heir was worthy to assume for himself the kingdom, for he is not inferior to his uncle, as his praises attest. Charibert is now with us, who in ruling over his people in the present moment brings back the joys of the past. He has shown himself so greatly devoted to his uncle that now a nephew is the protector of his uncle's wife and, remembering the name of Childebert with affection, he serves as both brother and father of that man's daughters, who safely sheltered by the calm governance of the king expect in a cousin the role of a father.

Maxima progenies, generosa luce coruscans,
  cuius ab excelsis gloria currit avis.
Nam quoscumque velim veterum memorare parentum,
30   stirpis honorificae regius ordo fluit,
cuius celsa fides eduxit ad astra cacumen
    atque super gentes intulit illa pedes,
calcavit hostes tumidos, erexit amicos,
    fovit subiectos, conteruitque feros.
35 Cur tamen hic repetam praeconia celsa priorum,
    cum potius tua laus ornet honore genus?
Illi auxere armis patriam, sed sanguine fuso;
    tu plus adquiris qui sine clade regis.
Quos prius infestis lassarunt bella periclis,
40   hos modo securos pacis amore foves.
Omnia laeta canunt felicia tempora regis,
    cuius in auspiciis floret opima quies,
per quem tranquille terrarum frugis abundat;
    devotis populis est tua vita seges.
45 Cum te nascentem meruerunt saecula regem,
    lumine maiori fulsit in orbe dies.
Posteritate nova tandem sua gaudia cernens,
    crescere se dixit prolis honore pater,
qui quamvis esset sublimi vertice rector,
50   altius erexit te veniente caput.
Laetus in heredis gremio sua vota reclinans,
    floruit inde magis spe meliore senes.
Ante alios fratres regali germine natus,
    ordine qui senior, sic pietate prior.
55 Praedicat hinc bonitas, illinc sapientia plaudit;
    inter utrumque decus te sibi quisque rapit.
De patruo pietas et de patre fulget acumen:

You are of the highest descent, brilliant with the light of
nobility, inheriting glory from your distinguished ancestors.
For no matter which of your family members I mention
from the past, the roll call is kingly of a glorious race, whose   30
sublime faith raised their heads to the stars and set under
their foot other peoples, trampled on proud enemies and
raised up friends, protected the subservient and crushed the
fierce. But why should I rehearse here the high glories of   35
your ancestors, when it is rather your praise that ornaments
your family with honor? They benefited their country with
arms, but at the cost of bloodshed; you achieve more by rul-
ing without slaughter. Those whom war once wearied with
its dangerous threats now you cherish in security with your   40
love of peace. All things sing with joy the happy times of the
king, under whose auspices prosperous tranquility flour-
ishes, and because of whom the fruits of the earth, grown in
peace, abound; for your devoted people your life is a harvest.

When the ages won the honor of your kingly birth, the   45
day shone with brighter light in the world. Your father, fi-
nally seeing cause for rejoicing in his new offspring, declared
that he grew in stature, receiving honor from his child, for
although he was a ruler of lofty eminence, he raised his head   50
higher when you came into the world. Happily laying his
wishes in the lap of his heir, he flourished all the more and
with higher hopes, though old. Born of the royal line before
your brothers, as you are oldest in order of years, so you are
first in piety.

Here goodness praises you, there wisdom acclaims you;   55
between them each of the two virtues claims you for itself.
Your uncle's piety, your father's intellect shine from you: in

unius in vultu vivit uterque parens.
Quas habuere ambo laudes tu colligis omnes
60   et reparas solus lege favente duos.
Semita iustitiae, gravitatis norma refulges,
      et speculum vitae dat pretiosa fides.
Tranquillis animis moderatio fixa tenetur,
      qui portum in proprio pectore semper habes.
65 Tempestas nullo penetrat tua corda tumultu;
      ne sensu titubes, anchora mentis adest.
Constantes animos non ventilat aura susurrans
      nec leviter facili mobilitate trahit.
Hinc bene disposito comitatur gloria cursu,
70   quod se mature mens moderata gerit.
Consilium vigilans alta radice retractas
      et res clausa aliis est manifesta tibi.
Publica cura movens proceres si congreget omnes,
      spes est consilii te monitore sequi.
75 Hinc quotiens felix legatio denique pergit,
      ingreditur caute quam tua lingua regit.
Quod tam mirifico floret patientia cultu,
      est tibi Daviticae mansuetudo vitae.
Iustitiae rector, venerandi iuris amator,
80   iudicium sapiens de Salomone trahis.
Tu melior fidei merito. Nam principis ampli
      Traiani ingenium de pietate refers.
Quid repetam maturum animum, qui tempore nostro
      antiqui Fabii de gravitate places?
85 Si veniant aliquae variato murmure causae,
      pondera mox legum regis ab ore fluunt.
Quamvis confusas referant certamina voces,

the face of one person each relative lives. You gather to
yourself all the qualities both men possessed and alone rep- 60
resent the two of them with the sanction of the law. You
shine as the path of justice, the model of authority, and pre-
cious faith gives the shape to your life. In the calm of your
spirit moderation is held fast, for you always have a haven in
your own breast. No storm penetrates your heart with its 65
rage; your mind is an anchor preventing your senses from
faltering. No whispering breeze shakes your resolute spirit
nor easily moves it with ready instability. Glory keeps you
company with well-regulated course, because your mind in 70
timely fashion shows moderation. You watchfully exercise
judgment with deep penetration, and matters obscure to
others are clear to you. If a matter of public concern impels
all leading men to meet, their hope for sound policy lies in
following your advice. For this reason whenever a fortunate 75
embassy goes on its way, it proceeds with care since your
tongue gives it instructions.

In you forbearance flowers in such a remarkable way that
you possess the mildness of the life of David. Dispenser of
justice, lover of what is revered as right, in your wisdom you 80
have the judgment of Solomon. You, though, are superior in
faith. But in charity you recall the character of the famous
emperor Trajan. Why should I linger over your maturity of
mind? For in the present day you win assent with the au-
thority of Fabius of old. If some cases arise with opinions 85
muttered at variance, the weight of the laws soon flows from
the mouth of the king. Although the parties give voice to

nodosae litis solvere fila potes.
Obtinet adveniens fructum cui iusta petuntur;
90 quem sua causa fovet praemia victor habet.
Cuius clara fides valida radice tenetur;
antea mons migrat quam tua verba cadant.
Spes promissa stat nullo mutabilis actu;
pollicitata semel perpetuata manent.
95 Illa domus proprio de pondere tuta tenetur
quae fundamento stat bene fixa suo.
Cum sis progenitus clara de gente Sigamber,
floret in eloquio lingua Latina tuo.
Qualis es in propria docto sermone loquella,
100 qui nos Romanos vincis in eloquio?
Splendet in ore dies detersa fronte serenus;
sinceros animos nubila nulla premunt.
Blanda serenatum circumdat gratia vultum;
laetitiam populus regis ab ore capit.
105 Muneribus largis replet tua gratia cunctos.
Ut mea dicta probes, plebs, mihi testis ades.
O bonitas immensa tui, quae divite censu
quod famulis tribuit, hoc putat esse suum!
Erigis abiectos, erectos lege tueris;
110 omnibus in totum factus es omne bonum.
Protegat Omnipotens pietatis munere regem
et dominum servet quem dedit esse patrem.
Cives te cupiant, tu gaudia civibus addas:
plebs placeat famulans, rex pietate regat.

a babble of sounds, you can untangle the threads of the knotty dispute. The petitioner whose claims are just gains his reward; he who has the best case wins the prize as victor. Your conspicuous good faith is firm-rooted and strong; mountains will move before your word fails. No action can change the hope that you promise; once your pledge is made it holds good forever. That house remains secure, held by its own weight, which stands firmly settled on its own foundation. Although you are Sicambrian, born of a glorious race, the Latin language flowers in your speech. What must your learned eloquence be like in your native language, who in your speech outdo us Romans in ours? The clear light of day shines with undimmed brow on your face; no clouds oppress your serenity of spirit. Winning charm wreathes your serene countenance; the people derive happiness from the face of their king. Your kindness satisfies everyone with generous gifts. To prove the truth of my words, people, bear me witness.

O how immense is your goodness, which from your great wealth considers as its own what it gives to your servants! You raise up the lowly, and once they are raised protect them with the law; to all in every way you are their entire good. May the Almighty protect you, the king, with the gift of his bounty, and preserve you, a lord to whom he gave the role of a father. May the citizens long for you, and you bring joy to the citizens; may the people please by their service and the king rule with his love.

3

De Theudechilde regina

Inclita progenies, regali stirpe coruscans,
    cui celsum a proavis nomen origo dedit,
currit in orbe volans generis nova gloria vestri
    et simul hinc frater personat, inde pater,
5   sed quamvis niteat generosa propago parentum,
    moribus ex vestris multiplicatur honor.
Cernimus in vobis quidquid laudatur in illis;
    ornasti antiquum, Theudechilde, genus.
Mens veneranda, decens, sollers, pia, cara, benigna;
10   cum sis prole potens, gratia maior adest.
Evitans odii causas micat ampla potestas;
    quae terrore minus, plus in amore venis.
Mitis ab ore sonus suavissima dicta resultat
    verbaque conloquii sunt quasi mella favi.
15   Femineum sexum quantum praecedis honore,
    tantum alias superas et pietatis ope.
Si novus adveniat, recipis sic mente benigna,
    ac si servitiis iam placuisset avis.
Pauperibus fessis tua dextera seminat escas.
20   ut segetes fructu fertiliore metas.
Unde foves inopes, semper satiata manebis,
    et quem sumit egens fit tuus ille cibus.
Pervenit ad Christum quidquid largiris egeno;
    etsi nemo videt, non peritura manent.

3

On Queen Theudechild

Renowned daughter, brilliant in your royal descent, to whom your ancestral line has bequeathed a glorious name, a new glory for your family wings its way in the world and together the names of your brother and father ring aloud, but 5 although the noble race of your kinsmen shines bright, by your character that distinction is further advanced. We see in you whatever is praised in them; you have brought honor to an ancient line, Theudechild. Your mind is dignified, refined, alert, pious, warm-heated, generous; though you win 10 power from your family, the greater charm is in you. You avoid reasons for hatred and radiate great power; the less you invite fear, the more you inspire love. The gentle tones from your mouth voice the sweetest expressions and the words of your speech are like honey in its comb. You so far 15 surpass other women in your charitable aid, as you outdo the feminine sex in your status. If a new person arrives, you receive him with so generous a spirit that it is as if he had already won your ancestors' favor by his services. Your hand sows seed by giving food to the poor and weary so you may 20 reap a harvest of more abundant fruit. In bringing support to the needy you always satisfy yourself and what the poor consume becomes your own food. Whatever you dispense to a poor man finds its way to Christ; although there

25 Cum venit extremus finis concludere mundum,
      omnia dum pereunt, tu meliora petis.
   Ecclesiae sacrae te dispensante novantur:
      ipsa domum Christi condis, et ille tuam.
   Tu fabricas illi terris, dabit ille supernis;
30   commutas melius sic habitura polos.
   Stat sine fraude tuum quod mittis ad astra talentum:
      quas bene dispergis has tibi condis opes.
   Quae Domino vivis summos non perdis honores;
      regna tenes terris, regna tenenda polis.
35 Sit modo longa salus pro munere plebis in orbe,
      felix quae meritis luce perennis eris.

4

De Berthichilde

Mens devota Deo, Bertchilde corde coruscans,
   pectore sub cuius Christus amore manet,
despiciens mortale malum, vitalia servans,
   unde fugis terras, hinc petis astra magis.
5 Immaculata micans nescis contagia mundi;
   sordibus humanis libera membra geris.
Digna pudicitiae debentur praemia sacrae,

are no witnesses, your reward remains imperishable. When 25
the last day comes to bring an end to the world, though all
things will perish, you will win a better place. With subsidies
from you holy churches are restored; you build an abode for
Christ, and he for you. You raise structures on earth, he will
give them on high; you benefit from the exchange, because 30
in this way you will occupy heaven. The talent you send to
the stars remains securely your own; the wealth that you dis-
burse in charity you keep in store for yourself. In living for
the Lord you do not lose your exalted status; you have a
kingdom here on earth, you will have one in heaven. May 35
you now enjoy long health in the world for the relief of the
people, who happy in your virtues will live forever in the
light.

4

On Berchild

With mind devoted to God and radiant in heart, in your
breast, Berchild, Christ resides in love. Scorning mortal suf-
fering, intent on what brings life, in fleeing the earth, you
seek instead the stars. Bright and without stain you know 5
nothing of worldly infection; you keep your body free of
human corruption. Due rewards are in store for your holy

virgo dicata Deo, hinc rapienda polo.
Ille tenet caelos cui tu conplexa videris;
10   quo tuus est sponsus, huc eris ipsa simul.
Non cupis auro humeros nec collum pingere gemmis,
      sed melius casto pectore pura micas.
Mutasti vestem, mutasti gentis honorem,
      cum thalamis Domini sponsa iuganda venis.
15   Quam meliore via meruisti vota tenere,
      quando creatori forma creata places!
Pauperibus largas das esurientibus escas,
      nescit habere famem qui tua tecta petit.
Qui sine veste iacet, tegmen pietate ministras;
20   unde calet nudus, frigora nulla times.
Te redimente pia captivi vincula laxant;
      quae solvis vinctos libera semper eris.
Distribuis censum nulli sua vota negando
      divitiasque tuas omnibus esse facis.
25   Colligis in caelis quidquid dispergis in arvis;
      semina nunc fundens post meliora metes.
Quidquid habet mundus fugitivo tramite transit;
      tempore tu modico semper habenda facis.
Hic tibi longaevis sit vita superstes in annis,
30   rursus in aeternum sit tibi vera salus.

chastity, a virgin dedicated to God, who will be transported from here to the sky. The one whose embrace you enjoy has his abode in heaven; where your bridegroom is, there you will be too.

You do not long to deck your shoulders with gold or neck with jewels, but have a better brilliance in the purity of your chaste heart. You have exchanged your clothing, you have put off your family's high status, in coming as a bride to be wed in the marriage chamber of the Lord. How much better the way you have merited to take marriage vows, in that you, a created image, win the favor of your creator!

You supply an abundance of food to the hungry poor; whoever approaches your dwelling cannot suffer hunger. Out of charity you provide clothing to whoever is unclothed and destitute; because the naked is warmed, you fear not the cold. Captives lose their bonds, when you in compassion ransom them; you who release the imprisoned will be always free. You share out your wealth, denying no one their desires, and you cause your riches to become the possession of all. You store up in heaven whatever you broadcast on earth; you sow the seeds now, hereafter to reap better things. The things of the world in fleeting course pass away; in this brief period you create what you will ever after enjoy. May your life continue here for many years to come, but then forever may you enjoy true salvation.

5

De Gelesuintha

Casibus incertis rerum fortuna rotatur
    nec figit stabilem pendula vita pedem.
Semper in ambiguo saeclum rota lubrica volvit
    et fragili glacie lapsibus itur iter.
5 Nulli certa dies, nulli est sua certior hora;
    sic sumus in statu debiliore vitro.
Dum gressu ancipiti trahit ignorantia fallens,
    huc latet ars foveae, quo putat esse viae.
Nescia mens hominum quid sit necis atque salutis,
10   lucifer an vitae mors sibi vesper erit.
His premimur tenebris ignari sorte futuri
    et vaga tam fragile haec tempora tempus habent.
Toletus geminas misit tibi, Gallia, turres:
    prima stante quidem fracta secunda iacet.
15 Alta super colles, speciosa cacumine pulchro,
    flatibus infestis culmine lapsa ruit.
Sedibus in patriae sua fundamenta relinquens,
    cardine mota suo non stetit una diu.
De proprio migrata solo, nova mersit harena,
20   exul et his terris, heu, peregrina iacet.
Quis valet ordiri tanti praesagia luctus?
    Stamine quo coepit texere flenda dolor?
Cum primum algentes iungi peteretur ad Arctos
    regia regali Gelesuintha toro—

5

On Galswintha

Fortune wheels along, subject to the whim of chance, and our life, ever hazardous, never finds secure footing. Always uncertain, the wheel of the years glides treacherously by; the journey we take is slippery and the ice is thin. No one 5 can be sure of the day, nor even of the hour; we humans live in a condition more fragile than glass. While treacherous ignorance leads us on with uncertain step, a pit is cunningly concealed where it thinks is a path. The minds of men are unaware of what brings destruction, what safety, whether 10 life's dawn will be their evening and death. This is the darkness we labor in, condemned to an uncertain future, and these our transient times have so slight a duration.

Toledo has dispatched to you, Gaul, its two towers; the first is still standing, but the second is shattered and fallen. Taller than mountains, well-favored, beautiful in height, 15 toppled by fierce winds it is dashed to the ground. Leaving behind its foundations in its home country, one of them, moved from its own clime, did not stand long. A refugee from its own native soil, on new sand it collapsed, and an 20 exile in this land, alas, the newcomer is laid low. Who can frame in words the first intimations of such sorrow? With what thread has grief begun to weave the tearful tale?

As soon as royal Galswintha was summoned to the cold

25 fixa Cupidineis cuperet huc frigora flammis
        viveret et gelida sub regione calens—
    hoc ubi virgo metu audituque exterrita sensit,
        currit ad amplexus, Goisuintha, tuos.
    Tum matris collecta sinu male sana reclinans,
30   ne divellatur se tenet ungue, manu.
    Bracchia constringens nectit sine fune catenam
        et matrem amplexu per sua membra ligat,
    illis visceribus retineri filia poscens
        ex quibus ante sibi lucis origo fuit,
35 committens secura eius se fasce levari,
        cuius clausa uteri pignore tuta fuit.
    Tum gemitu fit maesta domus, strepit aula tumultu,
        reginae fletu plorat et omnis honor.
    In populi facie lacrimarum flumina sordent,
40   infans, qui affectum nescit, et ipse gemit.
    Instant legati Germanica regna requiri,
        narrantes longae tempora tarda viae,
    sed matris moti gemitu sua viscera solvunt,
        et qui compellunt dissimulare volunt.
45 Dum natae amplexu genetrix nodata tenetur,
        praetereunt duplices, tertia, quarta dies.
    Instant legati nota regione reverti,
        quos his alloquitur Goisuintha gemens:
    "Si feritate trucis premerer captiva Geloni,
50   forsan ad has lacrimas et pius hostis erat;
    si nec corde pius, cupidus mihi cederet hostis,
        ut natam ad pretium barbara praeda daret;
    si neque sic animum velit inclinare cruentum,
        matri praestaret quo simul iret iter.

north for union with a royal bed—she would have wished   25
the chill here to be pierced by Cupid's flames and to live in
warmth though the land was icy—when the maiden got the
news, in fear and trembling at what she heard, she ran, Go-
iswintha, to your embrace. Then in her distress she rested,
gathered to her mother's breast, and lest she be parted clung   30
with her fingers and hands. Gripping the other's arms she
bound herself to her without rope and using her own limbs
she fastened her mother in an embrace, a daughter who de-
sired to be held by that flesh from which previously she had
received the beginnings of life, confidently trusting that she   35
would be relieved by encumbering the woman who had kept
her safe enclosed in the security of her womb. Then the
household was grief-stricken and lamenting, the palace in
uproar, and the entire court tearfully mourned for the prin-
cess. Rivers of tears disfigured the faces of the people and   40
even children, without understanding their feelings, cried.

The envoys pressed hard for a return to their German
kingdom, invoking the length and slowness of the journey,
but their hearts melted in compassion at the grieving moth-
er's cries and they were ready to suppress their calls for ur-
gency. While the mother was held entangled in her daugh-   45
ter's embrace, two, three, then four days pass. The envoys
pressed hard again to return to their home country, at which
a sobbing Goiswintha addressed them with these words:
"If I was suffering as a captive from the cruelty of a fierce
Gelonian, perhaps even such an enemy would show mercy   50
at these tears; and if he had no mercy in his heart, from
greed that enemy would consent as a barbarian profiteer to
sell my daughter for ransom; but if he was unwilling even to
soften his cruel heart this much, he would allow her mother

55 Nunc mora nulla datur pretio neque flectimus ullo;
   qui nihil indulget, saevius hoste nocet.
   Post uteri gemitus, post multa pericula partus,
   postque laboris onus, quod grave feta tuli,
   quae genui, natae matrem me non licet esse
60   ipsaque naturae lex mihi tota perit?
   Affectu ieiuna meo lacrimosa repellor,
   nec pietas aditum nec dat origo locum?
   Quid rapitis? Differte dies, dum disco dolores,
   solamenque mali sit mora sola mei.
65 Quando iterum videam, quando haec mihi lumina ludant,
   quando iterum natae per pia colla cadam?
   Unde, precor, tenerae gressum spectabo puellae
   oblectetque animos matris et ipse iocus?
   Post causas, quas regna gerunt, ubi maesta reclinem?
70   Quis colat affectu, lambiat ore caput?
   Extensis palmis quis currat ad oscula vel quae
   cervici insiliant pendula membra meae?
   Quem teneam gremio, blando sub fasce laborans,
   aut leviore manu verberer ipsa ioco?
75 Nec te ferre sinu, quamquam sis adulta, gravarer,
   quae mihi dulce nimis et leve pondus eras.
   Cur nova rura petas illic ubi non ero mater?
   an regio forsan non capit una duas?
   Quae genuere ergo, lacerentur viscera luctu;
80   gaudia cui pereunt, tempora fletus erunt.
   Plorans perdam oculos; duc et mea lumina tecum;
   Si tota ire vetor, pars mea te sequitur."

to join her on her journey. But as it is I win no delay and cannot persuade you with any payment; he who has no mercy inflicts crueler hurt than an enemy. After the groans of my labor, after the many dangers of childbirth, after the heavy burden of suffering I bore in my pregnancy, am I not to be allowed to be the mother of the daughter I bore, does the very law of nature entirely go for naught? Starved of my affection's object, am I to be driven off in tears? Do appeals to pity or the rights of birth give me no access or standing?

"Why do you hurry? Delay the day, while I learn to bear my sorrows and let time be the sole consolation for my suffering. When am I to see them again, when will these eyes sparkle for me, when will I again fall on the loving neck of my daughter? How, I pray, will I observe her movements as a young girl and how will her playfulness delight her mother's heart? After the affairs of kingship, where in my grief will I find rest? Who will cherish me with her love, kiss my head with her mouth? Who with hands outstretched will run for kisses or who will throw her clinging limbs around my neck? Whom am I to hold in my lap, a welcome burden to suffer, or who is to playfully slap me with a lighter touch of the hand?

"Though you be full grown, I would readily carry you in my arms, for you were to me a very sweet and light load. Why should you travel to new lands where, I, your mother, will be absent? Does one country perhaps have no room for two women? The flesh that bore you is torn apart with grief; when joys perish, weeping will be the only recourse. With mourning I will ruin my sight; take my eyes with you too. If the whole of me is forbidden to go, at least a part will accompany you."

Tum proceres, famuli, domus, urbs, rex ipse remugit,
    quaque petisses iter, vox gravis una gemit.
85 Progrediere fores tandem, sed turba morosa,
    solvere dum properat, se properando ligat.
Hinc tenet affectus, rapit inde tumultus euntes;
    sic per utrasque vices flebile fervet opus.
Alter abire monet, rogat alter amore redire;
90   sic variante fide hic trahit, ille tenet.
Dividitur populus per regna novella vetustus:
    stat pater, it genitus, stat socer itque gener.
Qui vidit strepitum, patriam migrare putaret
    et quasi captivum crederet ire solum.
95 Procedunt portis. Serraco in ponte retento
    protulit hoc fletu Gelesuintha caput:
"Sic gremio, Tolete, tuo nutribas, ut aegra
    excludar portis tristis alumna tuis?
Quoque magis crucier, prodens mea vulnera luctu,
100   stas felix regio. Cur ego praeda trahor?
Antea clausa fui, modo te considero totam;
    nunc mihi nota prius, quando recedo, ferox.
Hinc te dinumero currens per culmina visu;
    en ego de numero non ero sola tuo.
105 Crudeles portae, quae me laxastis euntem
    clavibus oppositis nec vetuistis iter,
antea vos geminas adamans petra una ligasset
    quam daret huc ullam ianua pansa viam.
Urbs, pia plus fueras, si murus tota fuisses,
110   me ire aut ne sineres, cingeret alta silex.

Then an outcry arose from court, servants, household, city, even the king himself, and wherever you made your way, there was one heartfelt cry of grief. Eventually all proceeded outside, but the reluctant crowd, while it hastened to move freely, only obstructed itself with its haste. Emotion held them back in their course, but the turmoil hurried them on, and so amid conflicting forces all was abuzz with the tearful task. One bade them depart, another lovingly urged her return; so with divided loyalties one impelled, and one restrained. An ancient people was split by the new royal powers: a father stayed, but a son left, a father-in-law stayed, but a son-in-law left. Whoever saw the turmoil would think that the country was migrating and believe that the whole land was going into captivity.

They went out from the gates. When her carriage was stopped on a bridge, Galswintha put out her head and spoke these tearful words: "Is this why, Toledo, you nurtured me in your bosom, so that I, your foster-child, though sick and grieving, should be expelled from your gates? To torture me the more—I reveal my wounds with my grief—you are a happy realm. Why am I being carried off as booty? Previously I was shut up within, now I view you as a whole; for the first time, as I leave, I recognize your harsh nature. Surveying your house tops, I number your people from here; but, see, I alone will not be one of your number. Cruel gates, who have opened for me as I pass and not been firmly locked to block my way, one adamantine stone should have bound your two doors together before they opened and gave any way through. It would have been kinder of you, my city, if you had been entirely walled, or if high rocks surrounded you to prevent me passing through.

383

Pergo ignota locis, trepidans quidnam antea discam:
　　gentem, animos, mores, oppida, rura, nemus?
Quem, precor, inveniam peregrinis advena terris,
　　quo mihi nemo venis civis, amice, parens?
115　Dic, si blanda potest nutrix aliena placere,
　　quae lavet ora manu vel caput ornet acu?
Nulla puella choro quae collactanea ludat.
　　Hic, mea blandities, hic, mea cura, iaces.
Si me non aliter, vel nuda sepulchra tenerent.
120　Non licet hic vivi? Hic mihi dulce mori.
Non fruor amplexu, neque visu plena recedo.
　　Quae me dimittis, dura Tolete, vale."
Sic accensi animi lacrimarum flumina rumpunt
　　fixus et inriguas parturit ignis aquas.
125　Hinc iter arripiunt genetrix, nata, agmina flentum,
　　nec piget obsequii mater anhela sequi.
Deducit dulcem per amara viatica natam:
　　inplentur valles fletibus, alta tremunt,
frangitur et densus vacuis ululatibus aer;
130　ipsa repercusso murmure silva gemit.
Dat causas spatii genetrix, ut longius iret,
　　sed fuit optanti tempus iterque breve.
Pervenit quo mater ait sese inde reverti,
　　sed quod velle prius, postea nolle fuit.
135　Rursus adire cupit, via qua fert invia matrem,
　　quam proceres retinent, ne teneretur iter.
Haerebant in se amplexae pariterque reflexae.
　　Incipit hic gemitu Goisuintha fero:

"I am journeying in ignorance of these lands, fearful at what I will learn about first: the people, their character and manners, town, country, or forest. Whom, pray, will I, a stranger in a foreign land, discover, where none of you come with me, citizen, friend, or kin? Tell me, can a foreign nurse 115 charm me and win me over, to wash my face with her hands and deck my hair with a pin? There will be no girl of my age to join me in play in the dance. Now, my sport, now, my delight, you are over. If there is no other way, even an un-marked grave could hold me. Can I not live here? Then here 120 it is sweet to die. Without enjoying your embrace, with-out satisfying my gaze I depart. Cruel Toledo, who send me away from you, farewell." In this way rivers of tears burst out from her enflamed heart, and the fire that pierced it brought forth running waters.

Then mother, daughter, and bands of mourners start on 125 their journey; her mother, yearning to follow, shows no re-luctance to attend her. She escorts her sweet daughter in her bitter progress: the valleys are filled with weeping and the heights tremble, the heavy air is broken by cries of unavail-ing lament, and the forest itself groans as it echoes the 130 sound.

The mother found reasons for extending her journey fur-ther, but despite her wishes time and her progress were short. She reached the point where she said she would turn back, but what once she wanted now was against her wishes. She was eager to go on where the way led her, though no 135 way for a mother, but the court nobles restrained her from continuing her course. Together both women clung to each other in an equally tight embrace. Then Goiswintha be-gan to speak with fierce lamentation: "For your citizens,

"Civibus ampla tuis, angusta, Hispania, matri
140   et regio soli tam cito clausa mihi,
Quae licet a Zephyro calidum percurris in Eurum,
    et de Tyrrheno tendis ad oceanum,
sufficiens populis quamvis regionibus amplis,
    quo est mea nata absens, terra mihi brevis es.
145 Nec minus hic sine te errans et peregrina videbor
    inque loco proprio civis et exul ero.
Quaeso quid inspiciant oculi, quem, nata, requirant,
    quae mea nunc tecum lumina ducis, amor.
Tu dolor unus eris. Quisquis mihi luserit infans,
150   amplexu alterius tu mihi pondus eris.
Currat, stet, sedeat, fleat, intret et exeat alter,
    sola meis oculis dulcis imago redis.
Te fugiente errans aliena per oscula curram
    et super ora gemens ubera sicca premam.
155 De facie infantum plorantia lumina lambam
    et teneras lacrimas insatiata bibam.
Tali potu utinam vel parte refrigerer ulla,
    aut plorata avidae mitiget unda sitim!
Quidquid erit, crucior; nulla hic medicamina prosunt;
160   vulnere distillo, Gelesuintha, tuo.
Qua, rogo, nata, manu cara haec coma pexa nitebit?
    Quis sine me placidas lambiat ore genas?
Quis gremio foveat, genibus vehat, ambiat ulna?
    Sed tibi praeter me non ibi mater erit.
165 Quod superest, timibundus amor hoc mandat eunti:
    sis, precor, o felix, sed cave—vade, vale.
Mitte avidae matri vel per vaga flabra salutem:

Spain, you are spacious, but for a mother you are but small
and your realm so suddenly has been denied to me alone. 140
Though you run from the West to the warmth of the East
and stretch from the Tyrrhenian Sea to the ocean, providing
ample space for your peoples with your spreading lands, for
me your territory is tiny, where my daughter is absent. Here 145
without you I will seem no less a wanderer and stranger, and
in my own home I will be both citizen and exile.

"What should my eyes look at, I ask, whom should they
seek, my daughter, you who now carry off with you, my
love, my powers of sight. You will be my one source of grief.
Whenever a child plays before me, though I embrace an- 150
other, you will be the weight in my arms. Whether one runs
or stands, sits, cries, goes in or goes out, yours will be the
only sweet image that comes before my eyes. With you gone
I will run to others' kisses in my distraction and sorrowfully
squeeze my dried-up breasts over their mouths. I will kiss 155
the weeping eyes on children's faces and drink their delicate
tears, without quenching my thirst. If only I could find some
measure of comfort from such a draft, or the water of tears
could moderate my greedy thirst! Whatever happens I am
in torment; for this no treatments provide help; from the 160
wound you cause I waste away, Galswintha. By what hand, I
ask, my daughter, will this dear hair be combed to a sheen?
Who in my absence is to kiss those gentle cheeks of yours,
who hug you on her lap, sit you on her knees, wrap you in
her arms? Without me you will have no mother there.

"For the rest, love mixed with fear has these words for 165
you as you go: may you be happy, I pray, but take care—go
your way, farewell. Send greetings to your impatient mother

si venit, ipsa mihi nuntiet aura boni."
Filia tum validis genetricis onusta querellis,
170   tristis, inops animi nec valitura loqui,
clausa voce diu, vix fauce solubile fandi,
   pauca refert—cordis vulnere lingua gravis:
"Maiestas si celsa Dei mihi tempora vellet
   nunc dare plus vitae, non daret ista viae.
175 Ultima sed quoniam sors inrevocabilis instat,
   si iam nemo vetat, qua trahit ira sequar.
Haec extrema tamen loquar et memoranda dolori:
   hinc tua non tua sunt. Goisuintha, vale."
Oscula sic rumpunt et fixa ori ora repellunt;
180   dum se non possunt, aera lambit amor.
Hinc pilente petens loca Gallica Gelesuintha
   stabat fixa oculis tristis eunte rota.
E contra genetrix post natam lumina tendens,
   uno stante loco, pergit et ipsa simul.
185 Tota tremens, agiles raperet ne mula quadrigas,
   aut equus inpatiens verteret axe rotas,
sollicitis oculis circumvolitabat amantem,
   illuc mente sequens qua via flectit iter.
saepe loquebatur quasi secum nata sederet
190   absentemque manu visa tenere sinu.
Prendere se credens in ventos bracchia iactat,
   nec natam recipit, sed vaga flabra ferit.
Inter tot comites unam spectabat euntem;
   sola videbat iter qua suus ibat amor.

even by the errant breezes; if it comes, may the wind bring
some good news to me."

The daughter then, oppressed by the forceful laments of
her mother, grief-stricken, her mind at a loss, and unable to 170
speak, her voice long muted and her throat scarcely capable
of talking, said a few words, though her tongue was heavy
from the wound to her heart: "If the high majesty of God
were now willing to grant me a greater length of life, he
would not give me this long journey. But since my final des- 175
tiny presses irrevocably on, if no one intervenes, I shall fol-
low where anger is taking me. Yet I shall speak these last
words addressed to your grief: hereafter what was yours is
yours no longer. Goiswintha, farewell!"

With this they break off their kisses and part mouths
that were joined; since they cannot kiss each other, love 180
kisses the air. On one side Galswintha, bound for the lands
of Gaul on her carriage, stood still with fixed gaze, grief-
stricken as the wheel moved on. Opposite her, her mother,
straining her eyes after her daughter, though she remained
in one place, went along with her too. Possessed by fear that 185
a mule would hurry away the swift chariot or a spirited horse
send the wheels racing on their axle, with anxious gaze she
hovered over her dearest, following in her heart every twist
and turn of the road. She often addressed her daughter as
though she sat there by her side, and though far from her 190
grasp, thought she held her in her lap. Believing she was
catching her, she stretched her arms to the winds, and in-
stead of holding her daughter clutched fleeting air. So many
companions, but she had eyes for the journey of just one;
only she could see the road on which her loved one trav-

195 Plus genetrix suspensa animo quam filia curru,
     haec titubans votis ibat et illa rotis,
donec longe oculo spatioque evanuit amplo
     nec visum adtingit, dum tegit umbra diem.
Ipsa putat dubios natae se cernere vultus,
200   et cum forma fugit, dulcis imago redit.
O nomen pietate calens, o cura fidelis!
     quamvis absenti quid nisi mater eras?
Fletibus ora rigans, lamentis sidera pulsans,
     singula commemorans dulcia, dura, pia,
205 mobilis, impatiens, metuens, flens anxia mater,
     quid sequeris lacrimis? Augurat altus amor?
Illa tamen pergit qua trita viam orbita sulcat.
     Quisque suis vacuos fletibus implet agros.
Inde Pyrenaeas per nubes transilit Alpes
210   quaque pruinosis Iulius alget aquis,
qua nive canentes fugiunt ad sidera montes
     atque super pluvias exit acutus apex.
Excipit hinc Narbo, qua litora plana remordens
     mitis Atax Rhodanas molliter intrat aquas.
215 Post aliquas urbes Pictavas attigit arces,
     regali pompa praetereundo viam,
inclitus ille quibus vere amplus Hilarius oris
     et satus et situs est ore tonante loquax.
Thrax, Italus, Scytha, Persa, Indus, Geta, Daca, Britannus
220   huius in eloquio spem bibit, arma capit.
Sol radio, hic verbo generalia lumina fundunt,
     montibus ille diem, mentibus iste fidem.
Hanc ego nempe novus conspexi praetereuntem
     molliter argenti turre rotante vehi,

eled. The mother was more caught up in her thoughts than 195
her daughter on the carriage—one trembling in prayer, the
other with the motion of the wheels—until her child dis-
appeared far from view over a long distance, no longer in
sight, as the shades of evening cloaked the day. But she still
thought she could see the faint features of her daughter, and 200
though her bodily form was gone, her sweet image returned.

O motherhood, a name of warm affection and faithful
devotion! Even to an absent child what were you but a
mother? Watering your face with your tears, assailing the
stars with laments, recalling all your memories, whether
sweet, harsh, or tender, wavering and indignant, fearful and 205
tearful, a mother in your anxiety, why do you pursue her with
tears? Does your profound love have foresight? But she goes
on her way where the worn track marks out a road. Each
woman fills the empty fields with her weeping.

From there she passed over the cloud-capped Pyrenees,
where July is chilled by frosty waters, where the mountains, 210
white with snow, soar up to the stars and sharp peaks extend
above the rain below. Next Narbonne received her, where
lapping its level shores the peaceful Aude gently mingles
with the waters of the Rhone. She journeyed through other 215
cities and came to the towers of Poitiers, in regal splendor
passing along her way, the place where the famous Hilary, a
man of true eloquence, was born and buried, thunderous in
his fluent speech. Thracian, Italian, Scythian, Persian, In-
dian, Goth, Dacian, and Briton from his words drink hope 220
and take up weapons. As the sun with its rays casts universal
light, so he with his preaching, one bringing day to moun-
tains, the other faith to men's minds. When I was newly ar-
rived there I saw her pass by, riding on a gently rolling tower

225 materno voluit pia quam Radegundis amore
    cernere ferventer, si daret ullus opem.
Saepe tamen missis dulci sibi dulcis adhaesit
    et placide coluit, quod modo triste dolet.
Toronicas terras Martini ad sidera noti
230   inde petit lento continuante gradu.
Vingennae volucer transmittitur alveus alno;
    turba comes rapidis alacris exit aquis.
Excipit inde repens vitrea Liger algidus unda,
    quo neque vel piscem levis harena tegit.
235 Pervenit qua se piscoso Sequana fluctu
    in mare fert, iuncto Rotomagense sinu.
Iungitur ergo toro regali culmine virgo
    et magno meruit plebis amore coli,
hos quoque muneribus permulcens, vocibus illos,
240   et licet ignotos sic facit esse suos,
utque fidelis ei sit gens armata, per arma
    iurat iure suo, se quoque lege ligat.
Regnabat placido conponens tramite vitam;
    pauperibus tribuens advena mater erat,
245 quaque magis possit regno superesse perenni,
    Catholicae fidei conciliata placet.
O dolor insignis, quid differs tempora fletus
    lugubresque vices plura loquendo taces?
Improba sors hominum, quae improviso abdita lapsu
250   tot bona tam subito morte volante voras.
Nam breve tempus habens consortia nexa iugalis,
    principio vitae funere rapta fuit.
Praecipiti casu volucri praeventa sub ictu
    deficit, et verso lumine lumen obit.

of silver. Holy Radegund with a mother's love fervently de- 225
sired to see her, if only someone would provide the means.
Lovingly in letters she held fast to her loved one, and paid
her kind attention; now the recollection causes bitter grief.
Next with slow but steady pace she traveled to Tours, land of 230
Martin, famed to the heavens. The rapid current of the Vi-
enne was crossed by boat, her company quickly emerging
from the swirling stream. Then soon the chill Loire, its wa-
ters running crystal clear, received her, where the smooth
silt cannot even conceal a fish. Her journey ended where the 235
Seine, its waves well-stocked with fish, rolls to the sea, curv-
ing by the town of Rouen.

The maiden of royal eminence was then joined in mar-
riage and gained the regard and great affection of the peo-
ple, winning some by her gifts, others by her words, and 240
making her own those who were unknown to her. To secure
the loyalty of the people under arms, by arms they swore af-
ter their practice, and she too bound herself by law. As queen
she conducted her life on a peaceful course; by giving to the
poor, though a foreigner, she became a mother, and so that 245
she could better live on in the eternal kingdom, she won ap-
plause by converting to the orthodox faith.

O untold grief, why do you put off the moment for weep-
ing and keep silent about painful events, though speaking so
much? Cruel are you, human destiny, who keep hidden, then
swoop unexpectedly and so suddenly devour so many good 250
things with the onset of death. For she enjoyed only briefly
the ties of marriage with a spouse; at the very beginning of
her life she was carried off by death. Overtaken by the swift
blow of sudden misfortune she passed away, and her lamp
was overturned, her light extinguished.

255 Infelix nutrix audito funere alumnae
        exanimum ad corpus vix animata volat.
     Ipsa inter famulas incumbens prima fideles,
        haec tandem potuit clausa dolore loqui:
     "Sic placidae matri promisi, pessima nutrix,
260   te longe incolumem, Gelesuintha, fore?
     Sic extincta meum mea cernunt lumina lumen?
        Pallida sic facies, qua rubor ante fuit?
     Dic aliquid miserans, miserae mihi redde loquellas.
        Quid referam ad matrem, si remeare licet?
265 Hoc sum per tantos peregrina secuta labores?
        Pro vice tale mihi munus, alumna, refers?
     Optabas pariter nobis vitam atque sepulchra;
        quae tecum vixi me sine passa mori.
     Ordo utinam vitae iuvenique senique fuisset:
270   te stante incolumi me prius ire neci."
     Vix planctus profert, vocem rapit alter ab ore,
        nec valet una loqui quod videt aula gemi.
     Interea vehitur tristi lacrimata feretro
        soluit et exequias obsequialis amor.
275 Ducitur, ornatur, deponitur, undique fletur,
        conditur et tumulo sic peregrina suo.
     Nascitur hic subito rerum mirabile signum:
        dum pendens lychnus lucet ad obsequium,
     decidit in lapidem nec vergit et integer arsit;
280   nec vitrum saxis nec perit ignis aquis.
     Fama recens resides germanae perculit aures,
        affectuque pio sic movet ora soror:
     "Hanc, rogo, germanae mandasti, cara, salutem?
        Scripta tuis digitis hoc mihi charta refert?

When her unhappy nurse heard of the death of her   255
charge, she flew, scarcely living, to the lifeless body. Bending
over it, first among faithful maidservants, she finally man-
aged to speak these words, constrained by grief: "Was it for
this that I, worst of nurses, made a promise to your kindly
mother that you would long remain safe, Galswintha? Do   260
my eyes, their light extinguished, see you lie so who were my
light? Is your face so pale, where once was the flush of red?
Say something in pity, give answer to me in my pitiable state.
What shall I say to your mother, if I am able to go home? Is   265
it for this that I endured so much suffering in a foreign land?
Is such the reward you pay me in exchange, my fosterling?
You used to hope that we would share life and the tomb to-
gether, but you have allowed yourself to die without me who
lived with you. If only the proper course of life had held for
young and old, for you to survive in good health and me to   270
meet my death first." Scarcely had she voiced her lament
and another took up the refrain, nor could one woman ex-
press the grief that the whole court saw.

Meanwhile to the accompaniment of tears she was car-
ried out on a sad bier and devoted love performed her fu-
neral rites. She was carried out, dressed in finery, laid in the   275
ground, wept for by all, and buried, though a foreigner, in
a tomb all her own. Suddenly a remarkable miracle came
about in that place: a lamp that hung there ministering light
fell to the stone floor, but intact continued burning; rock   280
did not break the glass nor liquid douse the flame.

The report, while still fresh, reached her sister's previ-
ously untroubled hearing and with loving affection she be-
gan to speak in this way: "Is this the greeting, I ask you,
my dear, you have sent to a sister? Is this the message a let-

285 Sollicitis oculis expectabam unde venires;
   quale precata fui, non agis illud iter.
Optavi Gallis te ut huc Hispania ferret:
   non te hic cara soror, non ibi mater habet.
Extremo obsequio non huc Brunichildis adivi;
290   si tibi nil vivae, mortis honora darem.
Cur peregrina tuos non clausi dulcis ocellos
   auribus aut avidis ultima verba bibi?
Officio tristi nihil impendi ipsa sorori,
   membra, manus, faciem nec manus ista tegit.
295 Non licuit fundi lacrimas nec ab ore resorbi,
   frigida nec tepido viscera fonte lavo.
Nutritas pariter, iunctas regionibus isdem,
   cur ad mortis iter dividis, alte dolor?"
Sicque relicta soror casu laceratur ademptae;
300   haec vocat, illa iacet nec repetita redit.
Germanae validos audit Germania fletus,
   quaque recurrit iter questibus astra ferit.
Nomine saepe vocans te, Gelesuintha, sororem,
   hoc fontes, silvae, flumina, rura sonant.
305 Gelesuintha, taces? Responde, ut muta sorori
   respondent, lapides, mons, nemus, unda, polus.
Anxia sollicitans ipsas interrogat auras,
   sed de germanae cuncta salute silent.
Nuntius hic subito fluvios transcendit et Alpes,
310   maerorisque gravis tam cito pinna volat.
Optandum fuerat, postquam loca cuncta replesset,
   tardius ad matrem hic dolor iret iter.
Sed quod fama refert qui plus amat et prius audit,
   ac dubium credit dante timore fidem.

ter written by your hand brings me? With anxious gaze I 285
watched for your approach; the journey you've taken is not
the one I prayed for. I wished that Spain would send you
here to Gaul, but neither your beloved sister here nor your
mother there now has you. I, Brunhild, was not present at
your last funeral rites; even if I did not pay you my respects 290
while living, I would have honored you in death. Why did I,
a foreigner and dear to you, not close your eyes or drink in
your last words with greedy ears? I contributed nothing to
the sad last duty for you, my sister, my hands did not shroud
your body, hands, or face. I could not shed any tears nor 295
drink them from your face, nor did I wash your cold flesh
with warm water. We were brought up together, sharing the
same native land. Why do you, profound grief, part us on the
road to death?" In this way the sister left behind was tor-
mented by the fate of the departed; she called out, but the 300
other lay dead and did not return when summoned. Ger-
many heard the sister's passionate laments; wherever she
made her way, she struck the stars with her cries. Often she
called on you by name, Galswintha, her sister, a name the
springs, forests, rivers, and countryside echo back. Galswin- 305
tha, are you silent? Reply, as mute nature replies to your sis-
ter—stones, mountain, forest, water, and sky. With anxious
inquiries she questioned even the breezes, but no reply was
heard about her sister's wellbeing.

The news then rapidly crossed rivers and mountain
ranges, so quickly did the wing laden with sorrow take flight. 310
It might have been hoped that these sad tidings, after
spreading through all other regions, would make their way
to the mother more slowly. But who most loves also first
hears what rumor reports and believes the doubtful tale,

315 Mox igitur matris iaculans dolor adtigit aures,
       anxia succiso poplite lapsa ruit.
     Audita de morte una mors altera pulsat,
       et paene incolumi corpore funus erat.
     Pallida suffuso tum Goisuintha rubore
320   molliter haec anima vix redeunte refert:
     "Siccine me tenero natae solabar amore,
       ut mea nunc gravius viscera vulnus aret?
     Si nostrum iam lumen obit, si nata recessit,
       quid me ad has lacrimas, invida vita, tenes?
325 Errasti, mors dura, nimis; cum tollere matrem
       funere debueris, sors tibi nata fuit.
     O utinam mersis crevissent flumina ripis,
       naufraga ceu fusis terra natasset aquis,
     alta Pyrenaei tetigissent sidera montes,
330   aut vitrea glacie se solidasset iter,
     quando relaxavi te, Gelesuintha, sub Arctum,
       ut nec raeda rotis, non equus isset aquis!
     Hoc ergo illud erat, quod mens praesaga timebat,
       non posse amplexu vellere, nata, meo?
335 Paruimus votis alienis, iussa sequentes:
       promissa existi non reditura mihi.
     Hoc erat altus amor, placida dulcedine natae
       quod teneris labiis ubera pressa dedi?
     Cur hinc lactis opem produxit vena mamillae?
340   Cur alimenta dedi nec habitura fui?
     Saepe soporantem furtiva per oscula suxi,
       ut leve dormires viscera subposui.
     Optasse extremum de te quid profuit illud,
       luderet ut gremiis parvula neptis avis?
345 Nec felix vota aut infelix funera vidi;

since fear inspires credence. As soon, therefore, as the shaft 315
of grief reached the mother's ears, in distress her knees
buckled and she collapsed to the ground. At the news of one
death a second death came knocking and though her body
was unharmed she was almost lifeless. Goiswintha was pale,
but with a red flush coming over her face; with difficulty she 320
came to, then softly spoke these words: "Is this the return
for my tender love of my daughter, that a crueler wound
now lacerates my flesh? If my light now has perished, if my
daughter is gone, why, hateful life, do you keep a hold on me
just for these tears? Cruel death, you were badly at fault; 325
when you should have ended a mother's life, your choice fell
on a daughter. If only rivers had risen and overflowed their
banks, as if the land was floundering, awash with floods of
water, if only the Pyrenees had risen to the stars, or the road 330
had frozen solid with crystalline ice, when I released you,
Galswintha, to travel north, so that your carriage could not
move on its wheels nor the horses for the water.

"Was this the reason, then, which aroused fear in my pre-
scient heart, why you were unable to break from my em-
brace, my daughter? We obeyed others' wishes, following 335
orders; you left as a betrothed, never to return to me. Did
my profound love, when I pressed my breasts with serene
joy to my daughter's tender lips, serve only for this? Why did
the flow from my nipples produce nurturing milk? Why did 340
I give sustenance, never to receive it in return? Often when
you were sleeping I planted furtive kisses, I held you close to
my body to lighten your sleep. What was the use of that last
wish that I had about you, that a little granddaughter play
on her grandparents' laps? I did not have the joy of seeing 345
your wedding or the misery of seeing your funeral; in the

perdidit heu nimius hoc labor, illud amor."
Partitis lacrimis soror hinc, inde anxia mater,
    vocibus haec Rhenum pulsat et illa Tagum.
Condolet hinc Batavus, gemit illinc Baeticus axis;
350   perstrepit hoc Vachalus, illud Hiberus aquis.
Tot lacrimas stillasse sat est, sed ab imbre vaporis
    non relevando sitim gutta ministrat opem.
Affectus si forte potest mitescere, dicam:
    non ea flenda iacet quae loca laeta tenet.
355 Dicite si quid ei nocuit quam tempore lapso
    mortis iter rapuit, vita perennis alit?
Quae modo cum Stephano caelesti consule pergit,
    fulget apostolico principe clara Petro?
Matre simul Domini plaudens radiante Maria,
360   rege sub aeterno militat illa Deo.
Conciliata placet, pretioso funere fulget;
    deposita veteri nunc stola pulchra tegit.
Atque utinam nobis illos accedere vultus
    cedat amore deus per mare, per gladios!
365 Vitae signa tenet, vitreo cum vase cadente
    non aqua restinxit nec petra fregit humi.
Tu quoque, mater, habes consultum dote Tonantis
    de nata et genero, nepte, nepote, viro.
Credite, Christicolae, vivam, quia credidit illa;
370   non hanc flere decet quam paradisus habet.

first case my great struggles suffered a loss, in the second my great love." In shared weeping, the sister in one place, the grieving mother in another assailed with their voices in one case the Rhine, in the other the Tagus. Here Batavia joined the grieving and there the Baetic realm lamented; here the 350 Waal and there the Ebro sounded with their waters. It is quite enough to shed so many tears, but from that storm of passion a drop does bring relief, though without assuaging the thirst.

If perhaps grief can be softened, I will speak out: there is no cause to mourn her in her grave, her home now is a joyful one. Tell me what harm she has suffered who after a 355 course of time was hurried on death's journey, but sustained by eternal life. She now steps forth with Stephen, consul of heaven, and shines brilliantly beside the prince of the apostles, Peter. Rejoicing in the company of Mary, radiant mother of our Lord, she serves now under God, the eter- 360 nal king. By her conversion she wins favor and rich in her death she shines bright; her old dress is put aside and a beautiful new one now clothes her. May God lovingly grant us the right to approach over sea and through swords those same countenances! She had a pledge of life, for when a glass 365 lamp fell, liquid did not put it out nor the stony ground break it. You too, mother, have consolation by the gift of the Lord in your daughter and son-in-law, granddaughter, grandson, and husband. Believe, Christians, that she lives, because she had belief; it is not right to mourn her, for paradise 370 now holds her.

6

De horto Ultrogothonis

Hic ver purpureum viridantia gramina gignit
  et paradisiacas spargit odore rosas.
Hic tener aestivas defendit pampinus umbras,
  praebet et uviferis frondea tecta comis,
5 pinxeruntque locum variato germine flores,
  pomaque vestivit candor et inde rubor.
Mitior hic aestas, ubi molli blanda susurro
  aura levis semper pendula mala quatit.
Haec magno inseruit rex Childebercthus amore;
10 carius ista placent quae manus illa dedit.
De cultore trahit mellitum planta saporem,
  forsan et hic tacitos miscuit ille favos.
Regis honore novis duplicata est gratia pomis,
  nare suavis odor, dulcis in ore sapor.
15 Qualiter ille hominum potuit prodesse saluti,
  cuius et in pomis tactus odore placet?
Felix perpetua generetur ab arbore fructus,
  ut de rege pio sit memor omnis homo.
Hinc iter eius erat cum limina sancta petebat,
20 quae modo pro meritis incolit ille magis.
Antea nam vicibus loca sacra terebat amatus,
  nunc tamen assidue templa beata tenet.
Possideas felix haec, Ultrogotho, per aevum,
  cum geminis natis tertia mater ovans.

6

On the garden of Ultrogotha

Here the radiance of spring gives birth to the green of new vegetation and diffuses the perfume of the roses of paradise. Here the young vine tendrils maintain shade in summer and offer a leafy canopy with their grape-laden foliage. Flowers 5 adorn the spot with their many-colored growth and the apples here are dressed both pale and red. Summer here is milder, where with a gentle murmur a soothing light breeze always shakes the hanging fruit.

King Childebert planted this place with great love; it is 10 all the more pleasing since that hand created it. From their gardener the plants take their honey-sweet savor; perhaps he secretly smuggled honeycombs in them. In honor of the king the fresh apples' attraction is doubled, a scent enticing to the nose, a taste sweet to the mouth. How greatly could 15 he advance the welfare of his people, whose touch even in apples produced a pleasing aroma? May a happy fruit be born from that tree forever, so that all retain the memory of that devoted king. From here he made his way when he visited holy precincts, which now for his virtues he inhabits 20 himself. For previously from time to time he lovingly frequented holy shrines, but now he lives forever in the halls of the blessed.

May you happily possess this plot throughout your life, Ultrogotha, and rejoice with your two children, their mother making a third.

7

Ad Cantumblandum villam de pomis dictum

Venimus ad Cantum felici tramite blandum,
   Aregium laetor quo reperisse patrem.
Quod petit instigans avido gula nostra barathro,
   excipiunt oculos aurea poma meos.
5 Undique concurrunt variato mala colore,
   credas ut pictas me meruisse dapes.
Vix digitis tetigi, fauce hausi, dente rotavi,
   migravitque alvo praeda citata loco.
Nam sapor ante placet quam traxit naris odorem;
10   sic vincente gula naris honore caret.

8

De Coco qui ipsi navem tulit

Cur mihi tam validas innectis, cura, querellas?
   Heu mea vel tandem desere corda, dolor.
Quid revocas casus? Iam me mea sarcina lassat.
   Quod iactare puto, cur duplicatur onus?

7

Recited at the Villa of Cantumblandum, on apples

It was a lucky journey that brought me to Cantumblandum, for there I rejoiced to encounter Father Aredius. My gluttony in its bottomless greed impelled me to reach for the golden apples there that caught my eye. On every side fruit with varied color crowds around so that you might think I'd won a painted feast. Scarcely had I touched them with my fingers, taken them in my mouth, rolled them against my teeth, than the booty I had stolen from its branch transferred itself to my stomach. For the taste gave me pleasure before my nose caught the scent; in this way gluttony won out and the nose was degraded.

8

On a cook who commandeered a boat

Why, my distress, do you devise for me such heavy woes? Grief, now finally, alas, take your leave of my heart. Why do you recall my sufferings? Already my burden exhausts me.

5 Tristius erro nimis, patriis vagus exul ab oris,
      quam sit Apollonius naufragus, hospes aquis.
   Venimus ut Mettis, cocus illic regius instans
      absenti nautas abstulit atque ratem.
   De flammis ardente manu qui diripit escas,
10   ille rati nescit parcere tutus aquis.
   Corde niger, fumo pastus, fuligine tinctus,
      et cuius facies caccabus alter adest,
   cui sua sordentem pinxerunt arma colorem,
      frixuriae, cocumae, scafa, patella, tripes,
15 indignus versu potius carbone notetur
      et piceum referat turpis imago virum.
   Res indigna nimis, gravis est iniuria facti:
      plus iuscella coci quam mea iura valent.
   Nec tantum codex quantum se caccabus effert,
20   ut mea nec mihi sit participata rates.
   Sed tamen auxilium solito porrexit amore
      qui Domini pascens Vilicus auget oves.
   Praestitit et gracili pavidus cum lintre cucurri,
      imbre, euro, fluvio sed madefactus ego.
25 Iactavi reliquos sequerentur ut inde pedestres,
      nam si nemo foris, nemo nec intus erat.
   Mergere mox habuit cunctos rapiente periclo;
      naufragii testis nemo superstes erat.
   Sic vicinus eram, postquam iactavimus omnes,
30   ictibus ut crebris lamberet unda pedes.
   "Obsequium," dixi "remove, modo nolo lavari,"
      sed tamen instabat lympha rigare pedes.
   Nauriacum veniens refero mea tristia regi.
      Risit et ore pio iussit adesse ratem.

Why is the load doubled that I'm trying to put off? A home- 5
less exile from my native shores, I wander in greater distress
than Apollonius, that shipwrecked stranger on the waves.

When I came to Metz, there the king's cook, an importu-
nate fellow, took from me in my absence both sailors and
boat. One who is used to snatching food with a hot hand
from the flames cannot refrain from safely stealing a boat 10
from the water. Black of heart, fed on smoke, and stained
dark with soot, he has a face that looks like one of his pans;
his utensils have colored his features with grime, his frying
pans, kettles, spoons, bowls, and tripods. He doesn't deserve 15
poetry. Let the mark that he bears be in charcoal, and let his
filthy appearance mirror his darkness of character. What an
indignity, what a serious affront to have happened: the soups
of a cook have usurped the rights due to me. The pen did
not carry as much weight as the pan, so that I did not have 20
the use of my boat.

But then Vilicus with his customary love brought me aid,
who pastures the sheep of the Lord and increases their num-
ber. He gave me help and I fearfully sped on a frail bark
though soaked through with rain, wind, and river. I ejected 25
everyone else, to follow me from there on foot, for if there
had been no one ashore, no one would have remained
aboard. All soon would have been drowned, carried off by
the danger; no one would have survived as witness to the
wreck. I was so low in the water, after I had thrown every-
one out, that the waves were constantly kissing my feet. "No 30
need for this attention," I said, "I don't need a wash now,"
but still the water insisted on lapping my feet.

When I reached Nauriac I told all my woes to the king.
He laughed and with kindly words bade a boat be readied.

35 Quaerunt nec poterant aliquam reperire carinam,
      donec cuncta cohors regia fluxit aquis.
  Restitit hic solus praestans solacia Gogo;
      quod tribuit cunctis non negat ille suis.
  Dulcius alloquitur comitem qui Papulus extat,
40   ut quamcumque mihi redderet ipse ratem.
  Omnia perlustrans vidit sub litore lintrem,
      nec tamen hic poterat sarcina nostra capi.
  Nauriacum interea fecit me stare parumper,
      ordinat et sumptus quos locus ipse dedit.
45 Quamvis parva ferat, satis est mihi sola voluntas;
      est nec parva quidem quam dat amator opem.
  Addidit et comis mihi pocula gratus amicus,
      in quantum poterat rure parare merum.
  Sic mihi iucundam direxti, Papule, proram.
50   Felix vive, vale, dulcis amice, comes.

9

Ad Dynamium de Massilia

  Expecto te, noster amor, venerande Dynami,
      quamvis absentem quem mea cura videt.
  Quae loca te teneant venientia flabra requiro;
      si fugias oculos, non fugis hinc animos.
5 Massiliae tibi regna placent, Germania nobis;

They looked, but were unable to find any vessel, while the 35
whole of the royal retinue was afloat on the waves. Only
Gogo was left there to bring me relief; he does not refuse his
friends what he grants to all. He kindly spoke to a count, by
the name of Papulus, and asked that he find some kind of 40
ship for me.

After looking everywhere, he saw on the river bank a
skiff, though it was not able to accommodate my baggage on
board. For a short while then he had me stay at Nauriac, and
arranged for the provisions that that location supplied. The 45
intention alone suffices for me, however slight its effects; in
fact no help is slight that is given out of love. In his kindness
to me my good friend also provided me drink, to the extent
that he could get wine in that country location. In this way,
Papulus, you provided me both with a boat and with amuse-
ment. Live happy and prosper, sweet friend and count. 50

9

To Dynamius of Marseille

I long for you, my dear one, worthy Dynamius, whom,
though absent, I see in my love. I inquire of the breezes that
come to me where you are located; though you may evade
my eyes, you do not evade my mind. The realm of Marseille 5
pleases you, Germany me; torn from my sight you are still

vulsus ab aspectu pectore iunctus ades.
Quo sine te tua pars hucusque oblita remansit
    nec revocas animo membra relicta tuo?
Si sopor obrepsit, tibi me vel somnia narrent,
10   nam solet unianimes ipsa videre quies.
Si vigilas, fateor, veniam tibi culpa negabit;
    nil unde excuses desidiosus habes.
Altera signiferi revolutis mensibus anni
    solis anhelantes orbita lassat equos,
15 cum mea discedens rapuisti lumina tecum,
    et modo nil sine te cerno patente die.
Vel mihi verba dares de fonte refusa loquaci,
    ut faceret tecum pagina missa loqui.
Sed tamen ut tandem venias huc carius hortor
20   et revocas oculis lumen, amice, meis.

10

Item ad Dynamium

Tempora, praecipiti vos invidistis amori,
    officium voti quae vetuistis agi
per lyricos modulos et fila loquacia plectris,
    qua citharis Erato dulce relidit ebur.
5 Ecce vaporiferum sitiens canis exerit astrum
    et per hiulcatos fervor anhelat agros.

present in my heart. How is it that part of you has hitherto remained apart and forgotten and you do not recall in your mind the portion abandoned? If sleep stole upon you, dreams at least would tell you of me, for sleep is accustomed to see those who are one in mind. If you are awake, I confess, your fault will admit no pardon; for your idle behavior there can be no excuse. With the passing months the circuit of the year through the zodiac is wearying the panting horses of the sun for the second time, since you, by departing, took away my light with you, and now without you in full daylight I can see nothing. You should have sent me word, a draft from your eloquent spring, so that the letter you sent would cause me to speak with you. But all the more affectionately I urge you at last to come here and bring back the light, my friend, to my eyes.

10

Again to Dynamius

Summertime, you held a grudge against my intemperate love by forbidding the fulfillment of my vow in lyric strains and strings responding to the plectrum, as Erato strikes the sweet ivory on the lyre. Look how the thirsty dog star raises its scorching light, and heat shimmers over the cracked

Hinc metuens saniem, ne quo iacularer ab igne,
  sanguine laxato bracchia nexa gero.
Labitur unde cruor, nodo manus inde tenetur
10 et dextram innocuam vena soluta ligat,
  ut sine temperie validi sitis urat amoris;
  causa meis votis obstitit ista gravis.
Nescio quam prosit ratio perfuncta medellae;
  me tamen inde nocet quod reticere facit.
15 Scribere si digitis sinerer, satis illa fuisset.
  Nunc mihi prima tui cura, secunda mei.
Ex studio studiis retrahor, silet unda Camenae;
  carne fluit sanies, ne riget ore latex.
Musicus ignis abest, algent in fonte sorores,
20 nam sanguis latices hinc gelat unde rigat.
Si qua calens animo recitanda poemata pangam,
  scis ipse hoc studium quam gravet arte labor.
Nam cruor ablatus magis otia lenta requirit,
  quo neque frigus hiat nec vapor ustus arat,
25 secretumque petit, neu flabilis aura flagellet,
  quo recreans animum stat viror, halat odor.
Ast ego posthabeo affectu mea seria vestro;
  cura tui faciem, nam mea terga tenet.
Post sudorem habui modo nam dare membra quieti;
30 ordine postposito tempora rumpit amor.
Duco parum propriam, tibi dum volo ferre salutem,
  sed mea prospicio, cum tua vota colo.
Nunc cape parva, cate et pollens duilance Dynami,
  clare decore tuo, care favore meo,

ground. Fearing an infection from this, lest I be struck by some fiery fever, I had my arms bound tight and my blood let flow. As my blood flowed freely, my hand was immobilized by a knot and the opened vein bound fast my helpless grasp, so that the thirst of my intense love scorched me without mitigation; that was the handicap that prevented me fulfilling my wishes.

I do not know how I benefited from completing the course of treatment, but it did do me harm by causing me to keep silent. If my fingers allowed me to write, that would have satisfied me. As it is, my first concern is for you, my second for myself. By one pursuit I am held back from others, the Muse's waters fall silent; corrupted blood flows from my flesh so streams cannot run from my mouth. The Muses' fire is absent, the sisters' spring is chilled, for blood in being shed freezes the flow.

If I do in the heat of my mind compose any poems for recital, you know yourself the effort such an artistic pursuit requires. The letting of blood demands rather leisurely ease, where the frost does not crack nor the scorching heat wither, and seeks a retreat to escape the whipping wind's blast, where greenery refreshes the mind and the air is fragrant. But I put behind me my serious concerns out of love of you; my feelings for you face forward, for myself are in the rear. After my sweating I should now have given my limbs to sleep, but neglecting that sequence my love breaks with the usual order. I slight my own welfare in wishing to send you a greeting, but look to my own wishes when cultivating my wishes for you.

Receive my small offering, learned Dynamius, powerful in justice's twin scales, held high by your own distinction,

35　partibus Italiae advecto mihi Rhenus et Hister
　　　　quem cecinere prius quam daret ipse locus,
　　insignem specie, celsum lare, lege sagacem,
　　　　omnibus aequalem spe, sale, pace, fide.
　　Incidit unde mihi, fateor, te sorte videndi
40　　　Arctoi gelida sub regione calor,
　　plusque libens vultus efferveo totus in illos
　　　　ad patriae reditus quam peregrina cohors,
　　visibus atque tuis issem velocius ac si
　　　　ad patris amplexus de Telamone satus.
45　Vix quoque tam cupidus vario sinuamine sulcat
　　　　rusticus arte solum, navita aplustre fretum.
　　Ex illo, celebrande, cliens stat pars mea tecum
　　　　et venis huc animae pars mediata meae,
　　antea corde mihi notus quam lumine visus,
50　　　quem mente adstringo, si neque tango manu.
　　Bracchia qui necdum circum tua colla cateno,
　　　　quod digiti nequeunt, alligat illud amor.
　　Longius inde absens ibi sed pertingo quod opto:
　　　　quo pede non venio, pectore totus eo.
55　Nos licet obstet Arar Rhodanusque, natamus amore,
　　　　nec vetat ire animum qui vetat ire gradum.
　　Legi etiam missos alieno nomine versus,
　　　　quo quasi per speculum reddit imago virum.
　　Fonte Camenali quadrato spargeris orbi;
60　　　ad loca quae nescis duceris oris aquis.
　　Hinc quoque non aliquo nobis abolende recedis,
　　　　quo fixus scriptis nosceris esse tuis.

held dear in my affection. When I traveled from the land of 35
Italy, the Rhine and the Danube sang of your fame before
proximity brought us together, distinguished as you are in
appearance, eminent in family, learned in law, well-disposed
to all in providing hope and eloquence, peace and good
faith. And so I experienced, I confess, from the good for-
tune of seeing you a sensation of heat in the icy regions of 40
the north. I more eagerly burned with a consuming desire
for your countenance than a company of travelers does to
return to their native land, and I would have journeyed more
rapidly to come in sight of you than the son of Telamon
would have for his father's embrace. Scarcely with as much 45
eagerness in their different ways does the farmer plow the
earth with his art and the sailor the sea at his stern. For that
reason, honorable sir, a part of me stays with you as a depen-
dent and you join me here as a half of my soul, known to me
in my heart before seen by my eyes, whom I embrace in my 50
mind, if not touch with my hand. Though I do not yet link
my arms round your neck, love provides the bond that fin-
gers cannot tie. I am far away from that place, but I still
achieve there what I desire; even if I do not journey thither
on foot, I do so entirely in heart. The Saône and Rhône may 55
block our way, but we swim them inspired by love; though
they stop our path, they cannot obstruct the movement of
minds.

I have also read verses transmitted under another's name
in which an image reflects the man as if in a mirror. From
the spring of the Muses you shower the four corners of the
world; you are channeled to places unknown to you by the 60
waters of your eloquence. And so, never to be forgotten by
me, you nowhere fade from mind, for you are acknowledged

Interiora mei penetrans possessor agelli,
    felix perpetue, dulcis amice, vale.
65 Spectans oris opem melioraque sideris optans,
    currat ut affatus, stet tibi longa salus.
Sacris Theodoro primo lare, sede Sapaudo,
    Felici egregio, quem dedit orbis honor,
Albino eximio, Heliae claroque Iovino
70   pro Fortunato redde salutis opus.
Haec tibi nostra chelys modulatur simplice cantu:
    sed tonet archetypo barbitus inde sopho.

to reside there by virtue of your writings. Possessor of my
little property, penetrator of my inner being, sweet friend,
be happy forever and fare well. Anticipating the balm of   65
your speech and hoping for a better season, I wish you pro-
longed good health so that your words may hurry to me. For
the saintly Theodorus, excelling in his family and Sapaudus,
in his see; for noble Felix, whom the honors of the world ex-
alt; for excellent Albinus; for Helias and famed Jovinus on   70
Fortunatus's behalf perform the task of greeting. My string
plays this refrain for you with simple melody, but in return
may your lyre resound with exemplary skill.

BOOK SEVEN

I

Ad Gogonem

Orpheus orditas moveret dum pollice chordas
    verbaque percusso pectine fila darent,
mox resonante lyra tetigit dulcedine silvas,
    ad citharae cantus traxit amore feras.
5 Undique miserunt vacuata cubilia dammas,
    deposita rabie tigris et ipsa venit.
Sollicitante melo nimio filomela volatu,
    pignora contemnens fessa cucurrit avis.
Sed quamvis longo spatio lassaverat alas,
10   ad votum veniens se recreavit avis.
Sic stimulante tua captus dulcedine, Gogo,
    longa peregrinus regna viator adit.
Undique festini veniant ut promptius omnes,
    sic tua lingua trahit sicut et ille lyra.
15 Ipse fatigatus huc postquam venerit exul,
    antea quo doluit te medicante caret.
Eruis adflictis gemitus et gaudia plantas;
    ne tamen arescant, oris ab imbre foves.
Aedificas sermone favos nova mella ministrans,
20   dulcis et eloquii nectare vincis apes.

I

To Gogo

When Orpheus drew his thumb over the web of strings and
their threads gave voice at the stroke of his plectrum, imme-
diately at the sound of his lyre he moved forests with the
sweetness, in response to the refrain of his music he swayed
wild animals with love. From every side lairs emptied and   5
sent out their does; even the tigress herself came, laying
aside her rage. Impelled by his song the nightingale with
lengthy flight, neglecting her children, though weary, sped
to him. But although by her long journey she had exhausted
her wings, by reaching her desire that bird won refreshment. 10

In like fashion attracted by your enticing sweetness,
Gogo, the traveler from abroad comes to your distant realm.
To make everyone hasten to you more eagerly from every
direction, your tongue carries the same allure as he had with
his lyre. After the weary exile has made his way here, the   15
grief he had before leaves him through your healing powers.
You root out laments from the afflicted and in their place
plant joys; to prevent their being parched you nurture them
with showers of speech. With your words you build honey-
combs, providing a new kind of honey, and with the nectar   20
of your sweet eloquence you surpass the bees. The powerful

Ubere fonte rigat labiorum gratia pollens,
    cuius ab arcano vox epulanda fluit.
Pervigili sensu dives prudentia regnat,
    fomite condito cui salis unda natat,
25 qui fulgore animi radios a pectore vibras,
    et micat interior lux imitata diem.
Sed vicibus mundum modo sol modo nubila complent,
    at tua semper habent corda serena diem.
Visceribus promptis templum pietatis haberis
30   muneribusque sacris es fabricata domus.
Forma venusta tibi proprio splendore coruscat
    ut mentis habitum vultus et ipse probet.
Omne genus laudum specie concludis in una
    nec plus est aliquid quam tua forma gerit.
35 Principis arbitrio Sigibercthi magnus haberis;
    iudicium regis fallere nemo potest.
Elegit sapiens sapientem et amator amantem,
    ac veluti flores docta sequestrat apes.
Illius ex merito didicisti talis haberi
40   et domini mores, serve benigne, refers.
Nuper ab Hispanis per multa pericula terris
    egregio regi gaudia summa vehis.
Diligis hunc tantum quantum meliora parasti;
    nemo armis potuit quod tua lingua dedit.
45 Haec bona si taceam, te nostra silentia laudant,
    nec voces spectes qui mea corda tenes.
Vera favendo cano neque me fallacia damnat;
    teste loquor populo, crimine liber ero.
Haec tibi longinquos laus ardua surgat in annos;
50   haec te vita diu servet et illa colat.

charm of your lips issues from an abundant spring, and from
its hidden source a voice fit to banquet on flows. In your vig-
ilant senses rich wisdom holds sway, and the flood of your
eloquence is awash with well-seasoned ardor. In the bril-   25
liance of your spirit you radiate sunbeams from your heart,
and within you shines a light that is just like the day. But the
world is alternately possessed now by sun, now by clouds,
while your heart always is unclouded in daylight. You are
deemed a temple of charity in the generosity of your heart,
and by your saintly gifts you are made into a sanctuary. Your   30
beguiling beauty shines so with its own brilliance that your
very countenance reveals your cast of mind. You contain in a
single figure all forms of praise, and there is nothing beyond
what your beauty displays.

By the choice of prince Sigibert you are deemed great;   35
no one can mislead the judgment of a king. In his wisdom
he has chosen a wise man and in affection an affectionate
one and he distinguishes you as a skilled bee does flowers.
From the example of his merits you have learned to be like
him and, kindly servant, you reflect the character of your   40
lord. Recently from the land of Spain after many a danger,
you brought the highest joy to the noble king. Your love for
him is measured by the benefits you won him; no one could
achieve with weapons what your tongue produced. If I keep   45
silent about your virtues, my silence speaks you praise, and
you need not await my speech, since you possess my heart.
The praise is true that I sing, no falsehood condemns me;
my words have the people as witness, I will be exempt from
any charge. May this your renown rise high for long years to
come; may life long preserve you here and the life to come   50
exalt you.

2

Ad eundem cum rogaretur
ad cenam

Nectar, vina, cibus, vestis, doctrina, facultas —
    muneribus largis tu mihi, Gogo, sat es;
tu refluus Cicero, tu noster Apicius extas;
    hinc satias verbis, pascis et inde cibis.
5 Sed modo da veniam: bubla turgente quiesco,
    nam fit lis uteri, si caro mixta fremat.
Hic, ubi bos recubat, fugiet, puto, pullus et anser;
    cornibus et pinnis non furor aequus erit.
Et modo iam somno languentia lumina claudo,
10   nam dormire meum carmina laeta probant.

3

Item ad eundem

Quas mihi porrexit modo pagina missa querellas,
    immunem culpae me loquor esse tuae.
Nam causam Remus tua plus praesentia laesit;
    quo vos peccastis crimine culpor ego.

2

Again to the same man,
for an invitation to dinner

Nectar, wine, food, clothing, learning, and wit—with your
generous presents, Gogo, you satisfy me. You are a Cicero
reborn, an Apicius for our times; like one you gratify with
words, like the other you nurture with food. But now, pray, 5
pardon, because of beef not digested I'm calling a halt, for
the belly is the site of dispute, if a mixture of meats growls
complaints. Here, where the ox reclines, the chicken and
goose will, I think, flee; between horns and feathers there
will be no equal fight. But now I am closing my drowsy eyes
in sleep; this playful poem gives proof of my sleepy state.   10

3

Again to the same man

As to the complaints that the letter you sent just now
brought me, I declare that I am undeserving of your cen-
sure. For it was rather your presence in Rheims that caused
the harm in this case; I am accused of a crime for which

5   Non tamen ex tali titulo dulcedo peribit;
      fructus amicitiae corde colente manet.

4

Item ad eundem

Nubila quae rapido perflante aquilone venitis,
    pendula sidereo quae movet axe rota,
dicite qua vegitet carus mihi Gogo salute,
    quid placidis rebus mente serenus agit,
5 si prope fluctivagi remoratur litora Rheni
    ut salmonis adeps rete trahatur aquis,
an super uviferi Mosellae obambulat amnem,
    quo levis ardentem temperet aura diem,
pampinus et fluvius medios ubi mitigat aestus:
10   vitibus umbra rigens, fluctibus unda recens.
Aut Mosa dulce sonans, quo grus, ganta, anser, olorque est,
    triplice merce ferax alite, pisce, rate,
an tenet herbosis qua frangitur Axona ripis,
    cuius aluntur aquis pascua, prata, seges?
15 Esera, Sara, Cares, Scaldis, Sate, Somena, Sura,
    seu qui Mettis adit de sale nomen habens?
Aut aestiva magis nemorum saltusque pererrans
    cuspide, rete feras hinc ligat, inde necat?
Ardenna an Vosagus cervi, caprae, helicis, uri

you were at fault. But our sweet affection will not perish on 5
these grounds; the fruits of friendship remain as long as the
heart cultivates them.

4

Again to the same man

Clouds who come on the blast of the fierce north wind,
who, suspended on high, circle in the starry heavens, tell me
what health my dear Gogo enjoys, what occupies his care-
free mind in tranquil times, if he lingers by the banks of 5
the wave-driven Rhine to catch in its waters with his net the
fat salmon, or roams by the grape-laden Moselle's stream,
where a gentle breeze tempers the blazing sun, where vine
and river moderate the midday heat: shade under the knit 10
vine-tendrils, water with fresh-flowing waves? Does the
Meuse, sweetly sounding, haunt of crane, goose, gander, and
swan, rich in its threefold wares in fish, fowl, and shipping,
detain him, or the Aisne where it breaks on grassy banks
and feeds pastures, meadows, and fields with its waters, or 15
the Oise, Saar, Chiers, Scheldt, Sambre, Somme, or Sauer, or
the river by Metz, which takes its name from salt? Or else
does he roam the summer groves and glens, and with his net
snare wild animals, with his spear kill them? Does the forest

20   caede sagittifera silva fragore tonat?
    Seu validi bufali ferit inter cornua campum,
       nec mortem differt ursus, onager, aper?
    An sua rura colens exusta novalia sulcat
       et rude cervici taurus aratra gemit?
25 Sive palatina residet modo laetus in aula,
       cui scola congrediens plaudit amore sequax?
    An cum dulce Lupo pietatis iura retractant
       consilioque pari mitia mella creant,
    quo pascatur inops, viduae solacia praestent,
30   parvus tutorem sumat, egenus opem?
    Quidquid agunt, pariter felicia vota secundent
       et valeant Christi regis amore frui.
    Vos precor, o venti, qui curritis atque reditis,
       pro Fortunato nuntia ferte suo.

5

De Bodegisilo duce

Pectore de sterili si flumina larga rigarem,
    non te sufficerem, dux Bodegisle, loqui.
Invasit nostram subito tua gratia mentem
    ut modo plus vester quam meus esse velim.
5 Quo primum placidos merui cognoscere vultus,
    oris ab unguento membra refecta gero.

crack and thunder in the Ardennes or Vosges with the death   20
of stag, goat, elk, or aurochs, shot by his arrows? Does he
strike between the horns the brow of the sturdy bison? Can
bear, wild ass, and boar no more delay their fate? Or does he
cultivate his property, furrowing the dried-out tilth, as the
bull groans at the plow's weight on his untrained neck? Does   25
he now sit joyfully in the hall of the palace, where a retinue
comes together to rejoice, attendant on him in their love?
Or does he join with my dear Lupus to follow the practice
of charity and create by their common counsel a soothing
honey, by which the poor are fed, widows gain comfort, the   30
young receive a guardian, and the needy aid?

Whatever they do, may they both prosper in their happy
intentions, and may they be able to enjoy the love of Christ
the king. But you, I pray, winds, who hurry to and fro, carry
them a message for their Fortunatus.

5

On Duke Bodegisel

If I could pour abundant streams from my barren heart, I
would not be adequate, Duke Bodegisel, to speak of you.
Your charm has suddenly so invaded my spirit that now I
would rather be yours than my own. Ever since I first won   5
sight of your calm countenance my body was refreshed by

Colloquio dulci satiasti pectus amantis,
    nam mihi devoto dant tua verba cibum.
Distribuunt epulas alii quae corpora supplent:
10   unde animum saties, das magis ipse dapes.
Non sic inficiunt placidissima mella Falernum,
    ceu tuus obdulcat pectora nostra sapor.
Qualiter oblectas quos semper amare videris,
    horae qui spatio me facis esse tuum?
15 Quae tibi sit virtus, si possem, prodere vellem,
    sed parvo ingenio magna referre vetor.
Exiguus titubo tantarum pondere laudum,
    sed melius gradior quem tua facta regunt.
Massiliae ductor felicia vota dedisti
20   rectoremque suum laude perenne refert.
Hic tibi consimili merito Germania plaudit,
    cuius ad laudem certat uterque locus.
De bonitate tua lis est regionis utraeque:
    te petit illa sibi, haec retinere cupit.
25 Iustitiam pauper numquam te iudice perdit
    nec poterit pretio vertere vera potens.
Non ligat immunem, non soluit poena nocentem,
    nil persona capit si sua causa neget.
Lumina cordis habes, animi radiante lucerna,
30   et tuus aeterna luce coruscat apex.
Ingenio torrente loquax de fonte salubri
    divitiasque pias ore fluente rigas.
Si videas aliquem defectum forte labore,
    Nilus ut Aegyptum, sic tua lingua fovet,
35 Qui patrias leges intra tua pectora condens
    implicitae causae solvere fila potes.
Assiduis epulis saturas, venerande, catervas,

the balm of your features. By your sweet conversation you satisfied the heart of one who loves you, for your words give me food in my devotion to you. Others provide dinners to sustain the body, but you give banquets to satisfy the soul. The finest honey does not so flavor Falernian as your savor sweetens my heart. What delight do you bring to those whom you continually love, when in the space of an hour you secure me for your own? If I could I would want to reveal what virtue is yours, but my talent is small and I'm forbidden to speak of large themes. My slight frame totters under the weight of such glories, but I make better progress when your actions guide me.

As governor of Marseille you gave a happy outcome to prayers; the city hymned its ruler with perpetual praise. Here too Germany applauds like merits in you; each place vies to sing your praise. The two regions wrangle over your bounty: one seeks to win you back, the other wishes to keep you. The poor will never lack for justice with you as judge, nor the powerful subvert what is true with a bribe. No punishment confines the innocent or frees the guilty, rank receives no favor if the case rejects it.

Your heart is illuminated with the rays from the lamp of your soul and your eminence shines bright with an eternal light. With eloquence like a torrent you give voice from a health-giving spring, and you pour forth generous riches in the flood of your speech. If you should see anyone worn out by suffering, your tongue brings relief, as the Nile does to Egypt. Because you store up in your heart the laws of your homeland, you can unravel the threads of an entangled case.

Revered sir, you content the masses with continual feed-

et repletus abit qui tua tecta petit.
Si venis in campos, ibi plebs pascenda recurrit
40   consequiturque suas te comitando dapes.
Vota feras cunctis per saecula longa superstes
et maneas populi semper in ore potens.

6

De Palatina, filia Galli Magni episcopi, uxore Bodegisili ducis

Lucifer ut nitidos producit in aethera vultus
clarior et laeto nuntiat ore diem,
ornat eundo polum, terris quoque lampada mittit,
atque inter stellas lumine regna tenet:
5   sic, Palatina, tuo diffundens lumina vultu
femineos vincis pulchrior ore choros,
aut tibi sic cedit muliebris turba decore,
ut solis radiis lumine luna minor.
Clara serenatos permutat forma colores,
10   lilia nunc reparans, nunc verecunda rosas.
Credite, nam si quis vultus conspexerit illos,
hic relegit flores quos dare verna solent.
Pingere non possunt pretiosam verba figuram
nec valet eloquium mira referre meum.
15   Gratior incessu, sensu reverenda pudico,

ing; whoever seeks out your house goes away replete. If you venture to the country, there the people throng to be fed, and by accompanying you they gain their own sustenance. 40 May you live for many long years and fulfill the wishes of all and remain always powerful on the lips of the people.

6

On Palatina, daughter of Bishop Gallomagnus and wife of Duke Bodegisel

As the morning star advances its bright countenance into the skies and in its greater brilliance heralds with joyous features the day, adorns the heavens with its course, but shines its lamp also on earth, and among the stars possesses royal status for its light, so you, Palatina, spreading wide the light 5 from your countenance, surpass the ranks of women in the greater beauty of your features, and the female population is as inferior to you in fairness of form as the moon is inferior in light to the rays of the sun. Your bright beauty alternates in its purity of color, at one time imaging lilies, at another, 10 in its modesty, roses. Believe me, whoever caught sight of those features, there sampled flowers that the spring is accustomed to bring. Words cannot depict so rare an appearance, nor my speech give an account of its wonders. Graceful in your bearing and admirable in modesty of feel- 15

talis in ingenio qualis in ore nitor.
Blandior alloquio, placidis suavissima verbis,
    dispiciamque lyram, si tua lingua sonat.
Pectore perspicuo sapientia provida fulget.
20   Ornatur sexus te radiante tuus.
Coniuge pervigili nituit magis aula mariti,
    floret et egregia dispositrice domus.
Iure quidem magna est quae est Galli filia Magni,
    sed merito natae crevit honore pater.
25 Non aliter poterat nisi munere clarior esse
    quae meruit celso digna placere viro.
Eligit e multis quam carus amaret amantem
    et iudex patriae iudicat ipse sibi.
Ambo pares iuncti longos maneatis in annos
30   et quaecumque volunt gaudia vestra ferant.

7

De Lupo duce

Antiqui proceres et nomina celsa priorum
    cedant cuncta, Lupi munere victa ducis.
Scipio quod sapiens, Cato quod maturus agebat,
    Pompeius felix, omnia solus habes.
5 Illis consulibus Romana potentia fulsit,
    te duce sed nobis hic modo Roma redit.

ing, your brilliance of character matches that of your features. Entrancing in conversation, most delightful in engaging speech, I detect the sound of a lyre whenever your tongue rings out. From your perceptive heart wisdom and foresight shine. Your sex is ornamented by your radiance. 20

Your husband's halls win greater luster from his wife's industry, and his house flourishes under your splendid stewardship. Quite rightly is the daughter of Gallomagnus magnified in status, but the father has grown in glory by the virtues of his child. She could not fail to excel in her dutifulness who was considered worthy to please an eminent husband. He chose from many whom he should affectionately love and be loved by, and a judge in his homeland he passed judgment for himself. May you both remain joined in marriage for many years and may the joys you anticipate all come to pass. 30

7

On Duke Lupus

Let the great men of antiquity and all the famous names of the past give way, surpassed by the merits of Duke Lupus. What Scipio in his wisdom, what the experienced Cato achieved, and the fortunate Pompey, you alone claim all yourself. Under their consulships Roman power shone bright, but with you as leader Rome has returned to us here 5

Te tribuente aditum cunctis fiducia surgit;
    libertatis opem libera lingua dedit.
Maestitiam si quis confuso in pectore gessit,
10   postquam te vidit, spe meliore manet.
Fundatus gravitate animi, quoque corde profundus,
    tranquilli pelagi fundis ab ore salem.
Sed facunda magis plebi tua munera prosunt;
    tu condis sensus, nam salis unda cibos.
15 Consilii radix, fecundi vena saporis,
    ingenio vivax, ore rotante loquax,
qui geminis rebus fulges in utroque paratus,
    quidquid corde capis prodere lingua potest.
Pectore sub cuius firmantur pondera regis,
20   pollet et auxilio publica cura tuo.
Subdis amore novo tua membra laboribus amplis;
    pro requie regis dulce putatur onus.
O felix animus patriae qui consulit actus
    et vivit cunctis mens generosa viris!
25 Legati adveniunt, te respondente ligantur,
    et iaculo verbi mox iacuere tui.
Lancea sermo fuit, quoque vox armata loquentis,
    auspicium palmae te Sigibercthus habet.
Responsum gentis sensu profertur ab illo
30   et votum populi vox valet una loqui.
Cuius ab ingenio sortita est causa triumphum,
    assertoris ope iustior illa fuit.
Nullus enim poterit proprias ita pandere causas,
    ceu tua pro cunctis inclita lingua tonat.
35 Nilus ut Aegyptum recreat, dum plenus inundat,
    sic tu colloquii flumine cuncta foves.
Iustitia florente favent te iudice leges,

and now. When you grant access everyone's confidence increases; freedom of speech brings with it the gift of freedom. If anyone's heart is disturbed with a feeling of sadness, after he has seen you, he lives in better hope. Firmly founded 10 on your seriousness of spirit and profound in your heart, you pour from your mouth the salt of a calm sea. But your gifts of eloquence go most to benefit the people; you season the mind, as a flood of salt does food. Root of good judgment, 15 font of rich flavoring, lively of intellect, eloquent and fluent in speech, who shine in twin talents, in each an adept, whatever you conceive in your heart your tongue is able to express. By your devotion the authority of the king is secured, and with your assistance the government of the state grows 20 strong. With uncommon love you subject your limbs to long hardships; to bring peace to the king the burden is felt to be sweet. O happy the spirit that watches over the concerns of the homeland, and noble the mind that lives for the service of all!

When ambassadors arrived they were immobilized by 25 your response and soon leveled by the javelin of your word. Your speech was a spear, your voice when you spoke was a weapon, in you Sigibert possesses an omen of victory. In those sentiments of yours the nation spoke its reply, and 30 that one voice could speak the will of the people. The cause claimed a triumph because of your intellect; by virtue of its spokesman it was more just. No one will be able to set forth his own case as well as your celebrated tongue speaks in thunderous tones for all.

As the Nile revives Egypt when it bursts its banks in 35 flood, so you with your river of eloquence bring comfort to all things. When you are judge, justice flourishes and the

437

causarumque aequo pondere libra manes.
Ad te confugiunt, te cingula celsa requirunt,
40   nec petis ut habeas, te petit omnis honor,
in cuius gremio nutritur adepta potestas,
    quo rectore datus crescere novit apex.
Quam merito retinet concessos semper honores
    per quem digna magis culmina culmen habent!
45 Antiquos animos Romanae stirpis adeptus,
    bella moves armis, iura quiete regis.
Fultus utrisque bonis, hinc armis, legibus illinc,
    quam bene fit primus cui favet omne decus!
Quae tibi sit virtus cum prosperitate superna,
50   Saxonis et Dani gens cito victa probat.
Bordaa quo fluvius sinuoso gurgite currit,
    hic adversa acies te duce caesa ruit.
Dimidium vestris iussis tunc paruit agmen.
    Quam merito vincit qui tua iussa facit!
55 Ferratae tunicae sudasti pondere victor
    et sub pulverea nube coruscus eras,
tamque diu pugnax acie fugiente secutus,
    Laugona dum vitreis terminus esset aquis.
Qui fugiebant iners, amnis dedit ille sepulchrum;
60   pro duce felici flumina bella gerunt.
Inter concives meruit te Gallia lumen,
    lampade qui cordis splendor ubique micas.
Sunt quos forma potens, sunt quos sapentia praefert;
    singula sunt aliis, sed bona plura tibi.
65 Occurrens dominis veneranda palatia comples
    et tecum ingrediens multiplicatur honor.
Te veniente novo domus emicat alma sereno
    et reparant genium regia tecta suum.

438

laws find favor; the scales of your judgment weigh cases impartially. Holders of high office hurry to you and seek you out; every honor looks to you, you do not look to have them 40 yourself. In your possession the power you have acquired is promoted; with you as its holder a position conferred grows in stature. How deservedly he lays claim to the offices continually granted him, by whom the eminence owed as his due gains further eminence! Possessing the ancient charac- 45 ter of the Roman race, you wage war with weapons, but govern in peace. Relying on two supports, on arms and the laws, how properly he enjoys primacy whom every glory serves!

Your speedy victory over the nations of Saxons and Danes goes to show what courage you possess, with favor from 50 on high. Where the river Bordaa meanders with winding stream, there the enemy were cut down and routed with you in command. Half the army then took their orders from you. How deserved their victory for doing your bidding! Victorious you sweated under the weight of iron mail; in a 55 cloud of dust you shone brilliantly forth. Long you continued the battle pursuing the fleeing host until the Laugona's glassy waters brought an end to their flight. The stream provided burial for the hapless fugitives; for the fortunate com- 60 mander rivers wage war.

Among your fellow citizens Gaul secured you as its light, who with the lamp of your heart shine your brilliance everywhere. There are those who excel in beauty of form and those who excel in wisdom; others possess individual virtues, but your virtues are manifold. In the presence of our 65 masters you make the august palace complete, and its glory is magnified by the glory that enters with you. With your coming the venerable halls shine with a new brightness, and

Nempe oculos recipit cum te videt aula redire,
70   quem commune ducum lumina lumen habent,
principis auxilium, patriae decus, arma parentum,
     consultum reliquis, omnibus unus amor.
Admiranda etiam quid de dulcedine dicam,
     nectare qui plenus construis ore favos?
75 Cara serenatum comitatur gratia vultum,
     fulget et interius perpetuata dies.
Qui satias escis, reficis sermone benignus,
     sepositis epulis sunt tua verba dapes.
Quis tibi digna loqui valeat, quem voce potente
80   rex pius ornatum praedicat esse suum?
Sit tibi summus apex illo regnante per aevum,
     vitaque sit praesens atque futura colat.

8

Ad eundem

Aestifer ignitas cum Iulius urit harenas
     siccaque pulvereo margine terra sitit,
languidior placidas vix pampinus explicat umbras,
     mollior et glaucas contrahit herba comas,
5 summissis foliis Phoebi regnante vapore
     vix sua defendit frigida tecta nemus.

the royal dwelling reacquires its true nature. For when it
sees you return the palace receives back its eyesight, since 70
the eyes of the dukes depend on you, their common light,
right hand of the ruler, glory of your country, bulwark of
your kin, consolation for others, for all their one love.

What too shall I say about your wonderful sweetness,
for full of nectar you shape honeycombs with your speech?
An attractive beauty graces your cloudless countenance, 75
while within perpetual daylight shines. You generously sat-
isfy with food and with your speech bring refreshment; even
apart from your dinners, your very words are a meal. Who
could worthily acclaim one whom in august tones the good 80
king declares to be an ornament to himself? May you hold
high eminence while he reigns long years; may you enjoy life
in the present devoted to what is to come.

8

To the same man

When the heat of July scorches the burning sands and the
dry earth is parched on the dusty riverbank, the withering
vine tendrils barely extend their welcome shade and the
weakened grass contracts its gray-green blades, leaves droop 5
on the trees as Phoebus's warmth holds sway, and forests
with difficulty preserve their cool depths. The heifer, scorn-

Pabula fastidens fugit aestu bucula saltus,
    ipse nec adflictis pascitur ervus equis.
Longius expositam linguam canis ore flagellat;
10   ilia lassa trahens tristis anhelat ovis.
Forte viator iter gradiens ferventibus horis
    uritur accensis sole premente comis.
Qui arescente solo, modico recreetur ut haustu,
    saepius irriguas anxius optat aquas
15 arboris aut tremulae viridante cacumine fuso
    frondibus oppositis temperet umbra sitim.
Prosperitate nova si iam prope lucus opacet
    et vitrei fontis sibilet unda recens,
huc properans placidis homo laetus sternitur arvis
20 volvit in herbosos et sua membra toros.
Vota secuta tenens gemino refovetur amoeno:
    hinc levat umbra diem, hinc fugat unda sitim.
Carmina siqua tenet, cantu modulante recurrit
    provocat et placidos blandior aura sonos,
25 Si sibi forte fuit bene notus Homerus Athenis
    aut Maro Traiano lectus in urbe foro,
vel si Davitico didicit sacra dogmata plectro,
    psallit honorificum fauce rotante melum.
Tangitur aut digito lyra, tibia, fistula, canna;
30 quisque suis Musis carmine mulcet aves.
Sic ego, curarum valido defessus ab aestu,
    noscens te salvum fonte refectus agor.
O nomen mihi dulce Lupi, replicabile semper
    quodque mei scriptum pagina cordis habet,
35 quem semel inclusum tabulis dulcedinis intus
    non abolenda virum pectoris arca tenet,
thesauros pietatis habens pretiosa voluntas,
    producens animo pura talenta suo.

ing its pasturage, flees the dells from heat, and the suffering
horses no longer feed on vetch. The dog extends his tongue
far out and laps it against his mouth; the distressed sheep   10
pants, heaving its weary flanks. Perhaps the traveler making
his way in the heat of the day is afire, the sun beating down
and scorching the hair on his head. He often anxiously
hopes to find running water when the ground is dried up, to
be refreshed by a mouthful, or in the green spreading can-   15
opy of shivering trees he hopes for some shade to assuage
his thirst by its barrier of leaves.

If by unlooked for good fortune a grove now provides
shade nearby and a fresh stream babbles from a crystalline
spring, hurrying there he joyfully hurls himself on the wel-
coming turf, and rolls his body around on the grassy couch.   20
Gaining fulfillment of his wishes, he is refreshed by a double
blessing: the shade moderates the daylight, water puts an
end to his thirst. If he knows any songs, he recalls them
in melodious voice, and the coaxing breeze calls forth his
charming strains. If he happened to know Homer well, fa-   25
mous in Athens, or Virgil, recited in the city in the forum of
Trajan, or if he'd learned the sacred teachings from the plec-
trum of David, he sings a song of praise with modulations of
his throat. Lyre, flute, pipe, and reed are played by his fin-
gers; each with its own muses charms the birds by its song.   30
In the same way I, wearied by the oppressive heat of cares,
learning you are well, am refreshed as by a spring.

O name of Lupus, sweet to me and ever on my lips, which
is held inscribed on the page of my heart, your person, when   35
once enclosed within on tablets of sweet love, the ark of
my heart keeps safe, and never will erase. Your rare good-
ness of heart, rich in the treasures of charity, produces from

Divitias quas mundus habet mens aurea vincit
40   gemmarumque decus corde micante refert.
Sensus aromaticus suaves diffundit odores,
       hoc tribuens animae quod bene tura solent.
Melle saporatum refluens a pectore verbum
       et sale conditum reddis ab ore sophum.
45   Post tenebras noctis stellarum lumina subdens
       lucifer ut radiis sic mihi mente nites.
Ut recreat mundum veniens lux solis ab ortu,
       illustrant animum sic tua verba meum.
Cum peregrina meos tenuit Germania visus,
50   tu pater et patriae consuliturus eras.
Quando merebar ovans placidos intendere vultus,
       mox geminata mihi fulsit in orbe dies.
Conserui quotiens vestro sermone loquellas
       credidi in ambrosiis me recubare rosis.
55   Omnibus una manens, sed plus tua gratia nobis,
       vinxit in affectu me properante suo.
Nunc quoque pro magnis quis digna rependat honoris?
       Materia vincor et quia lingua minor.
Sic post ascensum culmen supereminet altum:
60   hinc meus urguet amor, hinc tuus obstat honor.
Sed pro me reliqui laudes tibi reddere certent,
       et qua quisque valet te prece, voce sonet,
Romanusque lyra, plaudat tibi barbarus harpa,
       Graecus Achilliaca, crotta Britanna canat.
65   Illi te fortem referant, hi iure potentem,
       ille armis agilem praedicet, iste libris.
Et quia rite regis quod pax et bella requirunt,
       iudicis ille decus concinat, iste ducis.
Nos tibi versiculos, dent barbara carmina leudos:

your soul talents that are unalloyed. Your golden spirit tran-
scends the riches the world has to offer and mimics the   40
beauty of jewels in your glittering breast. Your fragrant feel-
ings spread abroad sweet perfumes, endowing your soul
with the fine properties of incense. Words flavored with
honey flood from your heart, and you give voice to an elo-
quence seasoned with salt. As after the darkness of night,   45
suppressing the light of the stars, the morning star shines
with its beams, so do you with your soul upon me. As the
light comes from the rising sun to restore the world, so your
words bring illumination to my spirit too. When the foreign
land of Germany occupied my vision, you were my father   50
and took thought for my fatherland. And when I was able
with joy to gaze at your calm features, immediately the light
of day shone in the world with redoubled brilliance. When-
ever I shared conversation with you and you spoke to me, I
believed I was reclining on ambrosial roses.

You show a single benevolence to all, but to me a kind-   55
ness still greater, that bound me with ties of affection as I
hastened to its embrace. But now who can repay your great
kindnesses as your honor merits? The subject is too much
for me and my eloquence is too slight. In like fashion after a
climb a high summit still looms above; my love urges me on,   60
but your greatness stands in the way. But in my place let oth-
ers vie to sound your praise, each doing his best to hymn you
in prayer or song. May the Roman acclaim you on his lyre,
the barbarian on his harp, the Greek in Achillean strain, the
Briton on his lute. May some call you brave, some strong in   65
the law, some skilled at arms and some in books. And be-
cause you manage well the needs of peace and war, may one
sing your fame as judge, another as duke. Let us give you

70 sic variante tropo laus sonet una viro.
  hi celebrem memorent, illi te lege sagacem,
   ast ego te dulcem semper habebo, Lupe.

9

Item ad Lupum ducem

Officiis intente piis, memorator amantis,
 prompte per affectum consuliture tuum,
carius absentis nimium miseratus amici,
 quando latente loco signa requirit amor,
5 unde meis meritis datur hoc, ut protinus esset
  spes Fortunati cura benigna Lupi?
Exul ab Italia nono, puto, volvor in anno
 litoris oceani contiguante salo.
Tempora tot fugiunt et adhuc per scripta parentum
10 nullus ab exclusis me recreavit apex.
Quod pater ac genetrix, frater, soror, ordo nepotum,
 quod poterat regio, solvis amore pio.
Pagina blanda tuo sub nomine missa benigne
 nectarei fontis me renovavit aquis.
15 Nec solum a vobis me dulcis epistula fovit;
 missus adhuc in rem portitor ecce venit.
Munera quis poterit, rogo, tot memor ore referre?

verses and barbarian songs give lays: so in varying style let a 70
single praise sound for one man. Some call you famous,
some skilled in the law, but to me you will always be sweet,
my Lupus.

9

Again to Duke Lupus

Devoted to your sacred duties, mindful of one who loves
you, quick to bring consolation with your affections, with
unusual kindness you showed great pity for an absent friend,
when in a remote location his love was seeking a sign from
you. How can this be attributed to my merits, that immedi- 5
ately the generous concern of Lupus answers Fortunatus's
hopes? I have lived an exile from Italy for nine years now by
my account, in a land where the salt–sea ocean borders the
coast. So much time has passed but still in letters from my
family not a single line has cheered me from those far away. 10
The role of father, mother, brother, sister, and host of neph-
ews, the role a country played, you perform with devoted
love. A charming page generously dispatched with your
name has revived me with the waters of its spring of nectar.
Not only has a sweet letter from you brought me comfort; a 15
letter carrier sent for the purpose has come here too. Who
will be able, I ask, to recount in speech your many gifts? The

Affectum dulcem pandere lingua nequit.
Sed tibi restituat rex cuncta supernus ab alto,
20   quae minimis fiunt qui docet esse suum.

10

Ad Magnulfum, fratrem Lupi

Quam cito fama volat pernicibus excita pinnis
    et loca cuncta suis actibus aucta replet!
Nam tibi cum Rhenus, mihi sit Liger ecce propinquus,
    hic, Magnulfe decens, magnus honore places.
5 Sic tuba praeconis Sigimundi missa cucurrit,
    ut tua diffuso sint bona nota loco.
Quod tamen in brevibus vix signat epistula verbis,
    non quia cuncta canit, nec reticere cupit.
Iuridico in primis pollens torrente relatu,
10   sic regis ut revoces facta vetusta novus,
cuius in officiis aequi cultoris aratro
    semine iustitiae plebs sua vota metit.
Nemo caret propriis, alienis nemo recumbit;
    sic facis ut populum non vacet esse reum.
15 Sollicitudo tua reliquis fert dona salutis,
    et labor unius fit populosa quies.

tongue cannot express such sweet affection. May the king in
heaven recompense you for all these things from on high,
who teaches that what is done to the least is his own.   20

10

To Magnulf, brother of Lupus

How quickly fame flies, carried onward by speedy wings,
and swelled by its movement fills every location! Though
you are by the Rhine and for me the Loire is a neighbor,
here, noble Magnulf, you gain favor, great in your glory. The   5
trumpeting of your promoter Sigimund has spread so rap-
idly abroad that your good qualities are known far and wide.
Yet what a letter can scarcely encompass in a few words, it
does not either want to remain silent about, because it can-
not sing of everything.

Among the most eminent in the torrent of your judicial
oratory, you so direct affairs that in this modern age you re-   10
call the deeds of the past. In your official duties you employ
the plowshare of impartial husbandry, and the people reap
their wishes from the seeds of your justice. No one is de-
prived of his own property, no one lays hand on another's;
you bring it about that the people do not find themselves
accused. Your conscientiousness brings the gift of wellbeing   15
to others, and the efforts of one bring a whole people re-

Aequalis, concors ut ab omnibus, alme, voceris,
    legibus hinc iudex, hinc bonitate parens.
Da paucis veniam, quoniam mihi portitor instat,
20   nam de fratre Lupi res monet ampla loqui.
Sic tribuat dominus, meritis reparetis ut illum,
    quem pariter tecum cordis amore colo.

II

Ad Iovinum illustrem ac patricium et rectorem provinciae

Prosaico quotiens direxi scripta relatu
    nullaque de vestro pocula fonte bibo,
quem prius inrigua recrearas ditior unda,
    nec modo Castaliis redditur haustus aquis!
5 Si me cura minor vestri tenuisset amoris,
    iam fuerat licitum stringere colla manu.
Nunc magis inde minus capio, quia diligo maius,
    et cum plus cupiam, vota negata gemam.
Qui sibi transfudit mea pectora pectore tuto,
10   cur, rogo, non pariter lumina lumen habent?
Vel quod, amice, licet scriptis fero, care, salutem,
    sed mihi qua relever pagina reddat opem.

pose. To win, kindly one, the titles of just and sympathetic from all, you are a judge according to the laws, but in generosity a parent.

Forgive my brevity, the letter carrier is pressing me hard, for the subject of Lupus's brother prompts me to speak at 20 length. May God grant to you that you reproduce him in your virtues, a man whom along with you I revere with the love of my heart.

II

To Jovinus, distinguished patrician and governor of Provence

How many times have I sent letters to you written in prose but drain no cups from your spring in return! In the past you refreshed me with the riches of your running waters, but now no draft is sent me from Castalian streams. Even if the 5 devotion of my love had less of a hold on me, I would have by now been permitted to clasp my hands round your neck. As it is, I receive still less in return because my love is greater, and since my longing is more, I grieve for my wishes denied.

When a person has transplanted my heart into the safety of his, why, I ask, do my eyes not enjoy the light of his sight? 10 At least, dear friend, since I send you greeting, if only in writing, let a page bring me the aid by which I may be relieved.

12

Item ad eundem

Tempora lapsa volant, fugitivis fallimur horis,
    ducit et in senium lubrica vita viros.
Fine trahit celeri sine fune volubilis axis
    nec retinet rapidas ad sua frena rotas,
5 cuncta movens secum momenta et pondera rerum,
    donec meta avidos sistere cogat equos.
Sic quoque dissimiles ad finem tendimus omnes,
    nemo pedem retrahit quo sibi limes erit.
Imperiale caput, regnum trahit, aeque senatum,
10   nec spectante die, cum venit, hora rapit.
Quid sunt arma viris? Cadit Hector et ultor Achilles;
    Aiax, in clipeo murus Achaeus, obit.
Quid satis est cupido, gremio quod condit avaro?
    Deliciis refluis Attalus auctus abest.
15 Quis non versutus recubet, dum fine supremo
    de Palamede potens ars in Ulixe perit?
Forma venusta fluit: cecidit pulcherrimus Astur,
    occubat Hippolytus nec superextat Adon.
Non agiles fugiunt; quo terminus instat eundum:
20   Nam cum fratre celer sorte Quirinus abit.
Quid, rogo, cantus agit? modulis blanditus acutis
    Orpheus et citharae vox animata iacet.
Docta recessuris quid prodest lingua sophistis,
    qui valuere loqui curva rotunda poli?

12

Again to the same man

Time passes by in full flight, we are beguiled by the fleet-
ing hours, and the slippery course of life brings men to old
age. The rolling axle, unchecked by rope, speeds to the end
and does not slow its whirling wheels for any bridle, carrying   5
with it in its course its full impetus and weight, until the fin-
ish line forces the eager horses to stop. So too we all, though
unlike, move toward our end; no one takes a step back from
where that boundary will be set. Emperors, kings, and the
senate, it carries all off and without a day's delay the hour,   10
when it comes, whisks them away.

What use are weapons for heroes? Hector fell, and Achil-
les, the avenger; Ajax died, whose shield was a wall for the
Greeks. How is the greedy man satisfied by what he stores
in his grasping embrace? Attalus, though lapped in abun-
dant luxury, passed away. What clever man is not to suc-   15
cumb, when at the very last the cunning of Ulysses perished,
though triumphing over Palamedes? Charm of appearance
is transient: Astur, beauty's epitome, died, Hippolytus met
his end, not even Adonis survives. The swift do not escape;
they must go to the bourn that awaits. For Quirinus, quick   20
to act, met his destiny, as did his brother. What role, I ask,
does song play? Orpheus charmed with his refined music,
but he and the inspired voice of his lyre lie silent now. How
did their learned tongue benefit scholars, destined, as they
were, to die, though they could describe the curved vault of

25 Archyta, Pythagoras, Aratus, Cato, Plato, Chrysippus,
    turba Cleantharum stulta favilla cubat.
quidve poema potest, Maro, Lysa, Menander, Homerus,
    quorum nuda tapho membra sepulchra tegunt?
Cum venit extremum, neque Musis carmina prosunt
30   nec iuvat eloquio detinuisse melos.
Sic, dum puncta cadunt, fugiunt praesentia rerum,
    et vitae tabulam tessera rapta levat.
Est tamen una salus, pia, maxima, dulcis et ampla,
    perpetuo trino posse placere Deo.
35 Hoc valet atque viget, manet et neque fine peribit,
    hinc quoque post tumulum nascitur almus honor.
Quod superest abitu, meritorum flore beato
    suavis iustorum flagrat odor tumulo;
Gratius aura fluens quam spiret aroma Sabaeum,
40   vincens quae pinguis balsama silva reflat.
Cinnama, calta, crocus, violae, rosa, lilia cedunt
    ut similis nullus nare bibatur odor.
Quid quod morte magis virtus generatur in illis
    dumque sepulchra tenent, languida membra fovent?
45 Multorum dubiam solidant pia funera vitam
    et redit ex tumulo vivificatus homo.
Nobilis urna tegit pretiosa talenta Tonantis
    ac terris recubat quod super astra volat.
Qui sub amore Dei sacro moderamine vivens
50   fit peregrinus humi, civis eundo poli.
Denique post illos qui fundamenta coruscant,
    postque Petri ac Pauli lumina prima fide,

the heavens? Archytas, Pythagoras, Aratus, Cato, Plato, and 25
Chrysippus, the company of Cleantheses are reduced to
senseless ash. What can poetry achieve, what Virgil, Lysa,
Menander, and Homer, whose bodies tombs enclose naked
and decaying in the grave? When the end is come, poetry
conveys no advantage even to the Muses, nor does it help to 30
have prolonged song with words. In this way, as the min-
utes fall away, the present circumstances flee, and when your
piece is taken it eliminates the board game of life.

Yet there is one means of salvation, sacred, most mighty,
sweet, and abundant, to be able to please the eternal and
three-form God. This carries power and force, this endures 35
and will never perish, from this even after the tomb honor
and blessing derive. This is what survives their passing, the
sweet scent of the just that by the happy flower of their vir-
tues breathes from their tombs. A more enticing aroma is
suffused than the fragrance of Sabaean perfumes, surpassing 40
the balsam that a luxuriant forest exudes. Cinnamon, mari-
gold, saffron, violets, rose, and lilies concede that no scent
like it is breathed in by the nose.

What of the fact that power is actually engendered in
such men by death, and while they occupy the tomb, they
bring strength to failing limbs? Their holy bodies make firm 45
the faltering lives of many, and people return from the tomb
restored to life. A noble urn encloses the precious talents of
the Lord and there resides on earth what flies beyond the
stars. He who for the love of God lives in holy temperance
becomes a stranger on earth, but in leaving it a citizen of 50
heaven. And so after those who provide the brilliant founda-
tions, and after the beacons of Peter and Paul, first in the
faith, what a number of saints spread their light, dispersed

quis numerus radiat sanctorum sparsus in orbe,
    quanta columnarum gratia fusa viget!
55 Per loca, per populos mundo sua sidera praesunt,
    quidquid ab oceanis circulus ambit aquis.
Arctos, meridies, oriens, occasus honorat
    lumina muneribus clarificata suis.
De reliquo nihil est quodcumque videtur in orbe,
60   nam tumor hic totus, fumus et umbra sumus.
Cur igitur muto trahitur data vita susurro,
    nec Fortunato pauca, Iovine, refers?
Tempora lapsa vides neque longa silentia rumpis,
    me quoque ne recrees ad mea damna taces.
65 Non ita rebar ovans, postquam Germania nostros
    contulerat visus, ut resileret amor.
Credideram potius, quantum se tenderet aetas,
    ut vestri affectus se duplicaret opus.
Heu magis, ut video, vota in contraria currunt;
70   tempora longantur, sed breviatur amor.
An quantum ex oculo, tantum tibi corde recedo
    et tam longe animo quam sumus ambo loco?
Non ego sic refero, quoniam tibi pectore nector;
    praedicat hoc aliter mens ubi dulce fovet.
75 Nam cui cara fides animum sociavit amici,
    quod minus est oculis flagrat amore magis,
et licet absentem paries, locus, aula retentet,
    corde suo illic est, est ubi forma placens.
Prospicit affectu quem vultu non videt ipso,
80   et vox longinqua de regione sonat.
Quid gerat aut ubi sit, tacito dare verba videtur;
    intra se loquitur pectore clausus amor.
Si volat aura levis, putat inde venire salutes;
    hoc fragor aure refert quod homo mente gerit.

456

in the world, how great the beauty and strength of these
far-flung columns! Among all countries and all peoples their 55
stars preside over the world, whatever regions the circling
waters of the ocean encompass. North, South, East, and
West join to give honor to lights that shine bright because of
their good deeds. For the rest all the sights of the world are
but nothing; here all is vanity, we are but smoke and shadow. 60

Why then do you pass your life speechless without a
whisper, and send not the slightest word to Fortunatus, Jovi-
nus? You see time is passing but do not break your long si-
lence; in failing to refresh me your silence does me harm.
This is not what I expected in my joy after Germany had 65
brought us together face to face, that our love would be si-
lenced. Rather I had believed that over the course of our
lives your loving attention would redouble. Alas, as I see, my
wishes are rather running in reverse; time is extended, but 70
your love contracts. Am I as distant from your heart as I am
from your sight and are we both as divorced in spirit as we
are in location? I make no such assertion, since my heart
is woven with yours; when a mind feels sweet affection it
makes a quite different claim. For when devoted fidelity has 75
won the heart of a friend, the less he sees him with his eyes
the more he burns with love, and though a wall, or other
place or palace keeps that man apart, in his heart he is there
where the beloved form is found. From affection he sees be-
fore him one whom he does not see face to face and that 80
voice sounds in his ears, though far away. He seems to ad-
dress a silent interlocutor, asking what he does, where he is;
love speaks with itself, confined in the chest. If a light breeze
comes up, he thinks that it brings a greeting; its sound
brings to the ear what he feels in the mind.

85 Hinc tuus ergo cliens ego, care colende, requiro,
        absentem faciunt quem loca, non animus,
    qui semper nostro memoralis haberis in ore.
        Scribimus et haec dum, non sine te loquimur.
    Affectu, studio, voto tua bracchia cingo
90   atque per amplexum pectora, colla ligo.
    Ingrederis mecum pariterque moveris amator,
        et quasi blanda loquens oscula libo labris.
    Ante oculos habeo, sed cara refugit imago;
        hic quoque quem habeo non retinere queo.
95 Alternis vicibus modo vadis et inde recurris:
        vix fugis ex oculis, ecce figura redis.
    Et cum terga dabis, facies mihi cernitur insons;
        si pede conversus, fronte regressus ades.
    Saepe etiam videor dare te pia dicta relatu;
100   illic forte taces, hic mihi verba refers.
    Hoc de te minus est, quia prendi non potes absens;
        nam velut illic es totus et hic meus es.
    Qualiter ambo simul paucis habitavimus horis
        non fugit ex oculis, dum manet ista dies.
105 Misimus o quotiens timidis epigrammata chartis
        et tua, ne recreer, pagina muta silet!
    Quis, rogo, reddat eas taciti quas perdimus horas?
        Tempora non revocat lux levis atque fugax.
    Dic homo note meus: quid agis? quid, amice, recurris?
110   Si tua rura colis, cur mea vota neges?
    Scribe vacans animo, refer alta poemata versu,
        et quasi ruris agrum me cole voce, melo.
    Per thoraca meum ducas, precor, oris aratrum,
        ut linguae sulcus sint sata nostra tuus,
115 pectoris unde seges gravidis animetur aristis,
        pullulet et nostrum farra novale ferax.

In this way I, your dependent, seek out you, my dear one, 85
for my devotion, whom location keeps apart from me, not
my emotions, and who are always called to mind in my
speech. When I write these very words, I do not speak in
your absence. With eager affection and devotion I wrap my
arms around yours and in my embrace I bind your chest and 90
neck. Where I walk you walk, where I go you go, lover, and
as if in sweet talk I take kisses from your lips. I have you in
my gaze, but your dear image is slipping away; I have it now,
but I can't hold it for long. In quick succession one moment 95
you're gone, the next you return: scarcely are you fled from
my eyes, look, now your figure returns. Even when you turn
you back, I can see your face all the same; if you turn around,
you come back and present me your front. Often I even
think that you are giving kind words in response; perhaps 100
you are silent where you are, but here you make a reply.

But this still falls short, because being absent you cannot
be held; as you are totally there, yet still you are here with
me. It will not be lost from my sight, for as long as the light
of life lasts, how we both spent time together for a few
hours. How often we exchanged verses on hesitant paper, 105
yet your page is silent now and unspeaking to give me no re-
freshment! Who, I ask, is to restore the hours we have lost
in silence? Each day's light is frail and fleeting, never recall-
ing time past. Tell me, my good friend, how are you and how
do you spend your time? If you are working the land, why do 110
you refuse my requests? Write when you have the free time,
send me fine poems in verse, and work on me too, like a
field, with voice and with song. Drive, I pray, through my
chest the plow of your words so that my field of grain is
the furrow of your tongue, so that the harvest of my heart 115
springs to life with swelling ears, and my fallow teems with

Nam mihi si loqueris, bone vir pietatis opimae,
    exsuperas labiis dulcia mella favis,
plusque liquore placet quem fert oleagina suco,
120   suavius et recreat quam quod aroma reflat.
Cum Aspasio pariter caris patre, fratre Leone
    longa stante die, dulcis amice, vale.

13

Ad Felicem socium

Ardua Pierio cui constant culmina fastu,
    vix humili valeo tangere claustra manu.
Sed quoniam patriae fuit aula sodalibus una,
    affectu fidens pulso, benigne, fores.

14

De Mummoleno

Dum mihi fessus iter gradior prope noctis in umbra,
    solis in occasu iam fugiente die,
cum super undarum viridantes gramine ripas
    pascua conspexi, pastus et ipse fui.

fertile crops. For if you speak to me, good sir, rich in kindness, you surpass sweet honey with your honeycomb lips, and that liquor gives more pleasure than the oil the olive tree gives and more sweetly refreshes than the scent of a perfume. Along with dear Aspasius, your father, and your brother Leo, sweet friend, fare well for many a day. 120

13

To his companion Felix

While you scale the lofty heights of Pierian splendor, I can scarcely touch your portals with my lowly hand. But since we shared one lecture hall in our native land, trusting in affection, I knock, kindly friend, on your door.

14

On Mummolenus

While I was wearily making my way almost in the darkness of night, and daylight was fleeing with the setting of the sun, I caught sight of pastures by the green grassy banks of

5   Huc oculis captus voto ducente trahebar
     deflectensque viam prosperiora peto.
  Mummolenus enim, qui celsa palatia regis
     altis consiliis crescere rite facit,
  inter concives merito qui clarior extat
10   quemque super proceres unica palma levat,
  nobilitate potens, animo bonus, ore serenus,
     ingenio sollers et probitate sagax,
  cui genus a proavis radianti luce coruscat
     —moribus ipse tamen vicit honore patres—
15 huc ergo adveniens epulis expletus opimis;
     quem vidisse mihi constitit esse cibum.
  Fercula magna quidem dapibus cumulata benignis,
     ac si colle tumens discus onustus erat.
  Undique montis opus, medium quasi vallis habebat,
20   quo meliore via piscis agebat iter.
  Ille natans oleum pro undis, pro caespite discum
     incoluit, cui pro gurgite mensa fuit.
  Attamen ante aliud data sunt mihi mitia poma,
     Persica quae vulgi nomine dicta sonant.
25 Lassavit dando (sed non ego lassor edendo),
     vocibus hinc cogens, hinc tribuendo dapes.
  Mox quasi parturiens subito me ventre tetendi,
     admirans uterum sic tumuisse meum.
  Intus enim tonitrus vario rumore fremebat;
30   viscera conturbans Eurus et Auster erat.
  Non sic Aeoliis turbatur harena procellis
     nec vaga per pelagus puppis adacta tremit,
  nec sic inflantur ventorum turbine folles,
     malleolis famulos quos faber ustus habet.
35 Alter in alterius ructabat mole susurros

a stream, and thereby was pastured myself. My eyes en- 5
tranced, I was drawn there following my wishes, and turning
aside I made my way to a happier place. For Mummolenus,
who causes by his high counsel the king's sublime palace to
prosper, who by his virtues stands out in distinction among
his fellow citizens, and whom unmatched glory raises above 10
the great, strong in his nobility, firm of character, cloudless
in countenance, skillful of intellect and discerning in his
morality, whose family from distant ancestors shines with
brilliant light—yet in his character he has surpassed his
forefathers in glory—satisfies whoever comes to him here 15
with a rich banquet; just the sight of him for me was as good
as a meal.

Large platters were piled high with generous helpings;
the dish was laden and piled up like a hillside. A mountain
reared on every side, with a kind of valley in the middle, a 20
convenient space for a fish to pursue its course. It swam in a
world where oil was water, where the dish was turf, and the
table took the place of the sea. Before anything else, though,
I was presented with delicate fruit that bear the name "Per-
sian" in common parlance. He grew weary with the giving 25
(but I did not grow weary of eating), as he urged me on with
his words, pressing on me more food. Soon enough my belly
suddenly grew large as if I was about to give birth, and I
marveled that my stomach had so swelled in size. Inside
thunderclaps sounded with varied reports; east wind and 30
south were throwing my belly into turmoil. Not so is the
sand stirred up by the storms of Aeolus nor a ship driven
adrift on the sea so shivered, not so are bellows inflated by
the blast of winds, the instruments the fire-scorched smith
uses to service his hammers. One food discharged belches, 35

et sine me mecum pugna superba fuit.
Sit tibi longa salus celsa cum coniuge, rector,
  et de natorum prole voceris avus.
Laudis honore potens felicia tempora cernas
40   et valeas dulces concelebrare iocos.

15

De Berulfo comite

Delicias, Berulfe, tuas spectando libenter
  me fateor duplicem sustinuisse famem.
Sic ego credebam, quarta satiarer ut hora;
  me nec ad octavam mensa benigna vocat.
5 Per vestras epulas didici ieiunia gestans;
  litania fuit prandia vestra magis.
Det tibi vota Deus, per quem—modo laeta notamus—
  haec quoque dum scribo, plus satiatus agor.

in conflict with the mass of another, and willy-nilly I was the site of a pitched battle.

May you enjoy long good health with your highborn wife, my lord, and from your children's children win the name of grandfather. Secure in the glory of your fame may you experience happy times and may you be able to enjoy sweet delights.   40

15

On Count Berulf

From the welcome sight of your delicacies, Berulf, I confess that I have experienced a twofold hunger. I expected I would get my fill at the fourth hour, but not even at the eighth did your hospitable table bid me come. From your   5 feasts I received training in enduring fasting; your banquet was rather a penitential act. May God grant you your wishes, for from you—now I report something happy—as I write these words, I find a greater satisfaction.

16

De Condane domestico

Temporibus longis regali dives in aula
  enituit meritis gloria, Conda, tuis.
Nam semel ut iuvenem vigili te pectore vidit,
  elegit secum semper habere senem.
5 Quis fuit ille animus vel quae moderatio sensus,
  cum fueris tantis regibus unus amor?
Mens generosa tibi pretioso lumine fulget,
  quae meritis propriis amplificavit avos.
Floret posteritas per quam sua crescit origo,
10 et facit antiquos surgere laude patres.
Nam si praefertur generis qui servat honorem,
  quanta magis laus est nobilitare genus?
Qui cupit ergo suum gestis attollere nomen,
  ille tuum velox praemeditetur opus.
15 A parvo incipiens existi semper in altum
  perque gradus omnes culmina celsa tenes.
Theudericus ovans ornavit honore tribunum.
  Surgendi auspicium iam fuit inde tuum.
Theudebercthus enim comitivae praemia cessit,
20 auxit et obsequiis cingula digna tuis.
Vidit ut egregios animos meliora mereri,
  mox voluit meritos amplificare gradus.
Instituit cupiens ut deinde domesticus esses;
  crevisti subito, crevit et aula simul.

16

On the majordomo Conda

For many long years in the royal palace, your glory, Conda. has richly shone because of your merits. For when that glory saw you but once as a young man vigilant of heart, it chose to keep you with it always till old age. What must have been your character, what your measured good sense, seeing that you were for so many kings their one common love? Your noble spirit shines with a precious light, which has brought additional luster to your ancestors by your special virtues. He is a flourishing descendant who lends stature to his lineage and makes forefathers from the past more prestigious by his glory. For if someone who preserves the status of his family is exalted, how much greater is the praise for one who ennobles them? Whoever then wishes to enhance his name by actions, let him with all speed think on your achievements.

From small beginnings you continually rose up on high, and at every stage you possessed a lofty eminence. Theuderic was pleased to confer on you the rank of tribune. That was already the first omen of your ascent. Theudebert bestowed on you the privileges of a count, and glorified the office as befitting your services. When he saw that outstanding personalities deserve more, he immediately wished to augment your well-merited status. Accordingly, he made you then majordomo; you gained in stature and the court along

25 Florebant pariter veneranda palatia tecum,
  plaudebat vigili dispositore domus.
 Theudebaldi etiam cum parva infantia vixit,
  huius in auxilium maxima cura fuit.
 Actibus eximiis sic publica iura fovebas
30 ut iuvenem regem redderes esse senem.
 Ipse gubernabas, veluti si tutor adesses,
  commissumque tibi proficiebat opus.
 Chlotharii rursus magna dominatus in aula,
  quique domum simili iussit amore regi.
35 Mutati reges, vos non mutastis honores
  successorque tuus tu tibi dignus eras.
 Tantus amor populi, sollertia tanta regendi
  ut hoc nemo volens subripuisset onus.
 Nunc etiam placidi Sigibercthi regis amore
40 sunt data servitiis libera dona tuis.
 Iussit et egregios inter residere potentes,
  convivam reddens proficiente gradu.
 Rex potior reliquis merito meliora paravit
  et quod maius habet hoc tua causa docet.
45 Sic tuus ordo fuit semper maiora mereri
  vitaque quam senior tam tibi crevit honor.
 Quae fuerit virtus, tristis Saxonia cantat;
  laus est arma truci non timuisse seni,
 pro patriae votis et magno regis amore
50 quo duo natorum funera cara iacent.
 Nec graviter doleas cecidisse viriliter ambos,
  nam pro laude mori vivere semper erit.
 Laetitiam vultus hilari diffundit ab ore
  et sine nube animi gaudia fida gerit.
55 Munificus cunctis largiris multa benignus

with you. In company with you the venerable palace flour- 25
ished, and the household rejoiced in its watchful overseer.

Also when Theudebald, while still a small child, was alive,
you showed the greatest care in assisting him. By your ex-
cellent actions you so administered the state that you ren- 30
dered the youthful king old. You yourself guided affairs, as if
you were his guardian, and the task prospered that was en-
trusted to you.

Once more you directed the mighty palace of Chlothar,
who instructed that his household be ruled with a like devo-
tion. Kings may have changed, but there was no change to 35
your glory and you were your own deserving successor. So
great was the love of the people, so great your own ability to
rule that no one would have been ready to snatch from you
this load. Now too by the love and generosity of King Sigib-
ert your services have freely been rewarded with gifts. He 40
bid you take your place among the distinguished and power-
ful, making you his banquet guest and advancing your sta-
tion. A king greater than others has rightly provided for you
better, and his superiority is proved by his treatment of you.

So it is your practice always to deserve something greater, 45
and as you advance in age, so you have advanced in honor.
Grieving Saxony rehearses the nature of your courage in
song; though old, you win praise for bravely showing no fear
of weapons, inspired by the wishes of your country and your
great love for the king, when two of your dear sons were 50
dead and lay in their grave. But do not grieve overmuch that
they both fell courageously, for to die for glory will be to live
forever.

Your countenance always spreads happiness from a joy-
ful expression and from an unclouded mind brings unfailing
good cheer. Generous to all, you lavish much in your kind- 55

et facis astrictos per tua dona viros.
Sit tibi longa salus placidis felicius annis
    atque suum reparet proles opima patrem.

17

Ad Gunduarium

Si prodi verbis affectus posset amantis,
    carmina plura tibi pagina nostra daret,
sed quod ab ore loqui nequeo quod pectore gesto,
    sit satis ex multis vel modo pauca dari.
5   Nam si respicias votum per verba canentis,
    malueram maius qui tibi parva fero.
Aspicimus sensum totum in dulcedine fusum,
    quo sine nube doli corda serena micant.
Puro fonte rigans nectar de fauce redundat,
10   cuius verba libens pectore, corde bibo.
Providus, exertus, vigilans, moderatus, honestus,
    condimentum animae mens tua semper habet.
Reginae egregiae patrimonia celsa gubernas;
    quae tibi commisit sensit ubique fidem.
15 Nemo piae poterat reginae carior esse,
    quam qui pro meritis talis et ipse foret.
Gunduari, longo vigeas placiturus in aevo,
    coniuge cum propria luce perenne manens.

ness, and win people's devotion by your giving of gifts. May you enjoy long health in peace and in happiness and may numerous offspring replicate their father.

17

To Gunduarius

If the affection of a loving friend could be expressed in words, my page would send you a larger number of verses, but because I cannot speak from my mouth what I hold in my heart, let it suffice that from many just a few words are offered. Certainly if you judge my feelings by the words of 5 my song, I would rather it was larger than the small offering I make you. I perceive that your whole mind is suffused with sweetness, since your heart shines clear with no cloud of deceit. Pouring from an unsullied spring nectar overflows from your throat; your words I gladly drink in with my breast and 10 my heart.

Provident, energetic, watchful, temperate, and principled, your mind always provides a seasoning for your soul. You manage the distinguished properties of the excellent queen; she who entrusted them to you understood your loyalty in everything. No one could be dearer to the dutiful 15 queen than he who in his virtues was such as she was. Gunduarius, may you prosper and win favor throughout a long life, with your wife enjoying the light for many a year.

18

Ad Flavum

Ad carum totiens mea pergit epistula Flavum;
    sic monet officii sedula cura loqui.
Nunc quoque prosaico, modo mittens carmina versu,
    blandior affatu debita solvit amor.
5 Quin tibi pauca ferat, qui vult iter ire viator
    nemo mihi tacite praetereundus abit,
fotus amicitiae te ut pagina saepe requirat;
    et si vir desit, portitor aura placet.
Attonitis animis ego per vaga nubila pendo
10   nullaque suscipio signa relata manu.
An tibi charta parum peregrina merce rotatur?
    Non amor extorquet quod neque tempus habet?
Scribere quo possis, discingat fascia fagum;
    cortice dicta legi fit mihi dulce tui.
15 An tua Romuleum fastidit lingua susurrum?
    Quaeso vel Hebraicis reddito verba notis.
Doctus Achaemeniis quae vis perscribito signis,
    aut magis Argolico pange canora sopho.
Barbara fraxineis pingatur rhuna tabellis,
20   quodque papyrus agit virgula plana valet.
Pagina vel redeat perscripta dolatile charta;
    quod relegi poterit, fructus amantis erit.

18

To Flavus

Frequently a letter from me makes its way to my dear Flavus; my attentive care for duty bids me to speak in this way. Now writing in prose, now sending poems in verse, my love pays its debt with beguiling speech. No traveler who wants 5 to be on his way is allowed to depart in silence unnoticed by me without carrying some few words for you, so that often a page of mine seeks the warmth of friendship from you, and if no man is available, the breeze serves me as carrier.

In eager anticipation I survey the wandering clouds, but I 10 receive no signs in writing from your hand. Is your supply of writing material bought from abroad too scant? Does not love contrive what the moment does not provide? For you to be able to write let the beech shed its covering; it will be sweet for me to read what you've written on bark. Does your 15 tongue disdain Romulean whisperings? Well then, I beg, send me your words in Hebrew script. If trained in the Persian language write down what you want in that, or otherwise compose poems with the learning of the Greeks. Let barbarous runes be depicted on ash-wood tablets and a flat 20 stick play the role of papyrus. Or let a message return to me inscribed on a carved writing surface; it will be thanks to my love that this will be legible.

19

Item ad Flavum et Euodium

Quam bene conveniunt genitor quos sustulit unus,
　　si simul hos unum pectus utrosque tenet!
Visceribus hisdem genitos Flavum Euodiumque
　　prorsus amore uno viscera nostra tegunt.
5　Alter in alterius mihi visu visus habetur,
　　et fratris speciem fratris imago dedit.
Unius ex facie facies mihi nota secundi;
　　sic speculo similem forma repressa refert.
Ergo pari voto paribus dans vota salutis,
10　　ambos inter ego tertius alter ero,
hoc cupiens, ut quos caris amplexibus idem
　　tres amor unus habet, nos quoque charta liget.

20

Ad Sigimundum

CARISSIMO ET OMNI GRATIA PRAEDICANDO
SIGIMUNDO FORTUNATUS SALUTEM

Fixus amore tuo, votis inhiantibus adstans,
　　quae tibi, care, salus, saepe requiro viros:
Quisque viator adest properans Aquilonis ab axe,

19

Again to Flavus and to Evodius

How well the children of one single father agree, if a single heart holds them both in union! My flesh embraces with just one single love Flavus and Evodius, born from the same flesh. Each appears to my sight when I see the other and one 5 brother's image presents the other brother's likeness. In the face of one man I recognize the face of the second, just as a shape is retained and reflects its likeness in a mirror. Therefore with equal good wishes wishing both of you equally health, I will make a third of your number along with you 10 two, desiring that letters also bind the three of us together whom one single love holds in the same affectionate embrace.

20

To Sigimund

FORTUNATUS SENDS GREETING TO MY DEAREST
SIGIMUND, WORTHY OF ALL THE WARMEST PRAISE

Transfixed by love of you, waiting with passionate longing, I often ask people how you are faring, my dear one. Every traveler who comes by hastening from northern climes,

quamvis festinum sollicitando moror.
5   Seu privata virum seu publica cura citabit,
     hinc, nisi perconter, nullus abibit iter.
    Quam vegetus membris? Quae te loca, care, coercent?
     Ordine disposito cuncta requirit amor.
    Si gravis arma tenens Italas terit hospes harenas
10   aut quae Francus habet pagina pandat age.
    Quid geris, oro, refer. Tamen ut queo longius opto
     vivas pars animae dimidiata meae.

21

Ad Sigimundum et Alagisilum

Nomina amicorum mihi dulcis epistula pandit:
    hinc Sigimunde nitens, hinc Alagisle decens.
Prosperitas felix ventorum flamina fudit,
    quando mihi caros nuntiat aura viros.
5   Testor utrumque caput, tantum mea vota iuvantur
    quantum fit florens laeta sub imbre seges.
Ne sitiam rabidis aestivo tempore flammis,
    nectarei fontis me recreastis aquis.
Post Italas terras mittis mihi, Rhene, parentes;
10   adventu fratrum non peregrinus ero.
Tempore belligero pacis nova gaudia surgunt,

whatever his hurry, I detain with my anxious questions. Whether his business is private or public affairs drive him on, no one will depart from here without my interrogations. How vigorous are you physically? What places possess you, my dear? In ordered sequence my love is curious about everything. Come, then, have your page relate if a foreigner formidable in arms oppresses the land of Italy or how things are for the Franks. Tell me, I beg, what you're doing. But as for me, I express what wishes I can, that you live for a long time, a half of my soul.

21

To Sigimund and Alagisil

A sweet letter is disclosing to me the names of my friends, the brilliant Sigimund and the noble Alagisil. Happy good fortune has directed the currents of winds, for a breeze brings news of these men who are dear to me. I swear by both of your persons that my desire is turned to as much joy as a flourishing crop revels in after a shower of rain. You have refreshed me with the waters of your spring of nectar so I am not parched by the scorching heat in the season of summer. After the land of Italy you, Rhine, send kinfolk to me; with the arrival of brothers I will be no stranger. In a time of war the joys of peace rise up afresh, because those whom my

hi quia venerunt quos meus optat amor.
Qui mihi festivae diei duplicastis honorem,
    sic vester crescat munere regis honor.

22

Ad Bosonem referendarium

Sic tegat Omnipotens radiantia culmina regis
    atque eius causas arma superna regant,
sic dominum ac servos divina potentia servet
    et patriae maneat hoc dominante salus,
5   sic placido regi summus pius Auctor ab alto,
    qui dedit ante Petro, porrigat ipse manum,
sic te longaevi comitetur gratia regis
    et florente illo gaudia fixa metas,
hoc rogo quam citius veniat quicumque iubetur,
10   ne gravet ultra animos hic mora tarda meos.
Nam festinato statuit quod certa voluntas,
    si votum adceleret, dulcius esse solet.
Illud enim nimium per verba precantia posco,
    commender domino te memorante meo.
15 Actibus excellens maneat per saecula felix
    et memor ipse mei, dulcis amice, vale.

love longs for have come. You have doubled for me the glory of a happy day; may in the same way your glory grow with bounty from the king.

22

To the referendary Boso

As I wish that the Almighty protect the brilliant eminence of the king and that the martial forces of heaven direct his affairs, that the divine power preserve the lord and his servants and that the homeland remain safe under his rule, that the most high and merciful Creator reach out his hand to the gracious king as he did before to Peter, that the favor of the king accompany you throughout his long life and that while he prospers you reap unwavering joys, so I ask that you order someone to come as quickly as possible so that no further delay here burden my spirits. For what fixed resolve has determined with good speed, if the resolve is quickly acted on, is accustomed to be all the sweeter. But this request I make with urgent words of prayer, that you make mention of me and commend me to my lord. May he continue to excel in his actions and prosper for years to come and may you, sweet friend, fare well and be mindful of me.

23

Ad Paternum

Nominis auspicio fulgent tua facta, Paterne,
    munere qui proprio te facis esse patrem.
Servitii nostri non immemor omnia praestas
    et tibi devotis das pia vota libens.
5 Ut bona distribuas modo qui tam promptus haberis,
    unde magis praestes amplificentur opes.

24

Versus in gavatis

a.   Qui legis in pulchro circumdata verba metallo,
        si venias purus, hoc imitaris opus.
    Nam velut argentum calida fornace probatur,
        sic se purgato pectore prodit homo.

b.   Qui venis ad caros conviva fidelis amicos,
        quod minus est epulis plus in amore capis.
    Non haec per pelagus peregrinus detulit hospes;
        sume libens patrii quod genuere lares.

23

To Paternus

Your actions shine brightly, Paternus, in accordance with the omen of your name, for you make yourself a father by the functions you perform. You furnish us with all we wish, not forgetful of our service, and willingly grant to those devoted to you their pious desires. Since you are so ready now 5 to distribute the good things you possess, may your wealth be enhanced so you can bestow still more.

24

Verses on bowls

a. You who read on the fine metal the words that encircle it, if you come in purity, you imitate this work. For as silver is put to the test in a heated furnace, so a human reveals his nature with his purified heart.

b. You who come to your dear friends as a well-disposed dinner guest, make up in love what is lacking in foodstuffs. No foreign visitor brought these things over the sea; receive with pleasure what a native estate has produced.

c.   Quamvis doctiloquax te seria cura fatiget,
        hac veniens festos misce, poeta, iocos,
    sic tamen ut propriam rationem servet honestus,
        nam solet incautus sermo movere manus.

d.   Vita brevis hominum, fugiunt praesentia rerum;
        tu cole quae potius non moritura manent.
    Erige iustitiam, sere pacem, dilige Christum,
        expete delicias quas sine fine geras.

e.   Pelle palatinas post multa negotia rixas;
        vivere iucunde mensa benigna monet.
    Causae, irae, strepitus sileant, fora, iurgia, leges;
        hic placeat requies, quam dat amica dies.

f.   Quem rogo, pacificos animos ad prandia defer;
        hostem quaere alibi, si tibi pugna placet.
    Deliciis mediis lites agitare recuses;
        arma tibi campus, mensa ministret olus.

g.   Si tibi magnanimus rigida virtute videris,
        secure ad calices fortia bella refers.
    Qui venit huc nostrae dapes cognoscere mensae,
        commendet positos gratia sola cibos.

c. Though a sober concern for eloquence wearies your mind, when you come here, poet, mix in some sportive play, yet in such a way that your respectable speech observes due measure, for careless words are accustomed to lead to violence.

d. The life of man is brief, the present world flees; cultivate rather what will not pass away. Establish justice, sow peace, and love Christ, seek the choice food that you may enjoy forever.

e. Now that all your business is over, banish the brawls of the palace; a generous table bids you live pleasurably. Let lawsuits, anger, and wrangling be silent, so too courts, disputes, and the law; here let peace prevail, the gift of this benevolent day.

f. You whom I invite, bring a peaceful frame of mind to the dinner; look elsewhere for an enemy, if fighting is what you like. In the middle of delicacies refuse to stir up disputes; let the battlefield equip you with weapons, the table with greens.

g. If you seem to yourself heroic, of courage invincible, here you can speak over cups of bold wars at your ease. When anyone comes here to try the fare of my table, let goodwill alone win favor for the food that is served.

25

Ad Galactorium comitem

Saepius optaram fieri me remige nauta,
  cursibus undifragis ut ratis iret aquis,
flatibus aut rapidis per dorsa Garonnica ferrer,
  Burdigalense petens ut celer actus iter,
5 velaque fluctivagum traherent Aquilone secundo,
  me quoque litoreo redderet aura sinu
qua pius antistes sacra Gundegisilus offert,
  culmine pro populi qui micat ara Dei;
tu quoque quo resides meritis, comes, ample serenis,
10 care Galactori, sedula cura mihi,
cui rite excellens rex Gunthechramnus honores
  maius adhuc debet, qui tibi magna dedit.
Cum tamen hoc vellem, timor obstitit et Himus ille
  qui cumulo rapidae mons fremit albus aquae.
15 Dulcedo invitat civilis et unda repugnat;
  sic vocat atque vetat hinc amor, inde pavor.
Plane hoc quod superest solvat vel epistula currens:
  littera, quod facerem, reddat amore vicem.
Maxime nunc igitur te, dulcis amice, saluto,
20 sperans a Domino te superesse diu,
cumque domo, sociis, antistite, coniuge, natis
  vive, comes, cui sint iura regenda ducis.

25

To Count Galactorius

Often I wished to be a sailor with myself at the oar, so my
boat would move on the waters, breasting the waves in its
course, or I would be carried by whirling winds on the cur-
rent of the Garonne to swiftly pursue my journey, heading
for Bordeaux, and sails would carry me with a favorable 5
wind afloat on waters and a breeze bring me to the curving
strand where the pious bishop Gundegisel makes his holy
offerings, who for the glory of his people shines as an altar of
God. You too, count, reside there, rich in your tranquil des-
erts, my dear Galactorius, object of my attentive devotion, 10
to whom rightly the excellent king Guntram owes still
greater honors, who has greatly honored you already. Yet
however much I wanted to come, fear checked me and that
Himalayan obstacle, the white mountain of swirling water
that roars in swelling peaks. Your sweet hospitality bids me 15
come, the wave bids me stay; so invite and deter me love and
timidity. Let a letter, at least, hurry to pay in full the debt
that remains; let my writing lovingly substitute for the ac-
tions I would have performed. Now, therefore, I greet you
especially, my sweet friend, hoping that by the will of the 20
Lord you live a long time, in the company of your house-
hold, friends, bishop, wife, and children, presently as count,
but soon with the rank of duke. May I be recommended to

Pontifici summo commender, opime, precatu,
    sic tua pars meritis sit data dextra polis.
25 Si superest aliquid quod forte tributa redundent:
    qui modo mitto apices, te rogo mitte pices.

the highest prelate, noble one, by your prayers, as for your merits may you equally be granted the right-hand side in heaven as your own.

If anything is left over from the abundant taxes you re- 25
ceive, please send pitch in return for the epistle I send.

BOOK EIGHT

I

Ex nomine suo ad diversos

Aonias avido qui lambitis ore Camenas
    Castaliusque quibus sumitur aure liquor,
quos bene fruge sua Demosthenis horrea ditant,
    largus et irriguis implet Homerus aquis;
5 fercula sive quibus fert dives uterque minister,
    Tullius ore cibum, pocula fonte Maro;
vos quoque qui numquam morituras carpitis escas,
    quos paradisiaco germine Christus alit,
facundo tonitru penetrati qui retinentur
10   nunc monitis Pauli, postea clave Petri,
Fortunatus ego hinc humili prece, voce saluto
    (Italiae genitum Gallica rura tenent).
Pictavis residens, qua sanctus Hilarius olim
    natus in urbe fuit, notus in orbe pater.
15 Eloquii currente rota penetravit ad Indos
    ingeniumque potens ultima Thyle colit,
perfundens cunctas vice solis nomine terras,
    cuius dona favens Persa, Britannus habet.
Christicolo Scythicas laxavit amore pruinas;
20   dogmate ferventi frigida corda calent.
Martinum cupiens voto Radegundis adhaesi,
    quam genuit caelo terra Thoringa sacro,

I

In his name to various people

You who drink in the Boeotian Muses with greedy mouth and whose ears absorb the waters of Castalia, whom the granaries of Demosthenes happily enrich with their harvest and copious Homer satisfies with his flowing streams; or you to whom two rich attendants serve up their offerings, Cicero food with his speech, Virgil drinks from his spring; you too who dine on food that is never to perish, whom Christ nourishes with the produce of paradise, who enraptured by thundering eloquence now are constrained by the precepts of Paul, but hereafter will be by the key of Peter, I Fortunatus send you greetings with humble prayer and voice (the land of Gaul is my home, though a son of Italy). I live in Poitiers, a city where once the saintly Hilary was born, though famed as a father throughout the world. On the rolling wheel of his eloquence he reached all the way to India and far-distant Thule reveres the powers of his intellect. With his name he spread abroad over every country like the sun, and Persian and Briton received his gifts with rejoicing. He melted Scythian frosts with his love for Christ; with the heat of his teaching chill hearts grew warm.

Eager for Martin I have attached myself to the wishes of Radegund, whom the land of Thuringia gave birth to under

491

germine regali pia neptis Herminefredi,
    cui de fratre patris Hamalafredus adest.
25 Mens ornata bonis fugitivos sprevit honores,
    sciens in solo firma manere Deo.
Regia lactineo commutans pallia cultu,
    vilior ancillae vestis amata tegit.
Splendida serraco quondam subvecta superbo,
30   nunc terit obsequio planta modesta lutum.
Quae prius insertis onerata est dextra zmaragdis
    servit inops famulis sedulitate suis.
Aulae celsa regens quondam, modo iussa ministrat;
    quae dominando prius, nunc famulando placet.
35 Paupertate potens et solo libera voto,
    clarius abiecto stat radiata loco.
Aurea fulcra tenens, iam tum sibi vilis honore,
    effugit extructum pulvere fusa torum.
Si contemnatur, tunc nobilis esse fatetur,
40   et putat esse minor, si datur ullus honor.
Parca cibo Eustochium superans, abstemia Paulam,
    vulnera quo curet dux Fabiola monet;
Melaniam studio reparans, pietate Blesillam,
    Marcellam votis aequiperare valens,
45 obsequio Martham renovat lacrimisque Mariam,
    pervigil Eugeniam, vult patiendo Theclam.
Sensibus ista gerit quidquid laudatur in illis;
    signa recognosco quae prius acta lego.
Omnia despiciens et adhuc in corpore constans,
50   spiritus hic vivit, sed caro functa iacet.
Terram habitans caelos intrat bene libera sensu
    atque homines inter iam super astra petit.
Cuius sunt epulae quidquid pia regula pangit,
    quidquid Gregorius Basiliusque docent,

blessed skies, of royal stock, devoted niece of Herminfred, whose cousin on her father's side is Amalfred. Her mind resplendent with virtues scorned fugitive glory, knowing how to remain firmly founded only on God. Exchanging her royal robes for a milk-white costume, she took on with pleasure a serving maid's humble attire. Once she traveled in style on a splendid carriage, but now her humble foot treads submissively on mud. The hand that in the past was laden with a setting of emeralds, stripped of its riches, attentively serves her own servants. She once ruled over the glories of the palace, now she follows orders; in the past her governance won favor, now her ministrations do. Empowered by her poverty and free only in her devotion, she enjoys a more brilliant status because of her lowly position. Her bedpost was golden, but she already then scorned its value, and flung herself in the dust to escape her heaped couch. If she is slighted, then she lays claim to nobility, and thinks herself diminished if she is paid any regard. In her frugal diet she surpasses Eustochium and in her self-restraint Paula; Fabiola sets an example of how to cure wounds. Mimicking Melania in her zeal and Blesilla in her piety, becoming the equal of Marcella in her prayers, she is a new Martha in her devotion and a new Mary with her tears, seeking to be a Eugenia in her vigils, a Thecla in her endurance. In her feelings she displays what won praise in them; I recognize the evidence of what I read was performed in the past. Scorning all things, though still existing in the body, her spirit lives here, but her flesh is dead and buried. Though residing on earth, she freely enters heaven with her senses, and while still among men already is on her way to the stars. Her banquet is whatever the holy canon prescribes: whatever Gregory and

55   acer Athanasius, quod lenis Hilarius edunt,
      quos causae socios lux tenet una duos,
   quod tonat Ambrosius, Hieronymus atque coruscat,
      sive Augustinus fonte fluente rigat,
   Sedulius dulcis, quod Orosius edit acutus:
60   regula Caesarii linea nata sibi est.
   His alitur ieiuna cibis, palpata nec umquam
      fit caro, sit nisi iam spiritus ante satur.
   Cetera nunc taceam, melius quia teste Tonante
      iudicioque Dei glorificanda manent.
65   Cui sua quisque potest sanctorum carmina vatum
      mittat in exiguis munera larga libris.
   Se putet inde Dei dotare manentia templa
      quisquis ei votis scripta beata ferat.
   Haec quoque qui legitis, rogo, reddite verba salutis,
70   nam mihi charta levis pondus amoris erit.

2

De itinere suo, cum ad domnum Germanum ire deberet et a domna Radegunde teneretur

Emicat ecce dies, nobis iter instat agendum;
   debita persolvens emicat ecce dies.
Me vocat inde pater radians Germanus in orbe;
   hinc retinet mater, me vocat inde pater.

Basil teach, the writings of fierce Athanasius and gentle Hilary, whom a single light holds as twin allies in the cause, the thunder of Ambrose and Jerome's lightning flash, the flowing spring of Augustine's abundant waters, the words of sweet Sedulius and incisive Orosius. The rule of Caesarius is her guide of conduct. These are the foods she feeds on when hungry; her flesh is never indulged until her spirit is already full first. 55 60

Let me keep silent now about her other virtues, because through the witness of the Lord and the judgment of God greater glory awaits them. Let all sacred poets, who can, send their verses, a generous offering, however slim the books; let all who send her holy writings as she wishes believe that in so doing they enrich an enduring temple of God. You who read this, I beseech, send also words of greeting in return; for me a page, however slight, will bear a heavy burden of love. 65 70

2

On his journey, when he was to travel to
Lord Germanus but was being held back
by Lady Radegund

Behold, the day shines out when I must go on a journey; paying a debt that is due, behold, the day shines out. There my father summons me, Germanus brilliant in the world; here my mother holds me back, there my father summons

5   Dulcis uterque mihi voto amplectente cohaesit,
      plenus amore Dei, dulcis uterque mihi.
   Carior haec animo, quamquam sit et ille beato;
      clarior ille gradu, carior haec animo.
   Mens tenet una duos aequali calce viantes;
10   ad pia tendentes mens tenet una duos.
   Proficit alterutro quidquid bene gesserit alter;
      unius omne bonum proficit alterutro.
   Sunt quia corde pares, iussus non ire recuso:
      obsequar ambobus, sunt quia corde pares.
15   Nec tamen hinc abeo, quamvis nova tecta videbo;
      corpore discedo nec tamen hinc abeo.
   Hic ego totus ero nec corde ac mente revellor;
      sic quoque dum redeo, hic ego totus ero.
   Porrigat arma mihi caelestia mater eunti:
20   ut sibi plus habeat, porrigat arma mihi.

3

In nomine domini nostri Iesu Christi et domnae Mariae matris eius de virginitate

   Culmina multa polos radianti lumine complent
      laetanturque piis agmina sancta choris.
   Carmine Davitico plaudentia bracchia texunt
      creditur et sacro tripudiare gradu.
5   Coetibus angelicis hominum sociata propago

me. Each is sweet to me and clings in an eager embrace, 5
filled by the love of God, each is sweet to me. She is dearer
to my soul, though to my happiness he too is dear; he is more
distinguished in status, she is dearer to my soul. One intent
possesses them both as they journey with equal step; di- 10
rected toward acts of holiness, one intent possesses them
both. Each derives benefit from every good deed of the
other; from every good action of one of them each derives
benefit. Because they are equal in heart, I do not refuse to
go as ordered; I will obey them both, because they are equal
in heart. Yet I do not leave here, though I will see fresh vis- 15
tas; I will depart in body, yet I do not leave here. I will be
entirely here, not separated in heart or mind; so too when I
return, I will be entirely here. May my mother provide me
with weapons of heaven for my journey; to secure them for 20
herself may she provide weapons for me.

3

In the name of our Lord Jesus Christ and the lady Mary his mother, on virginity

Many great figures fill the heavens with brilliant light, and
their sacred ranks rejoice in holy choirs. They entwine their
arms as they clap to the songs of David, and dance, it is
believed, with holy step. The human race in concert with 5

reddit honorificum laudis amore sonum:
Alternis vicibus divina poemata psallunt
    atque creatori mystica verba canunt.
Lucida sidereo caeli strepit aula tumultu
10   laudibus et Domini concutit astra fragor.
Hinc patriarcharum resonant modulamina vocum,
    inter quos Abrahae est maxima palma fide.
A quo acceperunt, reddunt dehinc verba prophetae,
    Moyses ante alios, dux mare teste, viros.
15 Inde favent fratres et celsa caterva piorum,
    lumen apostolicum praemeditante Petro,
qui valet ex meritis cineres animare sepultos
    et revocare diem voce iubente potest.
Hinc mercede pari sequitur pius ordo senatum,
20   in quibus est Stephanus victor honore prior,
quos saxis gladiisque, fame, site, frigore, flammis
    ereptos terris iungit in astra fides.
Casibus heu variis quos sic tulit ira furentis,
    etsi mors dispar, lux tamen una tenet.
25 Inde dei genetrix pia virgo Maria coruscat,
    virgineoque agni de grege ducit oves.
Ipsa puellari medio circumdata coetu
    luce pudicitiae splendida castra trahit.
Per paradisiacas epulas sua vota canentes,
30   ista legit violas, carpit et illa rosas.
Pratorum gemmas ac lilia pollice rumpunt
    et quod odoratum est flore comante metunt.
Euphemia illic, pariter quoque plaudit Agathe
    et Iustina simul consociante Thecla.
35 Hic Paulina, Agnes, Basilissa, Eugenia regnant

the company of angels lovingly offers up a glorious sound of
praise. Turn and turnabout they chant holy psalms and sing
mystical words to the Creator. The bright halls of heaven re-
sound with celestial clamor and the swell shakes the stars   10
with the praise of the Lord. On one side the harmonious
voices of the patriarchs ring out, among whom the supreme
palm goes to Abraham for his faith. The prophets render
to God the speech they received from him, and most of all
Moses, to whose leadership the sea bears witness. From an-   15
other side the brothers and sublime throng of the holy join
the praise, with Peter who set the pattern for the illumina-
tion brought by the apostles, who was able to resuscitate
the buried dead by his virtues and to bring back the light of
day by the bidding of his voice. Here holy ranks follow the
heavenly senate, sharing an equal reward, among whom is   20
Stephen, first to be honored as victor. These are they who
by stones, swords, hunger, thirst, cold, and flames were
snatched from the earth but united by faith in the stars. By
various fates, alas, the anger of a frenzied persecutor carried
them off, but though their deaths were dissimilar, yet one
light encompasses them all. Then the mother of God, the   25
holy virgin Mary, shines brightly and leads the sheep from
the virginal flock of the lamb. She herself, surrounded by
a company of maidens around her, heads a host that is radi-
ant with chastity's light. Hymning their marriages among
the banquets of paradise, one gathers violets, another picks   30
roses. They pluck with their thumbs the jewels of the mead-
ows and lilies, and harvest what is scented with full-petaled
flower. There Euphemia along with Agatha joins in the cele-
bration, and Justina, with Thecla to accompany her. Here   35
reign Paulina, Agnes, Basilissa, and Eugenia, and all whom

et quascumque sacer vexit ad astra pudor.
Felices quarum Christi contingit amore
    vivere perpetuo nomina fixa libro!
Has inter comites coniuncta Casaria fulget,
40   temporibus nostris Arelatense decus,
Caesarii monitis luci sociata perenni,
    si non martyrii, virginitatis ope.
Quos Liliola refert aequatis moribus ambos
    et claram heredem proxima palma manet
45 et quaecumque suos vigilans meditabitur actus,
    his erit egregio participanda gradu.
Concipiente fide Christi Radegundis amore
    Caesarii lambit regula quidquid habet,
cuius pontificis refluentia pectore mella
50   colligit et rivos insatiata bibit.
Quantum fonte trahit, tantum sitis addita crescit,
    et de rore Dei plus madefacta calet.
Nec sibi, sed cunctis generaliter unica vivens
    felix angustam pandit ad astra viam.
55 Sed tibi prae reliquis, mater pia, carior instat,
    te legit excelso consociare choro.
Res probat ipsa tamen, quoniam quae filia constas
    te matrem votis optat habere suam,
quamque suis genibus caram nutrivit alumnam
60   praeficit ecce suo constituendo loco,
et quae te semper baculi moderamine rexit
    prompta sub imperio vult magis esse tuo.
Proficit illa sibi, cum tu praeponeris illi;
    illa subit votum te potiente gradu.
65 Ecce diem festum tandem pietate Tonantis,
    quam precibus genetrix saepe rogabat, habet.

their holy chastity has raised to the stars. Happy are they who have won the right through the love of Christ to have their names inscribed in the eternal book! Among these companions as one of them Caesaria shines brightly, the glory of Arles in our own time. Through the precepts of Caesarius she enjoys perpetual light, by virtue of virginity, if not of martyrdom. Liliola in like conduct brings both of them to mind, and a similar palm awaits her, their glorious heir. Whatever woman attentively imitates their actions will share with the two of them their lofty status. With the receptiveness of faith, impelled by the love of Christ, Radegund laps up whatever the rule of Caesarius contains, she collects the honey that flows from the breast of that bishop and drinks the streams of his eloquence without being filled. The more she draws from that spring, the more her thirst intensifies and grows, and she becomes more ardent as she is moistened by God's dew. Though one person, she lives not for herself but in common for all, and happily reveals the narrow way to the stars.

But for you above all, reverent mother, she feels special affection, you she chooses to associate with her exalted band. The proof is in her actions, for though you are her daughter, she eagerly wishes to have you as her mother and the dear foster-child she brought up at her knees here she gives precedence to, establishing her in her position; she who always directed you with her guiding staff would rather of her own accord be under your command. She advances herself when you are given preference to her; she achieves her desire when you acquire status.

Behold at last the mother, thanks to the goodness of the Lord, now enjoys the happy day she often sought in her

Cuius respirant tacito praecordia pulsu
    angustosque animos gaudia larga replent.
Expectata nimis oculos ad tempora tendens,
70   semine laetitiae dona superna metit.
Optat adhuc supplex unum quod restat honoris,
    ut placeas Christo consocianda polo.
Qualiter haec capias labor esse videtur agentis,
    sed labor iste brevis fruge replendus erit.
75 Servitio Domini subdenda est ad iuga cervix,
    nec grave sed leve fit quidquid amore feres.
Non aliunde petas, in matre exempla require;
    aspicis ante oculos quod mediteris opus.
Cum qua festinas simul esse in luce perenni,
80   condecet hic simili currere lege viam.
Sit tibi dulce decus veneranda Casaria praesens,
    praesule Caesario non caritura tuo.
Illos corde sequens mandataque corpore conplens,
    ut teneas flores, has imiteris apes.
85 Respice qui voluit nasci se ventre puellae,
    et Domini summi qua caro carne venit:
Spiritus intactum venerabilis adtigit alvum,
    virgineam cupiens inhabitare domum,
hanc Deus ingrediens hominis quae nesciit usum,
90   sola suo nato conscia virgo viro.
Concipiente fide nullo se semine lusit,
    et quo factus homo est non fuit alter homo.
Virginitas felix quae partu est digna Tonantis,
    quae meruit dominum progenerare suum!
95 Templa Creatoris sunt membra pudica puellae
    et habitat proprius tale cubile Deus.
Quantum sponsa potest de virginitate placere,

prayers. Her heart thrills with an unheard beat, and abundant joys fill the confines of her spirit. Directing her gaze to the occasion so greatly anticipated, she reaps gifts from above from the seeds of her happiness. Still she begs as a suppliant for one last distinction, that you win Christ's favor to join him in heaven. To achieve this needs the effort of your agency, but that brief effort will be met with ample reward. Your neck should submit in service to the yoke of the Lord; a burden borne with love becomes not heavy but light. 75

Look no further, but take your example from your mother; you see before your eyes a regimen to imitate. It is fitting that you follow here a course on the same pattern she does, with whom you hasten to be together in eternal light. Let revered Caesaria be by your side, your sweet glory, accompanied by Caesarius, your protector. Following them in your heart and fulfilling their instructions with your body, to secure flowers you should imitate these bees. Consider who was willing to be born from the belly of a maiden, and from what flesh the flesh of the highest Lord came forth. The Holy Spirit made its way into an unsullied womb, desiring to occupy a virginal dwelling. God entered one who knew nothing of human unions, a solitary maiden who knew a man only in the birth of her son. It was faith that conceived, she trifled with no impregnation, and it was not by another man that a man was born. 80 85 90

Happy is the virginity found worthy of giving birth to the Lord, that won the right to bring forth its own master! The chaste body of a girl is the temple of the Creator, and God occupies such a bed as his own. How great is the preferment a bride can win for her virginity from him who preferred as 95

ipsa cui genetrix non nisi virgo placet?
Sarra, Rebecca, Rachel, Hester, Iudith, Anna, Noemi
100   quamvis praecipue culmen ad astra levent,
nulla tamen meruit mundi generare parentem:
    quae Dominum peperit, clausa Maria manet.
Intemerata Deum suspendit ad ubera natum
    et panem caeli munere lactis alit.
105 Hoc ergo in sponsae nunc viscera diligit ipse
    quod prius in matrem legit honore sacer.
Pectora liberius penetrat sibi cognita soli
    et quo nemo fuit laetior intrat iter,
haec sua membra putans quae nulla iniuria fuscat,
110   quae neque sunt alio participata viro.
Mitis in affectu pectus complectitur illud,
    promptus amore colens quo alter amator abest.
Cum sua regna Deus pariter velit omnibus esse,
    hoc commune tamen Christus habere fugit.
115 Per paradisiacas epulas cupit esse coheres;
    virgineam solus vult habitare domum.
Castra pudicitiae melius rex ipse tuetur,
    si sibi non violet turba dicata fidem;
ipse voluntatem si viderit esse fidelem,
120   proque suis famulis et Deus arma tenet.
Lorica, clipeo, galea praemunit amantem
    et stabilit solidum montis in arce gradum.
Ballista iaculans pro te mox exit in hostem,
    perdat ut adversos qui tibi bella movent.
125 Currit ad amplexus post proelia gesta triumphans,
    infigens labiis oscula casta sacris.
Blanditur, refovet, veneratur, honorat, obumbrat,
    et locat in thalamo membra pudica suo.
Siderei proceres, ad regia vota frequentes,

his mother none but a virgin? Sarah, Rebecca, Rachel, Esther, Judith, Anna, and Naomi, although they are elevated in their eminence to the stars, yet none deserved to bring to birth the father of the world. Mary, who gave birth to the Lord, remained a closed vessel. Unsullied she held at her breasts God, her son, and fed the bread of heaven with the gift of her milk.

Now therefore he loves in the body of his bride what previously in his holiness he chose to honor in his mother. He freely penetrates the heart known to him alone, and more gladly enters where no one has been before, thinking this to be his body which no taint darkens, which has not been shared with any other man. Gentle in his devotion he embraces that breast, quick in his loving attention when there is no second lover. Though God wants his kingdom to be equally available to everybody, yet this favor Christ resists maintaining in common. In the banquets of paradise he desires to share the inheritance, but he wants to occupy the dwelling of virgins alone. The king himself best protects the camp of chastity, if the ranks devoted to him do not break faith; if he sees that their sentiments are loyal, God himself takes up arms for his servants. With breastplate, shield, and helmet he comes to the defense of his devotee, and makes firm her step on the height of the mountain. With a ballista shot he quickly fires at the enemy to protect you and to destroy the opponents who wage war on you. He runs to your embrace in triumph after the battle is over, pressing chaste kisses on your holy lips. He soothes and caresses, adores, honors, and shelters you, and places your chaste body in his own bridal chamber.

The aristocracy of heaven, thronging to the royal mar-

130   certatim veniunt adglomerando chorum.
Quo praeter Cherubin, Seraphin reliquosque beatos
    aligeros comites, quos tegit umbra Dei,
bis duodena senum concursat gloria vatum,
    attonito sensu plaudere voce, manu.
135 His venit Helias, illis in curribus Enoch,
    et nati dono virgo Maria prior.
Iurisconsulti Pauli comitante volatu
    princeps Romana currit ab arce Petrus.
Conveniunt ad festa simul sua dona ferentes
140   hi quorum cineres urbs caput orbis habet.
Culmen apostolicum radianti luce coruscum
    nobilis Andream mittit Achaia suum.
Praecipuum meritis Ephesus veneranda Iohannem
    dirigit et Iacobos terra beata sacros,
145 laeta suis votis Hierapolis alma Phillipum,
    producens Thomam munus Edessa pium.
Inde triumphantem fert India Bartolomaeum,
    Matthaeum eximium Naddaver alta virum.
Hinc Simonem ac Iudam lumen Persida gemellum
150   laeta relaxato mittit ad astra sinu,
et sine rore ferax Aegyptus torrida Marcum,
    Lucae euangelica participante tuba.
Africa Cyprianum, dat Siscia clara Quirinum;
    Vincenti Hispana surgit ab arce decus.
155 Egregium Albanum fecunda Brittannia profert,
    Massilia Victor martyr ab urbe venit.
Porrigit ipsa decens Arelas pia dona Genesi,
    astris Caesario concomitante suo.
Ipse Parisiaca properat Dionysius urbe;
160   Augustiduno, Symphoriane, venis.

riage, eagerly assemble to join their numbers to the choir. 130
There in addition to the Cherubim, the Seraphim, and the
other blessed winged attendants, whom the shade of God
protects, the twice-twelve ancient prophets in their glory
hasten together, their spirits roused, to rejoice with voice
and hand. Elijah comes on one chariot, Enoch on another, 135
and by the gift of her son the virgin Mary takes precedence.
With Paul, the expert in the law, accompanying him on
his journey, the princely Peter hurries from the citadel of
Rome. Those whose ashes the city that heads the world pos-
sesses assemble for the festivities, bearing their gifts. Noble 140
Achaea dispatches its own Andrew, an eminent apostle, glit-
tering with brilliant light. Venerable Ephesus sends John,
distinguished by his merits, and the holy land two saintly
men named James, generous Hierapolis with joyful wishes 145
deputes Philip, and Edessa Thomas as its devoted gift. Next
India contributes triumphant Bartholomew, and lofty Nad-
aber that great man Matthew, while Persia sends Simon and
Jude, its twin lights, to the stars, happily unclasping its em- 150
brace, and scorching Egypt, fertile without raindrops, sends
Mark, in company with Luke, whose trumpet is the gospel.
Africa offers Cyprian, famed Siscia Quirinus, the glory of
Vincent ascends from the fastnesses of Spain. Fertile Britain 155
advances noble Alban, the martyr Victor comes from the
city of Marseille. Fair Arles provides as its holy offering
Genesius, whom its Caesarius accompanies to the stars. Di-
onysius hastens from the city of Paris; from Autun you, 160

Privatum Gabalus, Iulianum Arvernus abundans,
    Ferreolum pariter pulchra Vienna gerit.
Hinc simul Hilarium, Martinum Gallia mittit,
    te quoque, Laurenti, Roma, beata mihi.
165 Felicem meritis Vicetia laeta refundit
    et Fortunatum fert Aquileia suum,
Vitalem ac reliquos quos cara Ravenna sepultat,
    Gervasium, Ambrosium, Mediolane, meum.
Iustinam Patavi, Euphemiam huc Calchedon offert,
170   Eulalia Emerita tollit ab urbe caput.
Caeciliam Sicula profert, Seleucia Theclam;
    et legio felix Agaunensis adest.
Europae atque Asiae quis lumina tanta recurrat
    vel tua quis possit pignora, Roma, loqui?
175 Undique collectos diversis partibus orbis
    agminibus iunctis regia pompa trahit.
Intrant sidereo vernantes lumine portas;
    excipit hos proceres urbs patefacta poli.
Incedit sensim tum praetextata potestas
180   ordine, patricio sic potitura loco.
Nobilitas caeli, dives cruce, sanguine Christi,
    festinat festos concelebrare toros.
Paupertas terrae censu caeleste redundans
    consulibus tantis regia vota colit.
185 Undique distincte numerosa sedilia complent
    attonitique silent rege loquente patres.
Maiestas arcana Dei tum pondere fixo
    alloquitur proceres quos sua dextra regit:
"Haec mihi pollicitum servavit virgo pudorem
190   nec voluit placitam dilacerare fidem:
Sollicitis animis sponsi vestigia sectans

Symphorian, come. Javols contributes Privatus, the rich Auvergne Julian, and beautiful Vienne Ferreolus to their company. At the same time from here Gaul sends Hilary and Martin, and Rome, blessed in my eyes, dispatches you too, Lawrence. Joyful Vicenza submits Felix, fortunate in his merits, and Aquileia brings forth its own Fortunatus, Ravenna, dear to me, Vitalis and all the others there buried, and you, Milan, my Gervasius and my Ambrose. Padua's offering is Justina and Chalcedon's Euphemia; Eulalia raises her head from the city of Mérida. Sicily presents Cecilia, Seleucia Thecla, and the happy legion of Agaune joins up too. Who could enumerate so many bright lights of Europe and Asia, or who could recount your patrons, Rome? Gathered from every side, from various regions of the world, they progress in serried ranks with regal splendor. They enter gates that gleam with starry light; the city of heaven lies open and receives this nobility. Then gradually in robes of state the powerful company advances, observing due order, to occupy its place as patricians. The nobility of heaven, rich in the cross and blood of Christ, hastens to celebrate the joyful wedding. The poor on earth, now enriched by the wealth of heaven, pay honor to the royal marriage before so many consuls.

Spaced out on every side the fathers occupy the numerous seats, and are silent as their king begins to speak. Then the mysterious majesty of God with stern gravity addresses the nobles whom his right hand sways: "This virgin has preserved for me her chastity as promised and has shown no desire to break the pledge she undertook. With an anxious heart she has followed the steps of her bridegroom, and she

et mea vota petens inviolata venit.
Per tribulos gradiens spinae cavefecit acumen.
 sentibus in mediis nescia ferre vepres.
195 Vipera, serps, iaculus, basiliscus, emorrois, aspis
 faucibus horrificis sibila torsit iners.
Inde sagitta volans, hinc terruit arcus euntem,
 docta sed insidiis cautius ire suis.
Inter tot hostes nulli se subdidit insons;
200 vulnera suscepit, sed tolerando fugit.
Per tela et gladios tenuit mora nulla sequentem,
 sed tam dura nimis non nisi ferret amor.
Ad me aures, oculos, animos suspensa tetendit;
 cum terris iacuit, iam super astra fuit.
205 Singultus, gemitus, curas, suspiria, fletus
 saepius audivi non abolenda mihi.
Abscondens aliis, nulli confessa dolores
 intellecta mihi murmura clausa dedit.
Vidit forte meum quotiens in imagine vultum,
210 oscula dans labiis, lumine fudit aquas.
Pervigil incubuit, si forte alicunde venirem,
 marmore iam tepido frigida membra premens.
Haec gelifacta meum servavit in ossibus ignem;
 visceribus rigidis pectus amore calet.
215 Corpore despecto recubabat in aggere nudo,
 seque oblita iacens me memor ipsa fuit.
Fletibus adsiduis exhausto humore genarum
 siccatis oculis terra natabat aquis,
et quia me vivens carnali lumine quondam
220 cernere non potuit, misit amata precem.
Nam mihi sollicito nocturnis saepius horis
 scripta suis lacrimis pagina lecta fuit,

comes unsullied to seek marriage with me. She has walked upon burs but avoided the stick of the thorns; in the midst of brambles she could not feel the pricking. Viper, serpent, 195 tree snake, basilisk, hemorrois, and asp from their fearful jaws aimed their hisses in vain. Here the flight of an arrow, there a bow daunted her on her journey; schooled by their assaults she learned to travel with care. Among so many enemies in her innocence she succumbed to no one; she re- 200 ceived wounds, but endured them and escaped. Despite weapons and sword blows no delay kept her from following me; only love could endure such extreme suffering. In expectancy she directed her hearing, gaze, thoughts toward me; when she lay prostrate on the earth, she was already beyond the stars. Her sobs and groans, woes, sighs, and tears I 205 often heard, though I could not dispel them. Hiding her grief from others, confessing them to no one, she shared her troubles in secret, perceived by me alone. Whenever she happened to see my face in an image, she kissed it with her 210 lips, shed tears upon it from her eyes. She lay wide awake through the night in case I should happen to come, pressing her chilled limbs to the marble, which then took on warmth. Though she was ice-cold she retained her ardor for me in her bones; her heart was warm with love, though her flesh was frozen stiff. Scorning her body she stretched out on the 215 bare ground, forgetful of herself where she lay, but mindful of me. By her continual weeping the moisture on her cheeks was exhausted, and her eyes became dry, while the earth was awash with her tears, and because she could not see me with the eyes of the flesh while still alive, in her devotion she of- 220 fered a prayer. For often during the hours of night in distress

plena quidem variis tremulo sermone querellis,
    quod sine me solo maesta iaceret humo.
225 Cuius ab ore fluens nativo gutta liquore
    haec dedit in tremulis signa relata notis:
'Strata solo recubo lacrimans neque cerno quod opto,
    tristis in amplexu pectore saxa premo.
Sponso absente manens tam dura cubilia servo
230   nec mea quem cupiunt membra tenere queunt.
Dic ubi sis quem exspecto gemens, qua te urbe requiram
    quave sequar, nullis femina nota locis.
Ipsa venire velim, properans si possit in astris
    pendula sideream planta tenere viam.
235 Nunc sine te fuscis graviter nox occupat alis
    ipsaque sole micans est mihi caeca dies.
Lilia, narcissus, violae, rosa, nardus, amomum,
    oblectant animos germina nulla meos.
Ut te conspiciam per singula nubila pendo
240   et vaga per nebulas lumina ducit amor.
Ecce procellosos suspecta interrogo ventos,
    quid mihi de domino nuntiet aura meo.
Proque tuis pedibus cupio caementa lavare,
    et tua templa mihi tergere crine libet.
245 Quidquid erit tolerem, sunt omnia dulcia dura;
    donec te videam, haec mihi poena placet.
Tu tamen esto memor, quoniam tua vota requiro;
    est mihi cura tui, sit tibi cura mei.'
Haec referens avidis iactabat brachia palmis,
250   si posset plantas forte tenere meas.
Cum decepta sibi sine me sua dextra rediret,
    luminis instillans ora lavabat aquis.
Cum recubaret humo neque victa sopore quievit,

I read a page that was written by her in her tears, one full of various laments in wavering language, because alone without me she lay grief-stricken on the ground. From her face there flowed drops of the tears she was shedding, which produced this message recorded in uncertain script: 'I lie weeping on the ground but do not see what I wish for; sadly with my embrace I press my breast on the stone. So hard is the bed that I keep in my bridegroom's absence, and my arms cannot grasp the one whom they desire. Tell me where you are whom in grief I await, in what city shall I seek you, or where shall I follow you, a woman unused to venturing abroad. If my feet had the power, I would readily come in haste to the stars, and suspended in air make a journey to heaven. As it is, without you night with its sable wings weighs heavy, and the day itself, though brightened by the sun, is dark for me. Lilies, narcissus, violets, rose, nard, and balsam, none of these plants bring delight to my heart. To catch sight of you I hang on every cloud, and love leads my eyes astray in the mist. See, I look up and question the storm-driven winds, asking what news the breeze brings of my lord. In place of your feet I desire to wash paving stones with my tears, and I take pleasure in wiping dry your shrines with my hair. Let me endure whatever happens, all sufferings to me are sweet; until I see you, this punishment gives me pleasure. But you be mindful of me, for I seek marriage with you; you are the object of my love, may I be the object of yours.' When she said this she threw open her arms and reached out eagerly, in an attempt to somehow grasp my feet. When her hand was disappointed and returned without me, she bathed her face with drops of water from her eyes. As she lay on the ground without surrender-

consuliturus ei saepe simul iacui,
255 condolui pariter, lacrimarum flumina tersi,
oscula dans rutilis mellificata favis.
Nunc igitur regnet placitoque fruatur amore,
quae mihi iam pridem pectore iuncta fuit."
Assensu fremit aula poli residente senatu.
260 Nomen perpetuo scribitur inde libro.
Traditur aeternum mansura in saecula censum;
virginis in thalamos fundit Olympus opes.
Inseritur capiti radians diadema beryllis,
ordinibus variis alba, zmaragdus inest.
265 Alligat et nitidos amethystina vitta capillos,
margaritato flexilis arte sinu.
Sardonyche inpressum per colla monile coruscat,
sardia purpurea luce metalla micant.
Dextrae armilla datur carcedone, iaspide mixta,
270 aut hyacintheo sudat honore manus.
Brattea gemmatam cycladem fila catenant,
sidereis donis arte sigilla tument.
Pulchra topaziacis oneratur zona lapillis,
chrysolitha aurata fibula claudit acu,
275 veste superposita bis cocto purpura bysso,
qualem nupta Deo ferre puella potest.
His cumulata bonis thalamo regina sedebit,
atque poli solem sub pede virgo premet.
Cui tamen hoc opus est cum virginitatis honore
280 ut placeat sponso mens moderata suo.
Inconcussa gravem teneat patientia vultum,
viribus ira suis ne labefacta ruat,
neu faciles animos ventosa procella fatiget;
fluctibus in mediis anchora cordis agat.

ing to sleep or getting rest, I often lay down with her to
bring her consolation, I shared her grief and I wiped away   255
the rivers of tears, giving her kisses as sweet as golden hon-
eycombs. So now let her reign and enjoy the love that she
longs for, this woman who for a long time now has been
united to me in heart."

The palace of heaven with the senate in session roars in
approval. Her name then is inscribed in the eternal book.   260
Everlasting riches are granted her for long centuries to
come; heaven pours its wealth into the virgin's bridal cham-
ber. On her head is set a diadem brilliant with beryls, along
with pearls and emeralds in multicolored rows. A band of   265
amethyst encircles her shining hair, skillfully curved and
ringed with pearls. On her neck a necklace studded with
sardonyx glistens, and precious sard glitters with a purple
light. Her hand wears a bracelet of chalcedony, mingled with
jasper, and sweats with the brilliance of hyacinth it bears.   270
Gold threads interlace her jeweled robe, and on heaven's
gifts figures cunningly stand out in relief. Her lovely girdle is
studded with topaz gemstones, a chrysolite brooch snaps
shut with a golden pin. On top is her dress, linen twice-dyed   275
in purple, as befits a girl to wear who is the bride of God.
Endowed with these treasures she will sit as queen in the
bridal chamber, and as virgin will tread beneath her feet the
sun in the heavens.

She is obliged also to possess, along with the glory of her
virginity, a well-attuned mind to win the favor of her spouse.   280
Let an unwavering patience preserve a sobriety of expres-
sion, so that anger not burst upon her, carried away by its
own strength, and a windblown storm not wear out her sus-
ceptible mind; let her heart act as anchor in the midst of the

285 Virtutum speciale decus patientia fulget.
     Qua gradiaris iter Iob tibi signa dabit.
    Quidve loquar humilem, quem gratia celsa decorat,
     et quantum ima petit, surgit ad alta magis?
    Quo diversa nimis divisa est causa duobus:
290   qui iacet ille subit, qui tumet ipse cadit.
    Haec exempla quidem Ioseph Faraoque dederunt:
     tollitur ille lacu, mergitur iste freto.
    Est etiam laudis stipendia poscere tantum
     ne premat ipsa suum pestis avara sinum.
295 Contentus minimis, si non maiora requirat,
     pauper in angusto regnat habendo Deum.
    Sapphira vel mulier geminos largita minutos,
     illa tenendo perit, haec sua dando manet.
    O nimium felix quem non modo mollia frangunt,
300   iudice qui sese membra labore terit!
    Spernit opum laqueos, unguenta, toreumata, fluxus,
     ut custos animae sit rigor ipse suae,
    hoc etiam recolens, quid possit parcior usus:
     sobrietas Iudith vincere sola facit.
305 Quidve animum dulcem memorem quem gratia pascit,
     cum intra se populos viscera cara ferant?
    Pacificus gaudens unus complectitur omnes,
     stringit in affectu pectora cuncta suo.
    O nimium felix, florens bonitate voluntas,
310   qua sine nil populo nec placet ara Deo!
    Hoc opus, ut quotiens aliquo mens fertur amaro,
     firmet in adversis spes comitata fidem.
    Aspera non frangant, tumidos neque prospera reddant;
     sic mediocre tenens cautius itur iter.

waves. Among the virtues patience shines with a special dis-   285
tinction. Job will give you the sign of the path you should
take. Why should I mention the humble man whom sub-
lime glory honors, and the more he seeks abasement, the
higher he rises? How very different is the situation in the
two cases: he who lies low mounts up, he who gives him-   290
self airs sinks down. Joseph and the Pharaoh have provided
an example of this: one is removed from a pit, the other
is drowned in the sea. The reward of praise can only rightly
be claimed provided that the plague of greed not oppress
one's breast. A person who is content with little, requiring   295
no greater possessions, though poor and deprived, has a
kingdom by the possession of God. Take Sapphira and the
woman who presented her two mites; one by holding back
perished, the other by giving what she had lived on. O
greatly happy he whom not only does luxury not enervate,
but who of his own accord wears out his body with toil! He   300
spurns the snares of wealth, perfumes, couches, and flow-
ing robes, so that austerity acts as the guardian of his soul,
bearing in mind what the practice of restraint can achieve:
her sobriety alone assured Judith of victory. Why should I   305
mention the sweet soul that charity nourishes, seeing that a
loving heart embraces in itself the people? The bringer of
peace, though one person, joyfully envelops all and binds to-
gether all hearts by his affection. O greatly happy is the dis-
position that abounds in kindness, without which he is an   310
altar that pleases neither people nor God! It is necessary
that whenever the mind encounters some hardship, hope
strengthens it in adversity in company with faith. Let trou-
bles not break it nor good times render it arrogant; by pur-

315 Haec bona sumit homo, tribuat si gratia Christi,
     inspirante illo vel moderante gradum.
His ornata bonis radiantia lumina fundis;
     has retinens gemmas tu quoque gemma micas.
Virginitas felix nullis aequanda loquellis,
320   nec si centenus suppleat ora sonus.
Quod prius est, sine sorde nitet venerabilis orbi,
     naturae proprium non vitiando bonum,
corporis inlaesum servans pretiosa talentum,
     perpetuas retinens nescia furis opes.
325 Non premit incluso torpentia viscera fetu
     aut gravefacta iacet pignore maesta suo.
Inter anhelantes animae seu corporis aestus
     in dubio pendens stamine fessa salus,
quando suis iaculis uteri laesura tumescit
330   atque voluptatis morbida crescit hydrus.
Ultra hominis habitum tantum cutis effera turget,
     ut pudeat matrem hoc quod amore gerit.
Se fugiens propriis verecunda parentibus aufert,
     donec depositum sarcina solvat onus.
335 Quis gemitum partus verbis aequare valebit
     aut cui tot lacrimas carmine flere vacet,
cum sua secretum compago relaxat onustum
     atque dolore gravi viscera fascis agit?
Victa puerperio membrorum porta fatiscit,
340   exit et ad lucem fors sine luce puer.
Si vivat genitus genetrix se oblita requirit
     tristis et ad natum lumina lassa trahit.
Respicit expositum, nec iam sua mater, alumnum;
     quae vix dum peperit, haec modo funus habet.

BOOK 8

suing a middle course in this way its path is secure. A man 315
possesses these virtues if the grace of Christ bestows them,
providing inspiration and guidance for the journey.

Adorned by these virtues you radiate brilliant light; pos-
sessing these jewels you too shine as a jewel. The happy state
of virginity cannot adequately be expressed in words, not 320
even if a hundred voices filled as many mouths. Most im-
portant of all, it shines without stain, revered by the world,
without corrupting the virtue that is inherent by nature;
precious it preserves the wealth of her body unharmed, and
retains those riches forever untouched by a thief. The virgin 325
does not oppress her flesh, enervated by the child within, or
lie heavy in pregnancy, grieved by her own offspring. Amid
the seething turmoil of mind and body, enfeebled health
hangs by an uncertain thread, when the womb is hurt by
its own darts and swells up and the sick dropsy of pleasure 330
grows larger in size. The skin is so extremely distended be-
yond the human frame that the mother is ashamed of what
she bears out of love. She flees and in shame removes her-
self from her parents, until her burden has released and laid
aside its load. Who can adequately express in words the 335
cries of childbirth, or who is able to weep so many tears
in verse, when the frame releases the hidden load it carried,
and the burden wracks the flesh with grievous pain? Suc-
cumbing to childbirth the gate of the body lies open, and 340
an infant comes out to the light perhaps without life. The
mother, forgetful of herself, asks if her son is alive, and sadly
turns her weary eyes to the child. She looks at her fosterling
laid out, no longer now his mother; she had such difficulty

345 Nec mater fructu meruit nec virgo vocari;
      haec duo damna dolens se male nupta gemit.
Non validos . . . spes rapta dolores,
      nec fletu nati se fovet illa sui.
Non caras lacrimas infantis ab ore resorbet
350   aut teneras voces lacte fluente rapit.
Tristis decrepito damnat sua viscera luctu:
      quo iacuit natus, heu, dolet ille sinus.
Quid si vita manet pueri nec semper habenda,
      incipiat teneros ut dare voce sonos,
355 inperfecta rudis conlidens murmura linguae,
      cum matrem dulci fauce susurrus alit,
contingatque nefas, rapiatur pectore matris?
      Aetas ad damnum crevit adulta suum.
Triste flagellatis genetrix orbata capillis
360   defuncti in labiis ubera sicca premit.
Infundens lacrimas lamenta resuscitat ardens
      et gelidum corpus fonte tepente lavat.
Dilacerat faciem, crinem aufert, pectora tundit;
      heu dolor armatus sic sua membra ferit.
365 Si videt alterius natum, sua pignora deflet
      aequalemque suum tristis obisse gemit.
Alter si ploret, currat, stet, gaudeat infans,
      ante oculos nati ludit imago sui.
Quem semel effudit, per cuncta momenta requirit
370   nec miserae matris pendet ad ora puer.
Quid si aliud gravius, moriatur ut ipse iugalis?
      Quae nova nupta fuit iam viduata iacet.
De thalamo ad tumulum, modo candida tam cito nigra,
      ante quibus caluit frigida membra tenet,

bearing him and now she has only a corpse. She was not en-   345
titled by her offspring to be called a mother nor yet a virgin;
bemoaning these two losses she mourns her unhappy mar-
riage. The snatching away of her hope did not . . . her strong
grief, nor did she comfort herself with the tears of her son.
She did not drink the sweet tears from the face of her child
or dispel his tender cries with the flow of her milk. Sadly   350
with feeble lament she denounces her womb; the breast on
which that baby lay is, alas, stricken with grief. But what if
the child survives, though not forever, to begin to make gen-
tle sounds with his voice, lisping halting utterances from   355
his unpracticed tongue, when the whispers from his sweet
throat nourish his mother—and then a tragedy should hap-
pen and he is snatched from his mother's breast? The in-
crease in years has only added to the loss. Sadly the bereaved
mother with disheveled hair presses her dry breast to the   360
lips of the dead child. In a flood of tears she passionately re-
vives her laments and washes the icy body with a warming
spring. She tears at her face, pulls out her hair, and beats her
breasts; alas, her grief takes up arms and assaults her body
in this way. If she sees another's child, she laments her own,   365
and bitterly grieves that his age-mate has died. Whether an-
other child cries, runs, stands still, or rejoices, the image of
her own son plays before her eyes. The child she once gave
birth to at every moment she misses and no child is intent   370
on the wretched mother's face. What if something still
worse should happen, her husband himself should die? Now
the newlywed is reduced to being a widow. From bridal
chamber to burial, her white so quickly changed to black,

375 construit exequias perversaque vota celebrans
  exornat tumulum, heu, spoliando torum.
Saepe maritalem repetit miserando sepulchrum
  contemptaque domo funus amata colit.
Incumbit tumulo solacia cassa requirens;
380   cuius membra prius, nunc super ossa premit.
Fletibus inriguis, perituro carmine luget;
  funeris obsequio lumina perdit amor.
Quot mala plebeiae veniant quis pandere possit?
  vix bene reginae quae viduata manet.
385 "Non veto coniugium, sed praefero virginis alvum,"
  quod dat apostolica Paulus ab ore tuba.
Inclita virginitas, caelos quae dote mereris,
  cum thalamis Christi consocianda places.
Funera nulla gemis, sine limite gaudia sumis;
390   vivit amor semper nec tibi Christus obit.
Illic regna tenes, hic vincis et integra fulges,
  omni tuta loco, sanctificata Deo.
Haec tibi, cara Deo, meritis venerabilis Agnes,
  offero: quo placeas, tu faciendo colas,
395 iudicis ut iussu munus tribuatur utrisque:
  quando corona tibi, tunc mihi vel venia.
Opto per hos fluctus animas tu, Christe, gubernes
  arbore et antemna velificante crucis,
ut post emensos mundani gurgitis aestus
400   in portum vitae nos tua dextra locet.

she holds the cold body that previously gave her warmth, ar- 375
ranges a funeral and celebrating the reverse of her wedding
vows, adorns a tomb, alas, with the spoils of her marriage
bed. She often returns to her husband's grave with her la-
ments, and avoiding her house lovingly honors the dead. She
falls on his grave in search of an empty consolation; in the 380
past she clung tight to his body, now she clings to his bones.
With floods of tears she mourns in an ineffectual refrain;
in paying respect to the dead her love destroys her vision.
Who can recount the evils that come to an ordinary woman,
when scarcely can those of a widowed queen be properly
recounted? "I do not forbid marriage, but I prefer a virgin's 385
womb";—these are the words of Paul from the apostolic
trumpet of his voice. Glorious virginity, who win heaven as a
marriage gift, you are honored to share the bridal chamber
of Christ. You mourn no deaths, you enjoy happiness with-
out end; your love lives forever, for you Christ does not die. 390
There you have a kingdom, here you win victory and shine
in your purity, everywhere secure and sanctified by God.

I offer these words to you, Agnes, dear to God and re-
vered for your virtues: to please him, honor him with your
actions so that by the command of the judge a reward be 395
given to us both: when you receive a crown, I will at least re-
ceive pardon. I ask that you guide our souls, Christ, through
these waves with the tree of the cross as a mast carrying
the sails, so that after navigating the swell of the sea of the
world, your right hand may bring us to the harbor of life. 400

4

Ad virgines

Inter apostolicas acies sacrosque prophetas
  proxima martyribus praemia virgo tenet.
Splendida sidereo circumdata lumine pergens
  iungitur angelicis casta puella choris.
5 Fruge pudicitiae caeli dotanda talento
  aeterni regis ducitur in thalamis.
Pulchra corona caput triplici diademate cingit
  et gemmae exornant pectora, colla, comam.
Induitur teneris superaddita purpura membris
10 et candore nivis fulgida palla tegit.
Floribus aeternis oculos rosa, lilia pascunt
  et paradisiacus naribus intrat odor.
Unde magis, dulcis, hortamur ut ista requiras
  quae dedit Eugeniae Christus et alma Theclae.
15 Virgo Dei, fructus caeli, victoria mundi,
  ut semper regnes, has pete regis opes.
Sunt ibi chrysolithis fabricata palatia gemmis
  atque zmaragdineo ianua poste viret.
Limina sardonychum variato lumine florent
20 et hyacintheus circuit ordo domum.
Aurea tecta micant, plebs aurea fulget in aula
  et cum rege pio turba corusca nitet.
Ille puellarum locus est, quae lucis amore
  hic servant Domino corpore, mente fidem.
25 Despice quod terrae est et clara sedebis in astris,

4

To virgins

Among the ranks of the apostles and the holy prophets, a virgin wins a reward akin to that of the martyrs. Advancing in her radiance, surrounded by starry light, a chaste maiden keeps company with the angelic choirs. To be endowed with 5 a heavenly talent as the prize for her chastity, she is led into the bridal chamber of the eternal king. A beautiful crown circles her head with a triple diadem, and jewels adorn her breast, neck, and hair. A purple fabric is added to clothe her delicate limbs, and covering all a mantle brilliant with the 10 whiteness of snow. Roses and lilies feast her eyes with their perpetual flowers, and the fragrance of paradise makes its way into her nostrils. For this reason, sweet one, we urge you to seek those delights that Christ generously gave to Eugenia and Thecla. As virgin of God, fruit of heaven, victory 15 over the world, seek these riches from the king so that you may reign forever. There is there a palace made from chrysolite gemstones, and the doors glow green with emerald doorposts. The thresholds bloom with the variegated brightness of sardonyx, and a band of hyacinth circles the 20 house. The roofs gleam golden, a golden company shines in the hall, and with their loving king a glittering throng beams bright. That place awaits maidens who, for love of the light, keep faith here with their Lord in body and mind. Scorn 25

Christi ut sponsa placens regna superna colas.
Praesens vita nimis fugitivo tempore transit,
    virginis integritas glorificanda manet.
Paupertas te parva rogat cum divite Christo
30   ut venias nostro dulcis alumna sinu,
    quo patris auxilium Domino obtentura preceris
    atque tibi caelis regna beata pares,
ut pariter sanctae merearis iuncta Mariae
    gaudia perpetuo concelebrare choro.
35 Has quaecumque piis manibus susceperis arras
    non nuptura homini, sed sis amata Dei.

5

Ad domnam Radegundem

Regali de stirpe potens Radegundis in orbe,
    altera cui caelis regna tenenda manent,
despiciens mundum meruisti adquirere Christum,
    et dum clausa lates, hinc super astra vides.
5 Gaudia terreni conculcas noxia regni,
    ut placeas regi laeta favente polo.
Nunc angusta tenes, quo caelos largior intres:
    diffundens lacrimas gaudia vera metes.
Et corpus crucias, animam ieiunia pascunt.
10 Salve quam Dominus servat amore suus.

what is earthly and you will sit exalted among the stars to
dwell in the kingdom above as a pleasing bride of Christ.
The present life passes as time slips all too rapidly by, but
the virgin's purity is stable and glorious. Humble poverty
summons you, with Christ and his riches, to come to our   30
embrace as our sweet foster-child, so that you may pray to
the Lord to obtain the aid of the father, and win for your-
self a happy kingdom in heaven; so that you gain the honor
of joining the blessed Mary to share in joyful celebration
with an eternal choir. Whoever you are that make this   35
pledge with holy joining of hands will not be the bride of a
man, but the beloved of God.

5

To Lady Radegund

Radegund, of royal lineage, powerful in the earthly sphere,
whom a second kingdom awaits as your abode in heaven, re-
jecting the world your merits have gained you Christ, and
while you are concealed in seclusion, you see beyond the
stars. You trample on the poisoned joys of this earthly realm 5
so that joyfully you may win favor with your king to heaven's
applause. Now you are confined, to enter heaven uncon-
strained; you shed tears, but true joys will be your harvest.
You torture your body, but fasting nourishes your soul.
Greetings to you whom God protects with his love alone.   10

6

Ad eandem de violis

Tempora si solito mihi candida lilia ferrent
    aut speciosa foret suave rubore rosa,
haec ego rure legens aut caespite pauperis horti
    misissem magnis munera parva libens.
5   Sed quia prima mihi desunt, vel solvo secunda:
    profert qui violas, ferret amore rosas.
Inter odoriferas tamen has quas misimus herbas
    purpureae violae nobile germen habent.
Respirant pariter regali murice tinctae
10   et saturat foliis hinc odor, inde decor.
Hae quod utrumque gerunt pariter habeatis utraeque
    et sit mercis odor flore perenne decus.

7

Ad eandem de floribus
super altare

Frigoris hiberni glacie constringitur orbis
    totaque lux agri flore carente perit.
Tempore vernali, Dominus quo Tartara vicit,
    surgit aperta suis laetior herba comis.
5   Inde viri postes et pulpita floribus ornant,

6

To the same woman, on violets

If the seasons brought me their customary white lilies, or the beauty and sweet redness of the rose, I would have picked them in a field or humble garden plot, and gladly sent them as a meager gift to the great. But since I have not my   5
first wish, at least I offer a second: the man who brings you violets, in love would offer you roses. Still in this perfumed bouquet that we have sent, purple violets possess a nobility among flowers. Dyed with royal purple they exhale a scent, and from their petals fragrance and beauty fill the air. May   10
you two together share both properties of this flower; may the fragrance of your reward bloom with eternal beauty.

7

To the same woman, on flowers on an altar

The world is locked in the ice of winter chill, and all brightness is gone from the fields in the absence of flowers. In the season of spring, when the Lord conquered Tartarus, spreading blades emerge resplendent in their foliage. Then men   5

hinc mulier roseo complet odore sinum.
At vos non vobis, sed Christo fertis odores,
    has quoque primitias ad pia templa datis.
Texistis variis altaria festa coronis,
10   pingitur ut filis floribus ara novis.
Aureus ordo crocis, violis hinc blatteus exit,
    coccinus hinc rubricat, lacteus inde nivet.
Stat prasino venetus, pugnant et flore colores
    inque loco pacis herbida bella putas.
15 Haec candore placet, rutilo micat illa decore;
    suavius haec redolet, pulchrius illa rubet.
Sic specie varia florum sibi germina certant,
    ut color hic gemmas, tura revincat odor.
Vos quoque quae struitis haec, Agnes cum Radegunde,
20   floribus aeternis vester anhelet odor.

8

Item ad eandem pro floribus transmissis

O regina potens, aurum cui et purpura vile est,
    floribus ex parvis te veneratur amans.
Et si non res est, color est tamen ipse per herbas:
    purpura per violas, aurea forma crocus.

adorn doorposts and pedestals with blossoms, and women fill their laps with the fragrance of roses. But you bring scents not to yourself, but to Christ, and offer these first-fruits to his holy shrines. You have draped the festive altar with many-colored wreathes, adorned it with fresh flowers 10 like a tapestry. On one side runs the gold of saffron, on another purple violets, here the brilliance of scarlet, there the milky white of snow. Blue is matched with green, the colors wage a floral battle, and you would think there is a war of blossoms in a place of peace. One attracts with its white- 15 ness, another shines with ruddy glow; the first has a sweeter scent, but the red one is more beautiful. The sprays of blossom so contend in multicolored finery that their color outstrips jewels, their scent surpasses incense. May you too, whose work this is, Radegund and Agnes, be fragrant with 20 the scent of eternal blossoms.

8

Again to the same woman on the occasion of a gift of flowers

O powerful queen, who hold gold and purple as but cheap, your devotee shows his regard for you with these humble flowers. Though their blooms have not the same substance, yet their color is the same: purple for the violets, in saffron

5   Dives amore Dei vitasti praemia mundi;
      illas contemnens, has retinebis opes.
  Suscipe missa tibi variorum munera florum,
      ad quos te potius vita beata vocat.
  Quae modo te crucias, recreanda in luce futura,
10   aspicis hinc qualis te retinebit ager.
  Per ramos fragiles quos nunc praebemus olentes
      perpende hinc quantus te refovebit odor.
  Haec cui debentur precor ut, cum veneris illuc,
      meque tuis meritis dextera blanda trahat.
15   Quamvis te expectet paradisi gratia florum,
      isti vos cupiunt iam revidere foris,
  et licet egregio videantur odore placere,
      plus ornant proprias te redeunte comas.

9

Ad eandem cum se reclauderet

Mens fecunda Deo, Radegundis, vita sororum,
    quae ut foveas animam membra domando cremas,
annua vota colens hodie claudenda recurris;
    errabunt animi te repetendo mei.
5   Lumina quam citius nostris abscondis ocellis!

the appearance of gold. Rich in the love of God you have 5
shunned the rewards of the world; by rejecting the one
wealth you will secure another for yourself. Accept the gift
I send you of flowers of many colors; it is rather to these
that a blessed life is calling you. For the present you torment
yourself, to be restored in the light to come; you see from 10
this gift what kind of meadow awaits you. From the frail,
scented branches I now present you, judge what a fragrance
will refresh you there. I beg you to whom these pleasures are
due that, once you are there, you draw me after you too by
your merits with welcoming hand. Although the beauty of 15
paradise's flowers awaits you, these flowers now long to see
you outdoors once more, and although their special fra-
grance seems to give pleasure, their blossoms will be all the
finer when you return.

9

To the same woman, when she was in retreat

Radegund, mind fertile with God, life itself for the sisters,
who mortify and tame the flesh to cultivate the soul, in per-
formance of your yearly vows today you return to seclusion;
my spirit will wander astray in search of you. How quickly 5

Nam sine te nimium nube premente gravor.
Omnibus exclusis uno retineberis antro;
    nos magis includis, quos facis esse foris.
Et licet huc lateas brevibus fugitiva diebus,
10   longior hic mensis quam celer annus erit.
Tempora subducis, ceu non videaris amanti,
    cum vos dum cerno hoc mihi credo parum.
Sed tamen ex voto tecum veniemus in unum
    et sequor huc animo quo vetat ire locus.
15 Hoc precor, incolumem referant te gaudia paschae
    et nobis pariter lux geminata redit.

10

Ad eandem cum rediit

Unde mihi rediit radianti lumine vultus?
    Quae nimis absentem te tenuere morae?
Abstuleras tecum, revocas mea gaudia tecum,
    paschalemque facis bis celebrare diem.
5 Quamvis incipiant modo surgere semina sulcis,
    hic egomet hodie te revidendo meto.
Colligo iam fruges, placidos compono maniplos;
    quod solet Augustus, mensis Aprilis agit,
et licet in primis modo gemma et pampinus exit,

you hide away the light from my eyes! For without you I am
sorely distressed and under a cloud. You keep to a single cell,
all others excluded, but it is we who suffer enclosure when
you cause us to stay outside. Though you seclude yourself
from us here for a brief span of days, this month will be   10
longer than the swift course of a year. You take away all sense
of time, when you are not seen by your lover; even when I
see you, it seems too short to me. Yet still I will come to-
gether with you in my wishes, and follow in spirit where
your location forbids me to go. But this I pray, that the joys   15
of Easter restore you safely to us, and that a twofold light
returns to us once more.

10

To the same woman, when she returned

From where comes again this face of radiant light? What
kept you from me, absent for too long? You took my joys
with you, you bring them back again, and give me double
reason to celebrate Easter day. Though seeds are only now   5
beginning to shoot in the furrows, here, when I see you again
today, I reap a harvest. Now I collect the fruit, I stack the
peaceful sheaves; April now performs the customary tasks
of August, and though now the first buds and shoots appear

10   iam meus autumnus venit et uva simul.
      Malus et alta pirus gratos modo fundit odores,
        sed cum flore novo iam mihi poma ferunt.
      Quamvis nudus ager nullis ornetur aristis,
        omnia plena tamen te redeunte nitent.

II

Ad Gregorium episcopum pro infirmitate sua

      Venit ad aegrotum medici vox alma Gregori
        urbe ex Toronica, dum cubo rure toro,
      concite presbytero recitante Leone sereno,
        irem ut Martini sunt ubi festa pii.
5   Tum, fateor, morbi grave debilitate laborans,
        febre calens summa, iam rigor imus eram.
      Hinc fragili nimium forti languore redacto
        ilia lassa levans halitus aeger erat.
      Ibat anhelanti vapor aridus ora perurens,
10   ibat ab arcanis flatilis aura coquens.
      Fervor eram totus, tristis rogus, igne caminus,
        febris et in fibris stabat operta patens,
      donec Christus opem sudore undante refudit,
        fervidus et gelidas ignis abegit aquas.
15   Redditus ergo isti, pater alme, saluto saluti.
        Auxilium exili sis, rogo, pastor ovi.

on the vine, for me already autumn has come and with it the 10
grape. The apple and tall pear now spread their welcome
scents, but for me with their fresh blossoms they already
bring their fruit. Although the fields are bare, no ears of
grain showing, now you return, and all is plenty, all is bright.

11

To Bishop Gregory on his own sickness

The kindly message of Gregory the physician came to me
when sick from the city of Tours, as I lay on my bed in the
country, urgently delivered by the serene priest Leo, to go
to where the feast of Martin was being celebrated. Then, I 5
confess, I was suffering from the extreme infirmity of an ill-
ness, and burning with the highest fever was now chilled
deep within. So I was reduced to frailty by an overpowering
weakness, and labored breathing was heaving my wearied
flanks. The searing heat parched my mouth as I gasped for
breath, the air I breathed came baking from within me. I 10
was all aflame, a mournful funeral pyre, a fiery furnace, and
in my fibers fever hid, all too apparent, until Christ poured
forth his aid in a flood of sweating, and burning fire dis-
pelled the chilling waters. And so, restored to health, I wish 15
you health, kindly father. May you bring aid as a shepherd, I
beg, to your feeble sheep.

12

Ad eundem pro causa
abbatissae

Repsit quale nefas intra pia saepta synaxi
   —inconsulte dolor, rumpere verba vetas—
quale nec ante oculos patulas neque polluit aures
   nec facerent, vitio qui sua fana colunt!
5 Tu tamen, alme pater, pietatis amore labora
   ut sacer antistes, culmina cuius habes,
unde repraesentes Martinum in tempore sacrum,
   cursibus atque fide dando salutis opem.

12a

Epistula pro eadem re

Commendans humilitatem meam copiosissimae vestrae
dulcedini et mitissimae dominationi suggero ut causa uni-
versalis ecclesiae talem vos habens basidem ut nullus vento-
rum turbo succlinans, nulla procellarum propellens conge-
ries possit illic invenire quod quatiat, aut quod labefactet

12

To the same man, in the interests of the abbess

What a scandal has crept into the holy confines of the community—inconsolable grief, you forbid me from breaking out into speech—such as never previously defiled eyes or attentive ears, such as pagans who pollute their shrines with their worship would shrink from! You then, kindly father, 5 strive from your love of piety, like the holy bishop whose high office you possess, to make saintly Martin present in the here and now by bringing the means for salvation by your holy offices and by your faith.

12a

A letter on the same subject

Commending my humbleness to your most abundant sweetness and most gentle lordship I request that, as the cause of the entire church has in you such a foundation that no destructive gales of wind, no violent body of storms can find there anything to shake or discover anything to undermine,

reperiat, in causa qua conservus meus presbyter, prae-
sentium portitor, ad vos pro singulari praesidio confidens
occurrit (sicut ipse singula poterit explicare), memores com-
mendationis beatae dominae meae, filiae vel iam matris ves-
trae, domnae Radegundis, pro loci sui vel personae totius-
que regulae stabilitate quod petiit et verborum vel viscerum
supplicatione commisit, ita percipiatis infatigabiliter labo-
rare qualiter ipse vobis in retributione sempiterna restituat
qui videt pro auxilio indigentibus in causa iustitiae vester
apostolatus pastoraliter quod desudat.

13

Ad eundem

Antistes Domini, bone pastor et auctor honoris,
    rite decus generis quo est generosa fides,
Iustinam famulam pietate memento, beate,
    per te et commender, stirpe vel arce pater,
5 hinc referens grates, aviae quia reddita tandem
    ad vultus neptis dulcis imago venit.
Ista diu nostris votis dans gaudia, rector,
    inter avam et neptem tu mediator agas.

in this case on which a priest and my fellow servant, carrier of the present letter, hurries to you, trusting in your remarkable protection (as he himself can explain in detail), you be mindful of the charge of my blessed mistress, your daughter, or rather mother, the lady Radegund, that she sought from you for the security of her foundation, her person, and the entire monastic rule and entrusted to you with the prayers of mouth and heart, and undertake to work so tirelessly that God himself repays you with eternal recompense, who sees how your apostolic person labors as a shepherd in the cause of justice for those who need help.

13

To the same man

Bishop of the Lord, good shepherd and bestower of glory, rightly the pride of a family in which faith is ancestral, remember, blessed one, with benevolence your servant Justina. May I win favor through you, my father in kinship and status, giving thanks that finally a grandmother's sweet image has been restored to the sight of her granddaughter. May you fulfill with joy our long-cherished wishes, my lord, and act as intermediary between grandmother and granddaughter.

14

Ad eundem salutatoria

Alme, beate pater, lumen generale, Gregori,
    iure sacerdotum culminis arce caput,
reddo Deo grates de vobis prospera noscens,
    vestris nunc scriptis laetificatus agens.
5 Me quoque commendans humili prece, voce saluto,
    iugiter officio quem mea corda colunt.

15

Ad eundem salutatoria

Summe pater patriae, celsum et generale cacumen,
    forte decus generis, Toronicensis apex,
lumen ab Arvernis veniens feliciter arvis,
    qui illustrans populos spargeris ore pharus,
5 Alpibus ex illis properans mons altior ipsis,
    vir per plana sedens qui pia castra tegis;
neu noceant hostes qui sunt in ovile fideles,
    unicus in campis publica turris ades.
Vir date dulce caput regioni, care Gregori,

14

To the same man, in greeting

Gregory, kindly, benevolent father, and communal light, by
episcopal office head and lofty eminence, I give thanks to
God on learning that you are prospering, filled with joy as I
now am by your epistle. Commending myself, I greet with 5
humble words of prayer him whom my heart continually
honors with dutiful service.

15

To the same man, in greeting

Highest father of your country, lofty and universal emi-
nence, assured glory of your family, crown of Tours, you
come, bringing happiness, a light from the land of the Au-
vergne, your countenance a lighthouse beam to illuminate
your people, journeying from that mountainous land you are 5
a still higher peak, and settling on our plains you protect the
encampments of the holy; so that enemies do not hurt the
faithful in their sheepfold, you alone in the flatlands are the
people's tower. My dear Gregory, granted to this country as

10 Martini retinet quem sacra sella patrem,
  me Fortunatum humilem commendo patrono;
  sic tua vita diu hoc sit in orbe Deo.

16

Ad eundem salutatoria

Si qua mihi veniet quotiens occasio dulcis,
  opto, sacer, calamo solvere vota meo.
Summe pater patriae, toto venerabilis orbe,
  undique care mihi, fulgida cura Dei,
5 commendans humilem tibi me, sacer arce Gregori,
  pro famulo proprio, quaeso, precare Deum.

17

Item ad eundem
de ea re

Si cessent homines velociter ire, per austros
  ad te, care pater, carmina missa velim.
Nunc tamen est quoniam gerulus mihi, porrigo verbum,
  sed minus eloquio quam quod amore colo.

its sweet overseer, holy father, who occupy the sacred see of   10
Martin, to your patronage I commend myself, your humble
Fortunatus; so may you live long in this world for God.

16

To the same man, in greeting

Whenever the sweet opportunity arises for me, I wish, holy
sir, to express my desires with my pen. Highest father of
your country, revered throughout the whole world, in every
way dear to me, brilliant object of God's care, commending   5
my humble person to you, Gregory, sacred in status, I beg
you to pray for your servant to God.

17

Again to the same man
on the same matter

If men were no longer to make rapid journeys, I would
send, dear father, poems to you on the winds. But as it is,
since I have a carrier, I dispatch to you my words, though in

5   Dulcis, opime, decus nostrum, pie papa Gregori,
      versiculis brevibus solvo salutis opus.
    Sed memor ipse mei commenda, quaeso, Tonanti;
      sic te consocium reddat honore, throno.

18

Ad eundem de eadem re

Gurgitis in morem si lingua fluenta rigaret,
    turbine torrentis vel raperetur aquis,
ad tua praecipue praeconia summa, Gregori,
    dum non explerem flumine, gutta forem.
5 Munificumque patrem aequaret nec musa Maronis:
    fers, bone, quanta mihi quis valet ore loqui?
Hac brevitate, sacer, famulum commendo subactum
    me Fortunatum. Sit veniale, precor.

speech I fall short of expressing my loving devotion. Sweet 5
and noble one, my glory, holy father Gregory, in brief verses
I perform the task of greeting. But be mindful of me, and
commend me, I beg, to the Lord; so may he make you a
companion to his honor and throne.

18

To the same man on the same matter

Even if my tongue flowed eloquently like the flood of the
sea, or with its waters was swept along with the force of
a torrent, to laud your outstanding merits, my Gregory, I
would just be a drop, since I could not do you justice with a
stream. Not even the muse of Virgil could match your pater- 5
nal generosity; who can express in words how great are the
gifts you give me, kind sir? With these few words, holy one, I
commend myself, your humble servant Fortunatus. Be in-
dulgent to them, I pray.

19

Ad eundem pro villa praestita

Tramite munifico celebravit pagina cursum,
 carmine dulcifluo quam tuus edit amor,
in qua forte loci facta est collatio doni,
 qua Vigenna procax litore frangit aquas,
5 lapsibus et tumidis dum fertur nauta carinis,
 iugera culta videt, quando celeuma canit.
Grates, care, gero, pietatis fruge repleto,
 qui facis unde decens multiplicetur apex.
Et sine his mea sunt a te quaecumque tenentur:
10 grex habet omnis agris quod, bone pastor, habes.

20

Ad eundem precatoria
pro ipso agro

Munifici reparans Martini gesta, Gregori,
 texit ut ille habitu, nos alis ipse cibo.
Discipulus placidum sapiens imitando magistrum,
 ille ubi dux residet miles habebis opem.

19

To the same man, for the gift of a villa

Your page has made its way on its generous journey, the expression of your love in melodious verse, in which, as it happens, you have bestowed a gift on me, where the wanton Vienne breaks its waters on the riverbank and as the sailor is 5 carried along in his boat on the swelling current, he sees the cultivated farmland, while he chants the time for the stroke. Dear friend, I give you thanks, who are replete with the bounty of kindness, and whose actions augment the glory of your eminence. Even without this gift whatever is owned by you is mine; the whole flock possesses in land whatever you 10 possess, good shepherd.

20

To the same man, in the form of a prayer, for the same property

Reenacting the actions of Martin the munificent, as he covered men with clothing, you, Gregory, nourish us with food. A wise pupil imitating your gentle master, where that com-

5 Ut chlamydem ille prius, sic tu partiris agellum,
     ille tegendo potens tuque fovendo decens,
  ille inopem antiquum relevans, tu, care, novellum;
     fit dives merito paupere quisque suo.
  Quando reposcetur, vestris redit usibus arvum
10   et domino proprio restituemus agrum.
  Unde amplas refero grates, dulcissime rector,
     et repeto pangens haec, tua, pastor, ovis.
  Nec tantum reddo quantum tibi debeo, praesul:
     pro Fortunato sed, rogo, flecte Deum.

21

Ad eundem
pro pellibus transmissis

Egregio conpacta situ, phalerata rotatu,
    atque Sophocleo pagina fulta sopho
me arentem vestro madefecit opima rigatu,
    fecit et eloquio quod loquor esse tuo.
5 Dulcis, care, decens, facunde, benigne Gregori
    atque pater patriae, hinc sacer, inde cate,
muneribus, meritis, animis et moribus aequis,
    omnibus officiis unde colaris habens,
me Fortunatum tibi celso sterno pusillum

mander abides, you, his soldier, will have his support. As he 5
once shared his cloak, so you share an estate, he powerful in
clothing, you gracious in caring, he sustaining a needy man
in the past, you, dear one, in the present; each by his poor
man becomes rich in his deserts. When you ask for it back,
the land will return to your possession, and I will restore the 10
estate to its own proper master. For this I offer you abun-
dant thanks, sweetest lord, and as your sheep, my shepherd,
I redouble them in this poem. Even then I do not repay you
as much as I owe, good bishop; yet pray to God for Fortuna-
tus, I beg.

21

To the same man,
for sending him some hides

Composed with outstanding skill, embellished with oro-
tund style, and constructed with Sophoclean art, your rich
page moistened my barrenness with its irrigation, and
caused what I say to share your fluency. Sweet, dear, noble, 5
eloquent, and kindly Gregory, father of your country, both
saintly and learned, by your generosity, your virtues, your
equable temperament and character worthy to be honored
with every attention, I humble myself, the lowly Fortunatus,

10 commendo et voto supplice rite tuum,
   cui das unde sibi talaria missa ligentur
    pellibus et niveis sint sola tecta pedis.
  Pro quibus a Domino detur stola candida vobis;
   qui datis hoc minimis, inde feratis opes.

before your high station, and commend myself with suppli- 10
ant vow as rightly yours, for you have given me the means by
which the sandals you have sent can be laced, and the soles
of my feet covered by snow-white hides. In return for these
may a white robe be given to you by the Lord. You make this
gift to the lowliest; may you receive riches for it in reward.

BOOK NINE

I

Ad Chilpericum regem quando synodus Brinnaco habita est

Ordo sacerdotum venerandaque culmina Christi,
    quos dedit alma fides religione patres,
parvolus opto loqui regis praeconia celsi;
    sublevet exigui carmina vester amor.
5 Inclite rex armis et regibus edite celsis,
    primus ab antiquis culmina prima regens,
rector habens nascendo decus, moderando sed augens,
    de radice patris flos generate potens,
aequali serie vos nobilitando vicissim
10   tu genus ornasti, te genus ornat avi.
Excepisti etenim fulgorem ab origine gentis,
    sed per te proavis splendor honore redit.
Te nascente patri lux altera nascitur orbi
    nominis et radios spargis ubique novos.
15 Quem praefert Oriens, Libyes, Occasus et Arctus,
    quo pede non graderis, notus honore venis.
Quidquid habet mundus peragrasti nomine, princeps,
    curris et illud iter quod rota solis agit,
cognite iam ponto et rubro pelagoque sub Indo,

I

To King Chilperic, when a council was held at Berny

Order of bishops and revered eminences of Christ, whom kindly faith has granted to be fathers in holiness, I wish though small to speak the praise of a sublime king; may your love elevate the songs of my meager talent.

King famed in arms, and descendant of kings of high 5 fame, first of an ancient line ruling with the highest eminence, a ruler possessing glory by birth and increasing it by your governance, a mighty flower born from the root of your father, mutually by a reciprocal process conveying nobility, you have brought luster to your family, as your ances- 10 tors have to you. For indeed you have acquired brilliance from your family line, but from you distinction redounds in glory to your forbears. When you were born to your father a second sun was born to the world and you scatter everywhere the new sunbeams of your name. Libya and the 15 East, the West and the North sound your praises; you are honored in reputation where your feet never trod. You have traversed, prince, in name the entire expanse of the world, and you follow the course that the sun's chariot wheel runs. You are now well-known to the Red Sea and to the Indian

20 transit et oceanum fulgida fama sopho.
  Nomen ut hoc resonet non impedit aura nec unda;
    sic tibi cuncta simul, terra vel astra, favent.
  Rex bonitate placens, decus altum et nobile germen,
    in quo tot procerum culmina culmen habent,
25 auxilium patriae, spes et tutamen in armis,
    fida tuis virtus, inclitus atque vigor,
  Chilperice potens, si interpres barbarus extet,
    "adiutor fortis" hoc quoque nomen habes.
  Non fuit in vacuum sic te vocitare parentes;
30 praesagum hoc totum laudis et omen erat.
  Iam tunc indicium praebebant tempora nato,
    dicta priora tamen dona secuta probant.
  In te, dulce caput, patris omnis cura pependit;
    inter tot fratres sic amor unus eras.
35 Agnoscebat enim te iam meliora mereri;
    unde magis coluit, praetulit inde pater;
  Praeposuit genitor cum plus dilexit alumnum.
    Iudicium regis frangere nemo potest.
  Auspiciis magnis crevisti, maxime princeps,
40 hinc in amore manens plebis et inde patris.
  Sed meritis tantis subito sors invida rerum,
    perturbare parans regna quieta tibi,
  concutiens animos populorum et foedera fratrum,
    laedere dum voluit, prosperitate favet.
45 Denique iam capiti valido pendente periclo,
    quando ferire habuit, reppulit hora necem.
  Cum retinereris mortis circumdatus armis,
    eripuit gladio sors operante Deo.
  Ductus ad extremum remeas de funere vitae;

main, and your splendid fame for learning crosses even the   20
ocean. Neither wind nor wave prevents this name from
sounding clear; everything shows such favor to you, both
earth and stars.

King loved for your goodness, lofty in glory and noble
in race, in whom so many eminent worthies achieve a pre-
eminence, support of your country, under arms its hope   25
and protection, devoted in your courage to your people, and
famed for your energy, mighty Chilperic, if a barbarian pro-
vides the translation, you have also the name "brave helper."
It was no accident that your parents gave you this name; it   30
was entirely prescient and an omen of fame. Already then
that moment conferred on their son a first intimation, but
the gifts that followed proved the truth of past words. On
you, sweet head, your father's every care relied; among so
many brothers you were his only love. He recognized that   35
you already were the most promising; because he valued you
most, your father gave you preference. Your parent pro-
moted the child that was to him the dearest. No one can
contravene the judgment of a king. You grew, most mighty
prince, under high auspices, secure in the love of the people   40
and of your father.

But suddenly fate, envious of so great virtues, prepared
to throw into confusion your peaceful realm, agitating the
minds of the people and breaking pacts between brothers;
but when it wanted to harm, it blessed with good fortune.
For when danger was threatening your redoubtable person,   45
and was at the point of striking, the hour repulsed death.
When you were hemmed in, surrounded by weapons of
slaughter, by God's doing fortune snatched you from the
swords. Though reduced to extremity, you returned from

50   ultima quae fuerat fit tibi prima dies.
       Noxia dum cuperent hostes tibi bella parare,
         pro te pugnavit fortis in arma fides.
       Prospera iudicium sine te tua causa peregit
         et rediit proprio celsa cathedra loco.
55   Rex bone, ne doleas, nam te fortuna querellis
         unde fatigavit, hinc meliora dedit.
       Aspera tot tolerando diu modo laeta sequuntur
         et per maerores gaudia nata metis.
       Multimodas perpesse minas tua regna resumis,
60   namque labore gravi crescere magna solent.
       Aspera non nocuit, sed te sors dura probavit;
         unde gravabaris, celsior inde redis.
       Altior adsiduis crescis, non frangeris, armis,
         et belli artificem te labor ipse facit.
65   Fortior efficeris per multa pericula, princeps,
         ac per sudores dona quietis habes.
       Nil dolet amissum te rege superstite mundus,
         cui se servarunt debita regna gradu.
       Consuluit domui, patriae, populoque Creator,
70   quem gentes metuunt, te superesse virum.
       Ne ruat armatus per Gallica rura rebellis,
         nomine victoris hic es et ampla tegis,
     quem Geta, Vasco tremunt, Danus, Euthio, Saxo, Britannus,
         cum patre quos acie te domitasse patet.
75   Terror es extremis Fresonibus atque Suebis,
         qui neque bella parant, sed tua frena rogant.
       Omnibus his datus es timor illo iudice campo
         et terrore novo factus es altus amor.
       In te, rector, habet regio circumdata murum
80   ac levat excelsum ferrea porta caput.

death to life; what might have been the last became for you 50
the first of days. While your enemies desired to wage hostile
war against you, faith strong to arms combated on your side.
Your cause won a favorable judgment in your absence, and
the high throne returned to its proper place.

Good king, do not grieve, for the more fortune has wea- 55
ried you with its sufferings, the greater the blessings it has
bestowed. After long enduring so many hardships, joys now
follow, and you reap rejoicing engendered by grief. Having
endured multifarious dangers you recovered your kingdom,
for great things are accustomed to grow from grievous pain. 60
Harsh times did not hurt you, but cruel fortune proved you;
borne down by burdens you come back the taller. By con-
tinual warfare you grow in stature, not succumb, and strug-
gle only makes you a master of war. You are made bolder by 65
many perils, prince, and by the sweat of your brow you win
the gifts of peace.

The world grieves no loss while you remain as king, for
whom the kingdom due your rank is reserved. The Creator
looked to the interests of house, country, and people in se- 70
curing your survival, of whom all nations are in dread. You
are here with the title of victor, providing ample protection,
so armed rebels not run amok through the country of Gaul.
Goth, Basque, Dane, Euthian, Saxon, and Breton all fear
you, since with your father you decisively subdued them in
battle. You inspire dread in distant Frisians and Sueves, who 75
do not make war but sue for your governance. By the judg-
ment of the battlefield in all these you inspire terror, but by
a strange form of fear have become deeply loved. In you,
lord, the land possesses an encircling wall and an iron gate 80

Tu patriae radias adamantina turris ab austro
   et scuto stabili publica vota tegis.
Neu gravet haec aliquis, pia propugnacula tendis
   ac regionis opes limite forte foves.
85 Quid de iustitiae referam moderamine, princeps,
   quo male nemo redit, si bene iusta petit,
cuius in ore probo mensurae libra tenetur
   rectaque causarum linea currit iter.
Nec mora fit vero, falsus nihil explicat error,
90   iudiciisque tuis fraus fugit, ordo redit.
Quid quoscumque etiam regni dicione gubernas,
   doctior ingenio vincis et ore loquax,
discernens varias sub nullo interprete voces,
   et generum linguas unica lingua refert?
95 Erigit exiguos tua munificentia cunctos,
   et quod das famulo credis id esse tuum.
Qualiter hinc itidem tua se praeconia tendunt
   laudis et hoc cumulo concutit astra fragor.
Cui simul arma favent et littera constat amore;
100   hinc virtute potens, doctus et inde places.
Inter utrumque sagax, armis et iure probatus,
   belliger hinc radias, legifer inde micas.
De virtute pater, reparatur avunculus ore,
   doctrinae studio vincis et omne genus.
105 Regibus aequalis, de carmine maior haberis,
   dogmate vel qualis non fuit ante parens.
Te arma ferunt generi similem, sed littera praefert;
   sic veterum regum par simul atque prior.
Admirande mihi nimium rex, cuius opime

raises its head on high. You are a tower of adamant, shining from the South on your country, and with your sturdy shield you protect the will of the people. To protect it from threat, you devotedly draw up a line of defenses, and foster the region's prosperity by a fortified border.

Why should I speak, prince, of your administration of justice, from which no one returns disappointed, if his petition is just? The fair weighing of decisions is secured by your honest pronouncements, and the conduct of trials runs straight in its course. The truth is unhampered, false error finds no purchase, and in your judgments deceit is put to flight and order returns.

Why mention that you surpass in learning, intelligence, and eloquence of speech all who are subject to your royal jurisdiction, understanding different languages without a translator, and that your single tongue speaks various national tongues? Your generosity exalts all of mean station, and what you give to a servant you believe to be yours. In the same way as your praise spreads far and wide here, so with your mounting fame your acclaim strikes the stars. Simultaneously warfare reflects to your credit and letters are your love; strong in your courage in one, you please with your learning in the other. Wise in both endeavors, proved in weapons and the law, you are brilliant as a warrior, as a legislator a bright light. In courage you bring back your father to life, in eloquence your uncle, and you surpass the whole of your race in your devotion to knowledge. The equal of kings, but in poetry their superior, none of your family could match you in learning. Warfare makes you alike to your kin, but literature puts you above them; so at the same time you both equal past kings and you surpass them. My most admi-

110   proelia robor agit, carmina lima polit,
      legibus arma regis et leges dirigis armis;
         artis diversae sic simul itur iter.
      Discere si posset, rector, tua singula quisquis,
         ornarent plures quae bona solus agis.
115   Sed tamen haec maneant et crescant prospera vobis
         et liceat solio multiplicante frui
      coniuge cum propria, quae regnum moribus ornat
         principis et culmen participata regit,
      provida consiliis, sollers, cauta, utilis aulae,
120   ingenio pollens, munere larga placens,
      omnibus excellens meritis, Fredegundis opima,
         atque serena suo fulget ab ore dies,
      regia magna nimis curarum pondera portans,
         te bonitate colens, utilitate iuvans.
125   Qua pariter tecum moderante palatia crescunt,
         cuius et auxilio floret honore domus.
      Quaerens unde viro duplicentur vota salutis
         et tibi mercedem de Radegunde facit.
      Quae meritis propriis effulget gloria regis
130   et regina suo facta corona viro.
      Tempore sub longo haec te fructu prolis honoret,
         surgat et inde nepos, ut renoveris avus.
      Ergo Creatori referatur gratia digne,
         et cole, rex, Regem qui tibi praebet opem,
135   ut servet cumuletque bonum, nam rector ab alto
         omnia solus habet qui tibi multa dedit.
      Da veniam, victor, tua me praeconia vincunt;
         hoc quoque, quod superor, fit tibi maior honor.
      Parvulus opto tamen, sic prospera vota secundent,

rable king, by whose abundant qualities your strength fights   110
battles and your file smooths poems, you control arms with
laws and enforce laws with arms; so different skills together
travel the one course. If anyone, lord, could learn of each of
your virtues, the qualities you alone possess would be suffi-
cient to adorn many.

    May, then, these qualities remain and grow in prosperity   115
for you, and may you enjoy the increase of your throne in
company with your wife, who adorns your kingdom with her
character and shares in the direction of your high princely
position, prudent in counsel, resourceful, cautious, and ben-
eficial to the palace, powerful of intellect, winning favor by   120
her generosity with gifts, noble Fredegund, eminent in all of
the virtues, from whose countenance shines the clear light
of day, who bears the all too heavy burdens of royalty's cares,
supporting you with her kindness, aiding you with her ser-
vices. Under her shared governance with you the palace   125
prospers, and with her help your household flourishes in
glory. Seeking to double the wishes for her husband's wellbe-
ing, she also wins a reward from Radegund for you. She
shines by her own merits to the glory of the king and as   130
queen becomes her husband's crown. For a long period of
time may she grace you with the blessing of offspring, and
from them may a grandchild be born to bring you new life as
a grandfather. Therefore let due thanks be given to the Cre-
ator, and worship, king, the King who brings you his aid, so   135
that he preserve and increase your blessings, for the ruler on
high alone possesses all things, who has given you much.

    Grant pardon, victorious one, your praises defeat me; the
very fact that I'm bested wins you greater honor. Lowly
though I am, I wish—and so may good fortune favor my

140   ut veniant terris haec pia dona polis.
       Aera temperie faveant tibi, tempora pace,
          frugibus arva micent, foedera regna ligent.
       Edomites saevos, tuearis amore fideles,
          sis quoque catholicis religionis apex.
145   Summus honor regis, per quem donantur honores,
          cui longaeva dies constet et alma fides,
       regibus aurum alii aut gemmarum munera solvant,
          de Fortunato paupere verba cape.

2

Item ad Chilpericum et Fredegundem reginam

       Aspera condicio et sors irrevocabilis horae,
          quod generi humano tristis origo dedit,
       cum suadens coluber proiecit ab ore venenum
          morsu et serpentis mors fuit Eva nocens.
5   Sumpsit ab ipso ex tunc Adam patre terra dolorem
          et de matre gemens mundus amara capit.
       Praevaricando duo probro damnantur acerbo:
          ille labore dolet, haec generando gemit.
       Mors venit inde vorax, transmissa nepotibus ipsis,
10   heredesque suos tollit origo nocens.

wishes—that these bountiful gifts come from heaven to   140
earth. May the air bless you with mildness, your times bless
you with peace, may fields be bright with crops and kings
make binding pacts. May you subdue the cruel, protect with
love the faithful, and be for the Catholics the summit of
Christian faith. Most honored of kings, by whom honors are   145
distributed, may you enjoy long life and a sustaining faith.
Though others offer gold to kings or gifts of precious stones,
from Fortunatus, who is poor, receive words alone.

2

Again, to Chilperic and Queen Fredegund

Cruel is the condition and immutable the chance of the
hour, to which a bitter origin condemned the human race,
when a persuasive serpent spewed poison from its mouth,
and by the bite of the snake the guilty Eve became death.
From that moment the earth received suffering from its fa-   5
ther Adam, and from its mother the groaning world inher-
ited hardships. For their sins the two were condemned with
bitter reproach: he to pain in his labor, she to sorrow in
childbirth. This is the source of devouring death, be-
queathed to his descendants; original guilt passed sentence   10

Ecce hoc triste nefas nobis genuere parentes;
    coeperat unde prius, hinc ruit omne genus.
Primus Abel cecidit miserando vulnere caesus,
    ac fraterna sibi sarcula membra fodent.
15 Post quoque Seth obiit, sub Abel vice redditus isdem,
    et quamvis rediit, non sine fine fuit.
Quid Noe memorem, laudatum voce Tonantis,
    quem levis arca tulit, nunc gravis arva premit?
Sic quoque Sem et Iafeth, iustissima denique proles
20   sancta et progenies tale cucurrit iter.
Quid patriarcha Abraham vel Isac, Iacob quoque dignus,
    cum de lege necis nemo solutus adest?
Melchisedech etiam, Domini sacer ore sacerdos,
    Iob quoque seu geniti sic abiere sui.
25 Legifer ipse iacet Moyses Aaronque sacerdos,
    alloquiisque Dei dignus amicus obit.
Successorque suus, populi dux inclitus Iesus,
    quos legitis libris occubuere patres.
Quid Gedeon, Samson vel quisquis in ordine iudex?
30   Morti sub Domino iudice nemo fugit.
Israhelita potens David rex atque propheta
    est situs in tumulo cum Salomone suo.
Esaias, Danihel, Samuel, Ionasque beatus,
    vivens sub pelago, stat modo pressus humo.
35 Princeps clave Petrus, primus quoque dogmate Paulus,
    quamvis celsae animae, corpora terra tegit.
Semine ab humano cui nullus maior habetur,
    vir baptista potens ipse Iohannes obit.
Enoch Heliasque hoc adhuc spectat uterque:
40   qui satus ex homine est et moriturus erit.
Ipse Creator ovans surgens cito Christus ab umbris;

on his heirs. This, see, is the grievous wrong our parents en-
gendered for us; from that first beginning the whole race
came to ruin.

First Abel fell, struck down by a grievous wound, and a
brother's hoe broke up his limbs. Afterwards Seth too died,   15
granted to his parents instead of Abel, and although he took
his place, he was not exempt from that end. Why should
I mention Noah, praised by the Lord's thundering voice,
whom a frail ark carried, but now heavy earth envelopes?
So too Shem and Japheth, and after them their most just off-
spring and their saintly descendants ran just such a course.   20
Why mention the patriarch Abraham and Isaac, worthy Ja-
cob too, when no one is absolved from the law of mortal-
ity? Melchisedech also, holy priest by the Lord's declaration,
and Job and his sons as well, all departed in this way. Moses   25
the lawgiver himself lies in death and Aaron the priest; he
died who was worthy of conversing with God as a friend.
His successor, Joshua, famed leader of his people, and the
fathers you read of in the scriptures, all met their end.
Why mention Gideon, Samson, or any of the succession of
judges? When God is judge no one escapes from death. Da-   30
vid, powerful king and prophet of Israel, lies in his tomb
with his son Solomon; Isaiah too, Daniel, Samuel, and
blessed Jonah, who lived in the waves, but now lies under
the soil. Peter princely key-holder and Paul supreme in   35
teaching, although their souls are on high, have bodies cov-
ered by earth. The man to whom no one is thought superior
in the human race, the mighty John the Baptist himself
passed away. Enoch and Elijah still both await this fate: who   40
is born of man is destined to die. Christ the Creator himself
quickly rose in triumph from the shades; because he was

hic quia natus homo est, carne sepultus humo.
Quis, rogo, non moritur, mortem gustante salute,
    dum pro me voluit hic mea vita mori?
45 Dic mihi, quid poterunt Augusti aut culmina regum,
    membra Creatoris cum iacuere petris?
Bracchia non retrahunt fortes neque purpura reges;
    vir quicumque venit pulvere, pulvis erit.
Nascimur aequales morimurque aequaliter omnes:
50   una ex Adam est mors, Christus et una salus.
Diversa est merces, funus tamen omnibus unum:
    infantes, iuvenes, sic moriere senes.
Ergo quid hinc facimus nunc te rogo, celsa potestas,
    cum nihil auxilii possumus esse rei?
55 Ploramus, gemimus, sed nec prodesse valemus;
    luctus adest oculis, est neque fructus opis.
Viscera torquentur, lacerantur corda tumultu;
    sunt cari extincti, flendo cadunt oculi.
Ecce vocatur amor neque iam revocatur amator,
60   nos neque iam repetit quem petra mersa tegit.
Quamvis clamantem refugit mors surda nec audit,
    nec scit in affectum dura redire pium.
Sed, nolo atque volo, migrabo cum omnibus illuc;
    ibimus hinc omnes, nemo nec inde redit,
65 donec in adventu Domini caro mortua vivat,
    surgat et ex proprio pulvere rursus homo,
coeperit ut tegere arentes cutis uda favillas
    et vivi cineres de tumulis salient.
Ibimus ergo omnes alia regione locandi,
70   ibimus ad patriam quos peregrina tenent.
Ne cruciere igitur, pie rex, fortissime princeps,
    quod geniti pergunt quo petit omnis homo.

born as a man, in flesh he was buried in the earth. Who,
I ask, does not die, when even our salvation tastes death,
when my life was willing to die here on my behalf? Tell me,   45
what power will emperors have or high kingly status, when
the body of the Creator lay in a stone tomb? Muscular arms
do not rescue the strong nor purple kings; a man, whoever
he is, who comes of dust, will be dust again. We are born
equal and we all equally die; there is a single death from   50
Adam and a single salvation, Christ. The rewards are differ-
ent, but there is one demise for all; children, the young, and
the old, all die in this way.

So then I ask you now, lofty power, what do we do in this
case, since we have no power to find a remedy for this situa-
tion? We lament, we grieve, but we can be of no help; there   55
are tears in our eyes, but we get no benefit of relief. Our
flesh is tortured, our hearts are torn by distress, our dear
ones are dead, our eyes fail us with weeping. See, the loved
one is called but who loves him receives now no answer, and   60
he who is under the buried stone no longer returns to us.
Deaf however much you cry, death shrinks away and hears
nothing; implacable it has no capacity to acquire kindly feel-
ings. Still, whether I like it or not, I will travel with everyone
there; we all go from here, but from there no one returns,
until at the coming of the Lord the bodies of the dead re-   65
vive, and man again rises from his native dust, when moist
flesh begins to clothe the dried out embers, and quickened
ashes leap out of the tombs. We will all then go to take our
place in another country, we who have been living as strang-   70
ers will go to our native land.

Do not then torment yourself, good king, bravest of
princes, because your sons are going where all humans are

Quale placet figulo vas fictile, tale paratur;
    quando placet figulo, vasa soluta ruunt.
75 Quod iubet Omnipotens, non possumus esse rebelles,
    cuius ad intuitum sidera, terra tremunt.
Ipse creat hominem. Quid dicere possumus? Idem
    qui dedit et recipit; crimina nulla gerit.
Illius ecce sumus figmentum et spiritus inde est;
80   cum iubet, hinc imus qui sumus eius opus.
Si libet, in hora montes, freta, sidera mutat,
    cui sua facta favent; quid homo fumus agit?
Rex precor ergo potens, age quod tibi maxime prosit,
    quod prodest animae cum deitatis ope:
85 Esto virile decus, patienter vince dolores;
    quod non vitatur, vel toleretur onus.
Quod trahimus nascendo, sine hoc non transigit ullus,
    quod nemo inmutat, vel ratione ferat.
Consuleas dominae reginae et amantis amatae,
90   quae bona cuncta capit te sociante sibi;
materno affectu placare iubeto dolentem,
    nec simul ipse fleas nec lacrimare sinas.
Te regnante viro tristem illam non decet esse,
    sed magis ex vestro gaudeat alta toro.
95 Deprecor hoc etiam, vitam amplam coniugis optans,
    consuleas genitae, consuleas patriae.
Talis erit populus qualem te viderit omnis,
    deque tua facie plebs sua vota metet.
Denique Iob natos septem uno triste sub ictu
100   amittens laudes rettulit ore Deo.
David psalmographus genitum cum amisit amatum,
    mox tumulo posuit, prandia festa dedit.

bound. An earthenware vessel is made by the potter in the manner that pleases him; when it pleases the potter, the vessel is broken and smashed. We cannot resist what the Almighty orders, at whose gaze stars and earth tremble. He is the creator of man. What can we say? The same one who gave also takes back; he is committing no wrong. We are his creation, our breath comes from him; when he bids us we go from here, who are his handiwork. If he wishes, in an hour he transforms mountains, seas, and stars. All his creation does him honor; what can man do who is but smoke? Mighty king, then, I pray, do what most benefits you, what profits your soul, with divinity's aid. Display manly dignity, conquer your grief with resolve; let the burden which cannot be avoided at least be tolerated. We incur it with birth, no one lives life without it; what no one can alter, let him bear with reason.

Look to your lady queen, who enjoys your loving devotion, who receives all good things from your alliance with her; bid her moderate her grief from maternal affection, do not join her in tears or allow her to weep. While you, her husband, reign, it does not become her to be sad, but rather let her rejoice, exalted by your bed. I make this plea too, as I wish long life for your wife, that you look to your daughter and look to your country. The whole populace will be as they see you, and from your features the people will reap their desires. So Job losing seven sons in one grievous blow still rendered up praise to God with his voice. David the psalmist when he lost his beloved son, no sooner laid him in the tomb, then he gave a joyous meal. The twice blessed woman,

Femina bis felix pia mater Machabeorum
 natos septem uno funere laeta tulit,
105 prompta aiens Domino: "Semper tibi gloria, rector.
 Cum vis, summe pater, pignora mater habet."
Unde Deo potius referatur gratia nostro,
 germine de vestro qui facit ire polo,
eligit et gemmas de mundi stercore pulchras
110 de medioque luto ducit ad astra throno.
Messis vestra Deo placuit, quam in horrea condit
 dum spicis teneris dulcia grana metat.
Non paleas generas, frumenta sed integra gignis,
 nec recremanda focis, sed recreanda polis,
115 praesertim qui sic sancto baptismate puri
 hinc meruere rapi, fonte lavante novi.
Stantes ante Deum velut aurea vasa decoris
 aut quasi candelabris pulchra lucerna nitens,
immaculatae animae, radiantes semper honore,
120 vivorum retinent in regione locum
inque domo Domini plantati lumine vernant
 candida ceu rubeis lilia mixta rosis.
Iusserit et Dominus cum membra redire sepulta,
 vestibit genitos tunc stola pulchra tuos
125 aut palmata chlamys rutilo contexta sub auro,
 et variis gemmis frons diadema geret;
Utentes niveam per candida pectora pallam,
 purpureamque togam fulgida zona ligat.
Tunc pater et genetrix mediis gaudebitis illis,
130 cum inter sidereos cernitis esse viros.
Est tamen Omnipotens, Abrahae qui semen adauxit
 vobis atque dabit Iob quod amore dedit,

holy mother of the Maccabees, happily endured seven sons
suffering a single death, unhesitatingly saying to the Lord: 105
"Glory to you always, my king. A mother keeps her children,
highest father, for as long as you wish."

Therefore rather let thanks be given to our God, who
caused your children to ascend to heaven, and chose beauti-
ful jewels from the filth of the world, leading them from the 110
midst of the mire to his throne in the stars. Your harvest has
won favor with God; he has gathered it into his barns, as he
reaps the sweet kernels when the ears are still tender. You
bring forth no chaff, but give birth to unsullied grain, not to
be burned by the fires, but to be reborn in the skies, all the 115
more because they were cleansed by the holy waters of bap-
tism, and so were able to be carried from here made new by
washing in that font. Standing before God like fair golden
vessels, or like a beautiful lamp shining on its stand, unsoiled
souls, always radiant in glory, they occupy a place in the land 120
of the living, and planted in the house of the Lord they blos-
som with light like white lilies mingled with red roses. When
the Lord orders bodies to rise from their tombs, then a beau-
tiful robe will clothe your sons, and a palm-decorated cloak 125
picked out in gleaming gold, and their foreheads will bear a
diadem of multicolored stones. On their bright chests they
will bear a snow-white mantle with a brilliant belt holding
their purple togas. Then, father and mother, you will rejoice
in their company, when you see they are among the heroes 130
of heaven.

It is the Almighty, who increased the seed of Abraham,
and will give to you what he gave out of love to Job. Re-

restituens numerum natorum germine digno,
    progeniemque refert nobilitante fide.
135 Qui in solium David Salomonis contulit ortum,
    pro vice germani cum redit ipse patri,
ille tibi poterit de coniuge reddere natum,
    cui pater adludat, ubere mater alat,
qui medius vestri reptans per colla parentum
140   regibus et patriae gaudia longa paret.

3

Item ad Chilpericum et Fredegundem

Post tempestates et turbida nubila caeli,
    quo solet infesto terra rigere gelu,
post validas hiemes ac tristia frigora brumae,
    flamine seu rapidi rura gravante noti,
5 succedunt iterum vernalia tempora mundo
    grataque post glaciem provocat aura diem.
Rursus odoriferis renovantur floribus arva
    frondibus arboreis et viret omne nemus;
dulce saporatis curvantur robora pomis,
10   et redeunte sibi gramine ridet ager.
Sic quoque iam, domini, post tristia damna dolentes
    vos meliore animo laetificate, precor.
Ecce dies placidi revocant paschalia Christi,

storing from deserving stock the number of his children, he granted new offspring to the man ennobled by faith. He who bestowed on the throne of David the birth of Solo- 135 mon, when he came to his father in place of his brother, will be able to grant you a son from your wife, for the father to play with, the mother to feed at her breast, so that clamber- ing between you on the necks of his parents he win lasting 140 joys for your majesties and for the country.

3

Again to Chilperic and Fredegund

After storms and the heaving clouds in the sky, when the earth is accustomed to stiffen with treacherous ice, after se- vere winters and the biting cold of the season, when the south wind's raging blast oppresses the landscape, there fol- 5 lows again the coming of spring to the world, and after the chill a welcoming breeze summons the day. The fields are once more renewed by perfumed flowers, and every glade is green with trees in leaf, trunks are bent over by sweet- tasting fruit, and the land is cheered by the new growth of 10 grass. In this way too, my lords, though grieving after a sad loss, be joyful, I beg you, and in better spirits. Here, see, the tranquil days of Christ's Eastertide are returning, and the

orbs quoque totus item per nova vota fremit.
15 Gaudia plus faveant per celsa palatia regum
        et per vos famuli festa beata colant.
    Omnipotens nobis vestram addat in orbe salutem
        atque diu patriam culmina vestra regant.

4

Epitaphium super sepulchrum domni Chlodobercthi

Flere monent populum crudelia funera regum,
    cum caput orbis humo maesta sepulchra tegunt.
Hoc igitur tumulo recubans Chlodobercthus habetur,
    qui tria lustra gerens raptus ab orbe fuit,
5   de proavo veniens Chlodovecho celsa propago,
    Chlodacharique nepos Chilpericique genus,
quem de regina sumpsit Fredegunde iugali,
    auxerat et nascens Francica vota puer.
Quo patris et patriae dum spes adolesceret ampla,
10   accelerante die sors inimica tulit.
Sed cui nulla nocent queruli contagia mundi,
    non fleat ullus amor, quem modo cingit honor.
Nam puer innocuus vivens sine crimine lapsus
    perpetui regni se favet arce frui.

whole world too is abuzz with new hopes. May joys flourish 15
the more in the lofty palace of your majesties, and because
of you may your servants celebrate happy feasts. May the Al-
mighty grant us your good health in this world, and long may
your eminences rule over this country.

4

Epitaph on the Tomb of the lord Chlodobert

The cruel deaths of princes prompt the people to sorrow,
when a mournful grave covers a ruler of the world with
earth. So in this tomb is contained in repose Chlodobert,
who was carried off from the world when fifteen years old,
of lofty descent from his great-grandfather Clovis, grand- 5
son of Chlothar and son of Chilperic, whom he bore to his
queen and wife Fredegund, a boy whose birth had raised the
hopes of the Franks. When, then, the rich expectations of
father and country were coming to fruition, his last day has- 10
tened upon him and hostile fate took him off. But since no
contact with the fretful world now hurts him, let no one
who loves him grieve, as glory now surrounds him. For an
innocent youth, whose life was without the reproach of a
fault, rejoices to enjoy the citadel of the everlasting king-
dom.

5

Epitaphium Dagobercthi

Dulce caput, populi, Dagobercthe, perennis amore,
    auxilium patriae, spes puerilis obis,
germine regali nascens generosus, et infans
    ostensus terris, mox quoque rapte polis,
5 belligeri veniens Chlodovechi gente potenti,
    egregii proavi germen honore pari,
regibus antiquis respondens nobilis infans,
    Chilpericique patris vel Fredegunde genus.
Te veneranda tamen mox abluit unda lavacri;
10 hinc licet abreptum lux tenet alma throno.
Vivis honore ergo et cum iudex venerit orbis,
    surrecturus eris fulgidus ore nitens.

6

Ad Gregorium episcopum pro
metris Sapphicis

Pollente eloquio pervenit epistula cursu,
    sed voluit voto tarda venire meo.
Nec tamen offendit, quamvis remorata requirit,
    quem tenet adstrictum mente ligante virum,

5

Epitaph for Dagobert

Sweet personage, Dagobert, enduring in the love of the people, support to your country, their hope as a boy, noble and born from royal stock, you are dead, still a child, who were shown to the earth but immediately snatched up to heaven, descended from the mighty lineage of warlike Clovis, of 5 your noble great-grandfather's stock and equal in status, as a noble child bearing comparison with the kings of the past, the offspring of your father Chilperic and of Fredegund. Still, the sacred waters of baptism quickly washed you clean; though snatched away from here, you dwell in blessed light 10 by the throne. You live, then, in glory and when the judge of the world comes, you will rise up brightly shining and radiant in countenance.

6

To Bishop Gregory, written for Sapphic verses

Your letter has made its way to me, powerful in eloquence, though for my own wishes it came to me late. And although it seeks me out after some time, yet it does not offend a man

5 cum cupiam, talem qualis fuit ille Nazanzo
    Gregorium ut repares dogmate, sede parens.
  Quaeque iniunxisti, pater, ecce poemata misi,
    et mihi proficient, si tibi, care, placent.
  Hoc mandas etiam quo Sapphica metra remittam.
10   Da veniam, modici dum seges urguet agri.
  Dum meto, da spatium. Tibi mox parere parabo.
    Si saturer fructu, fors meliora cano.
  Condere si valeo, cum metro mitto libellum;
    quae cape tu voto quo tibi dictat amor.

7

Item ad Gregorium episcopum

  Corde iucundo, calamo venusto
  litteras mittis cupiente voto,
  blanda conscribens serie salutis,
    care Gregori,
5 exigens nuper nova me movere
  metra quae Sappho cecinit decenter,
  sic Dionaeos memorans amores,
    docta puella.
  Pindarus Graius, meus inde Flaccus
10 Sapphico metro modulante plectro
  molliter pangens citharista, blando
    carmine lusit.

whom it holds close with ties of affection, since I desire that 5
as father in your see you replicate in your teaching such a
Gregory as was the famous Nazianzene. See, father, I have
sent the poems that you instructed me to write, and they
will serve me well, if, dear one, they are pleasing to you. You
also bid me to send you verses in the Sapphic meter. Pardon 10
me, the harvest of my modest estate presses me hard. Give
me time, while I reap. I will soon be ready to obey you. If I
have my fill of produce, perhaps I will sing better. If I can
compose, I will send you a work in that meter; receive it
with the eagerness that your love dictates to you.

7

Again to Bishop Gregory

With friendly heart and charming pen you send me a letter
expressing a wish, writing kind words in the course of your
greeting, my dear Gregory, requesting that I now take on a 5
new task in the meter that Sappho sang so beautifully, tell-
ing thereby of the loves of Venus, a learned maiden. Pindar
in Greek and then my own Flaccus, their plectrums play- 10
ing a Sapphic meter, lyric poets of gentle verse, sported in
soothing song.

Cur mihi iniungis lyricos melodes,
voce qui rauca modo vix susurro?
15 Eloqui chordis mea dextra nescit
    pollice dulci.
Qui vel haec olim mihi si fuissent
nota prudentum docili Camena,
per tot oblitus fueram benignam
20   tempora Musam,
cum labor doctis sit, ut ista pangant,
dogma nec quisquam rapienter intret
et satis constent resonare paucis
    metra poetis.
25 Non leve est nautae rate transfretare
vincere aut vastum pelagus natatu.
Vix procelloso repetunt sub austro
    carbasa portum.
Arduum nobis iter et profundum,
30 quo iubes pergi, tamen ibo votis.
Si minus possum pedibus viare,
    ducor amore.
Praestitit, pastor, tua mi voluntas
codicem farsum tumido cothurno
35 quemque paupertas mea vix valebat
    tangere sensu.
Regiis verbis humili repugnat,
divites versus inopi recusans
et mihi Mopso reserare nolens
40   docta sophistis;
disputans multum variante milto
quaeque sunt rythmis vel amica metris,
Sapphicum quantum trimetrumve adornet
    dulcis epodus.

Why do you require from me lyrical strains, who only whisper with difficulty in a harsh voice? My hand has no skill 15 to speak on the strings sweetly plucked by the thumb. Or if these things had once been known to me, for poetic art can be learned by the wise, after so long a time I would have forgotten the Muses' blessing, for it is hard for the learned 20 to compose such things, and no one quickly acquires this knowledge, but it is well established that few are the poets who sing in this meter. It is no easy thing for a mariner to 25 cross the sea in a ship, or with his sailing to conquer the boundless deep. Sails only with a struggle regain the harbor under a southerly gale. The voyage you bid me follow is difficult and demanding, yet I will go as you wish. Even if I can't 30 make the journey on foot, I am impelled by love.

Your goodwill, my shepherd, has provided me with a volume packed full with swelling grandiloquence of the kind 35 my deficiency is scarcely able to comprehend with my senses. With its stately words it rejects the humble, denying to the poor the richness of verses, and refusing to reveal to me, a Mopsus, what is known to the learned, setting out 40 with many diverse rubrics what is fitting to rhythms or meters, and how Sapphics or the trimeter are refined by a charming epode.

45 Multus auctorum numerus habetur
plura dicentum modulo canoro,
quae volens isto memorare metro
    nomina frango,
maxime qui nunc resolutus arte
50 postque bis denos loquor istud annos,
clara quod scripsit citharam terendo
    Lesbia virgo.
Scire qui vult haec Libycas harenas
ante per litus numerare tendat,
55 cuncta quam metris ratione cauta
    carmine cingat.
Nam moras feci, remoratus ipse,
pluribus causis modo hinc et inde,
nec vacans legi placida quiete
60   dulce sophistae.
Scito nam, pastor, nec adhuc cucurri
ordinem totum religens libelli;
Sed satis, crede, est, satis est amanti
    sola voluntas.
65 Ergo laxatus celeri volatu
ad patrem sacrum comitante voto
et sibi nostrum renovans amorem
    perge, libelle.
Forte non possum piger ire gressu
70 quo vocat blandus meus ille vultus.
In vicem nostram, rogo te, libelle,
    redde salutem.
Sit memor fili pater, ore dulci
hunc precans qui nos, mare et astra fecit,
75 ac piis votis bene se colentem
    pectore servet,

A large number of authors are known who composed 45
many poems in tuneful song, but if I wished to recount them
in this meter, I would mutilate their names, especially since
now divorced from study, after twice ten years I recite the 50
verse which the famous Sappho wrote, playing her lyre, the
Lesbian maiden. He who wants to acquire this skill let him
first strive to number the Libyan sands on the shore, before 55
he expresses all in a poem in meter with careful art. And so I
have taken a long time, meeting delays for many reasons,
now this and now that, and have not been free to read in
peace and quiet the sweet lesson of the scholar. For know, 60
my shepherd, I have still not perused the whole length of
the book in my reading. But, believe me, the will alone is
enough, enough for a lover.

So released on a speedy flight to the holy father with my 65
good wishes, a fresh proof of my love for him, go on your
way, book. It happens in my sloth I cannot make my way
where that enchanting countenance summons me. In my 70
place I ask you then, my book, bring him greeting. May a
father remember his son, praying with sweet voice to the
one who created us, the sea, and the stars, that he protect 75
with his embrace one who dutifully worships him with holy

feminae carae, sibi mente nexae,
quem colunt, Agnes, Radegundis. Idem,
sicut exposcunt vice filiarum,
80   solve salutem.
Adde Iustinam pariter precantem,
nempe commendans famulam propinquam,
et refer quantum sibi cara profert
    neptis honorem.
85 Haec tibi promptus prece, voce, mente
solvo, vix implens, ego pauper arte,
sed tamen largo refluens amore,
    care Gregori.

Domine et dulcis ora pro me et tibi reputa qui me in Galliis
posito post tot annos . . .

8

Ad Baudoaldum episcopum

Summe sacerdotum, bonitatis opima facultas,
    culmen honore tuo, lumen amore meo,
officiis venerande sacris, pietatis alumne,
    pignore amicitiae corde tenende meae,
5 florens in studiis et sacra in lege fidelis,
    semper agens animae dona futura tuae,
te, pater, ergo precans terram, freta, sidera testor,
    ut velis ore sacro me memor esse tuum.

prayers; him too those devoted women Radegund and Ag-
nes, joined in spirit with him, likewise worship. For them
also, as they request in the manner of daughters, secure sal-   80
vation. To them add Justina, who likewise prays to you, rec-
ommend your servant and kinswoman, and recall how much
glory your dearly-loved niece wins for herself.

Ready in prayer, voice, and mind I make to you this offer-   85
ing, with difficulty completed, poor as I am in art, but over-
flowing with abundant love, my dear Gregory.

My sweet lord, pray for me and consider who, when I have
been in Gaul for so many years . . .

8

To Bishop Baudoald

Highest of bishops, rich resource of goodness, eminent in
your status, brilliant in my love, revered for your sacred of-
fice, fostered by holiness, who by the bond of friendship win
a place in my heart, flourishing in studies and faithful in the   5
sacred law, always pursuing the future rewards of your soul,
you, father, I therefore beseech, by the earth, sea, and stars,
that in your holy prayers you remember me, your own.

9

Ad Sidonium episcopum

Reddita ne doleas, felix Magantia, casus;
    antistes rediit qui tibi ferret opem.
Ne maerore gravi lacrimans orbata iaceres,
    te meruisse fame . . .
5 Porrigit ecce manum genitor Sidonius urbi,
    quo renovante loco prisca ruina perit,
iura sacerdoti sacro moderamine servans,
    per cuius studium crevit et ipse gradus.
Parturis assidue gravidos, Ecclesia, fructus,
10 quam vir apostolico iunctus amore regit.
Suscipit heredes caelesti germine natos,
    tali nupta viro quando marita placet.
Te vigili custode lupus non diripit agnos,
    te pascente gregem non ovis ulla perit.
15 Cautius in tuto per mitia pascua ducis,
    toxica ne noceant, florea rura paras.
Sis cibus ut populi, placide ieiunia servas
    et satias alios subtrahis unde tibi.
Nudos veste tegis, captivo vincula solvens,
20 deposito reddens libera colla iugo.
Exulibus domus es, sed et esurientibus esca:
    felix cui Christus debitor inde manet!
Te doctrina probum, providentia sacra modestum
    fecit et eloquio vincere mella tuo.

9

To Bishop Sidonius

Do not bewail your misfortunes, happy Mainz, for you are
restored; a bishop has returned to bring you aid. To free you
from lying bereft weeping in bitter grief, you have deserved
by your hunger . . . See, your father Sidonius stretches out   5
his hand to the city; the site is restored and the former ruin
vanishes. He wields the powers of bishop with holy author-
ity, and by his zeal the office itself has grown. Constantly,
Church, you bring to birth a teeming harvest, for he rules   10
you as your husband in a union of apostolic love. He receives
heirs born of heavenly stock, since a bride wed to such a
man wins favor.

   Under your vigilant stewardship no wolf carries off the
lambs, with you as shepherd of the flock not a single sheep
perishes. Cautiously you lead the way in safety though wel-   15
coming pastures; you find flowery fields so the poisonous
do no harm. To bring sustenance to your people you calmly
keep fast, and you satisfy others in depriving yourself. You
dress the naked in clothing, loose the chains from the cap-
tive, and set free necks that have thrown off their yoke. You   20
are a home to exiles and food for the hungry: happy is he
to whom Christ is in debt. Your learning made you honest,
your holy wisdom modest, and they caused you to outdo

25 Templa vetusta novans specioso fulta decore
    inseris hinc populis plus in amore Deum.
Ut plebem foveas et Rheni congruis amnes.
    Quid referat terris qui bona praebet aquis?
Hic quod fana micant, a te instaurata quod extant,
30   vivis in aeterno laude fluente tibi.
Haec habeas longos meritorum fruge per annos
    et crescente diu de grege vota feras.

10

Ad Ragnemodum episcopum

Summe pater patriae, dulci mihi nomine Rucco,
    interiora mei cordis amore tenens,
quidquid amicitiae veteris collegimus ambo
    crescit in affectum semper, opime, meum.
5 Nam mihi nulla meos oblivio tollit amantes;
    ante sit extremum, quam mihi desit amor.
Unde, beate pater, properans dependo salutem,
    optans longinquo te superesse gradu.
Hinc etiam genitae reddunt tibi pectore grates
10   munere pro niveo marmore de Pario,
quae, quotiens epulae disco tribuuntur in illo,
    in doni specie te pietate vident.
Nam pro gemmarum serie tibi reddat honorem
    cui data proficiunt crux veneranda throno.

honey in your speech. Rebuilding old churches, constructed 25
with eye-catching beauty, you thereby inspire your people
with greater love for God. To serve the populace you even
channel the course of the Rhine. What will he provide on
land who supplies blessings from water? Because of the
gleaming shrines here, and because they were rebuilt by you,
you will live for eternity on a full flood of praise. May this be 30
your life for long years as reward for your virtues, and may
you long gain your wish by the increase of your flock.

10

To Bishop Ragnemod

Highest father of the homeland, sweet name of Rucco to
me, who possess in love my innermost heart, whatever long-
standing friendship we have both shared continually grows
in my strength of feeling, noble one. For no forgetfulness 5
ever will take my loved ones from me; may my end come be-
fore my love fail me. And so, blessed father, I eagerly offer
you my greeting, with the hope that you live long in your of-
fice. Your daughters too offer you heartfelt thanks for the 10
snow-white present of Parian marble. Whenever meals are
served on that dish, at the sight of that gift in holy love they
will see you. Moreover may the venerable enthroned cross
grant you honor for the row of jewels that it enjoys as a gift
from you.

11

Ad Droctoveum abbatem

Vir venerande, sacer meritis et honore colende,
    Droctovee, mihi semper amore pater,
qui de discipulis Germani iure beati
    norma magisterii factus es ipse sui,
5 cuius pontificis sacra per vestigia currens
    despicis hic mundum, dum cupis ire polo,
perge libenter iter caeli mansurus in orbe,
    et pro me famulo, quaeso, precato Deum.

12

Ad Faramodum referendarium

Dulcis amice mihi, memorabile nomen amantis,
    promptus in officiis vir, Faramode, bonis,
si non ipse adii, te pagina missa salutet
    solvat et obsequium quod minus ipse gero.
5 Commendesque libens dominis me regibus, oro,
    et referas grates pro pietatis ope.
Inpenso affectu me pagina vestra requirat;
    hoc remeante tamen redde, benigne, vicem.

11

To Abbot Droctoveus

Venerable man, holy in your virtues, worthy of high honor, Droctoveus, always for me a father in love, who of the pupils of the truly blessed Germanus have become yourself the model of his teaching; following in the saintly footsteps of 5 this prelate you scorn the world here, as you long to mount to the sky. Joyfully make your way to the heavens, while still to remain on earth, and pray to God, I beg, for me, your servant.

12

To the referendary Faramod

My sweet friend, with the cherished name of a loved one, Faramod, quick to offer your good offices, seeing that I have not come in person, let the page I send give greeting and pay the duty that I fail to pay myself. Kindly recommend me, I 5 beg, to my lords the kings, and give them thanks for the wealth of their bounty. With urgent affection may a letter from you seek me out, and when this man returns, be generous and pay back the favor in kind.

13

Ad Lupum et Vualdonem diaconos

Corde parentali, iugi pietate colendi,
  hinc Lupe blande mihi, Waldo vel inde sacer,
ut bonitate pari simul estis honore ministri,
  sic mihi consimili semper amore rati.
5 Quod valeo facio: absens vel dependo salutem;
  si non possum oculis, vos peto litterulis.
Pontifici summo nos commendate, precamur,
  regibus et dominis ferte salutis opus.
Droctoveo dulci, clero et concivibus, oro,
10   quod praesens facerem, vos adhibete vicem.
Mummolus egregius veneretur Caesariusque
  et Constantino me memorate meo.

14

De basilicae
sancti Laurenti trabe

Laurenti, merito flammis vitalibus uste,
  qui fervente fide victor ab igne redis,
vir dilecte Deo terreno in corpore quondam,
  tunc quoque sidereus iam tibi sensus erat.

13

To Deacons Lupus and Waldo

Worthy of cherishing with a kinsman's affection and con-
stant devotion, Lupus with your charm and Waldo with your
holiness, as you both with equal benevolence hold the office
of deacon, so you are both always held in like love by me. I ⁵
do what I can: though absent at least I send you my greet-
ing; if I cannot seek you out with my eyes, I do with my let-
ter. Commend me to the eminent bishop, I pray, and convey
my duty of greeting to my lord kings. As for my dear Droc-
toveus, the clergy, and their fellow citizens, I beg, take my ¹⁰
place and do what I would do if present. Pay my respects to
noble Mummolus and to Caesarius, and remember me to
my Constantine.

14

On a beam of the church of
Saint Lawrence

Lawrence, who for your virtue were scorched by life-giving
flames, but by the heat of your faith rose up from the fire
as a victor, a man loved by God, while still in an earthly
body, already then in your senses you were among the stars.

5   Qui potuisti oculos tactu revocare sepultos,
      rursus et in vacua fronte referre diem
   luminis extinctas iterum accendisse lucernas
      credimus haec signo te faciente crucis.
   Addita nunc etiam populis miracula praestas,
10   ut fidei tribuas indubitanter opem.
   Dum tua templa novant breviori robore plebes,
      creveruntque trabes crevit et alma fides.
   Stipite contracto tua se mercede tetendit;
      quantum parva prius, postea caesa fuit.
15 Crescere plus meruit succisa securibus arbor
      et didicit sicca longior esse coma.
   Unde recisa fuit, populis fert inde salutem;
      si venit intrepidus, lumina caecus habet.
   Tu levita sacer, poena purgate fideli,
20   unde prius flammas, hinc modo lumen habes.
   Visa his temporibus venerandi antistitis acta,
      sed tamen aeterno sunt memoranda die.

15

De domo lignea

Cede Parum, paries lapidoso structe metallo;
   artificis merito praefero ligna tibi.
Aethera mole sua tabulata palatia pulsant,
   quo neque rima patet consolidante manu.

You who were able to recall with your touch eyes buried in 5
darkness and bring back the daylight once more to the un-
seeing brow, we believe that you reignited the lamps of vi-
sion that had gone out, performing this miracle by the sign
of the cross. Now too you offer up a further miracle for the
populace to grant them without hesitating the blessing of 10
faith. When the people were rebuilding your church, the
timber was too short, but a beam grew in length, and along
with it their loving faith. The wood was shrunken, but by
your bounty it lengthened; a piece was cut off as small as had
been its whole length before. A tree that was cut down by 15
axes was able to increase in size and learned to become
longer, though its foliage was withered and dry. From what
was cut off he brought healing to the people; a blind man
who approaches without fear regains sight. Saintly deacon,
washed clean by the pain you suffered for the faith, from 20
first experiencing flames you now enjoy the light. These ac-
tions of the venerable priest were witnessed in this present
time, but they deserve to be recounted for eternity.

15

On a palace of wood

Go back to Paros, walls built with materials of stone; be-
cause of an artist's skill I prefer wood to you. A many-storied
palace strikes the heavens with its size; no crack appears, for

5   Quidquid saxa, sablo, calces, argila tuentur,
      singula silva favens aedificavit opus.
   Altior in medio quadrataque porticus ambit
      et sculpturata lusit in arte faber.

16

Ad Chrodinum ducem

Inclite dux, meritis totum vulgate per orbem,
      quem nimis egregium splendida fama refert,
non ego praeteream praeconia celsa, Chrodine,
      ne videar solus magna silere bonis.
5   Itala terra tibi, pariter Germania plaudunt;
      laus tua cunctorum semper in ore sonat.
Clarus ab antiquis, digno generosior ortu,
      regibus et patriae qui placiturus eras.
Te tutorem alii nutritoremque fatentur
10   et fit certamen de pietate tua.
Ut habeant alii, nulli tua dona recusas;
      tu tibi plus auges quas bene fundis opes.
Cui possis praestare, libens exquiris et optas;
      ut sis apud cunctos, hos facis esse tuos.
15 Es generale bonum, nulli gravis, omnibus aequus;

handicraft has made it solid. Whatever roles stones, sand, 5
lime, and clay perform, that whole building a single forest
joyfully constructed. It is higher in the middle, surrounded
by a square colonnade, and ornamented by a craftsman's
skill in carving.

16

To Duke Chrodin

Famed duke, known throughout the whole world for your
virtues, whose great excellence brilliant fame spreads abroad,
I would not myself fail to mention your high praise, Chro-
din, lest I alone seem to keep silent about great matters be-
fore the good. Italy applauds your virtues and Germany like- 5
wise the same; your praise sounds always on the lips of all.
Distinguished by your ancestors, ennobled by high birth,
you were destined to win the favor of country and kings.
Others acclaim you as their protector and their sustainer
and rivalry grows up around the exercise of your bounty. To 10
provide possessions for others, you deny gifts to no one; in
wisely disposing of your wealth you thereby win more for
yourself. You eagerly seek out and long for people to receive
your largesse; in order to be close to all, you make them de-
voted to you. You are a universal good, harsh to no one, to 15

iustitiae socium nulla rapina tenet.
Mitis in alloquio, placidus, gravis atque modestus,
   omnia cui data sunt, ut decus omne geras.
Gentibus adstrictus, Romanis carus haberis,
20   felix qui populis semper in ore manes.

everyone fair; as devotee of justice you have no truck with extortion. Gentle in address, calm, sober and temperate, you have received all qualities to display every grace. You are embraced by the nations and held dear by the Romans; happy are you who will always be on the lips of the people.   20

BOOK TEN

Expositio orationis dominicae

Tanta pietatis profunda misericordia, filii dilectissimi, circa
genus humanum nostri patuit salvatoris, qua nos ereptos de
concatenatis mundi naufragiis ad portum perpetuae detulit
libertatis, ut nec verbis exsequi nec lingua patefieri neque
ipsa valeat cogitatione pulsari, cui parum videbatur de limo
quod condidit, quod cruore redemit, quod baptismo reno-
vavit, nisi ad salutis cumulum, mens nostra ne lapsum igno-
ranter incurreret, instrueret etiam qualiter exoraret, ne, si
non docuisset quemadmodum deberemus iustas voti preces
offerre, essemus aut certe temerarii aut erroris nube confusi
et nesciendo quae petere magis admitteremus peccatum,
potius quam purgare deberemus admissum, et unde expec-
tabamus posse venire suffragium, videremur incurrere de-
trimentum, cum de oratione incondita fieret periculi plus
2   causa quam voti. Inde retinentes eius mysteria et quam
multa sint in brevitate collata, propter aedificationem Ec-
clesiae paucis docemus explicare, quia tunc nobis melius

I

Explanation of the Lord's Prayer

So great was the profound mercy of our savior's kindness manifested for the human race, my dearest sons, by which he snatched us from the successive shipwrecks of the world and carried us to the harbor of eternal freedom, that it cannot be expressed in words or articulated by the tongue or even attained to in thought. It seemed too little to him that he created us from mud, redeemed us with his blood, and gave us new life with baptism, unless to ensure our complete salvation he also instructed us how to pray so our minds not incur a fault out of ignorance. He feared that if he had not taught us how we should present a proper plea for what we wanted, we would certainly be reckless, if not misled by a cloud of error, and not knowing what to ask for we would commit a sin rather than expiate one committed and suffer harm from where we hoped assistance would come, since an ill-framed prayer provides an occasion for danger rather than the fulfillment of a wish. So bearing in mind its mysteries and the many things that are contained in a brief compass, for the instruction of the Church we are teaching in a few words an explanation because these things will give 2

placebunt auditu, cum patuerint intellectu. Itaque ad ipsum veniamus sanctae orationis sermonem.

3   *Pater noster, qui es in caelis.* Ecce vox Domini praedicantis, de quo propheta dicit "nubes pluant iustum," arcanae scientiae lumen effudit et, ut nostram ariditatem sermonis
4   imbre reficeret, veluti fons aquae salientis erupit. Quis enim tantum secretum mysterii caelestis hominibus revelaret aut hoc docere vel praesumeret vel sciret? Numquid Abraham, Moyses, propheta vel angelus, nisi unigenitus, cui soli in maiestatis plenitudine pater est notus? Nam reliqui tantum meruerunt de Deo in terra cognoscere quantum ipse de caelo voluit ministrare. Filius enim, in quo pater est totus unitate substantiae, non confusione personae, subiectum habebat hoc nosse, non alterius munere, sed potestate natu-
5   rae. Ergo dicendo patrem nostrum esse in caelis peregrinationem nobis significat dum sumus in terris, iuxta illud "incola sum ego in terra." Unde videtur instruere, ut ad excelsa iugiter animum elevantes ea Deo tribuente festinemus peragere, quae nos in aeternae vitae beatitudinem placato patre, Christo duce faciant introire et promissa praemia filii valeant obtinere. Unde audito Deo patre nullus tam crudelis sit filius, ut non festinet ad veri genitoris amplexus.

6   Item congrue *pater noster,* quia homo renascendo per baptismum effectus est Dei filius, qui prius per praevaricationem factus fuerat inimicus et perditus. Ergo cuius gra-

more pleasure to the hearing when they are apparent to the understanding. Accordingly let us come to the actual words of the holy prayer.

Our father, who are in heaven. Here is the voice of the Lord speaking out, of whom the prophet says "Let the clouds rain down justice." It has poured forth the light of secret knowledge and burst forth like a spring of bubbling water to refresh our parched state with a shower of language. For who could have revealed so great a secret of heavenly mystery to men or would have dared or known how to communicate it? Abraham, Moses, a prophet, or an angel? No, rather the only begotten, who alone knew the father in the fullness of his majesty. For everyone else was able to know only as much about God on earth as he himself wished to make known from heaven. The son, however, in whom the father exists entirely by the unity of substance, not the intermingling of persons, has it in his power to know this not by the gift of another, but by the power of his nature. So in saying our father is in heaven he indicates to us our exile while we are on earth, according to the saying, "I am a foreigner on earth." Thereby he instructs us constantly to raise our minds to the things above and with God's support hasten to perform those things that with the favor of the father and Christ as our leader will cause us to enter the blessing of eternal life and attain the rewards promised by the son. Therefore let no one be so unnatural a son that when he has heard God the father he does not hurry to the embrace of his true progenitor.

Again we appropriately say *our father* because a man when reborn by baptism becomes the son of God, though previously by sin he had been hostile to him and lost. And so he

tia fruitur iam patrem libere confitetur. Sed licet non simus de eo patre sic filii quomodo persona domini nostri Iesu Christi, quia ille de ipsius est natus substantia, nos autem dignatus est creare de terra, attamen per gratiam unigeniti nos effici meruimus adoptivi, et ideo qui in Ecclesia Catholica ex aqua et spiritu sancto nascitur, inter Dei filios conputatur.

7   Item: *Pater noster qui es in caelis.* In hac confessione et Deum veneramur et mandata sequimur et fidem nostram exponimus et eos qui patrem in caelis denegant refutamus.

8   Item dicendo *pater noster* habemus quod in ipso diligere, agnoscendo Deum habemus pariter quod timere. Timeamus ergo quod iustus est, amemus quod pius est, ne quod ille sollicite contulit nos velimus perdere neglegenter et divina beneficia nostro sint excessu calcata.

9   Quisquis ergo patrem illum appellat, sicut decet filium sic vitam suam inmaculate dispenset, quia ipse est filius qui non contribulat genitorem, non exasperat coheredem, fratris caritatem non violat, testamentum conditoris non dissipat, sequitur monita, festinat implere mandata; quod si recalcitraverit, proiectus contumaciter de possessione discedit, nec aliqua iam fronte hereditatem repetit quem admissi culpa damnavit. Unde qui ad Deum patrem venimus Christi fratres dicimur, si in peccati crimine non versemur. Nam amittit nomen filii qui fuerit servus peccati.

10   Quod autem non singulariter pater meus, sed *pater noster* dicimus ad hoc pertinere cognoscitur, ut nullus pro se tan-

now freely recognizes him as father from whom he enjoys grace. But though we are not sons of that father in the same way as the person of our lord Jesus Christ, because he is born of that one's very substance, while he saw fit to create us from earth, still by the grace of the only begotten we have won the right to become adoptive sons, and so whoever is born in the Catholic Church of water and the Holy Spirit is accounted among God's sons.

Again: *Our father, who are in heaven.* In this declaration we pay honor to God, we follow his commandments, we avow our faith, and we refute those who deny a father in heaven. 7

Again by saying *our father* we have in him something to love and by recognizing him as God we have equally something to fear. Let us fear him then because he is just and love him because he is merciful, so that we will not carelessly throw away what his care has bestowed on us and that his divine benefactions are not trampled by our failings. 8

Whoever then calls him father let him conduct his life impeccably as befits a son, because he is a true son who causes his father no grief, does not harass his joint heir, does no violence to a brother's affection, does not ride roughshod over his creator's will, but follows his advice, and hurries to fulfill his instructions; but if he rebels, he will be thrown out and will insolently depart from the property and will not now have the face to reclaim his inheritance, since culpability for a crime has condemned him. Therefore we who have come to God as father are called the brothers of Christ, if we do not engage ourselves in the crime of sin. For he who is the servant of sin loses the name of son. 9

But the fact that we say not "my father," in the singular, but "our father" clearly relates to the practice whereby 10

tum, sed generaliter pro omnibus misericordem Dominum deprecetur, quatenus ab hoste perfido cuncti pariter libe-

11 rentur. Omnes enim qui in ecclesia conveniunt eodem se muro concludunt, quoniam, etsi multa membra sunt, tamen in uno Christi corpore continentur et ideo qui simul iungun-tur in templo separari non debent nec in voto. Nam sicut in membris nostris respicimus qualiter humerus humero, ma-nus manui, pes pedi subveniunt, ita congruum creditur ut monitis, orationibus, lacrimis nobis ipsis a nobis invicem succurratur, propter illud "invicem onera vestra portantes."

12 Denique frequenter alter pro alterius crimine confidenter obtinet qui pro se suggerere confunditur ex pudore, quia in suo facinore verecundia nil praesumit. Ergo unusquisque supplicet pro omnibus in commune, quoniam sicut in se di-visa domus non stabit, sic unita ruinae non subiacet; et bene Dominus, auctor pacis, sic docuit, ut quidquid unus peteret omnibus videretur proficere.

13 Item bene *pater noster* additur, quia nisi quis recte credat in Christo non potest habere patrem in caelo. Non est enim ipse pater Ariano, Iudaeo, Photino, Manichaeo, Sabellio, et reliquis pestibus veneno pravi cordis infectis et pessimae confessionis falce succisis, qui de filio quam iniuste a Deo patre nostro recensi sunt, ex patre suo diabolo frucore car-nat. Et ideo nobis pater in caelis est, qui recte filium confite-mur in terris.

14 *Sanctificetur nomen tuum.* Vigilanter considerandum est quid in hoc vocabulo admonitio divina significet, dicendo sanctificetur nomen tuum. Numquid invenitur superior a quo Deus pater sanctificari valeat, quasi ut nos videamur ali-

no one prays to merciful God just for himself but in general for everyone so that we all may equally be freed from the treacherous enemy. For all who come together in the church 11 enclose themselves with the same wall, since, although they are many limbs, yet they are brought together in the one body of Christ, and therefore those who are joined together in church should not be separated even in prayer. For just as in our bodies we see how shoulder assists shoulder, hand hand, and foot foot, so it is thought appropriate that by advice, prayers, and tears we mutually help each other in accordance with that saying "mutually bearing your burdens." Moreover frequently one person confidently wins a petition 12 for the fault of another who is ashamed to speak for himself because his inhibition at his crime prevents him from action. Therefore let each person pray for everyone else altogether, since just as a house divided against itself will not stand, so one united suffers no collapse and the Lord, the author of peace, rightly taught that whatever one person sought would benefit all.

Again *our father* is rightly added because unless a person 13 believes correctly in Christ, he cannot have a father in heaven. For he is not the father of the Arian, the Jew, the Photinian, the Manichaean, or the Sabellian, or of any other of those plagues corrupted by the poison of a false heart and cut down by the scythe of depraved belief . . . And therefore he is our father in heaven, since we correctly avow his son on earth.

May your name be made holy. We must diligently consider 14 what the divine instruction means by this wording, saying "may your name be made holy." Is some higher being discovered by whom God the father can be made holy, as though

quid illi orando praestare, cum magis ipse cuncta sanctifi-
cet? Sed sanctificetur, id est benedicatur, nomen tuum in-
cessanter omnibus linguis universis in locis, cuius dona sunt
hoc ipsum quod respiramus et vivimus.

15   *Santificetur nomen tuum.* Deus cum sit omnium elemento-
rum concentu laudandus et sanctus, ut in nobis nomen eius
sanctificetur, id est firmiter teneatur, optamus et in ea qua
16   nos abluit baptismi sanctitate vivamus. Ergo in hoc tempore
non novam sanctificationem requirimus, sed quam inconta-
minatam percepimus ut sine vitii macula conservemus. Nam
in homine fructus bonae conversationis sanctificatio Dei est.

17   Hoc quoque ordine nomen eius recte sanctificari dici-
mus, ut, si quis dono divinitatis vitam videat nobis esse sin-
ceram, gratias largitori referat et in nostris operibus sanc-
tum nomen eius extollat, quoniam recte omnis laus illi
redditur a quo vota complentur.

18   Item *sanctificetur nomen tuum.* Quia ipsa oratione non con-
tinetur expressum in nobis sanctificetur nomen tuum, vide-
mur non tantummodo pro nobis optare sanctificetur nomen
eius, sed et pro illis qui necdum ad baptismi meruerunt gra-
tiam pervenire. Nam in Christi plenissima caritate docemur
etiam pro inimicis orare, quia et ipse non amicos et fideles,
sed adversarios suos et culpabiles de mortis carcere libera-
vit.

19   *Adveniat regnum tuum.* Dubitare non licet Dominum
Deum semper hic et ubique regnare nec aliquando de regni
sorte sanctam trinitatem sumpsisse principium nec haberi
fine claudendum, re vera cum apud Deum stabilitate sua

we seem to benefit him in some way by praying, when rather it is he that makes everything holy? Rather may your name be made holy, that is, be blessed, unceasingly, in all languages and all places, for by your gifts we have our very breath and life.

May your name be made holy. Since God is to be praised 15 and held sacred by the chorus of all elements, we wish that in us his name be made holy, that is, firmly adhered to, and that we may live in the holiness of baptism with which he cleansed us. And therefore in the present time we do not 16 look for a new advent of holiness but to preserve without stain of fault the one we have received unsullied. For in humans the fruit of good conduct is the sanctification of God.

We rightly say that his name is made holy in this manner 17 too, that if anyone sees by the grace of God that our life is pure, he gives thanks to the donor and extols his holy name because of our actions, since rightly all praise is given to him by whom prayers are fulfilled.

Again *may your name be made holy.* Because in the prayer it 18 is not specifically said that your name be made holy *in us,* we wish not only for his name to be made holy on our own behalf, but also for those who have not yet had the fortune to achieve the grace of baptism. For in the great fullness of the charity of Christ we are taught to pray even for our enemies, because he himself freed from the prison of death not his friends and the faithful but his opponents and the culpable.

May your kingdom come. It is not possible to doubt that the 19 Lord God always reigns here and everywhere and that the Holy Trinity at no time made a beginning to its reign nor was it subject to being brought to an end, when in reality for God in his immutability time does not change and for him

tempora non mutentur, cui nec sol occidit neque nox in vice succedit. Sed dicimus adveniat regnum tuum, non ut illi aliunde obveniat, id est ut ei regnum praestetur a superiore persona, sed nobis scilicet ut illud adveniat, quod per mediatorem Christum poscimus repromissum ut cum illo regne-

20 mus liberi qui in mundo servivimus sub lege peccati. Ipse enim postulavit a patre dicens, "pater, ubi ego sum, et isti sint mecum" et alibi, "tunc iusti fulgebunt sicut sol in regno

21 patris eorum." Denique ob hoc evacuavit Tartaros, ut repleat caelos. Ergo hac ratione precamur ut regnum eius adveniat, non ut ipse, quod possidet, hoc adquirat, sed quod est nobis pollicitus ut persolvat.

22 Potest et sic intellegi *adveniat regnum tuum,* id est, veniat in corde nostro regni tui sincerum desiderium, ut possimus diaboli vincere blandimentum. Tunc enim in nobis serpentina falsitate subdolus hostis non praevalet, quando nos constanter respexerit divini regni desideria concepisse; id est, regnante Christo non possit in nostris corporibus regnare peccatum.

23 Item cum dicimus *adveniat regnum tuum,* admonemur ut nihil de terreni regni divitiis exspectemus qui omnem spem in futuri regni facultate plantamus.

24 Item *adveniat regnum tuum.* Agnoscimur his verbis eas increpare personas quae saeculi istam vitam diutius volunt protrahere, cum omnes iusti regnum illud ut festinanter veniat videntur optare.

25 Vel certe *adveniat regnum tuum,* hoc est, Christus nobis adveniat quem cotidie sanctorum chorus veneranter expec-

neither the sun sets nor the night in its turn succeeds it. We, however, say "may your kingdom come," not so that it come to him from someone else, that is, that his kingdom be bestowed on him by a higher person, but that there come to us what through Christ as intermediary we claim as promised that we will reign in freedom with him who have been slaves under the law of sin in the world. For he himself requested 20 of his father, saying, "father, where I am let them too be with me" and in another place, "then the just will shine like the sun in the kingdom of their father." Moreover for this rea- 21 son he emptied out Tartarus, to fill up the heavens. Therefore for this reason we pray that his kingdom may come, not that he gain what he already possesses but that he fulfill to us the promise he made us.

May your kingdom come can also be understood in this way, 22 that is, may a sincere desire for your kingdom come in our hearts, so that we can overcome the enticements of the devil. For the treacherous enemy does not prevail then with his serpentine deceit when he sees that we have resolutely conceived a desire for the heavenly kingdom; that is, when Christ reigns, sin cannot reign in our bodies.

Again when we say *may your kingdom come,* we are in- 23 structed to expect for nothing from the riches of the earthly realm but to ground all our hope in the resources of the future kingdom.

Again *may your kingdom come.* By these words we are seen 24 to be reproaching those people who want to drag out this present life longer, when all the just desire that kingdom to come quickly.

And certainly *may your kingdom come;* that is, may Christ 25 come to us, whom daily the choir of saints reverently awaits,

tat, in cuius promissione se confidunt iusti regnare, de cuius adventu apostolus ait, "tunc rapiemur simul in nubibus obviam Christo in aera et sic semper cum domino erimus."

26   Sed videamus qui rapientur cum beato Paulo in nubibus. Numquid homicidae, luxuriosi, fallaces, ebriosi, adulteri, rapaces, maledici? Tales enim nisi correpti fuerint, non solum quia non possunt in illo itinere participari cum sancto apostolo, cuius modo monita non secuntur, aut occurrere Christo vel paterna vel prosumunt, immo magis, si se a facie dei in fissuris petrarum valerent abscondere, super se cadere tunc montes optarent.

27   Ergo advertamus quibus illud regnum promittitur: "beati pauperes spiritu, quoniam ipsorum est regnum caelorum." In principio beatitudinum humiles corde praeposuit ac per hoc exclusit superbos et tumidos, ubi dicit pauperes spiritu
28   regnaturos. Deinde: "beati mites, beati qui lugent, beati qui esuriunt et sitiunt iustitiam, beati misericordes, beati pacifici, beati mundo corde," et reliqua. Ecce illi invitantur ad aeternam requiem qui tali desudaverint temporaliter in labore. Vere hoc est indeficienter regnare, coronam beatitudinis istis ornatam floribus possidere, Deum sine confusione mereri conspicere, quo praesente inveniet anima
29   quod amavit. Nam si in hoc saeculo dicit se ad praesens humana regnare fragilitas et paupertas, si quaedam illi blandiatur de falsa prosperitate fugitiva felicitas, quanto magis illud regnum quaerendum est ubi semper liliorum rosarumque

by whose promise the just are assured of their reign, of whose coming the apostle said, "then we will be snatched up together in the clouds to meet Christ in the air, and so we will always be with the Lord."

But let us see who will be snatched up with the blessed 26 Paul in the clouds. Surely not the murderers, the self-indulgent, the deceitful, the drunkards, the adulterers, the greedy, the slanderers? For unless such people are corrected, not only because they cannot share in that journey with the saintly apostle whose injunctions they now do not follow, or to meet Christ and . . . , but rather, if they could hide in the cracks of rocks from the face of God, they would then want mountains to fall on them.

So let us consider whom that kingdom is promised to: 27 "Blessed are the poor in spirit, for theirs is the kingdom of heaven." In the beginning of the beatitudes he gave preference to the humble in heart and thereby excluded the proud and self-important, when he said the poor in spirit would reign. And then: "Blessed are the meek, blessed are those 28 who mourn, blessed are those who hunger and thirst for justice, blessed are the merciful, blessed are the peacemakers, blessed the pure in heart," and so on. See, those who have struggled with such effort in this life are invited to eternal rest. Truly this is to reign endlessly, to possess a crown of blessedness adorned with these flowers, to be able to see God without consternation, in whose presence the soul will discover what it has loved. For if in this world human frailty 29 and poverty lay claim to rule for the time being, if fleeting happiness with deceitful good fortune gives to that frailty a certain allure, how much the more is that kingdom to be sought after, on which the still more alluring brilliance of lil-

blandior lux adridet, ubi pictura floris odoriferi non marces-
cit, ubi loci fecunditas neque nube premitur neque sole sic-
catur, ubi non finitur cum possessore possessio, ubi quid-
quid desiderat animus dat aspectus, ubi iustus gemmas
calcabit in plateis, quas modo reges non habent in coronis,
ubi mortalitas translata in inmortalitate cum angelis sorte
simili gloriatur, ubi hominibus et Deo fit una possessio. Ibi
desideretur consortium ubi tantae felicitatis gratia posside-
tur.

30   *Fiat voluntas tua sicut in caelo et in terra.* Quid est quod sic
petitur, ut fiat voluntas Dei? Numquid aliquis potuit eius
resistere voluntati, ut non faceret aliquando quod voluit
Omnipotens? Ergo non quia illum potest aliquid inpedire,
sed ut in nobis inpleatur eius voluntas operetur, quoniam
adversario resistente nos voluntatem eius inplere non possu-
mus, nisi ipsius patrocinio muniamur.

31   Si vero quaeritur quae sit Dei voluntas, habes decem
praecepta quae per Moysen Dei sunt voluntate vulgata;
habes Dei filium, qui patris voluntatem sciens quae erant
abscondita reseravit et quae obumbrabantur in luce transfu-
dit. Itaque voluntas Dei est agnita; excusatio non erit suc-
32   cursura. Nam qui de caelo descendit ad terras, quid aliud
suae voluntatis esse vult credi, nisi salva redemptione nos
debere caritatis et humilitatis ornamenta sectari, quoniam
et ipse hoc dignatus est facere ex caritate nimia, humilitate

ies and roses always smiles, where the vision of scented flowers never fades, where the fertility of the place is not oppressed by clouds or dried out by the sun, where possession is not limited by a possessor, where whatever the heart desires is present to the eyes, where the just will walk in the streets on jewels such as kings now do not have in their crowns, where mortality is transformed into immortality, and boasts of sharing the lot of angels, where there is one common possession for men and God. There is the community that should be longed for, where the gift of such happiness is possessed.

May your will be done as in heaven also on earth. What does it 30 mean to request in this way that God's will be done? Has anyone been able to resist his will so that at some time the Almighty did not do what he wanted? Therefore let him work not because anything can obstruct him, but so that his will is fulfilled by us, since against the opposition of the enemy we cannot fulfill his will, unless we are strengthened by his support.

But if the question is raised, what is the will of God, you 31 have the Ten Commandments, broadcast by Moses according to the will of God; you have the son of God, who knowing the will of his father made clear what was obscure and brought into the light what was in darkness. And so the will of God has been made known; there can be no recourse to an excuse. For what else did he who descended from heaven 32 to earth want to be believed as his will, except that besides redemption we should pursue the adornments of charity and humility, since he too performed his actions out of great charity and genuine humility? Next what does he who chose a virgin as his temple teach except to preserve the gifts of

sincera? Deinde qui templum sibi elegit in virgine, quid do-
cet nisi dona pudicitiae custodire? Qui iustitiam coluit, do-
lum in ore non habuit, misericordiam praebuit, culpas indul-
genti laxavit, mundo corde semper incessit, quid aliud nisi
quo nos post sua vestigia verbis traheret et exemplis?

33 Ideoque orandum est, ut, si perire nolumus, ipsius volun-
tas operetur in nobis iuxta apostolum dicentem, "qui in vo-
bis operatur et velle et operari pro bona voluntate"; sicut
alibi Dominus noster locutus est, "non vos me, sed ego elegi
vos." Alioquin homo Christum inveni.

34 Beatus Paulus voluntatem habebat ad Christum re vera,
cuius per ecclesias populum devastabat? Sed quando re-
demptor dignatus est in persecutore suo magis pius esse
quam iustus, ut ad meliora accederet, eum per caecitatis
amaritudinem castigavit et corporale lumen obduxit, ut ei
spiritales oculos aperiret, de quo dixit, "ego illi ostendam
quanta eum pro me pati oporteat."

35 Unde et ipsam bonam voluntatem pietas Christi contulit;
non fragilitas humana possedit. Audiamus ipsum Dominum
Iesum Christum in infirmitate carnis positum quid dixerit:
"pater, si possibile est, transeat a me calix iste. Verum tamen
non sicut ego volo, sed sicut tu." Filius Dei dicit, "verum non
quod ego volo, sed sicut tu, pater," et homo quare tam super-
bus sit, ut voluntatem sibi ex se esse dicat ad bonum et non
potius Dei munus esse testetur?

36 Quod si bona voluntas ex homine est sine Dei inspi-
ratione, dicat ergo Christianus in oratione, "Fiat voluntas
mea, quoniam bona est." Sed absit ut hoc aliquis confiteri
praesumat. Immo magis deprecetur ut fiat voluntas Dei in
homine, non hominis voluntas, quae bonum velle non habet

chastity? He who practiced justice, had no deceit in his speech, showed mercy, forgave the faults of whoever himself gave pardon, always conducted himself in purity of heart, what else was his purpose except to induce us by his words and examples to follow in his footsteps?

Therefore we must pray that, if we do not wish to perish, 33 his will work in us according to the words of the apostle, "he works in you his will and his works according to his good pleasure"; as our Lord said elsewhere, "you did not choose me, but I you." Otherwise I, a man, have discovered Christ.

Was the blessed Paul's will truly directed toward Christ 34 when from church to church he persecuted his people? But when the redeemer saw fit to be merciful toward his persecutor rather than just so that he could go on to better things, he punished him with the affliction of blindness, and darkened his bodily vision in order to open up the eyes of his spirit; he said of him, "I will show him how much he must suffer for me."

Therefore it is the mercy of Christ that bestowed the will 35 for good; human frailty did not possess it. Let us hear what the Lord Jesus Christ himself said, when in the weakness of the flesh: "Father, if it is possible, may this cup pass from me. But not as I wish, but as you." The son of God says "but not as I wish, but as you, father." How then can man be so arrogant as to say that the will for good comes from himself and not declare rather that it is the gift of God?

But if the will for good is from man without the inspira- 36 tion of God, let the Christian say in his prayer, "My will be done, since it is good." But far be it that anyone should dare to declare this. Rather let him pray that God's will be performed in man, not the will of man, which does not have the

nisi Dominus inspiret iuxta illud, "Deus meus, misericordia eius praeveniet me." Ergo non hominis voluntas praevenit Deum, sed Dei misericordia praevenit hominem, quoniam sicut scriptum est, "deus est qui iustificat impium"; item, "spiritus ubi vult spirat."

37   Igitur quare non unusquisque recognoscit tenebras suas, ne inluminatus tamquam lampas, quae aliunde succenditur, per ventositatem suae superbiae extinguatur et subducto splendore maneat in caecitatis caligine, dum, si quid bonum velle habet, sui esse putet arbitrii et non exinde gratias refe- rat conlatori, ne audiat quod dicitur: "qui autem non habet, et quod habet auferetur ab eo"? Hoc est, quod per gratiam praevenitur, nisi Deo illud adscripserit, per superbiam hoc amittet, quoniam iuxta scripturam ipsa voluntas a Domino praeparatur.

38   Audiamus in hac parte doctorem ubi dixit, "qui loquitur mendacium de suo loquitur." Quare non addidit et, "qui loquitur veritatem de suo loquitur," nisi ut hoc exemplo, quando veritatem aliquis loquitur, de Dei gratia, non de suo habuisse hoc bonum specialiter agnoscatur, quoniam de nostro solum habemus mendacium? Nam cum ipsa veritas Deus sit, qui loquitur de Deo, unde in homine mendace causa veritatis sit nisi ipsa veritas se ministret, hoc est, nisi in hominem ipsam bonam voluntatem Deus veritatis inspi- ret qui et velle tribuit et posse conplevit?

39   Sed si quis obiciat quod apostolus ait, "velle adiacet mihi," cum ipse dicit, "Deus qui in vobis operatur et velle et ope-

power to will what is good except with the Lord's inspiration, according to the saying, "my God, his mercy will go before me." The will of man, then, does not go before God, but the mercy of God goes before man, since, as is written, "it is God who justifies the unholy," and again, "the spirit breathes where it wishes."

Therefore why does not everyone recognize his own 37 darkness lest, like an illuminated lamp that is set alight from some other source, he is put out by the gale of his arrogance and, his brilliance suppressed, he remains in the gloom of blindness, when he thinks that whatever good thing he wills is under his control and does not offer thanks to his benefactor for it, lest he hear the saying, "who has not, even what he has will be taken from him"? That is, unless he attributes to God what is preceded by grace, he will lose it because of his pride, since according to scripture the will itself is supplied by the Lord.

Let us hear on this subject the teacher when he said "He 38 who tells a lie speaks on his own account." Why did he not add also "He who tells the truth speaks on his own account," except that by this illustration it is specifically understood that when someone speaks the truth he has acquired this good thing by the grace of God, not on his own account, since we have lying only from ourselves? For since it is God, the truth itself, who speaks about God, how does a reason for truth come about in a deceitful human unless the truth itself supplies it, that is, unless the God of truth who has bestowed on him will and endowed him with the power inspires the actual will for good.

But if anyone cites in refutation the words of the apostle, 39 "the will is present with me," he also says, "it is God who

rari pro bona voluntate"; ergo si quis dicat quia ipsam bonam voluntatem Deus non inspirat, quantum ad hanc intellegentiam, beatus apostolus discrepat sentiendo diversa. Sed absit ut ille vir pacificus, qui uno eodemque locatus est spiritu, in his dictis Ecclesiae generasset scandalum. Unde doctor gentium velle sibi adiacere dicebat, quoniam non solum inspiratus, sed etiam vas electionis fulgebat qui docuit dicens, "Deus est qui in vobis operatur et velle," deinde, "quid habes quod non accepisti?" ac si diceret, "quid boni est in te, nisi det ille qui fecit te?" Nam si bonam voluntatem Deus non confert, sed ex te est quod tu habes, iste mentitus est. Quid est quod habes, quod non acceperis? Unde tolle Dei voluntatem. Mox agnosco, si tu per te ad bonum habes aliquam voluntatem, cum nisi a Christo velut lucerna inlumineris, cotidie nesciendo quid elegerit divina potestas excedis. Dicamus humiliter quia nihil boni velle habemus, nisi singulis diebus Domino largiente sumamus, iuxta quod legitur: "omne datum bonum et omne donum perfectum desursum est," ut domni Pauli teneant dicta concordiam et nos omne bonum ad Dei referentes gratiam fidelem consequamur doctrinam. Nam qui cum apostolo Paulo, id est, oculo Ecclesiae, et cum beato Augustino eius sequace consonat, in eo ignorantiae caligo non regnat.

Quod autem de duabus viis, id est, spatiosa et angusta, dicitur, ut quis per quam elegerit gradiatur quid est? Per spatiosam laxatis frenis libere discurrimus famulando peccatis;

40

41

42

43

works in you his will and his works according to his good pleasure"; if anyone, then, says that God does not inspire the will for good, as far as this opinion is concerned, the blessed apostle disagrees, thinking differently. But perish the thought that that peaceable man, who always was reliant on one and the same spirit, created scandal in the Church by these words. Why then did the teacher of the gentiles say 40 the will was present to him, since he was not only inspired, but even shone as the chosen vessel, who taught, "it is God who works in you his will also" and, "what do you have that you did not receive?," as if he were saying, "what good is there in you unless he who made you gives it?" For if God 41 does not bestow the will for good, but if what you have is from yourself, he lied. What is this that you have that you have not received? Do away, then, with the will of God. I realize right away, if you have some will for the good on your own account, since you are not illuminated like a lamp except by Christ, every day you go astray in ignorance of what divine power chooses. Let us humbly say that we will wish 42 for no good thing unless we receive it by the gift of the Lord every day, according to the scripture: "every good gift and every perfect blessing is from above," so that the words of our master Paul remain in agreement and we, by referring every good thing to the grace of God, follow the teaching of the faith. For the mist of ignorance has no power over whoever accords with the apostle Paul, that is, the eye of the Church, and with the blessed Augustine, his follower.

As to the saying about the two ways, that is, the wide and 43 the narrow, what does it mean that each makes his way on the path he has chosen? On the wide one we career freely with slackened reins in subservience to sin; but on the nar-

in angusta vero consideremus apostolum dicentem: "voca-
44 tione qua vocati estis per Dominum Iesum Christum." Et
ideo non elegit aliquis neque ad viam pervenit nisi vocatus
fuerit ab ipso qui via est et vita et veritas. Sed in hac via cum
apostoli verbis et praeceptis euangelicis excurramus, dicen-
tes ad eos qui iam ex Iudaeis in Christo erant fide conversi,
"si vos filius liberaverit, tunc liberi eritis."

45   Et quando sit istud adtendite ipso Domino praedicante:
"si manseritis verbo meo, vere discipuli mei estis et cognos-
cetis veritatem et veritas liberabit vos"; ac per hoc hortatur,
ut sequendo illud quod dedit per gratiam nos ad veram
liberationem perducat. Unde tunc homo in bonum perfecte
liberum possidebit arbitrium quando omnino non poterit
servire peccato.

46   Item *fiat voluntas tua sicut in caelo et in terra,* id est, sicut in
caelis angeli, ita te homines venerentur in terris, et quemad-
modum illi concordia inculpabili, caritate devoti in laude
Dei videntur iugiter inhaerere, ita nos in suo timore et
amore iubeat sine labe purgare.

47   Item *fiat voluntas tua,* id est, sicut spiritus, qui de caelis
est, caelestia cogitat, ita caro, quae de terra est, terrena non
cupiat, sed quae sunt spiritus, haec intendat et quasi facta
48 concordia pariter ad caelos ascendat. Ergo sicut in caelo, id
est, in spiritu, ita in terra, id est, in carne, fiat Dei voluntas,
ut iam post adventum Christi non caro, quae mater est cri-
minis, spiritum festinet, sicut et Eva, decipere, sed Adam,
qui est in typo spiritus, carnem habeat famulantem, nec do-
minus ancillae, sed ancilla serviat dominanti.

row one let us ponder the words of the apostle speaking of "the vocation to which you have been called by the Lord Jesus Christ." Accordingly no one chose or came to this way 44 unless he was called by him who is the way and the life and the truth. But let us hasten on this path, following the words of the apostle and the teachings of the Gospels, saying to those who now have been converted in their faith from Jews through Christ, "if the son frees you, then you will be free."

Pay attention too when that will be, about which the Lord 45 himself declared: "If you keep to my word, you are truly my disciples, and you will know the truth and the truth will free you." By this he counsels that if we follow the instruction he gave by his grace he would lead us to true freedom. As a result a person will possess a will perfectly free for good when he can in no way be subject to sin.

Again *may your will be done as in heaven also on earth,* that is, 46 just as angels worship you in heaven, so may men on earth, and as they in unimpeachable accord and devoted affection continually band together in the praise of God, so may he bid that we be cleansed from stain in fear and love of him.

Again *may your will be done,* that is, as the spirit, which is 47 from heaven, thinks on heavenly things, so may the flesh, which is from the earth, not desire earthly things, but direct itself to the things of the spirit and once harmony is established ascend with it to heaven. Therefore as in heaven, that 48 is, in the spirit, so on earth, that is, in the flesh, may God's will be done, so that after the coming of Christ the flesh, which is the mother of sin, may not hurry to deceive the spirit like Eve, but may Adam, who is figurally the spirit, keep the flesh in servitude, and the master not serve the serving maid, but the serving maid the master.

49 *Sicut in caelo et in terra.* Homo ante baptismum carnalis esse describitur, post baptismum spiritalis efficitur ideoque pro illis qui adhuc sine lavacro loti sunt, a nobis oratur ut sicut nos videmur facti esse caelestes per baptismum, et illi, qui adhuc ab ecclesia peregrini sunt, tanto beneficio non fraudentur, sed per munificentiam Domini nobiscum dona similia consequantur, quia et cum illi consortes facti fuerint, nos facultatem non amittimus, sed augemus. Quare sit autem invidia, ut homo non oret pro homine, cum Christus, ut nos adquireret, suo sanguini non pepercit?

50 Item *fiat voluntas tua.* Voluntas patris erat quod filius praedicavit, quod operatus est, quod passus et mortuus est et resurrexit, sicut ait, "non veni voluntatem meam facere, sed voluntatem eius qui me misit, patris." Ergo orandum est ut nos similiter mereamur dicere, agere, sustinere, et in ipso resurgere, ut possimus cum ipso regnare.

51 Item *fiat voluntas tua.* Deus incommutabiliter bonus quid aliud nisi semper vult bonum, quamvis nos moles inpediat peccatorum? Ergo bene videmur optare, ut nobis ea contingant quae Deus vult, cum sciamus illum bonae voluntatis haberi.

52 *Panem nostrum cotidianum da nobis hodie.* Considerandum est quam mirabiliter orationis huius ornatus sit textus, ut nominatis aeternis temporalia peterentur. Nam tria ista quod poscimus—id est, sanctificetur nomen tuum, adveniat regnum tuum, fiat voluntas tua—propter aeterna consequenda hic sunt necessaria et hic incipiunt, sed perfecta in futura

As in heaven also on earth. A person before baptism is de- 49
scribed as of the flesh, but after baptism he becomes of the
spirit and therefore on behalf of those who still have not re-
ceived the cleansing of baptism we offer a prayer that just as
we are made citizens of heaven by baptism, they too, who
are still strangers to the church, should not be deprived of
such a benefit, but by the generosity of the Lord acquire
with us gifts like ours, for when they become our fellows,
there is no diminishment in our powers, but an increase.
Why then should there be jealousy so that one person not
pray for another, when Christ did not spare his own blood to
win us?

Again *may your will be done.* It was the will of the father 50
that his son preached, that he performed his mission, that
he suffered and died and rose again, as he said, "I have not
come to do my own will but the will of him who sent me,
the father." Therefore we should pray that we may be found
worthy to speak, act, endure, and rise in him in the same
way, so that we can reign with him.

Again *may your will be done.* What does God who is un- 51
changingly good always want except what is good, although
the mass of our sins impedes us? Therefore we rightly wish
that what God wants happen to us since we know that he
wills what is good.

Give us today our daily bread. We must examine how re- 52
markably the design of this prayer has been composed, in
that after enumerating eternal matters temporal concerns
are prayed for. For the three requests—that is, may your
name be made holy, may your kingdom come, may your will
be done—are necessary in this life and are the first to be
spoken here in order to acquire what is eternal, but in their

53 vita possideri credenda sunt et perpetua permanebunt. Ergo "panem nostrum da nobis" quantus animae et carni est necessarius, spiritaliter vel corporaliter, et "dimitte nobis debita nostra, sicut et nos dimittimus debitoribus nostris et ne nos inducas in temptationem, sed libera nos a malo" ad praesentis vitae opportunitates pertinere videntur. Denique nominis eius sanctificatio et regnum eius in spiritu et corpore nostro post resurrectionem perfecte manebunt.

54 Item *panem nostrum*. Quisquis ad veram salutem pervenire meruit, Christum esse panem vitae perpetuae non ignoret, quia dixit, "ego sum panis vivus qui de caelo descendi." Unde iste panis non est communis cum reliquo, quia ille corpora protegit, iste novit animas enutrire, et qui illum manducat esurit, qui autem isto fruitur nulla fame torquetur. Et ideo tanto magis iste cibus quaerendus est quanto plus reficit epulatus.

55 Quod vero cotidianum panem petimus, hoc insinuare videtur ut communionem eius corporis, si est possibile, omnibus diebus reverenter sumamus, quia, cum ipse vita nostra sit, nutrimento nostro peregrinos nos facimus, si ad eucharistiam tardi accedamus.

56 Item dum dicimus *panem nostrum da nobis hodie,* cognoscimus non nobis sufficere quod praeterito die Deum rogavimus, nisi et eo qui in praesenti est orationi vacemus,

57 propter illud, "sine intermissione orantes." Sive sic advertendum est, quod, postquam ad Christum pervenimus et mundum cum pompis suis reiecimus, non nobis necesse sit ad escam amplius quam cotidianus usus exigit ut quaeramus,

perfection should be believed a possession of the future life, when they will persist forever. Therefore "give us our bread," 53 to the extent that is necessary to the soul and the flesh, spiritually and bodily, and "forgive us our debts as we too forgive those who are in debt to us and do not lead us into temptation but free us from evil" all relate to the situations of the present life. The making holy of his name, however, and his kingdom will remain in perfection after the resurrection in our spirits and bodies.

Again *our bread*. Everyone who has successfully achieved 54 true salvation should not be unaware that Christ is the bread of eternal life, since he said, "I am the living bread who came down from heaven." Therefore this bread is not of the same nature as other bread, since the one sustains bodies, but this one is able to nourish souls, and whoever eats the one is hungry, but whoever enjoys this one is never tormented by hunger. And therefore this food is all the more to be sought after, the more it brings refreshment when eaten.

The fact that we pray for daily bread indicates that we 55 should receive dutifully communion of his body every day, if possible, since, because he himself is our life, we make ourselves alienated from our nourishment if we are slow in attending the Eucharist.

Again when we say *give us today our bread,* we recognize 56 that it is not enough for us to have petitioned God the previous day, unless we devote time to prayer on the present day too, in accordance with the saying "praying unceasingly." Or it is to be understood in this way, that after we have come 57 to Christ and rejected the world with its finery we do not need to request more food than each day's requirements demand, when in reality we are constantly awaiting the com-

re vera cum adventum Domini iugiter expectemus. Nam inpedimenta mundi faciunt homines miseros. Et sciamus panem illi sufficere cui Deus non deficit, quod Helia habitante in heremo ministravit.

58   *Et dimitte nobis debita.* Bene post escam quaesitam postulatur venia peccatorum, ut qui Dei cibo pascitur Deo vivat si ei dimittantur peccata, et congrue, ne se humana extollat superbia, petendo veniam videtur confiteri delicta, cum tamen, si purgari desiderat, saepius ad orationem recurrat.

59   Convenienter autem debita peccata dicuntur, quia et debentur et requirenda sunt. Nam sicut debitum a creditore requiritur, ita peccatum a Deo in die iudicii necesse est exigatur, nisi hic, dum vivimus, per pietatem eius indulgentiae ista nobis exactio condonetur. Et merito hic remittat cuncta rogamus ubi delicta committimus, quoniam in futuro sicut
60   peccare non licet ita non vacat paenitere. Sed addendo *sicut et nos dimittimus debitoribus nostris* qui pium se ostendit et legem inposuit, ut nisi quis peccanti culpas indulserit sibi indulgeri a Domino non expectet, propter illud, "in qua mensura mensurati fueritis remetietur vobis," item "misericordiam et iudicium cantabo tibi," quoniam qui in nobis pius est vult nos esse aliis miserentes. Unde merito de culpa vapulat qui magistri verba declinat. Summa est eleemosyna alteri remittere quod in te videatur peccasse.

61   Item *dimitte nobis debita.* Quid ergo? De baptismi fonte surgentes et corpore Christi communicantes mox nobis dimitti peccata? sed fragilitas nostra conservare puritatem la-

ing of the Lord. For the entanglements of the world make men wretched. We should be assured that he whom God does not fail has sufficient bread, for he provided food when Elijah was living in the desert.

And forgive us our debts. Forgiveness of sins is rightly 58 sought after a request for food so that he who is fed by God's food lives for God if his sins are forgiven, and appropriately by seeking pardon he confesses his sins so that human pride not puff him up, provided that, if he desires to be cleansed, he return frequently to prayer.

Sins are fittingly called debts, however, because they are 59 both owed and must be called in. For just as a debt is called in by a creditor, so must God seek requital for a sin at the day of judgment, unless here, while we are still alive, that requital is forgiven us by the mercy of his benevolence. And we rightly ask him to pardon everything here when we commit the faults, since in the future, as no sin will be possible, so there will be no scope for repentance. But by adding "as 60 we too forgive those who are in debt to us" he who shows himself merciful also imposed a rule, that no one should expect pardon from the Lord unless he pardoned the faults of a sinner, in accordance with the words "by the measure you have measured with it will be meted out to you," and again, "I will sing of mercy and judgment to you," since he who is merciful to us wants us to show pity to others. Therefore he is rightly punished for his fault who renounces the words of the teacher. It is the greatest almsgiving to forgive in another the sin he has committed against you.

Again *forgive our debts.* Why is that? After arising from 61 the font of baptism and sharing the body of Christ are our sins immediately to be forgiven us? But our frailty cannot

vacri non valet, quam de fonte percipit, nisi dignetur Dei gratia custodire. Et bene *sicut et nos dimittimus debitoribus nostris,* ut ostenderetur quia Deus pacis cum omnibus vult nos concordes.

62   *Ne nos inducas in temptationem.* Numquid Deus aliquem in laqueum temptationis inducit aut ab inimico cupiat subplantari, qui monet ne incidatur ... ?

2

Ad virum illustrem Salutarem

Inter humanae condicionis subripientia vulnera, quae semper incerto tramite nutantium animorum ac labentium temporum reddunt vota suspecta, nihil est in aliquo aliquid magis quod cruciet quam quemquam aut non videre quod cupiat aut videre quod perdat, cum trepidans animus in utroque non modico sub fasce succumbat, dum pendulus spectat diuturne quod habeat et, ut habere coeperit, mox amittat, scilicet afflictus donec impetret, elisus si perdit. Sed gravius hoc iaculo res illa percellitur, quod inter spectare vel spectata amittere illic spes tenditur, hic damnatur, illic dubius maeror an habeat, hic certus dolor est si relinquat.

preserve the purity of baptism, which we received from the font, unless the grace of God sees fit to preserve it. And rightly it is said *just as we too forgive our debtors,* to show that the God of peace wishes us to be in harmony with all.

Do not lead us into temptation. Does God lead anyone into 62 the snare of temptation or desire him to be tripped up by his enemy, who warns that no one should fall into . . . ?

2

To the distinguished gentleman Salutaris

Among the wounds that steal upon the human condition, which always in the uncertain course of wavering spirits and faltering times render desires suspect, there is nothing that causes more torment in anyone than either not to see what one longs for or to see what one will lose. In either case the fearful mind labors under no slight burden when in suspense it anticipates every day having something and, when it has it, anticipates soon losing it, tortured until it obtains it, but crushed if it loses it. But the blow suffered is more severe than this piercing pain in a situation when, poised between anticipation and losing what is anticipated, hope grows expansive or is dashed, and while grief is unsure whether it possesses something, the sadness is certain if it relinquishes it.

2   Habet hoc insitum natura praevaricatione protoplasti parentis ad nos decursa morte multata, ut saepe quod vix acquiritur mox linquatur. Serpentis inveterati dens a radice sic perculit ut nec arbor steterit quin stirpe mortis fixa vivat.

3   Misit hoc posteris hereditas parentalis, ut iacentes morti quaeramus vivere morituri. Vulnificavit cunctos infelicis arboris adquaesita possessio, quae blandientibus pomis prolem prius nocuit quam nutrivit; quo certe sub epuli specie mors intravit. Ferali tactu laesit hoc parentes et posteros, illos gustus, nos sucus, quoniam virulentae suasionis poculum, quod pater male sorbuit, in prolem transfudit et, ut ita dictum sit, quod a fonte manavit, in rivum defluxit.

4   Intulit hoc igitur illa mater de genere sed noverca de crimine, infelix cunctis Eva monades, quod certe sola sic extruit ut universa destrueret, cum veterata machinatione decipulae rudem virum perderet et periret. Sed proles quid boni faciat, si se in calumniam vel mali parentis extendat, aut ut illum iterum detrahendo remordeat qui semel morsu perierat, cum ipse sibi suffecerit suus lapsus, noster occasus?

5   Itaque puto incongruum si vel illum remorsero per quem gratis venit ingratum, cuius occasione vitalis alimoniae mors

Because of the sin of the firstborn parent which was pun- 2
ished by a death that is transmitted to us, it is inherent in
our nature that often what is with difficulty acquired is im-
mediately lost. The tooth of the ancient serpent so struck at
its root that the tree too did not stand without being grafted
onto a stock of death. The inheritance of our parents handed 3
this down to us their descendants that we would be subject
to death, but seek to live, though destined to die. Winning
possession of the accursed tree inflicted wounds on every-
one, for with its enticing fruit it brought harm to the human
race before it gave nourishment; thereby no doubt death
made its entrance in the guise of food. With its deadly con-
tagion it damaged both parents and progeny, them by its
taste and us by its juice, since the father transmitted to his
descendants the draft of poisonous persuasion that he to his
ruin drank down and, so to speak, what trickled from its
source flowed on as a stream.

That mother in respect of offspring but stepmother in 4
crime, Eve in her singularity a curse on all, brought it about
that she alone without doubt devised the destruction of ev-
erything, when with long-practiced contrivance of deceit
she brought to ruin her naïve husband and herself perished
too. But what good do we their descendants do if we occupy
ourselves in accusing our parent, whatever his wickedness,
or in again disparaging him bitingly carp at one who once
perished from a bite, since he procured for himself his own
fall and our death? And so I think it inappropriate to carp 5
even at one by whom an unwelcome fate came to us un-
earned, on whom on the pretext of providing him life-giving
nourishment death began to feed, for whom, when prom-

coepit depasci, cui dum oculorum apertio promittitur, lux
fugatur et divinitate promissa homo lapsus redit in terram.
Hinc est quod prolem genitam nocens esca traxit in prae-
dam.

6   Fecit ipsa captivitas nos prosperis exules, adversis con-
sortes, et tantum peregrinatio gravior, quam mors dura no-
tior. Nascitur ab Adam vetere usque ad novum hominem
7 vita nostra cum morte. Hinc se nec Abel exuit nec Enoch
effugiet neque Noe se subtraxit, qui diluvio mortem distulit,
non mutavit; hoc patriarcha non rennuit, hanc legem legifer
non avertit, propheta sustinuit et plus quam propheta suc-
cubuit; Sarra quoque, Rebecca, Rachel, Anna, Elisabeth, li-
8 cet sexus inferior, tamen hoc simul bibit amarum. Quid
conqueratur de reliquis, cum ipse triumphator mortis pro
parte qua caro factus est et morti subiectus est? Nec fuerat
plenus homo, si non sensisset et tumulum, nec Deus crede-
retur, nisi surgeret de sepulchro.

9   Hinc est quod loquor, carissime et fidae dilectionis mihi
voto conexe, eo quod tuos per apices natae sanctae transi-
tum conqueraris, vix singultu rumpente indicans calamo
tristi decennalis aetatis inruente funere pubertatis tenerae
floscula marcuisse, cum paene nuptiali retracta de limine
non ad patris votum thalamo datur sed tumulo, et diverso
cantico non toro traditur sed sepulchro, ad cuius forte vota

ised the opening of his eyes, the light was put to flight, and who, though divinity was promised, fell as a man back to earth. Because of this the deadly food sentenced his offspring to become prey.

That captivity has made us exiles from prosperity, comrades in suffering, our banishment all the more burdensome, as harsh death has become more familiar. From Adam up to present-day man our life comes to birth in consort with death. Abel did not avoid it, Enoch will not escape it, and Noah did not save himself from it, since he only delayed death in the flood, he did not alter it; the patriarch did not reject it, the lawgiver did not shun this law, the prophet endured it, the more than prophet suffered it; Sarah, too, and Rebecca, Rachel, Anna, and Elizabeth, though of the lesser sex, yet all drained this bitter draft. But why lament these others, when even the very victor over death was subject to death in that part that was made of flesh? He would not have been wholly a man, if he had not also experienced the tomb, and he would not be believed to be God, if he had not risen from the grave.

This is why I speak, my dearest friend, joined to me by vows of devoted affection, because in your letter you lament the passing of your saintly daughter, only with difficulty declaring with your sad pen as you burst out in sobbing that the flower of tender youth, ten years in age, has withered at the onset of death. Summoned back almost from the threshold of marriage she was handed over not, as her father wished, to the wedding chamber but to the tomb and to a different refrain she was committed not to the marriage bed but to the grave. Her fervent family were already flock-

iam festinans familia fervebat, sedule parentela excitabatur
et patria, mater erat prece suspensa, ipsa assurgebat cura
nutricis, iuncea pubertate, rosea modestate, festiva arte sui
sexus ornata.

10   Sed quo me rapit formae decor se prodere tam cito fugax,
quam caro mendax, cum defunctae si praedicetur gloria, ac-
11   crescant lamenta? Habuisti igitur istud pater, sed non tuum;
reddidisti potius commendatum. Ploratur velut amissum,
sed consideretur non perditum quod ad Christum redit in-
tactum.

12   An certe conquereris quasi solus ista perpessus sis, cum
casus hic vincat et reges? An felicior Augusto, fortior Alexan-
dro, favorabilior Traiano, sanctior es Theudosio? Cum hoc
habeat aequale tam miles quam princeps, patienter dolen-
dum est quod habes commune cum mundo.

13   Quantas autem feminas ab ipso primo complexu retraxit
ad tumulum, et pertulerunt dispendium agnito viro, non
habito! Quae bis lamentandae sunt, antea pudorem perdere,
14   sic perisse. Vnde quamvis conquereris talem te tali casu ami-
sisse subolem, nulli tamen novum est, ut non potuisset hoc
vitare puella quod venit per feminam. Illud potius inspice,
ut ista res funeris sit virtutis et ad illorum exempla te coae-
qua qui dolore victo surgunt ad palmam.

ing to her wedding, kin and country were busily gathering, her mother was caught up in prayer, while she herself was standing up attended by her nurse, slender in her youthfulness, blushing and bashful, adorned in finery by the skills of her sex.

But why am I being carried away by physical beauty, which 10 is as quick and fleeting in betrayal as flesh is deceitful, seeing that mourning only increases if the dead girl's glory is extolled? What you had as a father was not your own; rather 11 you have given back what was entrusted to you. Though it is mourned as if lost, do not consider what is returned unsullied to Christ as lost.

Are you perhaps lamenting as if you alone had suffered 12 such things, although this fate overcomes even kings? Are you more fortunate than Augustus, braver than Alexander, more favored than Trajan, more pious than Theodosius? Since the ruler is equally as subject to this as the soldier, you should show patience in your grief for what you have in common with the world.

How many women, moreover, has death carried off at the 13 very first embrace to the tomb, who have suffered loss after sleeping with their husband, but without keeping him! They are to be mourned twice over, for losing their chastity and then their life. Therefore, although you lament that you 14 have lost such a daughter, and by such a fate, yet no one finds it strange that a girl could not escape what came into the world by a woman. Rather consider this, that this fact of death has an element of virtue and follow the model of those who overcome grief and aspire to win a palm.

15   Habes itaque inter ipsa patientiae culmina primum velut in specula Iob censuram et normam, qui pro filiis Domino sic gratias retulit tamquam si tunc acceperit cum amisit. Qui vir experientiae voluntati divinae tradidit totum, ne ca-

16   deret. Quid vero? David fortis, licet Goliam subdiderit, non se velut faenum nutui caelesti substravit, cum filio amisso lavit, epulatus est, ne repugnet? Intellegens uni cedere qui cuncta formavit, servus fidelis timuit offensam boni Domini provocare vel murmure . . . quae ut iungeretur divinas ad nuptias, iugiter diffluebat pius pater per lacrimas. Potestis autem conicere quia talem non tolleret, nisi suis thalamis placuisset. Unde nosti abyssos divini consilii vel tuae natae qualis in corde concupiscentia latitavit? Fortassis hoc antea elegit quod meruit et illud prodiit quod optavit.

17   Qua de re, vir optime, esto tibi vix iudex et patere; hoc est, si per caritatem te temperes et te iudices, non offendis, praesertim cum te mitiget promissio redemptoris et praeco-nis Pauli vox simulata tonitrui, quia in ictu oculi resurgere maturabunt sepulti et vivent sub umbra Christi, de virgini-tate securi.

You have then as first among the leading examples of pa- 15
tience, as if set up on high, the rigorous model of Job, who
gave thanks to the Lord for his sons as if he received them
when he lost them. This man of many trials surrendered
wholly to God's will so as not to fall. What of this then? 16
David the brave, though he overcame Goliath, did he not
submit like straw to the will of heaven, when, so as not to
resist, though he had lost his son, he washed and dined? Un-
derstanding he should yield to the one who had created all
things, as a faithful servant he feared to offend the good
Lord even by the slightest muttering . . . Her pious father
continually dissolved into tears for her to be joined in divine
marriage. You can imagine that he would not have taken
such a one if she had not pleased his marriage chamber.
How do you know the depths of the divine plan and what
desire was concealed in your daughter's heart? Perhaps she
had previously chosen the course that she won and what she
desired came about.

Therefore, best of men, hard though it is, be a judge of 17
yourself and endure; that is, if in your affection you restrain
and judge yourself, you will not offend, especially since the
promise of the redeemer and the voice like thunder of the
herald Paul softens the blow, because in the twinkling of an
eye the buried will hasten to rise again and will live in the
shadow of Christ, untroubled because of their virginity.

3

Item alia

DOMINIS ILLUSTRIBUS CUNCTAQUE
MAGNIFICIS, OMNI DESIDERIO
COMPLECTENDIS SERVIENTIBUS
DOMINORUM

Si humanae consuetudinis isto se generaliter per omnes unus usus extendit et ab antiquis atavis ipso tradente genere et ad nos usque naturali quodammodo lege pervenit, eo quod post triticei panis oblectantem candorem vel suavitatem pascentem ad hordeaceae frugis aristosa cibaria fastidioso nimium dente, nare, fauce transitur (cum delectabilis escae dulcedine permutante ad convivium pergere, nisi fames urgueat, austeritas epuli non invitat), hinc est quod illustris ac magnifica celsitudinis vestrae gratia, copiosa cotidianae disciplinae doctrina superinundante refecta et ferventis ingenii studio lucubrante polita, post illum, ut dixerim, detersum eloquentiae vestrae nitorem et perspicue clarum exercitatione purgante ad linguae nostrae rubiginosam facundiam fastidiose vestri sensus fulgida lux inclinat, cum tale sit quod sermonis nostri rumores vacillantes auditis, ac si post epulas coturnicis aut fasidis viris delicatissimis

3

Again another letter

If a practice of human behavior that is one and common to all has made its way to this time and has reached as far as us too from our distant ancestors, transmitted by the human race itself by a kind of natural law, whereby after the delightful whiteness and nourishing sweetness of wheaten bread a change to the coarse fare of barley meal is vehemently shunned by tooth, nose, and throat (for a Spartan meal in place of the pleasure of delicious food does not attract one to come to a banquet, unless hunger is pressing), this is the reason why the illustrious and resplendent charm of your sublimity, reinforced by the overflowingly abundant expertise of your everyday regimen and refined by the long hours of study of your lively intellects, in the shining light of your minds prompts distaste at the rusted expressions of my tongue in comparison with the sheen of your eloquence that is, so to speak, scrubbed clean and made transparently clear through the purifying effect of practice. Indeed for you to hear the uneven mumbling of my speech is as if I should feed gourmet diners animal fodder after a banquet of quail

2 cibos ingeram pecuales. Sed inter haec una spe praesump-
tionis videor animari eo quod aliquatenus post regales deli-
cias esca desideretur ruralis et saepe rusticus offerat quod
3 animum potentis oblectat. Nam quamvis regum conviviis
auro intermicante purpurata palla coruscet, saepe tamen iu-
cunditate placere mensa plus adsolet vel adumbrata foliis
ordinatis ex palmite vel superiecto hederae corymbo cris-
pante. Igitur habet et de silva reductus pastor quod proferat.
Cui si desint reliqua, tamen dignantem convivam vel de lacte
dives invitat.

4 Quapropter dominationi, celsitudini et, teste Domino lo-
quor, profusae dulcedini vestrae salutes venerabiliter ac de-
siderantissime persolventes aeterni regis clementiam depre-
camur, ut domnis praecellentissimis feliciter regnantibus ac
vestrae potestatis officiis crescentibus ita fugitivae huius vi-
tae spatia producantur, ut illi piissimo tramite gubernando
et vos sine macula fidelissime serviendo creatoris ac re-
demptoris nostri desiderato pariter intretis in regno, spe-
rantes in Christo de vestrae caritatis affectu humilitatem
nostram peculiariter omnibus sanctis et Domini famulis,
sed etiam domnis regnantibus vel eorum fidelibus proflua
dulcedine commendetis, hoc fiducialiter deprecantes, ut
veneratorem vestrum, portitorem praesentium, hominem
domnae Radegundis matris vestrae, animae sanctae, vel
ea quae pro utilitate praedictae domnae suggesserit coram
Christo et eius angelis, tam pro sui necessitate quam prece
nostra proprium habere dignemini. Indubitabiliter intima-

or pheasant. But despite these circumstances I am moti- 2
vated by a single hope to be daring, because after the delica-
cies of a royal table to a certain extent country food is de-
sired and often the countryman can serve what pleases the
taste of the powerful. For although in the banquets of kings 3
a purple coverlet gleams, picked out with glittering gold, yet
often a table is accustomed to win more favor with its at-
tractiveness when shaded by a trellis of vine leaves or cov-
ered by curling clusters of ivy. And so even the shepherd
back from the forest has something to offer. If he has noth-
ing else, at least he is rich in milk to invite an acquiescent
guest.

Therefore, reverently and with deepest affection I send 4
my greetings to your lordships, to your sublimity, and, I de-
clare, as God is my witness, to your surpassing sweetness,
and I beseech the mercy of the eternal king that the length
of this fleeting life be so extended under the happy reign of
your most excellent lords and with the increasing responsi-
bilities of your own power that they by the most humane
tenor of their government and you by serving them most
faultlessly and faithfully may together enter the longed for
kingdom of our creator and redeemer, and I hope in Christ
that in the kindness of your feelings you will commend with
surpassing sweetness my humility to all the saints and ser-
vants of the Lord in particular, but also to the lord kings and
those faithful to them. I also confidently request that you
deign to receive as your own your devotee, the carrier of this
letter, a servant of lady Radegund, your mother and a pious
soul, along with the requests he makes before Christ and his
angels in the interests of that lady both because of his own
needs and because of my prayer. I have no hesitation in as-

mus ut quod pro causa illius apud praesentes domnos reges inpendetis apud aeternum regem centuplicato munere suis orationibus adquiratis.

4

Item alia

Celsitudinis vestrae legatis transcurrentibus omni caritate refectas nos insaturabili voto suscepisse gratificamur epistulas, in quibus ut, quod erat nostrae relevationis, consultum de vestri culminis incolumitate relegimus, inserendo commemorationem dulcissimae filiae quod est de maerore par-
2 timur. Denique quibus fuit in vivente participata laetitia, sint communes lacrimae necesse est in defuncta. Nec ratio suadet, ut sola tibi privilegium defendas in fletu, quae habuisti in cuius nos conpari ligaremur affectu, quoniam licet formata vestris ex visceribus processisset, tamen non minus adulta nostris in pectoribus habitavit, quippe quae producens partum ex utero transmiseras quasi in nostro gremio recepturum, ut cum a vobis esset, etsi non corde, tamen corpore recessura, nobis velut in vestra vicarietate fieret amplectenda.
3   Hinc est quod, <quod> matri de illa genitalis causa contulerat, mihi totum velut adoptivus amor explebat, quia, cum

serting that for the efforts you make in her interests before the present lords and kings you will win by her prayers from the eternal king a hundredfold reward.

4

Again another letter

I am delighted to have received with boundless joy from the traveling messengers of your highness a letter animated by every affection, in which I read the assurance of the good health of your eminence, which served to relieve my mind, but also shared your grief in the remembrance you included of your dearest daughter. For necessarily those who shared 2 joy in her when she was living should join the weeping now she is dead. Nor is it in accordance with reason that you should reserve the right to cry for yourself alone, for though she was yours, we were bound to her by equal affection, since though she was shaped by, and emerged from, your flesh, when grown she had no less a place in our hearts, seeing that having given birth to her from your womb you handed her over to be received as it were in our bosom, so that when she was to leave you, in body if not in heart, she was to be embraced by us as it were in your stead.

This is why my, so to speak, adoptive love performed ev- 3 erything the claim of birth bestowed on you over her as her

vobis genita, nobis tamen erat renata. Equidem optaveram
pro meritis eius illa superstite vobiscum loqui de gaudio ma-
gis quam tristis conlatio nasceretur ex fletu. Sed invida re-
rum series, quae illud celerius subripit quod magis placere
cognoverit, rem mihi desiderabilem paene uno momento et
offerre voluit et auferre. Vel quare nobis rem attulit quam
subducere festinavit, cum nihil sit in humana condicione
crudelius quam aut non videre quod habeat aut videre quod
perdat?

4   Sed quousque suum maerorem dolor inportunus exacuit
ac praeceps sine freno moderatae consolationis excurrit,
cum intellegat hoc temperari debere quod emendare nequi-
verit et aequanimiter toleret quod infectum facere non vale-
bit, praesertim cum in illa tot admiranda refulserint ut nec
apud homines in sermone defecerit et apud Deum de opere
5   praemia viventis expectet? Nam praeter reliqua bona quae
cum illa laudanda sunt (nec tamen clausa iacent in tumulo
dum volvuntur per ora cunctorum) hoc unum breviter ad-
sero: si fides et persecutio Christi martyrem facit, non habes
in tali filia quod deflere, quia illi et recte credere contigit et
perferre, et licet festinasset in iuventute sors debita, tamen
est innocentia secura de palma.

mother, since though born to you, she was reborn to me. Indeed such were her virtues, I would rather have spoken with you with rejoicing while she was still alive than have a mournful conversation arise from grief. But the envious passage of events, which steals away more quickly what it knows to be especially beloved, was ready almost in the same moment to present to me what I longed for and to take it away. Otherwise why did it bring me an object that it hastened to remove, when nothing is crueler in human experience that either not to see what one possesses or to see what one is losing?

But how long will persistent grief intensify its mourning 4
and run headlong unbridled by restraining consolation, when it understands that what it cannot mend must be moderated and that it should endure with composure what it cannot undo, especially because so many admirable qualities shone out in her that she will never fail to be on the tongues of men and from God she awaits for her works the rewards of the living? For beside the other good qualities 5
that are praiseworthy along with her (nor do they repine in the tomb when they are recounted on the lips of all) this one thing I briefly declare: if faith and persecution make a martyr for Christ, you have nothing to weep for in such a daughter, because she possessed both right belief and endurance, and though the destined fate hurried upon her in her youth, yet her innocence is assured of the palm.

5

In nomine Domini nostri Iesu Christi, incipiunt versus de oratorio Artannensi

Quisquis ad haec properas venerandi limina templi
   dona precaturus quae dat amore Deus,
haec in honore sacri Gabrielis culta coruscant,
   qui pia iussa Dei rite minister agit,
5 Zachariae veniens qui nuntia detulit astris,
   Elisabeth datus est quando propheta potens,
quique redemptorem e caelo regem omnipotentem
   post ait ut terris ventre Maria daret.
Quae sacer antistes nova tecta Gregorius effert,
10 ut sibi caelestes restituantur opes.

6

In nomine Domini nostri Iesu Christi versus ad ecclesiam Toronicam quae per Gregorium episcopum renovata est

Emicat Altithroni cultu venerabile templum,
   egregium meritis, nobilis arcis apex,
quo propria tunica dum operit Martinus egentem,
   gestorum serie fulgida signa dedit.

5

In the name of our Lord Jesus Christ, verses here begin on the oratory of Artannes

Whoever you are who hurry to the threshold of this sacred building to petition for the gifts that God from his love dispenses, this resplendent finery serves to honor saintly Gabriel, who dutifully performs God's holy orders as his servant, who coming to Zachariah brought the tidings from the stars, when a powerful prophet was granted to Elizabeth, and who afterward said that Mary would produce on earth from her womb an almighty king and redeemer from heaven. This new building the holy bishop Gregory is erecting so as to receive in return the riches of heaven.

6

In the name of our Lord Jesus Christ, verses for the Cathedral of Tours that was rebuilt by Bishop Gregory

The church of the All-high, imposing in its finery, shines bright, outstanding in its excellences, pinnacle of a noble city, where, when Martin clothed a poor man with his tunic,

5   Namque idem antistes, sacra dum mysteria tractat,
      lumina gemmarum est visus habere manu,
   ac de veste fuit quantum sua dextera nuda,
      tantum membra sibi gemma corusca tegit.
   Sanctus item Domini almum dum benediceret altar,
10   de capite est visus flammeus ire globus.
   Quae modo templa sacer renovata Gregorius effert
      et rediit priscus cultus honorque suus.
   Fulgida praecipui nituerunt culmina templi
      postque usus veteres praemicat aula rudis,
15 in senium vergens, melius revirescere discens,
      diruta, post casum firmius acta situ.
   Martini auxiliis operando Gregorius aedem
      reddidit iste novus quod fuit ille vetus.
   Clara supercilio Domini delubra nitescunt;
20   alma licet merito, sunt quoque celsa iugo,
   invida subruerat quam funditus ipsa vetustas,
      ut paries liquidis forte solutus aquis,
   quam pastor studuit renovare Gregorius aedem,
      nec cecidisse dolet quae magis aucta favet.

25 Ambianis tremulum cernens Martinus egenum,
      dimidiae chlamydis mox ope membra tegit.
   Sed coram angelicis turmis se hanc nocte silenti
      pauperis in specie Christus habere refert.
   O sacer antistes, meritis referende sub astris,
30   unde tegis nudum, hinc tua palla Deum!

   Inter opima Deus figulus quae vascula fecit
      Martinus meritis vas in honore nitet.
   Leprosi maculas pretiosa per oscula purgans,
      cui quod ab ore dedit pax medicina fuit.

he produced brilliant miracles in a series of deeds. For the ⁵
same bishop, as he was performing the sacred mysteries, was
seen to have on his hand the brightness of jewels, and the
sparkle of gems covered his limbs, as far as his arm was bare
of clothing. Again when the saint was blessing the venerable
altar of the Lord, a ball of flame was seen to come from his ¹⁰
head. This church holy Gregory now raises up restored; its
former finery and glory has been returned to it.

The roof of the splendid basilica has taken on a brilliant
glow, and after long use the shrine gleams again anew; once ¹⁵
decaying with age, it has learned to renew itself for the bet-
ter, a ruin once, but after its collapse more firmly established
in place. By the aid of Martin Gregory has brought to com-
pletion this church, and that new man has restored what the
former man was.

The sanctuary of the Lord shines bright on a hilltop, wel- ²⁰
coming in its own qualities, but eminent too in its high site.
Envious age had totally undermined its foundations, like a
wall that is eroded by flowing water, but Gregory the shep-
herd was eager to rebuild the church, nor does it grieve for
its fall but rather applauds its improvement.

When Martin saw at Amiens a trembling poor man, he ²⁵
quickly covered his body with half of his cloak. But in the
company of angels during the silence of the night, Christ
said he received this in the guise of the poor man. O saintly
bishop, worthy to rise to the stars for your virtues, in cloth- ³⁰
ing a naked man your cloak covers God!

Among the rich vessels that God the potter has made, with
his virtues the vessel that is Martin shines with special glory.
By his precious kisses he cleansed the stains of a leper; the

35 Ulcera morbosi curans sic fauce beatus,
        quod Iordanis agit tacta saliva facit.

    Quam generosa fides Martini in saecula civis,
        qui quocumque fuit, mors ibi perdit iter!
    Denique cum extincto catechumenus ore iaceret,
40   se superextendens effugat arma necis.
    Sic viduae genito laqueato, deinde reducto,
        est vir ubi iste Dei, non licet ire mori.

    Fanaticam pinum sanctus succidere cogens,
        iustum ibi subposuit rustica turba premi.
45 Caesa secure arbor cum iam daret alta ruinam,
        ad crucis imperium est ire coacta retro.
    Quis vigor hic fidei, validae dum pondera pini
        quo natura negat crux facit ire viam!

    Serpentis morsu tumido suprema regenti
50   hic digitum ut posuit, pestis iniqua fluit
    collecto morbo huc et ab ulcere pollice tracto,
        dumque venena cadunt, erigit ille caput.
    Unguentumque novum digitis traxisse venenum
        et tactu artificis sic superasse neces!

55 Dum latro extinctus falso coleretur honore,
        voce huc Martini cogitur umbra loqui,
    publice se referens scelerum pro mole peremptum
        se quoque nec iustum, sed magis esse reum.

kiss of peace he gave from his lips had medicinal power. The   35
blessed man in this way cured a sick man's sores with his
mouth; the touch of his spittle played the role that the river
Jordan performs.

How noble the faith of Martin, heaven's citizen forever,
since wherever he was, death there lost its way! For when
a catechumen lay dead, his breathing extinguished, stretch-   40
ing himself on him he put the forces of death to flight. So
too for a widow's son, who hanged himself but was restored,
where that man of God is, no one is allowed to die.

When the saint was insisting that a pine tree, an object of
pagan cult, be cut down, a crowd of countrymen stationed
the righteous man there to crush him. When the tall tree   45
was hacked at by an ax and now ready to fall, at the com-
mand of the cross it was compelled to turn back. How great
was the strength of his faith when the cross made the weight
of a sturdy pine take a course contrary to nature!

When he put his finger on a man who because of the swell-
ing from a snakebite was nearing death, the dangerous poi-   50
son flowed from him, as the venom collected there and was
drawn off from the wound by his touch; while the poison-
ing subsided, he raised up his head. A novel salve, to drain
venom with the fingers, and by his skilled touch so to con-
quer death!

When a dead robber was being venerated with false honors,   55
by the command of Martin his spirit was forced to speak
there, announcing in public that he was killed for the enor-
mity of his crimes, and that he was not righteous, but rather

O vox sancta, loqui defuncta cadavera cogens,
60   cui post fata iacens dat sua verba cinis!

Pergeret in fluvium dum vipera lapsa natatu
    et prope litorei tangeret ora soli,
Martini imperio liquidas revocatur ad undas
    transactumque viae lassa recurrit iter.
65 Quantus amor Domini tali sub corde calebat,
    quando venena potens ipsa retorquet aquis!

Martini meritis aliis quoque febre crematis
    sudores refluos pagina sicca dabat,
unde salutifero medicamine charta fovebat
70   atque graves ignes littera tinguit aquis.
Gratia quanta Dei huius sermone rigabat,
    febre ubi succensis fons suus ibat apex!

Alme, decus rerum, pie, summe, Gregorius, arcis,
    tu cui das sedem dat tibi templa sacer.
75 Nam veteri fuerant haec funditus eruta lapsu
    tecta labore novo quae modo culta cluunt—
Iure potestatis cui tu, bone conditor orbis,
    haec danti in terris culmina redde polis.

Victa vetustatis per tempora culminis arca
80   diruit ut melior surgeret aula solo,
quo sacra Martinus Domini mysteria tractans
    a capite igniferum misit in astra globum.
Ne tamen ipsa ruens miserando fine iaceret,
    pontificem meruit qui sibi ferret opem.
85 Quae rediviva micans instante labore Gregori,

a criminal. O saintly voice, that compels a dead body to
speak, and with which lifeless ashes in the grave exchange   60
words!

When a snake was swimming in a river, slipping through the
water, and was approaching the edge of the earthen bank, by
the command of Martin it returned to the flowing stream
and, though weary, retraced the path it had traveled before.
How ardent was the love of the Lord in such a heart, when   65
his power was able to turn back in water poison itself!

By the merits of Martin when others were suffering the
burning of fever, a dry letter reversed a flood of sweating; so
a sheet of paper brought relief with its healing medication
and writing put out raging fires with waters. How great was   70
the grace of God that flowed from this man's speech, when
his letters issued in a spring for those burning with fever.

Bountiful lord, glory of all, merciful, and supreme in status,
holy Gregory, to whom you give this see, gives you back a
church. For this structure had long ago completely fallen   75
into ruin, but now after the recent efforts it is celebrated for
its splendor. By virtue of your power, generous creator of
the world, grant him a high place in heaven who gave you
this building on earth.

Succumbing to the passing of time the structure of this edi-
fice collapsed so that a better church could rise from the   80
ground, where Martin, while performing the sacred myster-
ies of the Lord, had round his head a ball of fire that sped to
the stars. In order that it not collapse and be condemned to
a wretched end, it won for itself a bishop to bring it aid. Re-   85
stored to life and brilliance by the urgent efforts of Gregory,

POEMS

decidua in senio, floret honore novo.
Fundamenta igitur reparans haec prisca sacerdos
extulit egregius quam nituere prius.
Nunc placet aula decens, patulis oculata fenestris,
90   quo noctis tenebris clauditur arte dies.
Lucidius fabricam picturae pompa perornat,
ductaque qua fucis vivere membra putes.

Leprosum purgavit

Pannoniae satio misit tibi, Gallia, fructum
gignens caelestem terra maligna dapem,
95 Martinum inlustrem meritis, qui munere divo
culmen in aetheria sede senator habet.
Qui leprae maculas medicata per oscula purgat,
curat et infectum pura saliva virum.
Ad fluvium Domini cui non fuit ire labore,
100   quod Iordanis habet, sanctus ab ore dedit.
Qui sacer ipse mihi te, pastor, agente, Gregori,
Fortunato adimat tot maculosa reo.

Chlamys divisa

Dum chlamydem Martinus inops divisit egeno,
Christus ea memorat se bene veste tegi.
105 Dives paupertas, Dominum quae texit amictu,
cui Deus occurrit qui dedit astra faber!

Tunicam dedit

Noscere qui mavis Martini gesta beati,
hic poteris breviter discere mira viri.
Denique cum tunicam sacer ipse dedisset egenti

662

once decrepit and old, it now flourishes in new glory. For
the bishop, in restoring its former stability, has nobly raised
it to its previous splendor. Now the beauty of the church
gives pleasure, with its broad windows like eyes, by which   90
daylight is cunningly trapped in the darkness of night. The
splendor of paintings brilliantly adorns its structure, and
you would think the bodies alive that are depicted in colors.

He healed a leper

Seed sown in Pannonia has sent its harvest to you, Gaul, an
unfertile land, but one that produces heavenly food, Martin   95
renowned for his merits, who by the bounty of God holds
high station as senator in the heavenly abode. He cleansed
the stains of leprosy with his healing kisses; his purifying
spittle cured a man of infection. For one who could not
struggle all the way to the river of the Lord the saint pro-   100
vided from his mouth the power the Jordan possesses. May
this holy man by your agency, shepherd Gregory, take from
me, Fortunatus the sinner, my many stains.

The divided cloak

When Martin the needy divided his cloak with a poor man,
Christ declared that he was well-clothed by that garment.
Rich is the poverty that has covered the Lord with apparel   105
and has met God, who as craftsman created the stars!

He made a present of a tunic

You who want to know the actions of blessed Martin, will be
able here to learn in brief his miraculous deeds. For when

110   ac sibi pars tunicae reddita parva foret,
      quod non texerunt manicae per brachia curtae
         visa tegi gemmis est manus illa viri.
      O nimium felix cui contigit in vice lanae
         nobilium lapidum lumine membra tegi,
115 ut, cum adhuc cinere adspersus foret atque favillis,
         artifice angelico gemmeus iret homo!

Mortuos suscitavit

Quid Deus in famulis operetur opimus amator,
   Martini gestis magna probare potes,
ducere qui meruit de morte cadavera vitae
120   rettulit atque diem reppulit unde necem.

Pinus excisa

Dum caderet Martinum arbor pressura beatum,
   mox facit ipse crucem, pinus abacta redit.
Quis non virtuti divinae commodet aurem,
   dum trabe conversa dant quoque ligna fugam?

Idola prostrata

125 Idola dum cuperet Martinus sternere fulta,
      conterit haec caelis magna columna ruens.
   Auxilium ad iusti dignando militat aether.
      Quanta fides cuius currit ad arma polus!

the saint had given his tunic to a poor man and a small part- 110
tunic was given to him in its place, because the curtailed
sleeves on his arms provided no covering, his hand was seen
to be covered by jewels. O greatly happy is he who had the
good fortune to be clothed on his body with the brilliance of
precious stones in place of wool, so that, though he still was 115
scattered with cinders and ashes, he came forward bejew-
eled by angelic handiwork!

He raised the dead

From the actions of Martin you can judge the greatness of
the deeds that God in his generous love performs through
his servants, for he was able to bring back corpses from
death to life and where he expelled death he restored the 120
light of day.

A pine tree cut down

When a tree was falling and on the point of crushing the
blessed Martin, he made the sign of the cross and immedi-
ately the pine recoiled back. Who would not lend an ear to
the power of the divine when even timber changes its course
and wood takes to flight?

Idols thrown down

When Martin wished to overturn idols set on a pillar, a large 125
column descended from the skies and obliterated them.
The heavens wage war, seeing fit to bring aid to the righ-
teous. How great is his faith that can count on heavenly re-
inforcements!

665

Falsus martyr

Forte colebatur dum quis pro martyre latro,
130   Martini adventu se probat esse reum.
Virtutis merito fidei radiante corusco
    nec tacet extincti nec latet umbra rei.

7

Ad Childebercthum regem et Brunichildem reginam, de natali sancti Martini pontificis Toronici

Praecelsis dominis famulor dum corde pusillus
    fluminibusque vagis per vada pergo rate,
ecce supervenit venerandi in saecula civis
    Martini meritis luce perenne dies,
5 qui modo de Gallis totum mire occupat orbem,
    et virtus pergit quo pede nemo valet,
qui velut alta pharus lumen pertendit ad Indos,
    quem Hispanus, Maurus, Persa, Britannus amat.
Hunc Oriens, Occasus habet, hunc Africa et Arctos;
10   Martini decus est quo loca mundus habet,
quique per oceani discurrit marginis undas,

A false martyr

When a robber was receiving the veneration of a martyr, at 130
the coming of Martin he admitted that he was a malefactor.
Before the power of virtue, in the brilliant radiance of faith,
the ghost of the dead wrongdoer was neither silent nor un-
disclosed.

7

To King Childebert and Queen Brunhild, on the feast day of Saint Martin, bishop of Tours

While I, lowly as I am, was in devoted attendance on my
most high lords, and was passing by boat on the current
along meandering rivers, there came the feast day of the
revered saint, eternal citizen of heaven, Martin, by whose
merits that day enjoys perpetual light, who now in wonder- 5
ful fashion from Gaul wins for himself the whole world, and
whose powers advance where no one can travel on foot; who
like a lofty lighthouse extends his light to India, and is loved
by the Spanish, the Moor, the Persian, and Briton. The East
claims possession of him, the West, Africa, and the North;
the glory of Martin extends everywhere in the world, and 10
skirting the waters at the bounds of the ocean he circles

omnibus ut praestet, circuit orbis iter.
Per cinerem ascendens, per dura cilicia caelos,
    stat modo gemmatus, pauper in orbe prius,
15 quo patriarcharum decus est radiantque prophetae,
    quo est sacra turba senum bis duodena patrum,
inter apostolicum numerum rutilante senatu
    quo sedet ipse throno, rex sibi Christus amor,
quo excellit cum clave Petrus, cum dogmate Paulus,
20 fulget et in reliquis palma, corona, fides,
quo loca martyribus vernanti lumine florent
    atque libro vitae est scriptus honore cruor,
quo confessores gemmata palatia complent
    aeternumque tenent aurea tecta diem,
25 stat quoque post lacrimas ubi nunc Radegundis opima,
    forsan et Eugeniam nunc tenet illa manu.
Hos inter Martinus habet diademata pulcher
    atque sacris lumbis fulgida zona viret,
cantat et egregios Christi de morte triumphos
30 atque resurgenti plaudit amore Deo.
Hunc quoque Martinum colitis quem, regna, patronum;
    vos hunc in terris, vos memor ille polis.
Vos intra angelicas turmas canat ille sub astris,
    cui vos ante homines fertis honore diem.
35 Nomina vestra legat patriarchis atque prophetis
    cui hodie in templo diptychus edit ebur.
Reddat apostolicos proceres reliquosque patronos
    quem vos hic colitis vel pia festa datis.
Pergat et ad Christum pro vobis ille precator
40 cui vos in templis vota precando datis.
Ante poli referat sua haec sollemnia regem,
    dentur ut hinc vobis, regna, salutis opes,

the earth in order to do service to all. Having mounted to
heaven by ashes and by rough hair shirts, he now takes his
place bejeweled, though previously poor in the world, where   15
are found the glory of the patriarchs and the brilliance of
the prophets, where too is the holy company of twenty-four
elders, and among the group of the apostles, in the pres-
ence of the brilliant senate, where sits enthroned the king
Christ, their love, where Peter has preeminence with his key
and Paul with his teaching, and among the others palm,   20
crown, and faith shine bright, where the land flowers with
the blossoming light of martyrs, and their blood is inscribed
in the book of life in their honor, where confessors crowd
the jewel-encrusted palace, and the golden roofs enclose the
light of eternal day, where noble Radegund now takes her   25
place after our tears, and perhaps now holds Eugenia by the
hand. Among all these Martin in his finery wears a diadem
and a sparkling belt shines green round the holy man's waist;
there he sings of the glorious triumph of Christ over death,
and lovingly acclaims the resurrection of God.   30

   This too is the Martin whom, your majesties, you vener-
ate as your patron; you remember him on earth, he you in
heaven. May he sing of you in the stars among the angelic
host, as you celebrate his feast day in the company of men.
Today may he read your names before patriarchs and proph-   35
ets, as today the ivory diptych pronounces his name in
church. May he whom you venerate here and celebrate in
holy festivals win the noble apostles and all that company as
your patrons. May he to whom you offer suppliant prayers
in churches approach Christ too as intercessor on your   40
behalf. May he bring these devotions before the king of
heaven, so that in this way, your majesties, the boon of well-

deputet et Dominus vestrum hunc esse patronum,
ut modo qui colitur vos colat huius amor,
45 qui<que> dedit habitans miracula plurima terris,
distribuat vobis hic quoque mira potens.
Cuius gemmata est tunc dextera visa beati,
vos simul et vestros protegat illa manus.
Qui tunc promeruit revocare cadavera vitae
50 hic quoque pro vestra vota salute ferat.
Qui percusso homini abstraxit de carne venenum
noxia de vobis ipse venena vetet.
Qui serpentis iter fecit revocare retrorsum
ipse graves casus hinc fuget ire retro.
55 Qui de peste domum salvam dedit esse Lyconti,
haec domus incolumis floreat huius ope.
Cuius opima chlamys tremebundum texit egenum,
eius apostolici vos tegat ala viri.
Qui viduae matri revocavit ad ubera natum
60 ipse tibi hic tribuat pignora, mater, ava,
ut Childebercthus maneat cum prole novella,
rex sua regna tenens et nova regna trahens,
de genita ut videas genetrix, ut dulcius optas,
deque nuru cara quod tua vota rogant.
65 Unde hic felices habeant sua festa fideles
et Domini famulis sitis honoris apex,
quo tibi plus libeat, Brunichildis, habere patronum,
quando domum et dominos servat in orbe pius.
Sic quoque te erudiat, regat et sic tramite ducat
70 actibus ipsa piis ut sibi iuncta mices.

being be granted to you, and may the Lord regard him as
your patron, so that the love of him who is now being hon-
ored may protect you, and may he who while living on earth   45
performed many miracles now too through his power be-
stow on you marvelous things. May the hand of the blessed
man that appeared covered with jewels protect you and
yours. May he who then had the power to bring back the
dead to life, now too offer his prayers for your welfare. May   50
he who drew out poison from the body of a snakebite victim
banish insidious poison from you. May he who caused a ser-
pent to turn back in its course drive back away from here
burdensome misfortunes. May he who made the house of   55
Lycontius safe from disease keep this house secure and
flourishing through his aid. May the wing of that apostolic
man spread over you, as his beneficent cloak covered a trem-
bling poor man. May he who returned a son to the breast
of his widowed mother grant you now children, to be both   60
mother and grandmother, so that Childebert remain strong
with his new offspring, maintaining his kingdom secure and
adding new kingdoms to it, and so that you, his mother,
see from your daughter and beloved daughter-in-law, as you
dearly wish, what your prayers are seeking. Therefore may   65
the faithful in felicity here hold their festival, and may you
be supreme in honoring the servants of the Lord, so that
you may take all the more pleasure, Brunhild, in having such
a patron, when he preserves in his benevolence the house
and its lords. May he so educate you, direct you, and rule
your course that by your pious actions you shine in company   70
with him.

8

Ad eosdem in laude

Si praestaretur praeconia pandere regum,
    non mihi sufficeret nocte dieque loqui
qualiter hic populus dominorum pendet amore
    et vestris oculis lumina fixa tenet.
5 Vos, quibus et speculum et lux et dulcedo manetis,
    carum ornamentum his simul estis, honos.
Praecipuum donum placidum et placabile regnum
    ac vestro in statu est culmen in orbe pium.
Hicque parentela et patria et tutela coruscat,
10   hic decus atque gradus, hic pietatis opus,
hic tranquilla dies, hic spes iucunda fideli,
    postque Deum in vobis dona salutis habent.
Hic ego cum populo mea vota et gaudia iungo,
    quae pius amplificans crescere Christus agat.
15 Praestet cura Dei vos longa in sede tueri
    caelesti ac dono regna tenere diu.
Adquiratis adhuc nova vel possessa regatis
    ac pie participes has foveatis opes,
ut tibi quae floret de nato et germine, messem
20   maturam videas, mater honore micans,
sic ut et ex genito genitisque nepotibus amplis
    altera progenies inclita detur avae.

8

To the same couple in their praise

If it fell to my lot to celebrate the praises of our kings, for me to speak both night and day would not do full justice to how this people is possessed with love for its masters, and keeps its gaze fixed upon your eyes. For those to whom you 5 are their model, their light, and their sweetness, you are at the same time their beloved ornament and glory. Rule that is calm and peace-loving is a special gift, and in your practice here the height of all virtue is reached. Here your family, your country, and those you protect shine bright, here are 10 your glory and station, here your deeds of devotion, here is peaceful daylight, here hope embraced by the faithful, and second only to God they have the gift of wellbeing from you.

Here I too join with the people my prayers and my joys; may Christ in his goodness make them prosper and multiply. May the solicitude of God grant you lasting protection 15 on the throne and long duration of your reign by heavenly gift. May you go on winning new possessions and continue to rule your present ones, and maintain these riches by generously sharing them out, so that you, mother radiant in glory, may see come to maturity a harvest that flowers from 20 your son and descendants, and that from your son and the noble grandchildren born to him a second glorious generation may be bestowed on their grandmother. From Childe-

De Childeberctho, dulcedine, flore, salute,
    fructum habeas genetrix, plebs sua vota videns.
25 De nata atque nuru cumulet tibi dona creator
    cumque pio merito stes placitura Deo.
Hic ego promerear rediens dare verba salutis,
    congaudens dominis parvulus ipse piis.
Prospera sint regum, populorum gaudia crescant;
30   exultet regio, stet honor iste diu.

9

De navigio suo

Regibus occurrens ubi Mettica moenia pollent,
    visus et a dominis ipse retentor equo.
Mosellam hinc iubeor percurrere navita remo,
    accelerans tremulis pergere lapsus aquis.
5 Ascendensque ratem gracili trabe nauta cucurri,
    nec conpulsa notis prora volabat aquis.
Interea locus est per saxa latentia ripis;
    litore constricto plus levat unda caput.
Huc proram inplicitam rapuit celer impetus actam,
10   nam prope iam tumidas ventre bibebat aquas.
Ereptum libuit patulos me cernere campos
    et fugiens pelagus ruris amoena peto.

bert, your sweetness, your flower, and your safekeeping, may
you reap fruits as his mother, and the people see their wishes
fulfilled. From daughter and daughter-in-law may the Cre-   25
ator heap you with blessings, and may you find yourself
pleasing to God by your piety. May I have the honor when I
return here of offering words of greeting, humbly joining in
the rejoicing of my benevolent masters. May the rulers en-
joy prosperity and the joys of the people increase; may the   30
kingdom rejoice, and this glory continue a long time.

9

On his voyage

Meeting the royal pair where the walls of Metz stand strong,
I was received by my lords and parted from my horse. Then
I was bidden as a mariner to navigate the Moselle with oars,
hastening to direct my course through the whirling waters.
I embarked on the boat and speedily set sail on a slender   5
bark; even without the propulsion of winds, the prow flew
through the water. Then came a stretch between rocks hid-
den on each shore; as the banks drew closer, the water's level
rose higher. The rapid current snatched up our prow and
drove it on helplessly, for now it was well-nigh drinking the   10
swelling waters into its belly. I was relieved to escape and see
before me spreading plains; leaving the flood behind I wel-

Gurgite suscipior subter quoque fluminis Ornae,
　　quo duplicata fluens unda secundat iter.
15　Inde per exclusas cauta rate pergimus undas,
　　ne veluti piscem me quoque nassa levet.
Inter villarum fumantia culmina ripis
　　pervenio qua se volvere Sura valet.
Inde per extantes colles et concava vallis
20　ad Saram pronis labimur amnis aquis.
Perducor Treverum qua moenia celsa patescunt,
　　urbs quoque nobilium nobilis aeque caput.
Ducimur hinc fluvio per culmina prisca senatus,
　　quo patet indiciis ipsa ruina potens.
25　Undique prospicimus minitantes vertice montes,
　　nubila quo penetrans surgit acuta silex,
qua celsos scopulos praerupta cacumina tendunt
　　hispidus et tumulis crescit ad astra lapis.
Nec vacat huc rigidis sine fructibus esse lapillis:
30　denique parturiunt saxaque vina fluunt.
Palmite vestitos hic respicis undique colles
　　et vaga pampineas ventilat aura comas.
Cautibus insertis densantur in ordine vites
　　atque supercilium regula picta petit.
35　Culta nitent inter horrentia saxa colonis:
　　in pallore petrae vitis amoena rubet,
aspera mellitos pariunt ubi saxa racemos
　　et cote in sterili fertilis uva placet,
quo vineta iugo calvo sub monte comantur
40　et tegit umbrosus sicca metalla viror.
Inde coloratas decerpit vinitor uvas
　　rupibus adpensis pendet et ipse legens.
Delicias oculis habui dapibusque cibatus,
　　haec iucunda tenens, navita regna sequens.

comed the beauty of the countryside. Then I was carried
onward by the waters of the river Orne, where the current
flowing with redoubled force prospered the journey. Next   15
through narrowed waters we pass with cautious way, lest like
a fish I too be entangled by a net. Between the smoke-
wreathed roofs of villas on the riverbanks, I reach the spot
where the Sauer rolls its course. Then by a hollow valley be-
tween lofty hills we pass downstream to the river Saar.   20

I journey on to where the lofty walls of Trier come into
view, a city of noble inhabitants and a noble capital too.
From here the river takes me past the ancient structures
of the senate, where the very ruins show evidence of their
power. On every side we see the threatening mountain   25
peaks, where the pointed crags burst up through the clouds,
where sheer cliffs raise up high their rocky faces, and shaggy
stone outcrops surge upward to the stars. But here not even
solid stone can be unfruitful: the stones give birth and from   30
them wine flows. Here you see on every side hills clothed
with vine boughs, and the wandering breeze rustles the ten-
drils and foliage. Vines are planted in serried ranks on the
cliffs, and outlined in rows they mount to the brow of the
hill. Among the bristling rocks tracts cultivated by laborers   35
shine clear; on the bare, white stone the graceful vines show
red, where rough crags bring forth honey-sweet clusters,
and from barren flint the fertile grape gives pleasure. On
the ridge the vine leaves cloak the mountain's baldness and   40
green shade covers the solid rock. From there the harvester
picks the colored grapes, and in doing so he himself hangs
from the overhanging cliffs.

I had charms for my eyes and fine fare to eat, expe-
riencing these delights and voyaging in the train of royalty.

45   Hinc quoque ducor aquis qua se rate Contrua conplet,
      quo fuit antiquum nobilitate caput.
Tum venio qua se duo flumina conflua iungunt,
      hinc Rhenus spumans, inde Mosella ferax.
Omne per illud iter servibant piscibus undae;
50   regibus et dominis copia fervet aquis.
Ne tamen ulla mihi dulcedo deesset eunti,
      pascebar Musis, aure bibente melos.
Vocibus excussis pulsabant organa montes
      reddebantque suos pendula saxa tropos.
55   Laxabat placidos mox aerea tela susurros,
      respondit cannis rursus ab alpe frutex.
Nunc tremulo fremitu, modo plano musica cantu
      talis rupe sonat qualis ab aere meat.
Carmina divisas iungunt dulcedine ripas,
60   collibus et fluviis vox erat una tropis.
Quo recreet populum, hoc exquirit gratia regum,
      invenit et semper quo sua cura iuvet.
Antonnacensis castelli promptus ad arces
      inde peraccedens sarcina pergo ratis.
65   Sint licet hic spatiis vineta in collibus amplis,
      altera pars plani fertilis extat agri:
Plus tamen illa loci speciosi copia pollet,
      alter quod populis fructus habetur aquis.
Denique dum praesunt reges in sedibus aulae
70   ac mensae officio prandia festa colunt,
retibus inspicitur quo salmo fasce levatur,
      et numerat pisces, cum sit in arce sedens;
rex favet in mensa, resilit dum piscis ab unda,
      atque animos reficit quod sua praeda venit.
75   Illuc fausta videns, huc laeta palatia reddens
      pascens ante oculos post fovet ipse cibis.

From here I continued on the waters to Gondorf, packed   45
with boats, where there was a fortress of ancient nobility.
Then I reached the point where two rivers mingle their
streams, the one the foaming Rhine, the other the fruitful
Moselle. During the whole journey the waves paid court
with their fish; the waters teem with abundance for their   50
kings and lords. But so that no sweetness was denied me as I
traveled, I feasted on the Muses, drank in music with my
ears. The voices of the instruments rang out to strike the
mountains, and the overhanging rocks echoed back to them
their melody. Once the web of bronze strings let forth its   55
gentle whisper, the bushes on the mountainside replied with
reedy piping. The music now is quavering in sound, now has
a constant refrain; as it comes from the metal, so it resounds
from the rocks. Song joins with its sweetness the separate
shores; one voice unites hills and stream in music. The gra-   60
ciousness of royalty seeks out this diversion for the people,
and always finds the means to give pleasure by its care.

    Then quickly I draw near to the heights of the town of
Andernach, and continue on as cargo on board the ship.
While on one side vineyards stretch far over the hills, on the   65
other side are level tracts of fertile farmland. The splendid
vista of abundance makes a still greater impression, because
the people enjoy a second harvest from the rivers. For when
the royal pair sit enthroned in the banqueting hall and cele-   70
brate a joyful meal according to the etiquette of the table,
the nets are inspected where the weight of the salmon is
raised, and while he is enthroned on high, the ruler counts
the fish. The king spreads joy at the table, as the fish spring
from the wave, and refreshes spirits because his catch comes
to him unbidden. By seeing all is well appointed there and   75
by bringing joy to the palace, he first feasts the eyes, before

Praesentatur item mensae Rheni advena civis,
    turbaque quo residens gratificatur edens.
Ista diu Dominus dominis spectacula praestet,
80   et populis dulces detis habere dies.
Vultibus ex placidis tribuatis gaudia cunctis,
    vester et ex vestris laetificetur apex.

10

Versus de oratorio Artannensi

Magna beatorum retinet haec terra talenta;
    divinis opibus dives habetur humus.
Pars dextra angelico Gabrielis honore coruscat,
    gaudia qui mundo detulit ore sacro,
5 quando aeternalem concepit virgo salutem,
    dona redemptoris nuntius iste ferens.
Laeva est parte lapis tumuli, quem corpore Christus
    pressit morte brevi, victor eundo patri.
Hic quoque reliquiis micat ille Gregorius almis
10   qui probus igne redit nec pice mersus obit.
Sunt etiam Cosmas, Damianus et ipse, salubres
    non ferro artifices, sed medicante fide.
Est Iulianus item, gladio iugulatus amico,
    plebs quem Arverna colens arma salutis habet;
15 Martinusque sacer, retinet quem Gallicus orbis,

providing the nourishment of food. A citizen of the Rhine, though stranger here, is introduced to the table, and the seated throng dines on him with pleasure. May the Lord long grant such pageants for our lords, and may you provide 80 happy times for your people. By your tranquil countenance may you bestow joy on all, and may your royal dignity derive happiness from your subjects.

10

Verses on the oratory of Artannes

This spot possesses a great wealth of the blessed; the earth is rich with the riches of God. The right side shines brightly with the glory of the angel Gabriel, who brought joy to the world from his sacred lips, when a virgin conceived eternal 5 salvation, and who carried the message of the redeemer's bounty. On the left is a stone from the tomb that Christ with his body burdened briefly in death before returning in victory to his father. Here too that Gregory shines with his bountiful relics who by his virtue emerged unscathed from 10 fire and when plunged in pitch did not die. Also here are the physicians Cosmas and Damian, who practice not with a scalpel, but by the healing power of faith. Again there is Julian, whose throat was cut by a kindly sword–in honoring him the people of Auvergne win the weapons of salvation– and saintly Martin, whom the Gallic realm claims for itself, 15

cuius Christum operit dimidiata chlamys,
se tunica spolians nudum qui vestit egenum,
    unde datae sibi sunt alba, topazus, onyx,
quae meruere aliqui hoc in corpore cernere sancti,
20   gemmarumque sonus quod patefecit opus.
Additur hic meritis cum nomine Victor opimis,
    munere martyrii qui tenet alta poli;
hic veteris virtute viri nova palma Niceti,
    urbem Lugdunum qui fovet ore, sinu.
25 Horum pastor opem corde, ore Gregorius orat,
    vivat ut altithrono vir sine fine Deo.

II

In nomine Domini nostri
Iesu Christi versus facti in mensa
in villa sancti Martini
ante discriptores

Cum videam citharae cantare loquacia ligna
    dulcibus et chordis admodulare lyram
(quo placido cantu resonare videntur et aera)
    mulceat atque aures fistula blanda tropis,
5 quamvis hic stupidus habear conviva receptus,
    et mea vult aliquid fistula muta loqui.

whose halved cloak served to cover Christ, who stripped off his tunic to clothe a naked poor man, for which he received pearls, topaz, and onyx, which some were found worthy to see on the body of the saint, while the sound of the jew- 20 els revealed what had happened. Present here too is Victor, victorious in name and in his rich virtues, who as a reward for martyrdom possesses the heights of heaven; and here too Nicetius, whose palm is new but powers of long stand- ing, who protects the city of Lyon with voice and embrace. Gregory begs for the aid of all these with heart and with 25 speech, to live forever, though a man, with God the high-enthroned.

11

Verses composed in the name of our Lord Jesus Christ at table in a villa of Saint Martin in the presence of assessors of taxes

When I see the speaking wood of the lute sing aloud, and the lyre play in tune with its sweet-sounding strings in a gen- tle strain with which the bronze seems to resound, while the enchanting pipe soothes the ear with music, although I am 5 invited here merely as an unresponsive guest, yet my pipe too, though voiceless, wants to speak some words.

Ecce dies, in quo Christus surrexit ab imo,
    infernae legis rumpere vincla potens,
quando et vinctorum lacrimantia milia solvit
10   et revomunt multos Tartara fracta viros.
Additur hic aliud, quod Martini aula beati
    emicat haec ubi nunc prandia festa fluunt,
qui valuit gestis aures pulsare Tonantis
    obtinet et meritis quod petit alta fides,
15 qui pie restituit defuncta cadavera vitae
    atque Dei prompte praebet amicus opem;
cui successor ovans modo rite Gregorius extans,
    ille quod adquirit, hic regit ore, fide.
Qui rogat hic praesens, alibi licet insidet absens,
20   exhibet atque cibos pastor in urbe bonus.
Nunc igitur celebrate diem sollemniter omnes
    quos Deus omnipotens hic dedit esse pares,
quos sibi Martinus collegit amore benignus
    et facit ecce escas hic epulare suas.
25 Ergo sub incolumi Childebertho ac Brunichilde,
    quos tribuit celsos regna fovere Deus,
vos, quos miserunt, populum moderate fidelem
    et relevate inopes, si quis et extat egens,
ac bona de dominis noscendo et agendo benigna
30   sint quoque laetitiae pabula vestra fide.
Quos invitavit Martini mensa beati,
    sumite gaudentes quod dat amore dies.
Quae bonus antistes noscendo Gregorius expers
    plaudat et haec populus gaudia vestra canat;
35 cuius et haec domus est a Christo exoret amator
    reges, vos, populos ut tegat arce Deus.

This is the day when Christ rose up from the depths, powerful to break the bonds of the underworld's law, when he freed thousands of tearful prisoners, and Tartarus was broken and disgorged many men. A second reason is that it is the brilliant hall of blessed Martin where this festive banquet is now taking its course, he who was able to assail the ears of the Lord by his actions, and who obtains by his virtues whatever his profound faith seeks, who compassionately brought back the bodies of the dead to life, and as a friend of God readily offers his aid, whose joyful successor in due form now is Gregory; what his predecessor acquired he governs with words and faith. He who invites you is here present, though absent and located elsewhere, and as a good shepherd in his city he is the source of this food. Therefore all of you now celebrate this day with due ceremony, for the almighty God has here caused you to be equal, whom Martin has gathered to himself, benevolent in his love, and made to feast here on food of his own.

Therefore under the secure rule of Childebert and Brunhild, whom God has provided to protect the realm in their eminence, and whose emissaries you are, hold sway over a faithful people and relieve the poor, whoever there is that is needy; recognizing the goodness of your lords and acting with generosity in your fidelity may the happiness you bring serve to bring you sustenance. You who have been invited to the table of blessed Martin, receive joyfully what this day has lovingly to offer. May the good bishop Gregory, though absent, learn of these things and rejoice, and may the people sing of these your joys; and may he whose house this is win from Christ by his loving prayer that God on high protect the kings, the people, and you.

12

Pro puella a iudicibus capta

a. Ad Gregorium episcopum

Exemplo Domini mihi vel venerabilis orbi,
    qui minimas non vis perdere, pastor, oves,
sollicitis animis curam per pascua tendens,
    ne desint caulis, circuis ore greges.
5 Hic igitur gerulus genitam flens impie demptam,
    captivam subolem tempore pacis habens:
Martinique pii successor honore, Gregori,
    qui pater es populi, hanc, rogo, redde patri.
Iugiter ille sacris meritis illuminat orbos;
10   orbato hanc patri redde videndo diem.

b. Item pro eadem re ad Romulfum

Si rapidis oculis te semper, amice, viderem,
    sic quoque vix avidum me satiaret amor,
qui, si praesentis non possum cernere vultum,
    te mihi vel scriptis, care, saluto libens.
5 Hunc etiam famulum commendo, benigne, verenter
    et si iusta petit, hunc tua lingua iuvet.

12

For a girl imprisoned by judges

a. To Bishop Gregory

Shepherd, revered by me and the world, who after the ex-
ample of the Lord are not willing to lose even the least of
your sheep, in your anxious concern extending through the
pastures your care, you encircle the flocks with your speech
so the sheepfold suffers no loss. This letter carrier is weep-   5
ing for a daughter cruelly taken from him, for a child taken
captive in a time of peace. Gregory, successor to holy Martin
in office, I beg you, who are father of the people, return this
girl to her father. That saint by his holy virtues continually
brings light to the sightless; restore this girl to her childless   10
father so he may see the daylight.

b. Again on the same subject, to Romulf

If with my eager eyes I always had you in my sight, my friend,
yet still that affection would scarcely satisfy my hunger, for,
if I cannot see your countenance present here before me,
I readily greet you in writing at least, my dear one. I also   5
respectfully commend this servant to your generosity: may
your tongue bring him aid, if his petition is just. Having suf-

Qui tortus graviter genitam sibi luget abactam
    per vos ut redeat filia clausa rogat,
paupere ut audito, dum estis medicina dolenti,
10   et vestris curis sit pia cura Deus.

c. Item pro eadem re ad Gallienum

Officiis exerte tuis, moderamine sollers,
    sollicitus studiis, utilitate comes,
more mihi solito, dulcis, tibi debita solvo;
    qui colo devinctus, reddo salutis opus.
5 Sit commendatus homo quem male torsit iniquus,
    perdidit et genitam, heu, miser iste suam.
Huic da iustitiam de vulnere corporis emptam
    et pie captivam fac remeare suam.
Inter utramque necem cui lex et filia defit,
10   unus in ambabus rebus adesto salus.

d. Item pro eadem re ad Florentinum

Dum pergit hinc quisque viam, mea pagina currat,
    prodat ut eloquio quod sibi debet amor.
Nunc quoque care mihi, bone semper, amice fidelis,
    pectore devotus reddo salutis opus.
5 Commendo hunc etiam famulum, dure ante redactum,
    tortus qui legem nec meruisse gemit,
illa dolens gravius quam vulnera corpore fixa,

fered terrible tortures he mourns for the child taken from
him, and requests that his captive daughter be returned to
him by you, so that because you heard a poor man's petition
and were salve for the grieving, God too in his mercy will   10
make your concerns his.

c. Again on the same subject, to Gallienus

Energetic in your duties, skilled in your governance, zeal-
ous in your pursuits, a count in your service, in my custom-
ary fashion, my sweet sir, I am paying what I owe; bound in
devotion to you, I offer the duty of greeting. May I com-   5
mend to you a man whom a wicked person has cruelly tor-
tured and who in his wretchedness, alas, has lost his daugh-
ter. Grant to this man justice, bought by the wounds on
his body, and compassionately cause his captive daughter to
come back to him. He has suffered two deaths, the law and
his daughter are denied him; be you the one person who   10
brings relief in both cases.

d. Again on the same subject, to Florentinus

When anyone journeys from here, may my letters travel with
speed, to show by their words what I owe you in love. Now
too, dear sir, always kindly, loyal friend, in devotion of heart
I offer you the duty of greeting. I commend to you also this   5
servant, roughly handled in the past, who after being tor-
tured laments that he did not receive justice, though griev-
ing less intensely for those wounds that were inflicted on

quod sibi subducta est filia parva, rudis.
  Audiat hanc vocem pietas miserando benigne;
10   quae sibi cum tribuis, hinc tibi magna dabis.

13

Ad episcopos in commendatione peregrini

Pontifices summi, fidei via, semita vitae,
  quos dedit Omnipotens luminis esse duces
custodesque gregi caelestis contulit agnus,
  vos bene pastores ut foveantur oves,
5 ecce viator adest peragens iter inscius illud,
  finibus Italicis heu peregrina gemens.
Exulis auxilium, errantis via, norma salutis,
  ad reditum patriae sitis honore patres.
Semina iactetis mercedis ut ampla metatis
10   et redeat vobis centuplicata seges.
Fortunatus enim humilis commender opimis
  ac per vos Domino, culmina sancta, precor.

his body than that his small daughter, still young, has been snatched from him. May your compassion show pity in generously hearing this plea; what you grant to him will bring 10 great benefit to you.

13

To bishops in recommendation of a foreigner

Highest pontiffs, road of faith, pathway to life, whom the Almighty made guides to the light, and the lamb of heaven bestowed as guardians for the flock, good shepherds as you are in keeping watch over your sheep, behold, here is a trav- 5 eler journeying in ignorance of his way, bemoaning, alas, his condition, a foreigner from the land of Italy. Support of the exile, road for the wanderer, model of salvation, may you play the role of fathers to restore him to his fatherland. May you sow the seeds to reap an ample reward, and receive in 10 return a hundredfold harvest. May I Fortunatus, though humble, be commended to your excellencies, and by you, I pray, holy eminences, to the Lord.

14

De Platone episcopo

Provida disponunt reges solacia plebi
    pontificem dantes quem probat alma fides,
ut colat Hilarium, quem dat Martinus alumnum
    et confessoris protegat ala potens.
5 Dirigat hic populum successor honore beato
    et clerum ecclesiae qui moderetur ope.
Floreat arce decens rex Childebercthus in orbe
    cum genitis, populo, matre, sorore, iugo.
Gaudia laeta paret praesentia sancta Gregori
10 et geminas urbes adiuvet una fides.
Qui modo discipulo Platone antistite summo
    sollemnem Ecclesiae hic dedit esse diem.

15

Ad Armentariam matrem domni
Gregorii episcopi

Felix bis meritis sibi Machabaea vel orbi
    (nobilitas generis nobilior genitis),
quae septem palmas caelo transmisit ab alvo

14

On Bishop Plato

The kings in their providence are providing comfort for their people by granting them a bishop approved by beneficent faith, a man whom Martin presents as his foster-son, to venerate Hilary and for the powerful wing of that confessor to protect. May this successor in that blessed office guide 5 his people and the clergy of the church in exerting his sway. May King Childebert, glorious in his eminence, flourish in the world, along with his children, people, mother, sister, and wife. May the saintly presence of Gregory bring you happiness and rejoicing, and one devotion sustain your dou- 10 ble cities. He it is who has caused this day to be celebrated by the Church through his pupil Plato, now a most high bishop.

15

To Armentaria, mother of the lord bishop Gregory

Twice fortunate through her virtues was the mother of the Maccabees, in herself and in the world (the nobility of her birth was made still nobler by her offspring), who sent on to heaven seven palms of victory from her belly, and pro-

martyriique decus protulit ille uterus.
5 Tu quoque prole potens, recte Armentaria felix,
  nec minor ex partu quam prior illa sinu.
Illa vetus numero maior, tu maxima solo;
  quod poterant plures, unicus ecce tuus.
Fetu clara tuo, geniti circumdata fructu,
10 est tibi Gregorius palma, corona, decus.
Me Fortunatum humilem commendo verenter
  ac mihi caelestem quaeso preceris opem.

16

Pro comitatu eius Sigoaldo

Finibus Italiae cum primum ad regna venirem,
  te mihi constituit rex Sigibercthus opem,
tutior ut graderer tecum comitando viator
  atque pararetur hinc equus, inde cibus.
5 Implesti officium custos, revocaris amico,
  et mihi vel tandem iam mea cura redit.
Dic, meus, unde venis post tempora plurima, dulcis,
  magnus honore tuo, maior amore meo,
promptus in affectu, Sigoalde benigne, clientum
10 et Fortunato nomen, amice, pium?
Rex Childebercthus crescens te crescere cogat;
  qui modo dat comitis, det tibi dona ducis.
De domino tali videant sua vota fideles
  cursibus et fiat prospera vita via.

duced from her womb the glory of martyrdom. You too are 5
mighty in your son, Armentaria, deservedly fortunate, nor
are you inferior in your offspring to that former woman in
her womb. That woman of old was superior in number, you
are supreme with just one; what many could bestow on her, a
single son supplies for you. Famous for your progeny, en-
dowed with blessings from your child, you have in Gregory 10
your palm, crown, and your glory. I respectfully commend
myself, your humble Fortunatus, and beg that you pray for
heavenly aid for me.

16

To Sigoald, on his being made count

When first I came to this kingdom from the land of Italy,
King Sigibert appointed you to bring me aid, so that I might
move more safely as a traveler in your company, and acquire
both a horse and some provisions. You fulfilled your duty as 5
a protector, you are recalled to mind by a friend, and, even
after much time, my care for you now returns to me. Tell me,
my sweet friend, where do you come from after so much
time, great in your office, but greater still in my love, quick
in your affection for your dependents, generous Sigoald, a 10
name revered, my friend, by Fortunatus? May King Childe-
bert grow greater and in so doing cause you to grow; may he
who now honors you as count hereafter honor you as duke.
From such a lord may the faithful see their wishes fulfilled,
and life in its progress follow a prosperous course.

17

Ad Sigoaldum comitem, quod pauperes pro rege paverit

Actibus egregiis praeconia fulgida fulgent;
    laus tua, Christe, sonet, dum bona quisque gerit.
Unde genus hominum placeas tu, Summe, ministra,
    nam nisi tu dederis, prospera nullus agit.
5 Divitibus largus forte hinc et parcus egenis,
    se ut redimat dives quando fovetur egens.
Dulciter ista tui pia sunt commercia regni:
    dum escam sumit egens, divitis auget opes.
Pauper ventre satur satiat mercede potentem;
10   parva capit terris, praeparat ampla polis.
Divitibus plus praestat egens quam dives egenti;
    dat moritura cibi, sumit opima Dei,
dans terrae nummum missurus ad astra talentum,
    e modicis granis surgat ut alta seges.
15 Dent, iactent, spargant, commendent semina Christo,
    hic dare nec dubitent quae reditura manent.
Da; sic Christus erit tibi thesaurarius inde;
    praesta inopi quidquid reddere Christus habet,
hac animatus ope exposcens meliora Tonantis
20   nec dubitante fide quod Deus ista dabit.

17

To Count Sigoald, for having fed the poor on behalf of the king

From noble actions glory acquires brilliant luster; may your praise sound out, Christ, when anyone performs good deeds. Provide, O Most High, the occasions for the human race to please you, for unless you give the opportunity, no one will be fortunate in action. Perhaps this is why you are generous to the rich and frugal to the needy: so that the rich man can redeem himself when the poor is given support. In this way the transactions for your kingdom are sweetly conducted: while the poor man receives food, he increases the wealth of the rich man. In sating his stomach the poor man satisfies the powerful man with a reward; he receives small things on earth, but makes ready rich blessings in heaven. The poor man gives more to the rich than the rich man does to the poor; the rich man gives the transient gift of food, and wins the abundance of God; he expends coins on earth to transmit a talent to the stars, so that a harvest rises up high from insignificant seeds. Let them give, throw, scatter, and entrust the seeds to Christ, and have no hesitation in distributing what will come back to them again. Only give, then Christ will be your treasurer; provide for the needy all that Christ will return to you, and inspired by this promise seek better things from the Lord; let your faith have no doubt that God will grant them. It is for the prosperity and well-

Pro Childebercthi regis florente salute —
   surgat ut in solio qui fuit altus avo,
fiat ut hinc iuvenis validis robustior annis,
   ceu viguit proavus, sic sit in orbe nepos —
25 ergo suus famulus Sigoaldus amore fidelis
   pauperibus tribuit, regis ut extet apex.
Hinc ad Martini venerandi limina pergens
   auxilium domini dum rogat ipse sui
et dum illuc moderans rex pro regione laborat,
30 ut precibus sanctus hunc iuvet, illud agit.
Denique procedens . . . sacra festa tenere
   pauperibus Christi praebuit ipse dapem.
Dispensata placent alimenta per agmina Christi,
   pascitur et populus quem fovet arce Deus.
35 Plurima caecorum refovetur turba virorum,
   est quibus in tenebra lux Deus atque via.
Hinc alitur clodus quem dirigit ordine Christus
   quique sui Domini pendulus implet opus.
Quis referat tantos memorare sub ordine morbos,
40 occurrens pariter quos sua cura fovet?
Unde catervatim coeuntia milia pascens,
   erogat ut habeat, rex quoque cuncta regat.
Te Fortunatus, comes, hinc, Sigoalde, salutans,
   regis ut auxilium det meliora precor.

being of King Childebert—that he rise high on the throne
exalted by his grandfather and that thereby that young man
grow stronger and sturdier each year, and the grandson
wield worldly power as his great-grandfather once did—for   25
these reasons his faithful servant Sigoald out of affection
distributed alms to the poor, that the king's glory might be
exalted. Then proceeding to the threshold of the venerable
Martin, when he asked for assistance for his lord, while the
king was striving to govern in the interests of that realm, he   30
brought it about that the saint would aid the king with his
prayers. Next when going to celebrate the holy festival . . .
he furnished a meal for the poor of Christ. The nourish-
ment provided for the ranks of Christ won favor, and the
people whom God in heaven protects found sustenance. A   35
large number of blind men thereby found refreshment, for
whom God is their light and the path in their darkness. In
this way the lame were fed whom Christ set on the right
way, and who, though unsteady, fulfilled the behest of their
Lord. Who will be able to record in total the many illnesses   40
which his solicitude attended to and relieved? And so feed-
ing the thousands who collected together en masse, he paid
out to take in and to secure the king's rule over all, I, Fortu-
natus, with these words salute you, Count Sigoald, and beg
that the aid of the king bring greater blessings to you.

18

De prandio defensoris

Paschale hic hodie donum memorabile floret;
    defensor pascit, quo comes ipse favet.
Delicias Domini quas tempora, vota ministrant
    undique conveniunt flumine, fruge, polo.
5 Childebercthi etiam dominatio longa refulgens
    te, Sigoalde, diu sublevet arce, gradu.
Sit regio felix felicis regis amore
    atque boni comitis crescat honore fides.

19

Ad Galactorium comitem

Venisti tandem ad quod debebaris, amice,
    ante comes merito quam datus esset honor.
Burdegalensis eras et, cum defensor, amator;
    dignus habebaris haec duo digna regens.
5 Iudicio regis valuisti crescere iudex
    famaque quod meruit regia lingua dedit.
Debet et ipse potens, ut adhuc bene crescere possis,

18

On a meal given by a defender

Here today at Easter exceptional bounty abounds; a defender gives a feast in which the count himself rejoices. The delicacies of the Lord that the season and our prayers provide come in from every side, from river, crops, and sky. May also the lengthy and resplendent lordship of Childe- 5
bert long elevate you, Sigoald, in dignity and status. May the kingdom be fortunate in the love of a fortunate king, and the standing of a noble count increase in glory.

19

To Count Galactorius

You have finally attained what is your due, my friend, already a count in merit before you received the office. You were from Bordeaux, both defender of the city and its lover; performing these two esteemed roles you were held in high esteem. By the judgment of the king you were able to rise 5
to be judge, and what your reputation warranted the royal tongue bestowed. In order that you can rise further in sta-

praestet ut arma ducis, qui tibi restat apex,
ut patriae fines sapiens tuearis et urbes,
10   acquiras ut ei qui dat opima tibi,
Cantaber ut timeat, Vasco vagus arma pavescat
    atque Pyrenaeae deserat Alpis opem.
Aut (quasi grande loquor) facit hoc sacer unicus Auctor;
    a Domino erigitur parvus et altus homo.
15 De tirone ducis venit, et de milite princeps,
    ut reliquos taceam, Iustinianus erat.
Hoc et in ecclesia Christo tribuente refertur:
    de exorcista aliquo pontificalis honor.
Egregius merito Martinus testis habetur,
20   qui fuit ante sacer quam sacra iura daret.
Hoc agit Omnipotens, totum qui condidit orbem,
    magnaque sola putes quae facit ipse potens.
Laetior ergo, precor, maneas in culmine rector,
    maiora sperans, vir ratione sagax,
25 rege sub hoc florens aeternaque regna requirens
    . . .
Iustitia ac pietas tecum comitata coruscet:
    illa tuum pectus protegat, ista latus.
Alta fides etiam, dilectio fida nitescat,
30   et Fortunato sis, comes, amplus amor.

tus, he should use his power to grant you the arms of a duke, the only high rank that remains for you, so that in your wisdom you may protect the country's territory and its cities, and win possessions for him who lavishly gives honors to you, so that the Cantabrian is afraid and the wandering Basque dreads your arms, and abandons the stronghold of the Pyrenean mountains. Or rather our one holy Creator will bring this about (I speak of a great matter); by the Lord both the low and the high are raised up. A duke was once a raw recruit and an emperor a soldier; to mention no other, this was Justinian's case. This also is recorded in the church by the agency of Christ; an exorcist rose to the office of bishop. Martin who excels in his merits can serve as a witness, for he was saintly before he wielded sacred power. This is the work of the Almighty, who created the entire world; consider only those things great that he in his might performs. May you be happy, then, I pray, as a high ranking governor, hoping for greater things, a man of wisdom and discernment, thriving under this king and aspiring to the eternal kingdom . . . May justice and piety be your resplendent companions, the one protecting your chest, the other your flank. May your profound faith and your faithful affection shine bright, and, count, may your love be abundant for Fortunatus.

BOOK ELEVEN

Expositio symboli

Summam totius fidei catholicae recensentes, in qua et integritas credulitatis ostenditur et unius Dei omnipotentis, id est sanctae trinitatis, aequalitas declaratur et mysterium incarnationis filii Dei, qui pro salute humani generis a patre de caelo descendens de virgine nasci dignatus est, quo ordine vel quando pertulerit, quomodo sepultus surrexerit et in carne ipsa caelos ascendens ad dexteram patris consederit iudexque venturus sit, qualiter remissionem peccatorum sacro baptismate renatis contulerit et resurrectio humani generis in eadem carne in vitam aeternam futura sit, quia multa in symbolo paucis verbis conplexa sunt, mediocriter nobis sermo temperandus est, ne aut breviter dicendo non aperiat intellectum aut prolixitate verbi generetur fastidium.

2   Itaque resurgente Christo et ascendente in caelum, misso sancto spiritu, conlata apostolis scientia linguarum, adhuc in uno positi hoc inter se symbolum, unusquisque quod sensit dicendo, condiderunt, ut discedentes ab invicem hanc

I

Explanation of the creed

As I review the sum total of the whole Catholic faith, in which the entirety of belief is displayed and in which are asserted the equality of the one almighty God, that is of the Holy Trinity, and the mystery of the incarnation of the son of God, who, coming down from his father in heaven for the salvation of the human race saw fit to be born of a virgin, when and in what manner he suffered, how he was buried and rose again, and ascending in the flesh to heaven took his seat at the right of his father and is to come as a judge, how he granted forgiveness of sins to those reborn by holy baptism and how there will be resurrection of the human race into eternal life in the same body, because many things are encompassed in the creed in a few words, I must show restraint in my language and adopt a middle course, lest by speaking briefly my words fail to communicate meaning or by their diffuseness they produce boredom.

After Christ's resurrection, then, and his ascension to 2 heaven, the Holy Spirit came down and the knowledge of tongues was bestowed on the apostles. They were still together in one place and between them they composed this creed, each contributing his own opinion, so that when they

3   regulam per omnes gentes aequaliter praedicarent. Denique
symbolum Graece conlatio dicitur, quia hoc ipsi inter se per
sanctum spiritum salubriter contulerunt. Dicitur et indi-
cium, quod per hoc qui recte crediderit indicetur. Ergo
cunctis credentibus quae continentur in symbolo salus ani-
marum et vita perpetua bonis actibus praeparetur.

4   *Credo in Deum patrem omnipotentem.* Praeclarum in pri-
mordio ponitur fidelis testimonii fundamentum, quia salvus
esse poterit qui recte salutem crediderit, apostolo praedi-
cante, "credere oportet accedentem ad Deum"; item, "corde
creditur ad iustitiam"; et "credidi propter quod locutus
sum"; vel illud, "iustus ex fide vivit" et "nisi credideris, non
5   intellegetis." Ergo vel in rebus humanis nullum opus incipi-
tur, nisi labor omnis ad effectum venire credatur. Unde cre-
dendum est in Deum, a quo tam praesens vita quam futura
tribuitur.

6   Deus autem appellatio est substantiae sempiternae sive
timoris divini. Igitur Deus est sine principio, sine fine, sim-
7   plex, incorporeus, inconprehensibilis. Patrem autem cum
audis, agnosce quod habeat filium veraciter genitum, quo-
modo possessor dicitur qui aliquid possidet et dominus qui
alicui dominetur. Deus ergo pater secreti sacramenti voca-
bulum est, cuius vere filius est verbum et speculum et cha-
racter et imago vivens patris viventis, in omnibus patri simi-
lis, eiusdem naturae et in divinitate genitus, genitori per
8   omnia coaequalis. Nec quaeratur quomodo genuit filium,
quod et angeli nesciunt, prophetis est incognitum. Unde il-

separated from one another they would preach this rule in
unison through all the nations. For in Greek symbol means   3
contribution, because between them they contributed to it
by the aid of the Holy Spirit for the purpose of salvation. It
also means token because by it a token is given of who pos-
sesses correct belief. Therefore, for all who believe in what
the creed contains, let the salvation of their souls and eter-
nal life be acquired by good actions.

I believe in God the Father almighty. The basis of the decla-   4
ration of faith is excellently put at the beginning, because he
who has a proper belief in salvation will be able to be saved,
according to the preaching of the apostle, "he who comes to
God should believe," and again, "heartfelt belief attains jus-
tice," and "I believed and therefore I spoke," or that saying
"the just man lives by faith," and "unless you believe, you will
not understand." For even in human affairs no task is under-   5
taken unless it is believed that all the effort will reach an
outcome. Therefore we must believe in God, by whom both
the present and the future life is granted to us.

God moreover is the name for an eternal substance and   6
for the awe felt for the divine. Therefore God is without
beginning or end, simple, incorporeal, incomprehensible.
When you hear the name father, however, realize that he   7
has a properly born son, in the same way as someone who
possesses something is called a possessor and someone who
lords it over someone a lord. So God the Father is the ex-
pression of a hidden mystery, whose true son is the word
and the living mirror, impress, and image of the living father,
in everything like his father, born of the same nature and
divine, equal to his begetter in all things. Do not ask how   8
he begat a son, a matter of which even the angels have no

lud dictum est, "generationem eius quis enarrabit?" Quam secretam originem cum proprio filio novit ipse solus qui ge-

9 nuit. Nec a nobis Deus discutiendus est, sed credendus, qui in nobis ipsis nescimus quod sapimus, quomodo sapientia, ingenium aut intellectus consilium aut mens nostra generat

10 verbum. Sed, ut breviter dicamus, sufficit nos scire quia lux genuit splendorem, propheta testante: "in splendoribus sanctorum ex utero ante luciferum genui te"; et illud, "hic Deus noster, et non reputabitur alter ad eum"; et post, "in

11 terris visus est et inter homines conversatus est." Omnipotens vero dicitur eo quod omnia possit et omnium obtinet potentatum, quia pater omnia creavit per filium.

12 *Et in Iesum Christum.* Iesus Hebraice salvator dicitur. Hoc nomen digne convenit principi qui populo se sequenti possit salutem tribuere. Cuius figuram Iesus Navae gerens populum de deserto in terram repromissionis certum est induxisse, et iste de tenebris et terra ignorantiae se sequentes

13 ad caelos educit. Christus dicitur a chrismatis unctione, et hoc nomen pontificale est vel regale, quoniam reges unguebantur oleo corruptionis. Hic autem ab Spiritu Sancto oleo exultationis divinitus unctus est, propheta dicente: "Spiritus

14 Sanctus super me propter quod unxit me." Iesus ergo dicitur eo quod salvet populum, Christus, quod sit unctus pontifex in aeternum.

15 *Unicum Filium* ideo, ut nihil in hoc intellegas terrenum sive corporeum, ubi de uno est unus, de luce splendor, de

knowledge and the prophets are ignorant. Hence the saying "who will tell of his birth?" Only he who begat him, along with his son, knows of this hidden birth. Nor should we in-   9
quire about God but believe in him, for we are ignorant in our own persons of our own mental powers, how wisdom, intelligence, or understanding produce thought or how our mind generates speech. Rather, to put it briefly, it is suffi-   10
cient for us to know that the light brought forth brilliance, as the prophet bears witness: "Before the morning star I bore you from my womb in the brilliance of the saints"; and the saying, "this is our God and no one will be likened to him"; and after that, "he was seen on earth and lived among men." He is called almighty because he is able to do any-   11
thing and has power over everything, for as father he created all things through his son.

And in Jesus Christ. Jesus means "savior" in Hebrew. This   12
name fits very well a prince who can bring salvation to the people who follow him. It is established that Joshua, assuming this figure, led his people from the desert to the promised land, while Jesus brings those who follow him to heaven from darkness and the land of ignorance. He is called Christ   13
from the anointment of the chrism, a name that is priestly or royal, since kings were anointed with the oil of corruption. He, however, was divinely anointed by the Holy Spirit with the oil of rejoicing, according to the words of the prophet: "The Holy Spirit is on me because it has anointed me." He is called Jesus, therefore, because he saves his peo-   14
ple, and Christ, because he was anointed priest forever.

He is *his only Son* so that you understand there is nothing   15
earthbound or corporeal in this relationship, where the one is born from the one, brilliance from the light, the word

corde verbum, de mente sensus, de forte virtus, de sapientia sapiens, de aeterno natus est coaeternus, per omnia idem,

16 quod pater hoc filius. Nam unicus ideo, quia nec conparationem recipit cum reliquis creaturis nec similitudinem, quia omnium rerum summus ipse creator est. Homines autem filii dei vocantur per gratiam; ille solus filius genitus per naturam. Hucusque de deitate patris atque filii textus ordo secutus est.

17 *Qui natus est de Spiritu Sancto ex Maria virgine.* Ille qui de patre ante saecula natus est, postea de spiritu sancto eius templum in virgine fabricatum intellegendum est. Nam sicut in sanctificatione spiritus nulla fragilitas extitit, sic nec in partu eiusdem causa corruptionis apparuit, qui in caelis unus, in terris unicus, per portam virginis ingredi mundum

18 dignatus est. Hinc plurima prophetae de virginis conceptu et de partu locuti sunt. Unum tamen exemplum pro brevitate proponemus, de quo Ezechiel dicit: "Porta quae respicit ad orientem clausa erit et non aperietur et nemo transiet per eam, quoniam Dominus Deus Israhel ipse transibit per eam, et clausa erit."

19 Hoc tamen notandum est, quia dum Spiritus Sanctus est dominicae carnis creator, spiritus sancti hinc maiestas ostenditur. Quod vero Deus maiestatis de Maria in carne natus est, non est sordidatus nascendo de virgine qui non

20 fuit pollutus hominem condens de pulvere. Denique sol aut ignis si lutum inspiciat, quod tetigerit purgat et se tamen non inquinat; nec fuit Deo iniuriae causa misericordiae, neque sit incredibile quod est ipse natus de virgine qui Adam de pulvere et primam mulierem potuit de costa formare.

from the heart, thought from the mind, power from the powerful, wise from wisdom, coeternal from the eternal, identical in all things, as the father, so the son. For he is 16 unique because he admits of no comparison or similarity with other creatures, since he himself is the supreme creator of the entire world. Men are called the sons of God by grace; he alone is his son born according to nature. Up to this point the sequence of my text has pursued the subject of the divinity of the father and the son.

Who was born from the Holy Spirit, of the virgin Mary. He 17 who was born from the father before time, afterward, we must understand, had a temple built for him by the Holy Spirit in a virgin. For just as no flaw exists in the holiness of the Spirit, so no cause for corruption appeared in the birth of him who, one in the heavens and unique on earth, saw fit to enter the world by the gate of a virgin. That is why the 18 prophets said so much about conception and birth from a virgin. We will give just one example, however, for brevity's sake. On this subject Ezekiel said: "The gate that looks to the East will be closed and not be opened and no one will pass through it, since the Lord God of Israel himself will pass through it and it will be closed."

This too must be observed, that the majesty of the Holy 19 Spirit is demonstrated by its being the creator of the Lord's flesh. But as to the fact that the God of majesty was born in the flesh of Mary, he was not sullied by being born of a virgin, just as he was not defiled by creating man from dust. For 20 the sun or fire, if it looks on mud, purifies what it touches but is not itself polluted. In the case of God his act of compassion did him no harm, nor should it be incredible that he was born of a virgin who was able to shape Adam from dust and the first woman from a rib.

21 *Crucifixus sub Pontio Pilato.* Hinc multa prophetae qualiter confixus in cruce, foratis pedibus, aceto vel felle aut vino murrato potatus, spinis coronatus, lancea percussus, super veste eius sorte missa et in conspectu populi maligni manibus extensis in die pependerit praedixerunt quae diligens
22 lector inveniet. Tamen, ut breviter dicatur, in cruce suspensus est ut nos a damnatione ligni vetiti dissolveret; felle vero potatur ut amaritudinem praevaricati pomi et nimis acidi amputaret; spinis coronatur ut maledictae terrae vetustum crimen erueret; lancea percutitur ut per plagam lateris aqua fluente vel sanguine baptismum vel mysterium martyrii promulgaret; et, ut dicatur aliquid altius, in costa Christus percutitur ut vulnus nobis infixum per Evam, quae de costa viri formata fuerat, amputaret.

23 Ut tamen ad hoc intellegendum aliquantulum extendamur—sicut dicit scriptura: "cordis oculi aperti sint ad intellegendum quid sit altitudo, latitudo et profundum," quod est crucis significatio—quare Dominus in patibulo se pati elegerit quaeritur. Ratio tamen haec redditur: crux species tropaei est quod devictis hostibus solet fieri triumphanti et quia Dominus tria regna sibi subiecit, suspensus in aera victoriam de caelestibus et spiritalibus nequitiis est adeptus, expandens autem manus ad populos, palmam de terrenis, quod vero sub terra crux fixa est, ostendit eum et de Tartaro triumphare.

Crucified under Pontius Pilate. Of this the prophets made 21
many predictions that the careful reader will discover, how
he was crucified on the cross, his feet were pierced, he was
given vinegar and gall, or wine mixed with myrrh to drink,
crowned with thorns, and pierced by a spear, how lots were
cast for his clothing, and before the gaze of a wicked people
he hung, his hands extended, for a day. For, to put it briefly, 22
he hung on the cross to free us from the damnation in-
curred from the forbidden wood; he was given gall to drink
to drown the bitterness of the sharp-tasting fruit consumed
in sin; he was crowned with thorns to uproot the longstand-
ing charge against the accursed earth; he was pierced by the
spear to proclaim baptism and the mystery of martyrdom by
the water and blood flowing from the wound in his side;
and, to express a deeper meaning, Christ was pierced in the
rib so as to eradicate the wound inflicted on us by Eve, who
had been formed from the rib of a man.

To elaborate a little further in understanding this—as the 23
Scripture says, "let the eyes of the heart be opened to under-
stand what is the height, the breadth, and the depth," by
which is meant the cross—the question is raised why the
Lord chose to suffer on the gibbet in this way. This answer,
however, is provided: the cross is a kind of trophy such as is
accustomed to be set up for a general celebrating his tri-
umph after the enemy has been defeated. Because the Lord
subjected three realms to himself, by being raised in the air
he won a victory over the heavenly forces of spiritual wick-
edness, by stretching out his hands to the people he won the
palm for victory over the forces of earth, and because the
cross was set driven into earth, it revealed that he was tri-
umphing over Tartarus too.

24   Et quia de aliis brevitatis causa praeteriemus plurima, non generemus fastidium, si pro honore sanctae crucis nobis hic sermo distenditur, ut vobis aedificatio et illi crescat 25 praeconium. Ergo quia nec ipsa sidera in conspectu Dei pro humano crimine non erant pura et erat tota terra polluta, ideo suspensus est Christus in aera, ut simul terras et astra purgaret; aut quia ipse dixerat: "sicut Moyses exaltavit serpentem," ideo cruci suspenditur, ut adimplerentur verba quae creator praedixerat; aut quia inter caelum et terram grandis erat discordia, ut tolleret reconciliator se mediante scandalum, in aera suspenditur, ut se in medio posito inter caelum et terram inter hominem et Deum pax rediret post 26 odium; aut ideo quia ante gravis latro in cruce configebatur, ergo ad hoc elegit Christus principale supplicium, ut hominem absolveret originali peccato quod erat principale tormentum; aut ideo Dominus in cruce suspenditur, ut pro captivitate nostra pretium sui corporis mercator in statera 27 pensaret; aut ideo crucifigitur, quia mortui eramus per pomum et arborem, ut denuo crux et Christus, id est arbor et pomum, per ipsam similitudinem nos a morte liberaret. Pomum dulce cum arbore!

28   *Sub Pontio Pilato.* Bene hoc est additum, ut iudice cum tempore designato non esse videretur incertum, sub Herode rege, qui eo tempore tetrarcha erat, ad quem Pilatus misit Dominum vinctum, et per hoc inter iudices pax provenit post odium, et ligatus Dominus, magis legatarius, pax inter partes extitit et iudices a livore dissolvit.

And since I will pass over many other things for brevity's 24
sake, let me not cause boredom if this passage in honor of
the holy cross is extended by me to increase the instruc-
tion for you and celebration of it. Therefore Christ was sus- 25
pended in the air to purify the earth and the stars, because
not even the stars themselves in the eyes of the Lord were
free from sin because of the fault of humanity, and the whole
earth was defiled; or he was suspended from the cross to ful-
fill the words that the Creator had prophetically uttered,
because he himself said "just as Moses raised up a serpent";
or he was suspended in the air to remove a conflict as a me-
diator by his own intervention, because there was great dis-
harmony between heaven and earth, so that when he was
set between heaven and earth peace between man and God
would return after hatred; or because a terrible brigand 26
was previously nailed to the cross, Christ therefore chose
for himself the supreme punishment to free mankind from
original sin, which was the supreme torment; or the Lord
was hung on the cross so that as a merchant he should weigh
in the balance the value of his body as ransom for our captiv-
ity; or he was crucified because we had died by a fruit and a 27
tree, so that once again the cross and Christ, that is, a tree
and fruit, by their very similarity should free us from death.
Sweet fruit and tree!

Under Pontius Pilate. This is appropriately added so that by 28
specifying the judge and the time there can be no uncer-
tainty that it was when Herod was king, who was tetrarch at
that time, to whom Pilate sent the Lord in chains. In this
way peace ensued between the judges in place of hatred and
the Lord, more as an ambassador than a prisoner, was the
cause of peace between the parties and dissolved the judges'
mutual hostility.

29   *Descendit ad infernum.* Hinc prophetae plura dixerunt, unde est illud dictum, "vita mea in inferno adpropiavit," et "factus sum inter mortuos liber," et illud, "tu es qui venturus es," quod lector requirens inveniet. Sed descendens ad infernum iniuriam non pertulit, quod fecit causa clementiae, velut rex intrans carcerem, non ut ipse teneretur, sed ut noxii solverentur.

30   *Tertia die resurrexit.* De resurrectione eius idem prophetae plura locuti sunt, quod et Ionas ipse triduo in ventre ceti permanens designavit.

31   *Ascendit in caelum.* Hoc psalmographus, prophetae et apostolus meminit, unde illud dictum est, "ascendens in altum captivam duxit captivitatem." Ergo post passionem Dominus caelos ascendit, non ubi non erat Deus verbum, qui semper in caelis est, sed ubi adhuc verbum caro factum non sederat. Unde videntes angeli carnis naturam caelos intrare

32   stupuerunt dicentes, "Quis est iste rex gloriae?" Nam et ipsum sedere mysterium est carnis adsumptae et provectum sedis non divina, sed humana natura requirit. Inde et hoc dictum est: "Parata sedes tua, Domine," et "dixit Dominus domino meo, sede a dextris meis," et illud, "amodo videbis filium hominis sedentem a dextris virtutis."

33   *Iudicaturos vivos et mortuos.* Aliqui dicunt vivos iustos, mortuos vero iniustos, aut certe vivos quos in corpore invenerit adventus dominicus et mortuos iam sepultos, nos tamen intellegamus vivos et mortuos, hoc est animas et

34   corpora, pariter iudicandas. Nam de adventu Domini et Malachias ait, "ecce venit Dominus omnipotens," et Daniel,

He descended to hell. The prophets spoke much of this,   29
hence the sayings "my life has drawn near to hell," and "I
have become free among the dead," and "you are he who is
to come," which the reader who searches will discover. But
descending to hell he suffered no harm, because he acted
out of mercy, like a king entering a prison, not to be impris-
oned himself but so the guilty should be freed.

On the third day he rose again. The same prophets have spo-   30
ken much about his resurrection and even Jonah himself
embodied it by remaining three days in the whale's belly.

He ascended to heaven. The psalmist, the prophets, and the   31
apostle have made mention of this, hence the saying, "as-
cending on high he took captive captivity." And so the Lord
ascended to heaven after the passion, not that God the word
was not there, who is always in heaven, but that the word
made flesh had not yet taken its seat there. For this rea-
son the angels, when they saw the nature of flesh entering
heaven, were thunderstruck and said: "Who is this king of
glory?" For the very fact of sitting is a mystery of the incar-   32
nation, and human, not divine nature needs the support of a
seat. Hence come the sayings "your seat has been prepared,
Lord" and "the Lord said to my lord, sit on my right," and
"soon you will see the Son of man sitting on the right of
power."

To Judge the living and the dead. Some say the living are the   33
just and the dead the unjust, or perhaps the living are those
that the coming of the Lord finds in their bodies and the
dead those already buried, but let us understand the living
and the dead as souls and bodies, who are both to be judged.
For Malachi says of the coming of the Lord, "behold the   34
Lord almighty is coming," and Daniel, "behold in the clouds

"ecce in nubibus caeli quasi filium hominis," et illud, "sicut fulgor ab oriente, ita erit adventus filii hominis."

35   *Credo in Sanctum Spiritum.* In huius commemoratione mysterium trinitatis impletur: unus Pater, unus Filius, unus Spiritus Sanctus. Ut fiat distinctio personarum, vocabula secernuntur: Pater, ex quo omnia et qui non habet patrem; Filius ex patre genitus; Spiritus Sanctus de Dei ore proce-

36   dens et cuncta sanctificans. Ergo una divinitas in trinitate, quia dixit symbolum: "credo in Deum Patrem et in Iesum Christum et in Spiritum Sanctum." Ergo "in" ubi praepositio ponitur, ibi divinitas adprobatur, ut est "credo in Patrem, in Filium, in Spiritum Sanctum." Nam non dicitur "in sanctam Ecclesiam" nec dicitur "in remissionem peccatorum," sed "remissionem peccatorum" credit.

37   *Sanctam Ecclesiam.* Sancta, quia una est Ecclesia sine ruga, sicut una fides, unum baptisma, in qua unus Deus, unus Dominus, unus Spiritus Sanctus creditur; de qua in Canticis legitur: "una est columba mea." Nam haeretici congregant ecclesiam ubi ruga et perfidiae macula comprobatur.

38   *Remissionem peccatorum.* Nobis in hoc sermone sola credulitas sufficit, nec ratio requiritur ubi principalis indulgentia conprobatur. Ipse rex terrenus a nullo discutitur, si quodcumque largitur. Nam ille qui potuit de luto hominem facere, idem potens est etiam lutulentum purgare et valet innocentiam perditam restituere qui sepultos et membra perdita revocat ad salutem.

of heaven one like the Son of man," and there is the passage, "like lightning from the East, so will be the coming of the Son of man."

I believe in the Holy Spirit. By the mention of this the 35 mystery of the Trinity is brought to completion: one Father, one Son, one Holy Spirit. In order that there be a distinction of persons their names are differentiated: the Father, from whom are all things and who has no father; the Son, born from the Father; the Holy Spirit, proceeding from the mouth of God and making everything holy. And so there is 36 one divinity in the Trinity, because the creed had the expression: "I believe in God the Father and in Jesus Christ and in the Holy Spirit." For where the preposition "in" is used, it shows divinity, as "I believe in the Father, in the Son, in the Holy Spirit." For the wording is not believes "in the holy Church" or "in the remission of sins," but believes "the remission of sins."

The holy Church. Holy, because there is one Church, with- 37 out flaw, just as there is one faith and one baptism. In it one God, one Lord, and one Holy Spirit are believed in and of it is read in the Song of Songs: "my dove is the one and only." For heretics band together in a church in which flaws and the stain of unbelief are recognized to exist.

The remission of sins. On this point belief alone is sufficient 38 for us and no reasoning is required where there is recognized to be supreme forbearance. An earthly king is subject to no questioning, whatever benefit he bestows. But he who was able to make man from mud also has the power to cleanse that creature of mud and he who brings back to salvation the buried and their lost bodies is able to restore lost innocence.

39 *Resurrectionem carnis.* Summa perfectionis concluditur et caro ipsa quae cadit resurrectura erit immortalis ut maneat, licet resurrectio a paganis et a quibusdam haereticis non credatur. Tamen Esaias dicit, "surgent mortui et suscitabuntur," et Daniel ait, "resurgent tunc qui sunt in terrae pul-

40 vere." Christus dicit, "quod autem resurgent mortui non legistis?" et "non est Deus mortuorum sed viventium."Item apostolus dicit, "tu quod seminas non vivificatur, nisi prius moriatur," et dicit scriptura, "post resurrectionem erunt

41 sicut angeli dei." Ergo nec hoc credentibus inpossibile iudicetur, quia qui potuit hominem de terra conponere poterit hunc ex homine in angelum transformare et post hanc vitam

42 temporalem vitam aeternam tribuere. Ergo moritur homo quasi granum in sulco, ut resurgat cum spico et multiplicetur in fructu, adsimiletur et angelo. Quod ipse salutis auctor nobis tribuere dignetur, qui triumphato Tartaro cum Patre et Sancto Spiritu glorioso principatu intrans victor regnat in caelo. Amen.

2

Item aliud ad domnam Radegundem

Quo sine me mea lux oculis se errantibus abdit
 nec patitur visu se reserare meo?
Omnia conspicio simul—aethera, flumina, terram—
 cum te non video, sunt mihi cuncta parum.

The resurrection of the flesh. The height of perfection forms   39
the conclusion and the flesh that falls will rise again to be
immortal, although resurrection is not believed in by pagans
and certain heretics. For Isaiah says, "the dead will rise and
be awakened," and Daniel says, "those who are in the dust of
the earth will rise up then." Christ says, "have you not read   40
that the dead will rise again?" and "he is not the God of the
dead but of the living." Again the apostle says, "what you
sow will not receive life, unless it first dies," and the Scrip-
ture says, "after the resurrection they will be like angels of
God." Therefore this should not be thought impossible by   41
believers, because he who could form man of earth will be
able to transform man into an angel and to give him eternal
life after this temporal life. And so man dies like a seed in a   42
furrow, to grow again with an ear of grain and multiply in
fruit and become like an angel. May the author of our salva-
tion see fit to grant us this, who after triumphing over Tarta-
rus entered into glorious dominion with the Father and the
Holy Spirit and rules victorious in heaven. Amen.

2

Again another to Lady Radegund

Where does my light hide without me, away from wander-
ing eyes, and keep from revealing itself to my sight? I view
my fill of everything—heaven, rivers, earth—but when I do

5   Quamvis sit caelum nebula fugiente serenum,
      te celante mihi stat sine sole dies.
   Sed precor horarum ducat rota concita cursus
      et brevitate velint se celerare dies.
   Consultum nobis sanctisque sororibus hoc sit,
10   ut vultu releves quos in amore tenes.

3

Item aliud ad eandem
de natalicio abbatissae

Mater opima, decens, voto laetare beato,
     gaude; natalem filia dulcis habet.
Hanc tibi non uterus natam, sed gratia fecit,
     non caro, sed Christus hanc in amore dedit.
5   Quae sit in aeternum tecum, tibi contulit Auctor;
     perpetuam prolem dat sine fine Pater.
Felix posteritas quae nullo deficit aevo,
     quae cum matre simul non moritura manet!
Sit modo festa dies, sancto Radegundis honore;
10   Agnen hanc vobis agnus in orbe dedit.
Gaudia distensos pariter celebretis in annos
     et per vos populus vota superna colat,
virgineosque choros moderamina sancta docentes
     perpetuae vitae distribuatis opes.
15   Hinc longinqua salus teneat vos corpore iunctas,
     rursus in aeterno lumine iungat amor.

not see you, that everything is not enough for me. The sky 5
may be clear, with all mist dispersed, but when you are hid-
den from me, the sun is gone from the day. But, I pray, may
the swift wheel hurry on the coursing hours, and the days
fleet by at unaccustomed pace. May the holy sisters and I
receive this consolation, that you restore with your counte- 10
nance those who are yours in love.

3

Again another to the same woman
on the anniversary of the abbess

Bountiful and noble mother, rejoice in happy celebration,
be glad; it is your sweet daughter's birthday. Not the womb
but grace made her your daughter, not flesh but Christ gave
her in love to you. The Creator granted to you that she be 5
forever with you; the Father who is without end makes off-
spring be eternal. Happy are the ties that at no time will fail;
she with her mother together will suffer no death! Let this
day now be festive, holy and honored Radegund; the lamb 10
has given you Agnes here in this world. May you both cele-
brate joyful festivals for long years to come and may your
people learn through you to direct prayers on high; by teach-
ing your virgin choirs the ways of sanctity may you dispense
among them the riches of eternal life. May long health keep 15
you here united in body; then in eternal light may love unite
you once more.

4

Item aliud ad eandem,
ut vinum bibat

Si pietas et sanctus amor dat vota petenti,
    exaudi famulos munere larga tuos.
Fortunatus agens, Agnes quoque versibus orant
    ut lassata nimis vina benigna bibas.
5 Sic tibi det Dominus quaecumque poposceris ipsum,
    et tibi, sicut amas, vivat uterque rogans,
suppliciter petimus, si non offendimus, ambo,
    ut releves natos, mater opima, duos.
Non gula vos, sed causa trahat modo sumere vina,
10   talis enim potus viscera lassa iuvat.
Sic quoque Timotheum Paulus, tuba gentibus una,
    ne stomachum infirmet sumere vina iubet.

5

Item aliud ad abbatissam
de natali suo

Dulce decus nostrum, Christi sanctissima virgo,
    Agnes, quae meritis immaculata manes,
sic tibi conplacuit hodiernum ducere tempus,
    ut mihi nec solitam distribuisses opem,

4

Again another to the same woman, for her to drink wine

If devotion and holy love win petitioners their wishes, hear now your servants and be generous in your bounty. By Fortunatus's agency Agnes too begs in verse that you drink some soothing wine, for you are overweary. So may the Lord 5 grant you whatever you ask of him, and may both your petitioners live for you, as you love them, together we humbly ask you, if we give no offense, to relieve, good mother, your two children, we pray. Let not appetite, but reason persuade you now to take some wine, for such a draft brings succor to 10 the weary flesh. So too Paul, sole clarion of the nations, bid Timothy take some wine to treat the stomach's infirmity.

5

Again another poem to the abbess on her birthday

Sweet glory of mine, most holy virgin of Christ, Agnes, who by your merits live unstained, have you determined so to spend this day as not to grant me your accustomed relief,

5   nec dare nunc dominae modulamina dulcia linguae,
      cui dum verba refers pascitur ore tuo?
   Abstinuisse cibis etiam vos ipse probavi
      et quasi pro vobis est mihi facta fames.
   Audio, somnus iners radiantes pressit ocellos;
10   an nimias noctes anticipare volis?
   Cui non sufficiant haec tempora longa quietis,
      cum prope nox teneat quod duplicata dies?
   Nubila cuncta tegunt, nec luna nec astra videntur:
      si sis laeta animo, me nebulae fugiunt.
15 Gaudia vera colat quae nos haec scribere iussit
      et tecum faveat ducta sub arce poli.

6

Item aliud ad eandem

Mater honore mihi, soror autem dulcis amore,
      quam pietate, fide pectore, corde colo,
caelesti affectu, non crimine corporis ullo,
      non caro, sed hoc quod spiritus optat amo.
5   Testis adest Christus, Petro Pauloque ministris,
      cumque piis sociis sancta Maria videt,
te mihi non aliis oculis animoque fuisse,
      quam soror ex utero tu Titiana fores.
Ac si uno partu mater Radegundis utrosque

and not to bestow now on your mistress the sweet tones of 5
your voice, who is fed by the words that come from your
mouth? I have found out that you have also abstained from
eating, and, in sympathy with you, I too experienced hun-
ger. Drowsy sleep has overcome your bright eyes, so I am
told, or is it that you wish to forestall the long nighttime 10
hours? But for whom would these long hours of rest not suf-
fice, when one night lasts almost twice the time of daylight?
All is wreathed in cloud, no sign of moon or stars, but if you
are joyful in spirit, the darkness speeds from me. May she 15
who bid me write this enjoy true joy, and rejoice with you
when brought to the citadel of heaven.

6

Again another to the same woman

My mother in status, but sweet sister in love, whom I cher-
ish with loyalty and devotion in heart and in spirit, with a
holy affection, devoid of all bodily taint, I love what the
spirit, not the flesh desires. Christ is my witness, with Peter 5
and Paul, his servants, holy Mary sees too, with her devoted
companions, that I viewed you no differently with my eyes
and mind than if you had been my natural sister Titiana. For

10   visceribus castis progenuisset, eram,
      et tamquam pariter nos ubera cara beatae
        pavissent uno lacte fluente duos.
      Heu mea damna gemo, tenui ne forte susurro
        impediant sensum noxia verba meum.
15 Sed tamen est animus simili me vivere voto,
      si vos me dulci vultis amore coli.

7

Item aliud ad eandem

    Quae carae matri, quae dulci verba sorori
      solus in absenti cordis amore loquar?
    Quas locus excludit mens anxia voce requirit
      et simul ut videat per pia vota rogat.
5 Te peto, cara soror, matri pietate benigna
      quod minus impendi tu famulare velis.
    Illa decens tecum longo mihi vivat in aevo
      et tribus in Christo sit precor una salus.
    Nos neque nunc praesens nec vita futura sequestret,
10   sed tegat una salus et ferat una dies.
    Hic tamen, ut cupio, vos tempora longa reservent,
      ut soror et mater sit mihi certa quies.

me it is as if Radegund, our mother, in a single birth had   10
born us both from her chaste womb, and as if the blessed
woman's sweet breasts had nourished the two of us with one
flood of milk. Alas, I mourn my hurt, fearful that with in-
sinuating whispers carping words will inhibit my true feel-
ing. But still I desire to live with unchanged intent, if you are   15
willing for me to be cherished with sweet love.

7

Again another to the same woman

What words for my dear mother, what for my sweet sister
shall I speak alone and far away in the longing of my heart?
My troubled mind seeks them out with words, though loca-
tion parts us, and in so doing begs with devoted prayers for
sight of them. I ask you, dear sister, in your kindly devotion   5
to our mother, to perform for her the services I cannot give.
May that worthy woman, my hope is, enjoy long life with
you, and may all three of us, I pray, share one salvation in
Christ. Let neither the present life nor the life to come part
us, but let one salvation protect us and one day carry us off.   10
But still, as I wish, may long years keep you here, so that sis-
ter and mother may be my sure repose.

8

Item aliud ad eandem

Accessit votis sors iucundissima nostris,
   dum meruere meae sumere dona preces.
Profecit mihimet potius cibus ille sororum;
   has satias epulis, me pietate foves.
5 Qua probitate micans partes conponis utrasque!
   Me recreas animo has saturando cibo.
Pascunt membra dapes, animam dilectio nutrit;
   quae, cui plus opus es, dulcior esca venis.
Audiat Omnipotens et te pia vota petentem,
10   ut tibi perpetuos fundat in ore cibos.
Saecula longa simul cum matre superstite vernes
   et vestro freno stet chorus ille Deo.

9

Item ad eandem pro eulogiis
transmissis

Sollicita pietate iubes cognoscere semper,
   qualiter hic epulis te tribuente fover.
Haec quoque prima fuit hodiernae copia cenae,
   quod mihi perfuso melle dedistis holus,

8

Again another to the same woman

The happiest of outcomes has crowned my wishes, for my
prayers have been successful in securing a reward. Your feed-
ing of the sisters has instead benefited me; them you satisfy
with dinner, but me you cherish with kindness. With what 5
radiant honesty you reconcile both roles! You restore me in
spirit, while refreshing them with food. Banquets feed the
body, affection nurtures the soul; you are a sweeter delicacy
to him who needs you more. May the Almighty hear the
petition of your holy prayers, to pour into your mouth the 10
food of eternity. May you flourish for long ages with your
mother beside you and under your guidance may the com-
munity stand firm for God.

9

Again to the same woman for gifts
she had sent

With attentive devotion you bid me always inform you how
I enjoy here the banquets you provide. For today's dinner
first was the rich fare of vegetables you sent me, drenched in

5 nec semel aut iterum, sed terque quaterque cucurrit,
  cuius me poterat pascere solus odor.
Portitor ad tantos missus non sufficit unus;
  lassarunt totiens qui rediere pedes.
Praeterea venit missus cum collibus altis
10 undique carnali monte superbus apex,
deliciis cinctus quas terra vel unda ministrat;
  compositis epulis hortulus intus erat.
Haec ego nunc avidus superavi cuncta gulosus
  et mons et hortus ventre tenetur iners.
15 Singula nec refero, quia me tua munera vincunt;
  ad caelos victrix et super astra voles.

10

Item aliud de eadem re

Multiplices epulae concurrunt undique fusae;
  quid prius excipiam, me bonus error habet.
Carnea dona tumens argentea gavata perfert,
  quo nimium pingui iure natabat holus.
5 Marmoreus defert discus quod gignitur hortis,
  quo mihi mellitus fluxit in ore sapor.
Intumuit pullis vitreo scutella rotatu,
  subductis pinnis quam grave pondus habens!
Plurima de pictis concurrunt poma canistris,
10 quorum blandifluus me saturavit odor.

honey. They were served not once or twice, but three or four   5
times over, though I could have dined on their aroma alone.
For so many helpings one server was not sufficient; feet be-
gin to grow weary from returning so often. Next a course
came piled high into hillocks, with lofty peaks on every side,   10
rising on a mountain of meat, surrounded by the delicacies
which earth and water supply; the banquet was laid with a
little garden in its midst. And then in my greed I eagerly
swallowed it all: mountain and garden both lay heavy on my
stomach. I do not describe each detail, because your gener-   15
osity defeats me; may you wing victorious to heaven in flight
beyond the stars.

10

Again another poem on the same subject

Many different foodstuffs are showered on me from every
side; a happy hesitation grips me: which shall I reach for
first? A silver dish brings gifts of meat piled high, where
vegetables were swimming in an extra-rich sauce. A marble   5
platter serves what is grown in gardens, from which a honey-
sweet flavor pervades my palate. A circular salver of glass is
loaded high with chicken; though the wings are removed,
what a heavy weight it carries! Fruits in profusion surround
me, in gaily colored baskets, their sweet, insinuating aroma   10

Olla nigella nimis dat candida pocula lactis
  atque superba venit quae placitura fuit.
Haec dominae matri famulans, haec munera natae
  iunctus amore pio tertius ipse loquar.

II

Item aliud de floribus

Respice delicias, felix conviva, beatas,
  quas prius ornat odor quam probet ipse sapor.
Molliter arridet rutilantum copia florum;
  vix tot campus habet quot modo mensa rosas,
5 albent purpureis ubi lactea lilia blattis
  certatimque novo flagrat odore locus.
Insultant epulae, stillanti germine fultae.
  Quod mantile solet, cur rosa pulchra tegit?
Complacuit melius sine textile tegmine mensa,
10 munere quam vario suavis obumbrat odor;
Enituit paries viridi pendente corymbo;
  quae loca calcis habet, huc rosa pressa rubet.
Ubertas rerum tanta est, ut flore sereno
  mollia sub tectis prata virere putes.
15 Si fugitiva placent, quae tam cito lapsa recedunt,
  invitent epulae nos, paradise, tuae.
Daedalicis manibus nituit textura sororis;
  tantum digna fuit mater habere decus.

satisfying my appetite. A dark pail supplies many white drafts of milk and since it is destined to please it comes in state. In duty to my lady mother and to her daughter I shall describe these gifts, joined with them as a third in devoted love.

II

Again another poem, on flowers

Behold, happy guest, the rich delights before you, whose quality their scent recommends before taste confirms it. An abundance of brilliant flowers casts a gentle glow; scarcely can a field contain as many roses as this table now holds, where lilies gleam milk-white against the rich purple and the 5 place is suffused with a fresh blend of competing fragrances. The banquet puts on a fine show, cushioned on dewy flower buds. Why does a beautiful rose form the covering, normally the role of a cloth? The table has won more favor without a woven covering, for sweet fragrance wreathes it in var- 10 ied finery. Shining from the wall are green hanging clusters; where lime normally holds sway cling red masses of roses. Such was the richness of the scene that you would think gentle meadows were blooming indoors with brilliant blossoms. If fleeting things give such pleasure, which fail and 15 fade so fast, may your rich banquet, paradise, summon us to you. A sister's weaving shone with skill the equal of Daedalus's, but our mother was worthy to enjoy such finery.

12

Item aliud pro eulogiis

Munera direxi, sed non mea, crede fatenti;
    ad te quae veniunt sunt tua dona magis.
Melle superfusas cunctorum porrigis escas,
    cuius ab ore pio dulcia mella fluunt.
5 Copia quanta mihi maneat de munere vestro
    credite, dum spargit iam gula victa cibos.
Sed mihi da veniam, venerando corde benigna;
    quod praesumpsit amor sit veniale mihi.
Nunc Christum pro me chorus ille verendus adoret,
10   ne peccatorem me mea culpa gravet.

13

Item aliud pro castaneis

Ista meis manibus fiscella est vimine texta,
    credite mi, carae, mater et alma soror,
et quae rura ferunt, hic rustica dona ministro,
    castaneas molles, quas dedit arbor agris.

12

Again another poem, to accompany gifts

I have sent you gifts, though, I confess, they are not mine
to send, for the presents that are coming to you, believe
me, are already yours. You serve to everyone food that is
drenched with honey, for from your holy mouth sweet
honey flows. Be assured of how much abundance I enjoy   5
from your bounty, when my appetite is assuaged and itself
now distributes food. But grant me pardon, in the kindness
of your noble heart; love inspired my presumption, may it
find forgiveness. Now let that reverent choir pray to Christ
for me, that my faults not weigh heavy on me, a sinner.   10

13

Again another poem, to accompany
chestnuts

I wove this basket with my own hands from willow, believe
me, dear ones, mother and gentle sister. The gifts that the
country brings are my country gifts to you, tender chestnuts
that the trees let fall on the fields.

14

Item aliud pro lacte

Aspexi digitos per lactea munera fixos,
    et stat picta manus hic ubi crama rapis.
Dic, rogo, quis teneros sic sculpere compulit ungues?
    Daedalus an vobis doctor in arte fuit?
5 O venerandus amor, cuius faciente rapina
    subtracta specie venit imago mihi!
Spes fuit, haec quoniam tenui se tegmine rupit;
    nam neque sic habuit pars mihi parva dari.
Haec facias longos Domino tribuente per annos,
10   in hac luce simul matre manente diu.

15

Item aliud pro lacte

Quid tam dulce darent mihimet materque sororque,
    quam modo quod tribuunt congrue lactis opem,
sicut apostolico praecepit dogmate Paulus,
    cum infirmis animis lac iubet ipse dari?
5 Sollicitam mentem geritis de nomine nostro;
    de vobis semper sit pia cura Deo.

14

Again another poem, for milk

I saw fingerprints impressed on your gift formed of milk and
an image of your hand where you skimmed off the cream.
Tell me, I beg, who taught your slender figures so to mold?
Was Daedalus your instructor in this art? O admirable love,   5
whose image came to me without your presence by an act
of predation! It was an idle hope, for the slender skin soon
broke, and no part of you was left to me, however small. But
may you act like this for many years, if the Lord so grants,
and may our mother long remain in this light with you.   10

15

Again another poem, for milk

What could my mother and sister give to me as sweet as the
sustenance of milk they now fittingly proffer, according to
the apostolic precept taught by Paul, when he bid milk be
given to sickly spirits. You show yourself concerned about   5
my person; may God have merciful care for you always.

16

Item aliud pro prandio

Nescivi, fateor, mihi prandia lassa parari:
    sic animo merear posse placere tuo;
nec poterant aliqui vultu me avellere vestro,
    si non artificis fraus latuisset inops.
5 Quis mihi det reliquas epulas, ubi voce fideli
    delicias animae te loquor esse meae?
A vobis absens colui ieiunia prandens,
    nec sine te poterat me saturare cibus.
Pro summis epulis avido tua lingua fuisset,
10 replessent animum dulcia verba meum.
Ordine sed verso medicus fera vulnera gignit
    et fallax artem decipiendo probat.
Quem numquam saturat quidquid mare, terra ministrat,
    credebat solo me saturare meo.
15 Sed modo da veniam, quaeso, pietate parata,
    alterius facinus ne mihi constet onus.

16

Again another poem, for a meal

I did not know, I confess, that meals were being labored over for me, so may I deserve to win the favor of your heart, nor could anyone have torn me from your countenance, if a physician's unprofitable cunning had not deceived me. Who 5 could give me other foodstuffs, when in all honesty I declare that you are the sweet delicacy for my soul? Away from you, though dining, I practiced fasting and without you no food could satisfy my wants. In my hunger your speech would have been my finest fare, your sweet words would have sat- 10 isfied my spirit. But a doctor paradoxically caused savage wounds and deceitfully displayed his art by artfulness. Though I am never satisfied by what the sea and earth supply, he believed he could content me with just my own re- sources. But with your ready kindness grant me forgiveness 15 now, I beg, and let not another's crime be held against me.

17

Item aliud pro
munere suo

Composui propriis manibus hoc munus amoris,
    sed tibi vel dominae sit rogo dulce meae;
quamvis exiguo videantur inepta paratu,
    crescant affectu quae modo parva fero.
5 Si bene perpendas, apud omnes semper amantes
    muneribus parvis gratia maior inest.

18

Item aliud
pro prunellis

Transmissas epulas, quae pruna nigella vocantur,
    ne rogo despicias, quae mihi silva dedit.
Si modo dignaris silvestria sumere poma,
    unde placere queam dat meliora Deus.
5 Hoc quoque non metuas quod ramo umbrante pependit.
    Non tellus fungos, sed dedit arbor opes.
Non ego crudelis, qui matri incongrua praestem;
    ne dubites puros sumere fauce cibos.

17

Again another poem,
to accompany his own gift

I have prepared with my own hands this gift of love, but
to you and to my lady I beg it be sweet. Although it seem
clumsy and meager in quality, may affection make my small
offering grow larger. If you judge rightly, always with all lov-   5
ers, small gifts win the greater appreciation.

18

Again another poem,
to accompany plums

Though the forest gave me them, I beg you not to scorn the
food I send—black plums they are called. If you but deign to
receive these woodland fruits, God will give me better gifts
with which I can please you. Have no fear of what hung   5
from a shady branch. These are not mushrooms from the
earth, but a tree's rich bounty. I am not so cruel as to make
my mother unsuitable gifts; the food is safe, don't hesitate
to swallow it.

19

Pro aliis deliciis et lacte

Inter multiplices epulas ieiunia mittis
    atque meos animos plura videndo cremas.
Respiciunt oculi medicus quod non iubet uti,
    et manus illa vetat quod gula nostra rogat.
5 Attamen ante aliud cum lactis opima ministras,
    muneribus vincis regia dona tuis.
Nunc cum matre pia gaudens soror esto, precamur,
    nam nos laetitiae mensa benigna tenet.

20

Pro ovis et prunis

Hinc me deliciis, illinc me pascitis herbis;
    hinc ova occurrunt, hinc mihi pruna datur.
Candida dona simul praebentur et inde nigella.
    Ventre utinam pax sit sic variante cibo!
5 Me geminis ovis iussistis sero cibari.
    Vobis vera loquor, quattuor ipse bibi.
Atque utinam merear cunctis parere diebus
    sic animo, ceu nunc hoc gula iussa facit.

19

For milk and other delicacies

Your gift to me is to fast among numerous foodstuffs and you torture my spirit with the abundance it sees. My eyes see what the doctor forbids me enjoy, and his hand withholds what my appetite demands. Yet when, above all, you 5 furnish me with the richness of milk, you surpass with your gifts the bounty of kings. Now my sister and holy mother, be joyful, I pray, for we share a table that is rich in happiness.

20

For eggs and plums

You feed me now with delicate morsels and now with produce; now eggs are put before me, now I am given plums. At the same moment I am presented with white gifts and with black. I only hope my stomach will be at peace when its diet is so at variance! You commanded me to eat two eggs late in 5 the day. I will tell you the truth, I swallowed four. If only I were worthy so to obey you all my days in spirit, as my appetite in this case fulfilled your commands.

21

De absentia sua

Si me non nimium pluviatilis aura vetaret,
    dum nesciretis, vos repetisset amans,
nec volo nunc absens una detenter ut hora,
    cum mea tunc lux est quando videtur amans.

22

De convivio

Per pietatis opus, per qui pius imperat astris,
    per quod mater amat, frater et ipse cupit
ut, dum nos escam capimus, quodcumque loquaris,
    quod si tu facias, bis satiabor ego.

22a

Item de eadem re

Deliciis variis tumido me ventre tetendi,
    omnia sumendo, lac, holus, ova, butur.

21

On his absence

If the wind with its heavy rain did not prevent me, your devotee would have returned before you knew it. But I have no wish now to be kept apart for a single hour, since I only enjoy light when I see my dear love.

22

On a banquet

By the duty to be bountiful and by the bountiful ruler of the stars, by all our mother holds dear, a brother too requests that when I take food, you say a few words, for, if you do so, I shall twice be satisfied.

22a

Again on the same subject

I gorged my swelling stomach on various delights, eating everything, milk, vegetables, eggs, and butter. In this way fresh

Nunc instructa novis epulis mihi fercula dantur,
    et permixta simul dulcius esca placet.
5 Nam cum lacte mihi posuerunt inde buturum;
    unde prius fuerat, huc revocatur adeps.

23

Item versus in convivio factus

Inter delicias varias mixtumque saporem
    dum dormitarem dumque cibarer ego
(os aperiebam, claudebam rursus ocellos
    et manducabam somnia plura videns),
5 confusos animos habui, mihi credite, carae,
    nec valui facile libera verba dare.
Non digitis poteram, calamo neque pingere versus;
    fecerat incertas ebria Musa manus.
Nam mihi vel reliquis sic vina bibentibus apta
10   ipsa videbatur mensa natare mero.
Nunc tamen, ut potui, matri pariterque sorori
    alloquio dulci carmina parva dedi.
Etsi me somnus multis impugnat habenis,
    haec dubitante manu scribere traxit amor.

courses are served me of novel fare, and the mixture of foods is all the more sweet and pleasing. For butter is placed be- 5 fore me along with milk; its fatty richness is set beside what it previously came from.

23

Again verses composed at a banquet

Among varied delights and mingled flavors, as I nodded with sleep and as I continued eating (I was opening my mouth, then closing my eyes, and I went on chewing, as I saw many dreams), I was confused in my mind, believe me, 5 dear friends, and could not easily speak my words freely. Neither with fingers nor with pen could I trace out verses; my drunken Muse made my hands unsteady. For to me, like everyone else drinking so excellent a wine, the table itself 10 seemed awash with the vintage. But now, as best I can, to my mother and sister I have sent my humble poetry in a sweet address. Although sleep reins me in with many curbs, my love has impelled me to write this, however unsteady my hand.

23a

Item de eadem re

Blanda magistra suum verbis recreavit et escis
et satiat vario deliciante ioco.

24

Item de munere suo

Si non complestis quod hic completa vocatur,
haec, rogo suppliciter, suscipe, sume libens.
Nec parva spernas, nam si mea vota requiras,
munus in angustum cernitur amplus amor.

25

Ad easdem de itinere suo

Casibus innumeris hominum momenta rotantur
instabilique gradu pendula vita meat.
Ipsa futurarum titubans mens anxia rerum
ventura ignorat quid sibi lux pariat.

23a

Again on the same subject

My charming mistress refreshes her servant with words and food and satisfies me with a variety of delightful entertainments.

24

Again on his gift

If you have not completed what here is called compline, in all humility I beg you, receive, accept gladly, this gift. And do not scorn it as small, for if you consider my intentions, in a modest gift is seen an abundant love.

25

To the same women, about his journey

The course of human time rolls on with countless alarms, and life advances in suspense with uncertain tread. The mind, stumbling and anxious what the future holds in store,

5 Nam me digressum a vobis Eomundus amator
    illa suscepit qua bonitate solet.
Hinc citus excurrens Cariacae devehor aulae;
    Tincillacensi perferor inde loco.
Hinc sacer antistes rapuit me Domitianus,
10   ad sancti Albini gaudia festa trahens.
Inde relaxatus, per plura pericula fessum
    puppe sub exigua fluctus et imber agit,
quo gravis incumbens aquilo subverterat amnem
    et male curvatos extulit unda sinus.
15 Nec sua commotos capiebant litora fluctus;
    invadunt terras aequora fusa novas.
Pascua, rura, nemus, segetes, viburna, salictum
    viribus iratis una rapina tenet.
Huc mihi commisso per confraga murmura ponti
20   flatibus horrificis laxa fremebat hiems
surgebatque cadens per aquosa cacumina puppis,
    ascendens liquidas monte vagante vias,
quo rate suspensa modo nubila nauta tenebat,
    gurgite subducto rursus ad arva redit.
25 Fluctibus infestis pelagi spumante procella
    assidue rapidas prora bibebat aquas;
aequora lambebant inimica pace carinam,
    tristius amplexu nos nocitura suo.
Sed mora nulla vetat varias memorare querellas:
30   post referenda simul murmura corde tego.
Hoc mihi praecipue divina potentia praestet,
    ut cito felices vos revidere queam.

has no knowledge of what the coming day will bring. For in my case, when I left you, my friend Eomundus received me with his customary kindness. From there a rapid journey brought me to the halls of Cariac, and thence I traveled to the site of Tincillac. Next the holy bishop Domitianus caught me up, bringing me to the joyful festival of Saint Albinus. Leaving there I was exhausted by many dangers, as wave and rain carried me along in a tiny boat; a strong north wind lashed and whipped up the river, and the waves reared up threateningly in arching crests. Their banks could not contain the surging billows and a flood of water washed over the alien land. Pastures, country, forest, crops, shrubs, and willow brakes, all fell victim to the angry forces of a single inundation. I was launched there on the rough thunder of the deep, as the storm roared uncontrollably with violent blasts and the ship rose and fell on the peaks of the waves, climbing a watery trail on undulating mountains. One moment the boat reared up and the sailor reached for the clouds, the next the flood gave way and he sank toward the earth. As the storm foamed with the violent surge of waters, the ship's prow constantly drank in the raging flood. The waves licked the bark, but their kiss was hostile, not of peace, seeking to inflict severe harm on us by their embrace. But I cannot delay, haste forbids me tell my different trials; I keep in my heart my troubles, to be told in person in the future. May the power of God grant me this particular prayer, that I can quickly see you again, and that you prosper.

26

Item aliud

Passim stricta liget glacies concreta pruina
  nec levat adflictas flexilis herba comas.
Terra iacet crustata gelu sub cortice duro,
  mollis et arboreas nix tegit alta comas.
5 Proflua crustatum struxerunt flumina murum
  et densata gravem vestiit unda cutem.
Mole sua frenantur aquae, se lympha ligavit,
  obice sub proprio vix sibi praebet iter.
Fluminibus mediis nata est crystallina ripa,
10 nec cupimus subter, nec super itur iter.
Asperius tumuit glacies aquilone fremente.
  Cui dabit illa viam quae sibi pugnat aqua?
Sed si concipitur nunc spiritus ille caloris,
  qui tum in principio perferebatur aquis,
15 assiduis precibus si flectitis Omnipotentem,
  et mihi, ceu cupitis, prosperiora datis.
Nam vobis parere animo quodcumque iubetur
  posse utinam sic sit quam mihi velle placet.

26

Again another poem

The ice holds everywhere frozen tight in the grip of frost;
plants, normally pliant, cannot raise their heavy leaves. The
earth lies under a film of ice like a hard crust, and gentle
snow settles thickly on the foliage of the trees. Rivers once 5
flowing have piled up a frozen wall, and the water, grown
solid, is clothed in a heavy skin. The stream's own mass re-
strains the flood, the waters take themselves prisoner and
faced by their own obstruction hardly permit freedom of
passage. A bank springs up in midstream, all made of ice; we 10
have no desire to pass below it, yet cannot pass above it. The
ice piles up with fiercer cold as the north wind rages keenly.
To whom will water give passage that contests with itself?
But if that warming breath now comes into being which in
the beginning passed over the waters, and if with your con- 15
tinual prayers you move the Almighty, to me too, as you wish,
you bring happier times. For I wish I had the power, as I
have the desire and will, to obey you in spirit whatever
you bid.

APPENDIX

I

De excidio Thoringiae

Condicio belli tristis, sors invida rerum!
  Quam subito lapsu regna superba cadunt!
Quae steterant longo felicia culmina tractu
  victa sub ingenti clade cremata iacent.
5 Aula palatino quae floruit antea cultu,
  hanc modo pro cameris maesta favilla tegit.
Ardua quae rutilo nituere ornata metallo,
  pallidus oppressit fulgida tecta cinis.
Missa sub hostili domino captiva potestas;
10 decidit in humili gloria celsa loco.
Stans aetate pari famulorum turba nitentum
  funereo sordet pulvere functa die.
Clara ministrorum stipata corona potentum
  nulla sepulchra tenens mortis honore caret.
15 Flammivomum vincens rutilans in crinibus aurum
  strata solo recubat lacticolora manus.
Heu male texerunt inhumata cadavera campum,
  totaque sic uno gens iacet in tumulo.
Non iam sola suas lamentet Troia ruinas.
20 Pertulit et caedes terra Thoringa pares.
Hinc rapitur laceris matrona revincta capillis
  nec laribus potuit dicere triste vale.

I

On the destruction of Thuringia

The fortunes of war are painful and life's lottery is cruel!
How suddenly do proud kingdoms fall into ruin! Structures
that had stood tall and happy for many years succumb to
a great disaster and are leveled by flames. The hall that pre-
viously flourished with all the finery of a palace now is cov-
ered by mournful embers in place of vaulted roofing. Pale
ashes have overtaken the once bright ceilings that gleamed
on high in a sheath of bright metal. Power falls captive, sub-
jected to an enemy ruler; sublime glory is reduced to a hum-
ble station. A troop of elegant servants, all of similar age,
have met their end and in death are besmirched by dust.
The brilliant circle of attendants waiting on the powerful
receives no burial nor the honors due in death. The com-
pany whose hair outdoes in its brilliance flaming gold now
lies stretched out on the ground white as milk. Alas, unbur-
ied bodies make an ominous carpet for the plain; in this way
a whole nation lies in a single tomb. No longer does Troy
alone lament her destruction. The land of Thuringia too has
suffered a like disaster. The married woman, her hair torn,
was carried off bound from her home, and was unable to bid
her hearth a sad farewell. She was not permitted to plant

Oscula non licuit captivo infigere posti
    nec sibi visuris ora referre locis.
25 Nuda maritalem calcavit planta cruorem
    blandaque transibat fratre iacente soror.
Raptus ab amplexu matris puer ore pependit,
    funereas planctu nec dedit ullus aquas.
Sorte gravi minus est nati sic perdere vitam;
30   perdidit et lacrimas mater anhela pias.
Non aequare queo vel barbara femina fletum
    cunctaque guttarum maesta natare lacu.
Quisque suos habuit fletus, ego sola sed omnes;
    est mihi privatus publicus ille dolor.
35 Consuluit fortuna viris quos perculit hostis;
    ut flerem cunctis una superstes ago.
Nec solum extinctos cogor lugere propinquos;
    hos quoque, quos retinet vita benigna, fleo.
Saepe sub umecto collidens lumina vultu;
40   murmura clausa latent nec mea cura tacet.
Specto libens, aliquam si nuntiet aura salutem,
    nullaque de cunctis umbra parentis adest.
Cuius in aspectu tenero solabar amore
    solvit ab amplexu sors inimica meo.
45 An, quod in absenti te nec mea cura remordet,
    affectum dulcem cladis amara tulit?
Vel memor esto, tuis primaevis qualis ab annis,
    Hamalafrede, tibi tunc Radegundis eram,
quantum me quondam dulcis dilexeris infans
50   et de fratre patris nate, benigne parens.
Quod pater extinctus poterat, quod mater haberi,
    quod soror aut frater tu mihi solus eras.

kisses on her now captive doorpost, or to look back at the
locations that she would not see again. A naked foot has   25
trampled on the blood of a husband, and a charming sis-
ter passed by where her brother lies dead. A child, when
snatched from his mother's embrace, kept his eyes on hers;
no one shed tears in mourning at his death. It was the lesser
grief to lose the life of a son to cruel fate in this way; the   30
distraught mother also lost the chance to weep in maternal
devotion. I, a barbarian woman, cannot do justice to these
lamentations nor to the universal mourning, awash with a
lake of tears. Everyone had his own cause for grieving, I
alone shared them all; that universal grief was a grief that
was specific to me. Fortune provided consolation to the   35
men whom the enemy struck down; I alone was left surviv-
ing to weep for them all.

Nor must I only lament those of my kin who have died; I
weep too for those whom life in its goodness preserves. I of-
ten rub my eyes on my tear-drenched face; my groans are   40
concealed within, but my grief is far from silent. I eagerly
watch, to see if a breeze brings greeting, but no semblance
appears to me of all my kinsfolk. Hostile fate has parted
from my embrace the one in whose sight I enjoyed the con-
solation of a tender love. Has the bitter disaster removed all 45
sweetness of feeling, seeing that care for me does not tor-
ment you in my absence? At least remember what I, Rade-
gund, meant to you then from your earliest years, Amalfred,
how much you loved me once, a sweet child to me, son of   50
my father's brother, my loving cousin. Only you were to me
what my dead father could have been, or what a mother, sis-
ter, or brother. Caught up by your kindly arms and hanging,
ah me, on your calming kisses, I was soothed, though still

Prensa piis manibus heu blanda per oscula pendens
    mulcebar placido famine parva tuo.
55 Vix erat in spatium, quo te minus hora referret;
    saecula nunc fugiunt, nec tua verba fero.
Volvebam rabidas illiso in pectore curas
    ceu revocareris, quando vel unde, parens.
Si pater aut genetrix aut regia cura tenebat,
60   cum festinabas, iam mihi tardus eras.
Sors erat indicium, quia te cito, care, carerem;
    importunus amor nescit habere diu.
Anxia vexabar, si non domus una tegebat;
    egrediente foris rebar abisse procul.
65 Vos quoque nunc oriens et nos occasus obumbrat,
    me maris oceani, te tenet unda rubri,
inter amatores totusque interiacet orbis;
    hos dirimit mundus quos loca nulla prius.
Quantum terra tenet tantum divisit amantem;
70   si plus arva forent, longius isses iter.
Esto tamen, quo vota tenent meliora parentum,
    prosperior quam te terra Thoringa dedit.
Hinc potius crucior validis onerata querellis,
    cur mihi nulla tui mittere signa velis.
75 Quem volo nec video, pinxisset epistula vultum
    aut loca quem retrahunt ferret imago virum,
qua virtute atavos repares, qua laude propinquos,
    ceu patre de pulchro ludit in ore rubor.
Crede, parens, si verba dares, non totus abesses;
80   pagina missa loquens pars mihi fratris erat.
Cuncti munus habent, ego nec solacia fletus.
    O facinus, quae, dum plus amo, sumo minus!

little, by your gentle words. Scarcely an hour passed without ⁵⁵ my thinking of you; the ages now fly by and I receive no word. In my tortured heart crazed with anxiety I used to ask myself over and over, how you would return, when and from where, my kinsman. If concern for your father, mother, or royal house possessed you, though you hurried back, you ⁶⁰ would already be too late for me. Chance happenings gave evidence how quickly I would miss you, my beloved; the urgency of love does not know how to be patient. I was tormented by anxiety, if we were not under the one roof; if you just went outdoors, I thought you had gone far away. Now ⁶⁵ the East casts its protection over you and the West over me; I live by the ocean wave and you by the Red Sea. A whole continent is interposed between us lovers, and we who once were never separated are now worlds apart. The whole extent of the earth keeps my beloved from me; if there were ⁷⁰ more land, you would have journeyed still further. Wherever the wishes for better fortune of your kinsfolk reach out to you, may you enjoy greater prosperity than the land of Thuringia gave you.

Burdened by a weight of grief I am all the more tormented, because you send me no token of yourself. A letter ⁷⁵ could have depicted the features that I wish for but do not see, or an image convey the man whom location keeps afar, the virtue that equals your ancestors' and the glory a match for your kin, how the color plays over your face with your father's good looks. Believe me, cousin, if you sent me word, you would not be wholly apart; the page you sent would ⁸⁰ speak and bring part of my brother to me. Everybody receives their due, but I receive no solace for grief. How unjust that the more I love, the less I get back in return! If some

Si famulos alii pietatis lege requirunt,
    cur, rogo, praeterear sanguine iuncta parens?
85 Ut redimat dominus vernam, saepe ipse per Alpes
    frigore concretas cum nive rumpit aquas,
intrat in excisis umbrantia rupibus antra,
    ferventem affectum nulla pruina vetat,
et duce cum nullo, pede nudo, currit amator
90   atque suos praedae hoste vetante rapit.
Adversas acies et per sua vulnera transit,
    quod cupit ut capiat nec sibi parcit amor.
Ast ego pro vobis momenta per omnia pendens
    vix curae spatio mente quiete fruor.
95 Quae loca te teneant si sibilat aura, requiro,
    nubila si volitant pendula, posco locum:
bellica Persidis seu te Byzantion optat
    ductor Alexandrae seu regis urbis opes?
A Hierosolymae resides vicinus ab arce,
100 qua est genitus Christus virgine matre Deus?
Hoc quoque nulla tuis patefecit littera chartis,
    ut magis hinc gravior sumeret arma dolor.
Quod si signa mihi nec terra nec aequora mittunt,
    prospera vel veniens nuntia ferret avis!
105 Sacra monasterii si me non claustra tenerent,
    improvisa aderam qua regione sedes.
Prompta per undifragas transissem puppe procellas,
    flatibus hibernis laeta moverer aquis.
Fortior eductos pressissem pendula fluctus,
110   et quod nauta timet non pavitasset amans.
Imbribus infestis si solveret unda carinam,
    te peterem tabula remige vecta mari.
Sorte sub infausta si prendere ligna vetarer,

people, by the dictates of kindness, search for their servants, why am I passed over, I ask, a kinswoman united by blood? A master to ransom his servant often crosses the Alps in person, and breaks through the ice-bound waters amid the snow; he enters caves that provide shelter in hollowed-out crags—no frost puts an end to his fervent devotion—and without a guide and unshod, in his affection hastens on and rescues his men from captivity, though the enemy resist. He braves hostile forces and wounds to himself to secure his purpose; love spares no effort. But I, in suspense every moment because of my feelings for you, rarely enjoy peace of mind and a remission from care. If there is a whisper of breeze, I ask it where you are found; if the hanging clouds fleet by, I inquire about your location: does warlike Persia lay claim to you or does Byzantium; do you administer as governor the wealth of Alexandria? Or do you make your dwelling close to the citadel of Jerusalem, where Christ was born, a god from a virgin mother? No letter of your writing has brought me that news, so that my grief grows heavier and would take up arms.

But if neither earth nor sea sends me tokens of you, coming on favorable winds, a bird could bring me your news. If the sacred cloister of my convent did not prevent me, I would arrive unexpectedly in whatever region you dwell. Unhesitatingly I would have braved wave-smashing storms on a ship, and gladly traveled on the waters in the winter gales. Bravely I would have hung suspended on the mounting billows, and because of my love would not have feared what the sailor fears. If the waters broke up my boat in violent rainstorms, a plank would be my oarage to travel the sea looking for you. If cruel fate prevented me from grasping

ad te venissem lassa natante manu.
115 Cum te respicerem, peregrina pericla negassem—
    naufragii dulcis mox relevasses onus—
aut mihi si querulam raperet sors ultima vitam,
    vel tumulum manibus ferret harena tuis.
Ante pios oculos issem sine luce cadaver,
120   ut vel ad exequias commoverere meas.
Qui spernis vitae fletus, lacrimatus humares
    atque dares planctus qui modo verba negas.
Quid fugio memorare, parens, quid differo luctus?
    De nece germani cur, dolor alte, taces,
125 qualiter insidiis insons cecidisset iniquis
    oppositaque fide raptus ab orbe fuit?
Ei mihi, quae renovo fletus referendo sepultos
    atque iterum patior, dum lacrimanda loquor!
Ille tuos cupiens properat dum cernere vultus,
130   nec suus impletur dum meus obstat amor.
Dum dare dura mihi refugit, sibi vulnera fixit;
    laedere qui timuit, causa doloris adest.
Perculitur iuvenis tenera lanugine barbae,
    absens nec vidi funera dira soror.
135 Non solum amisi, sed nec pia lumina clausi
    nec superincumbens ultima verba dedi.
Frigida non calido tepefeci viscera fletu
    oscula nec caro de moriente tuli,
amplexu in misero neque collo flebilis haesi
140   aut fovi infausto corpus anhela sinu.
Vita negabatur. Quin iam de fratre sorori
    debuit egrediens halitus ore rapi?
Quae feci vivo, misissem listra feretro;

hold of a timber, I would come to you swimming with weary strokes of my hand. When I caught sight of you, I would deny the journey's dangers — immediately by your sweetness you would assuage the woes of shipwreck — or if the ultimate fate deprived me of my miserable life, at least the sand on my tomb would be heaped by your hand. I would pass as a lifeless corpse before your loving eyes, so that at my funeral at least you would feel emotion. You who scorned weeping in my lifetime would tearfully bury me, and would offer mourning who now fail to offer words.

What shall I shun to speak of, my cousin, why postpone grief? Why, my profound pain, are you silent about a brother's murder, how in his innocence he fell victim to cruel treachery and was snatched from the world on a charge of disloyalty? Wretch I am, who reawaken the tears I had laid to rest by recalling them, and suffer once more, as I speak of sorrowful events! When he was in eager haste to see your countenance, his desire was unfulfilled, since love for me stood in his way. In refusing to bring me suffering, he inflicted a wound on himself; his fear of causing hurt was the cause of grief. He was struck down while still young, his beard soft and downy, and I, his sister, was not there to see his mournful funeral. Not only did I lose him, I did not close his poor eyes, nor leaned over him to speak parting words. I gave no heat to his chill flesh with my warm tears, nor stole kisses from my dear departed one. I never tearfully clung to his neck in a sorrowing embrace, nor sobbing warmed his body at my unlucky breast. His life was at an end. Why should a sister not then catch with her mouth the departing breath of her brother? I would have sent gifts to your bier, as I sent you in your life; is it even forbidden for my

non licet extinctum vel meus ornet amor?
145 Impia, crede, tuae rea sum, germane, saluti:
    mors cui sola fui, nulla sepulchra dedi.
Quae semel excessi patriam, bis capta remansi
    atque iterum hostes fratre iacente tuli.
Tunc, pater ac genetrix et avunculus atque parentes,
150   quos flerem in tumulo reddidit iste dolor.
Non vacat ulla dies lacrimis post funera fratris.
    qui secum ad manes gaudia nostra tulit.
Sic miserae dulces consummavere parentes;
    regius hac serie sanguis origo fuit.
155 Quae mala pertulerim neque praesens ore referrem,
    nec sic laesa tuo consulor alloquio.
Quaeso, serene parens, vel nunc tua pagina currat,
    mitiget ut validam lingua benigna luem.
Deque tuis similis mihi cura sororibus haec est,
160   quas consanguineo cordis amore colo.
Nec licet amplecti quae diligo membra parentum.
    osculer aut avide lumen utrumque soror.
Si, velut opto, manent superis, rogo redde salutes
    proque meis votis oscula cara feras.
165 Ut me commendes Francorum regibus oro,
    qui me materna sic pietate colunt.
Tempore longaevo vitalibus utere flabris
    et mea de vestro vernet honore salus.
Christe, fave votis: haec pagina cernat amantes
170   dulcibus et redeat littera picta notis,
ut quam tarda spes cruciat per tempora longa,
    hanc celeri cursu vota secuta levent.

love to adorn you when dead? I am wicked, believe me, my 145
brother, guilty of failing to save you, I alone was the cause of
your death, but I gave you no burial. I quitted my homeland
only once, but went into captivity twice, and a second time
faced an enemy when my brother lay dead. Then that grief
brought back to me those who were to be mourned in the
tomb, my father and mother, my uncle, and all my kinsfolk. 150
No day has gone by without tears since the death of my
brother, who carried with him to the grave my good cheer.
In this way my sweet kinsfolk met their end and left me
wretched; the shedding of royal blood was the beginning of
this sequence of events.

I cannot recount in your presence the hardships I've en- 155
dured, nor receive consolation for this hurt of mine from
conversing with you. I ask, my serene cousin, that now at
least a letter of yours speed to me so that your kindly words
soothe my heavy heart-sickness. For your sisters too I have
the same affection; I am devoted to them as my kin with 160
heartfelt love. Yet I cannot embrace the bodies of my family
I love, nor greedily kiss their two eyes, sister to sister. If, as I
hope, they remain among the living, give them my greeting,
I ask, and convey loving kisses to them in accord with my
wishes. I request that you commend me to the kings of the 165
Franks, who honor me with the devotion due to a mother.
For many long years may you enjoy the breezes of life, and
may my welfare prosper through your glory. Christ, favor
my prayers: may this page see those whom I love, and a let- 170
ter return inscribed with their sweet handwriting, so that
with its swift dispatch the fulfillment of her wishes may re-
store this woman whom lingering hope has tormented for so
many years.

2

Item incipiunt versus

Gloria summa patris natique ac spiritus almi,
　　unus adorandus hac Trinitate Deus,
maiestas, persona triplex, substantia simplex,
　　aequalis, consors atque coaeva sibi,
5　virtus una manens idem, tribus una potestas
　　(quae pater haec genitus, spiritus ipsa potest),
personis distincta quidem, coniuncta vigore,
　　naturae unius, par ope, luce, throno,
secum semper erat Trinitas, sine tempore regnans,
10　nullius usus egens nec capiendo capax.
Gloria summa tibi, rerum sator atque redemptor,
　　qui das Iustinum iustus in orbe caput.
Rite super reges dominantem vindicat arcem
　　caelesti regi qui famulando placet.
15　Quam merito Romae Romanoque imperat orbi
　　qui sequitur quod ait dogma cathedra Petri,
quod cecinit Paulus passim, tuba milibus una,
　　gentibus et stupidis fudit ab ore salem,
cuius quadratum linguae rota circuit axem
20　eloquiique fide frigida corda calent.
Gloria summa tibi, rerum sator atque redemptor,
　　qui das Iustinum iustus in orbe caput.
Ecclesiae turbata fides solidata refulget
　　et redit ad priscum lex veneranda locum.

2

Again begin verses

Highest glory of the Father, the Son, and the fostering
Spirit, one God to be worshipped in this Trinity, majesty,
triple in person but single in substance, equal, consubstan-
tial, and coeternal, one and the same in power, a single ca-   5
pacity in all three (the Son and the Spirit can do what the
Father can do), separated in persons certainly, but united
in potency, of a single nature, equal in might, brilliance,
and kingship, the Trinity always coexisted, reigning beyond
time, not needing assistance, all-encompassing but receiv-   10
ing nothing.

Highest glory to you, world's creator and redeemer, who
in your justice give us Justin as supreme in the world. Rightly
he lays claim to eminence, to lord it over kings, who as his
servant wins the favor of the heavenly king. How deserv-   15
edly he holds sway over Rome and the whole Roman world
who follows the teaching that the seat of Peter propounds,
and that Paul blazoned everywhere, Paul who as sole clarion
to thousands poured from his mouth the salt of eloquence
to untutored pagans, and whose wheeling words circled the
four corners of the world and warmed chill hearts with faith   20
inspired by his language.

Highest glory to you, world's creator and redeemer, who
in your justice give us Justin as supreme in the world. The
faith of the Church, once in turmoil, again is resplendent
and firm, and the venerable law returns to its previous sta-

25 Reddite vota deo, quoniam nova purpura quicquid
    concilium statuit Calchedonense tenet.
Hoc meritis, Auguste, tuis et Gallia cantat,
    hoc Rhodanus, Rhenus, Hister, et Albis agit.
Axe sub occiduo audivit Gallicia factum,
30   Vascone vicino Cantaber ista refert.
Currit ad extremas fidei pia fabula gentes
    et trans Oceanum terra Britanna favet.
Quam bene cum Domino curam partiris amator!
    Ille tuas causas, tu facis ecce suas.
35 Dat tibi Christus opem, tu Christo solvis honorem;
    ille dedit culmen, reddis et ipse fidem.
Nil fuit in terris quod plus daret ille regendum,
    nec quod plus reddas quam valet alma fides.
Exilio positi patres pro nomine Christi
40   tunc rediere sibi, cum diadema tibi.
Carcere laxati, residentes sede priore,
    esse ferunt unum te generale bonum.
Tot confessorum sanans, Auguste, dolores
    innumeris populis una medella venis:
45 Thrax, Italus, Scytha, Phryx, Daca, Dalmata, Thessalus, Afer,
    quod patriam meruit, nunc tibi vota facit.
Haec tua laus, princeps, cum sole cucurrit in orbe;
    quo genus est hominum, huc tuus intrat honor.
Gloria summa tibi, rerum sator atque redemptor
50   qui das Iustinum iustus in orbe caput.
Cui meritis compar nubens felicibus annis
    obtinet augustum celsa Sophia gradum.
Quae loca sancta pio fixo colit, ornat amore
    et facit hoc voto se propiare polo.

tus. Give thanks to God that the new emperor adheres to 25
the tenets the Council of Chalcedon has propounded. This
action, Augustus, Gaul celebrates too in singing your merits,
this Rhone, Rhine, Danube, and Elbe proclaim. In the far
West Galicia has heard of your doings, and the Cantabrians 30
recount them with their neighbors the Basques. This tale of
piety and faith has quickly made its way to the most dis-
tant nations: beyond the Ocean the land of Britain voices its
praise. How well in your devotion you apportion your roles
with the Lord! He supports your interests and you support
his. Christ gives assistance to you, you pay him honor in re- 35
turn; he has given you eminence, you return to him faith.
There was no greater realm on earth that he could give you
to rule, nor anything more you could give back than the
power of true faith. The fathers that were driven into exile
for the name of Christ were then restored to themselves 40
when the diadem came to you. Freed from prison and reoc-
cupying their former sees, they declare that you, though one
person, are a blessing to all. By healing the suffering of so
many confessors, Augustus, you are the sole specific for un-
numbered peoples: Thracian, Italian, Scythian, Phrygian, 45
Dacian, Dalmatian, Thessalian, and African, all now offer
their devotion to you, because they have won from you a
homeland. This glory of yours, my prince, has traversed the
globe with the sun; wherever mankind is, there has your
praise penetrated.

　　Highest glory to you, world's creator and redeemer, who 50
in your justice give us Justin as supreme in the world. Your
equal in her virtues, enjoying happy married years, the sub-
lime Sophia holds an august position. She honors and adorns
the holy places with pious, unwavering love, and by this de-

55   Cuius opima fides orientis ab axe coruscans
     misit ad occasum fulgida dona Deo.
  Regina poscente sibi Radegunde Thoringa
     praebuit optatae munera sacra crucis,
  qua Christus dignans assumpta in carne pependit
60   atque cruore suo vulnera nostra lavat.
  Gloria summa tibi, rerum sator atque redemptor,
     quod tenet augustum celsa Sophia gradum.
  O pietas huc usque rigans de fonte benigno,
     cuius amor Christi fundit ubique fidem!
65   Ecce pari voto, Augusti, certatis utrimque:
     ipsa tuum sexum subrigis, ille suum:
  Vir Constantinum, Helenam, pia femina, reddis;
     sicut honor similis, sic amor ipse crucis.
  Illa invenit opem, tu spargis ubique salutem
70   implet et occasum quod prius ortus erat.
  Gloria summa tibi, rerum sator atque redemptor,
     quod tenet augustum celsa Sophia gradum.
  Per te crux Domini totum sibi vindicat orbem;
     quo nescita fuit, hoc modo visa tegit.
75   Accessit genti maior fiducia Christi,
     quando salutis opem spes oculata videt,
  sensibus et duplicata fides, cum munere vestro
     plus animae credant quod cruce teste probant.
  Hoc, Augusta, colens, quod apostolus instat aratro,
80   tu ligno, hic verbo laetificatis agrum.
  Haec iam fama favet qua se septentrio tendit;
     ortus et occasus militat ore tibi.
  Illinc Romanus, hinc laudes barbarus ipse,
     Germanus, Batavus, Vasco, Britannus agit.
85   Pars tua cum cruce sit florens, Augusta, per aevum,

votion brings herself nearer to heaven. Her rich faith shines 55
bright in eastern climes, and has sent its brilliant gifts to
the West in honor of God. At the request of Radegund, the
Thuringian queen, she has made a sacred gift of the trea-
sured cross, on which Christ, assuming flesh, was willing to
hang and wash clean our wounds with his own blood. 60

Highest glory to you, world's creator and redeemer, be-
cause the sublime Sophia enjoys imperial rank as Augusta.
O bounty that flows as far as here from a generous foun-
tain, and in its love of Christ everywhere pours forth true
faith! See, Augusti, in sharing the same wish you rival each 65
other: you lend glory to your sex and he to his. The man imi-
tates Constantine, you, holy woman, Helena; as like them in
glory as in love of the cross. She found that treasure, you dis-
tribute its saving power worldwide; and what previously be- 70
longed to the East spreads through the West.

Highest glory to you, world's creator and redeemer, be-
cause the sublime Sophia enjoys imperial rank as Augusta.
Through you the cross of the Lord lays claims to the whole
world; where once it was unknown, now it is seen and brings
protection. A nation acquires greater faith in Christ, when 75
hope sees with its own eyes the means of salvation, and the
faith that is perceived is redoubled, when because of your
bounty souls have greater belief in what they confirm with
the cross as a witness. Pursuing the same task, Augusta, as
the apostle performs with the plow, you make fertile the 80
land with wood, he with his word. You win fame for this
now in the far reaches of the North, and East and West are
loud in your service. Here the Roman, there the barbar-
ian voices your praise, joined by German, Batavian, Basque,
and Breton. May your region of the world, Augusta, long 85

777

    cui facis extremis crescere vota locis.
  Hanc prostrata solo supplex Radegundis adorat
    et vestro imperio tempora longa rogat,
  atque rigans lacrimis coniuncta sororibus optat,
90   ut hinc vestra fides gaudia larga metat.
  Felix Iustino maneas cum principe coniunx,
    ordine patricio cincta, Sophia, sacro.
  Romula regna regens tribuas sua iura senatu
    teque sibi dominam plebs trabeata colat.
95 Vota superna Deus votis felicibus addat
    nec vobis pereat quod Radegundis amat,
  assiduo cantu quae pulvere fusa precatur
    temporibus largis ut tibi constet apex.
  Voto, animo, sensu, studio bona semper agendo
100   sit tibi cura sui, sit memor illa tui.

3

Ad Artachin

  Post patriae cineres et culmina lapsa parentum,
    quod hostili acie terra Thoringa tulit,
  si loquar infausto certamine bella peracta,
    quas prius ad lacrimas femina rapta trahar?
5 Quid mihi flere vacet, pressam hanc funere gentem

flourish under the cross, for you caused devotion to it to increase in the most distant places. Radegund, lying prone on the ground, as suppliant pays honor to it, and requests long years for you both to reign; her face wet with tears, along with the sisters she prays that for this gift your faith 90 reap abundant rewards. May you continue, Sophia, in your happy marriage with Emperor Justin, encircled by the sacred patrician order. Ruling the realm of Romulus may you bestow their rights on the senate, and may the toga-wearing people honor you as their mistress. May God add to your 95 happy marriage his blessings from above, and may it not go for nothing that Radegund loves you, who, prostrate in the dust, prays in a continuous refrain that you maintain your lofty power for numerous years. Always working for good in wishes and thoughts, feelings and pursuits, may you have 100 concern for her, and she be mindful of you.

3

To Artachis

After a country reduced to ash and the glory of a family brought low–the fate that the land of Thuringia suffered from enemy forces–if I am to speak of the fortunes of war and ill-omened conflict, which cause for tears shall I, a captive woman, first turn to? What am I to weep over, this na- 5

an variis vicibus dulce ruisse genus?
Nam pater ante cadens et avunculus inde secutus,
    triste mihi vulnus fixit uterque parens.
Restiterat germanus apex, sed sorte nefanda
10   me pariter tumulo pressit harena suo.
Omnibus extinctis (heu viscera dura dolentis!)
    qui super unus eras, Hamalafrede, iaces.
Sic Radegundis enim post tempora longa requiror?
    Pertulit haec tristi pagina vestra loqui?
15 Tale venire diu expectavi munus amantis
    militiaeque tuae hanc mihi mittis opem?
Dirigis ista meo nunc serica vellera penso,
    ut, dum fila traho, soler amore soror?
Siccine consuluit valido tua cura dolori?
20   Primus et extremus nuntius ista daret?
Nos aliter lacrimis per vota cucurrimus amplis;
    non erat optanti dulcia amara dari.
Anxia sollicito torquebar pectora sensu;
    tanta animi febris his recreatur aquis.
25 Cernere non merui vivum nec adesse sepulchro;
    perferor exequiis altera damna tuis.
Cur tamen haec memorem tibi, care Artachis alumne,
    fletibus atque meis addere flenda tuis?
Debueram potius solamina ferre parenti,
30   sed dolor extincti cogit amara loqui.
Non fuit ex longa consanguinitate propinquus,
    sed de fratre patris proximus ille parens.
Nam mihi Bertharius pater, illi Hermenefredus;
    germanis geniti nec sumus orbe pari.
35 Vel tu, care nepos, placidum mihi redde propinquum

tion oppressed by bloodshed, or my sweet family brought
to ruin by various misfortunes? For my father fell first, and
my uncle followed soon thereafter; the death of each parent
transfixed me with a painful wound. I still had an illustrious
brother, but by a cruel fate when the earth weighed on him   10
in his tomb it weighed on me too. After all these deaths
(alas, how hardened is the heart of the grieving!) you who
alone were left, Amalfred, now lie in your grave. Is this the
greeting I, Radegund, receive after so long? How could your
letter bear to speak to me in my sadness such news? I long   15
awaited such a missive to arrive as the duty of a beloved; is
this the relief you send me from your loyal service? Do you
present me now this silken fleece to weave, to console me
for my cousin with love, as I draw out the threads? Is this
the consolation your devotion has to offer me for my violent
grief? Was this the first and last message I was to receive?   20
Quite otherwise were the wishes I harbored with copious
tears; when I wanted sweet things it was not right to receive
only bitter. My heart was tormented with anxiety in the agi-
tation of my feelings; so great was the fever of my mind it
was only fed by these waters. I was not able to see you alive   25
or attend your burial; by your funeral I suffered a second be-
reavement.

But why do I say this to you, Artachis, my dear fosterling,
and add to my weeping cause for you to weep too? Rather it
should be me who offers consolation to a kinsman, but grief   30
for the dead forces me to utter bitter words. His relation to
me was not from a distant bloodline, but he was my nearest
kin, son of my father's brother. For my father was Berthar
and his Hermanfred; we are children of brothers, but inhab-
ited different realms. In his stead, dear nephew, play the role   35

et sis amore meus quod fuit ille prius,
   meque monasterio missis, rogo, saepe requiras
   ac vestro auxilio stet locus iste Deo,
ut cum matre pia vobis haec cura perennis
40   possit in astrigero reddere digna throno.
Nunc Dominus tribuat vobis felicibus ut sit
   praesens larga salus, illa futura decus.

4

Versus ad Sigimundum

Christicolas animas haec conscia cura fatigat,
   ut circa cunctos stet sine labe salus.
Ast ego prae reliquis circum tua lumina pendens
   qui venit atque redit prompta requiro frequens.
5   Sollicitis oculis volitantia flabra recurro,
   quando vel unde tui nuntiet aura boni.
Hoc tibi praecipue mea, dulcis, epistula signet,
   quod dolor atque metus sit tuus ille meus
et quia nos animo cognoscis currere tecum,
10   det de te incolumi pagina missa fidem.

of my gentle relative yourself, and be in your love to me what he was before. May you often seek me out in the convent with your letters, I ask, and with your help may this place be firm in service to God, so that this continual attention can 40 bring you and your holy mother proper recompense at the heavenly throne. May the Lord now make you happy and bestow upon you the blessing of abundant well-being in the present and the glory of future salvation.

4

Verses to Sigimund

Christian souls are wearied by this engrossing care, that unblemished salvation come about for everyone. But I, in longing for your gaze before all else, am often quick to question travelers who come and go. With anxious looks I appeal to 5 the fleeting breezes to ask when or from where the wind will bring me good tidings of you. Sweet one, may my letter carry this special message to you, that you are the source of my suffering and fear, and because you know that I accompany you in spirit, may a letter come from you assuring me you 10 are well.

5

De Childebertho rege

Rex regionis apex et supra regna regimen,
    qui caput es capitum, vir capitale bonum,
ornamentorum ornatus, ornatius ornans,
    qui decus atque decens cuncta decenter agis,
5 primus et a primis, prior et primoribus ipsis,
    qui potes ipse potens, quem iuvat Omnipotens,
dulcia delectans, dulcis dilecta potestas,
    spes bona vel bonitas, de bonitate bonus,
digne nec indignans, dignos dignatio dignans,
10   florum flos florens, florea flore fluens,
Childeberche cluens, haec Fortunatus amore
    paupere de sensu pauper et ipse fero.
Audulfum famulum commendo supplice voto,
    me quoque. Sic nobis hic domineris apex.

6

De Brunichilde regina

Regia progenies, praecelsi et mater honoris,
    undique regnantum cincta decore pio,
Gallia cuius habet genus et Hispania fetum,
    masculus hinc moderans, inde puella regens,

5

On King Childebert

King, high ruler of the region and ruling over the realm, who are chief of chieftains and our blessing in chief, ornament of ornaments, an ornate adornment, who in glory gloriously glorify in all your actions, supreme, born from the supreme, superior to the superior, who have the power to be powerful with the help of the Almighty, savoring the sweet, a sweet and savored sovereignty, good in your goodness, a source of good hope and goodwill, worth worthily not scorning the worthful, but weighing them worthy, flourishing flower of flowers, flowing with floral flowering, celebrated Childebert, these words I, Fortunatus, present out of love, though poor myself and poor in abilities. With suppliant prayers I commend to you your servant Audulf, and myself as well. So may you reign supreme here over us.

6

On Queen Brunhild

Offspring of royalty and mother of a child of high station, surrounded on every side by pious and glorious rulers, Gaul claims your descendant and Spain the child of your womb,

5   auspicium felix sit prosperioribus annis;
     hic tegat Allobrogas, dirigat illa Getas,
   gentibus et geminis pariter tua germina regnent
     et tibi det fructus iste vel ille locus,
   quo te circumdet, pia, blanda corona nepotum,
10   de genito et genita bis genitalis ava.
   Illos auditu, hos visu laeta recensens,
     praesens hinc gaudens, inde sed aure favens,
   subque tuis cernens regiones mater utrasque
     cum populo et patria laetificeris ava.
15 Audulfum famulum commendo, me quoque secum;
     sic maneat cunctis gloria vestra nitens.

7

Item aliud ad Agiulfum

Nomen dulce mihi, mihi semper amabile nomen,
   omnibus unanimis, plus mihi mente nitens,
qui corde amplectens cunctos tibi reddis amantes
   (dum colis et coleris, carus haberis apex),
5   moribus excellens, Agiulfe, benigne sodalis,
    praecipuis dominis qui famulando places,
vir bonitate decens, concordia vincta per omnes,

your son governing here, your daughter reigning there. May   5
the omens be happy for more prosperous years; may he
oversee the Allobroges, she rule the Goths. May your off-
spring together rule over the twin nations, and both of the
locations produce progeny for you, so a charming crowd of
grandchildren encircle you in your piety, twice a prolific   10
grandmother by your son and your daughter. Becoming fa-
miliar with some by report, but others joyfully by sight, de-
lighting in the presence of one group, but rejoicing to hear
of the others, and seeing, as a mother, both realms under the
rule of your children, may you exult as a grandmother with
your people and country. I commend to you your servant   15
Audulf, and myself with him; so may your glory permanently
shine on all.

7

Again another poem, to Agiulf

Name sweet to me, name always dear to my affections, in
harmony with all, but especially treasured in mind by me,
who by embracing all in your heart make them devoted to
you (since you both give and receive respect, you are con-
sidered a beloved leader), outstanding in character, Agiulf,   5
a generous companion, who by your service win the favor
of distinguished lords, man of refined goodness, a guaran-

laetitiae facies, pectore fida fides,
   stet tuus amplus honor longe his regnantibus . . .
10   illorumque salus sit tibi, care, decus.
Supplico commender per te dominantibus altis;
   sic valeas felix, dum tenet ista dies.
Audulfum proprium commenda, magne, relatu;
   sic tua vita decens hoc sit in orbe manens.
15 Regale ad votum felicia cuncta sequantur
   detque Deus vobis tempora temporibus.

8

Item versus, epitaphium Nectarii

Triste sub hoc tumulo crudeli funere rapti
   Nectarii iuvenis membra sepulta iacent.
Ipse quater quinos valuit superesse per annos,
   quem fugiente die mors inimica tulit.
5 Hic Proculo genitore satus, sed sorte nefanda
   ante tenet lacrimas quam sua vota parens.
Gratus in aspectu, sensu moderatus opimo,
   qualem non puduit spem generasse patrem.
Sunt tamen ingenti solacia magna dolori,
10   quod quod in orbe venit non sine morte manet:
Haec via pauperibus, haec est et regibus una,
   sed vivit semper quem bene facta fovent.

tee of concord for all, with joyfulness in your face and firm
faith in your heart, may your full honors long continue un-
der these rulers, I pray, and may their welfare, my dear one, 10
bring glory to you. I request to be commended by you to
your lofty lords; so may you be strong and happy, as long as
this life persists. Commend too Audulf as your own, great
sir, by your report; so may your life continue to be glorious
in this world. May all good fortune attend on the desires of 15
the king, and may God grant you time upon time to live.

8

Again a poem, an epitaph for Nectarius

In this sad tomb lies buried the body of Nectarius, a young
man who was carried off by cruel fate. He had survived for
twenty years in all, when, his daylight fled, hostile death
bore him off. His father was Proculus, but by terrible mis- 5
fortune the parent experienced tears before achieving his
wishes. He was fair in appearance, prudent, with abundant
good sense, a son in whom a father would feel no shame to
invest his hopes. Yet there are great sources of consolation
for grief, however strong, because whatever comes into the 10
world must of necessity die. This path is trod by the poor
and by kings alike, but he lives forever whom good deeds
recommend.

9

Item aliud, incipiunt versus
pro pomis directis

Cardinis occidui regio quae sumpsit ab ortu,
    mittit amicalis dulcia poma manus.
Haec quoque, quae nostro pendentia vidimus horto,
    admonet affectus munera ferre pius.
5 Non animi metuant, haec sunt quod ab arbore carpta.
    Iam fraus nulla nocet quod paradisus habet.
Namque redemptrici postquam in cruce Christus adhaesit,
    per lignum rediit quod prius Eva tulit.
Iam meruit mulier purgari crimine sexus;
10   mors fuit illa vetus, virgo novella salus.
Et quia silvestrem tribuunt elementa paratum,
    misimus exiguum, quod dedit unda, cibum.
Deprecor ergo, pares vel poma vel ostrea fratri:
    eligat alterutrum, quod sibi maius amat.
15 Sed Dagaulfum haec rumpat cervesia tristis,
    faece lagunari turbida, tendat hydrops.
Faucibus in stupidis talem bibat ille liquorem,
    tam male sinceras qui vitiavit aquas.
At sicuti meritis exposcit opima voluntas,
20   dulcia vineti Dracco Falerna bibat.
Hoc tamen in Domino, qui te regat, oro benigne,
    rite salutetur mi Papiana soror.
Addo preces pariter, capias sic munera Christi,

9

Again another poem: here begin verses to accompany a gift of fruit

The hand of a friend sends you this sweet fruit that the regions of the West received from the East. These too that we saw hanging in our own garden our loving affection bids us to present as gifts. Don't let your hearts be afraid, because they were plucked from a tree. No harm now infects what has a place in paradise. For after Christ hung on the redeeming cross, what Eve first stole was restored by wood. A woman then was found worthy to be cleansed of the crime of her sex; the woman of old was death, the new virgin salvation. And because nature bestows on you produce from the woods, I have sent a small gift of food from the waters. I urge you then to present either fruit or oysters to your brother; let him choose whichever one he likes most. But as for Dagaulf, may this bitter beer, made cloudy by the bottle's dregs, cause him to burst, and dropsy swell his stomach. May such be the liquid he drinks down his insensible throat, who so foully defiled unpolluted waters. But as his unfailing goodwill requires together with his virtues, may Dracco drink vintage of sweet Falernian.

In the name of the Lord, who is your ruler, I ask you respectfully to greet properly my sister Papiana. In addition, I pray further, so may you receive the blessings of Christ, that

ne tibi post uxor, sed sit honesta soror.
25   Quid ventura dies portat nescimus in orbe:
        Quis morti obsistat, si furibunda ruit?
     Furem animae nemo ante videt quam tollere possit.
        nec placitum poterit dissimulare diem.
     Causa cavenda prius subito quam mergat ad umbras,
30   est ubi nemo parens nec levat ulla manus.
     Sed bene quod placuit constanti perfice voto,
        ne spatium rediens mors inimica neget.
     Nunc meliora tene, iam, quod fuit, inde recede
        et cape caelestes huc redivivus opes.
35   Per Dominum votis utraeque rogamus utrumque
        detur ut in nostro filia vestra sinu.
     Officio vestro ad nos migret cura parentum,
        vos generando utero, nos refovendo sinu.

10

Item aliud

Dulcibus alloquiis quae fabula fertur in aure?
   Si mihi iam placidas mensa benigna tenet,
placatos animos tabula redeunte notate,
   prodat ut affectum littera picta manu.
5 Dulcis amore pio pariter materque sororque
   gaudia festivo concelebrate sono.

hereafter she not be your wife but honored sister. We know 25
not in this world what the day to come will bring. Who can
resist death, if it attacks in full frenzy? No one sees this thief
of our breath before it can snatch life away, nor can anyone
disregard the day that is decreed. Death is a thing to beware
of before it suddenly dispatches us to the shades, where we 30
have no kin and no hand to relieve us. But fulfill with con-
stant resolve the course you have rightly decided on, lest
death come upon you as an enemy and brook no delay. Now
keep to the better course, depart from your ways of the past,
and reborn here receive the riches of heaven. By the Lord 35
with our prayers we both ask each of you that your daughter
be entrusted to our embrace. By your leave let the devotion
of parents be transferred to us from you; you gave birth to
her in the womb, we will cherish her in our bosom.

10

Again another poem

What tale with sweet tidings is brought to my hearing? If a
generous table now finds you well disposed to me, indicate
your reconciled feelings by return of tablet so that letters
drawn by your hand may reveal your affection. Mother and 5
sister, equally sweet to me in dutiful love, celebrate together
a joyful festival with glad sound.

11

Item aliud

Hodie festivum celebravi diem, in orbem
Domini natalem sacratum venisse diem.
Ubique in primis venerunt caseum . . .
dein veniunt lignea scutella rotata . . .
5 carnem, pullum simul discus ornatus undique . . .
temporis quae spatio cunctis feras cibos in ore
et a cunctis longum sem . . .
domina super te et te simul semper cum ipsa
quae die noctuque melliflua diffundis ab ore.

12

Item aliud

Dum volo carminibus notum percurrere plectrum,
   incipio solito pigrius ire pede,
nec mihi doctiloqua consentit harundine Musa,
   quae desueta suum pandere nescit opus.
5 Sed quamvis dubio trepident mea corda relatu,
   audacter solo promptus amore loquor.

II

Again another poem

Today I celebrated a day of festival, when the sacred birth-
day of our Lord came to the world. From all sides first comes
cheese . . . then come round wooden salvers . . . meat, 5
chicken as well; a platter adorned on every side . . . who in a
moment of time bring food to the mouths of all, and from
all long . . . mistress over you and always together with you,
who day and night pour from your lips honeyed eloquence.

12

Again another poem

As I seek to exercise my familiar lyre in song, I begin to
move slowly, on unusually sluggish feet, and the Muse with
her learned piping fails to come to me, as, out of practice,
she cannot compose her work. But although my heart wa- 5
vers, hesitant to speak, I speak out boldly, prompted by love

Cara, benigna, decens, dulcis, pia semper habenda,
   cuius in affectu stat mihi patris honor,
per quam, quae genuit, recolunt mea viscera matrem,
10   et mores aviae te renovante colo,
suppliciter humilis verbo trepidante saluto,
   commendans animam sed famulando meam,
et pariter natam, peperit quam gratia cordis,
   quas rex caelorum servet in orbe diu.

13

Item aliud

Sic vos Caesarii monitis honor ornet in orbe
   atque ambas caro cum patre Christus amet;
sic hic Caesaria et praecelsa Casaria surgat,
   ut per vos priscus hic reparetur honor;
5 gratia sic talis niteat, qua crescat in aevo
   per vos Pictavis Arelatense decus;
sic pie caelesti mereamur vivere regi
   et mea vobiscum membra sepulchra tegant;
si quod in offenso retinetur pectore murmur,
10   in vice laxatum sit veniale precor.
Pacem Christus amans, mira dulcedine plenus,
   pectora vestra sacer se mediante liget.
Obtineat pariter veneranda Casaria mecum,
   quae simul amplexu vos cupit esse pio.

alone. Dear, kind, fair, sweet, and holy as you always will be
to me, in whose love I feel the status of a father, in whom my
flesh recognizes the mother who bore me, and I revere the   10
character of a grandmother, reborn in you, humbly, as a sup-
pliant, with trembling words I greet you, entrusting my soul
as a servant to you, and with you your daughter, born to you
by heartfelt affection; may the king of heaven preserve you
long in this world.

13

Again another poem

So may your glory shine out in the world by the Rule of Cae-
sarius, and may Christ with his dear father love both of you;
so may Caesaria and noble Casaria rise in honor here so that
through you their former glory be revived here; so may such   5
grace shine that by it the fame of Arles may grow from age
to age at Poitiers by your doing; so may we deserve to live in
holiness for the heavenly king, and may one tomb cover my
body along with yours: if any murmured grievance is stored
up in your heart, let it be forgiven, I beg—each of you let it   10
go. Christ loves peace, he abounds in wonderful sweetness;
may he by his holy mediation bind your hearts together. Let
reverent Casaria obtain her prayer along with me, who
wants you to share a single loving embrace.

14

Item aliud

Quam prius inscribam fixam pietate parentem,
    quo geminae matres, extat et una soror?
Hanc praeponit honor, quae iunior extat in annis:
    his aetas gravior iure senile favet.
5 Sed mihi dulce tribus pariter mandare salutem,
    est quoniam vobis carus et unus amor.
Felix quae retinet pariter tria lumina mensa
    et paschale bonum multiplicare facit!
Angelico coetu sic participante fruantur
10   deliciae vobis in regione dei.

15

Item aliud

Nocte salutifera maneant materque sororque;
    hoc nati et fratris prospera vota ferant.
Angelicus coetus praecordia vestra revisat
    et regat alloquiis pectora cara suis.
5 Tempora noctis agunt ut hac brevitate salutem:
    sex modo versiculis vel duo ferte, precor.

14

Again another poem

What kinswoman's name shall I write first, cherished with devotion, when I have a pair of mothers and also one sister? Status gives preference to one, but she is younger in age; the others the burden of age promotes by right of seniority. But for me it is equally sweet to send greetings to all three, 5 since for you all I have a single, devoted love. Happy the table that possesses together three such lights and thereby makes the blessings of Easter multiply! So in the company of the angel band may you enjoy the delights of heaven in the 10 realm of God.

15

Again another poem

May my mother and sister abide safe through the night, and your son's and brother's prayers achieve this their wish. May a company of angels make their dwelling in your hearts, and with their converse guide the thoughts in your sweet breasts. It is the time of night and so my greeting is brief; for 5 these six slight verses, I beg, pay me back at least two.

16

Item aliud

Quamvis quod cuperem fugit me vespere facto,
    te mihi non totam nox tulit ista tamen.
Etsi non oculis, animo cernuntur amantes,
    nam quo forma nequit, mens ibi nostra fuit.
5 Quam locus ille pius qui numquam abrumpit amantes,
    quo capiunt oculis quos sua vota petunt,
in medio posito bonitatis principe Christo,
    cuius amore sacro corda ligata manent!
Hic quoque sed plures \<cape\> carmina iussa per annos:
10   hinc rapias tecum, quo tibi digna loquar.

17

Item aliud

Plaudite voce Deo, pia reddite vota, sorores,
    quod sic vobiscum gaudia tanta sedent.
Me foris excluso vos hanc retinetis amantes;
    quod commune placet, non simul esse licet.
5 Haec longaeva diu maneat per saecula nobis
    floreat et cunctis participanda bonis.

16

Again another poem

Although what I desired fled from me when evening came, yet that night did not take you entirely from me, for though not seen by the eyes, lovers are seen by the mind; my mind could be where my body cannot. How sacred is that place 5 that never separates lovers, where they see with their eyes whom their wishes long for, where set in their midst is Christ, prince of goodness, by whose holy love their hearts unite in a firm bond! But here too receive for many years the poems you request, and then take me with you from here, 10 since I will speak what is worthy of you.

17

Again another poem

Sisters, sing your praise of God, offer him your holy prayers, because so much good cheer resides with you now. Though I am kept outside, you keep within the woman you love; it is the common wish that we keep apart. May she live long re- 5 maining with you for many years, and prosper, sharing in all your good fortune.

18

Item aliud

Cuncti hodie festiva colunt; ego solus in orbe
  absens natali conqueror esse tuo,
qui si forte latens alia regione fuissem,
  ad vos debueram concitus ire magis.
5 Nunc alii tibi dant, ego munera nulla sorori,
  vel dare qui potui pomula, mora loci.
Sed quamvis absens specie, sum pectore praesens
  et rogo quae misi dona libenter habe.
Sic Deus omnipotens parcat matri atque sorori,
10 quae non egerunt me retinere sibi.
Haec pia festa diu multos, senis ipsa, per annos
  laeta matre simul, me quoque fratre colas.

19

Item aliud

Haec mihi festa dies longos superinstet in annos,
  gaudia magna ferens haec mihi festa dies.
Praestet amore Deus tam prospera vota per aevum,
  Martini meritis praestet amore deus.

18

Again another poem

Everybody today celebrates a holiday; only I in the whole world lament, for I am absent from your birthday. Even if perhaps I had been hidden away in some other country, I would have hurried to you all the more quickly, But as it is, others give you presents, but I give my own sister none, though I have native apples or blackberries to give. But though I am absent in person, I am present in spirit, and ask you gladly to receive the gifts I have sent. So may almighty God be merciful to my mother and sister, who did not strive to keep me with them. For many years may you celebrate this holy festival, till old yourself, in the company of your joyful mother and me, your brother.

19

Again another poem

This holiday may it continue for many long years, bringing me abundant joy, this holiday. May God in his love grant such favor to prayers forever, by the merits of Martin, may

5 Participata mihi vobiscum haec gaudia Christus
    servet in orbe diu participata mihi.
  Mitis in aure sonus suavi dulcedine tinnit,
    organa vocis habens mitis in aure sonus.
  Blandior esca favis vestra de fauce rigavit
10   et nova mella dedit blandior esca favis.
  Huc variante choro vox inde rotata cucurrit,
    sensibus angelicis huc variante choro.
  Carmina sancta diu vox illa ministret ab ore
    et recreent animos carmina sancta diu.

20

Item aliud

  Sollicitat famulum dominae sua cura benignae,
    qualiter a vobis laeta sit acta dies,
  nam dum plaudis ovans, mea sunt tua gaudia maius;
    tunc mihi vota favent, dum tibi membra vigent.
5 Ni vale iam fecit, spectet bona nostra parumper,
    nec sub nocte volet; stet veniente die.

God grant this in his love. These joys I share with you may 5
Christ preserve; may he long preserve in the world these
joys I share with you. A gentle sound in the ears rings with
enchanting sweetness; its instrument is the voice, a gentle
sound in the ears. Food more enticing than honeycombs
dripped from your lips, and produced a new honey, food 10
more enticing than honeycombs. To the accompaniment of
a choir a voice sang rolling cadences, sounds worthy of an-
gels, to the accompaniment of a choir. May songs of holiness
long be performed by her voice, and long may my spirits be
refreshed by songs of holiness.

20

Again another poem

Concern for his generous mistress prompts your servant to
inquire how you passed this happy day, for when you joyfully
rejoice, my happiness is all the greater; my prayers are an-
swered, when your body is healthy. If he has not already bid 5
farewell, let him delay a little our blessings, and not make his
journey by night, but stay till the coming of the day.

21

Item aliud

Sic hesterna dies totas mihi transtulit horas,
    ut matris vocem non meruisse querar.
Qualiter agnus amans genetricis ab ubere pulsus
    tristis et herbosis anxius errat agris
5 —nunc fugit ad campos feriens balatibus auras,
    nunc redit ad caulas, nec sine matre placent—
sic me de vestris absentem suggero verbis;
    vix tenet incluso nunc domus una loco.
Sed refero hinc grates placidae caraeque sorori,
10   quod me consuluit de pietatis ope.
Tu retines medium, medium me possidet illa;
    cum geminas video, tunc ego totus agor.
Nunc tibi, cara, precor Martinus, Hilarius adstent,
    et te vel natos spes tegat una Deus.

22

Item aliud

Si nequeo praesens, absens tibi solvo tributum,
    ut probet affectum, mater amata, meum.
Si non essem absens, facerem quodcumque iuberes;
    obsequiis parvis forte placeret iners.

21

Again another poem

Every hour yesterday passed for me in this way, with laments that I had not been able to hear my mother's voice. As a loving lamb, driven from its mother's teats, wanders grieving and distraught in grassy pastures –now it runs to the fields, assailing the breezes with its bleating, now it returns to the sheepfold, but without its mother finds no comfort there– so, I imagine myself, apart from your voice; scarcely now can a single house keep me contained. But I send thanks from here to my dear, gentle sister, because in her boundless charity she took thought for me. You possess half of me, she the other half; when I see you both, then I am wholly myself. Now I pray, dear mother, that Martin and Hilary attend you, and that God, your whole hope, protect you and your children.

22

Again another poem

If I cannot pay it in person, I pay you my offering from afar, to prove my devotion to you, my beloved mother. If I were not far away, I would do whatever you ordered; perhaps even

5 Pectore devoto set rustica lingua dedisset
      pastoris calamo matris in aure sonum.
   Imperiis famulans tererem mea membra diurnis,
      servirent dominae subdita colla suae.
   Nulla recusarent digiti, puteoque profundo
10   quae manus hoc scripsit prompta levaret aquas,
   protraheret vites et surcula figeret hortis,
      plantaret, coleret dulce libenter holus.
   Splendor erat tecum mea membra ardere coquina
      et nigra de puro vasa lavare lacu.
15 Hinc tibi nunc absens Marcelli munera misi,
      cui dedit excelsum vita beata locum,
   et si displiceant indigno verba relatu,
      complaceant animo signa superna tuo.
   Sis longaeva mihi cum nata et messe sororum,
20   virgineoque choro crescat ovile Dei.
   Si tua verba dares, essent plus dulcia quam si
      floribus electis mella dedisset apes.

23

Item aliud

Flumine nectareo meritis mihi dulcior Agnes,
   quam praesente deo pectore, mente colo,
aspice quam celeri mutantur cuncta rotatu,
   dum veluti pinnis tempora nostra volant.

a clumsy man would please by small services. With devout 5
heart but rustic tongue I would have played music on my
shepherd's pipe for my mother's ear. I would weary my body
every day in doing your bidding, and my neck would bow to
serve in submission its mistress. My fingers would refuse no
task; the hand that wrote this would willingly draw water 10
from a deep well, would lay out vines, set out the cuttings in
gardens, and gladly plant and cultivate your succulent vege-
tables. It would be a delight to warm my limbs with you
in the kitchen, and wash the blackened pots in a bowl of
clear water. But, as it is, I am far away and send as my gift 15
from here Marcellus, whose blessed life gave him a place on
high, and if my words displease because of their awkward
phrasing, still may his heaven-sent miracles win favor with
your mind. May you enjoy long life with your daughter and
your harvest of sisters, and may the sheepfold of God be in- 20
creased by their virgin company. If you send a reply, your
words would be sweeter than if bees had produced honey
from the choicest of flowers.

23

Again another poem

Agnes, sweeter to me for your virtues than a flood of nec-
tar, whom before God I honor in heart and mind, see how
all things change with rapid revolution, as our lives fly by

5 Casibus incertis scripulos nescimus et horas;
      cras sit homo an non sit quis dabit inde fidem?
  Arboris oppressit hodie nix alta cacumen
      duraque ramorum brachia curvat hiems.
  Crastina forte dies puro si fulserit ortu,
10   si qua pruina iacet, sole calente liquet.
  Sic quoque mens hominum dubio de fine salutis
      ignorat quantum vivere vita queat.
  Sed quoniam vario transcurrunt omnia lapsu,
      quem numquam perdas dilige corde sagax.
15 Sit tibi Christus honor, Christus spes, Christus amator,
      in solo semper fige salutis opem.
  Temporibus cunctis hunc per tua viscera volve;
      sic sponso servent membra pudica fidem.
  Si sopor obripiat, retinendo in pectore Christum
20   tempore sub noctis luminis arma geris.
  Illum mente colens muro tutaris opimo;
      et si latro furit, pax tua corda tegit.
  Huius in amplexu te totam effunde licenter;
      illum quisquis habet crimina nulla timet.
25 Hoc age ut, ad thalamos cum venerit arbiter orbis,
      visceribus puris immaculata mices.
  Lampade fulgenti tunc te veniente sorores
      excipiant laeto Thecla, Susanna choro.
  Haec modo dum redeo breviter mandata relinquo:
30   tu quoque, dum religis, me memorare velis.

as though on wings. Chance is uncertain, we know not the ⁵
minute and the hour; who can be sure whether a person will
be alive tomorrow or not? Today deep snow has laid its bur-
den on the treetops, and winter bends the sturdy limbs and
branches. But if tomorrow happens to dawn bright and
clear, all the ice on the ground will melt in the heat of the ¹⁰
sun. So too the minds of men, uncertain when their exis-
tence will end, do not know how long their life can continue.
But since all things pass with unpredictable course, be wise
and treasure in your heart the one whom you never will lose.
Let Christ be your glory, your hope, and your love; on him ¹⁵
alone always stake your means to salvation. At every mo-
ment meditate on him in your heart; in this way let your
chaste body keep faith with your bridegroom. If sleep steals
up upon you, keep Christ in your heart, and in the time of ²⁰
the night wield the weapons of light. If you honor him in
your mind, a sturdy wall protects you, and, despite the rob-
ber's fury, peace encompasses your heart. Surrender yourself
without reserve wholly to Christ's embrace; whoever pos-
sesses him need fear no rebuke. Do this so that, when the ²⁵
judge of the world enters the bridal chamber, you may shine
spotless, your flesh without stain. Then when you arrive
with bright shining lamp, may your sisters Thecla and Su-
sanna receive you in their happy choir. As I return, I leave
these brief precepts behind me; you too, when you read ³⁰
them, gladly remember me.

24

Item aliud

Anxius, afflictus curarum pondere curvor
   pectore confuso nec dare verba queo.
Murmure sub dubio laceror neque carmina laxo;
   nescio certa loqui mente vagante mihi.
5 Heu, tristem si vota velint audire fatentem,
   me subito ferrent nubila missa tibi.
Daedalico lapsu si pinnas sumere nossem,
   ad vos quantocius iam revolasset amans.
Novit enim Dominus, qui corda latentia pulsat,
10   quae mea, sed tacite, viscera cura domet.
Reddite, cum nequeo, dominae promissa benignae:
   nec tamen hic culpam crede fuisse meam.
Excusa, si forte potes, per sidera testor,
   me neque velle moras matris in aure feras.
15 Oret pro famulo; citius remeare parabo,
   et cum praesentor, verbere, voce domet.

24

Again another poem

Anxious and distressed, I am bent under a weight of cares, and cannot frame my words in the confusion of my heart. I am racked by inarticulate moans, no poems come; I cannot speak distinctly, for my mind is distraught. Alas, if they 5 wanted to hear me sadly confessing my wishes, the clouds would quickly come and carry me to you. If I knew how to grow wings and fly like Daedalus, your devotee would already have flown to you with all possible speed. For the Lord, who knocks upon the secrets of the heart, knows the 10 care that oppresses my being, though it is unavowed. Make my promises to my generous mistress, since I cannot, and do not believe that I was at fault in this. Beg forgiveness, if you can, I beseech by the stars, and bring to my mother's hearing that I wanted no delay. Let her pray for her servant; 15 I will try to return very soon, and in her presence let her chastise me with speech and with stripes.

25

Item aliud

Supplicibus votis referat mandata salutis
    matribus ac dominis pagina missa loquens,
dumque recusat iter nostrum tibi reddere vultus,
    affectum saltim sollicitudo probet,
5 nec sumus absentes, si nos oratio dulcis
    praesentes semper cordis amore tenet.

26

Item aliud

Matri natus ego, frater simul ipse sorori
    pectore devoto parvula dona fero.
Tertius unitus tria munera porto duabus;
    tam dulces animas dulcia poma decent.
5 Sed date nunc veniam mihi quod fano talis habetur:
    munera quae portet, charta canister erit.

25

Again another poem

May the page I send bring wishes for your good health, addressing suppliant prayers to my mothers and mistresses, and though my travels prevent me from showing you my face, let my anxious concern at least demonstrate my warm feelings. And, in fact, we are not apart if sweetness of speech 5 keeps us always present in the love of our hearts.

26

Again another poem

As a son to a mother, as a brother to a sister, I bear small gifts, but with a devoted heart. I bring three gifts to the two of you, with you I make up three; such sweet fruit matches the sweetness of your souls. But pardon me now that it is in 5 such a wrapping; a sheet of paper will serve as a container to carry these gifts.

27

Item aliud

Hoc tibi pro summo direxi munere signum,
  ut pariter fratres crux tegat una duos.
Alternis vicibus haec pectora nostra gubernet
  et commune bonum participetur amor.
5 Ad te quando venit, mecum magis ista manebit;
  plus mihi proficiet, cum tua corda tenet.
Sit huius species intra tua viscera semper,
  tunc ibi perpetuam Christus habebit opem.
In cruce sacrata qui tunc pietate pependit,
10 haec tibi cum pendet, porrigit ille manum.
Communem matrem venerando voce saluto,
  quae maneat vobis consociata diu.

28

Item aliud

Dulcis, opima, decens, cui tanta est cura laboris,
  ut tibi sit modico semine magna seges,
quae modo membra libens fugitivo tempore lassas,
  cum Christo dabitur perpetuanda quies.

27

Again another poem

As a most precious gift I send you this symbol, so that a single cross can equally protect two siblings. May it guide both our hearts with mutual exchange, and our love share this common blessing. When it comes to you, it will stay all the more with me; my profit will be the greater, when it possesses your heart. Let its image always be held in your bosom, for then Christ will maintain his continual protection there. He who once in his mercy hung on the holy cross will stretch out his hand to you, when this cross is hung up. In respectful tones I send my greetings to our common mother; may she live for a long time in your company.

28

Again another poem

My sweet, gracious, and excellent mother, who labor so hard to win an abundant harvest from a few seeds, and now gladly weary your limbs, as time hurries by, with Christ you will

5 Dextra ubi nempe paras sudando sororibus escas,
    undis et flammis hinc riget, inde calet.
Assiduis votis inter tua brachia volvor
    atque meos animos sarcina vestra terit.
Nunc faciendo focos epulasque coquendo recurris,
10   nec valeo matrem quippe iuvare piger.
Filia sed portet praesens onus omne vicissim
    et reddat pondus participando leve.
Det tibi auxilium mundi reparator utrisque
    atque diu pariter hanc foveatis opem.

29

Item aliud

Pergimus inclusas a gurgite cernere terras,
    qua vagus oceanus fertque refertque vices,
fluctibus assiduis cum surgit ad aethera pontus,
    huc feritate sua mobilis unda latrat.
5 Litus harena suum refugo nunc suscipit aestu,
    nunc, mare dum turget, naufraga terra latet.
Quo gelidas se esse, re . . . dicus occupat ardor,
    atque loco huc uno sunt tria dona Dei.
Quamvis sit sterilis, fructus fert illa beatos,
10   dum caelo dignos pascit harena viros.
Ast ego vel si qua sine vobis urbe tenerer,
    inter multa tamen milia solus eram.
Cernere vos laetas merear, materque sororque,
    cum venit excelsi cena beata Dei.

enjoy perpetual rest. Your hand, as you sweat in preparing 5
meals for the sisters, now freezes in cold water, now is
heated by flames. In constant prayers I share the labor of
your limbs, and the burden you bear oppresses my spirits.
Now you hasten to make the fire and cook the meal, and I in 10
my helplessness can bring no aid to my mother. But let your
daughter who is with you take turns in bearing every bur-
den, and make the weight light by sharing it with you. May
the Redeemer of the world grant both of you aid, and long
may you together enjoy his assistance.

29

Again another poem

We are going to view an island enclosed by the waves, where
the restless ocean tides ebb and flow, and when the sea rears
wave after wave to the sky, the seething waters howl there in
their fury. The sand now retakes its own shore as the tide 5
retreats; now, as the waves swell, the land disappears as
though shipwrecked. Though chill . . . warmth possessed it,
and in this one place are three gifts of God. Although it is
barren, the island bears happy fruit, for its sand nurtures 10
men worthy of heaven. But as for me, even if I were in a city,
without you I would be alone, though among many thou-
sands. May I have the pleasure of seeing you joyful, my
mother and sister, when the blessed feast of God most high

15   Si citius redeat frater Simplicius, oro,
      a me mandatae ferte salutis opus,
    et rogo per vestras me commendate sorores;
      sic faciat cunctas Christus amore suas.

30

Item aliud

Audivi, fateor, ieiunia longa parari:
    ad me si veniant, non toleranda gravent:
Expavesco famem quae iam vicina susurrat,
    ne parietis iter transeat illa celer.
5 Mox quoque diffugiens vacuis me abscondo cavernis,
    dum modo ieiuno non ego ventre domer.
Sed si nunc alios pietas et gratia pascit,
    de me nulla mihi causa timoris erit.

31

Item aliud

In brevibus tabulis mihi carmina magna dedisti,
    quae vacuis ceris reddere mella potes.
Multiplices epulas per gaudia festa ministras,
    sed mihi plus avido sunt tua verba cibus.

comes round. If brother Simplicius returns quickly, I beg,   15
give him my greeting that I now convey, and please com-
mend me in your sisters' prayers; so may Christ make them
all his in love.

30

Again another poem

I have heard, I confess, that a long fast is in store; if it comes
to me, it will be an unbearable burden. I am afraid of the
hunger that now whispers close by, lest it quickly penetrate
the walls of my dwelling. Soon I shall escape and hide myself   5
in empty caves, provided only that I do not first succumb
to a starving stomach. But if others now derive sustenance
from holiness and grace, I will have no reason to fear for my-
self.

31

Again another poem

On small tablets you have sent me magnificent poems, for
you can fill with honey the empty wax. You provide abun-
dant food in joyful celebrations, but I hunger more for the

5　Versiculos mittis placido sermone refectos,
　　　in quorum dictis pectora nostra ligas.
　　Omnia sufficiunt aliis quae dulcia tractas,
　　　at mihi sinceros det tua lingua favos.
　　Supplico me recolas inter pia verba sororum,
10　　verius ut matrem te mea vota probent,
　omnibus et reliquis te commendante reformer,
　　　ut per vos merear quod mea causa rogat.

Epistulae Austrasicae 14

Domino sancto, meritis apostolicis praedicando in Christo patri, Magnerico papae, Fortunatus humilis

Culmen honorificum, patrum pater, archisacerdos,
　　pontificale decus proficiente gradu,
quem fidei titulo merces erexit in altum,
　　ecclesiaeque caput distribuente deo,
5　discipule egregii, bone Magnerice, Niceti,
　　nominis auspicio magne canende tui,
clare sacro merito tanto informante magistro,
　　quem reparas operum fructificante loco,
cuius, opime, sequax sancta et vestigia servans,

food of your words. You send me verses composed in charm- 5
ing style, with whose words you bind together our hearts.
For others all the sweet things that you furnish them suffice,
but let your tongue give pure honeycombs to me. Mention
me in your holy conversations with the sisters, I beg, so that 10
my prayers show you all the more truly to be my mother. By
your recommendation to everyone else may I win new favor,
so that through you I gain what my circumstances seek.

Epistulae Austrasicae 14

Fortunatus in humility to Bishop Magneric, his Holy Lord, his father in Christ, praiseworthy for his apostolic merits

Honorable eminence, father of fathers, lofty bishop, glory
of the episcopate as your status advances, whom the reward
for your renowned faith has raised on high and the primacy
of the church, bestowed by God, good Magneric, pupil of 5
the excellent Nicetius, by the omen of your name bound to
be called great, famed for your holy worth, shaped by such a
great teacher, whom you replicate in fruitful performance of
good works, whose disciple you are, noble one, whose holy

10   rite minister agens ecce magister ades
        auctorisque pii successor dignus haberis
            heredisque sui frugiparensque manet.
        Crevit post obitum pater et te crescere fecit,
            dum capit ille polum, tu capis arce locum.
15   Grex alitur per te vice praecessoris, alumne,
            nec sua damna dolet, dum tua lucra tenet.
        Fratribus optandus, iucundus honore ministris
            carius et populis pastor amore places.
        Te panem esuriens, tectum hospes, nudus amictum,
20   te fessus requiem, spem peregrinus habet.
        Haec faciens intende magis, venerande sacerdos,
            ut commissa tibi dupla talenta feras.
        Pro Fortunato exorans quoque, dulcis amator,
            spem mihi dans veniae, sit tibi palma, pater.

footsteps you follow, by duly serving as a minister, see, you 10
stand forth as a teacher, and are deemed a worthy successor
to your holy father; he lives an heir to himself and a fertile
parent. Your father has grown after his death and caused you
to grow too; while he takes a place in heaven, you occupy a
high station. The flock is fed by you its fosterer in your fore- 15
runner's place, and does not grieve its loss while it acquires
from you gain. Admired by monks, by deacons honored and
beloved, the people love and cherish you as their dear shep-
herd. In you the hungry find food, the stranger shelter, the
naked clothing, the weary find in you rest, and the traveler 20
hope. By these acts, reverent bishop, strive all the more to
double the talents that have been entrusted to you. Pray for
Fortunatus too, I beg, my sweet friend, and in giving me
hope of pardon, may you, father, win the palm.

FIGURE POEMS

```
   DIVSAPEXCARNEEFFIGIANSGENETALIALIMI
   VITALITERRAECONPINGITSANGVINEGLVTEN
   LVCIFERAXAVRASANIMANTESAFFLVITILLIC
   CONDITVRENIXANSADAMFACTORISADINSTAR
 5 EXILVITPROTOPLASMASOLORESNOBILISVSV
   DIVESINARBITRIORADIANTILVMINEDEHINC
   EXMEMBRISADAEVASFITTVMVIRGINISEVVAE
   CARNECREATAVIRIDEHINCCOPVLATVREIDEM
   VTPARADYSSIACOBENELAETARETVRINHORTO
10 SEDDESEDEPIAPEPVLITTEMERABILEGVTTVR
   SERPENTISSVASVPOMISVCOATRAPROPINANS
   INSATIATRICIMORTIFAMESACCIDITILLINC
   GAVISVRVSOBHOCCAELIFLVISARCELOCATOR
   NASCIPRONOBISMISERARISETVLCERECLAVI
15 INCRVCECONFIGITALIMALAGMATEINVNCTIS
   VNASALVSNOBISLIGNOAGNISANGVINEVENIT
   IVCVNDASPECIESINTEPIABRACCHIACRISTI
   AFFIXASTETERVNTETPALMABEABILISINHAC
   CARACAROPOENASINMITESSVSTVLITHAVSTV
20 ARBORSVAVISAGRITECVMNOVAVITAPARATVR
   ELECTAVTVISVSICECRVCISORDINEPVLCHRA
   LVMENSPESSCVTVMGERERISLIVORISABICTV
   INMORTALEDECVSNECEIVSTILAETAPARASTI
   VNAOMNEMVITAMSICCRVXTVACAVSARIGAVIT
25 IMBRECRVENTAPIOVELISDASNAVITAPORTVM
   TRISTIASVMMERSOMVNDASTIVVLNERACLAVO
   ARBORDVLCISAGRIRORANSECORTICENECTAR
   RAMISDECVIVSVITALIACRISMATAFRAGRANT
   EXCELLENSCVLTVDIVAORTVFVLGIDAFRVCTV
30 DELICIOSACIBOETPERPOMASVAVISINVMBRA
   ENREGISMAGNIGEMMANTEMETNOBILESIGNVM
   MVRVSETARMAVIRISVIRTVSLVXARAPRECATV
   PANDEBENIGNAVIAMVIVAXETFERTILELVMEN
   TVMMEMORADFEROPEMNOBISEGERMINEDAVID
35 INCRVCEREXFIXVSIVDEXCVMPRAEERITORBI
```

Figure 1. Book 2, Poem 4

```
   EXTORQVETHOCSORTEDEIVENIABILESIGNVM
   RVSTICVLASLAVDESVIVENTIREDDEREFLATV
   INMEQVIREGITIRELVTVMPLASMABILENVMEN
   PORTIOVIVENTVMCVRATIOFAVSTAMEDELLAE
 5 EXCLVSORCVLPAETRINITASEFFVSACREATOR
   CVIVSHONORLVMENIVSGLORIAREGNACOAEVE
   C                I                C                      E
   R              H                T            O           C
   E            I                P              L           R
10 D          L                L                  L         I
   E        I                P                     S        S
   N      G                L                        L       T
   T    N                D                           I      E
   E  V                E                              G     T
15 S M                I                               N     V
   F P              C                                       O
   I               R                                        R
   D               I                                        V
   EXFIDEIMERITOMAGNVMPIEREDDISABRAHAM                       E
   I M             X                                      G  M
20 D A             E                              N       O
   E   I           T                                E     V
   C    V          V                            R        E
   V     S         E                           A         T
   V      O        L                         S           V
25 S       D       A                        T            R
   A        O      M                      I              C
   R         R     E                     S               A
   M          E    N                    H                V
   A           R   A                   O                 S
30 S            O   D                 O                   A
   A             S   O              N                     R
   L              E   R            O                      E
   V               T   N         R                        A
   T                    I A I                             T
35 SICPATERETGENITVSSICSCSSPIRITVSVNVS
```

Figure 2. Book 2, Poem 5

AVGVSTIDVNENSISOPVSTIBISOLVOSYAGRI ✠

```
   DIVSAPEXADAMVTFECITDATSOMNIADONEC
   AVVLSACOSTAPLASMATAESTEVANECINPAR
   FELICESPARITERDIPLOIDELVCISOPERTI
 5 ORECORVSCANTESINTERPIARVRAIVGALES
   RIPAEIVCVNDAENARIGRATAAVRAREDIBAT
   TVRISDELICIAESATVRABANTVBEREFLATV
   VNAFOVENSAMBOSFLOROSASEDEVOLVPTAS
   NOTABONISREGIOPASCEBATTEMPEBEATOS
10 ATCVMTAMMAGNOPOLLERENTMAIVSHONORE
   TOTAHOMINVMMIREPAREBATTERRADVORVM
   OCCVLTVSMENDAXMOXEXERITARMAVENENI
   SERPENSELATVSZELATORLARVEVSHOSTIS
   ATROXINNOCVOSEVINCENSFELLENOCENTI
15 CONLISITSVASVQVOSGRATIADIVABEARAT
   ETHOMODETERRATVMDENVODECIDITILLVC
   REPTANTISQ:DOLOEOOISEXCLVDITVRORTV
   HACNATIMORIMVRDAMNATILEGEPARENTVM
   ATDEVSEXCELLENSAIEETDELVMINELVMEN
20 ECAELISOLIODVMMVNERAPROVIDETVLTRO
   CASTAECARNERVDIVIVAXINTROIITAGNVS
   PRODIITINDESALVSMATVTINIVELVCERNA
   INTACTAEPARTVLVXERVITEXCITAMVNDVM
   APATREIVREDS̄HOMODEHINCCARNEVSALVO
25 VTNOSERIPERETVILISEDETRAHITAVCTOR
   OREGISVENALECAPVTQVODDECRVCEFIXIT
   TELOVOCEMANVMALFACTVSVERBEREFELLE
   ACTVHACSOLVISCAPTIVOSSORTECREATOR
   SEROVERADATAESTVITALISEMPTIOMORTE
30 YMNOSVNDEDEOLOQVORABSOLVENTEREATV
   ATVOSAETERNAESVFFVLTILAVDECORONAE
   GALLORVMRADIIVOBISQVOFVLGEATETNOX
   RVMPITELORAIVGISETSVMITISARMADIEI
   IPSAVELIBERTASVOSLIBERATATQ:BEABIT
```

Figure 3. Book 5, Poem 6a

Abbreviations

Bastiaensen = A. A. R. Bastiaensen, "La poésie de Venance Fortunat: Observations à propos d'une nouvelle édition," *Mnemosyne* 49 (1996): 168–81

Blomgren 1 = Sven Blomgren, *Studia Fortunatiana,* vol. 1 (Upsala, 1933)

Blomgren 2 = Sven Blomgren, "In Venantii Fortunati carmina adnotationes," *Eranos* 42 (1944): 100–134

Blomgren 3 = Sven Blomgren, "In Venantii Fortunati carmina adnotationes novae," *Eranos* 69 (1971): 104–50

Brower = Christopher Brower, ed., *Venantii Honorii Clementiani Fortunati presbyteri italici . . . carminum, epistolarum, expositionum libri XI* (Mainz, 1617)

CCSL = Corpus Christianorum. Series Latina

Epist. Austras. = Epistulae Austrasicae (see Malaspina, below)

Leo = Friedrich Leo, ed., *Venanti Honori Clementiani Fortunati presbyteri Italici opera poetica. Monumenta Germaniae Historica. Auctores Antiquissimi* 4.1 (Berlin, 1881)

Luchi = Michele Angelo Luchi, ed., *Venantii Honorii Clementiani Fortunati presbyteri italici . . . opera omnia quae extant,* 2 vols. (Rome, 1786–87)

Malaspina = Elena Malaspina, ed., *Il Liber epistolarum della cancelleria austrasica (sec. V–VI)* (Rome, 2001)

Meyer = Wilhelm Meyer, *Der Gelegenheitsdichter Venantius Fortunatus,*

Abhandlungen der königlichen Gesellschaft der Wissenschaften zu Göttingen, phil.-hist. Klasse, N. F. 4.5 (Berlin, 1901)

Nisard = Charles Nisard, *Le poète Fortunat* (Paris, 1890)

P = Parisinus Latinus 13048, Paris, Bibliothèque national de France

PCBE = André Marouze, Charles Pietri, and Luce Pietri, eds., *Prosopographie chrétienne du bas-empire,* 4 vols. in 6 bks. (Paris, 1982–2013)

PLRE = A. H. M. Jones, J. R. Martindale, and J. Morris, eds., *Prosopography of the Later Roman Empire,* 3 vols. in 4 bks. (Cambridge, 1971–1992)

Reydellet = Marc Reydellet, ed., *Venance Fortunat, Poèmes,* 3 vols. (Paris, 1994–2004)

Note on the Text

I follow Friedrich Leo's *Monumenta Germaniae Historica* edition of Venantius Fortunatus as my base text, with occasional minor changes of orthography and punctuation. In particular, following the series practice, I assimilate prefixes (for example, *compleo* not *conpleo*) and regularize nonclassical forms; I substitute *ph* for *f* where that letter represents the Greek *phi;* so too *lethargicus,* not *letargicus,* to represent the Greek letter *theta.* Other variations from Leo's text are listed in the Notes to the Text. Unless otherwise indicated, "Reydellet" next to a reading means that this is the reading of his edition, not that this is his conjecture. In most cases the changes Reydellet makes to Leo's text had already been proposed by Blomgren. Leo attributes some emendations to Mommsen. Although Mommsen did not himself publish an edition of Fortunatus, he appears to have provided assistance informally, for which he is thanked in the Preface to Leo's 1881 edition.

Notes to the Text

Praefatio

1 celebraturi *Reydellet*: celebrati *Leo*
3 augeret *Bastiaensen*: egerit *Leo*
6 quoniam humilem *Reydellet*: quoniam me humilem *Leo*
   repensurus *Reydellet*: repensus usi *Leo*

Book 1

3.12   fiat *Reydellet*: sciat *Leo*
16.79 cui *Leo in critical apparatus*: quo *Leo*
21.30 insidens *Reydellet*: insidiens *Leo*

Book 2

3.13   offert *Reydellet*: offers *Leo*
7.32   fudit *Reydellet*: fundit *Leo*
9.15   recoctum *Leo in corrections*: recocto *Leo*
9.36   quod *Reydellet*: quo *Leo*
16.107 glomerante *Roberts*: numerante *Leo*
16.129 sterilis *Reydellet*: steriles *Leo*
        honesti *Reydellet*: onusti *Leo*

Book 3

1.1   vobis *Reydellet*: a vobis *Leo*
2.3   erexit *Reydellet*: erigit *Leo*
3.10 vir es *Blomgren 1*: vires *Leo*
4.12 laudes *Reydellet*: laudis *Leo*

7.35   expositos *Reydellet*: expositas *Leo*
7.37–40   *as reordered by Meyer: with lines 37–38 preceding lines 39–40 Leo*
8.14   tuus *Blomgren 2*: tuo *Leo*
10.17   superinvehis *conjectured by Reydellet*: super invehis *Leo*
13.37   tua *Reydellet*: quam *Leo*
23a.24   plus *Reydellet*: plebs *Leo*

BOOK 4

1.15   quis *Leo in critical apparatus: Leo in text indicates lacuna*
4.30   vix *Leo in critical apparatus*: bis *Leo*
12.18   maesta *Leo in critical apparatus*: membra *Leo*
19.6   placito *Reydellet*: placido *Leo*

BOOK 5

1.5   commercium *Reydellet*: commercio *Leo*
2.28   inrigue *conjectured by Reydellet*: inriguae *Leo*
3.13   Egidii *Reydellet*: Aegidii *Leo*
4   antiphonam *Reydellet*: antiphona *Leo*
5.39   veternus *Reydellet*: veternos *Leo*
6.10   absoluturum *Reydellet*: absoluturo *Leo*
6.14   in directo *Nisard*: indirecto *Leo*
6a.17   Eoo is *Blomgren 2*: Eoois *Leo*
14.7   <lugent> *Blomgren 3 supplement*
            puellam *Blomgren 3*: puella *Leo*

BOOK 6

1   De domno Sigiberto rege *Reydellet*: De domno Sigiberctho rege
            et Brunichilde regina *Leo*
1.7   praemittens *Reydellet*: promittens *Leo*
1.77   de Theudeberctho pietas venit patrueli *Leo in critical apparatus*:
            perditheuberto pietas veniale *Leo*
1.83   generosior *Blomgren 3*: generosius *Leo*
1.84   <aevo> *Blomgren 3 supplement*

1a	Item de Sigiberto rege et Brunichilde regina *Reydellet*: De Sigiberctho rege et Brunichilde regina *Leo*
1a.11	Saxo et Thoringus *Leo in critical apparatus*: Saxone Thoringo *Leo*
1a.37	\<pia\> *Leo supplement in critical apparatus*: *Leo in text indicates lacuna*
2.106	ades *Leo in critical apparatus*: adest *Leo*
2.107	tui *Blomgren 3*: dei *Leo*
5.50	erat *Reydellet*: eras *Leo*
5.117	quae *Mommsen*: neque *Leo*
5.158	avidae *Reydellet*: avide *Leo*
5.268	mori *Reydellet*: mori es *Leo*
5.281	resides *Reydellet*: residis *Leo*
8.43	Nauriacum *Reydellet*: Nauriaco *Leo*
8.47	comis *Reydellet*: cum esca *Leo*

Book 7

2	rogaretur *Reydellet*: me rogaret *Leo*
2.10	laeta *Reydellet*: lenta *Leo*
3.3	Remus *Blomgren 3*: remus *Leo*
5.8	devoto *Reydellet*: de voto *Leo*
6.18	dispiciamque *Reydellet*: despiciamque *Leo*
8.59	post ascensum *Leo in critical apparatus*: per ascensum *Leo*
9.14	renovavit *Reydellet*: recreavit *Leo*
10.10	novus *Reydellet*: novis *Leo*
11.9	tuto *Reydellet*: toto *Leo*
12.14	refluis *Luchi*: resolvis *Leo*
12.20	abit *Reydellet*: obit *Leo*
12.28	tapho *Leo index*: tabo *Leo*
12.37	abitu *Blomgren 1*: obitu *Leo*
12.38	flagrat *Reydellet*: fragrat *Leo*
12.48	volat *Reydellet*: volet *Leo*
12.61	muto *Meyer*: metu *Leo*
17.3	gesto *Reydellet*: claudo *Leo*
25.13	et Himus *Reydellet*: aestibus *Leo*

Book 8

3.4	sacro *Reydellet*: sacros *Leo*
3.82	tuo *Reydellet*: suo *Leo*
3.198	docta sed *Reydellet*: doctast *Leo*
3.347	validos *Leo in critical apparatus*: validus *Leo*
5.10	salve *Reydellet*: solo *Leo*
6.6	violas *Reydellet*: vicias *Leo*
6.11	haec . . . gerit *Reydellet*: hae . . . gerunt *Leo*
	utraeque *Leo in index*: utraque *Leo*
8.3	ipse *Reydellet*: ipsa *Leo*
12a	percipiatis *Roberts*: praecipiatis *Leo*
15.9	vir *Reydellet*: huic *Leo*
17	Item ad eundem de ea re *Reydellet*: Ad eundem salutatoria *Leo*
18	Ad eundem de eadem re *Reydellet*: Ad eundem salutatoria *Leo*
19.7	repleto *Reydellet*: replete *Leo*

Book 9

1.143	saevos *Reydellet*: hostes *Leo*
2.65	in adventu *Reydellet*: ad adventum *Leo*
2.91	materno affectu *Reydellet*: maternum affectum *Leo*
9.6	loco *Reydellet*: locum *Leo*
9.24	fecit et *Reydellet*: facit *Leo*
13	Vualdonem *Reydellet*: Waldonem *Leo*
14.8	haec *Reydellet*: hic *Leo*
15.7	in medio *Leo in critical apparatus*: inmitior *Leo*

Book 10

1.1	potius quam *Reydellet*: potius cum *Leo*
1.12	confunditur *Leo in critical apparatus*: non confunditur *Leo*
1.36	hominem, quoniam *Roberts*: hominem non voluntatem, quoniam *Leo*
1.37	est, quod *Roberts*: est *Leo*
1.51	haberi *Reydellet*: haberis *Leo*

1.55	sit, nutrimento nostro peregrinos *Reydellet*: sit nutrimentum nostrum, peregrinos *Leo*
1.61	quam *Reydellet*: ut *Leo*
2.1	percellitur *Reydellet*: percellit *Leo*
2.10	quam *Reydellet*: quo *Leo*
2.12	habeat aequale *Leo in critical apparatus*: habeat obitu aequale *Leo*
2.16	quae *Leo in critical apparatus*: quem *Leo*
2.17	patere *Brower* : pater es *Leo*
3.4	utilitate praedictae *Leo in critical apparatus*: utilitate necessitate praedictae *Leo*
	necessitate *Leo in critical apparatus*: necessaria *Leo*
6.54	artificis *Reydellet*: artifici *Mommsen, Leo*
6.61	fluvium *Reydellet*: fluvio *Leo*
8.11	dies *Reydellet*: quies *Leo*
9.33	insertis *Reydellet*: insertae *Leo*
9.64	peraccedens *Blomgren 1*: per accedens *Leo*
12a.9	orbos *Reydellet*: orbes *Leo*
15.6	sinu *Reydellet*: suo *Leo*
17.44	auxilium det *Meyer*: auxilio des *Leo*

Book II

1.4	poterit qui *Reydellet*: non poterit quin *Leo*
1.42	glorioso principatu *Reydellet*: gloriosum principatum *Leo*
11.6	flagrat *Reydellet*: fragrat *Leo*

Appendix

1.16	lacticolora manus *Blomgren 3*: lacticolor amati *Leo*
1.132	qui *Reydellet*: quod *Leo*
1.133	perculitur *Reydellet*: percutitur *Leo*
1.154	hac *Reydellet*: ac *Leo*
1.159	tuis *Blomgren 3*: tui *Leo*
2	Item incipiunt versus *P*: Ad Iustinum et Sophiam Augustos *Leo*
2.60	lavat *Blomgren 3*: lavit *Leo*
2.100	illa *Reydellet*: ille *Leo*

7	Item aliud ad Agiulfum *P*: Ad Agiulfum *Leo*
8	Item versus epitaphium Nectarii *P*: Epitaphium Nectarii *Leo*
9	Item aliud, incipiunt versus pro pomis directis *P*: Versus pro pomis directis *Leo*
12.5	trepident mea corda *Reydellet*: trepidet mea chorda *Leo*
16.9	<cape> *Blomgren 1 supplement*
17.5	saecula *Nisard*: singula *Leo*
18.6	loci *Blomgren 3*: ioti *Leo*
21.12	agor *Reydellet*: ago *Leo*
26.5	talis *Nisard*: tali *Leo*
29.5	litus arena suum refugo nunc suscipit aestu *Blomgren 2*: litus harenosum refugit, nunc suscipit aestus *Leo*
29.7	quo gelidas se esse, re … dicus *P*: quo gelidum abscessit, rediens hoc *Leo*

Epist. Austras. 14 Domino s. m. a. p. i. C. p. M. p. F. humilis *Malaspina*: De Magnerico Treverensi episcopo *Leo*

Epist. Austras. 14.3 titulo merces *spelling regularized*: titulo mercis *Malaspina*: titulus meritis *Leo*

Epist. Austras. 14.12 manet *Blomgren 2*: manes *Leo*

Notes to the Translation

Preface

1   Fortunatus attributes a wide range of rhetorical qualities to the poets of old. The division *(partitio)* was the part of a speech in which the orator enumerated the main points of his argument. That process of analysis was known as classification *(distinctio)*. The words I have translated as "clauses" and "phrasing" *(cola* and *commata)* refer to greater or lesser divisions of a period or unit of verse. An epicheireme, broadly speaking, is a rhetorical syllogism. By "the charm of their concluding statements," Fortunatus may have in mind the practice of concluding a section of composition with an epigram.

4   Fortunatus ends his *Vita Sancti Martini* (4.630–703) by bidding his book travel from Gaul to Ravenna. It is generally taken to describe in reverse direction the course Fortunatus himself took when he first came to Gaul.

6   The word *arbitrem* seems to be corrupt. In my translation I have given an approximation of the likely sense. Blomgren 1 (110–11), followed by Reydellet, reads *arbitre,* but there is no convincing parallel for the dative (here, *meis frivolis*) with this word (the examples cited by Blomgren all involve datives of purpose with the gerundive).

Book 1

1.1   No bishop of Ravenna named Vitalis is recorded in this period. Fortunatus's addressee is generally identified with a bishop of Altinum (but see *PCBE* 2:2331–32 Vitalis 12 and 13).

1.6   Andrew, the disciple, brother of Peter.

2.14   Laurence, a deacon of Rome, was martyred by being bound to a
             gridiron that was then heated over a fire (see Prudentius, *Peri-
             stephanon* 2).

2.16   Vitalis was martyred in Bologna, but a later tradition identifies
             his place of death as Ravenna, where Fortunatus situated his
             tomb. According to one Passion he was executed by being bur-
             ied alive.

2.18   Martin clothed a beggar in his cloak at the city gate of Amiens.
             In a dream that night, Christ appeared to him wearing the
             cloak (Sulpicius Severus, *Vita Sancti Martini* 3).

2.20   Vigilius, bishop of Trento, according to tradition martyred circa
             400 by a group of pagans who were resisting the saint's mis-
             sionary activities (*PCBE* 2:2296–97 Vigilius 1).

2.22   Marturius and Sisennus were local martyrs of Trento, martyred
             in the course of missionary activities in 398 (*PCBE* 2:1424–25
             Martyrius 2 and 2:2087–88 Sisinnius 2).

2.23   An Alexander was martyred along with Marturius and Sisennus
             (*PCBE* 2:83–84 Alexander 3). Cecilia is the famous Roman
             saint.

2.25   Bishop John is not securely identified (*PCBE* 2:1098 Iohannes
             55).

3   Stephen the protomartyr (Acts 7:57–59).

3.6   1 Corinthians 10:4.

3.11   Palladius, identified as the bishop of Saintes by Reydellet (1:168),
             but see *PCBE* 4:1403 Palladius 9. The deacon is Stephen (see
             Acts 6:5).

4.5   Generally identified with Faustus, bishop of Auch (d. 585—
             PCBE 4:745 Faustus 4).

5   For the incident of Martin clothing a poor man, see Sulpicius
             Severus, *Dialogi* 2.1. The poem, without the two-line coda to
             Gregory and perhaps the preceding two lines seeking Martin's
             intercession for the poet, was presumably intended to be in-
             scribed in the cell where the miracle took place.

5.18   Fortunatus here combines two separate stories in Sulpicius
             Severus's *Dialogi,* the ball of fire that appears above Martin's
             head (2.2.1–2) and the jewels on his arms (3.10.6). He conflates

the same events in the collection of epigrams he wrote for Gregory of Tours's restored cathedral (10.6.1–10).

6.5 Leontius, bishop of Bordeaux, to whom (or to whose wife Placidina) Fortunatus dedicated fourteen of the poems of Book 1 (*PCBE* 4:1145–49). Fortunatus was later to write his epitaph (poem 4.10).

6.10 Sulpicius Severus (*Vita Sancti Martini* 18.3) records Martin's healing of a leper with a kiss at the city gates of Paris.

7 Fortunatus later wrote an epitaph for Basil at the request of his widow, Baudegund, in which he describes him as a royal confidant and frequent ambassador to Spain (4.18.11 and 15–16). It is likely he was from Poitiers. The church he restored seems to have been built on land reclaimed from a river (*PLRE* 3A:175 Basilius 4).

8 The Saint Vincent in question is Vincent of Agen, not the better-known saint of the same name from Saragossa celebrated in Prudentius, *Peristephanon* 5.

8.14 According to the Passion of the saint, his bodily remains were transported to *Pompeiacum,* identified with Mas d'Agenais (see Reydellet 1:171).

8.17 Fortunatus exploits the double meaning of *salus,* "health" or "salvation." His prayer is simultaneously for health in this life and salvation in the next. The following line, though, suggests he is primarily wishing for Leontius to continue his services to the church in this life.

9 Despite the *Item* in the title to this poem, the previous poem and this poem describe two different churches dedicated to Vincent of Agen.

9.1 Compare Psalm 18:5 and Romans 10:18.

9.10 The root of the word "Vernemet" is etymologically connected with the Latin *nemus* and implies a glade that is a place of cult.

10 Nazarius, martyr of Milan, whose remains were discovered by Saint Ambrose in 395.

10.8 That is, in heaven.

10.11 The Latin could also bear the meaning that the first church collapsed of its own accord.

11 Dionysius is the Parisian bishop and martyr (Saint Denis). Leon-

tius's church would have been in Bordeaux or on one of the properties Leontius owned in the region.

11.5　　Amelius is identified by Reydellet (1:173) with a bishop of Paris of that name in the second quarter of the sixth century (*PCBE* 4:132–33). But lines 7 and 8 would more naturally imply he was an episcopal predecessor of Leontius of Bordeaux.

12　　Saint Bibianus (Saint Vivien) was a fifth-century bishop of Saintes (*PCBE* 4:358–59).

12.6　　Gregory of Tours (*Historiae* 4.26) records friction between Emerius and Leontius. Leontius attempted to expel Emerius from his see on the grounds that his election was uncanonical, but he was restored by King Charibert.

12.22　　Compare Matthew 25:21.

13　　Eutropius (Eutropis) was the first bishop of Saintes. Gregory of Tours (*Gloria Martyrum* 55) reports a translation of Eutropius's body under Bishop Palladius of Saintes, when his martyrdom was revealed by marks on his skull, but this translation probably postdates Fortunatus's poem.

15.9　　For the Frankish campaign against Visigothic Spain, see Gregory of Tours, *Historiae* 3.29. The king in question was Childebert I.

15.25　　Leontius is the "flower" from the roots of (that is, descended from) his noble family.

15.63　　The "house of the church" is the cathedral of Bordeaux.

15.76　　See the dedicatory letter to Gregory (Preface 4), where, in describing his journey to Gaul, Fortunatus mentions all three rivers.

15.84　　Compare Matthew 6:20.

15.96　　Eparchius Avitus was briefly Roman emperor (455–56). Placidina was his great-great-granddaughter (*PLRE* 3B:1042).

15.110　　Fortunatus is apparently addressing the virgin Mary (see lines 55–58).

16　　The poem is an abecedarian. The first letters of the stanzas follow the sequence of the alphabet. It is in iambic dimeters. It apparently celebrates the successful restoration of Bishop Leontius to his see after an attempt to supplant him in his absence.

16.36 The bishops mentioned are Hilary of Poitiers, Martin of Tours, and Gregory of Nazianzus.

16.81 Χρς is a standard abbreviation for *Christus*. The Greek letter chi stands in for the Latin *X*.

16.85–87 My translation assumes that the hymn in question is the present one composed by Fortunatus. But the second and third lines of this stanza could also be translated "sound out a hymn in song / His is the praise who saved."

17.8 It is suggested that the object in question is an especially attractive seashell, which Fortunatus found on the island when he was prevented from taking to sea. But the circumstances of the poem are somewhat obscure.

18 The villa is identified with the modern Besson, south of Bordeaux.

19 The location of this villa has not been identified.

20 Praemiacum has been identified as Preignac, on the left bank of the Garonne.

20.6 The Latin word *Praemiacum* becomes *praemia* (prizes, rewards), when the fourth syllable is removed.

21.13 "Titan" is the sun.

21.22 Fortunatus plays on the name of the river (*Egircius* in Latin) and the Latin words for "sick" (*aeger*) and "is in need" (*eget*).

21.29 That is, in the summer, when the sun enters the constellation of Cancer.

Book 2

1 The first six poems of Book 2 take as their subject the cross. They were written in connection with Radegund's acquisition in 569 of a fragment of the cross from Constantinople for the convent she had founded.

1.8 Fortunatus has in mind Jesus's saving Peter from drowning (Matthew 14:30–31).

1.14 Compare Psalm 120:6.

1.15 Compare Psalm 1:3.

2 This famous hymn is composed in trochaic tetrameters catalectic, a meter associated in the ancient world with marching. It is

generally believed to have been written for the ceremonial procession that welcomed the fragment of the cross to Radegund's convent.

2.6   The wood of the cross and of the tree of the knowledge of good and evil.

2.10   Compare Galatians 4:4.

2.20   Compare John 19:34.

2.29   The cross is regularly represented as the mast of a ship, by which the Christian navigates the perils of the world.

3.22   "The cross that is shared," presumably because the fabric was decorated with crosses.

4   This is a figure poem, made up of thirty-five hexameter lines, each with thirty-five letters to the line. In most of the manuscripts the borders of the poem (the first and last lines and the hexameters constructed of the first and last letters of each line read from top to bottom) are rubricated, as are the sequences of letters that can be read within the poem that pick out the form of a cross. (For the layout of this poem and its interwoven texts, see the section Figure Poems in this volume.)

4.19   My translation takes the verb *sustulit* to be from *suffero* (endure). But it could also be from *tollo* (remove, abolish), which gives equally good sense: "he abolished cruel pains," that is, the cruel pains of death.

4.21   The "plan of the cross" (*ordo crucis*) consists in redemption by the wood of the cross from human sinfulness caused by the wood of the tree of the knowledge of good and evil.

4.26   That is, the nails that fixed Christ to the cross. But, as Reydellet (1:184) points out, the Latin word *clavus* can also mean "the helm (of a ship)," which picks up on the language of cross as sailor in the previous line.

5   A second figure poem containing the image of the cross. It includes eight 35-letter lines read horizontally, three vertically, and two diagonally. The first six lines of the poem are continuous, but otherwise each line is an independent unit of sense. This poem has no title in the manuscripts and appears to be an incomplete draft. The Latin of the first six lines is often un-

clear and I cannot be certain I have understood it correctly. (For the layout of this poem and its interwoven texts, see the section Figure Poems in this volume.)

One manuscript (*Sangallensis* 196) contains a third figure poem on the cross, but it is not in the manner of Fortunatus, though included in Reydellet's edition of his poetry.

The word *sanctus* appears in the last line of the poem in the abbreviated form *scs* in order to ensure the line has the right number of letters.

6   The second of Fortunatus's famous poems on the cross (see poem 2.2), written in iambic dimeters, the canonical meter for Christian hymns since Ambrose.

6.12   Compare John 19:34.

6.16   Psalm 95:10. The words *a ligno* are not in the Hebrew or Vulgate text but are commonly included in the verse when it is cited by patristic authors.

6.23   The cross is imagined as a balance or scales on which Christ's body counterbalances, and therefore ransoms, the sins of the world.

7   Saturninus, martyr and bishop of Toulouse. The poem forms a pair with 2.8 and was probably written for the same occasion, the dedication by Duke Launebod of a church in Toulouse to Saturninus (*PLRE* 3B:765–66).

8.3   The "victors" are the martyrs.

8.32   On Beretrud's charitable bequests and religious foundations, see Gregory of Tours, *Historiae* 9.35 (*PLRE* 3A:226; *PCBE* 4:339).

9.11–12   The insistent appeals of the Parisian clergy shape Fortunatus's will as hammer and anvil shape metal in a forge.

9.27   Germanus, bishop of Paris, died in 576 (*PCBE* 4:884–94). Fortunatus subsequently wrote his saint's life.

9.33   Fortunatus has in mind the description of priestly garments in Exodus 28 and 29.

9.64   In this allegory, church song is the equivalent of the process of threshing, the church the threshing floor, and the Christians of Germanus's congregation make up the harvest.

9.66   Compare Luke 12:37.

9.72 Compare Exodus 17:11.

10.17 Childebert I, son of Clovis, with his capital at Paris. He died in 558.

10.21 Melchisedech, biblical priest and king of Salem (Genesis 14:18–20).

11.7 Sidonius, bishop of Mainz (*PCBE* 4:1801 Sidonius 2; see also poem 9.9).

11.9 Berthoara, a daughter of Theudebert I (see below), grandson of Clovis. She is not referred to elsewhere.

11.15–20 Theudebert I, son of Theuderic, was king of the Franks between 533 and 547 (*PLRE* 3B:1228–30 Theodobertus 1). Fortunatus probably refers to an expedition into Italy in 539, seeking to benefit from the conflict between the Ostrogoths and the eastern empire.

12 Saint George, Palestinian martyr. The legend of his dragon-slaying is a later development.

13 Trasaricus is generally identified with Trisericus, bishop of Toul (*PCBE* 4:1894–95).

13.4 Compare Matthew 14:29.

13.7 Compare Sulpicius Severus, *Vita Sancti Martini* 3.1–4. After clothing a beggar with half of his cloak, Martin had a dream that night in which Christ appeared to him wearing the cloak.

13.10 Remedius (Saint Rémi), bishop of Rheims (late fifth and early sixth centuries), received veneration as a saint after his death (*PCBE* 4:1600–1604). Fortunatus means that Trasaricus's church contained relics of the apostles Peter and Paul, Martin of Tours, and Remedius of Rheims.

14 According to legend, the Theban legion, under their leader Maurice, refused the orders of the tetrarchic emperor Maximian to turn their weapons against their coreligionists and were martyred at Agaunum (modern Saint-Maurice d'Agaune in the Valais).

14.7 Reydellet (1:191) compares Philippians 1:21.

14.20 Exuperius, Candidus, Victor, and Innocentius. The first three names are provided by Eucherius of Lyon's *Passion of the Mar-*

tyrs of Agaune. A later interpolation refers to the subsequent discovery of the body of a fourth named martyr, Innocentius.

15   Leo argues persuasively that for metrical reasons and because of its untypical content this poem is not by Fortunatus.

15.2   Allobroges, originally a tribe in southeastern Gaul, but used by Fortunatus to stand for Gaul as a whole.

15.6   Arius, whose heresy the poet is referring to, was a Greek from Alexandria.

15.12   According to tradition Arius died when he expelled his bowels while on a toilet.

15.14   The protomartyr Stephen had a vision of God with Christ on God's right hand (Acts 7:55–56).

15.16   Hilary was condemned at the Council of Béziers in 356 for his resistance to Arianism and was subsequently exiled to Phrygia.

15.20   Hilary's twelve-book *De trinitate*. The poem may have been written to introduce a copy of that work.

16   Medard, bishop of Noyon, died circa 557 (*PCBE* 4:1311–12 Medardus 1). The poem apparently celebrates the consecration of a church in Soissons started by Chlothar I and completed by Sigibert to house the saint's remains.

16.18   Compare Matthew 7:13–14.

16.46   Fortunatus means that the saint gave grapes to the robber on his departure to take with him.

Book 3

1   Eufronius was Gregory's predecessor as bishop of Tours (*PCBE* 4:673–79 Eufronius 4). He was bishop from 556 to 573.

1.2   ". . . see himself exalted": Matthew 18:4.

2.6   Aventius is otherwise unknown, presumably a member of Eufronius's clergy (*PCBE* 4:238 Aventius 2).
        Felix, bishop of Nantes (see poems 3.4–3.10).

3.10   Compare John 1:47.

3.17   Compare Matthew 10:16: *estote . . . simplices sicut columbae*.

4   Felix was bishop of Nantes from 549 to 582 (*PCBE* 4:752–57 Felix

9). He is the recipient or dedicatee of the next seven composi-
tions in the collection and of poem 5.7.

4.3   Fortunatus's hyperbolic praise of Felix's prose style in this sec-
tion raises a number of questions. The reference to "the skill of
Pindar" does not imply Felix is writing in verse, just that he
shows similar artistry to Pindar's, in the same way Fortuna-
tus compares Gregory of Tours's prose style with Sophocles's
(8.21.2). The sense of *pedestri glutine suggillatus* is unclear. I
assume Fortunatus follows Prudentius's lead (*Peristephanon*
10.999) in understanding *suggillo* as equivalent in meaning to
suggero. The phrase means simply that the work is in prose. Per-
haps Felix's "more than native skill" suggests he rivals Greek
prose style. From the examples cited by Fortunatus in this let-
ter, Felix possessed an unusually elaborate epistolary style.

Echinades, a group of Greek islands in the Ionian Sea off the
coast of Acarnania.

4.4   The nature of Felix's compliment is not entirely clear. Presum-
ably he spoke of the shouts of praise Fortunatus's work re-
ceived and described Nantes, or more generally Brittany (see
section 6), as "the furthest corner of the world."

4.5   The font of Smyrna refers to Homer. Smyrna was one of the
towns that claimed to be his birthplace. In the *Iliad* (3.237)
Polydeuces (= Pollux) is described as a strong boxer.

4.9   Canobus was, according to Servius (*ad Georgica* 4.287), the
helmsman of Menelaus. By the Cheru(s)ci Fortunatus seems to
have in mind Saxons living in Felix's diocese. In myth the Sym-
plegades were rocks that clashed together to destroy any ship
that attempted to pass between them. The mythical boulders
figure in the story of the Argonauts. Oeta and Pindus are
mountains in Thessaly. The former was the location of the fu-
neral pyre of Hercules. The adjective "Tirynthian" alludes to
the city of Tiryns, with which the hero was often associated.

4.10   The Volsci, a central Italian people and fierce enemies of Rome
in its early history, are cited here as proverbially formidable
fighters.

4.11 Amphion was the mythical founder of Thebes, who moved stones by his lyre playing.

4.13 Fortunatus puns on the name Felix, while employing the conventional formula of blessing *felix qui . . . ,* "Happy he who . . ."

5 The poem is an acrostic. The first letters of each line, read vertically, spell "Fortunatus."

5.7 Gregory of Tours (*Historiae* 5.31) records a later initiative of Felix to control the depredations of the Bretons, apparently a continuation of earlier conflicts.

6.2 Compare 1 Kings 8:1.

6.12 The language suggests a figural relationship between Felix's dedication of the cathedral of Nantes and the Old Testament account of Solomon's temple.

6.14 Fortunatus puns on *Pauli* (of Paul) and *poli* (of the skies).

6.25 Domitianus was bishop of Angers (*PCBE* 4:583–83 Domitianus 4) and Victorius bishop of Rennes (*PCBE* 4:1959–60 Victorius 7).

6.27 Domnulus was bishop of Le Mans (*PCBE* 4:588–90 Domolus 2) and Romacharius bishop of Coutances (*PCBE* 4:1619).

6.35 Compare Virgil, *Aeneid* 4.298.

6.47 *Choraula* is literally a flute player, who accompanies a choir, but here it appears to be employed as a synonym for *chorus,* perhaps with the idea that the voices are flute-like in sound.

6.51 Compare 2 Chronicles 29:27.

6.52 Perhaps the building had two side aisles and a nave, hence the "threefold structure" (so Reydellet 1:94), though Fortunatus's language here and in line 27 is unspecific.

6.53 Compare Psalm 65:15.

7.18 For Allobroges as metonymy for Gaul, see 2.15.2.

7.51 Hilary, fourth-century bishop of Poitiers. Martin had come under his influence early in his ascetic career.

7.55 Ferreolus, martyr of Vienne.

8.18 Literally, "spring of salt." Fortunatus uses "salt" as a literary term not in its classical sense of "wit" but of spiritual substance that seasons a speech (see Colossians 4:6).

9.69   Compare Isaiah 40:12.

9.71   Compare John 20:7.

9.72   Compare John 1:3.

9.90   The concluding section of Fortunatus's poem celebrates the baptism on Easter Sunday of a group of Saxons recently converted by Felix.

9.96   Compare Matthew 25:22–23.

9.103   Gregory of Tours refers to pagan Saxons on the lower Loire (*Historiae* 2.19). Fortunatus plays on *Saxo* (Saxon) and *saxum* (stone).

9.104   The beast is Satan. By baptizing the Saxons, Felix turns them into sheep in his flock (83–84).

10   The river in question is generally identified as the Loire, but it is not named and, as Reydellet (1:104) points out, it could also be the Erdre.

11   Nicetius became bishop of Trier in 525/526 (*PCBE* 4:1373–77). The fact that Fortunatus wrote poems for him indicates he was still alive in 566, but the date of his death is unknown.

11.10   Matthew 25:40.

12.10   Mediolanus has been identified as Niederemmel, just downstream from Neumagen, but the identification is contested.

12.34   The tower apparently contained saints' relics, which served as weapons to protect Nicetius and his congregation.

12.36   The description of the ballista derives from Lucan 3.467–68. The ballista's shot is capable of causing multiple deaths without being halted in its course.

13   On Vilicus, bishop of Metz, see *PCBE* 4:1975–76 Vilicus 3.

13.41   Compare Matthew 25:18.

13a   The subject matter of 13a–d and the titles of 13c and 13d show that the poems were composed by Fortunatus for a banquet given by Vilicus.

14.2   Fortunatus plays on Carentinus's name and the Latin word *carus* (dear). On Carentinus see *PCBE* 4:423–24 Carentinus 2.

14.3–4 Fortunatus plays on the words *colonus* (cultivator) and the Latin name of Cologne (*Agripina Colonia*).

14.12   Matthew 19:19 and 22:39; Mark 12:31.

14.14   Compare 1 Corinthians 13:13.

15	On Aegidius, bishop of Reims, see *PCBE* 4:615–18 Egidius 4.
15.21	Matthew 4:4; Luke 4:4.
16	If Hilary is to be identified with the subject of poem 4.12, he was of noble family and a high officeholder before becoming a priest (*PCBE* 4:1012 Hilarius 9).
17	Bertram succeeded Leontius the Younger as the bishop of Bordeaux. He died in 585 (*PLRE* 3A:227; *PCBE* 4:341–45 Berthechramnus 1).
17.1	Fortunatus uses the word *raeda,* a word regularly used by classical authors, though of Gallic origin.
18.8	Fortunatus associates the forum of Trajan with the public reading of poetry (7.8.26). In late antiquity Claudian, Sidonius Apollinaris, and Merobaudes all had statues erected to them in the forum.
18.16	It appears that in trying to incorporate language from earlier poets in his verse, Bertram had composed lines that were metrically incorrect (they halt in their metrical feet).
19	It is unclear where Agricola was bishop (*PCBE* 4:89).
20	A "pyx" is a liturgical vessel for holding the host in the Eucharist. The Latin word *turris* suggests it had a tower-like shape. For Felix, bishop of Bourges, see *PCBE* 4:758–59 Felix 12.
20.6	Compare Genesis 4:4. The offering of Abel is regularly a figure of the Eucharist.
20.8	As Reydellet (1:198–99) points out, Fortunatus here combines two stories, of the widow's mite (Mark 12:42–44 and Luke 21:1–4) and the widow of Sarepta, who gave food to Elijah (1 Kings 17:8–16).
21	Avitus, bishop of Clermont from 571 to circa 594 (*PCBE* 4:265–68 Avitus 5).
21.11	The text in line 11 is problematic. In most manuscripts the line is lacking a syllable or two. Conjectures that fill the lacuna are not entirely convincing. I have translated the text as it stands. I think it is unlikely that the omitted word would have much altered the sense.
22a.8	"Our fathers," that is, bishops (see line 2).
23	On Ageric, bishop of Verdun, see *PCBE* 4:71–72 Agericus 1.

23.14   Presumably Ageric either built or completed work on baptisteries (or a baptistery). Fortunatus's language is unspecific, in part because of the verbal play in the Latin: *fontes . . . exples* and *fonte repletus.*

23a.17   Compare 2 Timothy 2:20–21.

24   The reference to Leontius of Bordeaux in line 19 suggests Anfion was a priest of that city (*PCBE* 4:141).

25   For Paternus see also 7.23 (*PCBE* 4:1432 Paternus 4).

25.2   That is, Paternus acts paternally.

25.6   The "corrected manuscript" referred to in the superscription is probably one written by Fortunatus himself (so Meyer, 29, n. 1). He here asks pardon for mistakes he has failed to catch in the attempt to correct the manuscript.

26   Rucco is Fortunatus's nickname for Ragnemod (9.10.1), who was to become bishop of Paris after Germanus's death in 576. Ragnemod died in 591 (*PCBE* 4:1585–86).

28.8   Hilary is presumably the addressee of poem 3.16. Anthemius is the addressee of the following poem (*PCBE* 4:150). The manuscripts waiver in the spelling of his name between "Anthemius" and "Anthimius." I have adopted the former in my translation.

30.2   The poem is in epanaleptic elegiac couplets; that is, the first half of the first line of the couplet and the second half of the second are identical (see too poem 8.2).

30.7   Compare Matthew 11:30.

Book 4

1   Eumerius, bishop of Nantes, was the predecessor, and probably father, of Felix of Nantes (see line 32). He died in 549 (*PCBE* 4:690–91 Eumerius 3).

1.26   Compare Matthew 13:8 and 23.

1.29   The cathedral of Nantes; see poem 3.6.

2   Gregory, bishop of Langres from 506/7–539/40, was the great-grandfather of Gregory of Tours (*PCBE* 4:910–14 Gregorius 1).

2.12   For Gregory's posthumous miracles, see Gregory of Tours, *Vita Patrum* 7.3–5.

3   Tetricus, son of Gregory of Langres; he succeeded his father as
         bishop of Langres (539/40–572/73; *PCBE* 4:1863–65).

3.2   The native land of the Christian is heaven. Life on earth is a
         temporary alienation from one's true home.

3.8   See 3.8.18.

4   Gallus was bishop of Clermont from circa 525 to circa 551 (*PCBE*
         4:849–53 Gallus 3). A number of the details of Gallus's life in
         this poem coincide with those given by Gregory of Tours, *Vita
         Patrum* 6.

4.13   Quintianus, bishop of Clermont, whom Gallus succeeded (see
         17–18; *PCBE* 4:1565–67).

4.16   Theuderic I, son of Clovis, king of the Franks from 513 to 534.

5   The elder Ruricius was bishop of Limoges from circa 485 to
         circa 506 (*PCBE* 4:1635–49 Ruricius 1). His grandson seems to
         have been bishop of the same city in the second quarter of the
         sixth century (*PCBE* 4:1650–51 Ruricius 2).

5.8   The Anicii were one of the most prestigious families of Rome in
         late antiquity. The connection of the Ruricii to this family is
         unclear.

5.9–10   This couplet is excluded by Leo on inadequate grounds and in-
         cluded in his *Appendix* as poem 32.

5.18   Matthew 6:19–21; Luke 12:33–34.

6   Exocius, successor of the younger Ruricius as bishop of Limoges
         (*PCBE* 4:725).

6.4   That is, died in his place.

6.19–22 One manuscript, *Parisinus lat.* 13048, contains this coda, in
         which Fortunatus seeks the bishop's heavenly intercession,
         though it omits verse 20. The concluding couplet is identical
         to that of poem 4.27. Verse 20 is supplied from that poem by
         Koebner, *Venantius Fortunatus,* 139–41, followed by Reydellet. I
         am not convinced the coda is in place here. When Fortunatus
         attaches such petitions to epitaphs, those epitaphs always ad-
         dress their subject in the second person. This is not the case in
         this poem. Leo omits the coda and includes verse 19 in his *Ap-
         pendix* as poem 33.

7   Chaletricus attended the Council of Tours in 567 (*PCBE* 4:459–

60). Fortunatus spells his name "Chalactericus" in the body of the text, presumably for metrical reasons.

7.16   That is, he sang in praise of God. Fortunatus may have in mind the common metaphor of the tongue as the plectrum that produces human speech and song.

8   There are records of Cronopius attending church councils in 506, 511, and 533 (*PCBE* 4:474–75).

8.24   A reference apparently to the suffering of the city under Visigothic rule (see Sidonius Apollinaris, *Epistulae* 7.6.7–9).

9   Leontius I attended the council of Orleans in 541 but probably had died by 552 (*PCBE* 4:1142–45 Leontius 15).

9.20   It is a familiar paradox of almsgiving that the performer of the charitable act retains what he has given in the form of spiritual benefits in the life to come.

9.38   Theudosius is otherwise unknown (*PCBE* 4:1881 Theodosius 4).

10   Leontius was bishop of Bordeaux from circa 552 until circa 570. His precise relationship to the elder Leontius, whom he succeeded, is unknown. He, his foundations, villas, and wife are the subject of poems 1.6 and 8 to 20.

10.26   Placidina, wife of Leontius (see poems 1.14, 15.93–110, and 17).

11   Victorianus was abbot of Saint Martin d'Asan in Spain (d. 558).

12   See poem 3.16.

12.4   Compare Genesis 3:19.

13.1   Fortunatus compares human life to a day. Whatever the length of that life, its light is short and transitory in the larger scheme of things.

13.6   Servilio will have held the office of *domesticus,* perhaps at the court of Metz.

14.10   For the metaphor see 3.8.18.

15.5   I have not been able to represent Fortunatus's play on *securus* (heedless, off his guard), and *securis* (ax).

17   Despite various conjectures, nothing certain is known of Arcadius beyond the evidence of this poem.

17.9   Compare Horace, *Carmina* 3.25.1–2, *Quo me, Bacche, rapis tui / plenum?*

18   Poem 1.7 celebrates a church built by Basil and his wife, Baudegund.

18.10   The mixed metaphor—language of water and irrigation in line 9, of light in line 10—does not strike me as in Fortunatus's manner. I suspect a couple of lines have dropped out.

23.6   That is, as treasure in heaven; see 4.5.18, 16.18, and 27.18.

23.14   Compare 1 Peter 2:5.

23.15   This John is perhaps identical with the addressee of poem 3.28.

25   Theudechild is generally identified with the queen of that name mentioned by Gregory of Tours (*Gloria confessorum* 40), the daughter of Theuderic I and Suavegotha (*PLRE* 3B:1233 Theudechildis 1). Poem 6.3 is also devoted to her.

25.10   She was sister of Theudebert I, daughter of Theuderic I, and granddaughter of Clovis.

25.11   The feminine form *(nudae)* shows that Fortunatus envisages women as especially benefiting from Theudechild's charity.

26   Fortunatus probably became acquainted with Vilithuta and her husband, Dagaulf, in Poitiers.

26.5   Compare Virgil, *Aeneid* 1.462.

26.7   Sometimes identified with the Dagaulf mentioned in Appendix 9.15, but the only evidence is the coincidence of name.

26.10   "With the setting of the light," a phrase normally used of sunset, here refers metaphorically to Vilithuta's death.

26.79   The second death (after death on earth) is failure to win eternal life and consignment to punishment (Revelation 20:6 and 14).

26.93   Both were believed to have been translated to heaven on chariots (see Genesis 5:24 and 2 Kings 2:11). The two are often paired.

26.94   Peter heads the apostles, Stephen the martyrs.

26.97   All three were virgin martyrs, Agnes and Agatha of Rome and Catania, respectively. Thecla of Iconium was the subject of apocryphal Acts, with widespread cult in both East and West.

26.103   Compare Hosea 10:8; Luke 23:30.

26.105   Compare Matthew 5:26.

26.107   Compare Matthew 3:12; Luke 3:17.

26.114   Compare Matthew 13:43.

26.118   Compare 1 Corinthians 3:13.

26.153   The transmitted text is short a foot. Leo is probably right that *omnis* is corrupt and that the line ended with another antitheti-

cal pair of epithets. He proposes *acer amoenus* (the fierce and the gentle) as an approximation of what might have been the original wording.

27.14   Namatius died in 559 after a relatively brief episcopate (*PCBE* 4:1349–50 Namatius 5). His predecessor was still bishop in 552.

28.18   *Tibi* (for you), has no obvious referent in the poem but seems to have an indefinite sense.

BOOK 5

1   Martin of Braga, born in Pannonia, but subsequently moved to Galicia, where he founded a monastery at Dumio and later (569) became bishop of Braga (in modern Portugal). The *primipilus* was the senior centurion in a Roman legion.

1.1   "Come to visit him in the breeze after midday," as he did Adam (Genesis 3:8).

1.2   Considerations of prose rhythm suggest the words "the great tidings of your letter" *(epistolae vestrae magna),* are corrupt, but no persuasive emendation has been proposed. The language of what follows is influenced by Judges 6:36–40 (see Sedulius, *Hymni* 1.43).

1.3   Salt and honey represent complementary qualities of Christian eloquence for Fortunatus. Salt seasons speech with substance and force, honey sweetens with charm.

1.5   Fortunatus is playing on the words *alumen* (alum) and *lumen* (light). On Spain as a source of alum, see Pliny, *Naturalis Historia* 35.184.

   For the fireproofing properties of alum, see Gellius 15.1.

1.6   For Fortunatus's critical language in this section, see the note on *Praefatio* 1.

1.7   Chrysippus (ca. 280–207 BCE) was the third head of the Stoic school in Athens, successor to Cleanthes (331–232 BCE; see below). Pittacus (ca. 650–570 BCE) was one of the seven sages. All three, along with Aristotle, are associated together by Juvenal (2.5–7).

   Probably Gregory of Nazianzus.

   "The company of Cleantheses" are presumably the proponents

of a severe moral doctrine like the Stoics (see *censura* above in this section). Fortunatus here plays on the words *clientela* and *Cleantharum*. Martin's writings show the influence of the Roman Stoic, Seneca the Younger.

1.8   See Luke 10:33–35.

I have been unable to represent the play on the words *dignissime, dignatio,* and *dignitatem*.

1.9   "A second intermediary," after Martin of Tours (see the next section).

1.10   "Lord Martin," that is, Martin of Tours.

Martin of Tours is recorded to have brought three people back to life (Sulpicius Severus, *Vita Sancti Martini* 7 and 8, *Dialogi* 2.4).

The church of Braga possessed relics of Martin of Tours (Gregory of Tours, *Gloria Martyrum* 1.11). Reydellet (2:164) draws attention to a striking coincidence in wording between Sidonius Apollinaris (*Epistulae* 7.1.7), Gregory of Tours (*Virt. Iuliani* 2, explicitly quoting Sidonius), and Fortunatus in this passage.

2.22   The Sueves ruled the kingdom of Galicia for most of the sixth century.

2.25   See 1 Kings 18:41–45. In Martin's case the rain is metaphorical, of his teaching.

2.29   Martin combated Arianism and converted the Suevian kingdom to orthodoxy.

2.30   The oleaster is the wild olive. Compare Romans 11:17.

2.33   Compare Matthew 21:19 and Mark 11:20.

2.50   For the metaphor see 3.8.18.

2.52–58   See Matthew 25:14–23.

2.62   More literally, "Peter's gate open."

2.67   Genesius, martyr of Arles.

2.68–70   Caesarius, bishop of Arles (502–542) and prior to that a monk at Lérins. His Rule, written for his sister's convent in Arles, was subsequently adopted by Radegund, probably in the late 560s, for the Convent of the Holy Cross.

3   The poem celebrates the entry of Gregory into Tours as its new bishop. Its dramatic date is September 573.

3.10   Fortunatus plays on Gregory's name and the Latin for "flock"

(*gregis*). I have not been able to represent this in my translation.

3.11 Julian of Brioude, an Arvernian martyr to whom Gregory and his family were especially devoted.

3.13 On Aegidius of Rheims see poem 3.15. The manuscripts spell his name variously "Egidius" or "Igidius."

3.31–32 Luke 16:22.

3.33–34 Matthew 25:20–23.

3.37 Athanasius, fourth-century bishop of Alexandria, like Hilary of Poitiers an opponent of Arianism.

3.39 Probably Gregory of Nazianzus.

3.40 Basil, bishop of Caesarea (370–379).

4 The *natalicium* in question is presumably the anniversary of Gregory's ordination as bishop.

5 Gregory of Tours was later to give his own version of the events that form the subject of this poem, which differs in some details from Fortunatus's (*Historiae* 5.11). The events took place in 576.

5.5 Here, "prophets" refers to Christian bishops and priests.

5.7 Compare Matthew 5:15, Mark 4:21, Luke 8:16.

5.15–16 Compare Matthew 25:20–23.

5.22 Blomgren 1 (123), followed by Reydellet, takes *inane cutis* of circumcision. I think the reference is to dropsy, used metaphorically of the effects of pride, as in Prudentius, *Peristephanon* 2.237–40.

5.25–26 Compare 2 Corinthians 3:13–15.

5.45 The lawgiver (*legifer*) is Moses.

5.47–48 Genesis 18:1–4. Luce Pietri, "Venance Fortunat," 134–35, traces Fortunatus's argument in this and the following lines to Book 4 (25–29) of Hilary of Poitiers's *De trinitate*.

5.49–50 Genesis 19:1–3 and 22–23.

5.51–52 Genesis 19.24: "*Igitur* Dominus *pluit super Sodomam et Gomorrham sulphur et ignem* a Domino *de caelo.*" Fortunatus interprets the two uses of the word *Dominus* in this verse as the two persons of the Trinity: the Father and the Son.

5.57 Fortunatus may have in mind Psalm 95:10 in the form *Dominus regnavit a ligno* (see 2.6.16).

5.58   Isaiah 7:14.

5.62   See lines 27–28.

5.69   Goffart, *Rome's Fall,* 313–14, argues that the Jewish community in Clermont included newcomers from Marseilles.

5.75   Christians claimed to be the "true Israel," as opposed to the alleged spurious authenticity of the Jews.

5.94   For the metaphor see 3.8.18.

5.105–6 That is, Pentecost, which fell on May 24 in 576.

5.113   Baptisms would normally take place at Easter.

5.129   Abraham's offering of his son Isaac (Genesis 22:1–19).

5.145   Avitus had been Gregory's teacher (*Vita Patrum* 2, *praefatio*).

6   For Syagrius see *PCBE* 4:1847–53 Syagrius 5. For the layout of the figure poem and its interwoven texts, see the section Figure Poems in this volume.

6.1   "My practice went to waste," seems to refer to practice in writing.

        Fortunatus plays on the words *vello* (to pluck, pull out) and *vellus* (fleece), and on *carmino* (to card; to compose poetry) and *carmen* (poem). I have been unable to represent the play in English. Metaphorically, Fortunatus's subject matter is the raw wool that he then "cards/composes" into verse.

        It is not clear why Fortunatus describes the person in question as a "fellow captive." Perhaps, as Reydellet (2:170) suggests, the poet considers his own silence a form of captivity.

6.2   The metaphor at the end of this section is from pressing grapes and storing the wine so produced.

6.4   "Fellow citizen," generally taken to mean the man in question was Poitiers. But could he have been from Italy? For an example of Fortunatus intervening on behalf of a fellow Italian, see poem 5.18.

6.6   "Your martyr," refers to Saint Symphorian of Autun. Fortunatus is afraid that the spiritual value of Syagrius's charitable act will be compromised if it is seen just as a commercial transaction. For the opposition between earthly cash *(nummus)* and heavenly talents, see 10.17.13.

6.7   *Ars Poetica* 9–10. For Pindaric Horace see, for instance, Sidonius Apollinaris (*Epistulae* 9.13.2, vs. 8–9), "Horace guided his lyric

steeds to Pindaric song" *(Flaccus lyricos Pindaricum ad melos / . . . flexit equos).*

6.8   "I wove a poem of just that number of verses and letters," that is, a poem of thirty-three lines and thirty-three letters to the line, conforming to the number of years of Christ's life.

6.11   "Fivefold," alluding to the three vertical and two diagonal verses that run through his composition.

6.14   "Two . . . read at the sides," refers to the acrostics and telestichs formed by the initial and final letters of each line.

6.15   The letter *M*, middle letter of the twenty-three letter Roman alphabet.

6.16   Arachne, cited by Fortunatus as the exemplary weaver (compare his *Vita Sancti Martini* 2.87).
         Exodus 28:6 and 35:35.

6a.9   Tempe, in origin a famous beauty spot in Thessaly, the valley of the river Peneus. Here used metonymically for a beautiful location.

6a.19   The word *aie* is a transliteration of the Greek ἀεί (always).

7   As Meyer, 87 observes, the word *Item* (Again), in the title is anomalous. It is used elsewhere when a poem is directed to the same addressee as the one that precedes it. The poem is also unusual because it is in hexameters.

7.1   The verb here is perhaps corrupt. It is alien to Fortunatus's normal practice to delay the object of a verb as long as he does here *(pondus* in line 4).

7.4   Compare Matthew 11:30.

7.8   The exact location of Felix's Cariacum estate (also referred to at 10.25.7) is unknown, but it was apparently by the river Loire.

8.9   By "the present servant" Fortunatus means the bearer of the letter.

8b   The book seems to have contained religious poetry composed by Gregory as well as by other poets.

9.7   Identified as Maroveus, bishop of Poitiers, who was at loggerheads with the Convent of the Holy Cross *(PCBE* 4:1261–64).

9.9   Literally, "by wish, by instruction, and by word sent." I take it Fortunatus is distinguishing between three modes of communication with Maroveus.

9.10   The content of the promise is unclear, perhaps to return to
         Poitiers within a certain period of time (see Reydellet 2:173).

9.13   "Your daughters" are Radegund and Agnes.

14.6   For this miracle of Martin, see Gregory of Tours, *Gloria confesso-
         rum* 7.

14.7   The line is metrically incomplete in the manuscripts. I print the
         conjecture of Blomgren 3 (120), adopted by Reydellet.

19   Aredius was founder and abbot of a monastery at Attanum
         (Saint-Yrieix) near Limoges. He died in 591 (*PCBE* 4:185–90).
         For details of his life, see Gregory of Tours, *Historiae* 10.29.

19.9   Aredius's mother, Pelagia, was a woman of some sanctity in her
         own right (see Gregory of Tours, *Gloria confessorum* 102; *PCBE*
         4:1460–61).

BOOK 6

1   Epithalamium for the Austrasian king Sigibert and his Visi-
         gothic bride, Brunhild. The marriage took place in Metz in
         566, making this the earliest datable poem from Fortunatus's
         time in Gaul.

1.7   Most manuscripts read *praemittens,* which gives little sense. My
         translation represents a possible meaning (compare Leo's criti-
         cal apparatus, *expectes praelibans*).

1.9–10 For the belief in the asexual reproduction of bees from vegeta-
         tion, see Virgil, *Georgics* 4.197–205.

1.20   Fortunatus plays on *duces,* "lords," and *decus,* literally, "glory."

1.23   Fortunatus is presumably addressing the royal couple and their
         entourage, described in the previous lines. His language is in-
         formed by the traditional classical idiom for poetic inspira-
         tion.

1.25   The rest of the poem is written in hexameters rather than For-
         tunatus's usual elegiac couplets. The hexameter is the tradi-
         tional meter in late antiquity for epithalamia.

1.75–79 A difficult passage. Chlothar I, with the aid of his brother
         Theuderic I and his nephew Theudebert, defeated the Thurin-
         gians probably in 531 (Gregory, *Historiae* 3.7) and subsequently
         put down the Saxons (in the mid-550s), who received help

from Thuringian allies (*Historiae* 4.10). It is not clear what action took place by the river Naab, in Bavaria. Fortunatus perhaps combines the two campaigns of Chlothar (so Reydellet 2:47). Verse 77 is corrupt. I have adopted Leo's suggested emendation (in his critical apparatus), *de Theudebertcho pietas venit patrueli,* though without a great deal of confidence in its correctness. I take it Fortunatus's point is that Sigibert possesses the military valor *(virtus)* of Chlothar, as demonstrated by the latter's military victories, but while Chlothar needed the aid of Theudebert, Sigibert embodies the qualities of both in one man.

1.112   There is no clear indication where Venus's speech ends. Because of the switch to third person and narrative in lines 113–15 and because line 112 makes an appropriate concluding *sententia,* I would finish the speech after 112. The succeeding second-person in line 116 *(carpis)* is somewhat anomalous.

1.118   In Fortunatus's writings *Germania* usually refers to Austrasia, sometimes Francia as a whole.

1.119   Or "by a single marriage"—the Latin can bear either sense.

1.124   Athanagild, king of the Visigoths (555–568; *PLRE* 3A:140–41 Athanagildus 1). Spain, his kingdom, was in Roman thought traditionally viewed as the extreme West.

1a.11–12 The campaign against the Saxons and Thuringians took place in the mid-550s (Gregory, *Historiae* 4.10 and 16). Sigibert's participation is nowhere else mentioned.

1a.29   Brunhild converted from Arianism (Gregory, *Historiae* 4.27).

1a.33   The two vows were her marriage and her conversion to orthodox Christianity.

2   Charibert, son of Chlothar I, ruled the western Frankish kingdom after his father's death (561–567), with his capital in Paris (*PLRE* 3A:283–84 Charibertus 1).

2.5   That is, the four compass points of north, south, east, and west.

2.19   Childebert I ruled the kingdom subsequently held by Charibert between 511 and 558. He was Charibert's uncle.

2.21–26   Childebert's wife was Ultrogotha, his daughters Chrodoberga and Chrodoswinth. They were exiled by Chlothar after Childebert's death (Gregory, *Historiae* 4.20) but recalled by Charibert.

2.60   Fortunatus refers to the law by which Charibert succeeded to
        the kingdom (so Reydellet 2:55). Childebert I (Charibert's un-
        cle) and Chlothar I (his father) had successively ruled the king-
        dom before him.

2.78   See Psalm 131:1, *Memento, Domine, David, et omnis mansuetudinis
        eius* (remember David, Lord, and all his mildness). The clausula
        of the line is unmetrical, requiring shortening of the initial syl-
        lable of *vitae*.

2.84   The Fabii represent old Roman virtue.

2.97   A Sicambrian is a Frank. Sicambria was a legendary home of the
        Franks.

2.107   I have with some hesitation accepted the emendation of Blom-
        gren 3 (122–23) *tui* for the manuscript reading *Dei*. Blomgren
        persuasively cites the similar sentiments in the panegyric for
        Chilperic (9.1.95–96).

3   Fortunatus also wrote Theudechild's epitaph (poem 4.25).

3.4   Theudechild's brother was Theudebert I, her father Theuderic
        I (*PLRE* 3B:1233 Theudechildis 1).

3.24   Theudechild performed her acts of charity in secret (4.25.15–16).

4.10   The Christian virgin is the bride of Christ.

5   Galswintha (*PLRE* 3A:503), daughter of the Visigothic king
        Athanagild and Goiswintha, and elder sister of Brunhild, mar-
        ried Chilperic I in 568 or 569. Fortunatus's poem probably
        dates to 570 or soon thereafter, shortly after Galswintha's
        death. Gregory (*Historiae* 4.28), in a later account of her mar-
        riage and death, records she was murdered on the orders of her
        husband.

5.10   The line is very obscure and the translation uncertain. I tenta-
        tively take it to mean that they do not know whether they will
        die young (in life's dawn).

5.13   "Two towers," that is, Brunhild and Galswintha.

5.17–19 Compare Luke 6:48–49.

5.27   There is a slight anacoluthon here. Lines 25 and 26 interrupt the
        sequence of thought. The first half of line 27 picks up on the
        content of 23 and 24.

5.32   That is, Galswintha uses her own limbs in place of physical con-
        straints to tie down her mother.

5.91   The "new royal powers" derive from Galswintha's newly aug-
mented royal status by her coming marriage to Chilperic.

5.145   That is, no less of a wanderer and stranger than Galswintha.

5. 175   "My final destiny," that is, of death. The words of Galswintha in
this speech are prophetic of her fate.

5.176   It is not clear whose anger is referred to here. Both Ovid (*Heroi-
des* 12.209) and Seneca (*Medea* 953) use a similar phrase of Me-
dea.

5.254   Fortunatus's metaphor here may be influenced by the miracle
that took place at Galswintha's tomb (lines 276–80), where a
lamp falls to the ground but is not extinguished.

5.277–80   Gregory gives a version of this miracle (*Historiae* 4.28).

5.290   Presumably Brunhild failed to pay her respects by not writing to
her or visiting her.

5.301   Fortunatus plays on *Germania* (Germany) and *germana* (sister).

5.346   Because she was not present at the wedding, Goiswintha did
not see her efforts in bringing up Galswintha brought to frui-
tion.

5.368   Respectively, Brunhild, Sigibert, Ingund, Childebert II, and
Leovigild. (Athanagild died in 567.)

6   Ultrogotha, widow of Childebert I; she died in 558 (*PLRE* 2:1182
and 3B:1391).

6.19–20   The "holy precincts" (*limina sancta*) of line 19 are, I take it,
shrines of saints, equivalent to the *loca sacra* of line 21. But in
line 20 Fortunatus exploits the ambiguity of the phrase, be-
cause the "holy precincts" Childebert now occupies are those
of heaven. The following couplet (21–22) repeats the sense of
these lines and points to their interpretation.

6.24   She had two daughters, Chrodoswintha and Chrodoberga.

7   The location of the villa is unknown. The reference to Aredius
in the second line (compare poem 5.19) suggests the region of
Limoges.

7.6   Fortunatus paradoxically reverses the normal sentiment. In-
stead of painted fruit looking so lifelike you would think it was
real, here real fruit looks so colorful you would think it had
been painted.

8   Presumably the events in this poem took place when Fortunatus was at the court in Metz shortly after his arrival in Gaul.

8.6   Apollonius of Tyre, the hero of the *Historia Apollonii Regis Tyri,* who was forced to flee his native land and suffered shipwreck and other misfortunes at sea.

8.19   "Pen," literally, "book, codex."

8.21   Vilicus, bishop of Metz (see poem 3.13).

8.23   Leo, following Mommsen, reads *cucurri* for the manuscript reading *cucurrit,* which improves the sequence of thought. I wonder whether there is a lacuna here in the manuscripts. Normally, *praestitit* would be followed by an object or noun clause of result. (As it is, *auxilium,* "help," has to be understood from the previous couplet.)

8.26   That is, on the more heavily laden boat all would have been shipwrecked (see the following couplet).

8.37   Gogo, a counselor of Sigibert, subsequently *nutricius* of Childebert II (see poems 7.1–4; *PLRE* 3A:541–42).

9   Dynamius (ca. 545–ca. 595) was a Gallo-Roman who pursued an administrative career in his native Provence, becoming *rector provinciae* (*PLRE* 3A:429–30 Dynamius 1). He was also a literary figure: two of his letters survive, along with a *Life of Maximus of Riez* and one line of his poetry.

10.33   Fortunatus puns on Dynamius's name. *Dunamis* in Greek means "power." Dynamius's legal expertise is praised in line 37.

10.44   The son of Telamon in question is generally identified as Ajax, but I wonder whether Fortunatus means to refer rather to Teucer, who was exiled by his father (Horace, *Carmina* 1.7.21–22) and so would have hurried back to a reconciliation.

10.57–58   Fortunatus appears to refer to verses of Dynamius circulating pseudonymously.

10.67–69   Theodorus is the bishop of Marseilles (*PCBE* 4:1876–79 Theodorus 7), Sapaudus archbishop of Arles (*PCBE* 4:1706–13 Sapaudus 4). Felix is probably the senator from Marseilles mentioned by Gregory of Tours (*Historiae* 4.46 and 6.7, *PLRE* 3A:481 Felix 3). Jovinus, *rector Provinciae* under Sigibert (572/73), is the addressee of two poems of Fortunatus (7.11 and 12; *PLRE*

3A:715–16 Iovinus 1). Albinus succeeded him as *rector Provinciae* (*PLRE* 3A:38 Albinus 2). Helias is unknown.

BOOK 7

1   For Gogo see 6.8.37.

1.1–2 Fortunatus's language is chosen to suggest an analogy with weaving. *Pecten,* here translated "plectrum," is also used of the comb that tamps down the threads *(fila)* in weaving. Fortunatus describes the lyre strings as set up like the warp of a web *(orditas).* It is perhaps also relevant that the thumb plays a crucial role in spinning (see 2.16.108).

1.24 A complicated combination of metaphors: more literally, "the wave of your salt swims with seasoned kindling." *Sal* (literally, "salt") is regularly used by Fortunatus of eloquence (see 3.8.18); hence, such eloquence can be described as "seasoned" *(condito).* But *sal* is also a regular metonymy for the sea. Fortunatus can then speak of "the wave of the salt sea" *(salis unda),* implying Gogo's eloquence has the force of sea waves. *Fomes* (literally, "kindling for a fire"), is elsewhere used by Fortunatus of heated prayers (3.21.12). Here too it seems to refer to heat, in this case of Gogo's eloquence.

1.41–42 Gogo was sent to Spain to escort Sigibert's Visigothic bride, Brunhild, to Metz.

2.1   Reydellet (2:87) takes the word *vestis* of the various hangings and coverings that decorate the banquet hall rather than of clothing.

2.3   Apicius, famous first-century CE gourmet and writer on culinary matters. His name became proverbial.

4.16 The river that "takes its name from salt" is the Seille, *Salia* in Latin. In the previous line Fortunatus enumerates rivers in northeastern Francia (Austrasia).

4.27 Lupus, duke under Sigibert and Childebert II and an influential figure at court (*PLRE* 3B:798–99 Lupus 1). Poems 7.7, 7.8, and 7.9 are addressed to him.

5	Bodegisil, duke first in Provence and then in Austrasia (see lines 19–24; *PLRE* 3A:235–36 Bodegesilus 1). He died in 585.
5.18	The second half of the poem enumerates Bodegisil's actions.
6	Gallomagnus was bishop of Troyes (*PLRE* 3A:501 Gallomagnus 1).
6.23	"Magnified in status," literally, "great" *(magna)*. Fortunatus plays on the name of her father, Gallo*magnus*.
7	For Lupus see 7.4.27.
11	The Latin noun *provincia* (translated here, "Provence") may refer to any territory outside Italy under the administration of Rome. But in a Gallic context and without further qualification, it signifies the region of southern France known today as Provence.
7.11–12	Fortunatus plays on the words *fundatus* (founded), *profundus,* (profound), and *fundis* (pour). For the metaphors in this line and line 14, see 3.8.18.
7.15	In the next poem (7.8.43) Fortunatus talks of Lupus's "words flavored with honey" *(melle saporatum . . . verbum)*. That is presumably what is meant here by "rich flavoring." This and the following line speak of Lupus's mental and verbal skills, the "twin talents" of verse 17.
7.49–50	Nothing further is known of this victory over Saxons and Danes.
7.58	*Laugona* is identified by Forcellini as the river Lahn.
7.65	"Our masters" are the royal couple Sigibert and Brunhild.
8.35–36	Fortunatus draws an analogy with the Ark of the Covenant and the tablets of the Law (Deuteronomy 10:3–5).
8.59	The idea is that in climbing a mountain, after each stage a new height to be scaled appears. So, in writing of Lupus, there is always a new honor to praise.
8.63–64	It is not clear what Fortunatus means by "Achillean strain" *(Achilliaca);* perhaps an epic-style poem roughly in the manner of the *Iliad*. The *harpa* and *crotta,* which I have translated "harp" and "lute," were stringed instruments, generically *citharae*. The *harpa* was oblong, the *crotta* triangular in shape.
9.7	Consequently the poem was written circa 574.

9.20   Compare Matthew 25:40.

10   Magnulf is only known from this poem (*PLRE* 3B:804 Magnul-
        fus).

10.4   Fortunatus plays on the name Magnulf and the Latin *magnus*
        (great).

10.5   Sigimund, addressee of poem 7.21 (with his brother Alagisil) and
        Appendix 4 (*PLRE* 3B:1149 Sigimundus).

12   For Jovinus see 6.10.69.

12.14   The name of three kings of Pergamum (241–197 and 158–133
        BCE). The third in particular was proverbial for his wealth.

12.15   I adopt the repunctuation of Blomgren 1 (128), with a comma
        after *recubet* and no punctuation at the end of line 15.

12.16   Ulysses brought about the death of Palamedes by planting in his
        tent a forged letter implicating him as a traitor.

12.17   Astur, a member of Aeneas's army, described in the *Aeneid*
        (10.180) as "most beautiful" *(pulcherrimus)*.

12.20   Quirinus is Romulus. It is not clear why he is called *celer* (quick);
        perhaps, as Reydellet suggests (2:186), for his alacrity in dispos-
        ing of his brother and rival Remus. There is a potential polem-
        ical point in insisting Romulus died a normal human death,
        since he is generally said to have experienced apotheosis.

12.25–26 Archytas was a fifth- and fourth-century BCE mathematician
        and philosopher—Horace refers to his speculations about the
        heavens (*Carmina* 1.28.4–6)—Aratus a third-century poet, au-
        thor of a didactic work on astronomy, the *Phaenomena*. For
        Chrysippus and Cleanthes see 5.1.7.

12.27   There is no known poet named Lysa, and no persuasive emen-
        dations have been suggested.

13   The addressee of the poem is identified with the Felix who be-
        came bishop of Treviso and whom Fortunatus describes as his
        "companion" *(socius)* in *Vita Sancti Martini* 4.666. He had been
        a fellow student of Fortunatus in Ravenna.

14   Mummolenus, Gallo-Roman, native of Soissons, and important
        figure at Sigibert's court (perhaps a duke; *PLRE* 3B:898–99
        Mummolenus 2).

14.23–24 The Persian fruit refers to peaches.

15	Berulf, later (580–585) duke of Tours, Poitiers, Angers, and Nantes (*PLRE* 3:229–30 Berulfus).
15.8	Perhaps writing to and thinking of Berulf provided Fortunatus with "greater satisfaction" than he received from the delayed meal. Reydellet (2:111) takes *Deum* as the antecedent of the relative clause.
16	Conda is only known from this poem. A high court official, rising to the rank of "majordomo" *(domesticus)*, administrator of the palace and royal estates, Fortunatus will have known Conda in his later years when he continued to be honored by Sigibert (39–42).
16.17	Theuderic I (511–533), son of Clovis. The duties of a tribune are unclear.
16.19	Theudebert I (533–547), son of Theuderic I.
16.27	Theudebald (547–555), son of Theudebert I, was still a child when he ascended to the throne (*PLRE* 3B:1227–28 Theodebaldus 1).
16.33	Chlothar I, son of Clovis (d. 561).
16.47	Perhaps he participated in a campaign of Chlothar against the Saxons in 555 (Gregory, *Historiae* 4.16; *PLRE* 3A:331).
18	Flavus, identified by Meyer (90) with a *referendarius* mentioned by Gregory of Tours (*Historiae* 5.45), but apart from the name the poem gives no support to this identification. A *referendarius* was one of the most important royal ministers, who dealt with various aspects of the king's affairs, including the financial.
18.15	"Romulean whisperings," that is, Latin.
18.21	That is, carved into wood.
20	See 7.10.5.
20.9–10	Apparently a reference to the Lombards.
20.12	Compare Horace, *Carmina* 1.3.8 and 2.17.5.
21.9–10	I take it the brothers referred to are Sigimund and Alagisil (so *PLRE* 3B:1149, *contra* Reydellet 2:118). Fortunatus's point seems to be that the brothers cause him no longer to be a stranger in Francia because they have recently been in his native Italy.
22	Boso is known only from this poem. For the role of the *referendarius,* see poem 7.18.

22.6   Matthew 14:31.

23   See poem 3.25.

25   Fortunatus celebrates Galactorius's appointment as count in poem 10.19 (*PLRE* 3:501). The poem must be misplaced at the end of Book 7, since the first seven books were published in or around 576, while this poem can have been written no earlier than 585, when Gundegisel succeeded Bertrand as bishop of Bordeaux (see line 7).

25.26   Fortunatus is playing on the words *apices,* "epistle"—more literally, "letters of the alphabet," and *pices,* "pitch."

BOOK 8

1   The poem appears to be a circular, addressed to a variety of recipients, seeking poetry on religious subjects for the convent at Poitiers.

1.1–2   Fortunatus playfully inverts the expected verbs in these two lines so that his addressees drink a sound and listen to a liquid. They drink in the Muses and absorb with their ears the waters of Castalia.

1.9   The verb *retinentur* (are possessed), is anomalously third rather than second person. The usage is ungrammatical in Latin.

1.23   King of the Thuringians Herminfred was killed and his kingdom conquered by the Franks in 531 (see Appendix 1). According to Gregory (*Historiae* 3.4) he killed his brother Berthar, Radegund's father.

1.35   "Free only in her devotion": the phrase is unclear. I tentatively suggest that in her self-abjection she is like a slave but that her self-subjugation paradoxically bestows freedom on her (see the next line).

1.41–46 Paula, along with her daughters Eustochium and Blesilla, were members of Jerome's circle in late fourth-century Rome. Paula and Eustochium established monasteries together in Bethlehem with Jerome as adviser after he had been driven from Rome. Marcella and Fabiola were also members of Jerome's circle. The Melania is probably Melania the Elder, founder of

BOOK 8

a monastery in Jerusalem. Martha is the biblical figure (Luke
10:38–40; John 12:2). Because of the reference to tears, the
Mary must be Mary Magdalene, who cried beside Christ's
tomb (John 20:11), not Martha's sister. Eugenia is the third-
century Roman martyr. Thecla of Iconium, according to the
apocryphal *Acts of Paul and Thecla,* was converted by the apostle
Paul and went on to suffer persecution and finally martyrdom.
Jerome heavily criticizes Fabiola for remarrying after divorce.
As Reydellet points out (2:189), this has relevance to Rade-
gund, who was separated from her husband, Chlothar. Fabiola
sets an example of how to pursue a life of Christian asceticism
after such a separation. Jerome refers to Fabiola's second mar-
riage as a "wound."

1.50   Fortunatus's *Life of Saint Radegund* emphasizes her practice of
mortification of the flesh.

1.54   Gregory is Gregory of Nazianzus, and Basil is Basil of Caesarea.

1.56   The common cause of Athanasius and Hilary is opposition to
Arianism.

1.59   Sedulius (second quarter of the fifth century) is the one poet in
this list. His *Carmen paschale* was very influential on Fortuna-
tus.

1.60   The date when the Convent of the Holy Cross (as it came to be
called) adopted the Rule of Caesarius is a matter of debate.
Conventionally, it has been put in the late 560s, though some
argue for an earlier date.

1.65–66   A difficult couplet. I adopt Meyer's punctuation (109) and imag-
ine that Fortunatus is asking his addressees, who are described
as devoted to poetry at the beginning of the poem, to send
their compositions, perhaps hymns, to be sung at the convent.
Fortunatus twice refers to the choir of sisters singing holy
songs (*carmina sancta* at 5.2.65–66 and Appendix 19.11–14).

2   For Germanus, bishop of Paris (d. 576), see poem 2.9. He was a
supporter of Radegund and her convent. For the epanaleptic
form see poem 3.30.

2.13–14   The conceit appears to be that he will not refuse to go to Paris
as Germanus has instructed him, but since Germanus and Ra-

873

degund are "equal in heart," as in, like-minded, to meet the wishes of one is to meet the wishes of them both. Fortunatus will travel to Paris but all the same he will remain spiritually present with Radegund in Poitiers.

3   The poem is generally believed to have been written for Agnes's assumption of the role of abbess, probably in the early 570s.

3.17–18   Peter brought Tabitha back to life (Acts 9:36–43).

3.20   The ranks of martyrs are led by the protomartyr Stephen (Acts 7:55–59).

3.33–36   For Thecla and Eugenia see 8.1.46. Reydellet notes (2:131) that six of these female martyrs, Euphemia (of Chalcedon), Agatha (of Catania, Sicily), Justina (of Padua), Paulina (of Rome), Agnes (of Rome), and Eugenia, are represented in the wall mosaic depicting a procession of female saints in the Basilica of Sant'Apollinare Nuovo in Ravenna. Thecla's high status makes her an appropriate member of Fortunatus's catalog, but the more obscure Basilissa is perhaps included because her name means "queen," and so she is especially appropriate to Radegund, herself a former queen.

3.38   The book of life that records the names of those who will be saved at the Last Judgment (Revelation 3:5). For its recording the names of martyrs, see Prudentius, *Peristephanon* 4.171–72 and 10.1131–35.

3.39–44   Caesarius, bishop of Arles, founded a convent in that city and composed a Rule for the foundation (*PCBE* 4:386–410 Caesarius 1). Its first abbess was his sister Caesaria (*PCBE* 4:381–83 Caesaria 1). The Caesaria mentioned here may be Caesarius's sister or her successor, also named Caesaria (*PCBE* 4:383–85 Caesaria 2). Liliola succeeded the younger Caesaria as abbess, perhaps in the late 550s and certainly by 561/62 (*PCBE* 4:1180–81).

3.55   "Holy mother," that is, Agnes.

3.73   *Agentis,* translated "of your agency," is a play on Agnes's name, the genitive of which is *Agnetis,* "of Agnes."

3.99   Biblical figures: Sarah the wife of Abraham, Rebecca of Isaac, Rachel of Jacob; Esther and Judith biblical heroines; Anna per-

haps the mother of Samuel, though there are various biblical
Annas; Naomi the mother-in-law of Ruth.

3.133 See Revelation 4:4 and 10.

3.135 See the identical line at 4.26.93.

3.137 Isidore (*Origines* 5.14) describes Paul's pronouncements as equiv-
alent to those of a legal expert *(iurisconsultus),* who would give
authoritative rulings on the questions posed to him.

3.148 Nadaber, a city in Ethiopia (see 5.2.9).

3.153–54 All three martyrs are subjects of poems in Prudentius's *Peristeph-
anon* (13, 7, and 5, respectively). Cyprian was martyred in Car-
thage; Quirinus in Siscia (Sisak) in ancient Pannonia (modern
Croatia); Vincent in Valencia, though born and venerated in
Saragossa.

3.155 Martyred under Diocletian at Verulamium (modern Saint Al-
bans).

3.161 For the circumstances surrounding the martyrdom of Privatus,
bishop of Javols, see Gregory, *Historiae* 1.34.

3.165 The word *Felicem* does double duty, for the proper noun "Felix,"
the name of the saint, and the adjective, "happy."

3.167 For Vitalis see 1.2.16.

3.172 For the martyrs of Agaune see poem 2.14.

3.179–80 Late Latin Christian authors often speak of the company of
heaven in terms of the Roman senate. The *toga praetexta,* which
I have translated "robes of state," was worn by Roman magis-
trates.

3.195 The hemorrois is a snake whose bite causes extensive bleeding
from many parts of the body (Lucan 9.806).

3.243–44 Compare Luke 7:38 and John 12:3. In Luke's gospel a woman
washes Christ's feet with her tears and wipes them with her
hair. The virgin in Fortunatus's poem, in the absence of Christ,
lets her tears fall on the paved floor of a chapel and wipes them
with her hair. In my translation I have added "with my tears" to
clarify the analogy.

3.291 Genesis 37:23–28; Exodus 14:27–28.

3.297–98 For Sapphira see Acts 5:1–10; for the woman who gave her two
mites, see Mark 12:42–44 and Luke 21:2–4.

3.304   Judith 12:19.

3.310   Fortunatus speaks of Bishop Gundegisel as "an altar of God who shines for the glory of his people" (7.25.8). Martin (*Mart.* 4.578) is an "altar for sinners" *(ara reorum)*. Fortunatus seems to think of the altar as a metaphor for the role of bishops or other holy persons in their mediation between God and humans.

3.329–30 Pregnancy is likened to dropsy because both cause a swelling of the body: according to Fortunatus pregnancy is a dropsy caused by pleasure.

3.347   No entirely satisfactory supplement for the lacuna has been proposed. Supplying *lenit sero* would give the sense "a delay in snatching away her hope did not alleviate her strong grief." The thought that the child did not live even for a short while coheres well with the following line, where the mother is denied even the consolation of hearing her child's weeping.

3.384   The point is that given her status, a queen might be imagined to suffer less, but even her suffering is beyond telling.

3.385–86 See 1 Corinthians 7:25–38 (especially 38).

4   Meyer (112) describes this as a recruitment letter, seeking to enlist new members of Radegund's convent.

5   The poem is an acrostic. The first letters of each line spell out Radegund's name *(Radegundes)*.

6   The last couplet shows the poem is addressed to Agnes also.

8.15–18 A reference to Radegund's custom of going into retreat in her cell for Lent (Fortunatus, *Vita Sanctae Radegundis* 22.52–53).

9.11   The meaning of this line is unclear. The normal meaning of *ceu* (as if), does not give good sense. Fortunatus seems to be making the point that Radegund's seclusion disturbs his sense of time: her absence seems longer than it is, just as at other times her presence seems shorter (line 12).

11.3   Gregory mentions a priest Leo of Tours in *Virt. Martini* 4.25.

12   This poem refers to the disturbances at the Convent of the Holy Cross in 589 after the deaths of Radegund and Agnes (Gregory, *Historiae* 9.39–43 and 10.15–17). The abbess was named Leubovera.

12.4   That is, pagans.

12a   This letter and the previous poem will have been sent together
         to Gregory. The syntax of the letter presents some difficulties.
         I take *causa . . . habens* as a hanging participle *(nominativus pen-*
         dens). The phrase *quod petiit et . . . commisit* (which she sought . . .
         and entrusted), is only loosely incorporated into the sentence.

13   The poem is spoken in the person of Justina, niece of Gregory
         of Tours, who became prioress of the convent (*PCBE* 4:1085–
         86).

13.5–6   Armentaria, Gregory's mother, is restored to Justina, her grand-
         daughter. Presumably Armentaria traveled to Poitiers for the
         meeting (*PCBE* 4:201–3 Armentaria 2).

18.5–6   Fortunatus presumably has in mind the gift of an estate on the
         Vienne referred to in the next two poems.

19.10   Compare John 16:15.

20   The description of the poem as "in the form of a prayer" *(precato-*
         ria) does not conform with its content, except for the last line.

20.1   On two occasions Martin clothed a poor beggar (Sulpicius
         Severus, *Vita Sancti Martini* 3 and *Dialogi* 2.1).

21.13   See Revelation 6:11, 7:9, 7:13.

Book 9

1   The poem was written in the context of a council of bishops
         summoned by King Chilperic in 580 to the royal villa of Berny-
         Rivière, where Gregory was accused of having spread slander-
         ous rumors about Queen Fredegund (Gregory of Tours, *Histo-*
         riae 5.49). The first four lines suggest it was commissioned by
         Gregory and the other bishops.

1.8   Compare Isaiah 11:1.

1.27–28 Fortunatus gives the translation of Chilperic's name. The first
         part of the name is related to the German *Hilfe*.

1.34   Chlothar, Chilperic's father, had seven sons by various mothers,
         four of whom survived him.

1.45–50 Chilperic was besieged in the city of Tournai by his brother Sig-

ibert and feared for his life until Sigibert himself was assassinated (Gregory of Tours, *Historiae* 4.50–51). Fortunatus is usually studiedly vague about Chilperic's fraught relations with his brothers, having recourse to generalizations and abstractions.

1.53   Perhaps an oblique reference to the assassination of Sigibert.

1.73   *Euthio* does not occur elsewhere. It is unclear whom Fortunatus is referring to.

1.103   "Your uncle" is presumably Charibert (see 6.2.97–100).

1.110   Horace (*Ars Poetica* 291) praises *limae labor* (the work of the file) in smoothing and refining poems. Gregory of Tours criticizes Chilperic's poetry (*Historiae* 5.44) for faulty metrics.

1.116   By the birth of sons (Reydellet 3:13).

1.128   Radegund either prays for Chilperic or sends him her good wishes and greetings (or both).

2   A poem of consolation to the royal couple for the deaths of two sons, Chlodobert and Dagobert, in 580, shortly after the council of Berny-Rivière (Gregory, *Historiae* 5.34 and 50).

2.4   I have been unable to preserve the paronomasia, *morsu* (bite) and *mors* (death); see 2.2.5.

2.3–14 Genesis 4:8.

2.15–16 Genesis 4:25.

2.23   Genesis 14:18.

2.26   See Exodus 19:3 and 34:1–3.

2.39   Both were taken up to heaven alive, escaping death (see 4.26.93).

2.42   With the frequent association of *homo,* "man," and *humo* (from *humus*), "earth."

2.48   Compare Genesis 3:19.

2.73–74 For the metaphor see, for instance, Psalm 2:9 and Ecclesiasticus 33:13.

2.82   Compare Wisdom 2:2 and 5:15.

2.96   Rigunth (*PLRE* 3B:1087–88).

2.99–100 Job 1:18–21.

2.101–2 2 Samuel 12:18–23.

2.103–6 2 Maccabees 7. Poem 10.15.1–4 explains that the mother of the Maccabees is "twice blessed," because of the nobility of her ancestry and the glorious martyrdom of her sons.

2.113–14   See Matthew 3:12 and Luke 3:17.

2.125   The palm-decorated tunic *(tunica palmata)* was an element of consular regalia in late antiquity.

2.132   Job had seven additional sons and three daughters (Job 42:13).

2.136   See 2 Samuel 12:24.

5   The poem is an acrostic, spelling out with the initial letters of each line the name *Dagobercthus.*

6   This poem serves as an introduction to the succeeding poem, which is in the Sapphic meter.

6.10   Perhaps a reference to the estate *(agellus)* Gregory had given the poet (poems 8.19 and 20). Fortunatus pleads the pressures of harvest time also in the dedicatory letter to his *Vita Sancti Martini* (1).

6.13   Fortunatus plays on two senses of *condo,* "to compose (a poem)" and "to store up," as in granaries.

7.9   Flaccus is the Roman poet Horace (Quintus Horatius Flaccus), likened by Fortunatus to Pindar (see note on 5.6.7).

7.39   Mopsus here is a proverbially bad poet. The associations are post-Virgilian. Calpurnius Siculus *(Eclogues* 3.59–60) refers to "the piercing voice of Mopsus, his crude songs, and the din of his raucous pipe" *(torrida Mopsi / vox et carmen iners et acerbae stridor avenae)* Nemesian *(Eclogues* 1.16) to his "discordant blasts" *(dissona flamina).*

7.44   The final adonic of the Sapphic stanza could be termed an epode. So too could the iambic dimeter that complemented the trimeter in epodic compositions. Both are shorter verses completing a metrical unit.

7.48   Because their names did not fit into the metrical scheme of the Sapphic meter.

7.81–84   For Justina see poem 8.13.

7.89   The manuscripts break off here. Leo, in the critical apparatus, compares lines 17 to 20 and 50 and suggests that the missing words reminded Gregory once more that Fortunatus was long out of practice with such compositions.

8   Bishop of Meaux *(PCBE* 4:331). The poem is identical to 5.12, addressed to Gregory.

9	For Sidonius of Mainz see poems 2.11 and 2.12.

9.4 The line is incomplete in the manuscripts. Leo suggested in his apparatus supplying *gaudia, crede, dapis.* The line would then mean "believe me, by your hunger for food, you have deserved rejoicing."

9.13–14 Fortunatus now turns to address Sidonius directly.

9.25 Fortunatus attributes to Sidonius the building of a baptistery (2.11) and a church of Saint George (2.12).

9.31 The line is metrically incomplete in the manuscripts. *habeas* is Leo's supplement.

10 See poem 3.26. Ragnemod became bishop of Paris after Germanus's death in 576.

10.1 Rucco is a familiar name for Ragnemod.

10.9 "Your daughters," refers to Radegund and Agnes.

10.13–14 I interpret this to mean that Ragnemod sent the convent a jeweled cross. The enthroned cross is a common iconographic motif (see, for instance, the dome of the Arian baptistery in Ravenna).

11 Droctoveus, abbot of Saint Vincent in Paris (*PCBE* 4:597–98).

12 Faramod may be the brother of Ragnemod, who unsuccessfully attempted to succeed his brother as bishop of Paris in 591 (Gregory of Tours, *Historiae* 10.26; *PLRE* 3A:477; *PCBE* 4:731).

12.5 That is, to Chilperic and Fredegund.

12.8 The man in question is the letter carrier.

13 Lupus and Waldo were probably deacons of Paris (*PCBE* 4:1212 Lupus 10).

13.9 For Droctoveus see poem 9.11.

13.11–12 Mummolus was an official at Chilperic's court, identified as a *praefectus* by Gregory (*Historiae* 6.35 and 7.15: *PLRE* 3:901 Mummolus 3). Caesarius and Constantine are otherwise unknown.

14 Gregory of Tours (*Gloria martyrum* 41) gives his own later version of the miracle, quoting some of Fortunatus's poem. He locates it at Brionae in Italy. For Lawrence see 1.2.14.

15.1 Paros, one of the Cyclades, was famous for its marble. I have been unable to represent the paronomasia of *Parum* and *paries* (wall).

15.7   I have adopted, with no great confidence, Leo's proposed emendation *in medio* for *inmitior* of the manuscripts, which gives no sense.

16   Chrodin (512–582), duke under Sigibert and Childebert II, praised for his generosity in almsgiving by Gregory of Tours (*Historiae* 6.20; *PLRE* 3:312–13).

16.19   "The nations" here means non-Roman tribes, preeminently in this context the Franks.

Book 10

1.2   Reydellet (3:40) persuasively argues that the sermon is intended for the clergy of Poitiers, whom Fortunatus addresses as "my dearest sons" at the beginning of the work. Presumably, it is to inform their preaching.

1.3   "Let the clouds rain down justice": Isaiah 45:8.

1.5   "I am a foreigner on earth": Psalm 119:19.

1.11   "Mutually bearing your burdens": see Galatians 6:2.

1.12   ". . . a house divided against itself will not stand": Matthew 12:25.

1.13   The Arians, Fotinians (followers of Photinus, a priest of Sirmium), and Sabellians were all heretics who challenged the Christological and Trinitarian teachings of the orthodox church.

    The text here is irredeemably corrupt. Fortunatus clearly contrasts his Christian audience, whose father is God, with the heretics, fathered by the devil.

1.18   "Pray even for our enemies": see Matthew 5:44 and Luke 6:28.

1.20   "Father, where I am let them too be with me": see John 17:24.

    "Then the just will shine like the sun in the kingdom of their father": Matthew 13:43.

1.25   "Then we will be snatched up together in the clouds to meet Christ in the air, and so we will always be with the Lord": see 1 Thessalonians 4:17.

1.26   The text is corrupt here. Leo suggests something like *vel paterna frui praesentia* (and to enjoy the father's presence), but the sentence still lacks a main verb.

"Cracks of rocks from the face of God, they would then want mountains to fall": compare Revelation 6:15–16.

1.27 "Blessed are the poor in spirit, for theirs is the kingdom of heaven": Matthew 5:3.

1.28 See Matthew 5:4–9.

1.33 "He works in you his will and his works according to his good pleasure": Philippians 2:13.

"You did not choose me, but I you": John 15:16.

"Otherwise I, a man, have discovered Christ": This sentence is oddly obtrusive. Leo, in his critical apparatus, suggests it should be deleted; Reydellet (3:49) proposes that it is a gloss.

1.34 "I will show him how much he must suffer for me": compare Acts 9:16.

1.35 "Father, if it is possible may this cup pass from me. But not as I wish, but as you": see Matthew 26:42, Mark 14:36, and Luke 22:42. Fortunatus's quotation does not correspond exactly to any of the Gospel texts in the Vulgate.

1.36 I have omitted *non voluntatem*. It is difficult in wording and sense and its elimination secures a perfectly balanced antithesis.

"My God, his mercy will go before me": Psalm 59:10.

"It is God who justifies the unholy": Romans 4:5.

"The spirit breathes where it wishes": see John 3:8.

1.37 "Who has not, even what he has will be taken from him": see Matthew 13:12.

1.38 The "teacher" is Jesus.

"He who tells a lie speaks on his own account": see John 8:44.

1.39 "The will is present with me": Romans 7:18. See 10.1.33.

1.40 "Chosen vessel": Acts 9:15.

"What do you have that you did not receive?": 1 Corinthians 4:7.

1.42 "Every good gift and every perfect blessing is from above": James 1:17.

1.43 "Two ways": Matthew 7:13–14.

"The vocation to which you have been called by the Lord Jesus Christ": see Ephesians 4:1.

1.44 "No one chose or came to the way unless he was called by him who is the way and the life and the truth": see John 14:6.

"If the son frees you, then you will be freed": John 8:36.

1.45 "If you keep to my word, you are truly my disciples, and you will know the truth and the truth will free you": John 8:31–32.

1.50 "I have not come to do my own will but the will of him who sent me": John 6:38.

1.54 "I am the living bread who came down from heaven": John 6:41.

1.56 "praying unceasingly": see 1 Thessalonians 5:17.

1.57 "Elijah was living in the desert": 1 Kings 19:3–8.

1.60 "By the measure you have measured with it will be meted out to you": Matthew 7:2.

"I will sing of mercy and judgment to you": Psalm 101:1.

1.62 The sermon breaks off here. Presumably an incomplete text was included among the writings Fortunatus left behind at his death.

2 *Vir illustris* (distinguished gentleman), denotes the highest rank of senator. Salutaris is otherwise unknown.

2.5 "Though divinity was promised": see Genesis 3:5.

2.7 "Enoch will not escape it": see 9.2.39.

The patriarch, lawgiver, and the prophets are Abraham, Moses, Isaiah, and John the Baptist.

For the biblical women see 8.3.99. Elizabeth is John the Baptist's mother.

2.16 For David's reaction to losing a son see 2 Samuel 12:20.

Leo suggests in his apparatus that the lacuna contained an *exemplum* of a father who wished for his daughter's death so that she could enjoy a heavenly marriage.

2.17 I have tried to make some sense of the beginning of this section, but it is not at all clear. Leo (in his critical apparatus) suspects the text is corrupt.

1 Corinthians 15:52.

3.1 The addressees are the servants of the *reges* referred to in section 4.

3.4 "Your most excellent lords": presumably Childebert II and Brunhild.

The transmitted text, *necessaria,* yields no sense. Leo, in his apparatus, suggests *necessitate* should be read here and omitted after *utilitate* in the previous clause. He understands it as a mis-

placed correction of the manuscript reading *necessaria*. I have translated accordingly.

4   The letter is written in the person of Radegund to the mother of a recently deceased girl who had been a member of the Poitiers convent. Elena Malaspina, "Letterati forestieri," 83, suggests that the addressee was the wife of Salutaris, addressee of poem 10.2.

5   See also poem 10.10 on the same building.

5.5–6   Luke 1:11–19.

5.7–8   Luke 1:26–33.

6   The poem contains two sets of epigrams (1–78 and 79–132) written to accompany images in Gregory's newly restored cathedral in Tours, which he completed in 589/90 (*Historiae* 10.31.18). There is a good deal of overlap in the content of the two sequences, suggesting they are alternative versions.

6.3–10   For the combination of these three miracles (Sulpicius Severus, *Dialogi* 2.1, 3.10.6, and 2.2.1–2), see poem 1.5.

6.25–28   See Sulpicius Severus, *Vita Sancti Martini* 3.1–4.

6.33–34   See Sulpicius Severus, *Vita Sancti Martini* 18.3–4.

6.36   The Jordan was believed to be able to cure leprosy (Gregory of Tours, *Gloria martyrum* 16 and 18).

6.39–40   See Sulpicius Severus, *Vita Sancti Martini* 7.

6.41–42   Martin restores a woman's dead son in Sulpicius Severus, *Dialogi* 2.4.4–9, though she is not said to be a widow. In a separate story (*Vita Sancti Martini* 8), Martin brought back to life a man who had hanged himself.

6.43–46   See Sulpicius Severus, *Vita Sancti Martini* 13. Martin makes the sign of the cross in order to check the falling pine in its course.

6.49–52   See Sulpicius Severus, *Dialogi* 2.2.4–7.

6.55–58   See Sulpicius Severus, *Vita Sancti Martini* 11.

6.61–64   See Sulpicius Severus, *Dialogi* 3.9.4.

6.67–70   See Sulpicius Severus, *Vita Sancti Martini* 19.1.

6.93   Martin was born in Sabaria, modern Szombathely, in Hungary.

6.110   Fortunatus seems to imagine that after giving his own tunic to the poor man, Martin received a rudimentary short-sleeved tunic in its place (see 1.5.9).

6.121–24 In Sulpicius Severus's account (*Vita Sancti Martini* 13.9), the miracle of the pine tree is immediately followed by conversion of the pagans who had resisted the tree's felling.

6.125–28 See Sulpicius Severus, *Dialogi* 3.9.1–2 (the heavenly reinforcements also owe something to *Vita Sancti Martini* 14.5).

7 This and the next two poems are evidence of a visit by Fortunatus to the Austrasian court, probably in 588. It is generally said that Fortunatus accompanied Gregory of Tours when he traveled to Metz in 588 (see *Historiae* 9.20), though while this is probable, it is not provable. (Fortunatus is not mentioned by Gregory.)

7.13 Sulpicius Severus (*Dialogi* 2.5.6) describes scattering ashes on himself and donning a hair shirt as Martin's "familiar expedients" *(nota praesidia)*.

7.16 Compare Revelation 4:4.

7.22 Compare Revelation 21:27.

7.25 Radegund died on August 13, 587.

7.55 See Sulpicius Severus, *Dialogi* 3.14.3–5. (For the other miracles referred to in this poem, see poem 10.6.)

7.59–64 Fortunatus prays that Childebert II will have new children by his wife Faileuba (he had two sons already) and that Brunhild will thereby acquire grandchildren from her daughter-in-law, as well as from her daughter Chlodosinda, who was promised in marriage to the Visigothic king Reccared.

8.19 At this point, Fortunatus turns from addressing the royal couple to address Brunhild specifically.

9 The poem recounts a journey Fortunatus took down river from Metz to Andernach in the company of Childebert II and his mother Brunhild (the "royal pair" of the first line) and members of the Austrasian court.

10 See also poem 10.5 on the same building.

10.4–7 Luke 1:26–38.

10.9–10 It is unclear whom Fortunatus is referring to here.

10.11 Cosmas and Damian, brothers and physicians, martyred near Cyrrhus, Syria, according to the legend, during the persecution of Diocletian.

10.13–14   Julian of Brioude (see 5.3.11).

10.19–20   In Sulpicius Severus's account (*Dialogi* 3.10.6), the ex-prefect Arborius testifies that he saw the jewels on Martin's hand and heard them clashing together.

10.21–22   Victor, martyr of Marseilles (see 8.3.156).

10.23–24   Nicetius of Lyon, great-uncle of Gregory of Tours, died in 573 (and so comparatively recently). Gregory attributes miracles to Nicetius during his lifetime (*Vita patrum* 8.4–5); hence, his "powers were of long standing" (*PCBE* 4:1369–73 Nicetius 5).

11   The poem was probably written on the occasion of an attempt in 589 to reimpose taxes on Tours, which Gregory successfully resisted (*Historiae* 9.30).

11.3   The "bronze" referred to here may be the bronze-stringed instrument referred to in 10.9.55 (perhaps a kind of harp).

11.11   Judging by the title of the poem, the "hall of blessed Martin" refers to a villa associated with Martin, perhaps as part of the church property.

11.19–20   Gregory is apparently absent from the banquet, though responsible for giving it.

11.34   "Your joys" is ambiguous. It could refer to the joy brought by the tax assessors (by relieving Tours of tax) or the joy provided for them in the dinner.

12b   Romulf was one of the tax assessors sent to Tours to organize tax collection (Gregory of Tours, *Historiae* 9.30; see the previous poem). Gregory styles him "count of the palace" (*comes palatii; PLRE* 3B:1094–95 Romulfus 1).

12c   Gallienus is otherwise unknown. He was probably a count at Tours (*PLRE* 3A:501; see line 2).

12d   Florentinus, like Romulf, was one of the tax assessors sent to Tours to organize tax collection (Gregory of Tours, *Historiae* 9.30, where he is described as the "mayor of the queen's palace," *maior domus reginae,* and his name is spelled "Florentianus"; *PLRE* 3A:487–88).

14   Formerly archdeacon of Tours, Plato was elected bishop of Poitiers in 591 (*PCBE* 4:1492–93 Plato 2). This is the latest datable poem of Fortunatus.

15.1–4   For the mother of the Maccabees and her seven martyred sons, see 9.2.103–6.

16   Sigoald is the addressee of this poem as well as the next two. Gregory makes one mention of him, as an envoy sent by Childebert II to Guntram (*Historiae* 7.14); otherwise, he is known only from these poems. This poem celebrates his appointment as count, perhaps of Poitiers (*PLRE* 3B:1150–51 Sigivaldus 3).

17.22   His grandfather was Chlothar.

17.24   His great-grandfather was Clovis.

17.31   Various attempts have been made to fill the lacuna. As Meyer says (130), probably some word identifying the festival has been omitted (he suggests *sancti* or *Paschae*).

18   The *defensor* (defender) was a civic official, whose original role was to defend the *plebs* against abuses by the powerful. By the Merovingian period that role had largely been taken over by bishops, and the *defensor* represented the interests of the church.

19   For Galactorius see poem 7.25.

19.11   The Cantabrians were a northern Spanish tribe.

19.16   The emperor Justinian (527–565). He came from a relatively humble background in Thrace and subsequently served among the *scolares* (the palace guard).

19.20   "He wielded sacred power," as bishop.

19.26   The pentameter is missing in all manuscripts.

19.27–28 The two virtues are imagined as bodyguards, protecting Galactorius's person.

Book 11

1   After its introductory section Fortunatus's interpretation of the creed derives largely from the *Expositio Symboli* of Rufinus of Aquileia (*CCSL* 20:125–82), written in 404.

1.2   "The Holy Spirit came down . . . ": Acts 2:1–4.

1.3   *symbolum* is the Latin word for "creed."

1.4   "He who comes to God should believe": Hebrews 11:6.
          "Heartfelt belief attains to justice": see Romans 10:10.

"I believed and therefore I spoke": 2 Corinthians 4:13.

"The just man lives by faith": Romans 1:17.

"Unless you believe, you will not understand": Isaiah 7:9 (a non-Vulgate version).

1.8   "Who will tell of his birth?": Isaiah 53:8.

1.10   "Before the morning star I bore you from my womb in the brilliance of the saints": Psalm 109:3.

"This is our God and no one will be likened to him": Baruch 3:36.

"He was seen on earth and lived among men": Baruch 3:38.

1.13   "oil of rejoicing": see Hebrews 1:9 and Psalm 44:8. It is contrasted with ordinary human oil, which is material and corruptible.

"The Holy Spirit is on me because it has anointed me": Isaiah 61:1.

1.18   "The gate that looks to the East will be closed and not be opened and no one will pass through it, since the Lord God of Israel himself will pass through it and it will be closed": see Ezekiel 44:1–2.

1.23   Fortunatus's biblical quotation combines Ephesians 1:18 and 3:18.

1.25   See John 3:14, "just as Moses raised up a serpent, so the Son of Man must be lifted."

1.28   "Dissolved the judges' mutual hostility": compare Luke 23:12.

1.29   "My life has drawn near to hell and I have become free among the dead": see Psalm 87:4–6.

"You are he who is to come": see Matthew 11:3.

1.31   "Ascending on high he took captive captivity": Ephesians 4:8.

"Who is this king of glory?": Psalm 23:8.

1.32   "Your seat has been prepared, Lord": Psalm 92:2.

"The Lord said to my lord, sit on my right": Psalm 109:1.

"Soon you will see the Son of man sitting on the right of power": Matthew 26:64.

1.34   "Behold the Lord almighty is coming": Malachi 3:1.

"Behold in the clouds of heaven one like the Son of man": Daniel 7:13.

888

> "Like lightning from the East, so will be the coming of the Son of man": see Matthew 24:27.

1.37 "My dove is the one and only": Song of Songs 6:8.

1.39 "The dead will rise and be awakened": Isaiah 26:19.

"Those who are in the dust of the earth will rise up then": Daniel 12:2.

1.40 "Have you not read that the dead will rise again?" and "He is not the God of the dead but of the living": see Matthew 22:31–32.

"What you sow will not receive life unless it first dies": 1 Corinthians 15:36.

"After the resurrection they will be like angels of God": see Matthew 22:30.

2.1–2 For Radegund's practice of Lenten retreat see 8.8.15–18.

3 That is, the anniversary of Agnes's consecration as abbess.

3.10 Fortunatus plays on *agnus* (lamb) and Agnes's name.

4.11–12 1 Timothy 5:23.

5.1 Compare Horace, *Carmina* 1.1.2, *dulce decus meum*.

5.15–16 "She who bid me write," refers to Radegund, the "mistress" of line 5.

14 Agnes apparently has sent Fortunatus a gift of a milk product, some form of stiffened cream that still bore the imprint of her fingers when he received it. The fingerprints, however, quickly disappeared.

15.3–4 1 Corinthians 3:2.

18.5 Fortunatus has in mind the fruit from the Tree of the Knowledge of Good and Evil in the Garden of Eden.

24.1 Compline was the last office of the day. Gifts could not be received after it.

25.5 Eomundus is not otherwise known.

25.7 Cariac, perhaps an estate belonging to Felix of Nantes. Poem 5.7, addressed to that bishop, speaks of the "beautiful estate of Cariacum" by the river Loire (8).

25.8 Saint Albinus had spent his early life at the monastery of Tincillac (Fortunatus, *Vita Sancti Albini* 5.13), where he later became abbot.

25.9   Domitianus, bishop of Angers (d. before 572), dedicatee of For-
        tunatus's *Vita Sancti Albini*. Albinus's festival was on March 1.

26.13–14   Genesis 1:2.

26.13–18   These lines are found only in one manuscript (*Parisinus lat.*
            13048), which alone also preserves the poems of the Appendix.

APPENDIX

1   The Thuringian kingdom was destroyed by the brothers Theu-
        deric and Chlothar in 531 (Gregory, *Historiae* 3.7). Radegund,
        niece of the Thuringian king Hermanfred, was taken prisoner
        and subsequently became the bride of Chlothar. The poem is
        written in the voice of Radegund, in an attempt to restore re-
        lations with her long-separated cousin Amalfred (see *PLRE*
        3A:50–51).

1.11   It was a particular refinement at a banquet to have servants of
        the same age (see Virgil, *Aeneid* 1.705).

1.31–32   This general grief at the destruction is to be distinguished from
           the tears mothers were not able to shed over the bodies of
           their children.

1.35–36   The point seems to be it would have been kinder to have died
           than to be left behind to weep alone for the dead.

1.50   Radegund's father was Berthar, brother of Hermanfred.

1.126   The phrase *oppositaque fide* (on a charge of disloyalty) is diffi-
         cult. It could equally mean "though asserting his loyalty." Rade-
         gund's brother, whose name we do not know, was killed on the
         orders of Chlothar (Gregory of Tours, *Historiae* 3.7).

1. 129–32   Radegund's brother apparently wanted to join Amalfred in the
             East but was held back by devotion to his sister.

1. 143   The sense of *listra* is uncertain. It is thought either to refer to
          funerary gifts or specifically to a kind of hem for a bier. In ei-
          ther case it is not clear why Radegund should also send her
          brother such a gift while he was still living (but *vivo* is an emen-
          dation of Leo's). My translation, "gifts," is a neutral place-
          holder.

1.159–60 One sister of Amalfred was betrothed to the Lombard king Audoin.

1.165–66 A puzzling couplet, not susceptible of easy emendation. The manuscript text implies that Amalfred is in contact with Frankish royalty and can thereby recommend Radegund to them.

2 The poem conveys Radegund's thanks to the emperor Justin II (565–578) and the empress Sophia for sending her relics, including a fragment of the holy cross (see Baudonivia, *Vita Sanctae Radegundis* 16 and 17). The poem was presumably written in 569, shortly after receipt of the relic.

2.18 For the metaphor see 3.8.18.

2.26 The Council of Chalcedon condemned Monophysitism and affirmed a creed accepted as orthodox in the West. In sixth-century theological disputes in the East, the council's decisions remained contentious.

2.30 For the Cantabrians see 10.19.11.

2.39–40 The bishops were exiled under Justinian for opposing his religious policies and his attempts to conciliate Monophysites.

2.69 According to legend Constantine's mother, Helena, discovered the holy cross.

2.79–80 The "wood" is, of course, the cross. The metaphor of plowing is frequently used of missionary activity. The apostle is Paul.

2.94 The manuscript reading, *plebs trabeata* is puzzling, virtually an oxymoron, since in late antiquity the *trabea* was an ornate garment worn by consuls. I have translated the phrase as the equivalent of the Virgilian *gens togata* (*Aeneid* 1.282), referring to the Romans.

3 The poem is in the voice of Radegund and addressed to Artachis, Radegund's nephew or grandnephew *(nepos)*. It responds to the news that Amalfred, addressee of Appendix 1, is dead. Some think Artachis was Amalfred's son.

3.7 Berthar and Hermanfred, respectively (see line 33). According to Gregory of Tours (*Historiae* 3.4) Hermanfred was responsible for the death of his brother.

3.24   "The waters" in question are Radegund's tears. The Latin could also mean that the fever was relieved by the tears, but since Radegund is describing the extremity of her grief, this seems unlikely. The paradox that fires are fed by water is very much in Fortunatus's manner.

3.26   The first bereavement was Amalfred's death, the second being unable to attend his funeral.

4   For Sigimund see poems 7.20 and 21.

5   One of three successive poems of recommendation for a certain Audulf. Its virtuoso use of alliteration and paronomasia has suggested to some that it is designed to appeal to the youthful taste of the king (he was born in 570). Such techniques are widespread in Fortunatus's poetry, though not in such a concentrated form (but see the concluding lines of the first book of the *Vita Sancti Martini,* especially 506, 508, and 510).

6.3–4   Childebert II, Brunhild's son, was king of Austrasia. The daughter is either Ingund, who was married to Hermenegild, son of the Visigothic king Leovigild, in 579 (*PLRE* 3A:620–21 Ingundis 2), or Chlodosind, engaged to the Visigothic king Reccared in 588 (Gregory of Tours, *Historiae* 9.16 and 20, *PLRE* 3A:298 Chlodosinda 2), though the marriage never took place.

6.6   For Allobroges, see 2.15.2.

7   Agiulf is otherwise unknown but was apparently influential at Childebert II's court.

7.9   The last two syllables of this line are missing in the manuscript. Blomgren 3 (137) proposed *oro* as the missing word, and I have translated accordingly.

8.5   Baudonivia (*Vita Sanctae Radegundis* 7) mentions a Proculus whom Radegund sent to carry a letter to Bishop Germanus of Paris. This may be our man, but there can be no certainty.

9   A puzzling poem. It may well be that Reydellet (3:192–93) is right to see in it two separate poems imperfectly joined together. The first half (1–20) is written to accompany a gift of fruit from the poet and includes invective against a certain Dagaulf. The second apparently is in the name of one of the women of the convent, Radegund or Agnes. Both (*utraeque,* 35)

	join in the final address. (The abuse with which the first half ends can hardly be attributed to either woman.) If this is the case, the first lines, at a minimum, of the second poem are lost.
9.2	Reydellet (3:193) suggests the fruit in question is cherries.
9.5–6	Compare 11.18.5.
9.15	A Dagaulf is the husband of Vilithuta, whose epitaph Fortunatus composed (4.26.7) Nothing in this poem suggests the two are identical.
9.18	We have no idea how Dagaulf "foully defiled unpolluted waters."
9.20	Dracco is otherwise unknown.
9.23–24	The language suggests that the addressee of the poem has recently become a bishop and should now live in chastity with his wife.
11	Apparently a rough draft or outline for a poem, describing a Christmas meal Fortunatus enjoyed but comparing it unfavorably with the sustenance derived from the addressee's words.
13.1	Caesarius, bishop of Arles (501/2–542). For the convent's adoption of his Rule, see 8.1.60 and 8.3.39–44.
13.3	Caesaria is the first abbess of the convent of Arles, sister of Caesarius. Casaria is presumably an alternative spelling of the same name and refers to Caesaria the Younger, also an abbess of the convent, who died probably in the late 550s and certainly by 561/62 (see 8.3.39–44).
14.2	The two mothers are Radegund and Agnes, Radegund by virtue of her age and status, Agnes by her position of abbess. For Fortunatus's awareness of the anomaly by which Agnes was Radegund's superior in rank in the convent, see *Vita Sanctae Radegundis* 33.75–77. Justina has been suggested for the sister (see poems 8.13 and 9.7.81), but this does not accord with line 4, which indicates she is advanced in years.
18.2	Presumably the anniversary of her consecration as abbess.
20.5–6	Fortunatus gives instructions for the letter carrier. The final couplet follows abruptly on what precedes, causing Leo to propose a lacuna.
21.11	"She," that is, Radegund.

22.15   Fortunatus refers to his prose *Vita Sancti Marcelli.*

23.28   For Thecla see 4.26.97 and 8.1.46. Susanna is the biblical fig-
            ure (Daniel 13), falsely accused of unchastity but vindicated by
            Daniel.

24   The poem, addressed to Agnes, expresses Fortunatus's mental
            distress and embarrassment at falling short in some way. It
            sounds as though Radegund has asked him to come to her but
            he has been unable to comply immediately, though he protests
            it was through no fault of his own.

27.1–2   The poem is written to accompany the gift of a cross or the im-
            age of the cross (*signum,* "symbol," could accommodate either
            meaning). The "two siblings" are Agnes and Fortunatus.

28.5–8   For Radegund's activities in the convent kitchen, see Fortuna-
            tus's *Vita Sanctae Radegundis* 23.57.

29.7   The transmitted text is corrupt. It apparently contained an an-
            tithesis between cold and warmth, the warmth presumably be-
            ing metaphorical, brought by the "three gifts of God," refer-
            ring to the "men worthy of heaven" (10).

30.5–6   Fortunatus is here joking. His reference to "empty caves" is for
            the sake of a contrast with an empty stomach.

Epist. Austras. 14 This poem is not included in manuscripts of Fortunatus
            but is found in the *Epistulae Austrasicae* (14) and in the *Vita Mag-
            nerici* of Abbot Eberuin (early 11th century). (Leo only had the
            latter text available to him.) Magneric was bishop of Trier in
            succession to Nicetius, who died in 566. The poem is num-
            bered *Appendix* 34 in Leo's edition, after two fragments, num-
            bered poems 32 and 33—a couplet and a single line—for which
            see 4.5.9–10 and 4.6.19–22.

Epist. Austras. 14.16 A difficult line. Presumably Nicetius is heir to himself
            because Magneric so replicates his virtues.

Epist. Austras. 14.22 Compare Matthew 25:14–23.

Bibliography

Editions and Translations

Di Brazzano, Stefano. *Venanzio Fortunato Opere 1,* Scrittori della Chiesa di Aquileia 8.1. Aquileia, 2001.

Cook, Geoffrey. *From the Miscellanea of Venantius Fortunatus: A Basket of Chestnuts.* Rochester, 1981.

George, Judith. *Venantius Fortunatus: Personal and Political Poems.* Translated Texts for Historians 23. Liverpool, 1995.

Leo, Friedrich, ed. *Venanti Honori Clementiani Fortunati presbyteri Italici opera poetica. Monumenta Germaniae Historica. Auctores Antiquissimi* 4.1. Berlin, 1881.

Pucci, Joseph. *Venantius Fortunatus, Poems to Friends.* Indianapolis, 2010.

Reydellet, Marc, ed. *Venance Fortunat, Poèmes.* 3 vols. Paris, 1994–2004.

Rogers, Barbara J. "The Poems of Venantius Fortunatus: A Translation and Commentary." PhD diss., Rutgers University, 1969.

Secondary Sources

Bastianesen, A. A. R. "La poésie de Venance Fortunat: Observations à propos d'une nouvelle édition." *Mnemosyne* 49 (1996): 168–81.

Blomgren, Sven. "Fortunatus cum elogiis collatus: De cognatione quae est inter carmina Venantii Fortunati et poesin epigraphicam Christianam." *Eranos* 71 (1973): 95–111.

Brennan, Brian. "'Being Martin': Saint and Successor in Sixth-Century Tours." *Journal of Religious History* 21 (1997): 121–35.

———. "The Career of Venantius Fortunatus." *Traditio* 41 (1985): 49–78.

———. "The Image of the Merovingian Bishop in the Poetry of Venantius Fortunatus." *JMed Hist* 18 (1992): 115–39.

Di Brazzano, Stefano. "Profilo biografico di Venanzio Fortunato." In *Venanzio Fortunato e il suo tempo,* 37–72. Treviso, 2003.

Elss, Hermann. *Untersuchungen über den Stil und die Sprache des Venantius Fortunatus.* Heidelberg, 1907.

George, Judith W. *Venantius Fortunatus: A Latin Poet in Merovingian Gaul.* Oxford, 1992.

———. "Venantius Fortunatus: The End Game." *Eranos* 96 (1998): 32–43.

Goffart, Walter. *Rome's Fall and After.* London, 1989.

Koebner, Richard. *Venantius Fortunatus: Seine Persönlichkeit und seine Stellung in der geistigen Kultur des Merowinger-Reiches,* Beiträge zur Kulturgeschichte des Mittelalters und der Renaissance 22. Leipzig, 1915.

Malaspina, Elena. "Letterati forestieri a servizio della corte austrasica (511–596)." In *Incontri di popoli e culture tra V e IX secolo: Atti delle V Giornate di studio sull' età romanobarbarica,* Benevento, 9–11 giugno 1997, 59–88. Naples, 1998.

———. "Il *lusus* poetico nella Gallia subromana." In *Arma virumque—: Studi di poesia e storiografia in onore di Luca Canal,* 197–233. Pisa, 2002.

Pietri, Luce. "Venance Fortunat, lecteur des pères latins." In *Chartae caritatis: Études de patristique et d'antiquité tardive en hommage à Yves-Marie Duval,* edited by Benoît Gain, Pierre Jay, and Gérard Nauroy, 127–41. Paris, 2004.

Reydellet, Marc. *La royauté dans la littérature latine de Sidoine Apollinaire à Isidore de Séville,* Bibliothèque des Écoles françaises d'Athènes et de Rome 243. Rome, 1981.

———. "Tours et Poitiers: Les relations entre Grégorie et Fortunat." In *Grégoire de Tours et l'espace gaulois,* Actes du congrès international, Tours, 3–5 Novembre 1994, edited by Nancy Gauthier and Henri Galinié, 159–76. Tours, 1997.

———. "Venance Fortunat et l'esthétique du style." In *Haut Moyen-Âge: Culture, éducation et société, Études offertes à Pierre Riché,* edited by M. Sot, 69–77. La Garenne-Colombes, 1990.

Roberts, Michael. *The Humblest Sparrow: The Poetry of Venantius Fortunatus.* Ann Arbor, Mich., 2009.

———. "Venantius Fortunatus' Elegy on the Death of Galswintha (*Carm.* 6.5)." In *Society and Culture in Late Antique Gaul: Revisiting the Sources,*

edited by Ralph W. Mathisen and Danuta Shanzer, 298–312. Aldershot, Eng., 2001.

Tardi, Dominique. *Fortunat: Étude sur un dernier représentant de la poésie latine dans la Gaule mérovingienne.* Paris, 1927.

Wood, Ian. "Administration, Law and Culture in Merovingian Gaul." In *The Uses of Literacy in Early Medieval Europe,* edited by Rosamond McKitterick, 63–81. Cambridge, 1990.

———. "The Audience of Architecture in Post-Roman Gaul." In *The Anglo-Saxon Church: Papers on History, Architecture, and Archaeology in Honour of Dr. H. M. Taylor,* edited by L. A. S. Butler and R. K. Morris, 74–79. London, 1986.

Index

Aaron, 2.9.31, 9.2.25

Abel, 3.20.6, 9.2.13, 9.2.15, 10.2.7

Abraham, 2.5 (on cross), 5.3.31, 5.5.45, 8.3.12, 9.2.21, 9.2.131, 10.1.4

Achaea, 8.3.142

Achilles, 3.10.5, 6.1.50, 7.8.64, 7.12.11

Adam, 2.4.4, 2.4.7, 2.11.2, 4.4.1, 5.1.1, 5.6a.1, 9.2.5, 9.2.50, 10.1.48, 10.2.6, 11.1.20

Adige (river), *Praef.*4

Adonis, 7.12.18

Adriatic, 1.15.74

Aegidius (bishop of Reims), 3.15, 3.15.1, 5.3.13

Aeolus, 7.14.31

Africa, 2.16.84, 8.3.153, 10.7.9, *App.* 2.45

Agatha (martyr), 4.26.97, 8.3.33

Agaune, 2.14, 8.3.172

Ageric (bishop of Verdun), 3.23, 3.23.4, 3.23a, 3.23a.7

Agiulf, *App.* 7, *App.* 7.5

Agnes (abbess), 2.4 (on cross), 3.21.11, 3.22a.14, 5.1.10, 5.2.63, 5.19.12, 8.3.393, 8.7.19, 9.7.78, 11.3.10, 11.4.3, 11.5.2

Agnes (martyr), 4.26.97, 8.3.35

Agricola (bishop), 3.19

Ajax, 7.12.12

Aisne (river), *Praef.*4, 7.4.13

Alagisil, 7.21, 7.21.2

Alamannia, *Praef.*4

Alban (martyr), 8.3.155

Albinus, 6.10.69

Albinus (saint), 11.25.10

Alexander, 10.2.12

Alexander (martyr), 1.2.23

Alexandria, *App.* 1.98

Allobroges, 2.15.2, 3.7.18, *App.* 6.6

Alps, *Praef.*4, 1.15.73, 2.14.14, 6.5.309, *App.* 1.85

Amalfred, 8.1.24, *App.* 1.48, *App.* 3.12

Ambrose, 5.1.7, 5.3.38, 8.1.57, 8.3.168

Amelius (bishop), 1.11.5

Amiens, 10.6.25

Amor, 6.1.45

Amphion, 3.4.11

Andernach, 10.9.63

Andrew (apostle), 1.1.6, 1.2, 1.2.11, 5.2.14, 8.3.142

Anfion, 3.24, 3.24.5

Anicii, 4.5.7

Anna, 8.3.99, 10.2.7

Anthemius, 3.28.5, 3.29, 3.29.1

Apicius, 7.2.3

Apollonius of Tyre, 6.8.6

Aquileia, 8.3.166

Aquitaine, *Praef.*4, 1.15.1, 3.8.13

Arabia, 4.26.126

Aracharius, 4.19, 4.19.3

Arachne, 5.6.16 (prose)

Aratus, 7.12.25

Arcadius (father of Placidina),
   1.15.95

Arcadius (young man), 4.17, 4.17.3

Archytas, 7.12.25

Ardennes, 7.4.19

Aredius (abbot), 5.19, 5.19.7, 6.7.2

Aristotle, 5.1.7

Arius/Arian, 2.15.12, 10.1.13

Arles, 5.2.69, 8.3.40, 8.3.157, *App.* 13.6

Armentaria, 10.15, 10.15.5

Armorica, 3.8.3

Artachis, *App.* 3, *App.* 3.27

Artannes, 10.5, 10.10

Asan, 4.11

Asia, 8.3.173

Aspasius, 7.12.121

Astur, 7.12.17

Athanagild (king), 6.1.124

Athanasius (bishop of Alexandria),
   5.3.37, 8.1.55

Athens, 7.8.25

Attalus, 7.12.14

Atticus, 4.16, 4.16.5

Aude (river), 6.5.214

Audulf, *App.* 5.13, *App.* 6.15, *App.* 7.13

Augusta, *App.* 2.79, *App.* 2.85

Augustine, 4.5.14, 5.1.7, 5.3.39,
   8.1.58, 10.1.42

Augustus, 10.2.12

Augustus (as title), *App.* 2.27, *App.*
   2.43, *App.* 2.65

Autun, 8.3.160

Auvergne/Arvernian, 5.5.17, 8.3.161,
   8.15.3, 10.10.14

Aventius, 3.2.6

Avernus, 2.16.19

Avitus (bishop of Clermont), 3.21,
   3.21.1, 3.22.2, 3.22a.2, 5.5, 5.5.1
   (prose), 5.5.13, 5.5.123

Avitus (emperor), 1.15.96

Avolus, 4.21, 4.21.1

Bacchus, *Praef.*5

Baetica, 6.5.349

Bartholomew (apostle), 5.2.13,
   8.3.147

Basil, 1.7, 1.7.7, 4.18, 4.18.6

Basil (bishop of Caesarea), 5.3.40,
   8.1.54

Basilissa, 8.3.35

Basque, 9.1.73, 10.19.11, *App.* 2.30,
   App. 2.84

Batavia, 6.5.349, *App.* 2.84

Baudegund, 1.7, 1.7.7, 4.18.21

Baudoald (bishop of Meaux), 9.8

Bavaria, *Praef.*4

Berchild, 6.4, 6.4.1

Beretrud, 2.8.25

Berny, 9.1

Berthar, *App.* 3.33

Berthoara, 2.11.9

Bertram (bishop of Bordeaux), 3.17, 3.17.7

Berulf (count), 7.15, 7.15.1

Bibianus (bishop of Saintes), 1.12, 1.12.1, 1.12.13

Bissonum, 1.18, 1.18.5

Blesilla, 8.1.43

Bobolenus (deacon), 4.15, 4.15.3

Bodegisil (duke), 7.5, 7.5.2, 7.6

Boeotia, 8.1.1

Bonosus, 5.1.11

Bordaa (river), 7.7.51

Bordeaux, 1.15.68, 1.16.3, 1.18.6, 4.9, 4.10, 7.25.4, 10.19.3

Bordelais, 1.18, 1.19, 1.20

Boso, 7.22

Bourges, 3.20

Brenta (river), *Praef.*4

Breuni, *Praef.*4

Britain, 6.5.219, 7.8.64, 8.1.18, 8.3.155, 10.7.8, *App.* 2.31

Brittany/Bretons, 3.5.7, 3.8.41, 3.26.5, 9.1.73, *App.* 2.84

Brumachius, 4.20, 4.20.2

Brunhild (queen), 5.3.15, 6.1.51, 6.1.101, 6.1a, 6.1a.31, 6.5.289, 10.7, 10.7.67, 10.11.25, *App.* 6

Byzantium, *App.* 1.97

Caesaria (abbess), 8.3.39, 8.3.81, *App.* 13.3

Caesarius, 9.13.11

Caesarius (bishop of Arles), 5.2.68, 5.3.40, 8.1.60, 8.3.41, 8.3.48, 8.3.82, 8.3.158, *App.* 13.1

Canobus, 3.4.9

Cantabrians, 10.19.11

Cantumblandum, 6.7, 6.7.1

Carentinus (bishop of Cologne), 3.14, 3.14.1

Cariacum, 5.7.8, 11.25.7

Casaria, *App.* 13.3, *App.* 13.13

Castalia, 7.11.4, 8.1.2

Cato, 7.7.3, 7.12.25

Cecilia (martyr), 1.2.23, 8.3.171

Chalcedon, 8.3.169, *App.* 2.26

Chaletricus (bishop of Chartres), 4.7, 4.7.5

Charibert (king), 6.2, 6.2.19

Chartres, 4.7

Cherubim, 8.3.131

Cherusci, 3.4.9

Chiers (river), 7.4.15

Childebert I, 2.10.17, 6.2.13, 6.2.23, 6.6.9

Childebert II, 10.7, 10.7.61, 10.8.23, 10.11.25, 10.14.7, 10.16.11, 10.17.21, 10.18.5, *App.* 5, *App.* 5.11

Chilperic (king), 9.1, 9.1.27, 9.2, 9.3, 9.4.6, 9.5.8

Chlodobert, 9.4, 9.4.3

Chlothar I, 7.16.33, 9.4.6

Chrodin (duke), 9.16, 9.16.3

Chrysippus, 5.1.7, 7.12.25

Cicero, 5.1.6, 7.2.3, 8.1.6

Cleanthes, 5.1.7, 7.12.26

Clermont, 4.4, 5.5

Clovis, 9.4.5, 9.5.5

Cologne, 3.14, 3.14.3

Conda, 7.16, 7.16.2

Constantine, 9.13.12

Constantine (emperor), *App.* 2.67

Cosmas (martyr), 10.10.11
Cronopius (bishop of Périgueux), 4.8, 4.8.5
Cupid, 6.1.38, 6.1.47, 6.1.65, 6.1.66, 6.5.25
Cyprian (martyr), 8.3.153

Dacia, 6.5.219, *App.* 2.45
Daedalus, 11.11.17, 11.14.4, *App.* 24.7
Dagaulf (husband of Vilithuta), 4.26.7
Dagaulf, *App.* 9.15
Dagobert, 9.5, 9.5.1
Dalmatia, *App.* 2.45
Damian (martyr), 10.10.11
Danes, 7.7.50, 9.1.73
Daniel, 9.2.33, 11.1.34, 11.1.39
Danube (river), *Praef.*4, 1.15.75, 6.10.35, *App.* 2.28
David (king), 2.4.34, 2.6.14, 2.9.19, 5.5.57, 6.2.78, 7.8.27, 8.3.3, 9.2.31, 9.2.101, 9.2.135, 10.2.16
Death, 2.7.39, 2.7.48, 2.8.18
Demosthenes, 8.1.3
Dhron (river), 3.12.7
Dionysius (martyr), 1.11, 1.11.11, 8.3.159
Domitianus (bishop of Angers), 3.6.25, 11.25.9
Domitius, 5.1.3
Domnulus (bishop of Le Mans), 3.6.27
Dracco, *App.* 9.20
Drava (river), *Praef.*4

Droctoveus (abbot), 9.11, 9.11.2, 9.13.9
Dynamius, 6.9, 6.9.1, 6.10, 6.10.33

Ebro (river), 6.5.350
Echinades, 3.4.3
Eden, 5.1.1
Edessa, 8.3.146
Egypt, 7.5.34, 7.7.35, 8.3.151
Elbe (river), *App.* 2.28
Elijah, 4.26.93, 5.2.25, 8.3.135, 9.2.39, 10.1.57
Elizabeth, 10.2.7, 10.5.6
Elysium, 5.1.1
Emerius (bishop of Saintes), 1.12.5
Eumerius (bishop of Nantes), 4.1, 4.1.5
Enn (river), *Praef.*4
Enoch, 4.26.93, 8.3.135, 9.2.39, 10.2.7
Eomundus, 11.25.5
Ephesus, 8.3.143
Erato (Muse), 6.10.4
Esther, 8.3.99
Ethiopia, 5.2.9
Eufrasia, 4.27, 4.27.3
Eufronius (bishop of Tours), 3.1, 3.1.3, 3.2, 3.3.4, 3.6.20
Eugenia (martyr), 8.1.46, 8.3.35, 8.4.14, 10.7.26
Eulalia (martyr), 8.3.170
Euphemia (martyr), 8.3.33, 8.3.169
Euphrates, 1.21.8
Europe, 8.3.173
Eusebia, 4.28, 4.28.5

Eusebius, 4.28.11

Eusebius (bishop), 1.12.3

Eustochium, 8.1.41

Euthian, 9.1.73

Eutropius (bishop of Saintes), 1.13, 1.13.3

Evantia, 4.12.17

Eve, 2.4.7, 3.9.99, 5.6a.2, 9.2.4, 10.1.48, 10.2.4, 11.1.22, *App.* 9.8

Evodius, 7.19, 7.19.3

Exocius (bishop of Limoges), 4.6, 4.6.8

Ezechiel, 11.1.18

Fabiola, 8.1.42

Fabius, 6.2.84

Falernian, 3.13c.4, 5.1.3, 7.5.11, *App.* 9.20

Faramod, 9.12, 9.12.2

Faustus (bishop of Auch), 1.4.5

Felix, 6.10.68

Felix, 7.13

Felix (bishop of Bourges), 3.20, 3.20.5

Felix (bishop of Nantes), 3.2.6, 3.4, 3.4.6, 3.5, 3.6, 3.6.9, 3.6.44, 3.7.23, 3.7.57, 3.8.4, 3.8.50, 3.9, 3.9.95, 3.9.102, 3.10, 3.10.5, 3.10.27, 4.1.31, 5.7, 5.7.2

Felix (martyr), 8.3.165

Ferreolus (martyr), 3.7.55, 8.3.162

Flaccus (Q. Horatius). *See* Horace

Flavus, 7.18, 7.18.1, 7.19, 7.19.3

Florentinus, 10.12d

Fortunatus, *Praef.*1.5.22, 2.4 (on cross), 2.14.29, 2.16.165, 3.1, 3.2, 3.4, 3.21, 3.21.16, 4.6.20, 4.7.26, 4.27.20, 5.1, 5.1.11, 5.2.60, 5.5, 5.5.138, 5.6, 5.7.12, 5.15.6, 5.16.5, 5.18, 5.18.9, 5.19.8, 6.10.70, 7.4.34, 7.9.6, 7.12.62, 8.1.11, 8.15.11, 8.18.8, 8.20.14, 8.21.9, 9.1.148, 10.6.102, 10.13.11, 10.15.11, 10.16.10, 10.17.43, 10.19.30, 11.4.3, *App.* 5.11, *Epist. Austras.* 14.23

Fortunatus (martyr), 8.3.166

Franks, 7.20.10, 9.4.8, *App.* 1.165

Fredegund (queen), 9.1.121, 9.2, 9.3, 9.4.7, 9.5.8

Frigia, 4.20.5

Frisians, 9.1.75

Gabriel, 10.5.3, 10.10.3

Galactorius (count), 7.25, 7.25.10, 10.19

Galicia, 5.1, 5.2.17, 5.2.22, 5.2.43, *App.* 2.29

Gallienus, 10.12c

Gallomagnus (bishop of Troyes), 7.6, 7.6.23

Gallus (bishop of Clermont), 4.4, 4.4.5

Galswintha (queen), 6.5, 6.5.24, 6.5.96, 6.5.160, 6.5.181, 6.5.260, 6.5.303, 6.5.305, 6.5.331

Garonne, *Praef.*4, 1.8, 1.15.71, 1.19.1, 1.20.17, 1.21.1, 7.25.3

Gaul, 1.9.10, 1.15.3, 1.21.8, 3.7.17, 3.7.23, 3.7.53, 3.8.5, 3.8.22, 3.17.1, 4.10.19, 4.16.9, 4.18.16, 5.2.15,

Gaul *(continued)*
  5.6a.32, 6.5.13, 6.5.181, 6.5.287,
  7.7.61, 8.1.12, 8.3.163, 9.7 (prose),
  10.6.93, 10.7.5, 10.10.15, *App.* 2.27,
  App. 6.3
Gelonians, 6.5.49
Genesius (martyr), 5.2.67, 8.3.157
George (martyr), 2.12, 2.12.1
Germanus (bishop of Paris), 2.9.27,
  2.9.71, 8.2, 8.2.3, 9.11.3
Germany, *Praef.*4, 6.1.118, 6.5.41,
  6.5.301, 6.9.5, 7.5.21, 7.8.49,
  7.12.65, 9.16.5, *App.* 2.84
Gers (river), 1.21, 1.21.3, 1.21.22
Gervasius (martyr), 8.3.168
Gideon, 9.2.29
Gogo, 6.8.37, 7.1, 7.1.11, 7.2.2,
  7.4.3
Goiswintha (queen), 6.5.28, 6.5.48,
  6.5.138, 6.5.178, 6.5.319
Goliath, 10.2.16
Gomorrah, 5.5.51
Gondorf, 10.9.45
Goths, 6.5.219, 9.1.73, *App.* 6.6
Greek (language), 3.4.13
Greece/Greeks, 2.15.6, 5.2.14,
  7.8.64, 7.12.12, 7.18.18
Gregory (bishop of Langres), 4.2,
  4.2.3
Gregory (bishop of Nazianzus),
  1.16.40, 5.1.7, 5.3.39, 8.1.54, 9.6.6
Gregory (bishop of Tours), *Praef.*,
  *Praef.*4, 1.5, 1.5.23, 2.3.13, 5.3,
  5.3.10, 5.3.17, 5.4, 5.4.1, 5.5, 5.5.137,
  5.8, 5.8.3, 5.8a.1, 5.9.1, 5.10.3, 5.11.1,
  5.13.1, 5.14.1, 5.16.3, 5.17.5, 8.11,

  8.11.1, 8.14.1, 8.15.9, 8.16.5, 8.17.5,
  8.18.3, 8.20.1, 8.21.5, 9.6, 9.6.6,
  9.7, 9.7.4, 9.7.88, 10.5.9, 10.6,
  10.6.11, 10.6.17, 10.6.23, 10.6.73,
  10.6.85, 10.6.101, 10.10.9,
  10.10.25, 10.11.17, 10.11.33, 10.12a,
  10.12a.7, 10.14.9, 10.15, 10.15.10
Gundegisel (bishop of Bordeaux),
  7.25.7
Gunduarius, 7.17, 7.17.17
Guntram (king), 7.25.11

Hebrew, 7.18.16, 11.1.12
Hector, 7.12.11
Helias, 6.10.69
Helena, *App.* 2.67
Hermanfred, 8.1.23, *App.* 3.33
Herod, 11.1.28
Hierapolis, 8.3.145
Hilary (priest), 3.16, 3.28.7, 4.12,
  4.12.7
Hilary of Poitiers (saint), 1.16.38,
  2.15, 2.15.1, 3.7.51, 5.1.7, 5.3.37,
  6.5.217, 8.1.13, 8.1.55, 8.3.163,
  10.14.3, *App.* 21.13
Himalayas, 7.25.13
Homer, 3.10.3, 6.1a.5, 7.8.25, 7.12.27,
  8.1.4
Hippolytus, 7.12.18
Horace, 5.6.7 (prose), 9.7.9

Illyria, 5.2.7
India, 5.2.13, 6.5.219, 8.1.15, 8.3.147,
  9.1.19, 10.7.7
Isaac, 9.2.21
Isaiah, 9.2.33, 11.1.39

Israel, 3.3.10, 3.6.2, 9.2.31, 11.1.18
Italy, 4.20.5, 6.5.219, 6.10.35, 7.9.7,
   7.20.9, 7.21.9, 8.1.12, 9.16.5,
   10.16.1, *App.* 2.45

Jacob, 9.2.21
James (apostle), 5.2.20, 8.3.144
Japheth, 9.2.19
Javols, 8.3.161
Jerome, 8.1.57
Jerusalem, *App.* 1.99
Jews, 1.3.7, 5.5, 5.5.19, 5.5.29, 5.5.35,
   5.5.73, 5.5.80, 5.5.109, 10.1.13,
   10.1.44
Job, 8.3.286, 9.2.24, 9.2.99, 9.2.132,
   10.2.15
John (apostle), 5.2.20, 8.3.143
John (bishop), 1.2.25
John (deacon), 3.28, 3.28.2
John (deceased infant), 4.22.7
John (son of Julian [merchant]),
   4.23.15
John the Baptist, 9.2.38
Jonah, 9.2.33, 11.1.30
Jordan (river), 10.6.36, 10.6.100
Joseph, 8.3.291
Joshua, 9.2.27, 11.1.12
Jovinus, 6.10.69, 7.11, 7.12.62
Judas (apostle), 8.3.149
Judith, 8.3.99, 8.3.304
Julian (martyr), 5.3.11, 8.3.161,
   10.10.13
Julian (merchant), 4.23, 4.23.1
Justin II (emperor), *App.* 2.12, *App.*
   2.22, *App.* 2.50, *App.* 2.91
Justina, 8.13.3, 9.7.81

Justina (martyr), 8.3.34, 8.3.169
Justinian (emperor), 10.19.16

Langres, 4.2, 4.3
Latin (language), 3.4.13, 6.2.98
Laugona (river), 7.7.58
Launebod (duke), 2.8, 2.8.21
Laurence (martyr), 1.2.13, 8.3.164,
   9.14, 9.14.1
Lazarus, 5.3.29
Lebanon, 3.7.2
Lech (river), *Praef.*4
Leo (brother of Jovinus),
   7.12.121
Leo (priest), 8.11.3
Leontius I (bishop of Bordeaux),
   4.9, 4.9.3
Leontius II (bishop of Bordeaux),
   1.6.5, 1.8.13, 1.8.16, 1.9.7, 1.10.7,
   1.11.9, 1.12.7, 1.13.1, 1.14, 1.14.1,
   1.15, 1.15.15, 1.16, 1.16.2, 1.16.92,
   1.18.11, 1.19.15, 1.20.19, 3.24.19,
   4.10, 4.10.5
Lérins, 5.2.69
Lesbos, 9.7.52
Libya, 9.1.15, 9.7.53
Liliola, 8.3.43
Limoges, 4.5, 4.6
Livenza (river), *Praef.*4
Loire (river), *Praef.*4, 3.4.9, 5.7.7,
   6.5.233, 7.10.3
Lot, 5.5.49
Luke (evangelist), 8.3.152
Lupus (deacon), 9.13, 9.13.2
Lupus (duke), 7.4.27, 7.7, 7.7.2, 7.8.33,
   7.8.72, 7.9, 7.9.6, 7.10.20

Lycontius, 10.7.55

Lyon, 10.10.24

Lysa, 7.12.27

Maccabees, 9.2.103, 10.15.1

Magneric (bishop of Trier), *Epist.
Austras.* 14, *Epist. Austras.* 14.5

Magnulf, 7.10, 7.10.4

Mainz, 2.11, 9.9.1

Malachi, 11.1.34

Manichaean, 10.1.13

Marcella, 8.1.44

Marcellus (saint), *App.* 22.15

Mark (apostle), 8.3.151

Mars, 6.1.20

Marseille, 6.9.5, 7.5.19, 8.3.156

Martha, 8.1.45

Martin (bishop of Braga), 5.1, 5.1.1,
5.2.17, 5.2.43, 5.2.59

Martin of Tours (saint), *Praef.*6,
1.2.17, 1.4, 1.4.2, 1.5, 1.5.4, 1.5.21,
1.6, 1.6.7, 1.7, 1.7.9, 1.16.39, 2.13.7,
3.1.3, 3.2.5, 3.3.23, 3.6.19, 3.7.52,
5.1.10, 5.1.11, 5.2.15, 5.3.11, 5.3.38,
5.4.1, 5.9.3, 5.11.7, 5.14.4, 5.14.17,
6.5.229, 8.1.21, 8.3.163, 8.11.4,
8.12.7, 8.15.10, 8.20.1, 10.6.3,
10.6.17, 10.6.25, 10.6.32, 10.6.37,
10.6.56, 10.6.63, 10.6.67, 10.6.81,
10.6.95, 10.6.103, 10.6.107,
10.6.118, 10.6.121, 106.125,
10.6.130, 10.7, 10.7.4, 10.7.10,
10.7.27, 10.7.31, 10.10.15, 10.11,
10.11.11, 10.11.23, 10.11.31, 10.12a.7,
10.14.3, 10.17.27, 10.19.19, *App.*
19.4, *App.* 21.13

Marturius (martyr), 1.2.21

Mary (mother of Jesus), 1.15.55,
1.15.57, 4.26.96, 6.5.359, 8.3, 8.3.25,
8.3.102, 8.3.136, 8.4.33, 10.5.8,
11.1.17, 11.1.19, 11.6.6

Mary Magdalene, 8.1.45

Matthew (apostle), 5.2.9, 8.3.148

Maurice (martyr), 2.14.5

Meaux, 3.27

Medard (bishop of Noyon), 2.16,
2.16.2

Mediolanus, 3.12.10

Melania, 8.1.43

Melchisedech, 2.10.21, 9.2.23

Menander, 7.12.27

Mérida, 8.3.170

Metz, 3.13, 3.13.9, 6.8.7, 7.4.16,
10.9.1

Meuse (river), *Praef.*4, 7.4.11

Milan, 8.3.168

Minerva, 4.28.8

Moor, 10.7.8

Mopsus, 9.7.39

Moselle (river), *Praef.*4, 3.12, 3.12.7,
3.12.24, 3.13.1, 3.13.7, 7.4.7, 10.9.3,
10.9.48

Moses, 2.9.72, 5.5.33, 5.5.131, 5.6.16
(prose), 8.3.14, 9.2.25, 10.1.4,
10.1.31, 11.1.25

Mummolenus, 7.14, 7.14.7

Mummolus, 9.13.11

Muse(s), *Praef.*4, *Praef.*5, 3.18.19,
6.10.17, 6.10.19, 6.10.59, 7.12.29,
8.1.1, 9.7.20, 10.9.52, 11.23.8, *App.*
12.3

Naab (river), 6.1.75

Nadaber, 8.3.148

Namatius (bishop of Vienne), 4.27.13

Nantes, 3.4, 3.4.9, 3.7, 3.10, 4.1, 5.7

Naomi, 8.3.99

Narbonne, 6.5.213

Nauriac, 6.8.33, 6.8.43

Nazarius (martyr), 1.10, 1.10.1

Nectarius, *App.* 8, *App.* 8.2

Nereids, 6.1.104

Nicasia, 4.24.12

Nicetius (bishop of Lyon), 10.10.23

Nicetius (bishop of Trier), 3.11, 3.11.1, 3.12.19, *Epist. Austras.* 14.5

Nile (river), 1.21.6, 7.5.34, 7.7.35

Noah, 9.2.17, 10.2.7

Noricum, *Praef.*4

Oeta, 3.4.9

Oise (river), 7.4.15

Orientius, 4.24, 4.24.5

Orne (river), 10.9.13

Orosius, 8.1.59

Orpheus, *Praef.*4, 7.1.1, 7.12.22

Padua, 8.3.169

Palamedes, 7.12.16

Palatina, 7.6, 7.6.5

Palladius (bishop of Saintes), 1.3.11

Pannonia, 5.2.21, 10.6.93

Papiana, *App.* 9.22

Papulus (count), 6.8.39, 6.8.49

Paris, 2.9, 2.9.17, 2.10, 3.26.4, 4.26.13, 6.2.9, 8.3.159

Paros, 9.10.10, 9.15.1

Paternus (abbot), 3.25, 3.25.2, 7.23, 7.23.1

Patrick, 4.22.8

Paul (apostle), 1.2.9, 2.1.8, 2.13.5, 2.14.7, 3.6.14, 3.7.4, 3.7.10, 3.7.11, 5.1, 5.2.7, 5.2.19, 5.3.35, 7.12.52, 8.1.10, 8.3.137, 8.3.386, 9.2.35, 10.1.26, 10.1.34, 10.1.42, 10.2.17, 10.7.19, 11.4.11, 11.6.5, 11.15.3, *App.* 2.17

Paula, 8.1.41

Paulina (martyr), 8.3.35

Périgueux, 4.8

Peripatetic school of philosophy, 5.1.7

Persia, 5.2.11, 6.5.219, 7.18.17, 8.1.18, 8.3.149, 10.7.8, *App.* 1.97

Peter (apostle), 1.2.7, 2.1.8, 2.13.3, 3.6.13, 3.7.4, 3.7.10, 3.13d.2, 4.5.12, 4.26.94, 4.27.22, 5.2.6, 5.2.19, 5.2.62, 5.3.35, 6.5.358, 7.12.52, 7.22.6, 8.1.10, 8.3.16, 8.3.138, 9.2.35, 10.7.19, 11.6.5, *App.* 2.16

Pharaoh, 8.3.291

Philip (apostle), 8.3.145

Phoebus, 3.23a.1, 7.8.5

Photinus, 10.1.13

Phrygia, *App.* 2.45

Piave (river), *Praef.*4

Pierian, 7.13.1

Pindar, 3.4.3, 5.6.7 (prose), 9.7.9

Pindus (mountain), 3.4.9

Pittacus, 5.1.7

Placidina (wife of Leontius I), 1.6.21, 1.12.14, 1.14.2, 1.15.93, 1.17, 4.10.26

Plato (bishop of Poitiers), 10.14, 10.14.11

Plato (philosopher), 5.1.7, 7.12.25

Po (river), *Praef.*4, 1.15.74

Poitiers, 2.15.2, 6.5.215, 8.1.13, *App.* 13.6

Polydeuces, 3.4.5

Pompey, 7.7.4

Pontius Pilate, 11.1.21, 11.1.28

Praemiacum, 1.20, 1.20.6

Praesidius, 4.14, 4.14.5

Privatus (martyr), 8.3.161

Proculus, *App.* 8.5

Prodomeres, 5.8b.9

Pyrenees, *Praef.*4, 6.1.113, 6.5.209, 6.5.329, 10.19.12

Pythagoras, 7.12.25

Quintianus (bishop of Clermont), 4.4.13

Quirinus (martyr), 8.3.153

Quirinus (Romulus), 7.12.20

Rachel, 8.3.99, 10.2.7

Radegund, 2.4 (on cross), 3.4.12, 3.21.11, 3.22a.14, 5.1.10, 5.2.63, 5.3.14, 5.19.12, 6.5.225, 8.1.21, 8.2, 8.3.47, 8.5, 8.5.1, 8.7.19, 8.9.1, 8.12a, 9.1.128, 9.7.78, 10.3.4, 10.7.25, 11.2, 11.3.9, 11.6.9, *App.* 1.48, *App.* 2.57, *App.* 2.87, *App.* 2.96, *App.* 3.13

Ragnemod (bishop of Paris), 3.26, 3.26.1, 9.10, 9.10.1

Ravenna, *Praef.*4, 1.1, 1.2, 8.3.167

Rebecca, 8.3.99, 10.2.7

Red Sea, 3.8.8, 9.1.19, *App.* 1.66

Remedius (bishop of Rheims), 2.13.9

Rheims, 3.15, 7.3.3

Rhine (river), *Praef.*4, 1.15.73, 6.5.348, 6.10.35, 7.4.5, 7.10.3, 7.21.9, 9.9.27, 10.9.48, 10.9.77, *App.* 2.28

Rhone (river), 2.14.13, 6.5.214, 6.10.55, *App.* 2.28

Romacharius (bishop of Coutances), 3.6.27

Rome/Roman, 2.8.11, 2.8.23, 3.4.10, 3.7.17, 3.8.20–22, 3.18.8, 4.5.8, 4.10.8, 4.26.14, 5.2.21, 6.2.7, 6.2.100, 7.7.5–6, 7.7.45, 7.8.63, 8.3.138, 8.3.164, 8.3.174, 9.16.19, *App.* 2.15, *App.* 2.83

Romulf, 10.12b

Romulus (city), 5.2.5, 7.18.15, *App.* 2.93

Romulus (legendary founder of Rome). *See* Quirinus

Rouen, 6.5.236

Rucco. *See* Ragnemod

Ruricii (bishops of Limoges), 4.5, 4.5.7

Saar (river), 7.4.15, 10.9.20

Sabaea, 7.12.39

Sabellius, 10.1.13

Saintes, 1.13.19, 1.15.60

Salutaris, 10.2

Sambre (river), 7.4.15

Samson, 9.2.29

Samuel, 9.2.33

Saone (river), 6.10.55

Sapaudus (bishop of Arles), 6.10.67

Sapphic meter, 9.6.9, 9.7.43

Sapphira, 8.3.297

Sappho, 9.7.6, 9.7.52

Sarah, 8.3.99, 10.2.7

Sarepta, 3.20.8

Saturninus (bishop of Toulouse), 2.7, 2.7.5, 2.8, 2.8.9

Sauer (river), 7.4.15, 10.9.18

Saxons, 3.9.103, 6.1a.11, 7.7.47, 7.16.47, 9.1.73

Scheldt (river), 7.4.15

Scipio, 7.7.3

Scythia, 5.2.7, 6.5.219, 8.1.19, *App.* 2.45

Sedulius, 8.1.59

Segor, 5.5.50

Seille (river), 3.13.5, 7.4.16

Seine (river), *Praef.*4, 3.26.5, 6.5.235

Seleucia, 8.3.171

Seraphim, 8.3.131

Servilio (priest), 4.13, 4.13.3

Seth, 9.2.15

Shem, 9.2.19

Sicambria, 6.2.97

Sicily, 8.3.171

Sidonius (bishop of Mainz), 2.11.7, 2.12.9, 9.9, 9.9.5

Sigibert (king), 2.16.161, 5.3.15, 6.1, 6.1.27, 6.1.51, 6.1.68, 6.1.131, 6.1a, 6.1a.7, 7.1.35, 7.7.28, 7.16.39, 10.16.2

Sigimund, 7.10.5, 7.20, 7.21, 7.21.2, *App.* 4

Sigoald (count), 10.16, 10.16.9, 10.17, 10.17.25, 10.17.43, 10.18.6

Simon (apostle), 8.3.149

Simplicius, *App.* 29.15

Sindulf (deacon), 3.30

Sion, 3.7.1

Sisennus (martyr), 1.2.21

Smyrna, 3.4.5

Sodom, 5.5.50

Solomon, 2.10.1, 3.6.1, 3.20.3, 6.2.80, 9.2.32, 9.2.135

Somme (river), 7.4.15

Sophia (empress), *App.* 2.52, *App.* 2.62, *App.* 2.72, *App.* 2.92

Sophocles, 8.21.2

Spain, 1.15.9, 4.18.16, 6.1.104, 6.1.111, 6.1.118, 6.1.127, 6.5.139, 6.5.287, 7.1.41, 8.3.154, 10.7.8, *App.* 6.3

Stephen (martyr), 1.3, 1.3.7, 2.15.14, 4.26.94, 6.5.357, 8.3.20

Stoic school of philosophy, 5.1.7

Sueves, 5.2.22, 9.1.75

Susanna, *App.* 23.28

Syagrius (bishop of Autun), 5.6, 5.6.1, 5.6a

Symphorian (martyr), 8.3.160

Symplegades, 3.4.9

Tagliamento, *Praef.*4

Tagus (river), 6.5.348

Tartarus, 2.6.24, 2.7.48, 3.9.33, 3.9.78, 3.9.85, 4.2.1, 4.5.3, 4.26.88, 8.7.3, 10.1.21, 10.11.10, 11.1.23, 11.1.42

Telamon, 6.10.44

Tempe, 5.6a.9

Tetricus (bishop of Langres), 4.3, 4.3.1

Thecla (martyr), 4.26.97, 8.1.46, 8.3.34, 8.3.171, 8.4.14, *App.* 23.28

Theodorus (bishop of Marseilles), 6.10.67

Theodosius (emperor), 10.2.12

Thessaly, *App.* 2.45

Theudebert I, 2.11.15, 6.1.77, 7.16.19

Theudechild (queen), 4.25, 4.25.8, 6.3, 6.3.8

Theuderic I, 4.4.16, 7.16.17

Theudosius, 4.9.38

Thomas (apostle), 5.2.11, 8.3.146

Thrace, 6.5.219, *App.* 2.45

Thule, 8.1.16

Thuringia, 6.1.75, 6.1a.11, 8.1.22, *App.* 1, *App.* 1.20, *App.* 1.72, *App.* 2.57, *App.* 3.2

Timothy, 11.4.11

Tincillac, 11.25.8

Tiryns, 3.4.9

Titan, 1.21.13

Titiana, 11.5.8

Toledo, 6.5.13, 6.5.97, 6.5.122

Toulouse, 2.7.11, 2.8.11

Tours, 2.3, 3.4.7, 5.3, 5.4.2, 5.8.5, 5.9.2, 5.10.2, 6.5.229, 8.11.2, 8.15.2, 10.6, 10.7

Trajan, 3.18.8, 6.2.82, 7.8.26, 10.2.12

Trasaricus, 2.13, 2.13.11

Trier, 3.11, 10.9.21

Troy, *App.* 1.19

Tyrrhenian Sea, 6.5.142

Ultrogotha, 6.6, 6.6.23

Ulysses, 7.12.16

Venus, 4.28.8, 6.1.49, 6.1.60, 6.1.64, 6.1.99, 6.1.103, 9.7.7

Verdun, 3.23, 3.23.1, 3.23a

Vereginis, 1.19, 1.19.2

Vernemet, 1.9, 1.9.9

Vicenza, 8.3.165

Victor (martyr), 8.3.156, 10.10.21

Victorianus (abbot), 4.11, 4.11.6

Victorius (bishop of Rennes), 3.6.25

Vienne (river), 6.5.231, 8.19.4

Vienne, bishop of. *See* Namatius

Vienne, martyr of. *See* Ferreolus

Vigilius (martyr of Trento), 1.2.19

Vilicus (bishop of Metz), 3.13, 3.13.17, 3.13.39, 6.8.22

Vilithuta, 4.26, 4.26.7

Vincent of Agen (saint), 1.8, 1.8.5, 1.9, 1.9.5

Vincent of Saragossa (saint), 8.3.154

Virgil, 5.1.6, 6.1a.5, 7.8.26, 7.12.27, 8.1.6, 8.18.5

Vitalis (bishop of Altinum), 1.1, 1.1.3, 1.2, 1.2.3, 1.2.25

Vitalis (martyr), 1.2.15, 8.3.167

Volsci, 3.4.10

Vosges, 7.4.19

Waal (river), 6.5.350

Waldo (deacon), 9.13, 9.13.2

Zachariah, 10.5.5